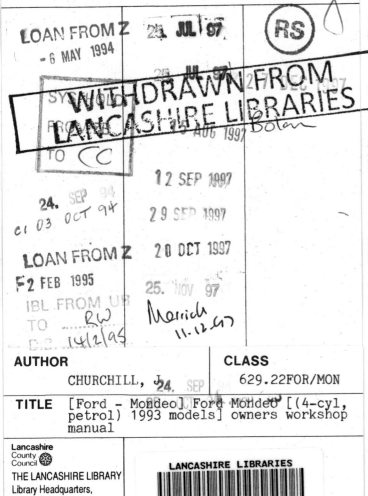
Ford Mondeo Owners Workshop Manual

Jeremy Churchill and AK Legg LAE MIMI

Models covered

All Ford Mondeo models with four-cylinder petrol engines, including special/limited editions
1597 cc, 1796 cc, and 1988 cc

Does not cover Diesel or V6 engines, or four-wheel-drive models

ABCDE
FGHIJ
KLMNO
PQRS

Haynes Publishing
Sparkford Nr Yeovil
Somerset BA22 7JJ England

Haynes Publications, Inc
861 Lawrence Drive
Newbury Park
California 91320 USA

06073873

Acknowledgements

Thanks are due to Champion Spark Plug, who supplied the illustrations showing spark plug conditions, to Holt Lloyd Limited who supplied the illustrations showing bodywork repair, and to Duckhams Oils, who provided lubrication data. Certain other illustrations are the copyright of the Ford Motor Company, and are used with their permission. Thanks are also due to Sykes-Pickavant Limited, who provided some of the workshop tools, and to all those people at Sparkford and Newbury Park who helped in the production of this manual.

A book in the **Haynes Owners Workshop Manual Series**

Printed by J.H. Haynes & Co. Ltd., Sparkford, Nr Yeovil, Somerset BA22 7JJ, England

ISBN 1 85010 923 0

British Library Cataloguing in Publication Data
A catalogue record for this book is available from the British Library.

We take great pride in the accuracy of information given in this manual, but vehicle manufacturers make alterations and design changes during the production run of a particular vehicle of which they do not inform us. No liability can be accepted by the authors or publishers for loss, damage or injury caused by any errors in, or omissions from, the information given.

Restoring and Preserving our Motoring Heritage

Few people can have had the luck to realise their dreams to quite the same extent and in such a remarkable fashion as John Haynes, Founder and Chairman of the Haynes Publishing Group.

Since 1965 his unique approach to workshop manual publishing has proved so successful that millions of Haynes Manuals are now sold every year throughout the world, covering literally thousands of different makes and models of cars, vans and motorcycles.

A continuing passion for cars and motoring led to the founding in 1985 of a Charitable Trust dedicated to the restoration and preservation of our motoring heritage. To inaugurate the new Museum, John Haynes donated virtually his entire private collection of 52 cars.

Now with an unrivalled international collection of over 210 veteran, vintage and classic cars and motorcycles, the Haynes Motor Museum in Somerset is well on the way to becoming one of the most interesting Motor Museums in the world.

A 70 seat video cinema, a cafe and an extensive motoring bookshop, together with a specially constructed one kilometre motor circuit, make a visit to the Haynes Motor Museum a truly unforgettable experience.

Every vehicle in the museum is preserved in as near as possible mint condition and each car is run every six months on the motor circuit.

Enjoy the picnic area set amongst the rolling Somerset hills. Peer through the William Morris workshop windows at cars being restored, and browse through the extensive displays of fascinating motoring memorabilia.

From the 1903 Oldsmobile through such classics as an MG Midget to the mighty 'E' Type Jaguar, Lamborghini, Ferrari Berlinetta Boxer, and Graham Hill's Lola Cosworth, there is something for everyone, young and old alike, at this Somerset Museum.

Haynes Motor Museum

Situated mid-way between London and Penzance, the Haynes Motor Museum is located just off the A303 at Sparkford, Somerset (home of the Haynes Manual) and is open to the public 7 days a week all year round, except Christmas Day and Boxing Day.

Contents

Spark plug condition and bodywork repair colour section between pages 1-2 and 1-3

Ford Mondeo 2.0 Ghia Saloon

Ford Mondeo 1.8 GLX Estate

About this manual

Its aim

The aim of this manual is to help you get the best value from your vehicle. It can do so in several ways. It can help you decide what work must be done (even should you choose to get it done by a garage), provide information on routine maintenance and servicing, and give a logical course of action and diagnosis when random faults occur. However, it is hoped that you will use the manual by tackling the work yourself. On simpler jobs, it may even be quicker than booking the vehicle into a garage and going there twice, to leave and collect it. Perhaps most important, a lot of money can be saved, by avoiding the costs a garage must charge to cover its labour and overheads.

The manual has drawings and descriptions to show the function of the various components, so that their layout can be understood. Then the tasks are described and photographed in a clear step-by-step sequence.

Its arrangement

The manual is divided into Chapters, each covering a logical sub-division of the vehicle. The Chapters are each divided into numbered Sections, which are headed in bold type between horizontal lines. Where required for ease of reference, some Sections are divided into sub-Sections, and in some cases into sub-sub-Sections; all such sub-divisions are indicated by appropriately-sized sub-headings. Each Section contains individual paragraphs which (except in the case of purely-descriptive "General description" Sections) are consecutively numbered; this numbering sequence is applied throughout the Section, regardless of any subdivision.

The manual is freely illustrated, especially in those parts where there is a detailed sequence of operations to be carried out. The reference numbers used in illustration captions indicate the Section, followed by the number of the paragraph within that Section, to which the

illustration refers; where more than one illustration applies to a particular paragraph, letters are added in alphabetical order to each illustration caption's reference number - for example, illustration "6.7C" is the third illustration referring to paragraph 7 of Section 6 of that Chapter.

Procedures, once described in the appropriate place in the text, are not normally repeated. When it is necessary to refer to another Chapter, the reference will be given as Chapter and Section number. Cross-references given without use of the word "Chapter" apply to other Sections in the same Chapter. For example, a cross-reference such as "see Section 8" means Section 8 in that Chapter.

There is an alphabetical index at the back of the manual, as well as a contents list at the front. Each Chapter is also preceded by its own individual contents list.

References to the "left" or "right" of the vehicle are in the sense of a person in the driver's seat facing forward.

Unless otherwise stated, nuts and bolts are removed by turning anti-clockwise, and tightened by turning clockwise.

We take great pride in the accuracy of information given in this manual, but vehicle manufacturers make alterations and design changes during the production run of a particular vehicle of which they do not inform us. No liability can be accepted by the authors or publishers for loss, damage or injury caused by any errors in, or omissions from, the information given.

Project vehicles

The main project vehicle used in the preparation of this manual, and appearing in many of the photographic sequences, was a 1993-model Ford Mondeo 2.0 Si Hatchback. Additional work was carried out and photographed on a 1993-model 2.0 Si Saloon and a 1993-model 2.0 Ghia Estate (with automatic transmission).

Introduction to the Ford Mondeo

Introduced in March 1993, the Ford Mondeo models are available in four-door Saloon, five-door Hatchback and five-door Estate configurations. All feature a high standard of equipment, with driver/passenger safety in accidents being a particularly high design priority; all models are fitted with features such as side impact bars in all doors, "anti-submarine" seats combined with "seat belt grabbers" and pre-tensioners, and an airbag fitted to the steering wheel. Vehicle security is enhanced, with an in-built alarm system and engine immobiliser being fitted as standard, as well as double-locking doors with shielded locks, and security-coded audio equipment.

The four-cylinder petrol engine is a new design, available in 1.6, 1.8 and 2.0 litre capacities. It is controlled by a sophisticated engine management system, which combines multi-point sequential fuel injection and distributorless ignition systems with evaporative emissions control, exhaust gas recirculation and a three-way regulated catalytic converter (with a pulse-air system for rapid warm-up) to ensure that the vehicle complies with the most stringent of the emissions control standards currently in force, and yet provides the levels of performance and fuel economy expected.

The transversely-mounted engine drives the front roadwheels through either a five-speed manual transmission with a cable-operated clutch, or through an electronically-controlled four-speed automatic transmission.

The fully-independent suspension is by MacPherson strut on all four roadwheels, located by transverse lower arms at the front, and by transverse and trailing arms at the rear; anti-roll bars are fitted at front and rear. The Estate rear suspension is of a different design, to give maximum loadspace inside the vehicle, with self-levelling suspension units available as an option. On some models, the suspension is electronically-controlled through the Adaptive Damping System.

The steering is power-assisted, the pump being belt-driven from the engine, and the rack-and-pinion steering gear mounted behind the engine.

The vacuum servo-assisted brakes are disc at the front, with drums at the rear on most models; disc rear brakes and an electronically-controlled Anti-lock Braking System (ABS) are available on some models, with a Traction Control System (TCS) available as a further option where ABS is fitted.

General dimensions and weights

Dimensions

Overall length:
Saloon, Hatchback	4481 mm
Estate	4631 mm

Overall width - including mirrors .... 1925 mm

Overall height - at kerb weight:
Saloon, Hatchback	1403 to 1435 mm
Estate	1416 to 1501 mm

Wheelbase .... 2704 mm

Front track - all models .... 1503 mm

Rear track:
Saloon, Hatchback	1486 to 1487 mm
Estate	1504 mm

Turning circle .... 10.9 m

Weights

Kerb weight:
1.6 Saloon, Hatchback models	1215 to 1250 kg
1.6 Estate models	1265 to 1275 kg

1.8 Saloon, Hatchback models:
Manual transmission	1225 to 1260 kg
Automatic transmission	1260 to 1280 kg

1.8 Estate models:
Manual transmission	1275 to 1285 kg
Automatic transmission	1305 kg

2.0 Saloon, Hatchback models:
Manual transmission	1250 to 1310 kg
Automatic transmission	1285 to 1340 kg

2.0 Estate models:
Manual transmission	1295 to 1335 kg
Automatic transmission	1330 to 1415 kg

Maximum gross vehicle weight:

Saloon, Hatchback:
1.6 models	1725 kg
1.8 Saloon models, automatic transmission	1750 kg
2.0 models, automatic transmission	1800 kg
All others	1775 kg

Estate:
1.6 models, 2.0 models with manual transmission	1900 kg
All others	1925 kg

Maximum roof rack load:
Estate models with integral roof rack	100 kg
All others	75 kg

Maximum towing weight .... 1500 kg

Trailer nose weight limit .... 75 kg

Jacking, towing and wheel changing

To change a wheel, remove the spare wheel and jack, apply the handbrake, and chock the wheel diagonally opposite the one to be changed. On manual transmission models, select first or reverse gear; on automatic transmission models, place the selector lever in "P". Make sure that the vehicle is located on firm level ground. Use the flat end of the wheelbrace carefully to remove the trim covering the wheel

nuts, then slightly loosen the wheel nuts with the brace **(see illustrations)**. Locate the jack head in the jacking point nearest to the wheel to be changed, ensuring that the channel in the jack head fits over the body flange **(see illustrations)** and turn its handle to raise the jack. When the wheel is clear of the ground, remove the nuts and lift off the wheel. Fit the spare wheel, and moderately tighten the nuts. Lower the

Use flat end of wheelbrace to remove trim covering roadwheel nuts

Slacken roadwheel nuts in diagonal sequence

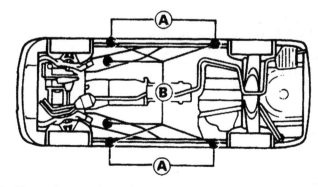

Jacking and supporting points

A   Jacking points (for vehicle jack in roadside use) - support points (for axle stands in servicing/overhaul work)
B   Jacking points (for trolley jack or workshop hoist in servicing/overhaul work) - additional support points

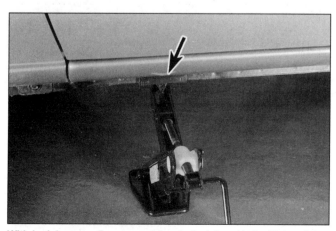

With jack base on firm ground, locate jack head in jacking point - indentations (arrowed) in sill identify jacking points

Tighten roadwheel nuts - preferably to specified torque wrench setting - securely, and in diagonal sequence

Front towing eye

vehicle, then tighten the nuts fully and refit the trim **(see illustration)**. With the spare wheel in position, remove the chock, and stow the jack and tools.

When jacking up the vehicle to carry out repair or maintenance tasks, position the jack as follows.

If the front of the vehicle is to be raised, either place the jack head under the sump, with a block of wood to prevent damage, or place a jacking beam across the two front points "B" shown in the accompanying illustration, and lift the vehicle evenly.

To raise the rear of the vehicle, place a jacking beam across the two rear points "B" shown in the accompanying illustration, and lift the vehicle evenly.

To raise the side of the vehicle, place the jack head under the appropriate point indicated in the accompanying illustration - if a trolley jack or similar is used on the points "A" provided for the vehicle's jack, make up a wooden spacer with a groove cut in it to accept the under-body flange, so that there is no risk of the jack slipping or buckling the flange. Never work under, around or near a raised vehicle unless it is adequately supported in at least two places with axle stands or suitable sturdy blocks.

The vehicle may be towed, for breakdown recovery purposes only, using the towing eyes positioned at the front and rear of the vehicle **(see illustrations)**. These eyes are intended for towing loads only, and must not be used for lifting the vehicle, either directly or indirectly.

If the vehicle is equipped with automatic transmission, the following precautions must be observed if the vehicle is to be towed, particularly if any kind of transmission fault is suspected. Preferably, a front-

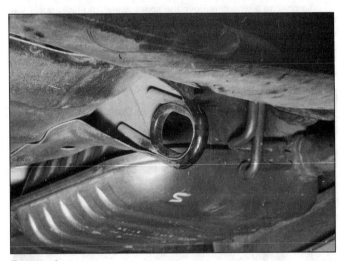

Rear towing eye

end-suspended tow should be used (ie with the front wheels off the ground). If this is not possible, place the selector lever in "N" and tow the vehicle - forwards only, never backwards - for a distance of no more than 30 miles (50 km), and at speeds no greater than 30 mph (50 km/h).

Buying spare parts and vehicle identification numbers

Buying spare parts

Spare parts are available from many sources; for example, Ford garages, other garages and accessory shops, and motor factors. Our advice regarding spare part sources is as follows.

Officially-appointed Ford garages - This is the best source for parts which are peculiar to your vehicle, and which are not generally available (eg complete cylinder heads, internal transmission components, badges, interior trim etc). It is also the only place at which you should buy parts if the vehicle is still under warranty. To be sure of obtaining the correct parts, it will be necessary to give the storeman the full Vehicle Identification Number, and if possible, to take the old parts along for positive identification. Many parts are available under a factory exchange scheme - any parts returned should always be clean. It obviously makes good sense to go straight to the specialists on your vehicle for this type of part, as they are best equipped to supply you.

Other garages and accessory shops - These are often very good places to buy materials and components needed for the maintenance of your vehicle (eg oil filters, spark plugs, bulbs, drivebelts, oils and greases, touch-up paint, filler paste, etc). They also sell general accessories, usually have convenient opening hours, charge lower prices, and can often be found not far from home.

Motor factors - Good factors will stock all the more important components which wear out comparatively quickly (eg exhaust systems, brake pads, seals and hydraulic parts, clutch components, bearing shells, pistons, valves etc). Motor factors will often provide new or reconditioned components on a part-exchange basis - this can save a considerable amount of money.

Vehicle identification numbers

Modifications are a continuing and unpublicised process in vehicle manufacture, quite apart from major model changes. Spare parts manuals and lists are compiled upon a numerical basis, the appropriate identification number or code being essential to correct identification of the component concerned.

When ordering spare parts, always give as much information as possible. Quote the vehicle model, year of manufacture, Vehicle Identification Number and engine numbers, as appropriate.

The *vehicle identification plate* is located on the engine compartment front crossmember **(see illustration)**. In addition to many other details, it carries the Vehicle Identification Number, maximum vehicle weight information, and codes for interior trim and body colours.

The *Vehicle Identification Number* is given on the vehicle identification plate. It is also stamped on the engine compartment bulkhead, behind the air intake plenum chamber, and into the body, so that it can be seen through the bottom left-hand corner of the windscreen **(see illustrations)**.

The *engine number*, consisting of two letters and five digits, with the three-letter engine code nearby, is stamped into a flat-machined surface on the cylinder block/crankcase's forward-facing flange, between the pulse-air filter housing and the transmission. To read the number without removing the engine compartment air intake resonator - see Chapter 4 - it is easiest to raise and support the front of the vehicle on axle stands, so that the number can be seen from underneath **(see illustration)**. If the number cannot be seen in this location, possible alternative sites are on a lower flange on the cylinder block's forward face, immediately above the sump mating surface, or on the left-hand end of the cylinder head, between the oil filler cap and ignition coil.

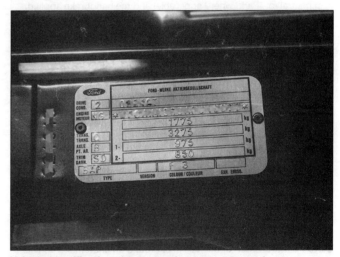

Vehicle identification plate on engine compartment front crossmember

Vehicle identification number on engine compartment bulkhead

Vehicle identification number in body, visible through bottom left-hand corner of windscreen

Engine number (arrowed) on front of cylinder block/crankcase - seen from beneath vehicle

Safety first!

However enthusiastic you may be about getting on with the job in hand, do take the time to ensure that your safety is not put at risk. A moment's lack of attention can result in an accident, as can failure to observe certain elementary precautions. There will always be new ways of having accidents, and the following points do not pretend to be a comprehensive list of all dangers; they are intended rather to make you aware of the risks and to encourage a safety-conscious approach to all work you carry out on your vehicle.

Essential DOs and DON'Ts

DON'T rely on a single jack when working underneath the vehicle. Always use reliable additional means of support, such as axle stands, securely placed under a structural part of the vehicle that you know will not give way.

DON'T attempt to loosen or tighten high-torque nuts (eg wheel hub nuts) while the vehicle is on a jack; it may be pulled off.

DON'T start the engine without first ascertaining that the transmission is in neutral (or 'Park' where applicable) and the handbrake applied.

DON'T suddenly remove the filler cap from a hot cooling system - cover it with a cloth and release the pressure gradually first, or you may get scalded by escaping coolant.

DON'T attempt to drain oil, automatic transmission fluid, or coolant until you are sure it has cooled sufficiently to avoid scalding you.

DON'T grasp any part of the engine, exhaust or catalytic converter without first ascertaining that it is sufficiently cool to avoid burning you.

DON'T allow brake fluid or antifreeze to contact vehicle paintwork.

DON'T syphon toxic liquids such as fuel, brake fluid or antifreeze by mouth, or allow them to remain on your skin.

DON'T inhale dust - it may be injurious to health (see *Asbestos* below).

DON'T allow any spilt oil or grease to remain on the floor - wipe it up straight away, before someone slips on it.

DON'T use ill-fitting spanners or other tools which may slip and cause injury.

DON'T attempt to lift a heavy component which may be beyond your capability - get assistance.

DON'T rush to finish a job, or take unverified short cuts.

DON'T allow children or animals in or around an unattended vehicle.

DON'T park vehicles with catalytic converters over combustible materials such as dry grass, oily rags, etc. if the engine has recently been run. As catalytic converters reach extremely high temperatures, any such materials in close proximity may ignite.

DON'T run vehicles equipped with catalytic converters without the exhaust system heat shields fitted.

DO wear eye protection when using power tools such as an electric drill, sander, bench grinder, etc., and when working under the vehicle.

DO use a barrier cream on your hands prior to undertaking dirty jobs - it will protect your skin from infection as well as making the dirt easier to remove afterwards; but make sure your hands aren't left slippery. Note that long term contact with used engine oil can be a health hazard.

DO keep loose clothing (cuffs, tie etc) and long hair well out of the way of moving mechanical parts.

DO remove rings, wristwatch etc, before working on the vehicle - especially the electrical system.

DO ensure that any lifting tackle or jacking equipment used has a safe working load rating adequate for the job, and is used precisely as recommended by the manufacturer.

DO keep your work area tidy - it is only too easy to fall over articles left lying around.

DO get someone to check periodically that all is well when working alone on the vehicle.

DO carry out work in a logical sequence and check that everything is correctly assembled and tightened afterwards.

DO remember that your vehicle's safety affects that of yourself and others. If in doubt on any point, get specialist advice.

IF, in spite of following these precautions, you are unfortunate enough to injure yourself, seek medical attention as soon as possible.

Asbestos

Certain friction, insulating, sealing, and other products - such as brake linings, brake bands, clutch linings, gaskets, etc - contain asbestos. *Extreme care must be taken to avoid inhalation of dust from such products since it is hazardous to health.* If in doubt, assume that they *do* contain asbestos.

Fire

Remember at all times that petrol is highly flammable. Never smoke, or have any kind of naked flame around, when working on the vehicle. But the risk does not end there - a spark caused by an electrical short-circuit, by two metal surfaces contacting each other, by careless use of tools, or even by static electricity built up in your body under certain conditions, can ignite petrol vapour, which in a confined space is highly explosive. The vapour produced by spilling oil or hydraulic fluid onto hot metal, such as an exhaust manifold, can also be flammable or explosive.

Whenever possible disconnect the battery earth (negative) terminal before working on any part of the fuel or electrical system, and never risk spilling fuel on to a hot engine or exhaust. Catalytic converters run at extremely high temperatures, and consequently can be an additional fire hazard. Observe the precautions outlined elsewhere in this section.

It is recommended that a fire extinguisher of a type suitable for fuel and electrical fires is kept handy in the garage or workplace at all times. Ideally, a suitable extinguisher should also be carried in the vehicle. Never try to extinguish a fuel or electrical fire with water. If a vehicle fire does occur, take note of the remarks below about hydrofluoric acid.

Note: *Any reference to a 'torch' appearing in this manual should always be taken to mean a hand-held battery-operated electric lamp or flashlight. It does NOT mean a welding/gas torch or blowlamp.*

Hydrofluoric acid

Hydrofluoric acid is extremely corrosive. It is formed when certain types of synthetic rubber, which may be found in O-rings, oil seals, brake hydraulic system seals, fuel hoses, etc., are exposed to temperatures above 400°C. The obvious circumstance in which this could happen on a vehicle is in the case of a fire. The rubber does not burn, but changes into a charred or sticky substance which contains the acid. *Once formed, the acid remains dangerous for years. If it gets onto the skin, it may be necessary to amputate the limb concerned.*

When dealing with a vehicle which has suffered a fire, or with components salvaged from such a vehicle, always wear protective gloves, and discard them carefully after use. Bear this in mind if obtaining components from a car breaker.

Fumes

Certain fumes are highly toxic, and can quickly cause unconsciousness and even death if inhaled to any extent, especially if inhalation takes place through a lighted cigarette or pipe. Petrol vapour comes into this category, as do the vapours from certain solvents such as trichloroethylene. Any draining or pouring of such volatile fluids should be done in a well-ventilated area.

When using cleaning fluids and solvents, read the instructions carefully. Never use materials from unmarked containers - they may give off poisonous vapours.

Never run the engine of a motor vehicle in an enclosed space such as a garage. Exhaust fumes contain carbon monoxide, which is extremely poisonous; if you need to run the engine, always do so in the open air, or at least have the rear of the vehicle outside the workplace. Although vehicles fitted with catalytic converters have greatly reduced toxic exhaust emissions, the above precautions should still be observed.

If you are fortunate enough to have the use of an inspection pit, never drain or pour petrol, and never run the engine, while the vehicle is standing over it; the fumes, being heavier than air, will concentrate in the pit, with possibly lethal results.

The battery

Batteries which are sealed for life require special precautions, which are normally outlined on a label attached to the battery. Such precautions are primarily related to situations involving battery charging and jump-starting from another vehicle.

Whatever the type of battery, never cause a spark, or allow a naked light, in close proximity to it. It will normally be giving off a certain amount of hydrogen gas, which is highly explosive.

Whenever possible, disconnect the battery earth (negative) terminal before working on the fuel or electrical systems.

If possible, loosen the filler plugs or cover when charging the battery from an external source. Do not charge at an excessive rate, or the battery may burst. Special care should be taken with the use of high charge-rate boost chargers to prevent the battery from overheating.

Take care when topping-up and when carrying the battery. The acid electrolyte, even when diluted, is very corrosive, and should not be allowed to contact clothing, eyes or skin.

Always wear eye protection when cleaning the battery, to prevent the caustic deposits from entering your eyes.

The vehicle electrical system

Take care when making alterations or repairs to the vehicle wiring. Electrical faults are the commonest cause of vehicle fires. Make sure that any accessories are wired correctly using an appropriately-rated fuse and wire of adequate current-carrying capacity. When possible, avoid the use of 'piggy-back' or self-splicing connectors to power additional electrical equipment from existing feeds; make up a new feed with its own fuse instead.

When considering the current which a new circuit will have to handle, do not overlook the switch, especially when planning to use an existing switch to control additional components - for instance, if spotlights are to be fed via the main lighting switch. For preference, a relay should be used to switch heavy currents. If in doubt, consult an auto electrical specialist.

Any wire which passes through a body panel or bulkhead must be protected from chafing with a grommet or similar device. A wire which is allowed to chafe bare against the bodywork will cause a short-circuit and possibly a fire.

Mains electricity and electrical equipment

When using an electric power tool, inspection light, diagnostic equipment, etc., which works from the mains, always ensure that the appliance is correctly connected to its plug and that, where necessary, it is properly earthed. Do not use such appliances in damp conditions and, again, beware of creating a spark or applying excessive heat in the vicinity of fuel or fuel vapour. Also ensure that the appliances meet the relevant national safety standards.

Ignition HT voltage

A severe electric shock can result from touching certain parts of the ignition system, such as the HT leads, when the engine is running or being cranked, particularly if components are damp or the insulation is defective. Where an electronic ignition system is fitted, the HT voltage is much higher and could prove fatal, especially to wearers of cardiac pacemakers.

Jacking and vehicle support

The jack provided with the vehicle is designed primarily for emergency wheel changing, and its use for servicing and overhaul work on the vehicle is best avoided. Instead, a more substantial workshop jack (trolley jack or similar) should be used. Whichever type is employed, it is essential that additional safety support is provided by means of axle stands designed for this purpose. Never use makeshift means such as wooden blocks or piles of house bricks, as these can easily topple or, in the case of bricks, disintegrate under the weight of the vehicle. Further information on the correct positioning of the jack and axle stands is provided in the 'Jacking, towing and wheel changing' section.

If removal of the wheels is not required, the use of drive-on ramps is recommended. Caution should be exercised to ensure that they are correctly aligned with the wheels, and that the vehicle is not driven too far along them so that it promptly falls off the other ends, or tips the ramps.

General repair procedures

Whenever servicing, repair or overhaul work is carried out on the vehicle or its components, it is necessary to observe the following procedures and instructions. This will assist in carrying out the operation efficiently, and to a professional standard of workmanship.

Joint mating faces and gaskets

When separating components at their mating faces, never insert screwdrivers or similar implements into the joint between the faces in order to prise them apart. This can cause severe damage, which results in oil leaks, coolant leaks, etc upon reassembly. Separation is usually achieved by tapping along the joint with a soft-faced hammer in order to break the seal. However, note that this method may not be suitable where dowels are used for component location.

Where a gasket is used between the mating faces of two components, ensure that it is renewed on reassembly, and fit it dry, unless otherwise stated in the repair procedure. Make sure that the mating faces are clean and dry, with all traces of old gasket removed. When cleaning a joint face, use a tool which is not likely to score or damage the face, and remove any burrs or nicks with an oilstone or fine file.

Make sure that tapped holes are cleaned with a pipe cleaner, and keep them free of jointing compound, if this is being used, unless specifically instructed otherwise.

Ensure that all orifices, channels or pipes are clear, and blow through them, preferably using compressed air. *Wear eye protection when using compressed air!*

Oil seals

Oil seals can be removed by levering them out with a wide flat-bladed screwdriver or similar implement. Alternatively, a number of self-tapping screws may be screwed into the seal, and these used as a purchase for pliers or some similar device in order to pull the seal free.

Whenever an oil seal is removed from its working location, either individually or as part of an assembly, it should be renewed.

The very fine sealing lip of the seal is easily damaged, and will not seal if the surface it contacts is not completely clean and free from scratches, nicks or grooves. If the original sealing surface of the component cannot be restored, and the manufacturer has not made provision for slight relocation of the seal relative to the sealing surface, the component should be renewed.

Protect the lips of the seal from any surface which may damage them in the course of fitting. Use tape or a conical sleeve where possible. Lubricate the seal lips with oil before fitting and, on dual-lipped seals, fill the space between the lips with grease.

Unless otherwise stated, oil seals must be fitted with their sealing lips toward the lubricant to be sealed.

Use a tubular drift or block of wood of the appropriate size to install the seal and, if the seal housing is shouldered, drive the seal down to the shoulder. If the seal housing is unshouldered, the seal should be fitted with its face flush with the housing top face (unless otherwise instructed).

Screw threads and fastenings

Seized nuts, bolts and screws are quite a common occurrence where corrosion has set in, and the use of penetrating oil or releasing fluid will often overcome this problem if the offending item is soaked for a while before attempting to release it. The use of an impact driver may also provide a means of releasing such stubborn fastening devices, when used in conjunction with the appropriate screwdriver bit or socket. If none of these methods works, it may be necessary to resort to the careful application of heat, or the use of a hacksaw or nut splitter device.

Studs are usually removed by locking two nuts together on the threaded part, and then using a spanner on the lower nut to unscrew the stud. Studs or bolts which have broken off below the surface of the component in which they are mounted can sometimes be removed using a proprietary stud extractor (sometimes called "easy-outs"). Always ensure that a blind tapped hole is completely free from oil, grease, water or other fluid before installing the bolt or stud. Failure to do this could cause the housing to crack, due to the hydraulic action of the bolt or stud as it is screwed in.

When tightening a castellated nut to accept a split pin, tighten the nut to the specified torque, where applicable, and then tighten further to the next split pin hole. Never slacken the nut to align the split pin hole, unless stated in the repair procedure.

When checking or retightening a nut or bolt to a specified torque setting, slacken the nut or bolt by a quarter of a turn, and then retighten to the specified setting. However, this should not be attempted where angular tightening has been used.

For some screw fastenings, notably cylinder head bolts or nuts, torque wrench settings are no longer specified for the latter stages of tightening, "angular tightening" being called up instead. Typically, a fairly low torque wrench setting will be applied to the bolts/nuts in the correct sequence, followed by one or more stages of tightening through specified angles.

Locknuts, locktabs and washers

Any fastening which will rotate against a component or housing in the course of tightening should always have a washer between it and the relevant component or housing.

Spring or split washers should always be renewed when they are used to lock a critical component such as a big-end bearing retaining bolt or nut. Locktabs which are folded over to retain a nut or bolt should always be renewed.

Self-locking nuts can be reused in non-critical areas, providing resistance can be felt when the locking portion passes over the bolt or stud thread. However, it should be noted that self-locking stiffnuts tend to lose their effectiveness after long periods of use, and in such cases should be renewed as a matter of course.

Split pins must always be replaced with new ones of the correct size for the hole.

When thread-locking compound is found on the threads of a fastener which is to be re-used, it should be cleaned off with a wire brush and solvent, and fresh compound applied on reassembly.

Special tools

Some repair procedures in this manual entail the use of special tools such as a press, two- or three-legged pullers, spring compressors etc. Wherever possible, suitable readily-available alternatives to the manufacturer's special tools are described, and are shown in use. In some instances, where no alternative is possible, it has been necessary to resort to the use of a manufacturer's tool, and this has been done for reasons of safety, as well as the efficient completion of the repair operation. Unless you are highly skilled and have a thorough understanding of the procedures described, never attempt to bypass the use of any special tool when the procedure described specifies its use. Not only is there a very great risk of personal injury, but expensive damage could be caused to the components involved.

Environmental considerations

When disposing of used engine oil, brake fluid, antifreeze etc, give due consideration to any detrimental environmental effects. Do not, for instance, pour any of the above liquids down drains into the general sewage system, or onto the ground to soak away. Many local council refuse tips provide a facility for waste oil disposal, as do some garages. If none of these facilities are available, consult your local Environmental Health Department for further advice.

With the universal tightening-up of legislation regarding the emission of environmentally-harmful substances from motor vehicles, most current vehicles have tamperproof devices fitted to the main adjustment points of the fuel system. These devices are primarily designed to prevent unqualified persons from adjusting the fuel/air mixture with the chance of a consequent increase in toxic emissions. If such devices are encountered during servicing or overhaul, they should, wherever possible, be renewed or refitted in accordance with the vehicle manufacturer's requirements or current legislation. Owners taking their vehicles abroad should note that some countries have strict legislation relating to vehicles driven without these tamperproofing measures in place!

Tools and working facilities

Introduction

A selection of good tools is a fundamental requirement for anyone contemplating the maintenance and repair of a motor vehicle. For the owner who does not possess any, their purchase will prove a considerable expense, offsetting some of the savings made by doing-it-yourself. However, provided that the tools purchased meet the relevant national safety standards and are of good quality, they will last for many years and prove an extremely worthwhile investment.

To help the average owner to decide which tools are needed to carry out the various tasks detailed in this manual, we have compiled three lists of tools under the following headings: *Maintenance and minor repair, Repair and overhaul*, and *Special*. Newcomers to practical mechanics should start off with the *Maintenance and minor repair* tool kit, and confine themselves to the simpler jobs around the vehicle. Then, as confidence and experience grow, more difficult tasks can be undertaken, with extra tools being purchased as, and when, they are needed. In this way, a *Maintenance and minor repair* tool kit can be built up into a *Repair and overhaul* tool kit over a considerable period of time, without any major cash outlays. The experienced do-it-yourselfer will have a tool kit good enough for most repair and overhaul procedures, and will add tools from the *Special* category when it is felt that the expense is justified by the amount of use to which these tools will be put.

Maintenance and minor repair tool kit

The tools given in this list should be considered as a minimum requirement if routine maintenance, servicing and minor repair operations are to be undertaken. We recommend the purchase of combination spanners (ring one end, open-ended the other); although more expensive than open-ended ones, they do give the advantages of both types of spanner.

Combination spanners:
  Metric - 8, 9, 10, 11, 12, 13, 14, 15, 17 & 19 mm
Adjustable spanner - 35 mm jaw (approx)
Transmission drain plug key (Allen type)
Spark plug spanner (with rubber insert)

Spark plug gap adjustment tool
Set of feeler gauges
Brake adjuster spanner (where applicable)
Brake bleed nipple spanner
Screwdrivers:
  Flat-bladed - approx 100 mm long x 6 mm dia
  Cross-bladed - approx 100 mm long x 6 mm dia
Combination pliers
Hacksaw (junior)
Tyre pump
Tyre pressure gauge
Oil can
Oil filter removal tool
Fine emery cloth
Wire brush (small)
Funnel (medium size)

Repair and overhaul tool kit

These tools are virtually essential for anyone undertaking any major repairs to a motor vehicle, and are additional to those given in the *Maintenance and minor repair* list. Included in this list is a comprehensive set of sockets. Although these are expensive, they will be found invaluable as they are so versatile - particularly if various drives are included in the set. We recommend the 1/2 in square-drive type, as this can be used with most proprietary torque wrenches. If you cannot afford a socket set, even bought piecemeal, then inexpensive tubular box spanners are a useful alternative.

The tools in this list will occasionally need to be supplemented by tools from the *Special* list.

Sockets (or box spanners) to cover range in previous list
Reversible ratchet drive (for use with sockets) **(see illustration)**
Extension piece, 250 mm (for use with sockets)
Universal joint (for use with sockets)
Torque wrench (for use with sockets)
Self-locking grips
Ball pein hammer
Soft-faced mallet (plastic/aluminium or rubber)

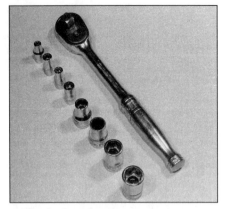

Sockets and reversible ratchet drive

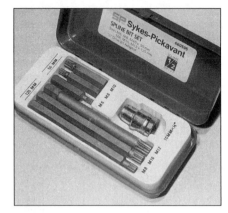

Spline bit set

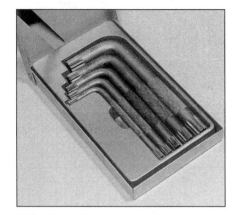

Spline key set

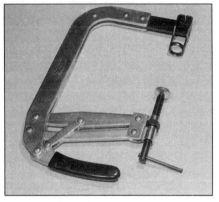

Valve spring compressor

Piston ring compressor

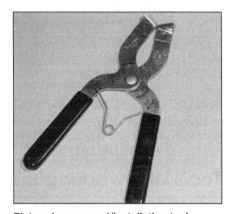

Piston ring removal/installation tool

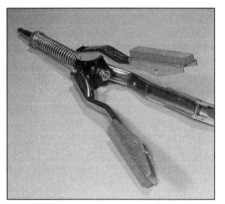

Cylinder bore hone

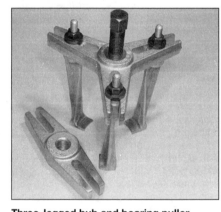

Three-legged hub and bearing puller

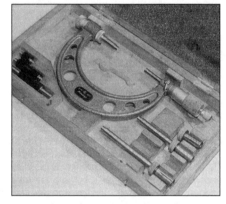

Micrometer set

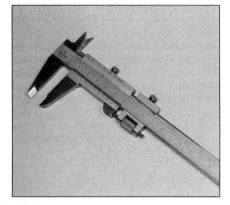

Vernier calipers

Dial test indicator and magnetic stand

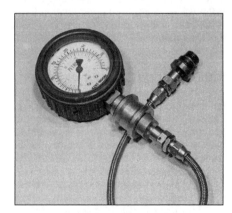

Compression testing gauge

Screwdrivers:
> *Flat-bladed - long & sturdy, short (chubby), and narrow (electrician's) types*
> *Cross-bladed - Long & sturdy, and short (chubby) types*

Pliers:
> *Long-nosed*
> *Side cutters (electrician's)*
> *Circlip (internal and external)*

Cold chisel - 25 mm
Scriber
Scraper
Centre-punch
Pin punch
Hacksaw
Brake hose clamp
Brake/clutch bleeding kit
Selection of twist drills
Steel rule/straight-edge
Allen keys (inc. splined/Torx type) **(see illustrations)**
Selection of files
Wire brush
Axle stands
Jack (strong trolley or hydraulic type)
Light with extension lead

Special tools

The tools in this list are those which are not used regularly, are expensive to buy, or which need to be used in accordance with their manufacturers' instructions. Unless relatively difficult mechanical jobs are undertaken frequently, it will not be economic to buy many of these tools. Where this is the case, you could consider clubbing together with friends (or joining a motorists' club) to make a joint purchase, or borrowing the tools against a deposit from a local garage or tool hire specialist. It is worth noting that many of the larger d-i-y superstores now carry a large range of special tools for hire at modest rates.

The following list contains only those tools and instruments freely available to the public, and not those special tools produced by the vehicle manufacturer specifically for its dealer network. You will find occasional references to these manufacturer's special tools in the text of this manual. Generally, an alternative method of doing the job without the vehicle manufacturer's special tool is given. However, sometimes there is no alternative to using them. Where this is the case and the relevant tool cannot be bought or borrowed, you will have to entrust the work to a franchised garage.

Valve spring compressor **(see illustration)**
Valve grinding tool
Piston ring compressor **(see illustration)**
Piston ring removal/installation tool **(see illustration)**
Cylinder bore hone **(see illustration)**
Balljoint separator
Coil spring compressors (where applicable)
Two-/three-legged hub and bearing puller **(see illustration)**
Impact screwdriver
Micrometer and/or vernier calipers **(see illustrations)**
Dial gauge/dial test indicator **(see illustration)**
Universal electrical multi-meter
Cylinder compression gauge **(see illustration)**
Hand-operated vacuum pump and gauge **(see illustration)**
Clutch plate alignment set **(see illustration)**
Brake shoe steady spring cup removal tool **(see illustration)**
Bush and bearing removal/installation set **(see illustration)**
Stud extractors **(see illustration)**
Tap and die set **(see illustration)**
Lifting tackle
Trolley jack

Vacuum pump and gauge

Clutch plate alignment set

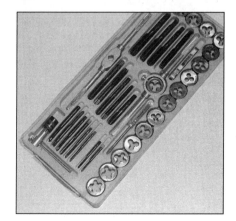

Brake shoe steady spring cup removal tool

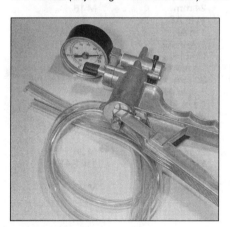

Bush and bearing removal/installation set

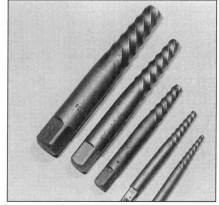

Stud extractor set

Tap and die set

Buying tools

For practically all tools, a tool factor is the best source, since he will have a very comprehensive range compared with the average garage or accessory shop. Having said that, accessory shops often offer excellent quality tools at discount prices, so it pays to shop around.

Remember, you don't have to buy the most expensive items on the shelf, but it is always advisable to steer clear of the very cheap tools. There are plenty of good tools around at reasonable prices, but always aim to purchase items which meet the relevant national safety standards. If in doubt, ask the proprietor or manager of the shop for advice before making a purchase.

Care and maintenance of tools

Having purchased a reasonable tool kit, it is necessary to keep the tools in a clean and serviceable condition. After use, always wipe off any dirt, grease and metal particles using a clean, dry cloth, before putting the tools away. Never leave them lying around after they have been used. A simple tool rack on the garage or workshop wall, for items such as screwdrivers and pliers, is a good idea. Store all normal spanners and sockets in a metal box. Any measuring instruments, gauges, meters, etc, must be carefully stored, somewhere they cannot be damaged or become rusty.

Take a little care when tools are used. Hammer heads inevitably become marked, and screwdrivers lose the keen edge on their blades from time to time. A little timely attention with emery cloth or a file will soon restore items like this to a good serviceable finish.

Working facilities

Not to be forgotten when discussing tools is the workshop itself. If anything more than routine maintenance is to be carried out, some form of suitable working area becomes essential.

It is appreciated that many an owner-mechanic is forced by circumstances to remove an engine or similar item without the benefit of a garage or workshop. Having done this, however, any repairs should always be done under the cover of a roof.

Wherever possible, any dismantling should be done on a clean, flat workbench or table at a suitable working height.

Any workbench needs a vice; one with a jaw opening of 100 mm (4 in) is suitable for most jobs. As mentioned previously, some clean dry storage space is also required for tools, as well as for any lubricants, cleaning fluids, touch-up paints and so on, which become necessary.

Another item which may be required, and which has a much more general usage, is an electric drill with a chuck capacity of at least 8 mm (5/16 in). This, together with a good range of twist drills, is virtually essential for fitting accessories.

Last, but not least, always keep a supply of old newspapers and clean, lint-free rags available, and try to keep any working area as clean as possible.

Spanner jaw gap and bolt size comparison table

Jaw gap – in (mm)	Spanner size	Bolt size
0.197 (5.00)	5 mm	M 2.5
0.216 (5.50)	5.5 mm	M 3
0.218 (5.53)	$\frac{7}{32}$ in AF	
0.236 (6.00)	6 mm	M 3.5
0.250 (6.35)	$\frac{1}{4}$ in AF	
0.275 (7.00)	7 mm	M 4
0.281 (7.14)	$\frac{9}{32}$ in AF	
0.312 (7.92)	$\frac{5}{16}$ in AF	
0.315 (8.00)	8 mm	M 5
0.343 (8.71)	$\frac{11}{32}$ in AF	
0.375 (9.52)	$\frac{3}{8}$ in AF	
0.394 (10.00)	10 mm	M 6
0.406 (10.32)	$\frac{13}{32}$ in AF	
0.433 (11.00)	11 mm	M 7
0.437 (11.09)	$\frac{7}{16}$ in AF	$\frac{1}{4}$ in SAE
0.468 (11.88)	$\frac{15}{32}$ in AF	
0.500 (12.70)	$\frac{1}{2}$ in AF	$\frac{5}{16}$ in SAE
0.512 (13.00)	13 mm	M8
0.562 (14.27)	$\frac{9}{16}$ in AF	$\frac{3}{8}$ in SAE
0.593 (15.06)	$\frac{19}{32}$ in AF	
0.625 (15.87)	$\frac{5}{8}$ in AF	$\frac{7}{16}$ in SAE
0.669 (17.00)	17 mm	M 10
0.687 (17.44)	$\frac{11}{16}$ in AF	
0.709 (19.00)	19 mm	M 12
0.750 (19.05)	$\frac{3}{4}$ in AF	$\frac{1}{2}$ in SAE
0.781 (19.83)	$\frac{25}{32}$ in AF	
0.812 (20.62)	$\frac{13}{16}$ in AF	
0.866 (22.00)	22 mm	M 14
0.875 (22.25)	$\frac{7}{8}$ in AF	$\frac{9}{16}$ in SAE
0.937 (23.79)	$\frac{15}{16}$ in AF	$\frac{5}{8}$ in SAE
0.945 (24.00)	24 mm	M 16
0.968 (24.58)	$\frac{31}{32}$ in AF	
1.000 (25.40)	1 in AF	$\frac{11}{16}$ in SAE
1.062 (26.97)	1 $\frac{1}{16}$ in AF	$\frac{3}{4}$ in SAE
1.063 (27.00)	27 mm	M 18
1.125 (28.57)	1 $\frac{1}{8}$ in AF	
1.182 (30.00)	30 mm	M 20
1.187 (30.14)	1 $\frac{3}{16}$ in AF	
1.250 (31.75)	1 $\frac{1}{4}$ in AF	$\frac{7}{8}$ in SAE
1.260 (32.00)	32 mm	M 22
1.312 (33.32)	1 $\frac{5}{16}$ in AF	
1.375 (34.92)	1 $\frac{3}{8}$ in AF	
1.418 (36.00)	36 mm	M 24
1.437 (36.49)	1 $\frac{7}{16}$ in AF	1 in SAE
1.500 (38.10)	1 $\frac{1}{2}$ in AF	
1.615 (41.00)	41 mm	M 27

Booster battery (jump) starting

When jump starting a vehicle using a booster battery, observe the following precautions:

(a)   Before connecting the booster battery, make sure that the ignition is switched off.

(b)   Ensure that all electrical equipment (lights, heater, wipers etc) is switched off.

(c)   Make sure that the booster battery is the same voltage as the discharged one in the vehicle.

(d)   If the battery is being jump-started from the battery in another vehicle, the two vehicles MUST NOT TOUCH each other.

(e)   Make sure that the transmission is in Neutral (manual transmission) or Park (automatic transmission).

Connect one jump lead between the positive (+) terminals of the two batteries. Connect the other jump lead first to the negative (-) terminal of the booster battery, and then to a good earthing point on the vehicle to be started, such as a bolt or bracket on the engine block, at least 45 cm (18 in) from the battery if possible. Make sure that the jump leads will not come into contact with the fan, drivebelt or other moving parts of the engine.

Start the engine using the booster battery, then with the engine running at idle speed, switch on the heater blower motor (to position 4/High) and heated rear window to reduce voltage peaks. (Do not switch on the headlights in place of the rear window heater - a high peak could blow the bulbs.) Disconnect the jump leads in the reverse order of connection.

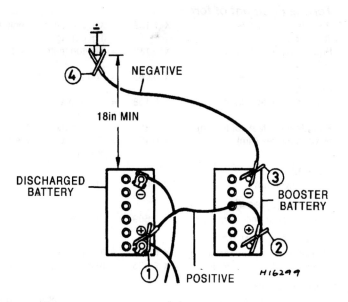

Jump start lead connections for negative-earth vehicles - connect leads in order shown

Conversion factors

Length (distance)

Inches (in)	25.4	= Millimetres (mm)	X 0.0394	= Inches (in)
Feet (ft)	0.305	= Metres (m)	X 3.281	= Feet (ft)
Miles	1.609	= Kilometres (km)	X 0.621	= Miles

Volume (capacity)

Cubic inches (cu in; in³)	X 16.387	= Cubic centimetres (cc; cm³)	X 0.061	= Cubic inches (cu in; in³)
Imperial pints (Imp pt)	X 0.568	= Litres (l)	X 1.76	= Imperial pints (Imp pt)
Imperial quarts (Imp qt)	X 1.137	= Litres (l)	X 0.88	= Imperial quarts (Imp qt)
Imperial quarts (Imp qt)	X 1.201	= US quarts (US qt)	X 0.833	= Imperial quarts (Imp qt)
US quarts (US qt)	X 0.946	= Litres (l)	X 1.057	= US quarts (US qt)
Imperial gallons (Imp gal)	X 4.546	= Litres (l)	X 0.22	= Imperial gallons (Imp gal)
Imperial gallons (Imp gal)	X 1.201	= US gallons (US gal)	X 0.833	= Imperial gallons (Imp gal)
US gallons (US gal)	X 3.785	= Litres (l)	X 0.264	= US gallons (US gal)

Mass (weight)

Ounces (oz)	X 28.35	= Grams (g)	X 0.035	= Ounces (oz)
Pounds (lb)	X 0.454	= Kilograms (kg)	X 2.205	= Pounds (lb)

Force

Ounces-force (ozf; oz)	X 0.278	= Newtons (N)	X 3.6	= Ounces-force (ozf; oz)
Pounds-force (lbf; lb)	X 4.448	= Newtons (N)	X 0.225	= Pounds-force (lbf; lb)
Newtons (N)	X 0.1	= Kilograms-force (kgf; kg)	X 9.81	= Newtons (N)

Pressure

Pounds-force per square inch (psi; lbf/in²; lb/in²)	X 0.070	= Kilograms-force per square centimetre (kgf/cm²; kg/cm²)	X 14.223	= Pounds-force per square inch (psi; lbf/in²; lb/in²)
Pounds-force per square inch (psi; lbf/in²; lb/in²)	X 0.068	= Atmospheres (atm)	X 14.696	= Pounds-force per square inch (psi; lbf/in²; lb/in²)
Pounds-force per square inch (psi; lbf/in²; lb/in²)	X 0.069	= Bars	X 14.5	= Pounds-force per square inch (psi; lbf/in²; lb/in²)
Pounds-force per square inch (psi; lbf/in²; lb/in²)	X 6.895	= Kilopascals (kPa)	X 0.145	= Pounds-force per square inch (psi; lbf/in²; lb/in²)
Kilopascals (kPa)	X 0.01	= Kilograms-force per square centimetre (kgf/cm²; kg/cm²)	X 98.1	= Kilopascals (kPa)
Millibar (mbar)	X 100	= Pascals (Pa)	X 0.01	= Millibar (mbar)
Millibar (mbar)	X 0.0145	= Pounds-force per square inch (psi; lbf/in²; lb/in²)	X 68.947	= Millibar (mbar)
Millibar (mbar)	X 0.75	= Millimetres of mercury (mmHg)	X 1.333	= Millibar (mbar)
Millibar (mbar)	X 0.401	= Inches of water (inH₂O)	X 2.491	= Millibar (mbar)
Millimetres of mercury (mmHg)	X 0.535	= Inches of water (inH₂O)	X 1.868	= Millimetres of mercury (mmHg)
Inches of water (inH₂O)	X 0.036	= Pounds-force per square inch (psi; lbf/in²; lb/in²)	X 27.68	= Inches of water (inH₂O)

Torque (moment of force)

Pounds-force inches (lbf in; lb in)	X 1.152	= Kilograms-force centimetre (kgf cm; kg cm)	X 0.868	= Pounds-force inches (lbf in; lb in)
Pounds-force inches (lbf in; lb in)	X 0.113	= Newton metres (Nm)	X 8.85	= Pounds-force inches (lbf in; lb in)
Pounds-force inches (lbf in; lb in)	X 0.083	= Pounds-force feet (lbf ft; lb ft)	X 12	= Pounds-force inches (lbf in; lb in)
Pounds-force feet (lbf ft; lb ft)	X 0.138	= Kilograms-force metres (kgf m; kg m)	X 7.233	= Pounds-force feet (lbf ft; lb ft)
Pounds-force feet (lbf ft; lb ft)	X 1.356	= Newton metres (Nm)	X 0.738	= Pounds-force feet (lbf ft; lb ft)
Newton metres (Nm)	X 0.102	= Kilograms-force metres (kgf m; kg m)	X 9.804	= Newton metres (Nm)

Power

Horsepower (hp)	X 745.7	= Watts (W)	X 0.0013	= Horsepower (hp)

Velocity (speed)

Miles per hour (miles/hr; mph)	X 1.609	= Kilometres per hour (km/hr; kph)	X 0.621	= Miles per hour (miles/hr; mph)

Fuel consumption*

Miles per gallon, Imperial (mpg)	X 0.354	= Kilometres per litre (km/l)	X 2.825	= Miles per gallon, Imperial (mpg)
Miles per gallon, US (mpg)	X 0.425	= Kilometres per litre (km/l)	X 2.352	= Miles per gallon, US (mpg)

Temperature

Degrees Fahrenheit = (°C x 1.8) + 32   Degrees Celsius (Degrees Centigrade; °C) = (°F - 32) x 0.56

It is common practice to convert from miles per gallon (mpg) to litres/100 kilometres (l/100km), where mpg (Imperial) x l/100 km = 282 and mpg (US) x l/100 km = 235

Fault diagnosis

Contents

Introduction

The vehicle owner who does his or her own maintenance according to the recommended service schedules should not have to use this section of the manual very often. Modern component reliability is such that, provided those items subject to wear or deterioration are inspected or renewed at the specified intervals, sudden failure is comparatively rare. Faults do not usually just happen as a result of sudden failure, but develop over a period of time. Major mechanical failures in particular are usually preceded by characteristic symptoms over hundreds or even thousands of miles. Those components which do occasionally fail without warning are often small and easily carried in the vehicle.

With any fault-finding, the first step is to decide where to begin investigations. Sometimes this is obvious, but on other occasions, a little detective work will be necessary. The owner who makes half a dozen haphazard adjustments or replacements may be successful in curing a fault (or its symptoms), but will be none the wiser if the fault recurs, and ultimately may have spent more time and money than was necessary. A calm and logical approach will be found to be more satisfactory in the long run. Always take into account any warning signs or abnormalities that may have been noticed in the period preceding the fault - power loss, high or low gauge readings, unusual smells, etc - and remember that failure of components such as fuses or spark plugs may only be pointers to some underlying fault.

The pages which follow provide an easy reference guide to the more common problems which may occur during the operation of the vehicle. These problems and their possible causes are grouped under headings denoting various components or systems, such as Engine, Cooling system, etc. The Chapter and/or Section which deals with the problem is also shown in brackets. Whatever the fault, certain basic principles apply. These are as follows:

Verify the fault. This is simply a matter of being sure that you know what the symptoms are before starting work. This is particularly important if you are investigating a fault for someone else, who may not have described it very accurately.

Don't overlook the obvious. For example, if the vehicle won't start, is there petrol in the tank? (Don't take anyone else's word on this particular point, and don't trust the fuel gauge either!) If an electrical fault is indicated, look for loose or broken wires before digging out the test gear.

Cure the disease, not the symptom. Substituting a flat battery with a fully-charged one will get you off the hard shoulder, but if the underlying cause is not attended to, the new battery will go the same way. Similarly, changing oil-fouled spark plugs for a new set will get you moving again, but remember that the reason for the fouling (if it wasn't simply an incorrect grade of plug) will have to be established and corrected.

Don't take anything for granted. Particularly, don't forget that a "new" component may itself be defective (especially if it's been rattling around in the boot for months), and don't leave components out of a fault diagnosis sequence just because they are new or recently fitted. When you do finally diagnose a difficult fault, you'll probably realise that all the evidence was there from the start.

1   Engine

Engine fails to rotate when attempting to start

- Battery terminal connections loose or corroded (Chapter 5).
- Battery discharged or faulty (Chapter 5).
- Broken, loose or disconnected wiring in the starting circuit (Chapter 5).
- Defective starter solenoid or switch (Chapter 5).
- Defective starter motor (Chapter 5).
- Starter pinion or flywheel ring gear teeth loose or broken (Chapter 5).
- Engine earth strap broken or disconnected (Chapter 5).
- Automatic transmission not in Park/Neutral position, or selector lever position sensor faulty (Chapter 7, Part B)

Engine rotates but will not start

- Fuel tank empty.
- Battery discharged (engine rotates slowly) (Chapter 5).
- Battery terminal connections loose or corroded (Chapter 5).
- Ignition components damp or damaged (Chapters 1 and 5).
- Broken, loose or disconnected wiring in the ignition circuit (Chapters 1 and 5).
- Worn, faulty or incorrectly-gapped spark plugs (Chapter 1).
- Major mechanical failure (eg camshaft drive) (Chapter 2, Part A).

Engine difficult to start when cold

- Battery discharged (Chapter 5).
- Battery terminal connections loose or corroded (Chapter 5).

- Worn, faulty or incorrectly-gapped spark plugs (Chapter 1).
- Other ignition system fault (Chapters 1 and 5).
- Engine management system fault (Chapters 1, 4, 5 and 6).
- Low cylinder compressions (Chapter 2, Part A).

Engine difficult to start when hot

- Air filter element dirty or clogged (Chapter 1).
- Engine management system fault (Chapters 1, 4, 5 and 6)
- Low cylinder compressions (Chapter 2, Part A).
- Faulty hydraulic tappet(s) (Chapter 2, Part A).

Starter motor noisy or excessively-rough in engagement

- Starter pinion or flywheel ring gear teeth loose or broken (Chapter 5).
- Starter motor mounting bolts loose or missing (Chapter 5).
- Starter motor internal components worn or damaged (Chapter 5).

Engine starts but stops immediately

- Loose or faulty electrical connections in the ignition circuit (Chapters 1 and 5).
- Engine management system fault (Chapters 1, 4, 5 and 6).
- Vacuum leak at the inlet manifold (Chapters 1, 4 and 6).

Engine idles erratically

- Idle speed control valve faulty (Chapter 4).
- Engine management system fault (Chapters 1, 4, 5 and 6)
- Air filter element clogged (Chapter 1).
- Vacuum leak at the inlet manifold or associated hoses (Chapters 1, 4 and 6).
- Worn, faulty or incorrectly-gapped spark plugs (Chapter 1).
- Faulty hydraulic tappet(s) (Chapter 2, Part A).
- Uneven or low cylinder compressions (Chapter 2, Part A).
- Camshaft lobes worn (Chapter 2).
- Timing belt incorrectly-tensioned (Chapter 2, Part A).

Engine misfires at idle speed

- Worn, faulty or incorrectly-gapped spark plugs (Chapter 1).
- Faulty spark plug HT leads (Chapter 1).
- Idle speed control valve faulty (Chapter 4).
- Incorrect ignition timing (Chapters 5 and 6).
- Engine management system fault (Chapters 1, 4, 5 and 6)
- Vacuum leak at the inlet manifold or associated hoses (Chapters 1, 4 and 6).
- Faulty hydraulic tappet(s) (Chapter 2, Part A).
- Uneven or low cylinder compressions (Chapter 2, Part A).
- Disconnected, leaking or perished crankcase ventilation hoses (Chapters 1 and 6).

Engine misfires throughout the driving speed range

- Fuel filter choked (Chapter 1).
- Fuel pump faulty or delivery pressure low (Chapter 4).
- Fuel tank vent blocked or fuel pipes restricted (Chapter 4).
- Vacuum leak at the inlet manifold or associated hoses (Chapters 1, 4 and 6).
- Worn, faulty or incorrectly-gapped spark plugs (Chapter 1).
- Faulty spark plug HT leads (Chapter 1).
- Faulty ignition coil (Chapter 5).
- Engine management system fault (Chapters 1, 4, 5 and 6)
- Uneven or low cylinder compressions (Chapter 2, Part A).

Engine hesitates on acceleration

- Worn, faulty or incorrectly-gapped spark plugs (Chapter 1).
- Engine management system fault (Chapters 1, 4, 5 and 6).
- Vacuum leak at the inlet manifold or associated hoses (Chapters 1, 4 and 6).

Engine stalls

- Idle speed control valve faulty (Chapter 4).
- Engine management system fault (Chapters 1, 4, 5 and 6).
- Vacuum leak at the inlet manifold or associated hoses (Chapters 1, 4 and 6).
- Fuel filter choked (Chapter 1).
- Fuel pump faulty or delivery pressure low (Chapter 4).
- Fuel tank vent blocked or fuel pipes restricted (Chapter 4).

Engine lacks power

- Incorrect ignition timing (Chapters 5 and 6).
- Engine management system fault (Chapters 1, 4, 5 and 6).
- Timing belt incorrectly fitted or incorrectly tensioned (Chapter 2, Part A).
- Fuel filter choked (Chapter 1).
- Fuel pump faulty or delivery pressure low (Chapter 4).
- Uneven or low cylinder compressions (Chapter 2, Part A).
- Worn, faulty or incorrectly-gapped spark plugs (Chapter 1).
- Vacuum leak at the inlet manifold or associated hoses (Chapters 1, 4 and 6).
- Brakes binding (Chapters 1 and 9).
- Clutch slipping (Chapter 8).
- Automatic transmission fluid level incorrect (Chapter 1).

Engine backfires

- Ignition timing incorrect (Chapters 5 and 6).
- Engine management system fault (Chapters 1, 4, 5 and 6).
- Timing belt incorrectly fitted or incorrectly tensioned (Chapter 2, Part A).
- Vacuum leak at the inlet manifold or associated hoses (Chapters 1, 4 and 6).

Oil pressure warning light illuminated with engine running

- Low oil level or incorrect oil grade (Chapter 1).
- Faulty oil pressure warning light switch (Chapter 2, Part A).
- Worn engine bearings and/or oil pump (Chapter 2).
- High engine operating temperature (Chapter 3).
- Oil pressure relief valve defective (Chapter 2, Part A).
- Oil pick-up strainer clogged (Chapter 2, Part A).

Engine runs-on after switching off

- Idle speed excessively high (Chapters 4 and 6).
- Engine management system fault (Chapters 1, 4, 5 and 6).
- Excessive carbon build-up in engine (Chapter 2, Part A).
- High engine operating temperature (Chapter 3).

Engine noises

Pre-ignition (pinking) or knocking during acceleration or under load

- Ignition timing incorrect (Chapters 5 and 6).
- Incorrect grade of fuel (Chapter 4).
- Vacuum leak at the inlet manifold or associated hoses (Chapters 1, 4 and 6).
- Excessive carbon build-up in engine (Chapter 2, Part A).

Whistling or wheezing noises

- Leaking inlet manifold gasket (Chapter 2, Part A).
- Leaking exhaust manifold gasket or downpipe-to-manifold joint (Chapters 1, 2 Part A, and 4).
- Leaking vacuum hose (Chapters 1, 4, 6 and 9).
- Blowing cylinder head gasket (Chapter 2, Part A).

Tapping or rattling noises

- Faulty hydraulic tappet(s) (Chapter 2, Part A).
- Worn valve gear or camshaft (Chapter 2, Part A).
- Worn timing belt or tensioner (Chapter 2, Part A).
- Ancillary component fault (water pump, alternator, etc) (Chapters 3 and 5).

Knocking or thumping noises

- Worn big-end bearings (regular heavy knocking, perhaps less under load) (Chapter 2, Part B).
- Worn main bearings (rumbling and knocking, perhaps worsening under load) (Chapter 2, Part B).
- Piston slap (most noticeable when cold) (Chapter 2, Part B).
- Ancillary component fault (water pump, alternator, etc) (Chapters 3 and 5).

---

2 Cooling system

Overheating

- Insufficient coolant in system (Chapter 1).
- Thermostat faulty (Chapter 3).
- Radiator core blocked or grille restricted (Chapter 3).
- Radiator electric cooling fan(s) or coolant temperature sensor faulty (Chapter 3).
- Engine management system fault (Chapters 1, 4, 5 and 6).
- Pressure cap faulty (Chapter 3).
- Auxiliary drivebelt worn or slipping (Chapter 1).
- Ignition timing incorrect (Chapters 5 and 6).
- Inaccurate coolant temperature gauge sender (Chapter 3).
- Air-lock in cooling system (Chapter 1).

Overcooling

- Thermostat faulty (Chapter 3).
- Inaccurate coolant temperature gauge sender (Chapter 3).

External coolant leakage

- Deteriorated or damaged hoses or hose clips (Chapter 1).
- Radiator core or heater matrix leaking (Chapter 3).
- Pressure cap faulty (Chapter 3).
- Water pump seal leaking (Chapter 3).
- Boiling due to overheating (Chapter 3).
- Core plug leaking (Chapter 2, Part B).

Internal coolant leakage

- Leaking cylinder head gasket (Chapter 2, Part A).
- Cracked cylinder head or cylinder bore (Chapter 2, Part B).

Corrosion

- Infrequent draining and flushing (Chapter 1).
- Incorrect antifreeze mixture, or inappropriate antifreeze type (Chapter 1).

---

3 Fuel and exhaust system

Excessive fuel consumption

- Unsympathetic driving style, or adverse conditions.
- Air filter element dirty or clogged (Chapter 1).
- Engine management system fault (Chapters 1, 4, 5 and 6).
- Ignition timing incorrect (Chapters 5 and 6).
- Tyres under-inflated (Chapter 1).

Fuel leakage and/or fuel odour

- Damaged or corroded fuel tank, pipes or connections (Chapter 1).
- Charcoal canister and/or connecting pipes leaking (Chapter 6).

Excessive noise or fumes from exhaust system

- Leaking exhaust system or manifold joints (Chapters 1, 2 Part A, and 4).
- Leaking, corroded or damaged silencers or pipe (Chapter 1).
- Broken mountings, causing body or suspension contact (Chapters 1 and 4).

4 Clutch

Pedal travels to floor - no pressure or very little resistance

- Broken clutch cable (Chapter 8).
- Incorrect clutch adjustment (Chapter 8).
- Broken clutch release bearing or fork (Chapter 8).
- Broken diaphragm spring in clutch pressure plate (Chapter 8).

Clutch fails to disengage (unable to select gears)

- Incorrect clutch adjustment (Chapter 8).
- Clutch disc sticking on transmission input shaft splines (Chapter 8).
- Clutch disc sticking to flywheel or pressure plate (Chapter 8).
- Faulty pressure plate assembly (Chapter 8).
- Clutch release mechanism worn or incorrectly assembled (Chapter 8).

Clutch slips (engine speed increases with no increase in vehicle speed)

- Incorrect clutch adjustment (Chapter 8).
- Clutch disc linings excessively worn (Chapter 8).
- Clutch disc linings contaminated with oil or grease (Chapter 8).
- Faulty pressure plate or weak diaphragm spring (Chapter 8).

Judder as clutch is engaged

- Clutch disc linings contaminated with oil or grease (Chapter 8).
- Clutch disc linings excessively worn (Chapter 8).
- Clutch cable sticking or frayed (Chapter 8).
- Faulty or distorted pressure plate or diaphragm spring (Chapter 8).
- Worn or loose engine/transmission mountings (Chapter 2, Part A).
- Clutch disc hub or transmission input shaft splines worn (Chapter 8).

Noise when depressing or releasing clutch pedal

- Worn clutch release bearing (Chapter 8).
- Worn or dry clutch pedal bushes (Chapter 8).
- Faulty pressure plate assembly (Chapter 8).
- Pressure plate diaphragm spring broken (Chapter 8).
- Broken clutch disc cushioning springs (Chapter 8).

5 Manual transmission

Noisy in neutral with engine running

- Input shaft bearings worn (noise apparent with clutch pedal released, but not when depressed) (Chapter 7, Part A).*
- Clutch release bearing worn (noise apparent with clutch pedal depressed, possibly less when released) (Chapter 8).

Noisy in one particular gear

- Worn, damaged or chipped gear teeth (Chapter 7, Part A).*

Difficulty engaging gears

- Clutch fault (Chapter 8).
- Worn or damaged gear linkage (Chapter 7, Part A).
- Incorrectly-adjusted gear linkage (Chapter 7, Part A).
- Worn synchroniser assemblies (Chapter 7, Part A).*

Jumps out of gear

- Worn or damaged gear linkage (Chapter 7, Part A).
- Incorrectly-adjusted gear linkage (Chapter 7, Part A).
- Worn synchroniser assemblies (Chapter 7, Part A).*
- Worn selector forks (Chapter 7, Part A).*

Vibration

- Lack of oil (Chapter 1).
- Worn bearings (Chapter 7, Part A).*

Lubricant leaks

- Leaking differential side gear oil seal (Chapter 7, Part A).
- Leaking housing joint (Chapter 7, Part A).*
- Leaking input shaft oil seal (Chapter 7, Part A).*
- Leaking selector shaft oil seal (Chapter 7, Part A).
- Leaking speedometer drive pinion O-ring (Chapter 7, Part A).

Although the corrective action necessary to remedy the symptoms described is beyond the scope of the home mechanic, the above information should be helpful in isolating the cause of the condition, so that the owner can communicate clearly with a professional mechanic.

6 Automatic transmission

Note: *Due to the complexity of the automatic transmission and its electronic control system, it is difficult for the home mechanic to properly diagnose and service this unit. For problems other than the following, the vehicle should be taken to a dealer service department or automatic transmission specialist.*

Fluid leakage

- Automatic transmission fluid is usually deep red in colour. Fluid leaks should not be confused with engine oil, which can easily be blown onto the transmission by airflow.
- To determine the source of a leak, first remove all built-up dirt and grime from the transmission housing and surrounding areas, using a degreasing agent, or by steam-cleaning. Drive the vehicle at low speed, so airflow will not blow the leak far from its source. Raise and support the vehicle, and determine where the leak is coming from. The following are common areas of leakage:

  (a) Housing joints (Chapters 1 and 7, Part B).
  (b) Dipstick tube (Chapters 1 and 7, Part B).
  (c) Transmission-to-fluid cooler pipes/unions (Chapters 3 and 7, Part B).
  (d) Speedometer drive pinion O-ring (Chapter 7, Part B).
  (e) Differential side gear oil seals (Chapter 7, Part B).

Transmission fluid brown, or has burned smell

- Transmission fluid level low, or fluid in need of renewal (Chapter 1).

General gear selection problems

- Chapter 7, Part B, deals with checking and adjusting the selector cable on automatic transmissions. The following are common problems which may be caused by a poorly-adjusted cable:

  (a) Engine starting in gears other than Park or Neutral.
  (b) Indicator on gear selector lever pointing to a gear other than the one actually being used.
  (c) Vehicle moves when in Park or Neutral.
  (d) Poor gear shift quality or erratic gear changes.

  Refer to Chapter 7, Part B for the selector cable adjustment procedure.

Transmission will not downshift (kickdown) with accelerator pedal fully depressed

- Low transmission fluid level (Chapter 1).
- Incorrect selector cable adjustment (Chapter 7, Part B).
- Engine management system fault (Chapters 1, 4, 5 and 6).

Engine will not start in any gear, or starts in gears other than Park or Neutral

- Incorrect selector lever position sensor adjustment (Chapter 7, Part B).
- Incorrect selector cable adjustment (Chapter 7, Part B).

Transmission slips, shifts roughly, is noisy, or has no drive in forward or reverse gears

- There are many probable causes for the above problems, but the home mechanic should be concerned with only one possibility - fluid level. Before taking the vehicle to a dealer or transmission specialist, check the fluid level and condition of the fluid as described in Chapter 1. Correct the fluid level as necessary, or change the fluid if needed. If the problem persists, professional help will be necessary.

7 Driveshafts

Clicking or knocking noise on turns (at slow speed on full-lock)

- Lack of constant velocity joint lubricant (Chapter 8).
- Worn outer constant velocity joint (Chapter 8).

Vibration when accelerating or decelerating

- Worn inner constant velocity joint (Chapter 8).
- Bent or distorted driveshaft (Chapter 8).

8 Braking system

Note: *Before assuming that a brake problem exists, make sure that the tyres are in good condition and correctly inflated, that the front wheel alignment is correct, and that the vehicle is not loaded with weight in an unequal manner. Apart from checking the condition of all pipe and hose connections, any faults occurring on the Anti-lock Braking System (ABS) should be referred to a Ford dealer for diagnosis - the same applies to the components of the Traction Control System (TCS).*

Vehicle pulls to one side under braking

- Worn, defective, damaged or contaminated front or rear brake pads/shoes on one side (Chapter 1).
- Seized or partially-seized front or rear brake caliper/wheel cylinder piston (Chapter 9).
- A mixture of brake pad/shoe lining materials fitted between sides (Chapter 1).
- Brake caliper mounting bolts loose (Chapter 9).
- Rear brake backplate mounting bolts loose (Chapter 9).
- Worn or damaged steering or suspension components (Chapter 10).

Noise (grinding or high-pitched squeal) when brakes applied

- Brake pad or shoe friction lining material worn down to metal backing (Chapter 1).
- Excessive corrosion of brake disc or drum (may be apparent after the vehicle has been standing for some time) (Chapter 1).
- Foreign object (stone chipping, etc) trapped between brake disc and splash shield (Chapter 1).

Excessive brake pedal travel

- Inoperative rear brake self-adjust mechanism (Chapter 9).
- Faulty master cylinder (Chapter 9).
- Air in hydraulic system (Chapter 9).

Brake pedal feels spongy when depressed

- Air in hydraulic system (Chapter 9).
- Deteriorated flexible rubber brake hoses (Chapter 9).
- Master cylinder mounting nuts loose (Chapter 9).
- Faulty master cylinder (Chapter 9).

Excessive brake pedal effort required to stop vehicle

- Faulty vacuum servo unit (Chapter 9).
- Disconnected, damaged or insecure brake servo vacuum hose (Chapter 9).
- Primary or secondary hydraulic circuit failure (Chapter 9).
- Seized brake caliper or wheel cylinder piston(s) (Chapter 9).
- Brake pads or brake shoes incorrectly fitted (Chapter 9).
- Incorrect grade of brake pads or brake shoes fitted (Chapter 1).
- Brake pads or brake shoe linings contaminated (Chapter 1).

Judder felt through brake pedal or steering wheel when braking

- Excessive run-out or distortion of front discs or rear drums (Chapter 9).
- Brake pad or brake shoe linings worn (Chapter 1).
- Brake caliper or rear brake backplate mounting bolts loose (Chapter 9).
- Wear in suspension or steering components or mountings (Chapter 10).

Brakes binding

- Seized brake caliper or wheel cylinder piston(s) (Chapter 9).
- Faulty handbrake mechanism (Chapter 9).
- Faulty master cylinder (Chapter 9).

Rear wheels locking under normal braking

- Rear brake shoe linings contaminated (Chapter 1).
- Faulty brake pressure regulator (Chapter 9).

9 Suspension and steering systems

Note: *Before diagnosing suspension or steering faults, be sure that the trouble is not due to incorrect tyre pressures, mixtures of tyre types, or binding brakes. Apart from checking the condition of all electrical connections, any faults occurring on the Adaptive Damping System should be referred to a Ford dealer for diagnosis.*

Vehicle pulls to one side

- Defective tyre (Chapter 1).
- Excessive wear in suspension or steering components (Chapter 10).
- Incorrect front wheel alignment (Chapter 10).
- Accident damage to steering or suspension components (Chapter 10).

Wheel wobble and vibration

- Front roadwheels out of balance (vibration felt mainly through the steering wheel) (Chapter 1).
- Rear roadwheels out of balance (vibration felt throughout the vehicle) (Chapter 1).
- Roadwheels damaged or distorted (Chapter 1).
- Faulty or damaged tyre (Chapter 1).
- Worn steering or suspension joints, bushes or components (Chapter 10).
- Roadwheel nuts loose (Chapter 1).

Excessive pitching and/or rolling around corners, or during braking

- Defective shock absorbers (Chapter 10).
- Broken or weak coil spring and/or suspension component (Chapter 10).
- Worn or damaged anti-roll bar or mountings (Chapter 10).

Wandering or general instability

- Incorrect front wheel alignment (Chapter 10).

- Worn steering or suspension joints, bushes or components (Chapter 10).
- Roadwheels out of balance (Chapter 1).
- Faulty or damaged tyre (Chapter 1).
- Roadwheel nuts loose (Chapter 1).
- Defective shock absorbers (Chapter 10).

Excessively-stiff steering

- Lack of steering gear lubricant (Chapter 10).
- Seized track-rod end balljoint or suspension balljoint (Chapter 10).
- Broken or slipping auxiliary drivebelt (Chapter 1).
- Incorrect front wheel alignment (Chapter 10).
- Steering rack or column bent or damaged (Chapter 10).

Excessive play in steering

- Worn steering column universal joint(s) or flexible coupling (Chapter 10).
- Worn steering track-rod end balljoints (Chapter 10).
- Worn rack-and-pinion steering gear (Chapter 10).
- Worn steering or suspension joints, bushes or components (Chapter 10).

Lack of power assistance

- Broken or slipping auxiliary drivebelt (Chapter 1).
- Incorrect power steering fluid level (Chapter 1).
- Restriction in power steering fluid hoses (Chapter 10).
- Faulty power steering pump (Chapter 10).
- Faulty rack-and-pinion steering gear (Chapter 10).

Tyre wear excessive

Tyres worn on inside or outside edges

- Tyres under-inflated (wear on both edges) (Chapter 1).
- Incorrect camber or castor angles (wear on one edge only) (Chapter 10).
- Worn steering or suspension joints, bushes or components (Chapter 10).
- Excessively-hard cornering.
- Accident damage.

Tyre treads exhibit feathered edges

- Incorrect toe setting (Chapter 10).

Tyres worn in centre of tread

- Tyres over-inflated (Chapter 1).

Tyres worn on inside and outside edges

- Tyres under-inflated (Chapter 1).

Tyres worn unevenly

- Tyres out of balance (Chapter 1).
- Excessive wheel or tyre run-out (Chapter 1).
- Worn shock absorbers (Chapter 10).
- Faulty tyre (Chapter 1).

10 Electrical system

Note: *For problems associated with the starting system, refer to the faults listed under **"Engine"** earlier in this Section.*

Battery will not hold a charge for more than a few days

- Battery defective internally (Chapter 5).
- Battery electrolyte level low (Chapter 1).
- Battery terminal connections loose or corroded (Chapter 5).
- Auxiliary drivebelt worn or incorrectly-adjusted (Chapter 1).
- Alternator not charging at correct output (Chapter 5).
- Alternator or voltage regulator faulty (Chapter 5).
- Short-circuit causing continual battery drain (Chapters 5 and 12).

Ignition (no-charge) warning light remains illuminated with engine running

- Auxiliary drivebelt broken, worn, or incorrectly-adjusted (Chapter 1).
- Alternator brushes worn, sticking, or dirty (Chapter 5).
- Alternator brush springs weak or broken (Chapter 5).
- Internal fault in alternator or voltage regulator (Chapter 5).
- Broken, disconnected, or loose wiring in charging circuit (Chapter 5).

Ignition (no-charge) warning light fails to come on

- Warning light bulb blown (Chapter 12).
- Broken, disconnected, or loose wiring in warning light circuit (Chapters 5 and 12).
- Alternator faulty (Chapter 5).

Lights inoperative

- Bulb blown (Chapter 12).
- Corrosion of bulb or bulbholder contacts (Chapter 12).
- Blown fuse (Chapter 12).
- Faulty relay (Chapter 12).
- Broken, loose, or disconnected wiring (Chapter 12).
- Faulty switch (Chapter 12).

Instrument readings inaccurate or erratic

Instrument readings increase with engine speed

- Faulty voltage regulator (Chapter 12).

Fuel or temperature gauges give no reading

- Faulty gauge sender unit (Chapters 3 or 4).
- Wiring open-circuit (Chapter 12).
- Faulty gauge (Chapter 12).

Fuel or temperature gauges give continuous maximum reading

- Faulty gauge sender unit (Chapters 3 or 4).
- Wiring short-circuit (Chapter 12).
- Faulty gauge (Chapter 12).

Horn inoperative, or unsatisfactory in operation

Horn fails to operate

- Blown fuse (Chapter 12).
- Cable or cable connections loose, broken or disconnected (Chapter 12).
- Faulty horn (Chapter 12).

Horn emits intermittent or unsatisfactory sound

- Cable connections loose (Chapter 12).
- Horn mountings loose (Chapter 12).
- Faulty horn (Chapter 12).

Horn operates all the time

- Horn push either earthed or stuck down (Chapter 12).
- Horn cable to horn push earthed (Chapter 12).

Windscreen/tailgate wipers inoperative or unsatisfactory in operation

Wipers fail to operate, or operate very slowly

- Wiper blades stuck to screen, or linkage seized or binding (Chapter 12).
- Blown fuse (Chapter 12).
- Cable or cable connections loose, broken or disconnected (Chapter 12).
- Faulty relay (Chapter 12).
- Faulty wiper motor (Chapter 12).

Wiper blades sweep over too large or too small an area of the glass
- Wiper arms incorrectly-positioned on spindles (Chapter 1).
- Excessive wear of wiper linkage (Chapter 1).
- Wiper motor or linkage mountings loose or insecure (Chapter 12).

Wiper blades fail to clean the glass effectively
- Wiper blade rubbers worn or perished (Chapter 1).
- Wiper arm tension springs broken, or arm pivots seized (Chapter 1).
- Insufficient windscreen washer additive to adequately remove road film (Chapter 1).

Windscreen/tailgate washers inoperative, or unsatisfactory in operation

One or more washer jets inoperative
- Blocked washer jet (Chapter 1).
- Disconnected, kinked or restricted fluid hose (Chapter 1).
- Insufficient fluid in washer reservoir (Chapter 1).

Washer pump fails to operate
- Broken or disconnected wiring or connections (Chapter 12).
- Blown fuse (Chapter 12).
- Faulty washer switch (Chapter 12).
- Faulty washer pump (Chapter 12).

Washer pump runs for some time before fluid is emitted from jets
- Faulty one-way valve in fluid supply hose (Chapter 12).

Electric windows inoperative, or unsatisfactory in operation

Window glass will only move in one direction
- Faulty switch (Chapter 12).

Window glass slow to move
- Incorrectly-adjusted door glass guide channels (Chapter 11).
- Regulator seized or damaged, or in need of lubrication (Chapter 11).
- Door internal components or trim fouling regulator (Chapter 11).
- Faulty motor (Chapter 12).

Window glass fails to move
- Incorrectly-adjusted door glass guide channels (Chapter 11).
- Blown fuse (Chapter 12).
- Faulty relay (Chapter 12).
- Broken or disconnected wiring or connections (Chapter 12).
- Faulty motor (Chapter 12).

Central locking system inoperative, or unsatisfactory in operation

Complete system failure
- Blown fuse (Chapter 12).
- Faulty relay (Chapter 12).
- Broken or disconnected wiring or connections (Chapter 12).

Latch locks but will not unlock, or unlocks but will not lock
- Faulty master switch (Chapter 11).
- Broken or disconnected latch operating rods or levers (Chapter 11).
- Faulty relay (Chapter 12).

One lock motor fails to operate
- Broken or disconnected wiring or connections (Chapter 12).
- Faulty lock motor (Chapter 11).
- Broken, binding or disconnected latch operating rods or levers (Chapter 11).
- Fault in door latch (Chapter 11).

MOT test checks

Introduction

Motor vehicle testing has been compulsory in Great Britain since 1960, when the Motor Vehicle (Tests) Regulations were first introduced. At that time, testing was only applicable to vehicles ten years old or older, and the test itself only covered lighting equipment, braking systems and steering gear. Current vehicle testing is far more extensive and, in the case of private vehicles, is now an annual inspection commencing three years after the date of first registration. Test standards are becoming increasingly stringent; for details of changes, consult the latest edition of the MOT Inspection Manual (available from HMSO or bookshops).

This section is intended as a guide to getting your vehicle through the MOT test. It lists all the relevant testable items, how to check them yourself, and what is likely to cause the vehicle to fail. Obviously, it will not be possible to examine the vehicle to the same standard as the professional MOT tester, who will be highly experienced in this work, and will have all the necessary equipment available. However, working through the following checks will provide a good indication as to the condition of the vehicle, and will enable you to identify any problem areas before submitting the vehicle for the test. Where a component is found to need repair or renewal, reference should be made to the appropriate Chapter in the manual, where further information will be found.

The following checks have been sub-divided into four categories, as follows:

(a) *Checks carried out from the driver's seat.*
(b) *Checks carried out with the vehicle on the ground.*
(c) *Checks carried out with the vehicle raised and with the wheels free to rotate.*
(d) *Exhaust emission checks.*

In most cases, the help of an assistant will be necessary to carry out these checks thoroughly.

Checks carried out from the driver's seat

Handbrake

Test the operation of the handbrake by pulling on the lever until the handbrake is in the normal fully-applied position. Ensure that the travel of the lever (the number of clicks of the ratchet) is not excessive before full resistance of the braking mechanism is felt. If so, this would indicate a fault in the rear brakes and/or handbrake mechanism.

With the handbrake fully applied, tap the lever sideways and make sure that it does not release, which would indicate wear in the ratchet and pawl. Release the handbrake, and move the lever from side to side to check for excessive wear in the pivot bearing. Check the security of the lever mountings, and make sure that there is no corrosion of any part of the body structure within 30 cm of the lever mounting. If the lever mountings cannot be readily seen from inside the vehicle, carry out this check later when working underneath.

Footbrake

Check that the brake pedal is sound, without visible defects such as excessive wear of the pivot bushes, or broken or damaged pedal pad. Check also for signs of fluid leaks on the pedal, floor or carpets, which would indicate failed seals in the brake master cylinder.

Depress the brake pedal slowly at first, then rapidly until sustained pressure can be held. Maintain this pressure, and check that the pedal does not creep down to the floor, which would again indicate problems with the master cylinder. Release the pedal, wait a few seconds, then depress it once until firm resistance is felt. Check that this resistance occurs near the top of the pedal travel. If the pedal travels nearly to the floor before firm resistance is felt, this would indicate incorrect brake adjustment, resulting in "insufficient reserve travel" of the footbrake. If firm resistance cannot be felt, ie the pedal feels spongy, this would indicate that air is present in the hydraulic system, which will necessitate complete bleeding of the system.

Check that the servo unit is operating correctly by depressing the brake pedal several times to exhaust the vacuum. Keep the pedal depressed, and start the engine. As soon as the engine starts, the brake pedal resistance will be felt to alter. If this is not the case, there may be a leak from the brake servo vacuum hose, or the servo unit itself may be faulty.

Steering wheel and column

Examine the steering wheel for fractures or looseness of the hub, spokes or rim. Move the steering wheel from side to side and then up and down, in relation to the steering column. Check that the steering wheel is not loose on the column, indicating wear in the column splines or a loose steering wheel retaining nut. Continue moving the steering wheel as before, but also turn it slightly from left to right. Check that there is no abnormal movement of the steering wheel, indicating excessive wear in the column upper support bearing, universal joint(s) or flexible coupling.

Windscreen and mirrors

The windscreen must be free of cracks or other damage which will seriously interfere with the driver's field of view, or which will prevent the windscreen wipers from operating properly. Small stone chips are acceptable. Any stickers, dangling toys or similar items must also be clear of the field of view.

Rear view mirrors must be secure, intact and capable of being adjusted. The nearside (passenger side) door mirror is not included in the test unless the interior mirror cannot be used - for instance, in the case of a van with blacked-out rear windows.

Seat belts and seats

Note: *The following checks are applicable to all seat belts, front and rear. Front seat belts must be of a type that will restrain the upper part of the body; lap belts are not acceptable. Various combinations of seat belt types are acceptable at the rear.*

Carefully examine the seat belt webbing for cuts, or any signs of serious fraying or deterioration. If the seat belt is of the retractable type, pull the belt all the way out, and examine the full extent of the webbing.

Fasten and unfasten the belt, ensuring that the locking mechanism holds securely, and releases properly when intended. If the belt is of the retractable type, check also that the retracting mechanism operates correctly when the belt is released.

Check the security of all seat belt mountings and attachments which are accessible, without removing any trim or other components, from inside the vehicle **(see illustration)**. Any serious corrosion, fracture or distortion of the body structure within 30 cm of any mounting point will cause the vehicle to fail. Certain anchorages will not be accessible or even visible from inside the vehicle; in this instance, further checks should be carried out later, when working underneath. If any part of the seat belt mechanism is attached to the front seat, then the

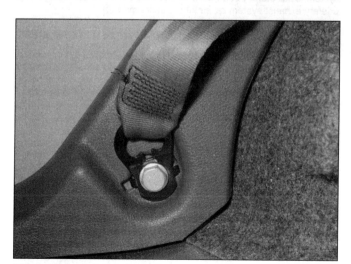

Check the security of all seat belt mountings

seat mountings are treated as anchorages, and must also comply as above.

The front seats themselves must be securely attached so that they cannot move unexpectedly, and the backrests must lock in the upright position.

Doors

Both front doors must be able to be opened and closed from outside and inside, and must latch securely when closed. In the case of a pick-up, the tailgate must be securely attached, and capable of being securely fastened.

Electrical equipment

Switch on the ignition, and operate the horn. The horn must operate, and produce a clear sound audible to other road users. Note that a gong, siren or two-tone horn fitted as an alternative to the manufacturer's original equipment is not acceptable.

Check the operation of the windscreen washers and wipers. The washers must operate with adequate flow and pressure, and with the jets adjusted so that the liquid strikes the windscreen near the top of the glass.

Operate the windscreen wipers in conjunction with the washers, and check that the blades cover their designed sweep of the windscreen without smearing. The blades must effectively clean the glass so that the driver has an adequate view of the road ahead, and to the front nearside and offside of the vehicle. If the screen smears or does not clean adequately, it is advisable to renew the wiper blades before the MOT test.

Depress the footbrake with the ignition switched on, and have your assistant check that both rear stop-lights operate, and are extinguished when the footbrake is released. If one stop-light fails to operate, it is likely that a bulb has blown or there is a poor electrical contact at, or near, the bulbholder. If both stop-lights fail to operate, check for a blown fuse, faulty stop-light switch, or possibly two blown bulbs. If the lights stay on when the brake pedal is released, it is possible that the switch is at fault.

Checks carried out with the vehicle on the ground

Vehicle identification

Front and rear number plates must be in good condition, securely fitted and easily read. Letters and numbers must be correctly spaced, with the gap between the group of numbers and the group of letters at least double the gap between adjacent numbers and letters.

The vehicle identification number on the plate under the bonnet must be legible. It will be checked during the test, as part of the measures taken to prevent the fraudulent acquisition of certificates.

Electrical equipment

Switch on the sidelights, and check that both front and rear sidelights and the number plate lights are illuminated, and that the lenses and reflectors are secure and undamaged. This is particularly important at the rear, where a cracked or damaged lens would allow a white light to show to the rear, which is unacceptable. Note in addition that any lens that is excessively dirty, either inside or out, such that the light intensity is reduced, could also constitute a fail.

Switch on the headlights, and check that both dipped beam and main beam units are operating correctly and at the same light intensity. If either headlight shows signs of dimness, this is usually attributable to a poor earth connection or severely-corroded internal reflector. Inspect the headlight lenses for cracks or stone damage. Any damage to the headlight lens will normally constitute a fail, but this is very much down to the tester's discretion. Bear in mind that with all light units, they must operate correctly when first switched on. It is not acceptable to tap a light unit to make it operate.

The headlights must not only be aligned so as not to dazzle other road users when switched to dipped beam, but also so as to provide adequate illumination of the road. This can only be accurately checked using optical beam-setting equipment, so if you have any doubts about the headlight alignment, it is advisable to have this professionally checked and if necessary reset, before the MOT test.

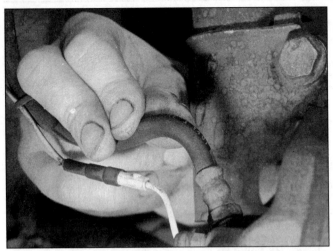

Check the braking system pipes and hoses for signs of damage or deterioration

Shake the roadwheel vigorously to check for excess play in the wheel bearings and suspension components

With the ignition switched on, operate the direction indicators, and check that they show amber lights to the front and to the rear, that they flash at the rate of between one and two flashes per second, and that the "tell-tale" on the instrument panel also functions. Operation of the sidelights and stop-lights must not affect the indicators - if it does, the cause is usually a bad earth at the rear light cluster. Similarly check the operation of the hazard warning lights, which must work with the ignition on and off. Examine the lenses for cracks or damage as described previously.

Check the operation of the rear foglight(s). The test only concerns itself with the statutorily-required foglight, which is the one on the offside (driver's side). The light must be secure, and emit a steady red light. The warning light on the instrument panel (or in the switch) must also work.

Footbrake

From within the engine compartment, examine the brake pipes for signs of leaks, corrosion, insecurity, chafing or other damage. Check the master cylinder and servo unit for leaks, security of their mountings, or excessive corrosion in the vicinity of the mountings. The master cylinder reservoir must be secure; if it is of the translucent type, the fluid level must be between the upper and lower level markings.

Turn the steering as necessary so that the right-hand front brake flexible hose can be examined. Inspect the hose carefully for any sign of cracks or deterioration of the rubber. This will be most noticeable if the hose is bent in half, and is particularly common where the rubber portion enters the metal end fitting **(see illustration)**. Turn the steering onto full-left then full-right lock, and ensure that the hose does not contact the wheel, tyre, or any part of the steering or suspension mechanism. While your assistant depresses the brake pedal firmly, check the hose for any bulges or fluid leaks under pressure. Now repeat these checks on the left-hand front hose. Should any damage or deterioration be noticed, renew the hose.

Steering mechanism and suspension

Have your assistant turn the steering wheel from side to side slightly, up to the point where the steering gear just begins to transmit this movement to the roadwheels. Check for excessive free play between the steering wheel and the steering gear, which would indicate wear in the steering column joints, wear or insecurity of the steering column-to-steering gear coupling, or insecurity, incorrect adjustment, or wear in the steering gear itself. Generally speaking, free play greater than 1.3 cm for vehicles with rack-and-pinion type steering (or 7.6 cm for vehicles with steering box mechanisms) should be considered excessive.

Have your assistant turn the steering wheel more vigorously in each direction, up to the point where the roadwheels just begin to turn. As this is done, carry out a complete examination of all the steering joints, linkages, fittings and attachments. Any component that shows

signs of wear, damage, distortion, or insecurity should be renewed or attended to accordingly. On vehicles equipped with power steering, also check that the power steering pump is secure, that the pump drivebelt is in satisfactory condition and correctly adjusted, that there are no fluid leaks or damaged hoses, and that the system operates correctly. Additional checks can be carried out later with the vehicle raised, when there will be greater working clearance underneath.

Check that the vehicle is standing level and at approximately the correct ride height. Ensure that there is sufficient clearance between the suspension components and the bump stops to allow full suspension travel over bumps.

Shock absorbers

Depress each corner of the vehicle in turn, and then release it. If the shock absorbers are in good condition, the corner of the vehicle will rise and then settle in its normal position. If there is no noticeable damping effect from the shock absorber, and the vehicle continues to rise and fall, then the shock absorber is defective and the vehicle will fail. A shock absorber which has seized will also cause the vehicle to fail.

Exhaust system

Start the engine, and with your assistant holding a rag over the tailpipe, check the entire system for leaks, which will appear as a rhythmic fluffing or hissing sound at the source of the leak. Check the effectiveness of the silencer by ensuring that the noise produced is of a level to be expected from a vehicle of similar type. Providing that the system is structurally sound, it is acceptable to cure a leak using a proprietary exhaust system repair kit or similar method.

Checks carried out with the vehicle raised and with the wheels free to rotate

Jack up the front and rear of the vehicle, and securely support it on axle stands positioned at suitable load-bearing points under the vehicle structure. Position the stands clear of the suspension assemblies, ensure that the wheels are clear of the ground, and that the steering can be turned onto full-right and full-left lock.

Steering mechanism

Examine the steering rack rubber gaiters for signs of splits, lubricant leakage or insecurity of the retaining clips. If power steering is fitted, check for signs of deterioration, damage, chafing, or leakage of the fluid hoses, pipes or connections. Also check for excessive stiffness or binding of the steering, a missing split pin or locking device, or any severe corrosion of the body structure within 30 cm of any steering component attachment point.

Have your assistant turn the steering onto full-left then full-right lock. Check that the steering turns smoothly, without undue tightness or roughness, and that no part of the steering mechanism, including a

Inspect the constant velocity joint gaiters for splits or damage

Check the handbrake mechanism - typical example shown - for signs of frayed or broken cables, or insecurity of the linkage

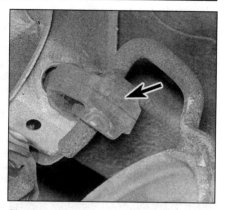

Check the condition of the exhaust system - typical example shown - paying particular attention to the mountings (arrowed)

wheel or tyre, fouls any brake flexible or rigid hose or pipe, or any part of the body structure.

On vehicles with four-wheel steering, similar considerations apply to the rear wheel steering linkages. However, it is permissible for a rear wheel steering system to be inoperative, provided that the rear wheels are secured in the straight-ahead position, and that the front wheel steering system is operating effectively.

Front and rear suspension and wheel bearings

Starting at the front right-hand side of the vehicle, grasp the road-wheel at the 3 o'clock and 9 o'clock positions, and shake it vigorously. Check for any free play at the wheel bearings, suspension balljoints, or suspension mountings, pivots and attachments. Check also for any serious deterioration of the rubber or metal casing of any mounting bushes, or any distortion, deformation or severe corrosion of any components. Look for missing split pins, tab washers or other locking devices on any mounting or attachment, or any severe corrosion of the vehicle structure within 30 cm of any suspension component attachment point.

If any excess free play is suspected at a component pivot point, this can be confirmed by using a large screwdriver or similar tool, and levering between the mounting and the component attachment. This will confirm whether the wear is in the pivot bush, its retaining bolt or in the mounting itself (the bolt holes can often become elongated).

Now grasp the wheel at the 12 o'clock and 6 o'clock positions, shake it vigorously and repeat the previous inspection **(see illustration)**. Rotate the wheel, and check for roughness or tightness of the front wheel bearing such that imminent failure of the bearing is indicated.

Carry out all the above checks at the other front wheel, and then at both rear wheels.

Roadsprings and shock absorbers

On vehicles with strut type suspension units, examine the strut assembly for signs of serious fluid leakage, corrosion or severe pitting of the piston rod, or damage to the casing. Check also for security of the mounting points.

If coil springs are fitted, check that the spring ends locate correctly in their spring seats, that there is no severe corrosion of the spring, and that it is not cracked, broken, or in any way damaged.

If the vehicle is fitted with leaf springs, check that all leaves are intact, that the axle is securely attached to each spring, and that there is no wear or deterioration of the spring eye mountings, bushes, and shackles.

The same general checks apply to vehicles fitted with other suspension types, such as torsion bars, hydraulic displacer units, etc. In all cases, ensure that all mountings and attachments are secure, that there are no signs of excessive wear, corrosion, cracking, deformation or damage to any component or bush, and that there are no fluid leaks, or damaged hoses or pipes (hydraulic types).

Inspect the shock absorbers for signs of serious fluid leakage. (Slight seepage of fluid is normal for some types of shock absorber, and is not a reason for failing.) Check for excessive wear of the mounting bushes or attachments, or damage to the body of the unit.

Driveshafts

With the steering turned onto full-lock, rotate each front wheel in turn, and inspect the constant velocity joint gaiters for splits or damage **(see illustration)**. Also check the gaiter is securely attached to its respective housings by clips or other methods of retention.

Continue turning the wheel, and check that each driveshaft is straight, with no sign of damage.

Braking system

If possible, without dismantling, check the brake pads and the condition of the discs. Ensure that the friction lining material has not worn excessively, and that the discs are not fractured, pitted, scored, or worn excessively.

Carefully examine all the rigid brake pipes underneath the vehicle, and the flexible hoses at the rear. Look for signs of excessive corrosion, chafing or insecurity of the pipes, and for signs of bulging under pressure, chafing, splits, or deterioration of the flexible hoses.

Look for signs of hydraulic fluid leaks at the brake calipers or on the brake backplates, indicating failed hydraulic seals in the components concerned.

Slowly spin each wheel, while your assistant depresses the footbrake then releases it. Ensure that each brake is operating, and that the wheel is free to rotate when the pedal is released. It is not possible to test brake efficiency without special equipment, but (traffic and local conditions permitting) a road test can be carried out to check that the vehicle pulls up in a straight line.

Examine the handbrake mechanism, and check for signs of frayed or broken cables, excessive corrosion, or wear or insecurity of the linkage **(see illustration)**. Have your assistant operate the handbrake, while you check that the mechanism works on each relevant wheel, and releases fully without binding.

Fuel and exhaust systems

Inspect the fuel tank, fuel pipes, hoses and unions (including the unions at the pump, filter and carburettor). All components must be secure, and free from leaks. The fuel filler cap must also be secure, and of an appropriate type.

Examine the exhaust system over its entire length, checking for any damaged, broken or missing mountings, security of the pipe retaining clamps, and condition of the system with regard to rust and corrosion **(see illustration)**.

Wheels and tyres

Carefully examine each tyre in turn, on both the inner and outer walls, and over the whole of the tread area. Check for signs of cuts, tears, lumps, bulges, separation of the tread, and exposure of the ply or cord due to wear or other damage. Check also that the tyre bead is correctly seated on the wheel rim, and that the tyre valve is sound and properly seated. Spin the wheel, and check that it is not excessively distorted or damaged, particularly at the bead rim.

Check that the tyres are of the correct size for the vehicle, and that they are of the same size and type on each axle. (Having a "space saver" spare tyre in use is not acceptable.) The tyres should also be inflated to the specified pressures (see Chapter 10 Specifications).

Using a suitable gauge, check the tyre tread depth. The current legal requirement states that the tread pattern must be visible over the whole tread area, and must be of a minimum depth of 1.6 mm over at least three-quarters of the tread width. It is acceptable for some wear of the inside or outside edges of the tyre to be apparent, but this wear must be in one even circumferential band, and the tread must be visible. Any excessive wear of this nature may indicate incorrect front wheel alignment, which should be checked before the tyre becomes excessively worn. See the appropriate Chapters for further information on tyre wear patterns and front wheel alignment.

Body corrosion

Check the condition of the entire vehicle structure for signs of corrosion in any load-bearing areas. For the purpose of the MOT test, all chassis box sections, side sills, crossmembers, pillars, suspension, steering, braking system and seat belt mountings and anchorages, should all be considered as load-bearing areas. As a general guide, any corrosion which has seriously reduced the metal thickness of a load-bearing area to weaken it, is likely to cause the vehicle to fail. Should corrosion of this nature be encountered, professional repairs are likely to be needed.

Body damage or corrosion which causes sharp or otherwise dangerous edges to be exposed will also cause the vehicle to fail.

Exhaust emission checks

Have the engine at normal operating temperature, and make sure that the preliminary conditions for checking idle speed and mixture (ignition system in good order, air cleaner element in good condition, etc) have been met.

Before any measurements are carried out, raise the engine speed to around 2500 rpm, and hold it at this speed for 20 seconds. Allow the engine speed to return to idle, and watch for smoke emissions from the exhaust tailpipe. If the idle speed is obviously much too high, or if

dense blue or clearly-visible black smoke comes from the tailpipe for more than 5 seconds, the vehicle will fail. As a rule of thumb, blue smoke signifies oil being burnt (worn valve stem oil seals, valve guides, piston rings or bores) while black smoke signifies unburnt fuel (dirty air cleaner element, mixture extremely rich, or other carburettor or fuel injection system fault).

If idle speed and smoke emission are satisfactory, an exhaust gas analyser capable of measuring carbon monoxide (CO) and hydrocarbons (HC) is now needed. The following paragraphs assume that such an instrument can be hired or borrowed - it is unlikely to be economic for the home mechanic to buy one. Alternatively, a local garage may agree to perform the check for a small fee.

CO emissions (mixture)

Current MOT regulations specify a maximum CO level at idle of 4.5% for vehicles first used after August 1983. The CO level specified by the vehicle maker is well inside this limit.

If the CO level cannot be reduced far enough to pass the test (and assuming that the fuel and ignition systems are otherwise in good condition) it is probable that the carburettor is badly worn, or that there is some problem in the fuel injection system. On carburettors with an automatic choke, it may be that the choke is not releasing as it should.

It is possible for the CO level to be within the specified maximum for MOT purposes, but well above the maximum specified by the manufacturer. The tester is entitled to draw attention to this, but it is not in itself a reason for failing the vehicle.

HC emissions

With the CO emissions within limits, HC emissions must be no more than 1200 ppm (parts per million). If the vehicle fails this test at idle, it can be re-tested at around 2000 rpm; if the HC level is then 1200 ppm or less, this counts as a pass.

Excessive HC emissions can be caused by oil being burnt, but they are more likely to be due to unburnt fuel. Possible reasons include:

(a) Spark plugs in poor condition or incorrectly-gapped.
(b) Ignition timing incorrect.
(c) Valve clearances incorrect.
(d) Engine compression low.

Note that excessive HC levels in the exhaust gas can cause premature failure of the catalytic converter (when fitted).

Chapter 1 Routine maintenance and servicing

Contents

Specifications

Engine

Direction of crankshaft rotation	Clockwise (seen from right-hand side of vehicle)
Oil filter	Champion C102

Cooling system

Coolant protection at standard 40% antifreeze/water mixture ratio:

Slush point	-25°C (-13°F)
Solidifying point	-30°C (-22°F)

Coolant specific gravity at standard 40% antifreeze/water
mixture ratio and 15°C/59°F - with no other additives in coolant ... 1.061

Fuel system

Idle speed - nominal	830 ± 50 rpm *
Air filter element	Champion U618
Fuel filter	Champion L218

* **Note:** *Given for reference only - not adjustable.*

Ignition system

Firing order .... 1-3-4-2 (No 1 cylinder at timing belt end of engine)
Spark plugs:
    Type... Champion RE7YCC
    Electrode gap .... 1.0 mm
Spark plug (HT) leads:
    Type... Champion type not available
    Maximum resistance per lead .... 30 000 ohms

Braking system

Note: *No minimum lining thicknesses are given by Ford - the following is given as a general recommendation. If the pad wear warning light comes on before the front brake pad linings reach the minimum thickness, the pads should nevertheless be renewed immediately.*
Minimum front or rear brake pad lining thickness .... 1.5 mm
Minimum rear brake shoe lining thickness .... 1.0 mm

Suspension and steering

Tyre pressures (cold):	**Front**	**Rear**
Normally-laden*..	2.1 bars (31 psi)	2.1 bars (31 psi)
Fully-laden*...	2.4 bars (35 psi)	2.8 bars (41 psi)

Note: *Normally laden means up to 3 persons. For sustained high speeds above 100 mph (160 km/h), increased pressures are necessary. Consult the driver's handbook supplied with the vehicle.*

Wiper blades

Windscreen:
    Driver's side.. Champion X 5303 (and SP 01 spoiler)
    Passenger's side .... Champion X 5103
Tailgate:
    Hatchback.. Champion X 5103
    Estate .... Champion type not available

Torque wrench settings

	Nm	**lbf ft**
Auxiliary drivebelt cover fasteners.....................................	5 to 10	4 to 7
Auxiliary drivebelt automatic tensioner Torx screws.............	23	17
Engine oil drain plug	25	18
Manual transmission filler/level plug..................................	35	26
Radiator undershield screws	7	5
Spark plugs...	15	11
Roadwheel nuts...	85	63
Seat belt mounting bolts	28	21

Are your plugs trying to tell you something?

Normal.
Grey-brown deposits, lightly coated core nose. Plugs ideally suited to engine, and engine in good condition.

Heavy Deposits.
A build up of crusty deposits, light-grey sandy colour in appearance.
Fault: Often caused by worn valve guides, excessive use of upper cylinder lubricant, or idling for long periods.

Lead Glazing.
Plug insulator firing tip appears yellow or green/yellow and shiny in appearance.
Fault: Often caused by incorrect carburation, excessive idling followed by sharp acceleration. Also check ignition timing.

Carbon fouling.
Dry, black, sooty deposits.
Fault: over-rich fuel mixture.
Check: carburettor mixture settings, float level, choke operation, air filter.

Oil fouling.
Wet, oily deposits. Fault: worn bores/piston rings or valve guides; sometimes occurs (temporarily) during running-in period.

Overheating.
Electrodes have glazed appearance, core nose very white – few deposits. Fault: plug overheating. Check: plug value, ignition timing, fuel octane rating (too low) and fuel mixture (too weak).

Electrode damage.
Electrodes burned away; core nose has burned, glazed appearance. Fault: pre-ignition. Check: for correct heat range and as for 'overheating'.

Split core nose.
(May appear initially as a crack). Fault: detonation or wrong gap-setting technique. Check: ignition timing, cooling system, fuel mixture (too weak).

WHY DOUBLE COPPER IS BETTER FOR YOUR ENGINE.

Unique Trapezoidal Copper Cored Earth Electrode — 50% Larger Spark Area — Copper Cored Centre Electrode

Champion Double Copper plugs are the first in the world to have copper core in both centre <u>and</u> earth electrode. This innovative design means that they run cooler by up to 100°C – giving greater efficiency and longer life. These double copper cores transfer heat away from the tip of the plug faster and more efficiently. Therefore, Double Copper runs at cooler temperatures than conventional plugs giving improved acceleration response and high speed performance with no fear of pre-ignition.

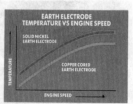

Champion Double Copper plugs also feature a unique trapezoidal earth electrode giving a 50% increase in spark area. This, together with the double copper cores, offers greatly reduced electrode wear, so the spark stays stronger for longer.

 FASTER COLD STARTING

 FOR UNLEADED OR LEADED FUEL

 ELECTRODES UP TO 100°C COOLER

 BETTER ACCELERATION RESPONSE

 LOWER EMISSIONS

 50% BIGGER SPARK AREA

 THE LONGER LIFE PLUG

Plug Tips/Hot and Cold.
Spark plugs must operate within well-defined temperature limits to avoid cold fouling at one extreme and overheating at the other.
Champion and the car manufacturers work out the best plugs for an engine to give optimum performance under all conditions, from freezing cold starts to sustained high speed motorway cruising.
Plugs are often referred to as hot or cold. With Champion, the higher the number on its body, the hotter the plug, and the lower the number the cooler the plug.

Plug Cleaning
Modern plug design and materials mean that Champion no longer recommends periodic plug cleaning. Certainly don't clean your plugs with a wire brush as this can cause metal conductive paths across the nose of the insulator so impairing its performance and resulting in loss of acceleration and reduced m.p.g.
However, if plugs are removed, always carefully clean the area where the plug seats in the cylinder head as grit and dirt can sometimes cause gas leakage.
Also wipe any traces of oil or grease from plug leads as this may lead to arcing.

DOUBLE COPPER

This photographic sequence shows the steps taken to repair the dent and paintwork damage shown above. In general, the procedure for repairing a hole will be similar; where there are substantial differences, the procedure is clearly described and shown in a separate photograph.

First remove any trim around the dent, then hammer out the dent where access is possible. This will minimise filling. Here, after the large dent has been hammered out, the damaged area is being made slightly concave.

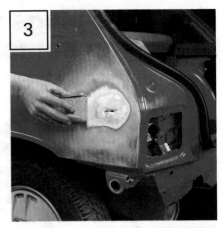

Next, remove all paint from the damaged area by rubbing with coarse abrasive paper or using a power drill fitted with a wire brush or abrasive pad. 'Feather' the edge of the boundary with good paintwork using a finer grade of abrasive paper.

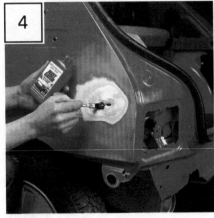

Where there are holes or other damage, the sheet metal should be cut away before proceeding further. The damaged area and any signs of rust should be treated with Turtle Wax Hi-Tech Rust Eater, which will also inhibit further rust formation.

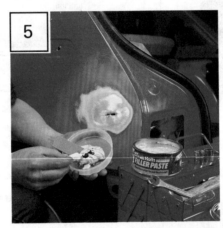

For a large dent or hole mix Holts Body Plus Resin and Hardener according to the manufacturer's instructions and apply around the edge of the repair. Press Glass Fibre Matting over the repair area and leave for 20-30 minutes to harden. Then ...

... brush more Holts Body Plus Resin and Hardener onto the matting and leave to harden. Repeat the sequence with two or three layers of matting, checking that the final layer is lower than the surrounding area. Apply Holts Body Plus Filler Paste as shown in Step 5B.

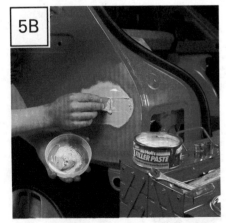

For a medium dent, mix Holts Body Plus Filler Paste and Hardener according to the manufacturer's instructions and apply it with a flexible applicator. Apply thin layers of filler at 20-minute intervals, until the filler surface is slightly proud of the surrounding bodywork.

For small dents and scratches use Holts No Mix Filler Paste straight from the tube. Apply it according to the instructions in thin layers, using the spatula provided. It will harden in minutes if applied outdoors and may then be used as its own knifing putty.

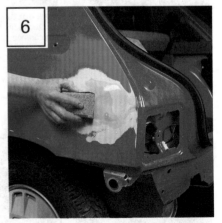

Use a plane or file for initial shaping. Then, using progressively finer grades of wet-and-dry paper, wrapped round a sanding block, and copious amounts of clean water, rub down the filler until glass smooth. 'Feather' the edges of adjoining paintwork.

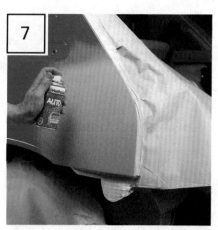

7

Protect adjoining areas before spraying the whole repair area and at least one inch of the surrounding sound paintwork with Holts Dupli-Color primer.

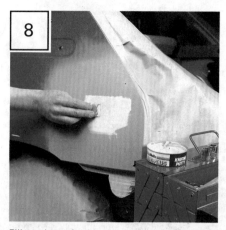

8

Fill any imperfections in the filler surface with a small amount of Holts Body Plus Knifing Putty. Using plenty of clean water, rub down the surface with a fine grade wet-and-dry paper – 400 grade is recommended – until it is really smooth.

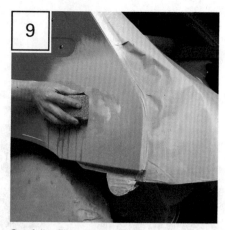

9

Carefully fill any remaining imperfections with knifing putty before applying the last coat of primer. Then rub down the surface with Holts Body Plus Rubbing Compound to ensure a really smooth surface.

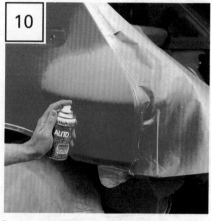

10

Protect surrounding areas from overspray before applying the topcoat in several thin layers. Agitate Holts Dupli-Color aerosol thoroughly. Start at the repair centre, spraying outwards with a side-to-side motion.

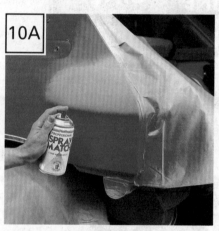

10A

If the exact colour is not available off the shelf, local Holts Professional Spraymatch Centres will custom fill an aerosol to match perfectly.

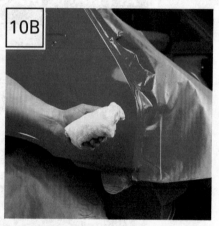

10B

To identify whether a lacquer finish is required, rub a painted unrepaired part of the body with wax and a clean cloth.

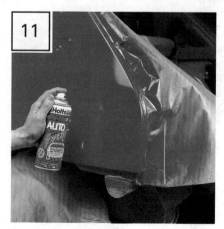

11

If *no* traces of paint appear on the cloth, spray Holts Dupli-Color clear lacquer over the repaired area to achieve the correct gloss level.

12

13

The paint will take about two weeks to harden fully. After this time it can be 'cut' with a mild cutting compound such as Turtle Wax Minute Cut prior to polishing with a final coating of Turtle Wax Extra.

14

When carrying out bodywork repairs, remember that the quality of the finished job is proportional to the time and effort expended.

THE **I.C.E.**
IN-CAR ENTERTAINMENT MANUAL
Choosing □ Installing □ Improving

AUTOMOBILE
**ELECTRICAL &
ELECTRONIC
SYSTEMS**
ESSENTIAL THEORY & PRA

The Car
**BODYWORK
REPAIR**
Manual
NEW EDITION

CAR BODYWORK
MAINTENANCE
FROM PAINTING &
SPRAYING
THROUGH TO
WATERPROOFING
AND RUST
PREVENTION

HAYNES No1 for DIY

Haynes publish a wide variety of books besides the world famous range of *Haynes Owners Workshop Manuals*. They cover all sorts of DIY jobs. Specialist books such as the *Improve and Modify* series and the *Purchase and DIY Restoration Guides* give you all the information you require to carry out everything from minor modifications to complete restoration on a number of popular cars. In addition there are the publications dealing with specific tasks, such as the *Car Bodywork Repair Manual* and the *In-Car Entertainment Manual*. The *Household DIY* series gives clear step-by-step instructions on how to repair everyday household objects ranging from toasters to washing machines.

Whether it is under the bonnet or around the home there is a Haynes Manual that can help you save money. Available from motor accessory stores and bookshops or direct from the publisher.

The Home
**ELECTRICA
APPLIANC**
Manu

The
**WASHING
MACHINE**
Manual

ALL GINE
Manual

AEG, Ariston,
ASEA, Beko,
Beaker, Bendix,
Blomberg, Bosch,
Burco, Candy,
Caravelle,
Carlton, Colston,

**SU
CARBUR**
Tuning □ Overhaul
Type H □ HD □ HS □
Owners W

**WEBER
CARBUR**
Tuning - Overhaul -
Popular carburettor
Owners W

**WEBER
CARBURETTOR**
Theory □ Specifications □ Fault diagnosis
Dismantling □ Repairs □ Service adjustments
Popular carburettor types □ 1979 to 1991
Repair & Service

FORD VEHICLE
CARBURETTOR
Theory □ Specifications □ Fault diagnosis
Dismantling □ Repairs □ Service adjustments
Ford □ Pierburg □ Solex □ Weber □ 1978 to 1999
Repair & Service

AUTOMOTIVE
**FUEL
INJECTION**
SYSTEMS
A Technical Guide

GUIDE TO PU
**ALFA
G I**
HISTORY

GUIDE TO PURCHASE
PORS

JAGUAR E-TYP
SIX-CYLINDER
RESTORATION
—& ORIGINALITY GUIDE

GUIDE TO PURCHASE & D.I.Y. RESTORATION
**MG MIDGET
&
AUSTIN-HEALEY
SPRITE**

Improve & Modify
GOLF VW **& JETTA**
INCLUDING GTi

GUIDE TO PURCHASE
**SPITZ
VITESS**

the guide to
PURCHASE & DIY RESTORATION
MINI
ALL MODELS

GUIDE TO PURCHASE & D.I.Y. RESTORATION
All Mk I & Mk II Models

& D.I.Y. RESTORATION
**BEETLE
PORTER**
BUILDING A BEETLE SPECIAL

Improve & Modify
MGB
Including
MGC & MGB V8s

Modify
TA

the guide to
PURCHASE & DIY RESTORATION
FORD
CAPRI
ALL MODELS FROM 1
KIM HENSON
History • Buying • Specification
Mechanics • Interior • Electrics • M

the guide to
PURCHASE & DIY RESTORATION
**MORRIS
MINOR & 1000**
383 COM
LINDSAY PORTER
History Buying Specification
Mechanics Interior Electrics

Improve & Modify
ESCORT & ORION
INCLUDING XR3 & XR3i
Porter & Pollard
Lindsay Porter & Dave Pollard

Lubricants, fluids and capacities

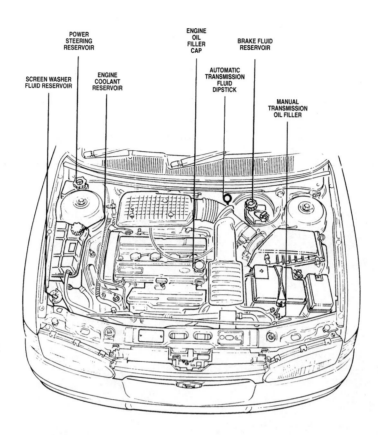

Lubricants and fluids

Component or system	Lubricant type/specification	Duckhams recommendation
Engine	Multigrade engine oil to specification API SG/CD or better, viscosity range 5W/50 to 10W/30	Duckhams QXR, QS, Hypergrade Plus, or Hypergrade
Manual transmission	Gear oil to Ford specification ESD-M2C-186-A	Duckhams Uni-Matic
Automatic transmission	Transmission fluid to Ford specification ESP-M2C-166-H	Duckhams Uni-Matic
Power steering	Transmission fluid to Ford specification ESP-M2C-166-H	Duckhams Uni-Matic
Cooling system	Soft water, and antifreeze (ethylene glycol-based, suitable for use in mixed-metal cooling systems) to Ford specification ESD-M97B-49-A	Duckhams Universal Antifreeze and Summer Coolant
Braking system	Hydraulic fluid to Ford specification ESD-M6C-57-A, Super DOT 4 or equivalent Clutch Fluid	Duckhams Universal Brake and Clutch Fluid
Driveshaft joints	Long-life grease to Ford specification SQM-1C 9004-A	Duckhams LBM 10

Capacities

Engine oil:
At oil and filter change .... 4.25 litres
Dry - at engine overhaul .... 4.50 litres
Difference between dipstick
minimum and maximum level notches............................... 0.5 to 1.0 litre
Cooling system:
Manual transmission models .... 6.6 litres
Automatic transmission models.. 7.1 litres
Fuel tank .... 61.5 litres
Manual transmission.. 2.6 litres
Automatic transmission:
Total, including fluid cooler .... 7.2 litres
Drain and refill .... 3.6 litres

Maintenance schedule

1 Introduction

This Chapter is designed to help the home mechanic maintain the Ford Mondeo models for peak performance, economy, safety and long life.

On the following pages is a master maintenance schedule, followed by Sections dealing specifically with each item on the schedule. Visual checks, adjustments, component replacement and other helpful items are included. Refer to the accompanying illustrations of the engine compartment and the underside of the vehicle for the location of various components.

Servicing your Mondeo in accordance with the mileage/time maintenance schedule and the following Sections will provide it with a planned maintenance programme, which should result in a long and reliable service life. This is a comprehensive plan, so maintaining some items but not others at the specified service intervals will not produce the same results.

As you service your Mondeo, you will discover that many of the procedures can - and should - be grouped together, because of the nature of the particular procedure you're performing, or because of the close proximity to one another of two otherwise-unrelated components.

For example, if the vehicle is raised for any reason, you should inspect the exhaust, suspension, steering and fuel systems while you're under the vehicle. When you're checking the tyres, it makes good sense to check the brakes and wheel bearings, especially if the roadwheels have already been removed.

Finally, let's suppose you have to borrow or hire a torque wrench. Even if you only need to tighten the spark plugs, you might as well check the torque of as many critical fasteners as time allows.

The first step of this maintenance programme is to prepare yourself before the actual work begins. Read through all the Sections which are relevant to the procedures you're planning to carry out, then make a list of, and gather together, all the parts and tools you will need to do the job. If it looks as if you might run into problems during a particular segment of some procedure, seek advice from your local parts man or dealer service department.

2 Maintenance schedule

General

The manufacturer's recommended maintenance schedule for these vehicles is as described below - note that the schedule starts from the vehicle's date of registration. These are the minimum maintenance intervals recommended by the factory for Mondeos driven daily, but subjected only to "normal" use. If you wish to keep your vehicle in peak condition at all times, you may wish to perform some of these procedures even more often. Because frequent maintenance enhances the efficiency, performance and resale value of your vehicle, we encourage you to do so. If your usage is not "normal", shorter intervals are also recommended - the most important examples of these are noted in the schedule. These shorter intervals apply particularly if you drive in dusty areas, tow a caravan or trailer, sit with the engine idling or drive at low speeds for extended periods (ie, in heavy traffic), or drive for short distances (less than four miles) in below-freezing temperatures.

When your vehicle is new, it should be serviced by a Ford dealer service department to protect the factory warranty. In many cases, the initial maintenance check is done at no cost to the owner. Note that this first free service (carried out by the selling dealer 1500 miles or 3 months after delivery), although an important check for a new vehicle, is not part of the regular maintenance schedule, and is therefore not mentioned here.

Coolant renewal

Ford state that, where antifreeze to specification ESD-M97B-49-A (the type with which the vehicle's cooling system would have been filled on production at the factory) is used, it will last the lifetime of the vehicle. This is subject to it being used in the recommended concentration, unmixed with any other type of antifreeze or additive, and topped-up when necessary using only that antifreeze mixed 50/50 with clean water. If any other type of antifreeze is added, the lifetime guarantee no longer applies; to restore the lifetime protection, the system must be drained and thoroughly reverse-flushed before fresh coolant mixture is poured in.

If the vehicle's history (and therefore the quality of the antifreeze in it) is unknown, owners who wish to follow Ford's recommendations are advised to drain and thoroughly reverse-flush the system, as outlined in Section 28, before refilling with fresh coolant mixture. If the appropriate quality of antifreeze is used, the coolant can then be left for the life of the vehicle.

If any antifreeze other than Ford's is to be used, the coolant must be renewed at regular intervals to provide an equivalent degree of protection; the conventional recommendation is to renew the coolant every two years.

The above assumes the use of a mixture (in exactly the specified concentration) of clean, soft water and of antifreeze to Ford's specification or equivalent. It is also assumed that the cooling system is maintained in a scrupulously-clean condition, by ensuring that only clean coolant is added on topping-up, and by thorough reverse-flushing whenever the coolant is drained (Section 28).

Daily, when refuelling, or before any long journey

Check the engine oil level, and top-up if necessary (Section 3)
Check the brake fluid level, and top-up if necessary (Section 3). If repeated topping-up is required, check the system for leaks or damage at the earliest possible opportunity (Sections 12 and 22)
Check the windscreen/tailgate washer fluid level, and top-up if necessary (Section 3)
Check the tyre pressures, including the spare (Section 4)
Visually check the tyres for excessive tread wear, or damage (Section 4)
Check the operation of all (exterior and interior) lights and the horn, wipers and windscreen/tailgate washer system (Sections 6 and 8). Renew any blown bulbs (Chapter 12), and clean the lenses of all exterior lights

Monthly

Repeat all the daily checks, then carry out the following:
Check the coolant level, and top-up if necessary (Section 3)
Check the battery electrolyte level, where applicable (Section 3)
Check the power steering fluid level, and top-up if necessary (Section 5)
Visually check all reservoirs, hoses and pipes for leakage (Section 12)
Check the operation of the air conditioning system (Section 14)
Check the operation of the handbrake (Section 23)
Check the aim of the windscreen/tailgate/headlight washer jets, correcting them if required (Section 6)
Check the condition of the wiper blades, renewing them if worn or no longer effective - note that the manufacturer recommends renewing the blades as a safety precaution, irrespective of their apparent condition, at least once a year (Section 6)

Standard service - every 10 000 miles or 12 months, whichever occurs first

Repeat all the monthly checks, then carry out the following:
Check the electrical system (Section 8)
Check the battery (Section 9)
Check the seat belts (Section 10)
Check the auxiliary drivebelt (Section 11)
Check under the bonnet for fluid leaks and hose condition (Section 12)
Check the condition of all engine compartment wiring (Section 13)
Check the condition of all air conditioning system components (Section 14)
Change the engine oil and filter (Section 15)
Check the manual transmission oil level (Section 16)
Check the adjustment of the clutch pedal (Section 17)
Lubricate the automatic transmission linkage (Section 18)
Check the steering, suspension and roadwheels (Section 19)
Check the driveshaft rubber gaiters and CV joints (Section 20)
Check the exhaust system (Section 21)
Check the underbody, and all fuel/brake lines (Section 22)
Check the brake system (Section 23)
Check the doors and bonnet, and lubricate their hinges and locks (Section 24)
Check the security of all roadwheel nuts (Section 25)
Road test (Section 26). Check the level of the automatic transmission fluid with the engine still hot, after the road test (Section 7)

Note: *If the vehicle is used regularly for very short (less than 10 miles), stop/go journeys, the oil and filter should be renewed between services (ie, every 5000 miles/6 months). Seek the advice of a local Ford dealer if in doubt on this point.*

Note: *When carrying out this Service, if the 20 000-mile interval has been reached, in addition, carry out the procedure listed under the 20 000-mile heading below.*

Every 20 000 miles

Carry out all operations listed above, plus the following:
Renew the ventilation system pollen filter (Section 27)

Extended service - every 30 000 miles or 3 years, whichever occurs first

Carry out all operations listed above, plus the following:
Renew the air filter element (Section 29). Note that this task must be carried out at more frequent intervals if the vehicle is used in dusty or polluted conditions
Check the Positive Crankcase Ventilation (PCV) system, and clean the filter (Section 30)
Renew the spark plugs (Section 31)

Note: *When carrying out this Service, if the appropriate time/mileage interval has been reached, in addition, carry out the procedure(s) listed under the following 60 000-mile and 3-year headings:*

Every 60 000 miles

Carry out all operations listed above, plus the following:
Renew the timing belt (Section 32)
Renew the fuel filter (Section 33)

Every 3 years (regardless of mileage)

Carry out all applicable operations listed above, plus the following:
Renew the brake fluid (Section 34)

Engine compartment components

1 Spark plugs (Section 31)
2 Engine oil filler cap (Section 3)
3 Brake fluid reservoir (Section 3)
4 Auxiliary fusebox (Chapter 12)
5 Air cleaner assembly (Section 29)
6 Battery (Section 9)
7 Cooling system expansion tank (Section 28)
8 Ventilation system pollen filter - under cowl grille panel (Section 27)

9 Air intake resonator (Chapter 4)
10 Radiator top hose (Section 12)
11 Cooling system expansion tank filler cap (Section 3)
12 Air intake plenum chamber (Chapter 4)
13 Engine oil dipstick (Section 3)
14 Vehicle Identification Number (VIN) plate
15 Windscreen/tailgate washer fluid reservoir (Section 3)
16 Auxiliary drivebelt (Section 11)
17 Power steering fluid reservoir (Section 5)

Front underbody view

1   Radiator bottom hose (Section 12)
2   Exhaust gas oxygen sensor (Chapter 6)
3   Braking system, fuel and emission control
     system lines (Section 22)
4   Front disc brake (Section 23)
5   Manual transmission drain plug (Chapter 7, Part A)
6   Front suspension subframe (Chapter 2, Part B)

7   Manual transmission filler/level plug (Section 16)
8   Radiator undershield (Section 28)
9   Catalytic converter (Section 21)
10   Exhaust system rubber mountings (Section 21)
11   Engine oil drain plug (Section 15)
12   Engine oil filter (Section 15)

Rear underbody view - Saloon and Hatchback models

1   Silencers (Section 21)
2   Rear brakes (Section 23)
3   Exhaust system rubber mounting (Section 21)
4   Handbrake cables (Section 23)

5   Suspension struts and springs (Section 19)
6   Fuel tank filler neck (Section 22)
7   Fuel filter (Section 33)

Rear underbody view - Estate models

1   *Silencers (Section 21)*
2   *Rear brakes (Section 23)*
3   *Exhaust system rubber mounting (Section 21)*
4   *Handbrake cables (Section 23)*
5   *Suspension springs (Section 19)*

6   *Suspension shock absorbers (Section 19)*
7   *Fuel tank filler neck (Section 22)*
8   *Evaporative emissions control system charcoal canister (Chapter 6)*

Maintenance procedures

3 Fluid level checks (Daily/Monthly - see schedule)

General

1   Fluids are an essential part of the lubrication, cooling, braking and other systems. Because these fluids gradually become depleted and/or contaminated during normal operation of the vehicle, they must be periodically replenished. See *"Lubricants and fluids and capacities"* at the beginning of this Chapter before adding fluid to any of the following components. **Note:** *The vehicle must be on level ground before fluid levels can be checked.*

Engine oil

2   The engine oil level is checked with a dipstick located at the front of the engine; it can be identified by its yellow/black plastic grip **(see illustration)**. The dipstick extends through a metal tube, from which it protrudes down into the sump at the bottom of the engine.
3   The oil level should be checked before the vehicle is driven, or about 5 minutes after the engine has been switched off. If the level is checked immediately after driving the vehicle, some of the oil will remain in the engine upper components, producing an inaccurate dipstick reading.
4   Pull the dipstick from the tube, and wipe all the oil from the end with a clean rag or paper towel; note the dipstick's maximum and minimum levels, indicated by notches **(see illustration)**. Insert the clean dipstick all the way back into its metal tube, and pull it out again. Observe the oil on the end of the dipstick; its level should be between these two notches.
5   Do not allow the level to drop below the minimum level notch, or oil starvation may cause engine damage. Conversely, overfilling the engine (adding oil above the maximum level notch) may cause oil-fouled spark plugs, oil leaks or oil seal failures.
6   The yellow/black plastic oil filler cap is screwed into the left-hand front end of the cylinder head cover; unscrew it to add oil **(see illustration)**. When topping-up, use only the correct grade and type of oil, as given in the Specifications Section of this Chapter; use a funnel if necessary to prevent spills. It takes approximately 0.5 to 1.0 litre of oil to raise the level from the dipstick's minimum level notch to its maximum level notch. After adding the oil, refit the filler cap hand-tight. Start the engine, and allow it to idle while the oil is redistributed around the engine - while you are waiting, look carefully for any oil leaks, particularly around the oil filter or drain plug. Stop the engine; check the oil level again, after the oil has had enough time to drain from the upper block and cylinder head galleries.
7   Checking the oil level is an important preventive maintenance step. A continually-dropping oil level indicates oil leakage through damaged seals and from loose connections, or oil consumption past worn piston rings or valve guides. If the oil looks milky in colour, or has water droplets in it, the cylinder head gasket may be blown - the engine's compression pressure should be checked immediately (see Chapter 2A). The condition of the oil should also be checked. Each time you check the oil level, slide your thumb and index finger up the dipstick before wiping off the oil. If you see small dirt or metal particles clinging to the dipstick, the oil should be changed (Section 15).

Coolant

Warning: *Do not allow antifreeze to come in contact with your skin or painted surfaces of the vehicle. Flush contaminated areas immediately with plenty of water. Don't store new coolant, or leave old coolant lying around, where it's accessible to children or pets - they're attracted by its sweet smell. Ingestion of even a small amount of coolant can be fatal! Wipe up garage-floor and drip-pan spills immediately. Keep antifreeze containers covered, and repair cooling system leaks as soon as they're noticed.*
8   All vehicles covered by this manual are equipped with a sealed, pressurised cooling system. A translucent plastic expansion tank, located on the right-hand side of the engine compartment, is connected by a hose to the thermostat housing. As the coolant heats up during engine operation, surplus coolant passes through the connecting hose into the expansion tank; a connection to the radiator bottom hose union allows coolant to circulate through the tank and back to the water pump, thus purging any air from the system. As the engine cools, the coolant is automatically drawn back into the cooling system's main components, to maintain the correct level.
9   While the coolant level must be checked regularly, remember therefore that it will vary with the temperature of the engine. When the engine is cold, the coolant level should be between the "MAX" and "MIN" level lines on the tank, but once the engine has warmed up, the level may rise to above the "MAX" level line.
10   For an accurate check of the coolant level, the engine must be

3.2 The engine oil dipstick (arrowed) is located at the front of the engine - note yellow/black plastic grip

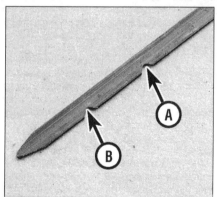

3.4 The oil level should be at or near the maximum level notch (A) - if not, add enough oil to correct the level. It takes approximately 0.5 to 1.0 litre of oil to raise the level from the minimum level notch (B) to the maximum

3.6 The yellow/black oil filler cap is screwed into the cylinder head cover. Always make sure the area around the opening is clean before unscrewing the cap, to prevent dirt from contaminating the engine

3.10 The cooling system expansion tank is located on the right-hand side of the engine compartment. The coolant level must be between the tank "MAX" and "MIN" level lines (arrowed) when the engine is cold

3.13 Remove the cap to add coolant only when the engine is cold - top-up to the "MAX" level line using the specified coolant mixture

3.17 Topping-up the windscreen washer reservoir

cold. The level must be between the "MAX" and "MIN" level lines on the tank **(see illustration)**. If it is below the "MIN" level line, the coolant must be topped-up as follows.

11   First prepare a sufficient quantity of coolant mixture, using clean, soft water and antifreeze of the recommended type, in the specified mixture ratio. If you are using antifreeze to Ford's specification or equivalent (see the note at the beginning of Section 2 of this Chapter), mix equal quantities of water and antifreeze to produce the 50/50 mixture ratio specified when topping-up; if using any other type of antifreeze, follow its manufacturer's instructions to achieve the correct ratio. If only a small amount of coolant is required to bring the system up to the proper level, plain water can be used, but repeatedly doing this will dilute the antifreeze/water solution in the system, reducing the protection it should provide against freezing and corrosion. To maintain the specified antifreeze/water ratio, it is essential to top-up the coolant level with the correct mixture, as described here. Use only ethylene/glycol type antifreeze, and *do not* use supplementary inhibitors or additives. **Warning:** *Never remove the expansion tank filler cap when the engine is running, or has just been switched off, as the cooling system will be hot, and the consequent escaping steam and scalding coolant could cause serious injury.*

12   If topping-up is necessary, wait until the system has cooled completely (or at least 10 minutes after switching off the engine, if lack of time means it is absolutely necessary to top-up while the engine may still be warm). Wrap a thick cloth around the expansion tank filler cap, and unscrew it one full turn. If any hissing is heard as steam escapes, wait until the hissing ceases, indicating that pressure is released, then slowly unscrew the filler cap until it can be removed. If more hissing sounds are heard, wait until they have stopped before unscrewing the filler cap completely. At all times, keep your face, hands and other exposed skin well away from the filler opening.

13   When the filler cap has been removed, add coolant to bring the level up to the "MAX" level line **(see illustration)**. Refit the cap, tightening it securely.

14   With this type of cooling system, the addition of coolant should only be necessary at very infrequent intervals. If topping-up is regularly required, or if the coolant level drops within a short time after replenishment, there may be a leak in the system. Inspect the radiator, hoses, expansion tank filler cap, radiator drain plug and water pump. If no leak is evident, have the filler cap and the entire system pressure-tested by your dealer or suitably-equipped garage; this will usually show up a small leak not otherwise visible. If significant leakage is found at any time, use an antifreeze hydrometer to check the concentration of antifreeze remaining in the coolant.

15   Coolant hydrometers are available at most automotive accessory shops. If the specific gravity of a sample taken from the expansion tank (when the engine is switched off and fully cooled down) is less than that specified, the coolant mixture strength has fallen below the mini-

mum. If this is found, either the coolant strength must be restored by adding neat antifreeze to Ford's specification (if that is what is in the system) or by draining and flushing the system, then refilling it with fresh coolant mixture of the correct ratio (if any other type of antifreeze is being used).

16   When checking the coolant level, always note its condition; it should be relatively clear. If it is brown or rust-coloured, the system should be drained, flushed and refilled. If antifreeze has been used which does not meet Ford's specification, its corrosion inhibitors will lose their effectiveness with time; such coolant must be renewed regularly, even if it appears to be in good condition, usually at the intervals suggested at the beginning of Section 2 of this Chapter.

Windscreen/tailgate and headlight washer fluid

17   Fluid for the windscreen/tailgate washer system (and where applicable the headlight washer system) is stored in a plastic reservoir, which is located at the right front corner of the engine compartment. In milder climates, plain water can be used to top-up the reservoir, but the reservoir should be kept no more than two-thirds full, to allow for expansion should the water freeze. In colder climates, the use of a specially-formulated windscreen washer fluid, available at your dealer or any car accessory shop, will help lower the freezing point of the fluid **(see illustration)**. *Do not* use regular (engine) antifreeze - it will damage the vehicle's paintwork.

Battery electrolyte

18   On models not equipped with a sealed battery (see Section 9), check the electrolyte level of all six battery cells. The level must be approximately 10 mm above the plates; this may be shown by maximum and minimum level lines marked on the battery's casing **(see illustration)**. If the level is low, use a coin to release the filler/vent cap, and add distilled water. Install and securely retighten the cap. **Caution:** *Overfilling the cells may cause electrolyte to spill over during periods of heavy charging, causing corrosion or damage. Refer also to the warning at the beginning of Section 9.*

Brake fluid

19   The brake fluid reservoir is located on the top of the brake master cylinder, which is attached to the front of the vacuum servo unit. The "MAX" and "MIN" marks are indicated on the side of the translucent reservoir, and the fluid level should be maintained between these marks at all times **(see illustration)**.

20   The brake fluid inside the reservoir is readily visible. With the vehicle on level ground, the level should normally be on or just below the "MAX" mark.

21   Progressive wear of the brake pads and brake shoe linings causes the level of the brake fluid to gradually fall; however, when the brake pads are renewed, the original level of the fluid is restored. It is

3.18 On non-sealed batteries, keep the electrolyte level of all the cells in the battery between the maximum and minimum levels (arrowed) - ie, 10 mm above the plates. Use only distilled water, and never overfill

3.19 Brake fluid reservoir, showing "MAX" and "MIN" marks

3.22 Topping-up the brake fluid reservoir

4.2A The TWI mark on the side of the tyre shows the position of the tread wear indicator bands

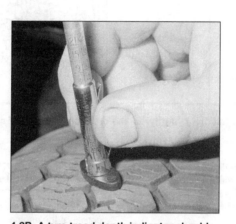

4.2B A tyre tread depth indicator should be used to monitor tyre wear - they are available at accessory shops and service stations, and cost very little

4.3 Check the tyre pressures regularly using an accurate gauge

not therefore necessary to top-up the level to compensate for this minimal drop, but the level must never be allowed to fall below the minimum mark.

22 If topping-up is necessary, first wipe the area around the filler cap with a clean rag before removing the cap. When adding fluid, pour it carefully into the reservoir, to avoid spilling it on surrounding painted surfaces **(see illustration)**. Be sure to use only the specified hydraulic fluid (see *"Lubricants, fluids and capacities"* at the start of this Chapter) since mixing different types of fluid can cause damage to the system. **Warning:** *Brake hydraulic fluid can harm your eyes and damage painted surfaces, so use extreme caution when handling and pouring it. Wash off spills immediately with plenty of water. Do not use fluid that has been standing open for some time, as it absorbs moisture from the air. Excess moisture can cause corrosion and a dangerous loss of braking effectiveness.*

23 When adding fluid, it is a good idea to inspect the reservoir for contamination. The system should be drained and refilled if deposits, dirt particles or contamination are seen in the fluid.

24 After filling the reservoir to the correct level, make sure that the cap is refitted securely, to avoid leaks and the entry of foreign matter.

25 If the reservoir requires repeated replenishing to maintain the correct level, this is an indication of an hydraulic leak somewhere in the system, which should be investigated immediately.

Power steering fluid

26 See Section 5 of this Chapter.

4 Tyre and tyre pressure checks (Daily)

1 Periodic inspection of the tyres may spare you from the inconvenience of being stranded with a flat tyre. It can also provide you with vital information regarding possible problems in the steering and suspension systems before major damage occurs.

2 The original tyres on this vehicle are equipped with tread wear indicator (TWI) bands, which will appear when the tread depth reaches approximately 1.6 mm. Most tyres have a mark around the tyre at regular intervals to indicate the location of the tread wear indicators, the mark being TWI, an arrow, or the tyre manufacturer's symbol **(see illustration)**. Tread wear can also be monitored with a simple inexpensive device known as a tread depth indicator gauge **(see illustration)**.

3 Ensure that tyre pressures are checked regularly and maintained correctly (see the Specifications at the beginning of this Chapter for pressures). Checking should be carried out with the tyres cold, and *not* immediately after the vehicle has been in use. If the pressures are checked with the tyres hot, an apparently-high reading will be obtained, owing to heat expansion. *Under no circumstances* should an attempt be made to reduce the pressures to the quoted cold reading in this instance, or effective under-inflation will result. Most garage forecourts have a pressure line which combines a gauge to check and adjust the tyre pressures, but they may vary in accuracy, due to general misuse and abuse. It therefore pays to carry a good-quality tyre pressure gauge in the vehicle, to make the regular checks required and ensure pressure accuracy **(see illustration)**.

Condition	Probable cause	Corrective action	Condition	Probable cause	Corrective action
Shoulder wear	• Underinflation (wear on both sides) • Incorrect wheel camber (wear on one side) • Hard cornering	• Check and adjust pressure • Repair or renew suspension parts • Reduce speed	**Feathered edge** **Toe wear**	• Incorrect toe setting	• Adjust front wheel alignment
Centre wear	• Overinflation	• Measure and adjust pressure	**Uneven wear**	• Incorrect camber or castor • Malfunctioning suspension • Unbalanced wheel • Out-of-round brake disc/drum	• Repair or renew suspension parts • Repair or renew suspension parts • Balance tyres • Machine or renew disc/drum

4.4 This chart will help you determine the condition of your tyres, the probable cause(s) of abnormal wear, and the corrective action necessary

4   Note any abnormal tread wear **(see illustration)**. Tread pattern irregularities such as feathering, flat spots, and more wear on one side than the other, are indications of front wheel alignment and/or balance problems. If any of these conditions are noted, they should be rectified as soon as possible.

5   Under-inflation will cause overheating of the tyre, owing to excessive flexing of the casing, and the tread will not sit correctly on the road surface. This will cause a consequent loss of adhesion and excessive wear, not to mention the danger of sudden tyre failure due to heat build-up.

6   Over-inflation will cause rapid wear of the centre part of the tyre tread, coupled with reduced adhesion, harder ride, and the danger of damage occurring in the tyre casing.

7   Regularly check the tyres for damage in the form of cuts or bulges, especially in the sidewalls. Remove any nails or stones embedded in the tread, before they penetrate the tyre to cause deflation. If removal of a nail reveals that the tyre has been punctured, refit the nail, so that its point of penetration is marked. Then immediately change the wheel, and have the tyre repaired by a tyre dealer. Do not drive on a tyre in such a condition. If in any doubt as to the possible consequences of any damage found, consult your local tyre dealer for advice.

8   General tyre wear is influenced to a large degree by driving style - harsh braking and acceleration, or fast cornering, will all produce more rapid tyre wear. Interchanging of tyres may result in more even wear; however, it is worth bearing in mind that if this is completely effective, the added expense is incurred of replacing simultaneously a complete set of tyres, which may prove financially restrictive for many owners.

9   Front tyres may wear unevenly as a result of wheel misalignment. The front wheels should always be correctly aligned according to the settings specified by the vehicle manufacturer.

10   Don't forget to check the spare tyre for condition and pressure.

11   Legal restrictions apply to many aspects of tyre fitting and usage, and in the UK this information is contained in the Motor Vehicle Construction and Use Regulations. It is suggested that a copy of these regulations is obtained from your local police, if in doubt as to current legal requirements with regard to tyre type and condition, minimum tread depth, etc.

5   Power steering fluid level check (Monthly)

1   The power steering fluid reservoir is located on the right-hand rear corner of the engine compartment.

2   For the fluid level check, the power steering system should be at its normal operating temperature, so it is best to carry out the check after a run.

3   Position the vehicle on level ground, with the front wheels pointing straight ahead, and switch off the engine.

4   Check that the fluid level is up to the "MAX" mark on the reservoir **(see illustration)**.

5   If topping-up is required, first use a clean rag to wipe the filler cap and the surrounding area, to prevent foreign matter from entering the system. Unscrew and remove the filler cap.

6   Top-up the level to the "MAX" mark, using the grade of fluid specified at the beginning of this Chapter **(see illustration)**. Be careful not to introduce dirt into the system, and do not overfill. The need for frequent topping-up indicates a leak, which should be investigated.

7   Refit the filler cap.

6   Windscreen/tailgate washer system and wiper blade check (Daily/Monthly - see schedule)

1   The windscreen wiper and blade assembly should be inspected at the specified intervals for damage, loose components, and cracked or worn blade elements.

2   Road film can build up on the wiper blades and affect their efficiency, so they should be washed regularly with a mild detergent solution.

3   The action of the wiping mechanism can loosen bolts, nuts and fasteners, so they should be checked and tightened, as necessary, at the same time as the wiper blades are checked.

4   If the wiper blade elements are cracked, worn or warped, or no longer clean adequately, they should be replaced with new ones.

5.4 Power steering fluid reservoir, showing "MAX" and "MIN" marks

5.6 Topping-up the power steering fluid reservoir

6.6 Releasing the catch to remove a windscreen wiper blade

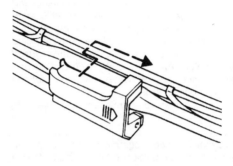

6.7 Tailgate wiper blade removal

7.4 Removing the automatic transmission dipstick from its tube

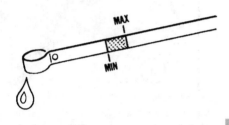

7.6A "MIN" and "MAX" marks on the dipstick

7.6B Adding automatic transmission fluid through the dipstick tube

5   Lift the wiper arm and blade away from the glass.
6   To remove the windscreen wiper blade, release the catch on the arm, then turn the blade through 90° and withdraw the blade from the end of the arm **(see illustration)**.
7   To remove the tailgate wiper blade, push the wiper blade forward, and at the same time depress it against the spring pressure, then withdraw it from the end of the arm **(see illustration)**.
8   If the metal part of the wiper blade is in good condition, it may be possible to renew the rubber insert separately. The insert can be obtained from a car accessory shop and, according to type, it may need to be cut to the correct length before sliding into the clips.
9   Refit the wiper blade assembly using a reversal of the removal procedure, making sure that it fully engages with the spring clip.

10   Check that the washer jets direct the fluid onto the upper part of the windscreen/tailgate/rear window/headlight, and if necessary adjust the small sphere on the jet with a pin.

7   Automatic transmission fluid level check (every 10 000 miles or 12 months)

1   The level of the automatic transmission fluid should be carefully maintained. Low fluid level can lead to slipping or loss of drive, while overfilling can cause foaming, loss of fluid and transmission damage.
2   The transmission fluid level should only be checked when the transmission is hot (at its normal operating temperature). If the vehicle has just been driven over 10 miles (15 miles in a cold climate), and the fluid temperature is 160 to 175°F, the transmission is hot. **Caution:** *If the vehicle has just been driven for a long time at high speed or in city traffic in hot weather, or if it has been pulling a trailer, an accurate fluid level reading cannot be obtained. In these circumstances, allow the fluid to cool down for about 30 minutes.*
3   Park the vehicle on level ground, apply the handbrake, and start the engine. While the engine is idling, depress the brake pedal and move the selector lever through all the gear ranges three times, beginning and ending in "P".
4   Allow the engine to idle for one minute, then (with the engine still idling) remove the dipstick from its tube **(see illustration)**. Note the condition and colour of the fluid on the dipstick.
5   Wipe the fluid from the dipstick with a clean rag, and re-insert it into the filler tube until the cap seats.
6   Pull the dipstick out again, and note the fluid level. The level should be between the "MIN" and "MAX" marks. If the level is on the "MIN" mark, stop the engine, and add the specified automatic transmission fluid through the dipstick tube, using a clean funnel if necessary **(see illustrations)**. It is important not to introduce dirt into the

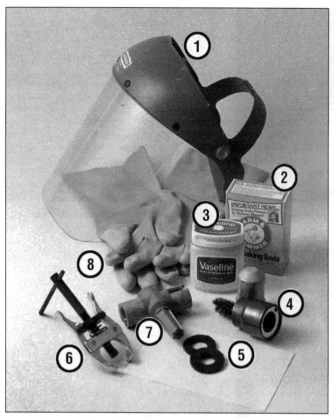

9.1 Tools and materials required for battery maintenance

1 *Face shield/safety goggles - When removing corrosion with a brush, the acidic particles can easily fly up into your eyes*
2 *Baking soda - A solution of baking soda and water can be used to neutralise corrosion*
3 *Petroleum jelly - A layer of this on the battery terminals will help prevent corrosion*
4 *Battery terminal/lead cleaner - This wire brush cleaning tool will remove all traces of corrosion from the battery terminals and lead clamps*
5 *Treated felt washers - Placing one of these on each terminal, directly under the lead clamps, will help prevent corrosion*
6 *Puller - Sometimes the lead clamps are very difficult to pull off the terminals, even after the nut has been completely slackened. This tool pulls the clamp straight up and off the terminal without damage*
7 *Battery terminal/lead cleaner - Here is another cleaning tool which is a slightly different version of number 4 above, but does the same thing*
8 *Rubber gloves - Another safety item to consider when servicing the battery; remember, that's acid inside the battery!*

transmission when topping-up.
7   Add the fluid a little at a time, and keep checking the level as previously described until it is correct.
8   The need for regular topping-up of the transmission fluid indicates a leak, which should be found and rectified without delay.
9   The condition of the fluid should also be checked along with the level. If the fluid at the end of the dipstick is black or a dark reddish-brown colour, or if it has a burned smell, the fluid should be changed. If you are in doubt about the condition of the fluid, purchase some new fluid, and compare the two for colour and smell.

8   Electrical system check (every 10 000 miles or 12 months)

1   Check the operation of all external lights and indicators (front and rear).
2   Check for satisfactory operation of the instrument panel, its illumination and warning lights, the switches and their function lights.
3   Check the horn(s) for satisfactory operation.
4   Check all other electrical equipment for satisfactory operation.
5   Check all electrical wiring in the engine compartment for correct routing, and for any signs of physical or heat-damage or chafing.

9   Battery check, maintenance and charging (every 10 000 miles or 12 months)

Warning: *Certain precautions must be followed when checking and servicing the battery. Hydrogen gas, which is highly flammable, is always present in the battery cells, so keep lighted tobacco and all other open flames and sparks away from the battery. The electrolyte inside the battery is actually dilute sulphuric acid, which will cause injury if splashed on your skin or in your eyes. It will also ruin clothes and painted surfaces. When disconnecting the battery, always detach the negative (earth) lead first and connect it last!*
Note: *Before disconnecting the battery, refer to Section 1 of Chapter 5.*

General

1   A routine preventive maintenance programme for the battery in your vehicle is the only way to ensure quick and reliable starts. Before performing any battery maintenance, make sure that you have the proper equipment necessary to work safely around the battery **(see illustration)**.
2   There are also several precautions that should be taken whenever battery maintenance is performed. Before servicing the battery, always turn the engine and all accessories off, and disconnect the lead from the negative terminal of the battery - see Chapter 5, Section 1.
3   The battery produces hydrogen gas, which is both flammable and explosive. Never create a spark, smoke, or light a match around the battery. Always charge the battery in a well-ventilated area.
4   Electrolyte contains poisonous and corrosive sulphuric acid. Do not allow it to get in your eyes, on your skin, or on your clothes. Never ingest it. Wear protective safety glasses when working near the battery. Keep children away from the battery.
5   Note the external condition of the battery. If the positive terminal and lead clamp on your vehicle's battery is equipped with a plastic cover or rubber protector, make sure that it's not torn or damaged. It should completely cover the terminal. Look for any corroded or loose connections, cracks in the case or cover, or loose hold-down clamps. Also check the entire length of each lead for cracks and frayed conductors.
6   If corrosion, which looks like white, fluffy deposits **(see illustration)** is evident, particularly around the terminals, the battery should be removed for cleaning. Slacken the lead clamp nuts with a spanner, being careful to remove the negative (earth) lead first, and slide them off the terminals **(see illustration)**. Then unscrew the hold-down clamp nuts, remove the clamp, and lift the battery from the engine compartment.
7   Clean the lead clamps thoroughly, using a soft wire brush or a terminal cleaner, with a solution of warm water and baking soda. Wash the terminals and the top of the battery case with the same solution, but make sure that the solution doesn't get into the battery. When cleaning the leads, terminals and battery top, wear safety goggles and rubber gloves, to prevent any solution from coming in contact with your eyes or hands. Wear old clothes too - even when diluted, sulphuric acid splashed onto clothes will burn holes in them. If the terminals have been extensively corroded, clean them up with a terminal cleaner **(see illustrations)**. Thoroughly wash all cleaned areas with plain water.

9.6A Battery terminal corrosion usually appears as light, fluffy powder

9.6B Removing a lead from the battery terminal - always remove the earth lead first, and connect it last!

9.7A When cleaning the lead clamps, all corrosion must be removed - the inside of the clamp is tapered to match the terminal, so don't remove too much material

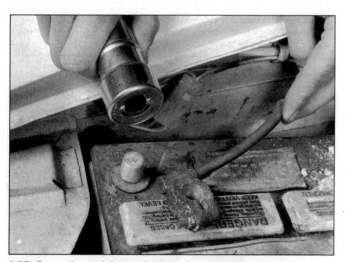

9.7B Regardless of the method used to clean the terminals, a clean, shiny surface should result

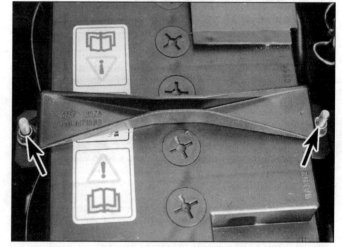

9.8 Make sure the battery hold-down nuts (arrowed) are tight

8   Make sure that the battery tray is in good condition and the hold-down clamp nuts are tight **(see illustration)**. If the battery is removed from the tray, make sure no parts remain in the bottom of the tray when the battery is refitted. When refitting the hold-down clamp nuts, do not overtighten them.

9   Information on removing and installing the battery can be found in Chapter 5. Information on jump starting can be found at the front of this manual. For more detailed battery checking procedures, refer to the Haynes "Automobile Electrical and Electronic Systems Manual".

Cleaning

10   Corrosion on the hold-down components, battery case and surrounding areas can be removed with a solution of water and baking soda. Thoroughly rinse all cleaned areas with plain water.

11   Any metal parts of the vehicle damaged by corrosion should be covered with a zinc-based primer, then painted.

Charging

Warning: *When batteries are being charged, hydrogen gas, which is very explosive and flammable, is produced. Do not smoke, or allow open flames, near a charging or a recently-charged battery. Wear eye protection when near the battery during charging. Also, make sure the charger is unplugged before connecting or disconnecting the battery from the charger.*

12   Slow-rate charging is the best way to restore a battery that's discharged to the point where it will not start the engine. It's also a good

way to maintain the battery charge in a vehicle that's only driven a few miles between starts. Maintaining the battery charge is particularly important in winter, when the battery must work harder to start the engine, and electrical accessories that drain the battery are in greater use.

13   It's best to use a one- or two-amp battery charger (sometimes called a "trickle" charger). They are the safest, and put the least strain on the battery. They are also the least expensive. For a faster charge, you can use a higher-amperage charger, but don't use one rated more than 1/10th the amp/hour rating of the battery (ie no more than 5 amps, typically). Rapid boost charges that claim to restore the power of the battery in one to two hours are hardest on the battery, and can damage batteries not in good condition. This type of charging should only be used in emergency situations.

14   The average time necessary to charge a battery should be listed in the instructions that come with the charger. As a general rule, a trickle charger will charge a battery in 12 to 16 hours.

---

10 Seat belt check (every 10 000 miles or 12 months)

---

1   Check the seat belts for satisfactory operation and condition. Inspect the webbing for fraying and cuts. Check that they retract smoothly and without binding into their reels.

2   Check that the seat belt mounting bolts are tight, and if necessary tighten them to the specified torque wrench setting.

1

11.3 Removing the auxiliary drivebelt cover - it is secured by a fastener at each end (arrowed) - from inside the right-hand front wheel arch

11 Auxiliary drivebelt check and renewal (every 10 000 miles or 12 months)

General

1   The auxiliary drivebelt is of the flat, multi-ribbed (or "polyvee") type, and is located on the right-hand end of the engine. It drives the alternator, water pump, power steering pump and (when fitted) the air conditioning compressor from the engine's crankshaft pulley.
2   The good condition and proper tension of the auxiliary drivebelt is critical to the operation of the engine. Because of their composition and the high stresses to which they are subjected, drivebelts stretch and deteriorate as they get older. They must, therefore, be regularly inspected.

Check

3   With the engine switched off, open and support the bonnet, then locate the auxiliary drivebelt on the right-hand end of the engine, under the engine right-hand mounting bracket. (Be very careful, and wear protective gloves to minimise the risk of burning your hands on hot components, if the engine has recently been running.) For improved access, jack up the front right-hand side of the vehicle, support it securely on an axle stand, remove the roadwheel, then remove the auxiliary drivebelt cover (two fasteners) from inside the wheel arch **(see illustration)**.
4   Using an inspection light or a small electric torch, and rotating the engine when necessary with a spanner applied to the crankshaft pulley bolt, check the whole length of the drivebelt for cracks, separation of the rubber, and torn or worn ribs **(see illustration)**. Also check for fraying and glazing, which gives the drivebelt a shiny appearance. Both sides of the drivebelt should be inspected, which means you will have to twist the drivebelt to check the underside. Use your fingers to feel the drivebelt where you can't see it. If you are in any doubt as to the condition of the drivebelt, renew it (go to paragraph 7).

Drivebelt tension

5   The auxiliary drivebelt is tensioned by an automatic tensioner; regular checks are not required, and manual "adjustment" is not possible.
6   If you suspect that the drivebelt is slipping and/or running slack, or that the tensioner is otherwise faulty, it must be renewed. To do this, remove the drivebelt as described below, then unbolt the tensioner (two Torx-type screws accessible from underneath, via the wheel arch) from the alternator mounting bracket **(see illustration)**. On fitting the new tensioner, ensure it is aligned correctly on its mountings, and tighten the screws to the specified torque wrench setting.

Renewal

7   Open the bonnet. Jack up the front right-hand side of the vehicle and support it securely on an axle stand, remove the roadwheel, then

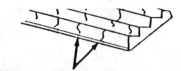
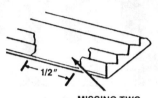

CRACKS RUNNING ACROSS "V" PORTIONS OF BELT

ACCEPTABLE

MISSING TWO OR MORE ADJACENT RIBS 1/2" OR LONGER

CRACKS RUNNING PARALLEL TO "V" PORTIONS OF BELT

UNACCEPTABLE

11.4 Check the auxiliary drivebelt for signs of wear like these. Very small cracks across the drivebelt ribs are acceptable. If the cracks are deep, or if the drivebelt looks worn or damaged in any other way, renew it

11.6 The auxiliary drivebelt is tensioned by an automatic tensioner; Torx screws (arrowed) secure it to alternator mounting bracket

remove the auxiliary drivebelt cover (two fasteners) from inside the wheel arch.
8   If the existing drivebelt is to be refitted, mark it, or note the maker's markings on its flat surface, so that it can be installed the same way round.
9   Reaching up between the body and the engine (above and to the rear of the crankshaft pulley), apply a spanner to the hexagon in the centre of the automatic tensioner's pulley. Rotate the tensioner pulley clockwise to release its pressure on the drivebelt, then slip the drivebelt off the crankshaft pulley, and release the tensioner again **(see illustration)**. Working from the wheel arch or engine compartment as necessary, and noting its routing, slip the drivebelt off the remaining pulleys and withdraw it.
10   Check all the pulleys, ensuring that their grooves are clean, and removing all traces of oil and grease. Check that the tensioner works properly, with strong spring pressure being felt when its pulley is rotated clockwise, and a smooth return to the limit of its travel when released.
11   If the original drivebelt is being refitted, use the marks or notes made on removal, to ensure that it is installed to run in the same direction as it was previously. To fit the drivebelt, arrange it on the grooved pulleys so that it is centred in their grooves, and not overlapping their raised sides (note that the flat surface of the drivebelt is engaged on the idler, tensioner and water pump pulleys) and routed correctly **(see**

11.9 Rotate the tensioner pulley clockwise to release its pressure on the drivebelt, then slip the drivebelt off the crankshaft pulley

illustrations). Start at the top, and work down to finish at the crankshaft pulley; rotate the tensioner pulley clockwise, slip the drivebelt onto the crankshaft pulley, then release the tensioner again.

12   Using a spanner applied to the crankshaft pulley bolt, rotate the crankshaft through at least two full turns clockwise to settle the drivebelt on the pulleys, then check that the drivebelt is properly installed.

13   Refit the auxiliary drivebelt cover and roadwheel, then lower the vehicle to the ground.

12 Underbonnet check for fluid leaks and hose condition (every 10 000 miles or 12 months)

Caution: *Renewal of air conditioning hoses must be left to a dealer service department or air conditioning specialist who has the equipment to depressurise the system safely. Never remove air conditioning components or hoses until the system has been depressurised.*

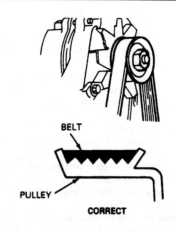

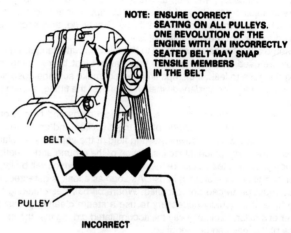

BELT

PULLEY

CORRECT

NOTE: ENSURE CORRECT SEATING ON ALL PULLEYS. ONE REVOLUTION OF THE ENGINE WITH AN INCORRECTLY SEATED BELT MAY SNAP TENSILE MEMBERS IN THE BELT

BELT

PULLEY

INCORRECT

11.11A When installing the auxiliary drivebelt, make sure that it is centred - it must not overlap either edge of the grooved pulleys

11.11B Auxiliary drivebelt routing

  1   *Power steering pump*
  2   *Idler pulley*
  3   *Alternator*
  4   *Automatic tensioner*
  5   *Air conditioning compressor (when fitted)*
  6   *Crankshaft pulley*
  7   *Water pump pulley*

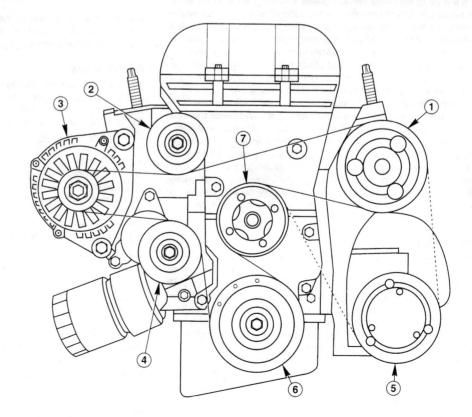

General

1   High temperatures in the engine compartment can cause the deterioration of the rubber and plastic hoses used for engine, accessory and emission systems operation. Periodic inspection should be made for cracks, loose clamps, material hardening and leaks.

2   Carefully check the large top and bottom radiator hoses, along with the other smaller-diameter cooling system hoses and metal pipes; do not forget the heater hoses/pipes which run from the engine to the bulkhead, and those to the engine oil cooler (where fitted). Inspect each hose along its entire length, replacing any that is cracked, swollen or shows signs of deterioration. Cracks may become more apparent if the hose is squeezed **(see illustration)**. If you are using non-Ford specification antifreeze, and so have to renew the coolant every two years or so, it's a good idea to renew the hoses at that time, regardless of their apparent condition.

3   Make sure that all hose connections are tight. A leak in the cooling system will usually show up as white- or rust-coloured deposits on the areas adjoining the leak; if the spring clamps that are used to secure the hoses in this system appear to be slackening, they should be renewed to prevent the possibility of leaks.

4   Some other hoses are secured to their fittings with clamps. Where clamps are used, check to be sure they haven't lost their tension, allowing the hose to leak. If clamps aren't used, make sure the hose has not expanded and/or hardened where it slips over the fitting, allowing it to leak.

5   Check all fluid reservoirs, filler caps, drain plugs and fittings etc, looking for any signs of leakage of oil, transmission and/or brake hydraulic fluid, coolant and power steering fluid. If the vehicle is regularly parked in the same place, close inspection of the ground underneath it will soon show any leaks; ignore the puddle of water which will be left if the air conditioning system is in use. As soon as a leak is detected, its source must be traced and rectified. Where oil has been leaking for some time, it is usually necessary to use a steam cleaner, pressure washer or similar, to clean away the accumulated dirt, so that the exact source of the leak can be identified.

Vacuum hoses

6   It's quite common for vacuum hoses, especially those in the emissions system, to be colour-coded, or to be identified by coloured stripes moulded into them. Various systems require hoses with different wall thicknesses, collapse resistance and temperature resistance. When renewing hoses, be sure the new ones are made of the same material.

7   Often the only effective way to check a hose is to remove it completely from the vehicle. If more than one hose is removed, be sure to label the hoses and fittings to ensure correct installation.

8   When checking vacuum hoses, be sure to include any plastic T-fittings in the check. Inspect the fittings for cracks, and check the hose where it fits over the fitting for distortion, which could cause leakage.

9   A small piece of vacuum hose (quarter-inch inside diameter) can be used as a stethoscope to detect vacuum leaks. Hold one end of the hose to your ear, and probe around vacuum hoses and fittings, listening for the "hissing" sound characteristic of a vacuum leak. **Warning:** *When probing with the vacuum hose stethoscope, be very careful not to come into contact with moving engine components such as the auxiliary drivebelt, radiator electric cooling fan, etc.*

Fuel hoses

Warning: *There are certain precautions which must be taken when inspecting or servicing fuel system components. Work in a well-ventilated area, and do not allow open flames (cigarettes, appliance pilot lights, etc.) or bare light bulbs near the work area. Mop up any spills immediately, and do not store fuel-soaked rags where they could ignite.*

10   Check all fuel hoses for deterioration and chafing. Check especially for cracks in areas where the hose bends, and also just before fittings, such as where a hose attaches to the fuel filter.

11   High-quality fuel line, usually identified by the word "Fluoroelastomer" printed on the hose, should be used for fuel line renewal. Never, under any circumstances, use unreinforced vacuum line, clear plastic tubing or water hose for fuel lines.

12   Spring-type clamps are commonly used on fuel lines. These

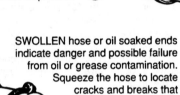

ALWAYS CHECK hose for chafed or burned areas that may cause an untimely and costly failure.

SOFT hose indicates inside deterioration. This deterioration can contaminate the cooling system and cause particles to clog the radiator.

HARDENED hose can fail at any time. Tightening hose clamps will not seal the connection or stop leaks.

SWOLLEN hose or oil soaked ends indicate danger and possible failure from oil or grease contamination. Squeeze the hose to locate cracks and breaks that cause leaks.

12.2 Hoses, like drivebelts, have a habit of failing at the worst possible time - to prevent the inconvenience of a blown radiator or heater hose, inspect them carefully as shown here

clamps often lose their tension over a period of time, and can be "sprung" during removal. Replace all spring-type clamps with screw clamps whenever a hose is replaced.

Metal lines

13   Sections of metal piping are often used for fuel line between the fuel filter and the engine. Check carefully to be sure the piping has not been bent or crimped, and that cracks have not started in the line.

14   If a section of metal fuel line must be renewed, only seamless steel piping should be used, since copper and aluminium piping don't have the strength necessary to withstand normal engine vibration.

15   Check the metal brake lines where they enter the master cylinder and ABS hydraulic unit (if used) for cracks in the lines or loose fittings. Any sign of brake fluid leakage calls for an immediate and thorough inspection of the brake system.

13 Engine compartment wiring check (every 10 000 miles or 12 months)

1   With the vehicle parked on level ground, apply the handbrake firmly and open the bonnet. Using an inspection light or a small electric torch, check all visible wiring within and beneath the engine compartment.

2   What you are looking for is wiring that is obviously damaged by chafing against sharp edges, or against moving suspension/transmission components and/or the auxiliary drivebelt, by being trapped or crushed between carelessly-refitted components, or melted by being forced into contact with the hot engine castings, coolant pipes, etc. In almost all cases, damage of this sort is caused in the first instance by incorrect routing on reassembly after previous work has been carried out.

3   Depending on the extent of the problem, damaged wiring may be

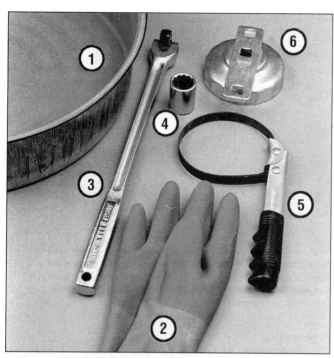

15.2 These tools are required when changing the engine oil and filter

1   **Drain pan** - It should be fairly shallow in depth, but wide to prevent spills
2   **Rubber gloves** - When removing the drain plug and filter, it is inevitable that you will get oil on your hands (the gloves will prevent burns from hot oil)
3   **Breaker bar** - Sometimes the oil drain plug is pretty tight, and a long breaker bar is needed to loosen it
4   **Socket** - To be used with the breaker bar or a ratchet (must be the correct size to fit the drain plug)
5   **Filter wrench** - This is a metal band-type wrench, which requires clearance around the filter to be effective
6   **Filter wrench** - This type fits on the bottom of the filter, and can be turned with a ratchet or breaker bar (different size wrenches are available for different types of filters)

repaired by rejoining the break or splicing-in a new length of wire, using solder to ensure a good connection, and remaking the insulation with adhesive insulating tape or heat-shrink tubing, as appropriate. If the damage is extensive, given the implications for the vehicle's future reliability, the best long-term answer may well be to renew that entire section of the loom, however expensive this may appear.
4   When the actual damage has been repaired, ensure that the wiring loom is re-routed correctly, so that it is clear of other components, and not stretched or kinked, and is secured out of harm's way using the plastic clips, guides and ties provided.
5   Check all electrical connectors, ensuring that they are clean, securely fastened, and that each is locked by its plastic tabs or wire clip, as appropriate. If any connector shows external signs of corrosion (accumulations of white or green deposits, or streaks of "rust"), or if any is thought to be dirty, it must be unplugged and cleaned using electrical contact cleaner. If the connector pins are severely corroded, the connector must be renewed; note that this may mean the renewal of that entire section of the loom - see your local Ford dealer for details.
6   If the cleaner completely removes the corrosion to leave the connector in a satisfactory condition, it would be wise to pack the connector with a suitable material which will exclude dirt and moisture, preventing the corrosion from occurring again; a Ford dealer may be able to recommend a suitable product.
7   Check the condition of the battery connections - remake the connections or renew the leads if a fault is found (Chapter 5). Use the

same techniques to ensure that all earth points in the engine compartment provide good electrical contact through clean, metal-to-metal joints, and that all are securely fastened. (In addition to the earth connection at the engine lifting eye, and that from the transmission to the body/battery, there are one or two earth points behind each headlight assembly, and one below the power steering fluid reservoir.)
8   Refer to Section 31 for details of spark plug (HT) lead checks.

14 Air conditioning system check (Monthly/every 10 000 miles or 12 months)

Warning: *The air conditioning system is under high pressure. Do not loosen any fittings or remove any components until after the system has been discharged. Air conditioning refrigerant must be properly discharged into an approved type of container, at a dealer service department or an automotive air conditioning repair facility capable of handling R134a refrigerant. Always wear eye protection when disconnecting air conditioning system fittings.*
1   The following maintenance checks should be performed on a regular basis, to ensure that the air conditioner continues to operate at peak efficiency:

(a)   *Check the auxiliary drivebelt. If it's worn or deteriorated, renew it (see Section 11).*
(b)   *Check the system hoses. Look for cracks, bubbles, hard spots and deterioration. Inspect the hoses and all fittings for oil bubbles and seepage. If there's any evidence of wear, damage or leaks, renew the hose(s).*
(c)   *Inspect the condenser fins for leaves, insects and other debris. Use a "fin comb" or compressed air to clean the condenser.* **Warning:** *Wear eye protection when using compressed air!*
(d)   *Check that the drain tube from the front of the evaporator is clear - note that it is normal to have clear fluid (water) dripping from this while the system is in operation, to the extent that quite a large puddle can be left under the vehicle when it is parked.*

2   It's a good idea to operate the system for about 30 minutes at least once a month, particularly during the winter. Long term non-use can cause hardening, and subsequent failure, of the seals.
3   Because of the complexity of the air conditioning system and the special equipment necessary to service it, in-depth fault diagnosis and repairs are not included in this manual. For more complete information on the air conditioning system, refer to the Haynes "Automotive Heating and Air Conditioning Manual".
4   The most common cause of poor cooling is simply a low system refrigerant charge. If a noticeable drop in cool air output occurs, the following quick check will help you determine if the refrigerant level is low.
5   Warm the engine up to normal operating temperature.
6   Place the air conditioning temperature selector at the coldest setting, and put the blower at the highest setting. Open the doors - to make sure the air conditioning system doesn't cycle off as soon as it cools the passenger compartment.
7   With the compressor engaged - the clutch will make an audible click, and the centre of the clutch will rotate - feel the inlet and outlet pipes at the compressor. One side should be cold, and one hot. If there's no perceptible difference between the two pipes, there's something wrong with the compressor or the system. It might be a low charge - it might be something else. Take the vehicle to a dealer service department or an automotive air conditioning specialist.

15 Engine oil and filter change (every 10 000 miles or 12 months)

1   Frequent oil changes are the best preventive maintenance the home mechanic can give the engine, because ageing oil becomes diluted and contaminated, which leads to premature engine wear.
2   Make sure that you have all the necessary tools before you begin this procedure **(see illustration)**. You should also have plenty of rags or newspapers handy, for mopping up any spills. To avoid any

1

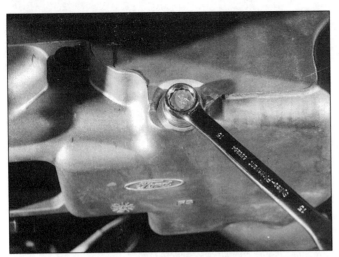

15.7 Use the correct-size spanner or socket to remove the oil drain plug and avoid rounding it off

15.9 Since the oil filter is usually on very tight, you'll need a special wrench for removal. DO NOT use the wrench to tighten the new filter. Pack rag under the filter before removal to minimise the mess

possibility of scalding, and to protect yourself from possible skin irritants and other harmful contaminants in used engine oils, it is advisable to wear gloves when carrying out this work.

3   Access to the underside of the vehicle is greatly improved if the vehicle can be lifted on a hoist, driven onto ramps, or supported by axle stands. **Warning:** *Do not work under a vehicle which is supported only by an hydraulic or scissors-type jack, or by bricks, blocks of wood, etc.*

4   If this is your first oil change, get under the vehicle and familiarise yourself with the position of the engine oil drain plug, which is located at the rear of the sump. The engine and exhaust components will be warm during the actual work, so try to anticipate any potential problems while the engine and accessories are cool.

5   The oil should preferably be changed when the engine is still fully warmed-up to normal operating temperature, just after a run (the needle on the temperature gauge should be in the "Normal" sector of the gauge); warm oil and sludge will flow out more easily. Park the vehicle on firm, level ground, apply the handbrake firmly, then select 1st or reverse gear (manual transmission) or the "P" position (automatic transmission). Open the bonnet and remove the engine oil filler cap from the cylinder head cover, then remove the oil level dipstick from its tube (see Section 3).

6   Raise the front of the vehicle, and support it securely on axle stands. Remove the front right-hand roadwheel to provide access to the oil filter; if the additional working clearance is required, remove also the auxiliary drivebelt cover (two fasteners). **Warning:** *To avoid personal injury, never get beneath the vehicle when it is supported by only by a jack. The jack provided with your vehicle is designed solely for raising the vehicle to remove and refit the roadwheels. Always use axle stands to support the vehicle when it becomes necessary to place your body underneath the vehicle.*

7   Being careful not to touch the hot exhaust components, place the drain pan under the drain plug, and unscrew the plug **(see illustration)**. If possible, try to keep the plug pressed into the sump while unscrewing it by hand the last couple of turns. As the plug releases from the threads, move it away sharply, so the stream of oil issuing from the sump runs into the pan, not up your sleeve! Allow the oil to drain into the drain pan, and check the condition of the plug's sealing washer; renew it if worn or damaged.

8   Allow some time for the old oil to drain, noting that it may be necessary to reposition the pan as the oil flow slows to a trickle; when the oil has completely drained, wipe clean the drain plug and its threads in the sump and refit the plug, tightening it to the specified torque wrench setting.

9   Using a suitable filter removal tool, unscrew the oil filter from the right-hand rear of the cylinder block; be prepared for some oil spillage **(see illustration)**. Check the old filter to make sure that the rubber sealing ring hasn't stuck to the engine; if it has, carefully remove it. Withdraw the filter through the wheel arch, taking care to spill as little

oil as possible.

10   Using a clean, lint-free rag, wipe clean the cylinder block around the filter mounting. If there are no specific instructions supplied with it, fit a new oil filter as follows. Apply a light coating of clean engine oil to the filter's sealing ring **(see illustration)**. Screw the filter into position on the engine until it seats, then tighten it through a further half- to three-quarters of a turn *only*. Tighten the filter by hand only - do not use any tools.

11   Remove the old oil and all tools from under the vehicle, refit the roadwheel, and lower the vehicle to the ground.

12   Refill the engine with oil, using the correct grade and type of oil, as given in the Specifications Section of this Chapter. Pour in half the specified quantity of oil first, then wait a few minutes for the oil to fall to the sump. Continue adding oil a small quantity at a time, until the level is up to the lower notch on the dipstick. Adding approximately 0.5 to 1.0 litre will raise the level to the dipstick's upper notch.

13   Start the engine. The oil pressure warning light will take a few seconds to go out while the new filter fills with oil; do not race the engine while the light is on. Run the engine for a few minutes, while checking for leaks around the oil filter seal and the drain plug.

14   Switch off the engine, and wait a few minutes for the oil to settle in the sump once more. With the new oil circulated and the filter now completely full, recheck the level on the dipstick, and add more oil as necessary.

15   Dispose of the used engine oil safely, with reference to *"General repair procedures"* in the preliminary Sections of this manual.

16 Manual transmission oil level check (every 10 000 miles or 12 months)

1   The manual transmission does not have a dipstick. To check the oil level, raise the vehicle and support it securely on axle stands, making sure that the vehicle is level. On the lower front side of the transmission housing, you will see the filler/level plug. Unscrew and remove it. If the lubricant level is correct, the oil should be up to the lower edge of the hole.

2   If the transmission needs more lubricant (if the oil level is not up to the hole), use a syringe, or a plastic bottle and tube, to add more **(see illustration)**. Stop filling the transmission when the lubricant begins to run out of the hole.

3   Refit the filler/level plug, and tighten it to the specified torque wrench setting. Drive the vehicle a short distance, then check for leaks.

4   A need for regular topping-up can only be due to a leak, which should be found and rectified without delay.

15.10 Lubricate the filter's sealing ring with clean engine oil before installing the filter on the engine

16.2 Topping-up the manual transmission oil

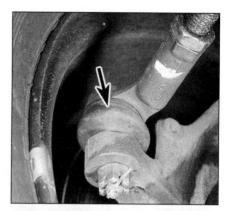

19.2A Check the condition of the track rod balljoint dust cover (arrowed)

19.2B Check the condition of the lower arm balljoint dust cover (arrowed)

19.2C Check the condition of the steering rack gaiters

19.4 Checking for wear in the front suspension and hub bearings

17 Clutch pedal adjustment (every 10 000 miles or 12 months)

The procedure is described in Chapter 8, Section 3.

18 Automatic transmission linkage lubrication (every 10 000 miles or 12 months)

1   Apply the handbrake, then jack up the front of the vehicle and support on axle stands. Remove the left-hand front wheel.
2   Apply a little oil to the cable end fitting on the selector lever on the left-hand side of the transmission (refer to Chapter 7, Part B if necessary).
3   Refit the wheel, and lower the vehicle to the ground.

19 Steering, suspension and roadwheel check (every 10 000 miles or 12 months)

Front suspension and steering check

1   Apply the handbrake, then raise the front of the vehicle and support it on axle stands.
2   Visually inspect the balljoint dust covers and the steering gear gaiters for splits, chafing or deterioration **(see illustrations)**. Any wear of these components will cause loss of lubricant, together with dirt and water entry, resulting in rapid deterioration of the balljoints or steering gear.

3   Check the power-assisted steering fluid hoses for chafing or deterioration, and the pipe and hose unions for fluid leaks. Also check for signs of fluid leakage under pressure from the steering gear rubber gaiters, which would indicate failed fluid seals within the steering gear.
4   Grasp the roadwheel at the 12 o'clock and 6 o'clock positions, and try to rock it **(see illustration)**. Very slight free play may be felt, but if the movement is appreciable, further investigation is necessary to determine the source. Continue rocking the wheel while an assistant depresses the footbrake. If the movement is now eliminated or significantly reduced, it is likely that the hub bearings are at fault. If the free play is still evident with the footbrake depressed, then there is wear in the suspension joints or mountings.
5   Now grasp the wheel at the 9 o'clock and 3 o'clock positions, and try to rock it as before. Any movement felt now may again be caused by wear in the hub bearings or the steering track rod balljoints. If the outer track rod balljoint is worn, the visual movement will be obvious. If the inner joint is suspect, it can be felt by placing a hand over the rack-and-pinion rubber gaiter, and gripping the track rod. If the wheel is now rocked, movement will be felt at the inner joint if wear has taken place.
6   Using a large screwdriver or flat bar, check for wear in the suspension mounting bushes by levering between the relevant suspension component and its attachment point. Some movement is to be expected as the mountings are made of rubber, but excessive wear should be obvious. Also check the condition of any visible rubber bushes, looking for splits, cracks or contamination of the rubber.
7   With the vehicle standing on its wheels, have an assistant turn the steering wheel back-and-forth, about an eighth of a turn each way. There should be very little, if any, lost movement between the steering wheel and roadwheels. If this is not the case, closely observe the joints and mountings previously described, but in addition, check the steering column universal joints for wear, and also check the rack-and-pinion steering gear itself.

1

Rear suspension check

8   Chock the front wheels, then raise the rear of the vehicle and support it on axle stands.
9   Check the rear hub bearings for wear, using the method described for the front hub bearings (paragraph 4).
10   Using a large screwdriver or flat bar, check for wear in the suspension mounting bushes by levering between the relevant suspension component and its attachment point. Some movement is to be expected as the mountings are made of rubber, but excessive wear should be obvious.

Roadwheel check and balancing

11   Periodically remove the roadwheels, and clean any dirt or mud from the inside and outside surfaces. Examine the wheel rims for signs of rusting, corrosion or other damage. Light alloy wheels are easily damaged by "kerbing" whilst parking, and similarly, steel wheels may become dented or buckled. Renewal of the wheel is very often the only course of remedial action possible.
12   The balance of each wheel and tyre assembly should be maintained, not only to avoid excessive tyre wear, but also to avoid wear in the steering and suspension components. Wheel imbalance is normally signified by vibration through the vehicle's bodyshell, although in many cases it is particularly noticeable through the steering wheel. Conversely, it should be noted that wear or damage in suspension or steering components may cause excessive tyre wear. Out-of-round or out-of-true tyres, damaged wheels and wheel bearing wear/maladjustment also fall into this category. Balancing will not usually cure vibration caused by such wear.
13   Wheel balancing may be carried out with the wheel either on or off the vehicle. If balanced on the vehicle, ensure that the wheel-to-hub relationship is marked in some way prior to subsequent wheel removal, so that it may be refitted in its original position.

20 Driveshaft rubber gaiter and CV joint check (every 10 000 miles or 12 months)

1   The driveshaft rubber gaiters are very important, because they prevent dirt, water and foreign material from entering and damaging the constant velocity (CV) joints. External contamination can cause the gaiter material to deteriorate prematurely, so it's a good idea to wash the gaiters with soap and water occasionally.
2   With the vehicle raised and securely supported on axle stands, turn the steering onto full-lock, then slowly rotate each front wheel in turn. Inspect the condition of the outer constant velocity (CV) joint rubber gaiters, squeezing the gaiters to open out the folds. Check for signs of cracking, splits, or deterioration of the rubber, which may allow the escape of grease, and lead to the ingress of water and grit into the joint **(see illustration)**. Also check the security and condition of the retaining clips. Repeat these checks on the inner CV joints. If any damage or deterioration is found, the gaiters should be renewed as described in Chapter 8.
3   At the same time, check the general condition of the outer CV joints themselves, by first holding the driveshaft and attempting to rotate the wheels. Repeat this check on the inner joints, by holding the inner joint yoke and attempting to rotate the driveshaft.
4   Any appreciable movement in the CV joint indicates wear in the joint, wear in the driveshaft splines, or a loose driveshaft retaining nut.

21 Exhaust system check (every 10 000 miles or 12 months)

1   With the engine cold (at least three hours after the vehicle has been driven), check the complete exhaust system, from its starting point at the engine to the end of the tailpipe. Ideally, this should be done on a hoist, where unrestricted access is available; if a hoist is not available, raise and support the vehicle on axle stands.
2   Check the pipes and connections for evidence of leaks, severe

20.2 Check the driveshaft gaiters by hand for cracks and/or leaking grease

corrosion, or damage. Make sure that all brackets and rubber mountings are in good condition, and tight; if any of the mountings are to be renewed, ensure that the replacements are of the correct type **(see illustration)**. Leakage at any of the joints or in other parts of the system will usually show up as a black sooty stain in the vicinity of the leak. Holts Flexiwrap and Holts Gun Gum exhaust repair systems can be used for effective repairs to exhaust pipes and silencer boxes, including ends and bends. Holts Flexiwrap is an MOT-approved permanent exhaust repair. Holts Firegum is suitable for the assembly of all exhaust system joints. **Note:** *Exhaust sealants should not be used on any part of the exhaust system upstream of the catalytic converter - even if the sealant does not contain additives harmful to the converter, pieces of it may break off and foul the element, causing local overheating.*
3   At the same time, inspect the underside of the body for holes, corrosion, open seams, etc. which may allow exhaust gases to enter the passenger compartment. Seal all body openings with silicone or body putty.
4   Rattles and other noises can often be traced to the exhaust system, especially the rubber mountings. Try to move the system, silencer(s) and catalytic converter. If any components can touch the body or suspension parts, secure the exhaust system with new mountings.
5   Check the running condition of the engine by inspecting inside the end of the tailpipe; the exhaust deposits here are an indication of the engine's state of tune. The inside of the tailpipe should be dry, and should vary in colour from dark grey to light grey/brown; if it is black and sooty, or coated with white deposits, the engine is in need of a thorough fuel system inspection.

22 Underbody and fuel/brake line check (every 10 000 miles or 12 months)

1   With the vehicle raised and supported on axle stands or over an inspection pit, thoroughly inspect the underbody and wheel arches for signs of damage and corrosion. In particular, examine the bottom of the side sills, and any concealed areas where mud can collect. Where corrosion and rust is evident, press and tap firmly on the panel with a screwdriver, and check for any serious corrosion which would necessitate repairs. If the panel is not seriously corroded, clean away the rust, and apply a new coating of underseal. Refer to Chapter 11 for more details of body repairs.
2   At the same time, inspect the PVC-coated lower body panels for stone damage and general condition.
3   Inspect all of the fuel and brake lines on the underbody for damage, rust, corrosion and leakage. Also make sure that they are correctly supported in their clips. Where applicable, check the PVC coating on the lines for damage.

21.2 If any of the exhaust system rubber mountings are to be renewed, ensure that the replacements are of the correct type - their colour is a good guide. Those nearest to the catalytic converter are more heat-resistant than the others

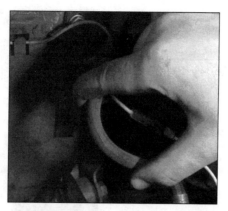

23.10 Checking the condition of a flexible brake hose

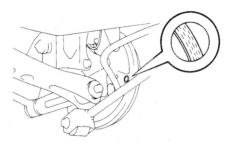

23.13 Prise the rubber plugs from the backplates to inspect the leading brake shoe linings

23 Brake check (every 10 000 miles or 12 months)

Note: *For detailed photographs of the brake system, refer to Chapter 9.*
1   The work described in this Section should be carried out at the specified intervals, or whenever a defect is suspected in the braking system. Any of the following symptoms could indicate a potential brake system defect:
   (a)   *The vehicle pulls to one side when the brake pedal is depressed.*
   (b)   *The brakes make scraping or dragging noises when applied.*
   (c)   *Brake pedal travel is excessive.*
   (d)   *The brake fluid requires repeated topping-up.*
2   A brake pad wear warning light is fitted, and it is illuminated when the thickness of the front (or rear) disc brake pad linings reach the minimum amount. However, a physical check should be made to confirm the thickness of the linings, as follows.

Disc brakes
3   Jack up the front or rear of the vehicle, as applicable, and support it on axle stands. Where rear brake pads are fitted, also jack up the rear of the vehicle and support on axle stands.
4   For better access to the brake calipers, remove the wheels.
5   Look through the inspection window in the caliper, and check that the thickness of the friction lining material on each of the pads is not less than the recommended minimum thickness given in the Specifications. **Note:** *Bear in mind that the lining material is normally bonded to a metal backing plate.*
6   If it is difficult to determine the exact thickness of the pad linings, or if you are at all concerned about the condition of the pads, then remove them from the calipers for further inspection (refer to Chapter 9).
7   Check the remaining brake caliper(s) in the same way.
8   If any one of the brake pads has worn down to, or below, the specified limit, *all four* pads at that end of the car must be renewed as a set (ie all the front pads or all the rear pads).
9   Measure the thickness of the discs with a micrometer, if available, to make sure that they still have service life remaining. If any disc is thinner than the specified minimum thickness, renew it (refer to Chapter 9). In any case, check the general condition of the discs. Look for excessive scoring and discolouration caused by overheating. If these conditions exist, remove the relevant disc and have it resurfaced or renewed (refer to Chapter 9).
10   Before refitting the wheels, check all brake lines and hoses (refer to Chapter 9). In particular, check the flexible hoses in the vicinity of the calipers, where they are subjected to most movement. Bend them between the fingers (but do not actually bend them double, or the casing may be damaged) and check that this does not reveal previously-hidden cracks, cuts or splits **(see illustration).**

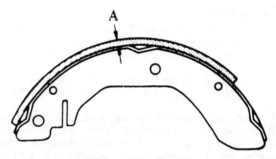

23.14 If the lining is bonded to the brake shoe, measure the lining thickness from the outer surface to the metal shoe, as shown here; if the lining is riveted to the shoe, measure from the lining outer surface to the rivet head

Rear drum brakes
11   Chock the front wheels, then jack up the rear of the vehicle and support on axle stands.
12   For better access, remove the rear wheels.
13   To check the brake shoe lining thickness without removing the brake drums, prise the rubber plugs from the backplates, and use an electric torch to inspect the linings of the leading brake shoes **(see illustration).** Check that the thickness of the lining material on the brake shoes is not less than the recommendation given in the Specifications.
14   If it is difficult to determine the exact thickness of the brake shoe linings, or if you are at all concerned about the condition of the shoes, then remove the rear drums for a more comprehensive inspection (refer to Chapter 9) **(see illustration).**
15   With the drum removed, check the shoe return and hold-down springs for correct installation, and check the wheel cylinders for leakage of brake fluid. Check the friction surface of the brake drums for scoring and discoloration. If excessive, the drum should be resurfaced or renewed.
16   Before refitting the wheels, check all brake lines and hoses (refer to Chapter 9). On completion, apply the handbrake and check that the rear wheels are locked. The handbrake is self-adjusting, and no manual adjustment is possible.

24 Door and bonnet check and lubrication (every 10 000 miles or 12 months)

1   Check that the doors, bonnet and tailgate/boot lid close securely. Check that the bonnet safety catch operates correctly. Check the operation of the door check straps.

2   Lubricate the hinges, door check straps, the striker plates and the bonnet catch sparingly with a little oil or grease.

25 Roadwheel nut tightness check (every 10 000 miles or 12 months)

1   Apply the handbrake.
2   Remove the wheel covers, using the flat end of the wheelbrace supplied in the tool kit (on models with the RS trim kit, it will be necessary to unscrew the retaining bolts with the special key).
3   Check that the roadwheel nuts are tightened to the specified torque wrench setting.
4   Refit the wheel covers.

26 Road test (every 10 000 miles or 12 months)

Check the operation and performance of the braking system

1   Make sure that the vehicle does not pull to one side when braking, and that the wheels do not lock prematurely when braking hard.
2   Check that there is no vibration through the steering when braking.
3   Check that the handbrake operates correctly, without excessive movement of the lever, and that it holds the vehicle stationary on a slope.
4   With the engine switched off, test the operation of the brake servo unit as follows. Depress the footbrake four or five times to exhaust the vacuum, then start the engine. As the engine starts, there should be a noticeable "give" in the brake pedal as vacuum builds up. Allow the engine to run for at least two minutes, and then switch it off. If the brake pedal is now depressed again, it should be possible to detect a hiss from the servo as the pedal is depressed. After about four or five applications, no further hissing should be heard, and the pedal should feel considerably harder.

Steering and suspension

5   Check for any abnormalities in the steering, suspension, handling or road "feel".
6   Drive the vehicle, and check that there are no unusual vibrations or noises.
7   Check that the steering feels positive, with no excessive sloppiness or roughness, and check for any suspension noises when cornering and driving over bumps.

Drivetrain

8   Check the performance of the engine, transmission and driveshafts.
9   Check that the engine starts correctly, both when cold and when hot.
10   Listen for any unusual noises from the engine and transmission.
11   Make sure that the engine runs smoothly when idling, and that there is no hesitation when accelerating.
12   On manual transmission models, check that all gears can be engaged smoothly without noise, and that the gear lever action is not abnormally vague or "notchy".
13   On automatic transmission models, make sure that all gearchanges occur smoothly without snatching, and without an increase in engine speed between changes. Check that all the gear positions can be selected with the vehicle at rest. If any problems are found, they should be referred to a Ford dealer.
14   Listen for a metallic clicking sound from the front of the vehicle as the vehicle is driven slowly in a circle with the steering on full-lock. Carry out this check in both directions. If a clicking noise is heard, this indicates wear in a driveshaft joint, in which case renew the joint if necessary.

27.3 Remove screws (arrowed) to release cowl grille panel . . .

Clutch

15   Check that the clutch pedal moves smoothly and easily through its full travel, and that the clutch itself functions correctly, with no trace of slip or drag. If the movement is uneven or stiff in places, check that the cable is routed correctly, with no sharp turns.
16   Inspect both ends of the clutch inner cable, both at the gearbox end and inside the car, for signs of wear and fraying.
17   Check the pedal stroke as described in Chapter 8, Section 3, and adjust if necessary.

Instruments and electrical equipment

18   Check the operation of all instruments and electrical equipment.
19   Make sure that all instruments read correctly, and switch on all electrical equipment in turn, to check that it functions properly.

27 Ventilation system pollen filter renewal (every 20 000 miles)

1   The air entering the vehicle's ventilation system is passed through a very fine pleated-paper air filter element, which removes particles of pollen, dust and other airborne foreign matter. To ensure its continued effectiveness, this filter's element must be renewed at regular intervals.
2   Remove the left-hand side windscreen wiper arm (Chapter 12).
3   Prise off their trim caps, then unscrew the two screws securing the windscreen edge of the cowl grille panel; open the bonnet and remove the remaining three retaining screws **(see illustration)**.
4   Peel back the rubber seal and withdraw the cowl grille panel.
5   Releasing the clip at each end, lift out the pollen filter housing, and withdraw the element **(see illustrations)**.
6   Wipe out the ventilation system intake and the filter housing, removing any leaves, dead insects etc.
7   If carrying out a routine service, the element must be renewed regardless of its apparent condition. If you are checking the element for any other reason, inspect its front surface; if it is very dirty, renew the element. If it is only moderately dusty, it can be re-used by blowing it clean from the rear to the front surface with compressed air. **Warning:** *Wear eye protection when using compressed air!* Because it is a pleated-paper type filter, it cannot be washed or re-oiled. If it cannot be cleaned satisfactorily with compressed air, discard and renew it.
8   Refitting is the reverse of the removal procedure; ensure that the element and housing are securely seated, so that unfiltered air cannot enter the passenger compartment.

28 Coolant renewal

Note: *If the antifreeze used is Ford's own, or of similar quality, the coolant need not be renewed for the life of the vehicle. If the vehicle's*

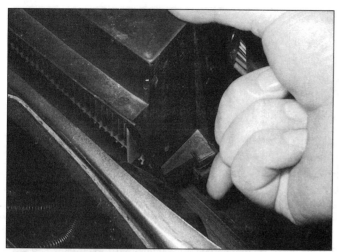

27.5A . . . release clips to lift out pollen filter housing . . .

27.5B . . . then withdraw pollen filter element

28.3A Remove the screws (arrowed) and withdraw the radiator undershield . . .

28.3B . . . to unscrew the radiator drain plug (arrowed) and empty the cooling system. Try to protect yourself from coolant splashing into your eyes or onto your skin, catching as much of it as possible in the drain tray

history is unknown, if antifreeze of lesser quality is known to be in the system, or simply if you prefer to follow conventional servicing intervals, the coolant should be changed periodically (typically, every 2 years) as described here. Refer also to the information at the beginning of Section 2 of this Chapter.

Warning: *Do not allow antifreeze to come in contact with your skin or painted surfaces of the vehicle. Flush contaminated areas immediately with plenty of water. Don't store new coolant, or leave old coolant lying around, where it's accessible to children or pets - they're attracted by its sweet smell. Ingestion of even a small amount of coolant can be fatal! Wipe up garage-floor and drip-pan spills immediately. Keep antifreeze containers covered, and repair cooling system leaks as soon as they're noticed.*

Warning: *Never remove the expansion tank filler cap when the engine is running, or has just been switched off, as the cooling system will be hot, and the consequent escaping steam and scalding coolant could cause serious injury.*

Coolant draining

Warning: *Wait until the engine is cold before starting this procedure.*

1   To drain the system, first remove the expansion tank filler cap (see Section 3).

2   If the additional working clearance is required, raise the front of the vehicle and support it securely on axle stands.

3   Remove the radiator undershield (eight or nine screws), then place a large drain tray underneath, and unscrew the radiator drain plug; direct as much of the escaping coolant as possible into the tray **(see illustrations)**.

System flushing

4   With time, the cooling system may gradually lose its efficiency, as the radiator core becomes choked with rust, scale deposits from the water, and other sediment (refer also to the information at the start of Section 2). To minimise this, as well as using only good-quality antifreeze and clean soft water, the system should be flushed as follows whenever any part of it is disturbed, and/or when the coolant is renewed.

5   With the coolant drained, refit the drain plug and refill the system with fresh water. Refit the expansion tank filler cap, start the engine and warm it up to normal operating temperature, then stop it and (after allowing it to cool down completely) drain the system again. Repeat as necessary until only clean water can be seen to emerge, then refill finally with the specified coolant mixture.

6   If only clean, soft water and good-quality antifreeze (even if not to Ford's specification) has been used, and the coolant has been renewed at the suggested intervals, the above procedure will be sufficient to keep clean the system for a considerable length of time. If, however, the system has been neglected, a more thorough operation will be required, as follows.

7   First drain the coolant, then disconnect the radiator top and bottom hoses. Insert a garden hose into the top hose, and allow water to circulate through the radiator until it runs clean from the bottom outlet.

8   To flush the engine, insert the garden hose into the thermostat water outlet, and allow water to circulate until it runs clear from the

1

bottom hose. If, after a reasonable period, the water still does not run clear, the radiator should be flushed with a good proprietary cleaning agent, such as Holts Radflush or Holts Speedflush.

9   In severe cases of contamination, reverse-flushing of the radiator may be necessary. To do this, remove the radiator (Chapter 3), invert it, and insert the garden hose into the bottom outlet. Continue flushing until clear water runs from the top hose outlet. A similar procedure can be used to flush the heater matrix.

10   The use of chemical cleaners should be necessary only as a last resort. Normally, regular renewal of the coolant will prevent excessive contamination of the system.

Coolant filling

11   With the cooling system drained and flushed, ensure that all disturbed hose unions are correctly secured, and that the radiator drain plug is securely tightened. Refit the radiator undershield, noting that it is located by three clips at its front edge; tighten the retaining screws securely **(see illustration)**. If it was raised, lower the vehicle to the ground.

12   Prepare a sufficient quantity of the specified coolant mixture (see below); allow for a surplus, so as to have a reserve supply for topping-up.

13   Slowly fill the system through the expansion tank; since the tank is the highest point in the system, all the air in the system should be displaced into the tank by the rising liquid. Slow pouring reduces the possibility of air being trapped and forming air-locks.

14   Continue filling until the coolant level reaches the expansion tank "MAX" level line, then cover the filler opening to prevent coolant splashing out.

15   Start the engine and run it at idle speed, until it has warmed-up to normal operating temperature and the radiator electric cooling fan has cut in; watch the temperature gauge to check for signs of overheating. If the level in the expansion tank drops significantly, top-up to the "MAX" level line, to minimise the amount of air circulating in the system.

16   Stop the engine, allow it to cool down *completely* (overnight, if possible), then uncover the expansion tank filler opening and top-up the tank to the "MAX" level line. Refit the filler cap, tightening it securely, and wash off any spilt coolant from the engine compartment and bodywork.

17   After refilling, always check carefully all components of the system (but especially any unions disturbed during draining and flushing) for signs of coolant leaks. Fresh antifreeze has a searching action, which will rapidly expose any weak points in the system.

18   **Note:** *If, after draining and refilling the system, symptoms of overheating are found which did not occur previously, then the fault is almost certainly due to trapped air at some point in the system, causing an air-lock and restricting the flow of coolant; usually, the air is trapped because the system was refilled too quickly. In some cases, air-locks can be released by tapping or squeezing the various hoses. If the problem persists, stop the engine and allow it to cool down completely, before unscrewing the expansion tank filler cap or disconnecting hoses to bleed out the trapped air.*

Antifreeze mixture

19   If the antifreeze used is not to Ford's specification, it should always be renewed at the suggested intervals. This is necessary not only to maintain the antifreeze properties, but also to prevent the corrosion which would otherwise occur as the corrosion inhibitors become progressively less effective. Always use an ethylene glycol-based antifreeze which is suitable for use in mixed-metal cooling systems.

20   If the antifreeze used is to Ford's specification, the levels of protection it affords are indicated in the Specifications Section of this Chapter. To give the recommended standard mixture ratio for this antifreeze, 40% (by volume) of antifreeze must be mixed with 60% of clean, soft water; if you are using any other type of antifreeze, follow its manufacturer's instructions to achieve the correct ratio. It is best to make up slightly more than the system's specified capacity, so that a supply is available for subsequent topping-up.

21   Before adding antifreeze, the cooling system should be completely drained, preferably flushed, and all hoses checked for condition

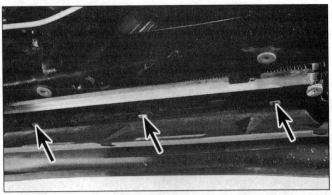

28.11 Ensure radiator undershield is located securely in three clips at front edge (arrowed) when refitting

and security. As noted earlier, fresh antifreeze will rapidly find any weaknesses in the system.

22   After filling with antifreeze, a label should be attached to the expansion tank, stating the type and concentration of antifreeze used, and the date installed. Any subsequent topping-up should be made with the same type and concentration of antifreeze. If topping-up using antifreeze to Ford's specification, note that a 50/50 mixture is permissible, purely for convenience.

23   Do not use engine antifreeze in the windscreen/tailgate washer system, as it will damage the vehicle's paintwork. A screen wash additive such as Turtle Wax High Tech Screen Wash should be added to the washer system in its maker's recommended quantities.

General cooling system checks

24   The engine should be cold for the cooling system checks, so perform the following procedure before driving the vehicle, or after it has been shut off for at least three hours.

25   Remove the expansion tank filler cap (see Section 3), and clean it thoroughly inside and out with a rag. Also clean the filler neck on the expansion tank. The presence of rust or corrosion in the filler neck indicates that the coolant should be changed. The coolant inside the expansion tank should be relatively clean and transparent. If it is rust-coloured, drain and flush the system, and refill with a fresh coolant mixture.

26   Carefully check the radiator hoses and heater hoses along their entire length; renew any hose which is cracked, swollen or deteriorated (see Section 12).

27   Inspect all other cooling system components (joint faces, etc.) for leaks. A leak in the cooling system will usually show up as white- or rust-coloured deposits on the area adjoining the leak. Where any problems of this nature are found on system components, renew the component or gasket with reference to Chapter 3.

28   Clean the front of the radiator with a soft brush to remove all insects, leaves, etc, embedded in the radiator fins. Be careful not to damage the radiator fins, or cut your fingers on them.

29 Air filter element renewal (every 30 000 miles or 3 years)

1   The air filter element is located in the air cleaner assembly on the left-hand side of the engine compartment. Release the clips, and lift the air cleaner cover **(see illustrations)**. If the additional working clearance is required, unclip the cover from the air mass meter, and withdraw it completely.

2   Lift out the element, and wipe out the housing **(see illustration)**. Check that no foreign matter is visible, either in the air intake or in the air mass meter.

3   If carrying out a routine service, the element must be renewed regardless of its apparent condition; note that the small foam filter in the rear right-hand corner of the air cleaner housing must be cleaned

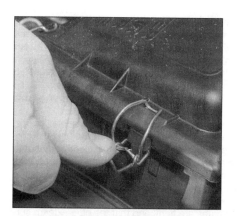

29.1A Release the wire clips to detach the cover from the air cleaner assembly . . .

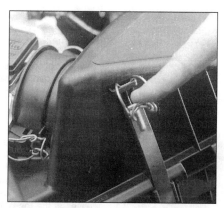

29.1B . . . noting the long clip normally hidden by the battery . . .

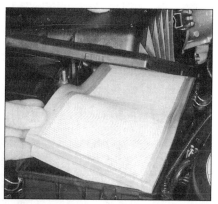

29.2 . . . lift the element out of the housing, and wipe out its interior before fitting the new element

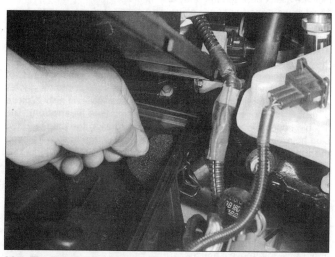

30.5 The Positive Crankcase Ventilation (PCV) system filter in the air cleaner assembly must be cleaned whenever the air filter element is renewed

whenever the air filter element is renewed (see Section 30).

4   If you are checking the element for any other reason, inspect its lower surface; if it is oily or very dirty, renew the element. If it is only moderately dusty, it can be re-used by blowing it clean from the upper to the lower surface with compressed air. **Warning:** *Wear eye protection when using compressed air!* Because it is a pleated-paper type filter, it cannot be washed or re-oiled. If it cannot be cleaned satisfactorily with compressed air, discard and renew it. **Caution:** *Never drive the vehicle with the air cleaner filter element removed. Excessive engine wear could result, and backfiring could even cause a fire under the bonnet.*

5   Refitting is the reverse of the removal procedure. Ensure that the element and cover are securely seated, so that unfiltered air cannot enter the engine.

30 Positive Crankcase Ventilation (PCV) system check and filter cleaning (every 30 000 miles or 3 years)

1   The Positive Crankcase Ventilation (PCV) system components are located at the front of the engine, underneath the exhaust manifold and air intake resonator. Refer to Chapter 6 for further information.

2   Check that all components of the system are securely fastened, correctly routed (with no kinks or sharp bends to restrict flow) and in sound condition; renew any worn or damaged components.

3   If oil leakage is noted, disconnect the various hoses and pipes,

and check that all are clear and unblocked. Remove the air cleaner assembly cover, air mass meter and resonator, then check that the hose from the cylinder head cover to the air cleaner housing is clear and undamaged. Disconnect the rubber T-piece both from the union on the inlet manifold left-hand end, and from the metal crankcase breather pipe under the ignition coil. Connect a spare, clean, length of hose to the breather pipe. Suck on the end of the hose, then blow through it - little or no restriction to airflow should be felt in either direction. A similar test can be applied to check that the inlet manifold passages are clear - air should be heard hissing out of the plenum chamber mouth as you blow.

4   The PCV valve is designed to allow gases to flow out of the crankcase only, so that a depression is created in the crankcase under most operating conditions, particularly at idle. Therefore, if either the oil separator or the PCV valve are thought to be blocked, they must be renewed (see Chapter 6). In such a case, however, there is nothing to be lost by attempting to flush out the blockage using a suitable solvent. The PCV valve should rattle when shaken.

5   While the air filter element is removed (see Section 29), wipe out the housing, and withdraw the small foam filter from its location in the rear right-hand corner of the housing **(see illustration)**. If the foam is badly clogged with dirt or oil, it must be cleaned by soaking it in a suitable solvent, and allowed to dry before being refitted.

31 Spark plug renewal (every 30 000 miles or 3 years)

Spark plug check and renewal

1   It is vital for the correct running, full performance and proper economy of the engine that the spark plugs perform with maximum efficiency. The most important factor in ensuring this is that the plugs fitted are appropriate for the engine. The suitable type is given in the Specifications Section at the beginning of this Chapter, on the Vehicle Emissions Control Information (VECI) label located on the underside of the bonnet (only on models sold in some areas) or in the vehicle's Owner's Handbook. If these sources specify different plugs, purchase the spark plug type specified on the VECI label (where appropriate), as that information is provided specifically for your engine. If this type is used and the engine is in good condition, the spark plugs should not need attention between scheduled renewal intervals. Spark plug cleaning is rarely necessary, and should not be attempted unless specialised equipment is available, as damage can easily be caused to the firing ends.

2   Spark plug removal and refitting requires a spark plug socket, with an extension which can be turned by a ratchet handle or similar. This socket is lined with a rubber sleeve, to protect the porcelain insulator of the spark plug, and to hold the plug while you insert it into the spark plug hole. You will also need a wire-type feeler gauge, to check and adjust the spark plug electrode gap, and a torque wrench to

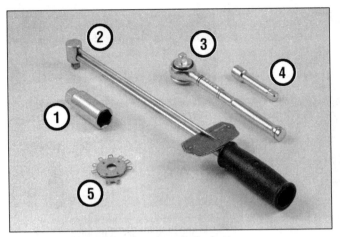

31.2 Tools required for changing spark plugs

1   **Spark plug socket** - *This will have special padding inside, to protect the spark plug porcelain insulator*
2   **Torque wrench** - *Although not essential, use of this tool is the best way to ensure that the plugs are tightened properly*
3   **Ratchet** - *Standard hand tool to fit the plug socket*
4   **Extension** - *Depending on the other tools available, you may need an extension to reach the plugs*
5   **Spark plug gap gauge** - *This gauge for checking the gap comes in a variety of styles. Make sure the gap for your engine is included*

tighten the new plugs to the specified torque **(see illustration)**.
3   To remove the spark plugs, first open the bonnet; the plugs are easily reached at the top of the engine. Note how the spark plug (HT) leads are routed and secured by clips along the channel in the cylinder head cover. To prevent the possibility of mixing up spark plug (HT) leads, it is a good idea to try to work on one spark plug at a time.
4   If the marks on the original-equipment spark plug (HT) leads cannot be seen, mark the leads 1 to 4, to correspond to the cylinder the lead serves (No 1 cylinder is at the timing belt end of the engine). Pull the leads from the plugs by gripping the rubber boot sealing the cylinder head cover opening, not the lead, otherwise the lead connection may be fractured.
5   It is advisable to soak up any water in the spark plug recesses with a rag, and to remove any dirt from them using a clean brush, vacuum cleaner or compressed air before removing the plugs, to prevent any dirt or water from dropping into the cylinders. **Warning:** *Wear eye protection when using compressed air!*
6   Unscrew the spark plugs, ensuring that the socket is kept in alignment with each plug - if the socket is forcibly moved to either side, the porcelain top of the plug may be broken off. If any undue difficulty is encountered when unscrewing any of the spark plugs, carefully check the cylinder head threads and tapered sealing surfaces for signs of wear, excessive corrosion or damage; if any of these conditions is found, seek the advice of a Ford dealer as to the best method of repair.
7   As each plug is removed, examine it as follows - this will give a good indication of the condition of the engine. If the insulator nose of the spark plug is clean and white, with no deposits, this is indicative of a weak mixture.
8   If the tip and insulator nose are covered with hard black-looking deposits, then this is indicative that the mixture is too rich. Should the plug be black and oily, then it is likely that the engine is fairly worn, as well as the mixture being too rich.
9   If the insulator nose is covered with light tan to greyish-brown deposits, then the mixture is correct, and it is likely that the engine is in good condition.
10   If you are renewing the spark plugs, purchase the new plugs, then check each of them first for faults such as cracked insulators or damaged threads. Note also that, whenever the spark plugs are renewed as a routine service operation, the spark plug (HT) leads should

be checked as described below.
11   The spark plug electrode gap is of considerable importance as, if it is too large or too small, the size of the spark and its efficiency will be seriously impaired. The gap should be set to the value given in the Specifications Section of this Chapter. New plugs will not necessarily be set to the correct gap, so they should always be checked before fitting.
12   Special spark plug electrode gap adjusting tools are available from most motor accessory shops **(see illustration)**.
13   To set the electrode gap, measure the gap with a feeler gauge, and then bend open, or closed, the outer plug electrode until the correct gap is achieved **(see illustration)**. The centre electrode should never be bent, as this may crack the insulation and cause plug failure, if nothing worse. If the outer electrode is not exactly over the centre electrode, bend it gently to align them.
14   Before fitting the spark plugs, check that the threaded connector sleeves at the top of the plugs are tight, and that the plug exterior surfaces and threads are clean. Brown staining on the porcelain, immediately above the metal body, is quite normal, and does not necessarily indicate a leak between the body and insulator.
15   On installing the spark plugs, first check that the cylinder head thread and sealing surface are as clean as possible; use a clean rag wrapped around a paintbrush to wipe clean the sealing surface. Apply a smear of copper-based grease or anti-seize compound to the threads of each plug, and screw them in by hand where possible. Take extra care to enter the plug threads correctly, as the cylinder head is of aluminium alloy - it's often difficult to insert spark plugs into their holes without cross-threading them. To avoid this possibility, fit a short piece of rubber hose over the end of the spark plug **(see illustration)**. The flexible hose acts as a universal joint, to help align the plug with the plug hole. Should the plug begin to cross-thread, the hose will slip on the spark plug, preventing thread damage.
16   When each spark plug is started correctly on its threads, screw it down until it just seats lightly, then tighten it to the specified torque wrench setting **(see illustration)**. If a torque wrench is not available - and this is one case where the use of a torque wrench is strongly recommended - tighten each spark plug through *no more than 1/16 of a turn*. *Do not* exceed the specified torque setting, and *NEVER* overtighten these spark plugs - their tapered seats mean they are almost impossible to remove if abused.
17   Reconnect the spark plug (HT) leads in their correct order, using a twisting motion on the boot until it is firmly seated on the end of the spark plug and on the cylinder head cover.

Spark plug (HT) lead check

18   The spark plug (HT) leads should be checked whenever the plugs themselves are renewed. Start by making a visual check of the leads while the engine is running. In a darkened garage (make sure there is ventilation) start the engine and observe each lead. Be careful not to come into contact with any moving engine parts. If there is a break in the lead, you will see arcing or a small spark at the damaged area.
19   The spark plug (HT) leads should be inspected one at a time, to prevent mixing up the firing order, which is essential for proper engine operation. Each original lead should be numbered to identify its cylinder. If the number is illegible, a piece of tape can be marked with the correct number, and wrapped around the lead (the leads should be numbered 1 to 4, with No 1 lead nearest the timing belt end of the engine). The lead can then be disconnected.
20   Check inside the boot for corrosion, which will look like a white crusty powder. Clean this off as much as possible; if it is excessive, or if cleaning leaves the metal connector too badly corroded to be fit for further use, the lead must be renewed. Push the lead and boot back onto the end of the spark plug. The boot should fit tightly onto the end of the plug - if it doesn't, remove the lead and use pliers carefully to crimp the metal connector inside the boot until the fit is snug.
21   Using a clean rag, wipe the entire length of the lead to remove built-up dirt and grease. Once the lead is clean, check for burns, cracks and other damage. Do not bend the lead sharply, because the conductor might break.
22   Disconnect the lead from the ignition coil by pressing together the plastic retaining catches and pulling the end fitting off the coil terminal.

31.12 Spark plug manufacturers recommend using a wire-type gauge when checking the gap - if the wire does not slide between the electrodes with a slight drag, adjustment is required

31.13 To change the gap, bend the outer electrode only, as indicated by the arrows, and be very careful not to crack or chip the porcelain insulator surrounding the centre electrode

31.15 A length of rubber hose will save time and prevent damaged threads when installing the spark plugs

31.16 Spark plugs have tapered seats - do not overtighten them on refitting, or you will not be able to get them out again without risking damage to the plugs and cylinder head

31.22 Measure the resistance of the spark plug (HT) leads - if any exceeds the specified maximum value, renew all the leads as a set

33.5 Squeeze together fuel filter pipe union locking lugs, then pull pipes off filter stubs - note colour-coding to ensure pipes are correctly reconnected

Check for corrosion and for a tight fit. If a meter with the correct measuring range is available, measure the resistance of the disconnected lead from its coil connector to its spark plug connector **(see illustration)**. If the resistance recorded for any of the leads exceeds the value specified, all the leads should be renewed as a set. Refit the lead to the coil, noting that each coil terminal is marked with its respective cylinder number, so that there is no risk of mixing up the leads and upsetting the firing order.

23   Inspect the remaining spark plug (HT) leads, ensuring that each is securely fastened at the ignition coil and spark plug when the check is complete. If any sign of arcing, severe connector corrosion, burns, cracks or other damage is noticed, obtain new spark plug (HT) leads, renewing them as a set. If new spark plug leads are to be fitted, re-move and refit them one at a time, to avoid mix-ups in the firing order.

32 Timing belt renewal (every 60 000 miles)

Refer to Chapter 2, Part A.

33 Fuel filter renewal (every 60 000 miles)

Warning: *Petrol is extremely flammable, so extra precautions must be taken when working on any part of the fuel system. Do not smoke, or allow open flames or bare light bulbs, near the work area. Also, do not work in a garage if a natural gas-type appliance with a pilot light is*

present. While performing any work on the fuel system, wear safety glasses, and have a suitable (Class B) fire extinguisher on hand. If you spill any fuel on your skin, rinse it off immediately with soap and water.

1   The fuel filter is located at the front right-hand corner of the fuel tank, just forward of the vehicle's right-hand rear jacking point. The fil-ter performs a vital role in keeping dirt and other foreign matter out of the fuel system, and so must be renewed at regular intervals, or when-ever you have reason to suspect that it may be clogged. It is always unpleasant working under a vehicle - pressure-washing or hosing clean the underbody in the filter's vicinity will make working conditions more tolerable, and will reduce the risk of getting dirt into the fuel sys-tem.

2   Relieve any residual pressure in the system by removing the fuel pump fuse (No 14) and starting the engine; allow the engine to idle un-til it dies. Turn the engine over once or twice on the starter, to ensure that all pressure is released, then switch off the ignition. **Warning:** *This procedure will merely relieve the increased pressure necessary for the engine to run - remember that fuel will still be present in the system components, and take precautions accordingly before disconnecting any of them.*

3   Noting the comments made in Section 1 of Chapter 5, disconnect the battery earth terminal.

4   Jack up the rear right-hand side of the vehicle, and support it se-curely on an axle stand.

5   Using rag to soak up any spilt fuel, release the fuel feed and outlet pipe unions from the filter, by squeezing together the protruding lock-ing lugs on each union, and carefully pulling the union off the filter stub **(see illustration)**. Where the unions are colour-coded, the feed and

33.7A When installing the new filter, ensure the arrow showing direction of fuel flow points towards the engine . . .

33.7B . . . secure pipe unions as described - do not overtighten clamp screw (arrowed)

outlet pipes cannot be confused; where both unions are the same colour, note carefully which pipe is connected to which filter stub, and ensure that they are correctly reconnected on refitting.

6   Noting the arrows and/or other markings on the filter showing the direction of fuel flow (towards the engine), slacken the filter clamp screw and withdraw the filter. Note that the filter will still contain fuel; care should be taken, to avoid spillage and to minimise the risk of fire.

7   On installation, slide the filter into its clamp so that the arrow marked on it faces the correct way, then slide each pipe union on to its (correct) respective filter stub, and press it down until the locking lugs click into their groove **(see illustrations)**. Tighten the clamp screw carefully, until the filter is just prevented from moving; do not over-tighten the clamp screw, or the filter casing may be crushed.

8   Refit the fuel pump fuse and reconnect the battery earth terminal, then switch the ignition on and off five times, to pressurise the system. Check for any sign of fuel leakage around the filter unions before lowering the vehicle to the ground and starting the engine.

34 Brake fluid renewal (every 3 years)

The procedure is similar to that for the bleeding of the hydraulic system as described in Chapter 9, except that the brake fluid reservoir should be emptied by syphoning, and allowance should be made for the old fluid to be removed from the circuit when bleeding a section of the circuit.

Chapter 2 Part A
In-car engine repair procedures

Contents

Specifications

General

Engine type.. Four-cylinder, in-line, double overhead camshafts
Engine code:
    1.6 litre models.. LIF
    1.8 litre models.. RKA
    2.0 litre models.. NGA

Capacity:
    1.6 litre models... 1597 cc
    1.8 litre models... 1796cc
    2.0 litre models... 1988 cc
Bore:
    1.6 litre models... 76.0 mm
    1.8 litre models... 80.6 mm
    2.0 litre models... 84.8 mm
Stroke - all models... 88.0 mm
Compression ratio:
    1.6 litre models... 10.3:1
    1.8 and 2.0 litre models... 10.0:1
Compression pressure - at starter motor speed,
engine fully warmed-up .... Not available
Firing order .... 1-3-4-2 (No 1 cylinder at timing belt end)
Direction of crankshaft rotation .... Clockwise (seen from right-hand side of vehicle)

Cylinder head

Hydraulic tappet bore inside diameter .... 28.395 to 28.425 mm

Camshafts and hydraulic tappets

Camshaft bearing journal diameter .... 25.960 to 25.980 mm
Camshaft bearing journal-to-cylinder head running clearance .... 0.020 to 0.070 mm
Camshaft endfloat .... 0.080 to 0.220 mm
Hydraulic tappet diameter .... 28.400 mm

Lubrication

Engine oil type/specification.. See Chapter 1
Engine oil capacity... See Chapter 1
Oil pressure... No information available at time of writing
Oil pump clearances.. No information available at time of writing

Torque wrench settings

	Nm	lbf ft
Cylinder head cover bolts:		
Stage 1	2	1.5
Stage 2	7	5
Camshaft toothed pulley bolts	68	50
Camshaft bearing cap bolts:		
Stage 1	10	7
Stage 2	19	14
Cylinder head bolts:		
Stage 1	25	18
Stage 2	45	33
Stage 3	Angle-tighten a further 105°	
Timing belt cover fasteners:		
Upper-to-middle (outer) cover bolts	4	3
Cover-to-cylinder head or block bolts	7	5
Cover studs-to-cylinder head or block	9 to 11	6.5 to 8
Timing belt tensioner bolt	38	28
Timing belt tensioner backplate locating peg	8 to 11	6 to 8
Timing belt tensioner spring retaining pin	10	7
Timing belt guide pulley bolts	35 to 40	26 to 30
Water pump pulley bolts	10	7
Water pump bolts	See Chapter 3	
Auxiliary drivebelt idler pulley	48	35
Inlet manifold nuts and bolts	18	13
Alternator mounting bracket-to-cylinder block bolts	47	35
Cylinder head support plates:		
Front plate Torx screws - to power ..steering pump/air conditioning compressor mounting bracket and cylinder head	47	35
Rear plate/engine lifting eye - to alternator mounting bracket and cylinder head bolts	47	35
Front engine lifting eye bolt	16	12
Inlet and exhaust manifold studs-to-cylinder head	10 maximum	7 maximum
Exhaust manifold heat shield bolts:		
Shield-to-cylinder head	7	5
Shield/dipstick tube	10	7
Shield/coolant pipe-to-manifold	23	17
Exhaust manifold nuts	16	12
Air conditioning refrigerant pipe-to-exhaust manifold bolts	10	7

Crankshaft pulley bolt..	108 to 115	80 to 85
Oil pump-to-cylinder block bolts..	10	7
Oil pick-up pipe-to-pump screws...	10	7
Oil baffle/pump pick-up pipe nuts..	19	14
Oil filter adaptor-to-pump..	18 to 25	13 to 18
Oil pressure warning light switch...	27	20
Oil level sensor	27	20
Sump bolts	21 to 22	15 to 16
Coolant pipe-to-sump bolt	10	7
Flywheel/driveplate bolts...	110 to 112	81 to 83
Crankshaft left-hand oil seal carrier bolts.................................	22	16
Transmission-to-engine bolts..	40	30
Engine/transmission front mounting:		
Mounting bracket-to-transmission.....................................	Not available	
Mounting-to-subframe bolts/nuts - stage 1	10	7
Mounting-to-subframe bolts/nuts - stage 2	48	35
Mounting centre bolt	120	89
Engine/manual transmission rear mounting:		
Mounting bracket-to-transmission 12 mm fasteners..........	78 to 84	58 to 62
Mounting bracket-to-transmission 10 mm fasteners..........	48	35
Mounting-to-subframe bolts and nut - stage 1	10	7
Mounting-to-subframe bolts and nut - stage 2	48	35
Mounting centre bolt	120	89
Engine/automatic transmission rear mounting:		
Mounting bracket-to-transmission.......................................	48 to 49	35 to 36
Mounting-to-subframe bolts - stage 1	10	7
Mounting-to-subframe bolts - stage 2	48	35
Mounting centre bolt	120	89
Engine/transmission left-hand mounting:		
Bracket-to-transmission nuts..	83	61
Mounting centre bolt	Not available	
Mounting-to-body bolts	Not available	
Engine/transmission right-hand mounting:		
Bracket-to-engine and mounting nuts	83 to 90	61 to 66
Mounting-to-body bolts	84	62

Note: *Refer to Part B of this Chapter for remaining torque wrench settings.*

2A

1 General information

How to use this Chapter

This Part of Chapter 2 is devoted to repair procedures possible while the engine is still installed in the vehicle, and includes only the Specifications relevant to those procedures. Since these procedures are based on the assumption that the engine is installed in the vehicle, if the engine has been removed from the vehicle and mounted on a stand, some of the preliminary dismantling steps outlined will not apply.

Information concerning engine/transmission removal and refitting, and engine overhaul, can be found in Part B of this Chapter, which also includes the Specifications relevant to those procedures.

General description - engine

The engine, also known by Ford's internal code name "Zetec" (formerly "Zeta"), is of four-cylinder, in-line type, mounted transversely at the front of the vehicle, with the (clutch and) transmission on its left-hand end **(see illustrations)**.

Apart from the plastic timing belt covers and the cast-iron cylinder block/crankcase, all major engine castings are of aluminium alloy.

The crankshaft runs in five main bearings, the centre main bearing's upper half incorporating thrustwashers to control crankshaft end-float. The connecting rods rotate on horizontally-split bearing shells at their big-ends. The pistons are attached to the connecting rods by gudgeon pins which are an interference fit in the connecting rod small-end eyes. The aluminium alloy pistons are fitted with three piston rings: two compression rings and an oil control ring. After manufacture, the cylinder bores and piston skirts are measured and classified into three

grades, which must be carefully matched together, to ensure the correct piston/cylinder clearance; no oversizes are available to permit re-boring.

The inlet and exhaust valves are each closed by coil springs; they operate in guides which are shrink-fitted into the cylinder head, as are the valve seat inserts.

Both camshafts are driven by the same toothed timing belt, each operating eight valves via self-adjusting hydraulic tappets, thus eliminating the need for routine checking and adjustment of the valve clearances. Each camshaft rotates in five bearings that are line-bored directly in the cylinder head and the (bolted-on) bearing caps; this means that the bearing caps are not available separately from the cylinder head, and must not be interchanged with caps from another engine.

The water pump is bolted to the right-hand end of the cylinder block, inboard of the timing belt, and is driven with the power steering pump and alternator by a flat "polyvee"-type auxiliary drivebelt from the crankshaft pulley.

When working on this engine, note that Torx-type (both male and female heads) and hexagon socket (Allen head) fasteners are widely used; a good selection of bits, with the necessary adaptors, will be required, so that these can be unscrewed without damage and, on re-assembly, tightened to the torque wrench settings specified.

General description - lubrication system

Lubrication is by means of an eccentric-rotor trochoidal pump, which is mounted on the crankshaft right-hand end, and draws oil through a strainer located in the sump. The pump forces oil through an externally-mounted full-flow cartridge-type filter - on some versions of the engine, an oil cooler is fitted to the oil filter mounting, so that clean oil entering the engine's galleries is cooled by the main engine cooling

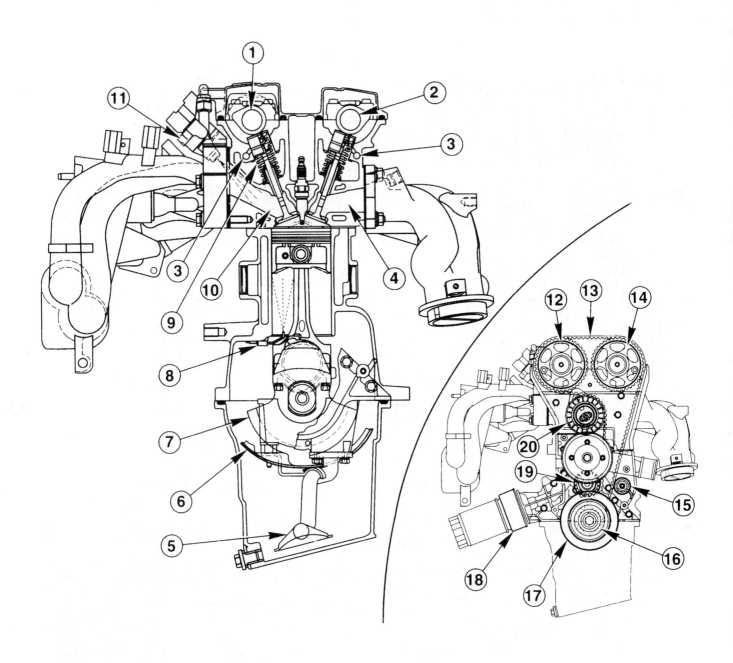

1.3A Longitudinal cross-section through engine - inset showing timing belt details

1	Inlet camshaft	11	Fuel injector
2	Exhaust camshaft	12	Inlet camshaft toothed pulley
3	Oil galleries	13	Timing belt
4	Exhaust port	14	Exhaust camshaft toothed pulley
5	Oil strainer and pick-up pipe	15	Timing belt (front) guide pulley
6	Oil baffle	16	Crankshaft toothed pulley - behind
7	Crankshaft	17	Crankshaft pulley
8	Piston-cooling oil jet (where fitted)	18	Oil cooler (where fitted)
9	Inlet valve	19	Timing belt (rear) guide pulley
10	Inlet port	20	Timing belt tensioner

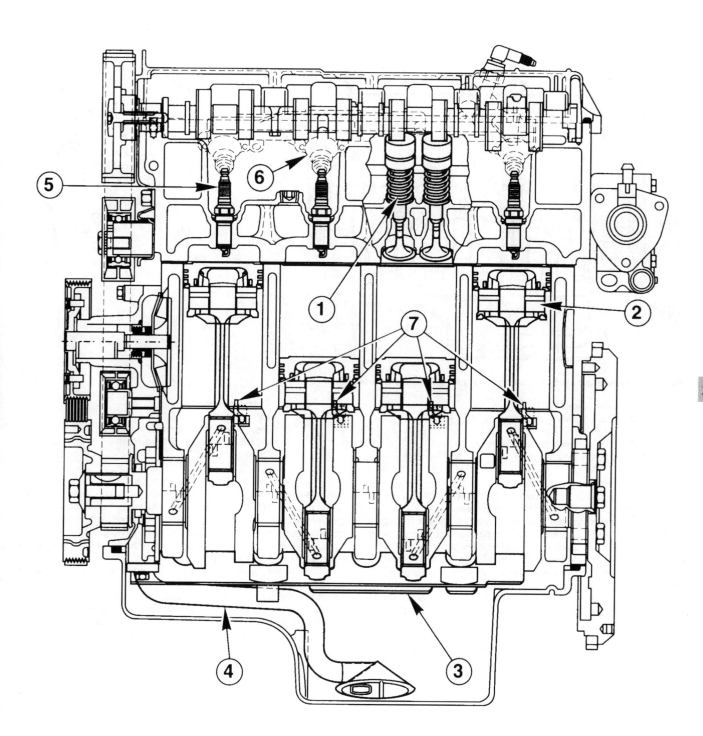

2A

1.3B Lateral cross-section through engine

1	Exhaust valve	5	Spark plug
2	Piston	6	Fuel injector
3	Oil baffle	7	Piston-cooling oil jets (where fitted)
4	Oil strainer and pick-up pipe		

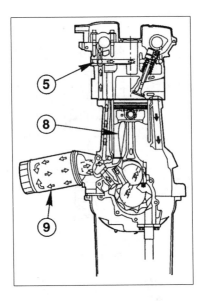

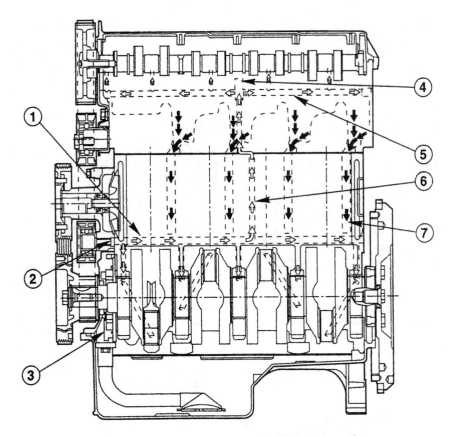

1.10 Engine lubrication system - inset showing longitudinal cross-section

1	Main oil gallery	6	Cylinder head oil supply
2	From oil filter	7	Oil return
3	Oil pump	8	Piston-cooling oil spray (where fitted)
4	Cylinder head oil-retaining valve	9	Oil filter - oil cooler not shown here
5	Cylinder head oil gallery		

system. From the filter, the oil is pumped into a main gallery in the cylinder block/crankcase, from where it is distributed to the crankshaft (main bearings) and cylinder head **(see illustration)**.

The big-end bearings are supplied with oil via internal drillings in the crankshaft. On some versions of the engine, each piston crown is cooled by a spray of oil directed at its underside by a jet. These jets are fed by passages off the crankshaft oil supply galleries, with spring-loaded valves to ensure that the jets open only when there is sufficient pressure to guarantee a good oil supply to the rest of the engine components; where the jets are not fitted, separate blanking plugs are provided, so that the passages are sealed, but can be cleaned at overhaul **(see illustration)**.

The cylinder head is provided with two oil galleries, one on the inlet side and one on the exhaust, to ensure constant oil supply to the camshaft bearings and hydraulic tappets. A retaining valve (inserted into the cylinder head's top surface, in the middle, on the inlet side) prevents these galleries from being drained when the engine is switched off. The valve incorporates a ventilation hole in its upper end, to allow air bubbles to escape from the system when the engine is restarted.

While the crankshaft and camshaft bearings and the hydraulic tappets receive a pressurised supply, the camshaft lobes and valves are lubricated by splash, as are all other engine components.

Valve clearances - general

It is necessary for a clearance to exist between the tip of each valve stem and the valve operating mechanism, to allow for the expansion of the various components as the engine reaches normal operating temperature.

On most older engine designs, this meant that the valve clearances (also known as "tappet" clearances) had to be checked and adjusted regularly. If the clearances were allowed to be too slack, the engine would be very noisy, its power output would suffer, and its fuel consumption would increase. If the clearances were allowed to be too tight, the engine's power output would be reduced, and the valves and their seats could be severely damaged.

The engines covered in this manual, however, employ hydraulic tappets which use the lubricating system's oil pressure automatically to take up the clearance between each camshaft lobe and its respective valve stem. Therefore, there is no need for regular checking and adjustment of the valve clearances, but it is essential that *only* good-quality oil of the recommended viscosity and specification is used in the engine, and that this oil is always changed at the recommended intervals. If this advice is not followed, the oilways and tappets may become clogged with particles of dirt, or deposits of burnt (inferior) engine oil, so that the system cannot work properly; ultimately, one or more of the tappets may fail, and expensive repairs may be required.

On starting the engine from cold, there will be a slight delay while full oil pressure builds up in all parts of the engine, especially in the tappets; the valve components, therefore, may well "rattle" for about 10 seconds or so, and then quieten. This is a normal state of affairs, and is nothing to worry about, provided that all tappets quieten quickly and stay quiet.

After the vehicle has been standing for several days, the valve components may "rattle" for longer than usual, as nearly all the oil will have drained away from the engine's top end components and bearing surfaces. While this is only to be expected, care must be taken not to damage the engine under these circumstances - avoid high speed run-

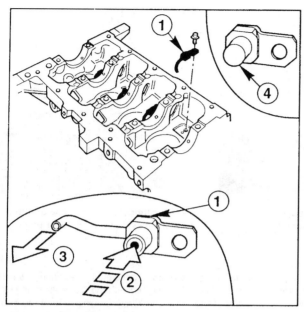

1.11 Piston-cooling oil jet details

1   Oil jets (when fitted)
2   Oil flow - only when valve opens at set pressure
3   Oil spray
4   Blanking plug (when fitted)

ning until all the tappets are refilled with oil and operating normally. With the vehicle stationary, hold the engine at no more than a fast idle speed (maximum 2000 to 2500 rpm) for 10 to 15 minutes, or until the noise ceases. *Do not run the engine at more than 3000 rpm until the tappets are fully recharged with oil and the noise has ceased.*

If the valve components are thought to be noisy, or if a light rattle persists from the top end after the engine has warmed up to normal operating temperature, take the vehicle to a Ford dealer for expert advice. Depending on the mileage covered and the usage to which each vehicle has been put, some vehicles may be noisier than others; only a good mechanic experienced in these engines can tell if the noise level is typical for the vehicle's mileage, or if a genuine fault exists. If any tappet's operation is faulty, it must be renewed (Section 13).

2   Repair operations possible with the engine in the vehicle

The following major repair operations can be accomplished without removing the engine from the vehicle. However, owners should note that any operation involving the removal of the sump requires careful forethought, depending on the level of skill and the tools and facilities available; refer to the relevant text for details.

(a)   Compression pressure - testing.
(b)   Cylinder head cover - removal and refitting.
(c)   Timing belt covers - removal and refitting.
(d)   Timing belt - renewal.
(e)   Timing belt tensioner and toothed pulleys - removal and refitting.
(f)   Camshaft oil seals - renewal.
(g)   Camshafts and hydraulic tappets - removal and refitting.
(h)   Cylinder head - removal, overhaul and refitting.
(i)   Cylinder head and pistons - decarbonising.
(j)   Sump - removal and refitting.
(k)   Crankshaft oil seals - renewal.
(l)   Oil pump - removal and refitting.
(m)   Piston/connecting rod assemblies - removal and refitting (but see note below).

(n)   Flywheel/driveplate - removal and refitting.
(o)   Engine/transmission mountings - removal and refitting.

Clean the engine compartment and the exterior of the engine with some type of degreaser before any work is done. It will make the job easier, and will help to keep dirt out of the internal areas of the engine.

Depending on the components involved, it may be helpful to remove the bonnet, to improve access to the engine as repairs are performed (refer to Chapter 11 if necessary). Cover the wings to prevent damage to the paint; special covers are available, but an old bedspread or blanket will also work.

If vacuum, exhaust, oil or coolant leaks develop, indicating a need for component/gasket or seal replacement, the repairs can generally be made with the engine in the vehicle. The intake and exhaust manifold gaskets, sump gasket, crankshaft oil seals and cylinder head gasket are all accessible with the engine in place.

Exterior components such as the intake and exhaust manifolds, the sump, the oil pump, the water pump, the starter motor, the alternator and the fuel system components can be removed for repair with the engine in place.

Since the cylinder head can be removed without lifting out the engine, camshaft and valve component servicing can also be accomplished with the engine in the vehicle, as can renewal of the timing belt and toothed pulleys.

In extreme cases caused by a lack of necessary equipment, repair or renewal of piston rings, pistons, connecting rods and big-end bearings is possible with the engine in the vehicle. However, this practice is not recommended, because of the cleaning and preparation work that must be done to the components involved, and because of the amount of preliminary dismantling work required - these operations are therefore covered in Part B of this Chapter.

3   Compression test - description and interpretation

1   When engine performance is down, or if misfiring occurs which cannot be attributed to the ignition or fuel systems, a compression test can provide diagnostic clues as to the engine's condition. If the test is performed regularly, it can give warning of trouble before any other symptoms become apparent.
2   The engine must be fully warmed-up to normal operating temperature, the oil level must be correct, the battery must be fully charged, and the spark plugs must be removed. The aid of an assistant will be required also.
3   Disable the ignition system by unplugging the ignition coil's electrical connector, and remove fuse 14 to disconnect the fuel pump.
4   Fit a compression tester to the No 1 cylinder spark plug hole - the type of tester which screws into the plug thread is to be preferred.
5   Have the assistant hold the throttle wide open and crank the engine on the starter motor; after one or two revolutions, the compression pressure should build up to a maximum figure, and then stabilise. Record the highest reading obtained.
6   Repeat the test on the remaining cylinders, recording the pressure developed in each.
7   At the time of writing, no compression specifications were available from Ford, but a typical reading would be in excess of 12 bars. All cylinders should produce very similar pressures; any difference greater than 10% indicates the existence of a fault. Note that the compression should build up quickly in a healthy engine; low compression on the first stroke, followed by gradually-increasing pressure on successive strokes, indicates worn piston rings. A low compression reading on the first stroke, which does not build up during successive strokes, indicates leaking valves or a blown head gasket (a cracked head could also be the cause). Deposits on the undersides of the valve heads can also cause low compression.
8   If the pressure in any cylinder is considerably lower than the others, introduce a teaspoonful of clean oil into that cylinder through its spark plug hole, and repeat the test.
9   If the addition of oil temporarily improves the compression pressure, this indicates that bore or piston wear is responsible for the pres-

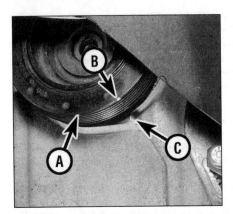

4.9A Do not use crankshaft pulley's first pair of notches "A" - align second pair of notches "B" with raised rib on sump "C" . . .

4.9B . . . using a straight edge extended out from the sump (arrowed) if greater accuracy is required

5.4 Disconnecting crankcase breather hose from cylinder head cover union

sure loss. No improvement suggests that leaking or burnt valves, or a blown head gasket, may be to blame.

10   A low reading from two adjacent cylinders is almost certainly due to the head gasket having blown between them; the presence of coolant in the engine oil will confirm this.

11   If one cylinder is about 20 percent lower than the others and the engine has a slightly rough idle, a worn camshaft lobe or faulty hydraulic tappet could be the cause.

12   If the compression is unusually high, the combustion chambers are probably coated with carbon deposits. If this is the case, the cylinder head should be removed and decarbonised.

13   On completion of the test, refit the spark plugs, then reconnect the ignition system and fuel pump.

---

4   Top Dead Centre (TDC) for No 1 piston - locating

General

1   Top Dead Centre (TDC) is the highest point in its travel up-and-down its cylinder bore that each piston reaches as the crankshaft rotates. While each piston reaches TDC both at the top of the compression stroke and again at the top of the exhaust stroke, for the purpose of timing the engine, TDC refers to the piston position (usually No 1 piston) at the top of its compression stroke.

2   It is useful for several servicing procedures to be able to position the engine at TDC.

3   No 1 piston and cylinder are at the right-hand (timing belt) end of the engine (right- and left-hand are always quoted as seen from the driver's seat). Note that the crankshaft rotates clockwise when viewed from the right-hand side of the vehicle.

Locating TDC

4   Remove all the spark plugs (Chapter 1).

5   Disconnect both battery leads - see Chapter 5, Section 1 - unless the starter motor is to be used to turn the engine.

6   Apply the handbrake and ensure that the transmission is in neutral, then jack up the front right-hand side of the vehicle and support on an axle stand. Remove the roadwheel.

7   Remove the auxiliary drivebelt cover (see Chapter 1) to expose the crankshaft pulley and timing marks.

8   It is best to rotate the crankshaft using a spanner applied to the crankshaft pulley bolt; however, it is possible also to use the starter motor (switched on either by an assistant using the ignition key, or by using a remote starter switch) to bring the engine close to TDC, then finish with a spanner. If the starter is used, be sure to disconnect the battery leads immediately it is no longer required.

9   Note the two pairs of notches in the inner and outer rims of the crankshaft pulley. In the normal direction of crankshaft rotation (clockwise, seen from the right-hand side of the vehicle) the first pair of

notches are irrelevant to the vehicles covered in this manual, while the second pair indicate TDC when aligned with the rear edge of the raised mark on the sump. Rotate the crankshaft clockwise until the second pair of notches align with the edge of the sump mark; use a straight edge extended out from the sump if greater accuracy is required **(see illustrations)**.

10   Nos 1 and 4 cylinders are now at TDC, one of them on the compression stroke. Remove the oil filler cap; if No 4 cylinder exhaust cam lobe is pointing to the rear of the vehicle and slightly downwards, it is No 1 cylinder that is correctly positioned. If the lobe is pointing horizontally forwards, rotate the crankshaft one full turn (360) clockwise until the pulley notches align again, and the lobe is pointing to the rear and slightly down. No 1 cylinder will then be at TDC on the compression stroke.

11   Once No 1 cylinder has been positioned at TDC on the compression stroke, TDC for any of the other cylinders can then be located by rotating the crankshaft clockwise 180 at a time and following the firing order (see Specifications).

12   An alternative method of locating TDC is to remove the cylinder head cover (see Section 5) and to rotate the crankshaft (clockwise, as described in paragraph 8 above) until the inlet valves for the cylinder concerned have opened and just closed again. Insert a length of wooden dowel (approximately 150 mm/6 in long) or similar into the spark plug hole until it rests on the piston crown, and slowly further rotate the crankshaft (taking care not to allow the dowel to be trapped in the cylinder) until the dowel stops rising - the piston is now at the top of its compression stroke, and the dowel can be removed.

13   There is a "dead" area around TDC (as the piston stops rising, pauses and then begins to descend) which makes difficult the exact location of TDC by this method; if accuracy is required, either establish carefully the exact mid-point of the dead area, or refer to the timing marks (paragraph 9 above).

---

5   Cylinder head cover - removal and refitting

1   Unplug the two electrical connectors and disconnect the vacuum hose (where fitted), then remove the air cleaner assembly cover with the air mass meter, the resonator and the plenum chamber (see Chapter 4).

2   Disconnect the accelerator cable from the throttle linkage as described in Chapter 4. Where fitted, disconnect also the cruise control actuator cable (see Chapter 12).

3   Remove the timing belt upper cover (see Section 9).

4   Disconnect the crankcase breather hose from the cylinder head cover union **(see illustration)**.

5   Unplug the HT leads from the spark plugs and withdraw them, unclipping the leads from the cover.

6   Working progressively, unscrew the cylinder head cover retaining bolts, noting the spacer sleeve and rubber seal at each, then withdraw the cover **(see illustration)**.

5.6 Removing cylinder head cover

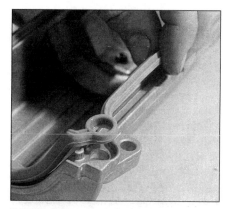

5.8 Ensure gasket is located correctly in cover groove

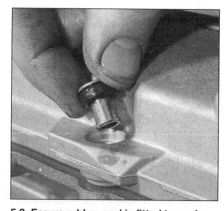

5.9 Ensure rubber seal is fitted to each cover bolt spacer, as shown

7   Discard the cover gasket; this *must* be renewed whenever it is disturbed. Check that the sealing faces are undamaged, and that the rubber seal at each retaining bolt is serviceable; renew any worn or damaged seals.

8   On refitting, clean the cover and cylinder head gasket faces carefully, then fit a new gasket to the cover, ensuring that it locates correctly in the cover grooves **(see illustration)**.

9   Refit the cover to the cylinder head, then insert the rubber seal and spacer sleeve at each bolt location **(see illustration)**. Start all bolts finger-tight, ensuring that the gasket remains seated in its groove.

10   Working in a diagonal sequence from the centre outwards, and in two stages (see Specifications), tighten the cover bolts to the specified torque wrench setting.

11   Refit the HT leads, clipping them into place so that they are correctly routed; each is numbered, and can also be identified by the numbering on its respective coil terminal.

12   Reconnect the crankcase breather hose, and refit the timing belt upper cover. Reconnect and adjust the accelerator cable, then refit the air cleaner assembly cover with the air mass meter, the resonator and the plenum chamber (see Chapter 4).

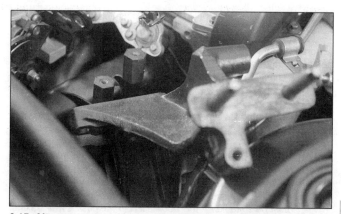

6.15 Alternator mounting bracket must be unbolted from rear of cylinder block to permit access to inlet manifold nut

6   Inlet manifold - removal and refitting

Warning: *Petrol is extremely flammable, so take extra precautions when disconnecting any part of the fuel system. Don't smoke, or allow naked flames or bare light bulbs in or near the work area. Don't work in a garage where a natural gas appliance (such as a clothes dryer or water heater) is installed. If you spill petrol on your skin, rinse it off immediately. Have a fire extinguisher rated for petrol fires handy, and know how to use it.*

Removal

1   Park the vehicle on firm, level ground, apply the handbrake firmly, and slacken the nuts securing the right-hand front roadwheel.

2   Relieve the fuel system pressure (see Chapter 4).

3   Disconnect the battery negative (earth) lead - see Chapter 5, Section 1.

4   Unplugging the two electrical connectors and disconnecting the vacuum hose (where fitted), remove the air cleaner assembly cover with the air mass meter, the resonator and the plenum chamber (see Chapter 4).

5   Disconnect the accelerator cable from the throttle linkage as described in Chapter 4 - where fitted, disconnect also the cruise control actuator cable (see Chapter 12).

6   Disconnect the crankcase breather hose from the cylinder head cover union.

7   Unbolt the upper part of the exhaust manifold heat shield; unclip the coolant hose to allow it to be withdrawn. Slacken the sleeve nut securing the EGR pipe to the manifold, remove the two screws securing the pipe to the ignition coil bracket, then unscrew the sleeve nut securing the pipe to the EGR valve - see Chapter 6 for full details if required.

8   Remove the two screws securing the wiring "rail" to the top of the manifold - this is simply so that it can be moved as required to reach the manifold bolts. Unplug their electrical connectors to disconnect the camshaft position sensor and the coolant temperature sensor, then unclip the wiring from the ignition coil bracket, and secure it to the manifold.

9   Remove the three screws securing the wiring "rail" to the rear of the manifold. Releasing its wire clip, unplug the large electrical connector (next to the fuel pressure regulator) to disconnect the wiring of the manifold components from the engine wiring loom.

10   Marking or labelling them as they are unplugged, disconnect the vacuum hoses as follows:

(a)   *One from the rear of the throttle housing (only the one hose - there is no need to disconnect the second hose running to the fuel pressure regulator).*

(b)   *One from the union on the manifold's left-hand end.*

(c)   *The braking system vacuum servo unit hose (see Chapter 9 for details).*

(d)   *One from the Exhaust Gas Recirculation (EGR) valve.*

11   Equalise the pressure in the fuel tank by removing the filler cap, then undo the fuel feed and return lines connecting the engine to the chassis (see Chapter 4). Plug or cap all open fittings.

12   Unbolt the power steering high-pressure pipe and the earth lead from the cylinder head rear support plate/engine lifting eye, then unscrew the bolt securing the support plate/lifting eye to the alternator mounting bracket.

13   Unscrew the six nuts securing the engine/transmission right-hand mounting bracket, then withdraw the bracket.

14   Remove the alternator (see Chapter 5).

15   Unbolt the alternator mounting bracket from the rear of the cylinder block and withdraw it, together with the cylinder head rear support plate/engine lifting eye **(see illustration)**.

2A

6.16 Withdrawing inlet manifold - take care not to damage delicate components

6.17A Always renew inlet manifold gasket - do not rely on sealants

6.17B Check all disturbed components - braking system vacuum servo unit hose (arrowed) shown here - for leaks on reassembly

16   Unscrew the bolts and nuts securing the manifold to the cylinder head and withdraw it **(see illustration)**. Take care not to damage vulnerable components such as the EGR pipe and valve as the manifold assembly is manoeuvred out of the engine compartment.

Refitting

17   Refitting is the reverse of the removal procedure, noting the following points:

(a)   *When using a scraper and solvent to remove all traces of old gasket material and sealant from the manifold and cylinder head, be careful to ensure that you do not scratch or damage the material of either; the cylinder head is of aluminium alloy, while the manifold is a plastics moulding - any solvents used must be suitable for this application. If the gasket was leaking, have the mating surfaces checked for warpage at an automotive machine shop. While it may be possible to have the cylinder head gasket surface skimmed if necessary, to remove any distortion, the manifold must be renewed if it is found to be warped, cracked - check with special care around the mounting points for components such as the idle speed control valve and EGR pipe - or otherwise faulty.*

(b)   *Provided the relevant mating surfaces are clean and flat, a new gasket will be sufficient to ensure the joint is gas-tight.* **Do not use any kind of silicone-based sealant on any part of the fuel system or inlet manifold.**

(c)   *Fit a new gasket, then locate the manifold on the head and install the nuts and bolts* **(see illustration)**.

(d)   *Tighten the nuts/bolts in three or four equal steps to the torque listed in this Chapter's Specifications. Work from the centre outwards, to avoid warping the manifold.*

(e)   *Refit the remaining parts in the reverse order of removal - tighten all fasteners to the torque wrench settings specified.*

(f)   *When reassembling the engine/transmission right-hand mounting, renew the self-locking nuts, and do not allow the mounting to twist as the middle two of the bracket's six nuts are tightened.*

(g)   *Before starting the engine, check the accelerator cable for correct adjustment and the throttle linkage for smooth operation.*

(h)   *When the engine is fully warmed up, check for signs of fuel, intake and/or vacuum leaks* **(see illustration)**.

(i)   *Road test the vehicle, and check for proper operation of all disturbed components.*

7   Exhaust manifold - removal, inspection and refitting

Warning: *The engine must be completely cool before beginning this procedure.*

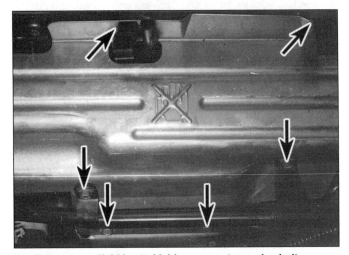

7.5 Exhaust manifold heat shield upper part securing bolts (arrowed)

Note: *In addition to the new gasket and any other parts, tools or facilities needed to carry out this operation, a new plastic guide sleeve will be required on reassembly.*

Removal

1   Disconnect the battery negative (earth) lead - see Chapter 5, Section 1.

2   Unbolt the resonator support bracket from the engine compartment front crossmember, slacken the two clamp screws securing the resonator to the air mass meter and plenum chamber hoses, then swing the resonator up clear of the thermostat housing (see Chapter 4).

3   Drain the cooling system (see Chapter 1).

4   Disconnect the coolant hose and the coolant pipe/hose from the thermostat housing; secure them clear of the working area.

5   Unbolt the exhaust manifold heat shield, and withdraw both parts of the shield **(see illustration)**. Apply penetrating oil to the EGR pipe sleeve nut, and to the exhaust manifold mounting nuts (also to the pulse-air system sleeve nuts, if they are to be unscrewed).

6   Unscrew the sleeve nut securing the EGR pipe to the manifold, remove the two screws securing the pipe to the ignition coil bracket, then slacken the sleeve nut securing the pipe to the EGR valve - see Chapter 6 for full details if required.

7   While the manifold can be removed with the pulse-air system components attached - unbolt the filter housing and disconnect its vacuum hose if this is to be done - it is easier to remove the pulse-air assembly first, as described in Chapter 6 **(see illustration)**.

8   Unplugging the oxygen sensor electrical connector to avoid

7.7 Pulse-air system (sleeve nuts arrowed) need not be removed unless required - assembly can be withdrawn with exhaust manifold

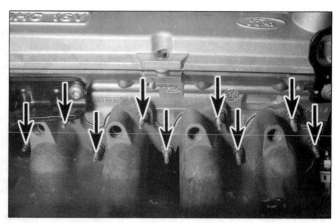

7.9A Unscrew nuts (arrowed) to remove exhaust manifold . . .

7.9B . . . studs can be unscrewed also, if required, to provide additional working space

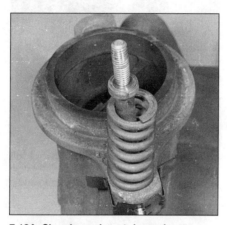

7.13A Showing exhaust downpipe-to-manifold securing bolts - note coil spring, and shoulder on bolt

7.13B Renew exhaust system downpipe-to-manifold gasket to prevent leaks

2A

straining its wiring, unscrew the nuts to disconnect the exhaust system front downpipe from the manifold (see Chapter 4).

9   Remove the nuts and detach the manifold and gasket (see illustration). Take care not to damage vulnerable components such as the EGR pipe as the manifold assembly is manoeuvred out of the engine compartment. When removing the manifold with the engine in the vehicle, additional clearance can be obtained by unscrewing the studs from the cylinder head; a female Torx-type socket will be required (see illustration).

10   Always fit a new gasket on reassembly, to carefully-cleaned components (see below). *Do not* attempt to re-use the original gasket.

Inspection

11   Use a scraper to remove all traces of old gasket material and carbon deposits from the manifold and cylinder head mating surfaces. If the gasket was leaking, have the manifold checked for warpage at an automotive machine shop, and have it resurfaced if necessary. **Caution:** *When scraping, be very careful not to gouge or scratch the delicate aluminium alloy cylinder head.*

12   Provided both mating surfaces are clean and flat, a new gasket will be sufficient to ensure the joint is gas-tight. *Do not* use any kind of exhaust sealant upstream of the catalytic converter.

13   Note that the downpipe is secured to the manifold by two bolts, with a coil spring, spring seat and self-locking nut on each. On refitting, tighten the nuts until they stop on the bolt shoulders; the pressure of the springs will then suffice to make a leakproof joint (see llustrations).

14   Do not overtighten the nuts to cure a leak - the bolts will shear; re-

new the gasket and the springs if a leak is found. The bolts themselves are secured by spring clips to the manifold, and can be renewed easily if damaged (see illustration).

7.14 Release spring clip to extract securing bolt from manifold, when required

7.15 Fit plastic guide sleeve to stud arrowed when refitting exhaust manifold

8.4A Unscrew pulley bolt to release crankshaft pulley

8.4B Ensure pulley is located on crankshaft Woodruff key on reassembly

9.1 Remove bolts (arrowed) to release timing belt upper cover

9.7 Slacken water pump pulley bolts and remove pulley

9.8 Remove fasteners (arrowed) to release timing belt middle cover

Refitting

15   Refitting is the reverse of the removal procedure, noting the following points:

(a)   *Position a new gasket over the cylinder head studs, and fit a new plastic guide sleeve to the stud nearest to the thermostat housing, so that the manifold will be correctly located (see illustration). Do not refit the manifold without this sleeve.*

(b)   *Refit the manifold, and finger-tighten the mounting nuts.*

(c)   *Working from the centre out, and in three or four equal steps, tighten the nuts to the torque wrench setting given in the Specifications Section of this Chapter.*

(d)   *Refit the remaining parts in the reverse order of removal. Tighten all fasteners to the specified torque wrench settings.*

(e)   *Refill the cooling system (see Chapter 1).*

(f)   *Run the engine, and check for exhaust leaks. Check the coolant level when fully warmed-up to normal operating temperature.*

8   Crankshaft pulley - removal and refitting

1   Remove the auxiliary drivebelt - either remove the drivebelt completely, or just secure it clear of the crankshaft pulley, depending on the work to be carried out (see Chapter 1).

2   If necessary, rotate the crankshaft until the timing marks align (see Section 4).

3   The crankshaft must now be locked to prevent its rotation while the pulley bolt is unscrewed. Proceed as follows:

(a)   *If the engine/transmission is still installed in the vehicle:*
        (1) If the vehicle is fitted with manual transmission, select top gear, and have an assistant apply the brakes hard.
        (2) If the vehicle is fitted with automatic transmission, unbolt the small metal cover plate from the sump, and use a large

screwdriver or similar to lock the driveplate ring gear teeth while an assistant slackens the pulley bolt; take care not to damage the teeth or the surrounding castings when using this method.

(b)   *If the engine/transmission has been removed but not yet separated:*
        (1) If the vehicle is fitted with manual transmission, remove the starter motor (see Chapter 5) and lock the flywheel using the method outlined in (2) above.
        (2) If the vehicle is fitted with automatic transmission, see (2) above.

(c)   *If the engine/transmission has been removed and separated, use the method shown in illustration 21.11.*

4   Unscrew the pulley bolt and remove the pulley **(see illustrations)**.

5   Refitting is the reverse of the removal procedure; ensure that the pulley's keyway is aligned with the crankshaft's locating key, and tighten the pulley bolt to the specified torque wrench setting.

9   Timing belt covers - removal and refitting

Upper cover

1   Unscrew the cover's two mounting bolts and withdraw it **(see illustration)**.

2   Refitting is the reverse of the removal procedure; ensure the cover edges engage correctly with each other, and note the torque wrench setting specified for the bolts.

Middle cover

3   Unscrew the six nuts securing the engine/transmission right-hand mounting bracket, then withdraw the bracket.

4   Slacken the water pump pulley bolts.

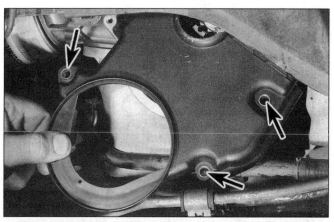

9.11 Removing timing belt lower cover - bolt locations arrowed

9.14 Timing belt inner shield fasteners (arrowed)

5   Remove the timing belt upper cover (see paragraph 1 above).
6   Remove the auxiliary drivebelt (see Chapter 1).
7   Unbolt and remove the water pump pulley **(see illustration)**.
8   Unscrew the middle cover fasteners (one bolt at the front, one at the lower rear, one stud at the top rear) and withdraw the cover **(see illustration)**.
9   Refitting is the reverse of the removal procedure. Ensure the cover edges engage correctly with each other, and note the torque wrench settings specified for the various fasteners. When reassembling the engine/transmission right-hand mounting, renew the self-locking nuts, and do not allow the mounting to twist as the middle two of the bracket's six nuts are tightened.

Lower cover

10   Remove the crankshaft pulley (see Section 8).
11   Unscrew the cover's three securing bolts and withdraw it **(see illustration)**.
12   Refitting is the reverse of the removal procedure; ensure the cover edges engage correctly with each other, and note the torque wrench settings specified for the various fasteners.

Inner shield

13   Remove the timing belt, its tensioner components and the camshaft toothed pulleys (see Sections 10 and 11).
14   The shield is secured to the cylinder head by two bolts at the top, and by two studs lower down; unscrew these and withdraw the shield **(see illustration)**.
15   Refitting is the reverse of the removal procedure; note the torque wrench settings specified for the various fasteners.

10 Timing belt - removal, refitting and adjustment

Note: *To carry out this operation, a new timing belt (where applicable), a new cylinder head cover gasket, and some special tools (see text) will be required. If the timing belt is being removed for the first time since the vehicle left the factory, a tensioner spring and retaining pin must be obtained for fitting on reassembly.*
1   With the vehicle parked on firm level ground, open the bonnet and disconnect the battery negative (earth) lead - see Chapter 5, Section 1 **(see illustration)**.
2   Unbolt the power steering high-pressure pipe from the cylinder head rear support plate/engine lifting eye, and from the front support plate/pump bracket.
3   Unscrew the six nuts securing the engine/transmission right-hand mounting bracket, then withdraw the bracket.
4   Slacken the water pump pulley bolts.
5   Remove the cylinder head cover (see Section 5).
6   Remove the spark plugs, covering their holes with clean rag, to prevent dirt or other foreign bodies from dropping in (see Chapter 1).
7   Remove the auxiliary drivebelt (see Chapter 1).

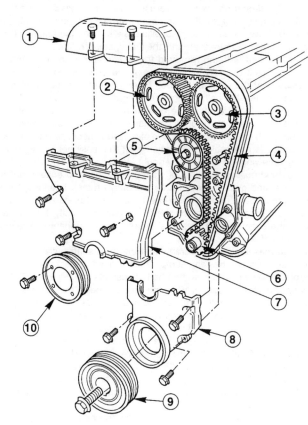

10.1 Timing belt and cover details

1	Timing belt upper cover	5	Timing belt tensioner
2	Inlet camshaft toothed pulley	6	Crankshaft toothed pulley
3	Exhaust camshaft toothed pulley	7	Timing belt middle cover
4	Timing belt	8	Timing belt lower cover
		9	Crankshaft pulley
		10	Water pump pulley

8   Rotate the crankshaft clockwise until the second pair of notches in the pulley rim align with the edge of the sump mark, so that Nos 1 and 4 cylinders are at TDC (see Section 4).
9   Unbolt and remove the water pump pulley and the auxiliary drivebelt idler pulley.
10   Obtain Ford service tool 21-162, or fabricate a substitute from a strip of metal 5 mm thick (while the strip's thickness *is* critical, its length and width are not, but should be approximately 180 to 230 mm by 20 to 30 mm). Check that Nos 1 and 4 cylinders are at Top Dead Centre (TDC) - No 1 on the compression stroke - by resting this tool on the cylinder head mating surface, and sliding it into the slot in the left-

hand end of both camshafts **(see illustration)**. The tool should slip snugly into both slots while resting on the cylinder head mating surface; if one camshaft is only slightly out of alignment, it is permissible to use an open-ended spanner to rotate the camshaft gently and carefully until the tool will fit.

11   If both camshaft slots (they are machined significantly off-centre) are below the level of the cylinder head mating surface, rotate the crankshaft through one full turn clockwise and fit the tool again; it should now fit as described in the previous paragraph.

12   With the camshaft aligning tool remaining in place, remove the crankshaft pulley. *Do not* use the locked camshafts to prevent the crankshaft from rotating - use only the locking methods described in Section 8.

13   Remove the timing belt lower and middle covers (see Section 9).

14   With the camshaft aligning tool still in place, slacken the tensioner bolt, and use an Allen key inserted into its centre to rotate the tensioner clockwise as far as possible away from the belt; retighten the bolt to secure the tensioner clear of the timing belt **(see illustration)**.

15   If the timing belt is to be re-used, use white paint or similar to mark its direction of rotation, and note from the manufacturer's markings which way round it is fitted. Withdraw the belt **(see illustration)**. *Do not* rotate the crankshaft until the timing belt is refitted.

16   If the belt is being removed for reasons other than routine renewal, check it carefully for any signs of uneven wear, splitting, cracks (especially at the roots of the belt teeth) or contamination with oil or coolant. Renew the belt if there is the slightest doubt about its condition. As a safety measure, the belt must be renewed as a matter of course at the intervals given in Chapter 1; if its history is unknown, the belt should be renewed irrespective of its apparent condition whenever the engine is overhauled. Similarly, check the tensioner spring (where fitted), renewing it if there is any doubt about its condition. Check also the toothed pulleys for signs of wear or damage, and ensure that the tensioner and guide pulleys rotate smoothly on their bearings; renew any worn or damaged components. If signs of oil or coolant contamination are found, trace the source of the leak and rectify it, then wash down the engine timing belt area and related components, to remove all traces of oil or coolant.

17   On reassembly, temporarily refit the crankshaft pulley, to check that the pulley notches and sump rib are aligned as described in paragraph 8 above, then ensure that both camshafts are aligned at TDC by the special tool (paragraph 10). If the engine is being reassembled after major dismantling, both camshaft toothed pulleys should be free to rotate on their respective camshafts; if the timing belt alone is being renewed, both pulleys should still be securely fastened.

18   A holding tool will be required to prevent the camshaft toothed pulleys from rotating while their bolts are slackened and retightened; either obtain Ford service tool 15-030A, or fabricate a substitute as follows. Find two lengths of steel strip, one approximately 600 mm long and the other about 200 mm, and three bolts with nuts and washers; one nut and bolt forming the pivot of a forked tool, with the remaining nuts and bolts at the tips of the "forks", to engage with the pulley

10.10 Fit camshaft aligning tool to ensure engine is locked with Nos 1 and 4 cylinders at TDC

spokes as shown in the accompanying illustrations. **Note:** *Do not use the camshaft aligning tool (whether genuine Ford or not) to prevent rotation while the camshaft toothed pulley bolts are slackened or tightened; the risk of damage to the camshaft concerned and to the cylinder head is far too great. Use only a forked holding tool applied directly to the pulleys, as described.*

19   If it is being fitted for the first time, screw the timing belt tensioner spring retaining pin into the cylinder head, tightening it to the specified torque wrench setting. Unbolt the tensioner, hook the spring on to the pin and the tensioner backplate, then refit the tensioner, engaging its backplate on the locating peg **(see illustrations)**.

20   In all cases, slacken the tensioner bolt (if necessary), and use an Allen key inserted into its centre to rotate the tensioner clockwise as far as possible against spring tension, then retighten the bolt to secure the tensioner **(see illustration)**.

21   Fit the timing belt; if the original is being refitted, ensure that the marks and notes made on removal are followed, so that the belt is refitted the same way round, and to run in the same direction. Starting at the crankshaft toothed pulley, work anti-clockwise around the camshaft toothed pulleys and tensioner, finishing off at the rear guide pulley. The front run, between the crankshaft and the exhaust camshaft toothed pulleys, *must* be kept taut, without altering the position either of the crankshaft or of the camshaft(s) - if necessary, the position of the camshaft toothed pulleys can be altered by rotating each on its camshaft (which remains fixed by the aligning tool). Where the pulley is still fastened, use the holding tool described in paragraph 18 above to prevent the pulley from rotating while its retaining bolt is slackened - the pulley can then be rotated on the camshaft until the belt will slip into place; retighten the pulley bolt.

22   When the belt is in place, slacken the tensioner bolt gently until the spring pulls the tensioner against the belt; the tensioner should be

10.14 Slacken tensioner bolt, and use Allen key to rotate tensioner away from timing belt . . .

10.15 . . . then withdraw timing belt

10.19A Fitting tensioner spring retaining pin

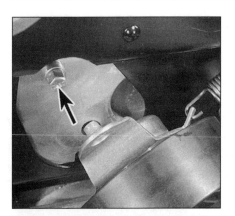

10.19B Hook spring onto tensioner and refit as shown - engage tensioner backplate on locating peg (arrowed) . . .

10.20 . . . then use Allen key to position tensioner so that timing belt can be refitted

10.22 Slacken tensioner bolt to give initial belt tension

retained correctly against the timing belt inner shield and cylinder head, but must be just free to respond to changes in belt tension **(see illustration)**.

23   Tighten both camshaft toothed pulley bolts (or check that they are tight, as applicable) and remove the camshaft aligning tool. Temporarily refit the crankshaft pulley, and rotate the crankshaft through two full turns clockwise to settle and tension the timing belt, returning the crankshaft (pulley notches) to the position described in paragraph 8 above. Refit the camshaft aligning tool; it should slip into place as described in paragraph 10. If all is well, proceed to paragraph 26 below.

24   If one camshaft is only just out of line, fit the forked holding tool to its toothed pulley, adjust its position as required, and check that any slack created has been taken up by the tensioner; rotate the crankshaft through two further turns clockwise, and refit the camshaft aligning tool to check that it now fits as it should. If all is well, proceed to paragraph 26 below.

25   If either camshaft is significantly out of line, use the holding tool described in paragraph 18 above to prevent its pulley from rotating while its retaining bolt is slackened - the camshaft can then be rotated (gently and carefully, using an open-ended spanner) until the camshaft aligning tool will slip into place; take care not to disturb the relationship of the pulley to the timing belt. Without disturbing the pulley's new position on the camshaft, tighten the pulley bolt to its specified torque wrench setting **(see illustration)**. Remove the camshaft aligning tool, rotate the crankshaft through two further turns clockwise and refit the tool to check that it now fits as it should.

26   When the timing belt has been settled at its correct tension, and the camshaft aligning tool fits correctly when the crankshaft pulley notches are exactly aligned, tighten the tensioner bolt to its specified torque wrench setting **(see illustration)**. Fitting the forked holding tool to the spokes of each pulley in turn, check that the pulley bolts are

tightened to their specified torque wrench setting. Remove the camshaft aligning tool, rotate the crankshaft through two further turns clockwise, and refit the tool to make a final check that it fits as it should.

27   The remainder of the reassembly procedure is the reverse of removal, noting the following points:

   (a) Tighten all fasteners to the torque wrench settings specified.

   (b) When reassembling the engine/transmission right-hand mounting, renew the self-locking nuts, and do not allow the mounting to twist as the middle two of the bracket's six nuts are tightened.

11 Timing belt tensioner and toothed pulleys - removal, inspection and refitting

Tensioner

Note: *If the tensioner is being removed for the first time since the vehicle left the factory, a tensioner spring and retaining pin must be obtained for fitting on reassembly.*

1   While it is possible to reach the tensioner once the timing belt upper and middle covers only have been removed (see Section 9), the whole procedure outlined below must be followed, to ensure that the valve timing is correctly reset once the belt's tension has been disturbed.

2   Release the tension from the timing belt as described in Section 10, paragraphs 1 to 14.

3   Unscrew the tensioner bolt and withdraw the tensioner, unhooking the spring, if fitted **(see illustration)**. Check the tensioner and spring as described in paragraph 16 of Section 10.

2A

10.25 Using forked holding tool while camshaft toothed pulley bolt is tightened

10.26 When setting is correct, tighten tensioner bolt to specified torque wrench setting

11.3 Removing timing belt tensioner

11.8 Note "FRONT" marking on outside face of crankshaft toothed pulley - note which way round thrustwasherbehind is fitted

11.13 Tighten timing belt guide pulley bolts to specified torque settings on refitting

12.5 Using socket and toothed pulley bolt to install camshaft oil seal

4   On reassembly, if it is being fitted for the first time, screw the timing belt tensioner spring retaining pin into the cylinder head, tightening it to the specified torque wrench setting. Hook the spring onto the pin and the tensioner backplate, then refit the tensioner, engaging its backplate on the locating peg.

5   Use an Allen key inserted into its centre to rotate the tensioner clockwise as far as possible against spring tension, then tighten the bolt to secure the tensioner.

6   Reassemble, checking the camshaft alignment (valve timing) and setting the timing belt tension, as described in paragraphs 22 to 27 of Section 10.

Camshaft and crankshaft toothed pulleys

7   While it may be possible to remove any of these pulleys once their respective covers have been removed, the complete timing belt removal/refitting procedure (see Section 10) must be followed, to ensure that the valve timing is correctly reset once the belt's tension has been disturbed.

8   With the timing belt removed, the camshaft toothed pulleys can be detached once their retaining bolts have been unscrewed as described in paragraphs 18 and 21 of Section 10. The crankshaft toothed pulley can be pulled off the end of the crankshaft once the crankshaft (grooved) pulley and the timing belt have been removed. Note the "FRONT" marking identifying the pulley's outboard face, and the thrustwasher behind it; note which way round the thrustwasher is fitted (see illustration). Note the pulley-locating Woodruff key; if this is loose, it should be removed for safe storage with the pulley.

9   Check the pulleys as described in paragraph 16 of Section 10.

10   Refitting is the reverse of the removal procedure.

Timing belt guide pulleys

11   Remove the timing belt covers (see Section 9).

12   Unbolt and withdraw the pulley(s); check their condition as described in paragraph 16 of Section 10.

13   Refitting is the reverse of the removal procedure; tighten the pulley bolts to the specified torque wrench setting (see illustration).

12 Camshaft oil seals - renewal

Note: *While it is possible to reach either oil seal, once the respective toothed pulley has been removed (see Section 11) to allow the seal to be prised out, this procedure is not recommended. Not only are the seals very soft, making this difficult to do without risk of damage to the seal housing, but it would be very difficult to ensure that the valve timing and the timing belt's tension, once disturbed, are correctly reset. Owners are advised to follow the whole procedure outlined below.*

1   Release the tension from the timing belt as described in Sec-

tion 10, paragraphs 1 to 14. **Note:** *If the timing belt is found to be contaminated by oil, remove it completely as described, then renew the oil seal (see below). Wash down the engine timing belt area and all related components, to remove all traces of oil. Fit a new belt on reassembly.*

2   If the timing belt is still clean, slip it off the toothed pulley, taking care not to twist it too sharply; use the fingers only to handle the belt. *Do not* rotate the crankshaft until the timing belt is refitted. Cover the belt, and secure it so that it is clear of the working area and cannot slip off the remaining toothed pulley.

3   Unfasten the pulley bolt and withdraw the pulley (see Section 11).

4   Unbolt the camshaft right-hand bearing cap, and withdraw the defective oil seal. Clean the seal housing, and polish off any burrs or raised edges, which may have caused the seal to fail in the first place.

5   To fit a new seal, Ford recommend the use of their service tool 21-009B, with a bolt (10 mm thread size, 70 mm long) and a washer, to draw the seal into place when the camshaft bearing cap is bolted down; a substitute can be made using a suitable socket (see illustration). Grease the seal lips and periphery to ease installation, and draw the seal into place until it is flush with the housing/bearing cap outer edge. Refit the bearing cap, using sealant and tightening the cap bolts as described in Section 13.

6   For most owners, the simplest answer will be to grease the seal lips, and to slide it on to the camshaft (until it is flush with the housing's outer edge). Refit the bearing cap, using sealant and tightening the cap bolts as described in Section 13 (see illustration). Take care to ensure that the seal remains absolutely square in its housing, and is not distorted as the cap is tightened down.

7   Refit the pulley to the camshaft, tightening the retaining bolt loosely, then slip the timing belt back onto the pulley (refer to paragraphs 18 and 21 of Section 10) and tighten the bolt securely.

8   The remainder of the reassembly procedure, including checking the camshaft alignment (valve timing) and setting the timing belt tension, is as described in paragraphs 22 to 27 of Section 10.

13 Camshafts and hydraulic tappets - removal, inspection and refitting

Removal

1   Release the tension from the timing belt as described in Section 10, paragraphs 1 to 14.

2   Either remove the timing belt completely (Section 10, paragraphs 15 and 16) or slip it off the camshaft toothed pulleys, taking care not to twist it too sharply; use the fingers only to handle the belt. Cover the belt, and secure it so that it is clear of the working area. *Do not* rotate the crankshaft until the timing belt is refitted.

3   Unfasten the pulley bolts as described in Section 10, paragraphs 18 and 21, and withdraw the pulleys; while both are the same

12.6 Alternatively, seal can be inserted when camshaft bearing cap is unbolted

13.3 Using forked holding tool while camshaft toothed pulley bolt is slackened

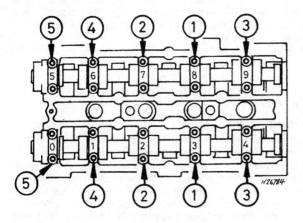

13.4 Camshaft bearing cap slackening sequence

Note: *View from front of vehicle, showing bearing cap numbers*

13.5A Note locating dowels when removing camshaft bearing caps

2A

and could be interchanged, it is good working practice to mark them so that each is refitted only to its original location **(see illustration)**.
4   Working in the sequence shown, slacken progressively, by half a turn at a time, the camshaft bearing cap bolts **(see illustration)**. Work only as described, to release gradually and evenly the pressure of the valve springs on the caps.
5   Withdraw the caps, noting their markings and the presence of the locating dowels, then remove the camshafts and withdraw their oil seals. The inlet camshaft can be identified by the reference lobe for the

camshaft position sensor; therefore, there is no need to mark the camshafts **(see illustrations)**.
6   Obtain sixteen small, clean containers, and number them 1 to 16. Using a rubber sucker, withdraw each hydraulic tappet in turn, invert it to prevent oil loss, and place it in its respective container, which should then be filled with clean engine oil **(see illustrations)**. Do not interchange the hydraulic tappets, or the rate of wear will be much increased. Do not allow them to lose oil, or they will take a long time to refill on restarting the engine, resulting in incorrect valve clearances.

13.5B Inlet camshaft has lobe for camshaft position sensor

13.6A Removing hydraulic tappets

13.6B Hydraulic tappets must be stored as described in text

Inspection

7   With the camshafts and hydraulic tappets removed, check each for signs of obvious wear (scoring, pitting etc) and for ovality, and renew if necessary.

8   Measure the outside diameter of each tappet **(see illustration)** - take measurements at the top and bottom of each tappet, then a second set at right-angles to the first; if any measurement is significantly different from the others, the tappet is tapered or oval (as applicable) and must be renewed. If the necessary equipment is available, measure the inside diameter of the corresponding cylinder head bore. Compare the measurements obtained to those given in the Specifications Section of this Chapter; if the tappets or the cylinder head bores are excessively worn, new tappets and/or a new cylinder head will be required.

9   If the engine's valve components have sounded noisy, particularly if the noise persists after initial start-up from cold, there is reason to suspect a faulty hydraulic tappet. Only a good mechanic experienced in these engines can tell whether the noise level is typical, or if renewal of one or more of the tappets is warranted. If faulty tappets are diagnosed, and the engine's service history is unknown, it is always worth trying the effect of renewing the engine oil and filter (see Chapter 1), using *only* good-quality engine oil of the recommended viscosity and specification, before going to the expense of renewing any of the tappets - refer also to the advice in Section 1 of this Chapter.

10   Visually examine the camshaft lobes for score marks, pitting, galling (wear due to rubbing) and evidence of overheating (blue, discoloured areas). Look for flaking away of the hardened surface layer of each lobe **(see illustration)**. If any such signs are evident, renew the component concerned.

11   Examine the camshaft bearing journals and the cylinder head bearing surfaces for signs of obvious wear or pitting. If any such signs are evident, renew the component concerned.

12   Using a micrometer, measure the diameter of each journal at several points **(see illustration)**. If the diameter of any one journal is less than the specified value, renew the camshaft.

13   To check the bearing journal running clearance, remove the hydraulic tappets, use a suitable solvent and a clean lint-free rag to clean carefully all bearing surfaces, then refit the camshafts and bearing caps with a strand of Plastigage across each journal **(see illustration)**. Tighten the bearing cap bolts to the specified torque wrench setting (do not rotate the camshafts), then remove the bearing caps and use the scale provided to measure the width of the compressed strands **(see illustration)**. Scrape off the Plastigage with your fingernail or the edge of a credit card - don't scratch or nick the journals or bearing caps.

14   If the running clearance of any bearing is found to be worn to beyond the specified service limits, fit a new camshaft and repeat the check; if the clearance is still excessive, the cylinder head must be renewed.

15   To check camshaft endfloat, remove the hydraulic tappets, clean

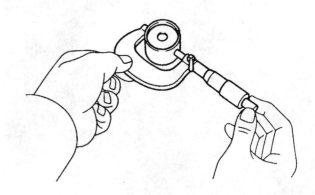

13.8 Use a micrometer to measure diameter of hydraulic tappets

the bearing surfaces carefully, and refit the camshafts and bearing caps. Tighten the bearing cap bolts to the specified torque wrench setting, then measure the endfloat using a DTI (Dial Test Indicator, or dial gauge) mounted on the cylinder head so that its tip bears on the camshaft right-hand end.

16   Tap the camshaft fully towards the gauge, zero the gauge, then tap the camshaft fully away from the gauge, and note the gauge reading. If the endfloat measured is found to be at or beyond the specified service limit, fit a new camshaft and repeat the check; if the clearance is still excessive, the cylinder head must be renewed.

Refitting

17   On reassembly, liberally oil the cylinder head hydraulic tappet bores and the tappets **(see illustration)**. Note that if new tappets are being fitted, they must be charged with clean engine oil before installation. Carefully refit the tappets to the cylinder head, ensuring that each tappet is refitted to its original bore, and is the correct way up. Some care will be required to enter the tappets squarely into their bores.

18   Liberally oil the camshaft bearings and lobes **(see illustration)**. Ensuring that each camshaft is in its original location, refit the camshafts, locating each so that the slot in its left-hand end is approximately parallel to, and just above, the cylinder head mating surface **(see illustration)**.

19   Ensure that the locating dowels are pressed firmly into their recesses, and check that all mating surfaces are completely clean, unmarked and free from oil. Apply a thin film of suitable sealant (Ford recommend Loctite 518) to the mating surfaces of each camshaft's right-hand bearing cap **(see illustration)**. Referring to paragraph 6 of Section 12, some owners may wish to fit the new camshaft oil seals at this stage.

13.10 Check the cam lobes for pitting, wear and score marks - if scoring is excessive, as is the case here, renew the camshaft

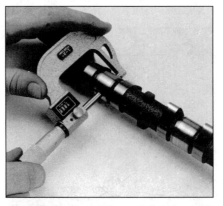

13.12 Measure each journal diameter with a micrometer - if any journal measures less than the specified limit, renew the camshaft

13.13A Lay a strip of Plastigage on each camshaft journal

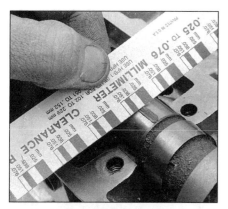

13.13B Compare the width of the crushed Plastigage to the scale on the envelope to determine the running clearance

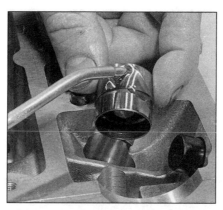

13.17 Oil liberally when refitting hydraulic tappets

13.18A Apply engine assembly lubricant or molybdenum disulphide-based grease to the cam lobes and journals before refitting a camshaft

13.18B Use camshaft position sensor lobe to identify inlet camshaft on refitting - locate camshafts as described in text

13.19 Apply sealant to mating surface of camshaft right-hand bearing caps

13.20 Etched marks on camshaft bearing caps must be arranged as shown, and face outwards

2A

13.21A Keep caps square to cylinder head at all times when tightening down

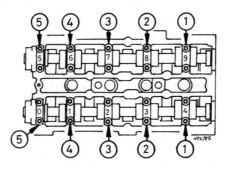

13.21B Camshaft bearing cap tightening sequence

Note: *View from front of vehicle - locate bearing caps according to etched numbers, aligned as described in text*

13.21C Fit camshaft aligning tool to set TDC position . . .

20   All camshaft bearing caps have a single-digit identifying number etched on them **(see illustration)**. The exhaust camshaft's bearing caps are numbered in sequence 0 (right-hand cap) to 4 (left-hand cap), the inlet's 5 (right-hand cap) to 9 (left-hand cap); see illustration 13.21B for details. Each cap is to be fitted so that its numbered side faces outwards, to the front (exhaust) or to the rear (inlet).

21   Ensuring that each cap is kept square to the cylinder head as it is tightened down, and working in the sequence shown, tighten the camshaft bearing cap bolts slowly and by one turn at a time, until each cap touches the cylinder head **(see illustrations)**. Next, go round again in the same sequence, tightening the bolts to the first stage torque wrench setting specified, then once more, tightening them to the second stage setting. Work only as described, to impose gradually and evenly the pressure of the valve springs on the caps. Fit the camshaft aligning tool; it should slip into place as described in paragraph 10 of Section 10 **(see illustration)**.

13.24 . . . while camshaft toothed pulleys are refitted

14.8A Release wire clip to unplug engine wiring loom connector from inlet manifold

14.8B Unplug connectors (arrowed) to disconnect ignition coil wiring

22   Wipe off all surplus sealant, so that none is left to find its way into any oilways. Follow the sealant manufacturer's instructions as to the time needed for curing; usually, at least an hour must be allowed between application of the sealant and starting the engine.

23   If using Ford's recommended procedure, fit new oil seals to the camshafts as described in paragraph 5 of Section 12.

24   Using the marks and notes made on dismantling to ensure that each is refitted to its original camshaft, refit the toothed pulleys to the camshafts, tightening the retaining bolts loosely **(see illustration)**. Slip the timing belt back onto the pulleys (refer to paragraph 21 of Section 10) and tighten the bolts securely - use the forked holding tool described in paragraph 18 of Section 10.

25   The remainder of the reassembly procedure, including checking the camshaft alignment (valve timing) and setting the timing belt tension, is as described in paragraphs 17 to 27 of Section 10.

14 Cylinder head - removal and refitting

Removal

Note: *The following text assumes that the cylinder head will be removed with both inlet and exhaust manifolds attached; this simplifies the procedure, but makes it a bulky and heavy assembly to handle - an engine hoist will be required, to prevent the risk of injury, and to prevent damage to any delicate components as the assembly is removed and refitted. If it is wished first to remove the manifolds, proceed as described in Sections 6 and 7 of this Chapter; amend the following procedure accordingly.*

1   Relieve the fuel system pressure (see Chapter 4).

2   With the vehicle parked on firm level ground, open the bonnet and disconnect the battery negative (earth) lead - see Chapter 5, Section 1.

3   Whenever you disconnect any vacuum lines, coolant and emissions hoses, wiring loom connectors, earth straps and fuel lines as part of the following procedure, always label them clearly, so that they can be correctly reassembled. Masking tape and/or a touch-up paint applicator work well for marking items. Take instant photos, or sketch the locations of components and brackets.

4   Unplugging the two electrical connectors, disconnecting the vacuum hose (where fitted) and disconnecting the crankcase breather hose from the cylinder head cover, remove the complete air cleaner assembly with the air mass meter, the resonator and the plenum chamber (see Chapter 4).

5   Equalise the pressure in the fuel tank by removing the filler cap, then undo the fuel feed and return lines connecting the engine to the chassis (see Chapter 4). Plug or cap all open fittings.

6   Disconnect the accelerator cable from the throttle linkage as described in Chapter 4 - where fitted, disconnect also the cruise control actuator cable (see Chapter 12). Secure the cable(s) clear of the engine/transmission.

7   Unbolt the power steering high-pressure pipe from the cylinder head rear support plate/engine lifting eye, and from the front support plate/pump bracket. Releasing its wire clip, unplug the power steering pressure switch electrical connector, then unbolt the earth lead from the cylinder head rear support plate/engine lifting eye.

8   Remove the three screws securing the wiring "rail" to the rear of the manifold. Releasing its wire clip, unplug the large electrical connector (next to the fuel pressure regulator) to disconnect the engine wiring from the main loom **(see illustration)**. Unplug the electrical connectors on each side of the ignition coil, and the single connector from beneath the front of the thermostat housing, to disconnect the coil and coolant temperature gauge sender wiring **(see illustration)**.

9   Marking or labelling them as they are unplugged, disconnect the vacuum hoses as follows:

(a) *One from the rear of the throttle housing (only the one hose - there is no need to disconnect the second hose running to the fuel pressure regulator).*

(b) *One from the union on the inlet manifold's left-hand end* **(see illustration).**

(c) *The braking system vacuum servo unit hose (see Chapter 9 for details).*

(d) *Disconnect all vacuum hoses from the Exhaust Gas Recirculation system components - one from the EGR valve and two from the EGR pipe. (Note that these last two are of different sizes, as are their pipe stubs, so that they can only be connected the correct way round.)*

10   Unbolt both parts of the exhaust manifold heat shield; unclip the coolant hose to allow the upper part to be withdrawn. Either remove the dipstick and tube, or swing them out of the way.

11   Unscrew the single bolt securing the pulse-air filter housing to the engine/transmission front mounting bracket, then disconnect its vacuum hose.

12   Drain the cooling system (see Chapter 1).

13   Disconnect all coolant hoses from the thermostat housing **(see illustration)**.

14   Unscrew the two nuts to disconnect the exhaust system front downpipe from the manifold (Chapter 4); disconnect the oxygen sensor wiring, so that it is not strained by the weight of the exhaust system.

15   Remove the auxiliary drivebelt (see Chapter 1).

16   Support the weight of the engine/transmission using a trolley jack, with a wooden spacer to prevent damage to the sump.

17   Unscrew the six nuts securing the engine/transmission right-hand mounting bracket, then withdraw the bracket. Unbolt the auxiliary drivebelt's idler pulley **(see illustration)**.

18   Unbolt the cylinder head front and rear support plates **(see illustrations)**.

19   Remove the timing belt and both camshafts (see Sections 1 and 13); if the cylinder head is to be dismantled, withdraw the hydraulic tappets.

20   Remove the timing belt inner shield (see Section 9).

21   Working in the *reverse* of the sequence shown in illustra-

14.9 Disconnect vacuum hoses (arrowed) as described in text

14.13 Disconnect all coolant hoses (arrowed) from thermostat housing

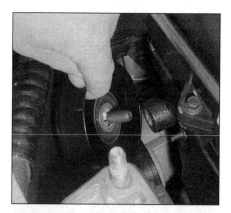

14.17 Unbolt auxiliary drivebelt idler pulley

14 18A Remove cylinder head front . . .

14.18B . . . and rear support plates

14.22 Using an engine hoist to lift off the cylinder head complete with manifolds

2A

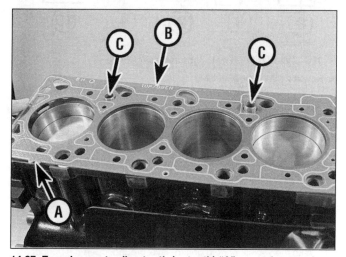

14.27 Ensuring protruding tooth (or teeth) "A" are at front and marking "B" is upwards, locate new cylinder head gasket on dowels "C"

tion 14.32C, slacken the ten cylinder head bolts progressively and by one turn at a time; a Torx key (TX 55 size) will be required. Remove each bolt in turn, and ensure that new replacements are obtained for reassembly; these bolts are subjected to severe stresses and so must be renewed, regardless of their apparent condition, whenever they are disturbed.

22 Lift the cylinder head away; use assistance if possible, as it is a heavy assembly **(see illustration)**. Remove the gasket, noting the two dowels, and discard it.

Refitting

23 The mating faces of the cylinder head and cylinder block must be perfectly clean before refitting the head. Use a hard plastic or wood scraper to remove all traces of gasket and carbon; also clean the piston crowns. Take particular care, as the soft aluminium alloy is easily damaged. Also, make sure that the carbon is not allowed to enter the oil and water passages - this is particularly important for the lubrication system, as carbon could block the oil supply to any of the engine's components. Using adhesive tape and paper, seal the water, oil and bolt holes in the cylinder block. To prevent carbon entering the gap between the pistons and bores, smear a little grease in the gap. After cleaning each piston, use a small brush to remove all traces of grease and carbon from the gap, then wipe away the remainder with a clean rag. Clean all the pistons in the same way.

24 Check the mating surfaces of the cylinder block and the cylinder head for nicks, deep scratches and other damage. If slight, they may be removed carefully with a file, but if excessive, machining may be the only alternative to renewal.

25 If warpage of the cylinder head gasket surface is suspected, use a straight edge to check it for distortion. Refer to Part B of this Chapter, Section 7, if necessary.

26 Wipe clean the mating surfaces of the cylinder head and cylinder block. Check that the two locating dowels are in position in the cylinder block, and that all cylinder head bolt holes are free from oil.

27 Position a new gasket over the dowels on the cylinder block surface, so that the "TOP/OBEN" mark is uppermost, and the tooth (or teeth, according to engine size) protruding from one edge point to the front of the vehicle **(see illustration)**.

28 Temporarily refit the crankshaft pulley, and rotate the crankshaft anti-clockwise so that No 1 cylinder's piston is lowered to approximately 20 mm before TDC, thus avoiding any risk of valve/piston contact and damage during reassembly.

29 As the cylinder head is such a heavy and awkward assembly to

14.30 Refitting cylinder head - note fabricated guide studs (arrowed)

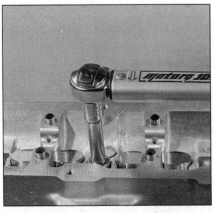

14.32A Tightening cylinder head bolts (to first and second stages) using torque wrench . . .

14.32B . . . and to third stage using angle gauge

refit with manifolds, it is helpful to make up a pair of guide studs from two 10 mm (thread size) studs approximately 90 mm long, with a screwdriver slot cut in one end - two old cylinder head bolts with their heads cut off would make a good starting point. Screw these guide studs, screwdriver slot upwards to permit removal, into the bolt holes at diagonally-opposite corners of the cylinder block surface (or into those where the locating dowels are fitted, as shown); ensure that approximately 70 mm of stud protrudes above the gasket.

30   Refit the cylinder head, sliding it down the guide studs (if used) and locating it on the dowels **(see illustration)**. Unscrew the guide studs (if used) when the head is in place.

31   Fit the new cylinder head bolts dry (*do not oil* their threads); carefully enter each into its hole and screw it in, by hand only, until fingertight.

32   Working progressively and in the sequence shown, use first a torque wrench, then an ordinary socket extension bar and an angle gauge, to tighten the cylinder head bolts in the stages given in the Specifications Section of this Chapter **(see illustrations)**. Note: *Once tightened correctly, following this procedure, the cylinder head bolts do not require check-tightening, and must **not** be re-torqued.*

33   Refit the hydraulic tappets (if removed), the camshafts, their oil seals and pulleys (see Sections 10, 11, 12 and 13, as appropriate). Temporarily refit the crankshaft pulley, and rotate the crankshaft clockwise to return the pulley notches to the position described in paragraph 8 of Section 10.

34   Refit the timing belt and covers, checking the camshaft alignment (valve timing) and setting the timing belt tension, as described in Section 10.

35   The remainder of reassembly is the reverse of the removal procedure, noting the following points:

(a)   *Tighten all fasteners to the torque wrench settings specified.*

(b)   *When reassembling the engine/transmission right-hand mounting, renew the self-locking nuts, and do not allow the mounting to twist as the middle two of the bracket's six nuts are tightened.*

(c)   *Refill the cooling system, and top-up the engine oil.*

(d)   *Check all disturbed joints for signs of oil or coolant leakage, once the engine has been restarted and warmed-up to normal operating temperature.*

15 Sump - removal and refitting

Removal

Note: *To carry out this task with the engine/transmission installed in the vehicle requires the assistance of at least one person, plus the equipment necessary to raise and support the front of the vehicle (high enough that the sump can be withdrawn from underneath), and to lift*

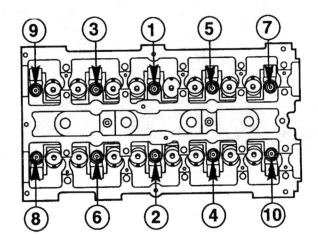

14.32C Cylinder head bolt tightening sequence

Note: *View from rear of vehicle*

and support the complete engine/transmission unit 2 to 3 inches from its mountings while the vehicle is raised. Precise details of the procedure will depend on the equipment available - the following is typical.

The full procedure outlined below must be followed, so that the mating surfaces can be cleaned and prepared to achieve an oil-tight joint on reassembly, and so that the sump can be aligned correctly; depending on your skill and experience, and the tools and facilities available, it may be that this task can be carried out only with the engine removed from the vehicle.

Note that the sump gasket must be renewed whenever it is disturbed.

1   With the vehicle parked on firm level ground, open the bonnet and disconnect the battery negative (earth) lead - see Chapter 5, Section 1.

2   Drain the engine oil, then clean and refit the engine oil drain plug, tightening it to the specified torque wrench setting. Although not strictly necessary as part of the dismantling procedure, owners are advised to remove and discard the oil filter, so that it can be renewed with the oil (see Chapter 1).

3   Drain the cooling system (see Chapter 1).

4   Disconnect the radiator bottom hose from the radiator union and from the (heater) coolant pipe. Unbolt the coolant pipe from the sump; if they will prevent sump removal, disconnect or release the coolant hoses from the oil cooler unions (where fitted).

5   Unscrew the two bolts securing the power steering system pipes to the right-hand side of the subframe.

6   Unplug the electrical connector(s) to disconnect the oxygen sen-

15.12 Equipment must be available to raise and support engine/transmission unit while vehicle is raised, to allow sump removal

sor and, where fitted, the oil level sensor wiring - unclip the connectors to release the wiring where necessary.

7 Where the vehicle is fitted with automatic transmission, trace the fluid cooler lines from the transmission to the radiator, and release them from any clips etc, so that they have as much movement as possible.

8 Remove the auxiliary drivebelt cover (see Chapter 1).

9 Unscrew the nuts to disconnect the exhaust system front downpipe from the manifold, then either unhook all the system's rubber mountings and withdraw the complete exhaust system from under the vehicle, or remove only the downpipe/catalytic converter (see Chapter 4 for details).

10 Unscrew the sump-to-transmission bolts, also any securing the engine/transmission lower adaptor plate.

11 Unplugging the two electrical connectors, disconnecting the vacuum hose (where fitted) and disconnecting the crankcase breather hose from the cylinder head cover, remove the complete air cleaner assembly with the air mass meter, the resonator and the plenum chamber (see Chapter 4).

12 Take the weight of the engine/transmission unit using the lifting eyes provided on the cylinder head; bolt on additional lifting eyes where required **(see illustration)**. Remove completely the engine/transmission front mounting, unscrew the rear mounting's centre bolt, and unbolt the left-hand mounting from the body. Unscrew the six nuts securing the right-hand mounting bracket, and withdraw the bracket.

13 Being careful to watch the wiring, coolant hoses, fluid cooler pipes or gearchange linkage and transmission support rods (where ap-

propriate), and the radiator electric cooling fan, to ensure that nothing is trapped, stretched or damaged, lift the engine/transmission unit by 2 to 3 inches and support it securely.

14 Progressively unscrew the sump retaining bolts. Break the joint by striking the sump with the palm of the hand, then lower the sump and withdraw it with the engine/transmission lower adaptor plate; note the presence of any shims between the sump and transmission.

15 Remove and discard the sump gasket; this must be renewed as a matter of course whenever it is disturbed.

16 While the sump is removed, take the opportunity to remove the oil pump pick-up/strainer pipe and to clean it (see Section 16).

Refitting

17 On reassembly, thoroughly clean and degrease the mating surfaces of the cylinder block/crankcase and sump, then use a clean rag to wipe out the sump and the engine's interior. If the oil pump pick-up/strainer pipe was removed, fit a new gasket and refit the pipe, tightening its screws to the specified torque wrench setting. Fit the new gasket to the sump mating surface so that the gasket fits into the sump groove **(see illustration)**.

18 If the sump is being refitted with the engine/transmission still connected and in the vehicle, proceed as follows:

(a) *Check that the mating surfaces of the sump, the cylinder block/crankcase and the transmission are absolutely clean and flat. Any shims found on removal of the sump must be refitted in their original locations.*

(b) *Apply a thin film of suitable sealant (Ford recommend Hylosil 102) to the junctions of the cylinder block/crankcase with the oil pump and the crankshaft left-hand oil seal carrier. Without delay - the sump bolts must be fully tightened within 10 to 20 minutes of applying the sealant - offer up the sump and engine/transmission lower adaptor plate, and refit the bolts, tightening them lightly at first **(see illustration)**.*

(c) *Ensuring that the engine/transmission lower adaptor plate is correctly located, firmly press the sump against the transmission, and tighten the transmission-to-sump (ie, engine) bolts to the specified torque wrench setting.*

(d) *Without disturbing the position of the sump, and working in a diagonal sequence from the centre outwards, tighten the sump bolts to the specified torque wrench setting.*

(e) *Proceed to paragraph 20.*

19 If the sump is being refitted with the engine and transmission separated (in or out of the vehicle), proceed as follows:

(a) *Apply a thin film of suitable sealant (Ford recommend Hylosil 102) to the junctions of the cylinder block/crankcase with the oil pump and the crankshaft left-hand oil seal carrier **(see illustration)**. Without delay - the sump bolts must be fully tightened within 10 to 20 minutes of applying the sealant - offer up the sump to the cylinder block/crankcase, and insert the sump bolts, tightening them lightly at first.*

2A

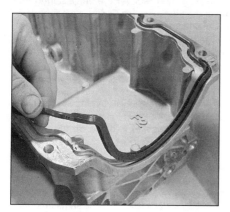

15.17 Ensure gasket is located correctly in sump groove

15.18 Engine/transmission lower adaptor plate (arrowed) must be refitted with sump

15.19A Apply sealant (arrowed) as directed when refitting sump

15.19B Checking alignment of sump with cylinder block/crankcase

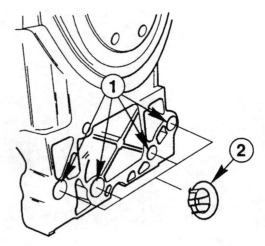

15.19C Sump-to-cylinder block/crankcase alignment shims

1 *Fitting points on sump*	2 *Shim*

(b) *Using a suitable straight edge to check alignment across the flat-machined faces of each, move the sump as necessary so that its left-hand face - including any shims found on removal - is flush with that of the cylinder block/crankcase* **(see illustration)**. *Without disturbing the position of the sump, and working in a diagonal sequence from the centre outwards, tighten the sump bolts to the specified torque wrench setting.*

(c) *Check again that both faces are flush before proceeding; if necessary, unbolt the sump again, clean the mating surfaces, and repeat the full procedure to ensure that the sump is correctly aligned.*

(d) *If it is not possible to achieve exact alignment by moving the sump, shims are available in thicknesses of 0.25 mm (colour-coded yellow) or 0.50 mm (colour-coded black) to eliminate the discrepancy* **(see illustration)**.

20   The remainder of reassembly is the reverse of the removal procedure, noting the following points.

(a) *Tighten all fasteners to the torque wrench settings specified.*

(b) *Always renew any self-locking nuts disturbed on removal.*

(c) *Lower the engine/transmission unit into place, and reassemble the rear, left-hand and right-hand mountings. Do not yet release the hoist; the weight of the engine/transmission unit must not be taken by the mountings until all are correctly aligned.*

(d) *Fitting the Ford service tool in place of the front mounting, tighten the engine/transmission mounting fasteners to their specified torque wrench settings, and in the sequence described in Part B of this Chapter, Section 4, paragraphs 49 and 50.*

(e) *Refill the cooling system (see Chapter 1).*

(f) *Refill the engine with oil, remembering that you are advised to fit a new filter (see Chapter 1).*

(g) *Check for signs of oil or coolant leaks once the engine has been restarted and warmed-up to normal operating temperature.*

16 Oil pump - removal, inspection and refitting

Removal

Note: *While this task is theoretically possible when the engine is in place in the vehicle, in practice, it requires so much preliminary dismantling, and is so difficult to carry out due to the restricted access, that owners are advised to remove the engine from the vehicle first. Note, however, that the oil pump pressure relief valve can be removed with the engine in situ - see paragraph 8.*

In addition to the new pump gasket and other replacement parts required, read through Section 15, and ensure that the necessary tools and facilities are available.

1   Remove the timing belt (see Section 10).

2   Withdraw the crankshaft toothed pulley and the thrustwasher behind it, noting which way round the thrustwasher is fitted (see Section 11).

3   Remove the sump (see Section 15).

4   Undo the screws securing the oil pump pick-up/strainer pipe to the pump, then unscrew the nut and withdraw the oil pump pick-up/strainer pipe. Discard the gasket.

5   Unbolt the pump from the cylinder block/crankcase **(see illustration)**. Withdraw and discard the gasket, and remove the crankshaft right-hand oil seal. Thoroughly clean and degrease all components, particularly the mating surfaces of the pump, the sump, and the cylinder block/crankcase.

Inspection

6   Unscrew the Torx screws, and remove the pump cover plate; noting any identification marks on the rotors, withdraw the rotors **(see illustration)**.

7   Inspect the rotors for obvious signs of wear or damage, and renew if necessary; if either rotor, the pump body, or its cover plate are scored or damaged, the complete oil pump assembly must be renewed.

8   The oil pressure relief valve can be dismantled, if required, without disturbing the pump. With the vehicle parked on firm level ground, apply the handbrake securely and raise its front end, supporting it securely on axle stands. Remove the front right-hand roadwheel and auxiliary drivebelt cover (see Chapter 1) to provide access to the valve.

9   Unscrew the threaded plug, and recover the valve spring and plunger **(see illustrations)**. If the plug's sealing O-ring is worn or damaged, a new one must be obtained, to be fitted on reassembly.

10   Reassembly is the reverse of the dismantling procedure; ensure the spring and valve are refitted the correct way round, and tighten the threaded plug securely.

Refitting

11   The oil pump must be primed on installation, by pouring clean engine oil into it, and rotating its inner rotor a few turns.

12   Using grease to stick the new gasket in place on the cylinder block/crankcase, and rotating the pump's inner rotor to align with the flats on the crankshaft, refit the pump and insert the bolts, tightening them lightly at first **(see illustration)**.

13   Using a suitable straight edge and feeler gauges, check that the pump is both centred *exactly* around the crankshaft, and aligned squarely so that its (sump) mating surface is exactly the same amount - between 0.3 and 0.8 mm - below that of the cylinder block/crankcase on each side of the crankshaft. Being careful not to disturb the gasket, move the pump into the correct position, and tighten its bolts to the

16.5 Unscrew bolts (arrowed) to remove oil pump

specified torque wrench setting **(see illustration)**.
14   Check that the pump is correctly located; if necessary, unbolt it again, and repeat the full procedure to ensure that the pump is correctly aligned.
15   Fit a new crankshaft right-hand oil seal (see Section 20).

16   Using grease to stick the gasket in place on the pump, refit the pick-up/strainer pipe, tightening its screws and nut to their specified torque wrench settings **(see illustration)**.
17   The remainder of reassembly is the reverse of the removal procedure, referring to the relevant text for details where required.

17   Oil cooler - removal and refitting

1   Drain the cooling system (see Chapter 1). Disconnect the coolant hoses from the oil cooler.
2   Unscrew the oil filter (see Chapter 1) - catch any escaping oil in a drip tray.
3   Unscrew the filter adaptor from the oil pump, and withdraw the oil cooler; note how its unions are aligned, and be prepared for oil loss from the cooler.
4   Refitting is the reverse of the removal procedure, noting the following points:

(a)   *Renew all O-rings and seals disturbed on removal.*
(b)   *Align the cooler's unions as noted on removal, and tighten the adaptor to the specified torque wrench setting.*
(c)   *Refill the cooling system (see Chapter 1).*
(d)   *Refit the oil filter, then check the engine oil level, and top-up as necessary (see Chapter 1).*
(e)   *Check for signs of oil or coolant leaks once the engine has been restarted and warmed-up to normal operating temperature.*

2A

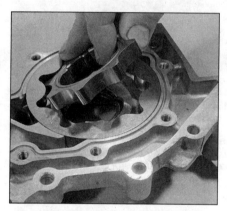
16.6 Withdrawing oil pump inner rotor

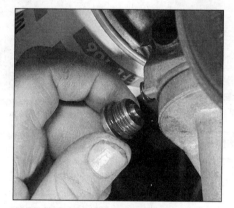
16.9A Unscrew threaded plug - seen through right-hand wheel arch . . .

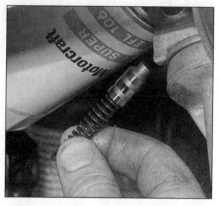
16.9B . . . to withdraw oil pressure relief valve spring and plunger

16.12 Use new gasket when refitting oil pump

16.13 Oil pump must be centred on crankshaft, and square to cylinder block/crankcase-to-sump mating surface - use straight edge and feeler gauges to check that pump surface is an equal amount (within permissible limits) below crankcase surface on both sides of crankshaft

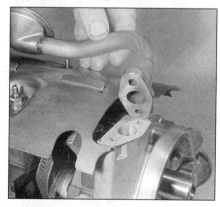
16.16 Use new gasket when refitting oil pick-up pipe to pump

2A-26   Chapter 2 Part A In-car engine repair procedures

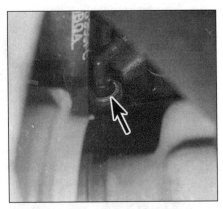

18.3 Remove screws (arrowed) to remove oil level sensor cover . . .

18.4 . . . disconnecting wiring from sensor

19.1 Oil pressure warning light switch (arrowed) is screwed into rear of cylinder block, above right-hand driveshaft support bearing

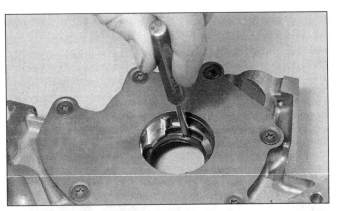

20.2 Driving out crankshaft right-hand oil seal

20.5 Socket of correct size can be used to replace Ford service tool, drawing new seal into place as described

18 Oil level sensor - removal and refitting

1   With the vehicle parked on firm level ground, open the bonnet and disconnect the battery negative (earth) lead - see Chapter 5, Section 1.
2   Raise the front of the vehicle, and support it securely on axle stands.
3   Undo the two screws, and remove the sensor's cover from the front of the sump **(see illustration)**.
4   Unplug the wiring from the sensor **(see illustration)**. Where necessary, unplug the electrical connector to disconnect the sensor wiring, and unclip the connector to release the wiring from the vehicle.
5   Unscrew the sensor, and quickly plug the sump aperture to minimise oil loss; note the sensor's seal.
6   Refitting is the reverse of the removal procedure; renew the sensor's seal if it is worn or damaged, and tighten the sensor to the specified torque wrench setting. Check the engine oil level, and top-up as necessary (see Chapter 1) - check for signs of oil leaks once the engine has been restarted and warmed-up to normal operating temperature.

19 Oil pressure warning light switch - removal and refitting

1   The switch is screwed into the rear of the cylinder block, above the right-hand driveshaft's support bearing **(see illustration)**.
2   With the vehicle parked on firm level ground, open the bonnet and disconnect the battery negative (earth) lead - see Chapter 5, Section 1.
3   Raise the front of the vehicle, and support it securely on axle stands.
4   Unplug the wiring from the switch, and unscrew it; be prepared for some oil loss.
5   Refitting is the reverse of the removal procedure; apply a thin

smear of suitable sealant to the switch threads, and tighten it to the specified torque wrench setting. Check the engine oil level, and top-up as necessary (see Chapter 1). Check for signs of oil leaks once the engine has been restarted and warmed-up to normal operating temperature.

20 Crankshaft oil seals - renewal

Note: *Don't try to prise these seals out without removing the oil pump or seal carrier - the seals are too soft, and the amount of space available is too small, for this to be possible without considerable risk of damage to the seal housing and/or the crankshaft journal. Follow exactly the procedure given below.*

Right-hand seal

1   Remove the oil pump (see Section 16).
2   Drive the oil seal out of the pump from behind **(see illustration)**.
3   Clean the seal housing and crankshaft, polishing off any burrs or raised edges, which may have caused the seal to fail in the first place.
4   Refit the oil pump (see Section 16). Grease the lips and periphery of the new seal, to ease installation.
5   To fit a new seal, Ford recommend the use of their service tool 21-093A, with the crankshaft pulley bolt, to draw the seal into place; an alternative can be arranged using a socket of suitable size, with a washer to match the crankshaft pulley bolt **(see illustration)**.
6   If such tools are not available, press the seal squarely into place by hand; tap it in until it is flush with the pump housing, using a soft-faced mallet and a socket with an outside diameter only slightly smaller than the seal's **(see illustration)**. This approach requires great care, to ensure that the seal is fitted squarely, without distortion or damage.
7   Wash off any traces of oil. The remainder of reassembly is the reverse of the removal procedure, referring to the relevant text for details

20.6 If seal is tapped into place as shown, exercise great care to prevent seal from being damaged or distorted

20.12 Unscrew bolts (arrowed) to remove crankshaft left-hand oil seal carrier . . .

20.13 . . . and ensure that carrier is properly supported when driving out used oil seal - note notches provided in carrier for drift

20.15 Use new gasket when refitting left-hand oil seal carrier

20.16 Oil seal carrier must be centred on crankshaft, and square to cylinder block/crankcase-to-sump mating surface - use straight edge and feeler gauges to check that carrier surface is an equal amount (within permissible limits) below crankcase surface on both sides of crankshaft

20.18 Using guide made from thin sheet of plastic to slide oil seal lips over crankshaft shoulder

2A

where required. Check for signs of oil leakage when the engine is restarted.

Left-hand seal

8   Remove the transmission (see the relevant Part of Chapter 7).
9   Where appropriate, remove the clutch (Chapter 8).
10   Unbolt the flywheel/driveplate (see Section 21).
11   Remove the sump (see Section 15).
12   Unbolt the oil seal carrier **(see illustration)**. Remove and discard its gasket.
13   Supporting the carrier evenly on wooden blocks, drive the oil seal out of the carrier from behind **(see illustration)**.
14   Clean the seal housing and crankshaft, polishing off any burrs or raised edges, which may have caused the seal to fail in the first place. Clean also the mating surfaces of the cylinder block/crankcase and carrier, using a scraper to remove all traces of the old gasket - be careful not to scratch or damage the material of either - then use a suitable solvent to degrease them.
15   Use grease to stick the new gasket in place on the cylinder block/crankcase, then offer up the carrier **(see illustration)**.
16   Using a suitable straight edge and feeler gauges, check that the carrier is both centred *exactly* around the crankshaft, and aligned squarely so that its (sump) mating surface is exactly the same amount - between 0.3 and 0.8 mm - below that of the cylinder block/crankcase on each side of the crankshaft. Being careful not to disturb the gasket, move the carrier into the correct position, and tighten its bolts to the

specified torque wrench setting **(see illustration)**.
17   Check that the carrier is correctly located; if necessary, unbolt it again, and repeat the full procedure to ensure that the carrier is correctly aligned.
18   Ford's recommended method of seal fitting is to use service tool 21-141, with two flywheel bolts to draw the seal into place. If this is not available, make up a guide from a thin sheet of plastic or similar, lubricate the lips of the new seal and the crankshaft shoulder with grease, then offer up the seal, with the guide feeding the seal's lips over the crankshaft shoulder **(see illustration)**. Press the seal evenly into its housing by hand only, and use a soft-faced mallet gently to tap it into place until it is flush with the surrounding housing.
19   Wipe off any surplus oil or grease; the remainder of the reassembly procedure is the reverse of dismantling, referring to the relevant text for details where required. Check for signs of oil leakage when the engine is restarted.

---

21 Flywheel/driveplate - removal, inspection and refitting

Removal

1   Remove the transmission (see the relevant Part of Chapter 7). Now is a good time to check components such as oil seals and renew them if necessary.

2   Where appropriate, remove the clutch (Chapter 8). Now is a good time to check or renew the clutch components and pilot bearing.

3   Use a centre-punch or paint to make alignment marks on the fly-wheel/driveplate and crankshaft, to ensure correct alignment during refitting.

4   Prevent the flywheel/driveplate from turning by locking the ring gear teeth, or by bolting a strap between the flywheel/driveplate and the cylinder block/crankcase. Slacken the bolts evenly until all are free.

5   Remove each bolt in turn, and ensure that new replacements are obtained for reassembly; these bolts are subjected to severe stresses, and so must be renewed, regardless of their apparent condition, when-ever they are disturbed.

6   Noting the reinforcing plate (automatic transmission-equipped models only), withdraw the flywheel/driveplate; do not drop it - it is very heavy.

Inspection

7   Clean the flywheel/driveplate to remove grease and oil. Inspect the surface for cracks, rivet grooves, burned areas and score marks. Light scoring can be removed with emery cloth. Check for cracked and broken ring gear teeth. Lay the flywheel/driveplate on a flat surface, and use a straight edge to check for warpage.

8   Clean and inspect the mating surfaces of the flywheel/driveplate and the crankshaft. If the crankshaft left-hand seal is leaking, renew it (see Section 20) before refitting the flywheel/driveplate.

9   While the flywheel/driveplate is removed, clean carefully its in-board (right-hand) face, particularly the recesses which serve as the reference points for the crankshaft speed/position sensor. Clean the sensor's tip, and check that the sensor is securely fastened.

Refitting

10   On refitting, ensure that the engine/transmission adaptor plate is in place (where necessary), then fit the flywheel/driveplate to the crankshaft so that all bolt holes align - it will fit only one way - check this using the marks made on removal. Do not forget the reinforcing plate (where fitted).

21.11 Note method used to lock flywheel/driveplate while (new) bolts are tightened

11   Lock the flywheel/driveplate by the method used on dismantling. Working in a diagonal sequence to tighten them evenly, and increasing to the final amount in two or three stages, tighten the new bolts to the specified torque wrench setting **(see illustration)**.

12   The remainder of reassembly is the reverse of the removal proce-dure, referring to the relevant text for details where required.

22 Engine/transmission mountings - inspection and renewal

General

1   The engine/transmission mountings seldom require attention, but broken or deteriorated mountings should be renewed immediately, or

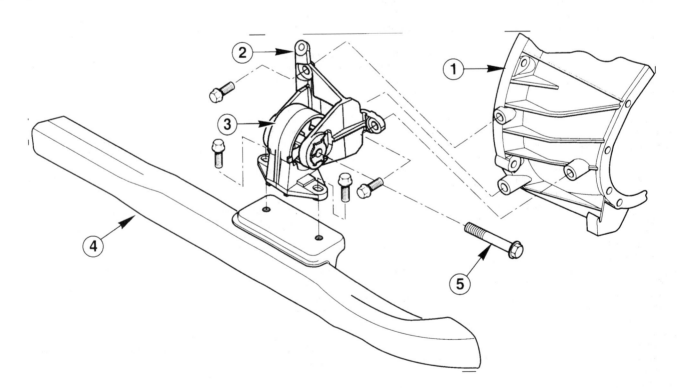

22.8 Engine/transmission front mounting - manual transmission shown, automatic equivalent similar

1	*Transmission*	*3*	*Mounting*	*5*	*Mounting centre bolt*
2	*Mounting bracket*	*4*	*Front suspension subframe*		

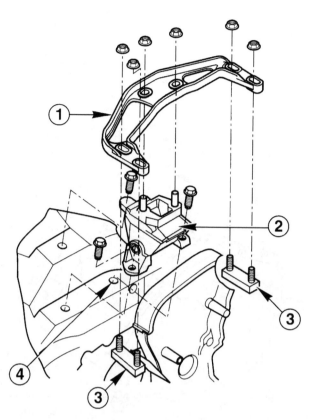

22.10 Engine/transmission right-hand mounting - standard type

1 Bracket
2 Mounting
3 Brackets bolted to cylinder block/crankcase
4 Vehicle body

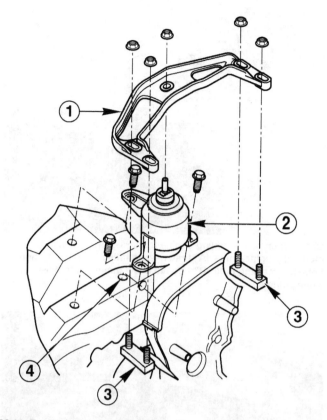

22.11 Engine/transmission right-hand mounting - hydraulic type (where fitted)

1 Bracket
2 Hydraulic mounting
3 Brackets bolted to cylinder block/crankcase
4 Vehicle body

the added strain placed on the driveline components may cause damage or wear.

2   While separate mountings may be removed and refitted individually, if more than one is disturbed at a time - such as if the engine/transmission unit is removed from its mountings - they must be reassembled and their fasteners tightened in a strict sequence.

3   On reassembly, the weight of the engine/transmission unit must not be taken by the mountings until all are correctly aligned. Fitting the Ford service tool in place of the front mounting, tighten the engine/transmission mounting fasteners to their specified torque wrench settings, and in the sequence described in Part B of this Chapter, Section 4, paragraphs 49 and 50.

Inspection

4   During the check, the engine/transmission unit must be raised slightly, to remove its weight from the mountings.

5   Raise the front of the vehicle, and support it securely on axle stands. Position a jack under the sump, with a large block of wood between the jack head and the sump, then carefully raise the engine/transmission just enough to take the weight off the mountings. **Warning:** *DO NOT place any part of your body under the engine when it is supported only by a jack!*

6   Check the mountings to see if the rubber is cracked, hardened or separated from the metal components. Sometimes the rubber will split right down the centre.

7   Check for relative movement between each mounting's brackets and the engine/transmission or body (use a large screwdriver or lever to attempt to move the mountings). If movement is noted, lower the engine and check-tighten the mounting fasteners.

Renewal

Front mounting

8   Unbolt the resonator support bracket from the engine compartment front crossmember, slacken the two clamp screws securing the resonator to the air mass meter and plenum chamber hoses, then swing the resonator up clear of the thermostat housing (see Chapter 4). Unbolt the pulse-air filter housing from the mounting bracket, then unfasten the bolts/nuts securing the mounting to the subframe, unscrew the centre bolt and withdraw the mounting; note the location of the wiring connector bracket. The mounting's bracket can be unbolted from the transmission if required **(see illustration)**.

9   On refitting, ensure that the mounting-to-transmission bolts are securely tightened, then refit the mounting and wiring connector bracket. Tighten first the mounting-to-subframe bolts/nuts, noting that these are to be tightened in two stages to the final specified torque wrench setting. Finally tighten the mounting's centre bolt, again to the specified torque wrench setting.

Right-hand mounting

10   Unscrew the nuts and withdraw the bracket; note that these nuts are self-locking, and must therefore be renewed whenever they are disturbed. Unbolt the mounting from the body **(see illustration)**.

11   Where hydraulic-type mountings are fitted - there are only five nuts securing the bracket, and the mounting is clearly identifiable from its shape - take care never to tilt these more than 5 from the vertical **(see illustration)**.

12   On refitting, renew the self-locking nuts, and tighten all fasteners to the torque wrench settings specified. When tightening the nuts,

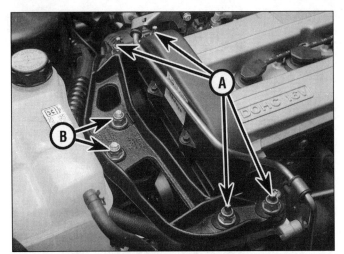

22.12 When reassembling engine/transmission right-hand mounting, tighten nuts "A" first, release lifting equipment, then tighten remaining nuts "B" - do not allow mounting to twist when doing so

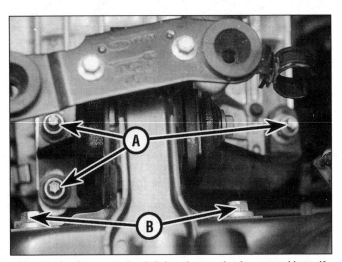

22.15 Engine/transmission left-hand mounting is secured by self-locking nuts "A" to transmission, by bolts "B" to body

tighten first the four bracket-to-engine nuts, then release the hoist or jack to allow the engine/transmission's weight to rest on the mounting. Do not allow the mounting to twist as the last two of the nuts are tightened **(see illustration)**.

Left-hand mounting
13   Unplugging the two electrical connectors, disconnecting the vacuum hose (where fitted) and disconnecting the crankcase breather hose from the cylinder head cover, remove the complete air cleaner assembly with the air mass meter, the resonator and the plenum chamber (see Chapter 4).
14   Unscrew the three nuts to release the mounting from the transmission, then unbolt it from the body **(see illustration)**. Note that the nuts are self-locking, and must therefore be renewed whenever they are disturbed. Unscrew the centre bolt to dismantle the mounting, if necessary to renew components.
15   On refitting, renew the self-locking nuts, and do not allow the mounting to twist as the nuts are tightened **(see illustration)**. Tighten all fasteners to the specified torque wrench settings.

Rear mounting
16   Where the vehicle is fitted with automatic transmission, a separate damper may be fitted beneath the subframe, which must be unbolted to reach the mounting's fasteners **(see illustration)**.

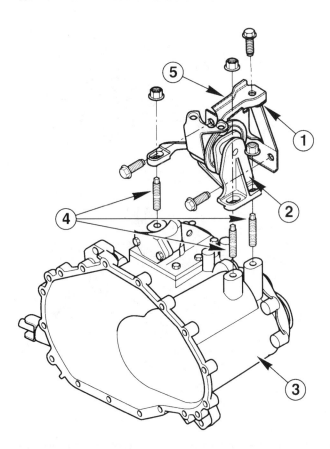

22.14 Engine/transmission left-hand mounting - manual transmission shown, automatic equivalent similar

1	Mounting bracket	4	Studs
2	Mounting	5	Fastening plate -
3	Transmission		where fitted

22.16 Where vehicle is fitted with automatic transmission, additional damper may be fastened to underside of engine/transmission rear mounting, as shown

17   Unbolt the mounting from the subframe, then unscrew the mounting's centre bolt. If required, unbolt the mounting's bracket from the transmission **(see illustrations)**.
18   On refitting, ensure that the mounting-to-transmission bolts are securely tightened, then refit the mounting. Tighten first the mounting-

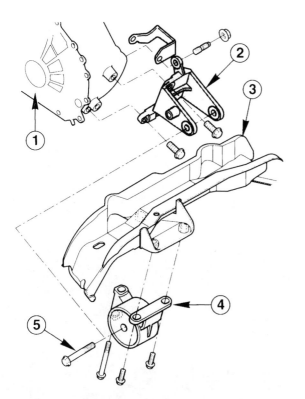

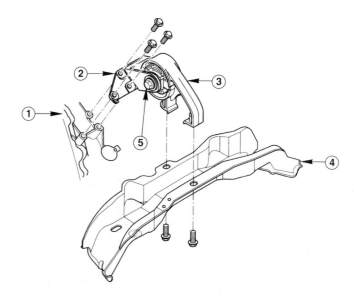

22.17A Engine/transmission rear mounting - manual transmission type

1   Transmission
2   Mounting bracket
3   Front suspension subframe
4   Mounting
5   Mounting centre bolt

22.17B Engine/transmission rear mounting - automatic transmission type

1   Transmission
2   Mounting bracket
3   Mounting
4   Front suspension subframe
5   Mounting centre bolt

to-subframe bolts, noting that these are to be tightened in two stages to the final specified torque wrench setting. Finally tighten the mounting's centre bolt, again to the specified torque wrench setting.

2A

Notes

Chapter 2 Part B Engine removal and general engine overhaul procedures

Contents

2B

Specifications

Cylinder head

Maximum permissible gasket surface distortion	0.10 mm
Valve seat included angle	90°
Valve guide bore	6.060 to 6.091 mm

Valves - general

	Inlet	Exhaust
Valve lift	7.500 to 7.685 mm	7.610 to 7.765 mm
Valve length	96.870 to 97.330 mm	96.470 to 96.930 mm
Valve head diameter:		
1.6 litre engine	26.0 mm	24.5 mm
1.8 and 2.0 litre engines	32.0 mm	28.0 mm
Valve stem diameter	6.028 to 6.043 mm	6.010 to 6.025 mm
Valve stem-to-guide clearance	0.017 to 0.064 mm	0.035 to 0.081 mm

Cylinder block

Cylinder bore diameter - 1.6 litre engine:	
Class 1	76.000 to 76.010 mm
Class 2	76.010 to 76.020 mm
Class 3	76.020 to 76.030 mm
Cylinder bore diameter - 1.8 litre engine:	
Class 1	80.600 to 80.610 mm
Class 2	80.610 to 80.620 mm
Class 3	80.620 to 80.630 mm
Cylinder bore diameter - 2.0 litre engine:	
Class 1	84.800 to 84.810 mm
Class 2	84.810 to 84.820 mm
Class 3	84.820 to 84.830 mm

Pistons and piston rings

Piston diameter - 1.6 litre engine:	
Class 1	75.975 to 75.985 mm
Class 2	75.985 to 75.995 mm
Class 3	75.995 to 76.005 mm
Piston diameter - 1.8 litre engine:	
Class 1	80.570 to 80.580 mm
Class 2	80.580 to 80.590 mm
Class 3	80.590 to 80.600 mm
Piston diameter - 2.0 litre engine:	
Class 1	84.770 to 84.780 mm
Class 2	84.780 to 84.790 mm
Class 3	84.790 to 84.800 mm
Oversizes - all engines	None available
Piston-to-cylinder bore clearance	No information available at time of writing
Piston ring end gaps - installed:	
Top compression ring - 1.6 and 1.8 litre engines	0.30 to 0.50 mm
Top compression ring - 2.0 litre engine	0.26 to 0.50 mm
Second compression ring	0.30 to 0.50 mm
Oil control ring - 1.6 litre engine	0.25 to 1.00 mm
Oil control ring - 1.8 litre engine	0.38 to 1.14 mm
Oil control ring - 2.0 litre engine	0.40 to 1.40 mm

Gudgeon pin

Diameter:	
White colour code/piston crown marked "A"	20.622 to 20.625 mm
Red colour code/piston crown marked "B"	20.625 to 20.628 mm
Blue colour code/piston crown marked "C"	20.628 to 20.631 mm
Clearance in piston	0.010 to 0.016 mm
Connecting rod small-end eye internal diameter	20.589 to 20.609 mm
Interference fit in connecting rod	0.011 to 0.042 mm

Crankshaft and bearings

Main bearing shell standard inside diameter - installed	58.011 to 58.038 mm
Main bearing journal standard diameter	57.980 to 58.000 mm
Main bearing journal-to-shell running clearance	0.011 to 0.058 mm
Main bearing shell undersizes available	0.02 mm, 0.25 mm
Big-end bearing shell standard inside diameter - installed	46.926 to 46.960 mm
Crankpin (big-end) bearing journal standard diameter	46.890 to 46.910 mm
Crankpin (big-end) bearing journal-to-shell running clearance	0.016 to 0.070 mm
Big-end bearing shell undersizes available	0.02 mm, 0.25 mm
Crankshaft endfloat	0.090 to 0.310 mm

Torque wrench settings

	Nm	lbf ft
Main bearing cap bolts and nuts	80	59
Big-end bearing cap bolts:		
Stage 1	18	13
Stage 2	Angle-tighten a further 90°	
Piston-cooling oil jet/blanking plug Torx screws	10	7
Cylinder block and head oilway blanking plugs:		
M6 x 10	8 to 11	6 to 8
M10 x 11.5 - in block	24	17
1/4 PTF plug - in block	25	18
Power steering pump/air conditioning compressor mounting bracket-to-cylinder block bolts	47	35
Exhaust manifold heat shield mounting bracket-to-cylinder block bolts	32	24
Crankcase breather system:		
Oil separator-to-cylinder block bolts	10	7
Pipe-to-cylinder head bolt	23	17
Water pump bolts	See Chapter 3	
Driveshaft support bearing bracket-to-cylinder block bolts	48	35
Transmission-to-engine bolts	See Part A of this Chapter	
Engine/transmission mounting fasteners	See Part A of this Chapter	
Front suspension subframe bolts	130	96

Note: *Refer to Part A of this Chapter for remaining torque wrench settings.*

1 General information

How to use this Chapter

This Part of Chapter 2 is devoted to engine/transmission removal and refitting, to those repair procedures requiring the removal of the engine/transmission from the vehicle, and to the overhaul of engine components. It includes only the Specifications relevant to those procedures. Refer to Part A for additional Specifications, if required.

General information

The information ranges from advice concerning preparation for an overhaul and the purchase of replacement parts, to detailed step-by-step procedures covering removal and installation of internal engine components and the inspection of parts.

The following Sections have been written based on the assumption that the engine has been removed from the vehicle. For information concerning in-vehicle engine repair, as well as removal and installation of the external components necessary for the overhaul, see Part A of this Chapter and Section 5 of this Part.

When overhauling this engine, it is essential to establish first exactly what replacement parts are available. At the time of writing, components such as the piston rings are not available separately from the piston/connecting rod assemblies; pistons, gudgeon pins and valve guides are not available separately, and very few under- or oversized components are available for engine reconditioning. In most cases, it would appear that the easiest and most economically-sensible course of action is to replace a worn or damaged engine with an exchange unit.

2 Engine overhaul - general information

It's not always easy to determine when, or if, an engine should be completely overhauled, as a number of factors must be considered.

High mileage is not necessarily an indication that an overhaul is needed, while low mileage doesn't preclude the need for an overhaul. Frequency of servicing is probably the most important consideration. An engine that's had regular and frequent oil and filter changes, as well as other required maintenance, will most likely give many thousands of miles of reliable service. Conversely, a neglected engine may require an overhaul very early in its life.

Excessive oil consumption is an indication that piston rings, valve seals and/or valve guides are in need of attention. Make sure that oil leaks aren't responsible before deciding that the rings and/or guides are worn. Perform a cylinder compression check (Part A of this Chapter, Section 3) to determine the extent of the work required.

Loss of power, rough running, knocking or metallic engine noises, excessive valve train noise and high fuel consumption rates may also point to the need for an overhaul, especially if they're all present at the same time. If a full service doesn't remedy the situation, major mechanical work is the only solution.

An engine overhaul involves restoring all internal parts to the specification of a new engine. **Note:** *Always check first what replacement parts are available before planning any overhaul operation; refer to Section 1 of this Part.* Ford dealers, or a good engine reconditioning specialist/automotive parts supplier may be able to suggest alternatives which will enable you to overcome the lack of replacement parts.

During an overhaul, it is usual to renew the piston rings, and to rebore and/or hone the cylinder bores; where the rebore is done by an automotive machine shop, new oversize pistons and rings will also be installed - all these operations, of course, assume the availability of suitable replacement parts. The main and big-end bearings are generally renewed and, if necessary, the crankshaft may be reground to restore the journals. Generally, the valves are serviced as well, since they're usually in less-than-perfect condition at this point. While the engine is being overhauled, other components, such as the starter and alternator, can be renewed as well, or rebuilt, if the necessary parts can be found. The end result should be an as-new engine that will give

many trouble-free miles. **Note:** *Critical cooling system components such as the hoses, drivebelt, thermostat and water pump MUST be replaced with new parts when an engine is overhauled. The radiator should be checked carefully, to ensure that it isn't clogged or leaking (see Chapter 3). Also, as a general rule, the oil pump should be renewed when an engine is rebuilt.*

Before beginning the engine overhaul, read through the entire procedure to familiarise yourself with the scope and requirements of the job. Overhauling an engine isn't difficult, but it is time-consuming. Plan on the vehicle being off the road for a minimum of two weeks, especially if parts must be taken to an automotive machine shop for repair or reconditioning. Check on availability of parts, and make sure that any necessary special tools and equipment are obtained in advance. Most work can be done with typical hand tools, although a number of precision measuring tools are required, for inspecting parts to determine if they must be replaced. Often, an automotive machine shop will handle the inspection of parts, and will offer advice concerning reconditioning and replacement. **Note:** *Always wait until the engine has been completely dismantled, and all components, especially the cylinder block/crankcase, have been inspected, before deciding what service and repair operations must be performed by an automotive machine shop. Since the block's condition will be the major factor to consider when determining whether to overhaul the original engine or buy a rebuilt one, never purchase parts or have machine work done on other components until the cylinder block/crankcase has been thoroughly inspected. As a general rule, time is the primary cost of an overhaul, so it doesn't pay to install worn or sub-standard parts.*

As a final note, to ensure maximum life and minimum trouble from a rebuilt engine, everything must be assembled with care, in a spotlessly-clean environment.

3 Engine/transmission removal - methods and precautions

If you've decided that an engine must be removed for overhaul or major repair work, several preliminary steps should be taken.

Locating a suitable place to work is extremely important. Adequate work space, along with storage space for the vehicle, will be needed. If a workshop or garage isn't available, at the very least, a flat, level, clean work surface made of concrete or asphalt is required.

Cleaning the engine compartment and engine/transmission before beginning the removal procedure will help keep tools clean and organized.

The engine can only be withdrawn by removing it complete with the transmission; the vehicle's body must be raised and supported securely, sufficiently high that the engine/transmission can be unbolted as a single unit and lowered to the ground; the engine/transmission unit can then be withdrawn from under the vehicle and separated. An engine hoist or A-frame will therefore be necessary. Make sure the equipment is rated in excess of the combined weight of the engine and transmission. Safety is of primary importance, considering the potential hazards involved in removing the engine/transmission from the vehicle.

If this is the first time you have removed an engine, a helper should ideally be available. Advice and aid from someone more experienced would also be helpful. There are many instances when one person cannot simultaneously perform all of the operations required when removing the engine/transmission from the vehicle.

Plan the operation ahead of time. Arrange for, or obtain, all of the tools and equipment you'll need prior to beginning the job. Some of the equipment necessary to perform engine/transmission removal and installation safely and with relative ease, and which may have to be hired or borrowed, includes (in addition to the engine hoist) a heavy-duty trolley jack, a strong pair of axle stands, some wooden blocks, and an engine dolly (a low, wheeled platform capable of taking the weight of the engine/transmission, so that it can be moved easily when on the ground). A complete set of spanners and sockets (as described in the front of this manual) will obviously be needed, together with plenty of rags and cleaning solvent for mopping-up spilled oil, coolant

2B

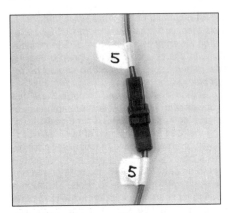

4.5A Whenever any wiring is disconnected, mark or label it as shown, to ensure correct reconnection . . .

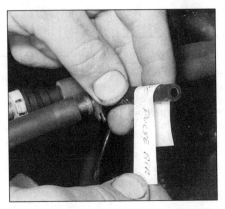

4.5B . . . vacuum hoses and pipes should be similarly marked

4.7 Note colour-coding of unions when disconnecting fuel feed and return lines

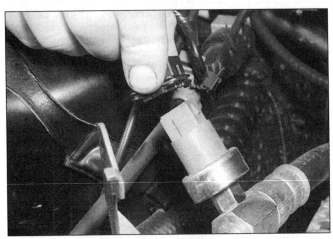

4.9A Unplug the power steering pressure switch electrical connector . . .

4.9B . . . unbolt the power steering high-pressure pipe . . .

and fuel. If the hoist is to be hired, make sure that you arrange for it in advance, and perform all of the operations possible without it before-hand. This will save you money and time.

Plan for the vehicle to be out of use for quite a while. A machine shop will be required to perform some of the work which the do-it-your-selfer can't accomplish without special equipment. These establish-ments often have a busy schedule, so it would be a good idea to consult them before removing the engine, to accurately estimate the amount of time required to rebuild or repair components that may need work.

Always be extremely careful when removing and installing the en-gine/transmission. Serious injury can result from careless actions. By planning ahead and taking your time, the job (although a major task) can be accomplished successfully.

4 Engine/transmission - removal and refitting

Warning: *Petrol is extremely flammable, so take extra precautions when disconnecting any part of the fuel system. Don't smoke, or allow naked flames or bare light bulbs in or near the work area, and don't work in a garage where a natural gas appliance (such as a clothes dryer or water heater) is installed. If you spill petrol on your skin, rinse it off immediately. Have a fire extinguisher rated for petrol fires handy, and know how to use it.*
Note: *Read through the entire Section, as well as reading the advice in the preceding Section, before beginning this procedure. The engine and transmission are removed as a unit, lowered to the ground and re-moved from underneath, then separated outside the vehicle.*

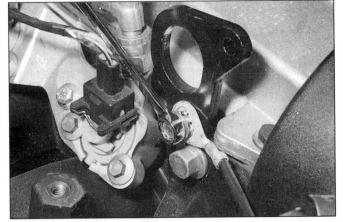

4.9C . . . and the earth lead from the cylinder head rear support plate/engine lifting eye

Removal

1   Park the vehicle on firm, level ground, apply the handbrake firmly, and slacken the nuts securing both front roadwheels.
2   Relieve the fuel system pressure (see Chapter 4).
3   Disconnect the battery negative (earth) lead - see Chapter 5, Section 1. For better access the battery may be removed completely (see Chapter 5).
4   Place protective covers on the wings and engine compartment front crossmember, then remove the bonnet (see Chapter 11).

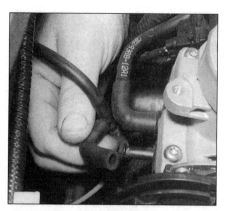

4.10A Disconnect vacuum hose shown from rear of throttle housing . . .

4.10B . . . vacuum hose (arrowed) from union on left-hand end on inlet manifold . . .

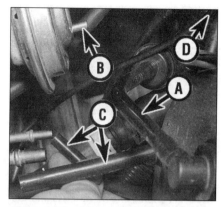

4.10C . . . also brake servo hose (A), EGR valve hose (B), EGR pipe hoses (C) - noting their different sizes - and pulse-air filter vacuum line (D)

4.11 Unbolt the engine/transmission-to-body earth lead - hidden behind wiring loom guide - from location (arrowed) on the transmission's top surface

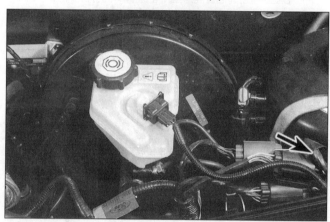

4.13A Unplug three large electrical connectors (arrowed) . . .

2B

5   Whenever you disconnect any vacuum lines, coolant and emissions hoses, wiring loom connectors, earth straps and fuel lines as part of the following procedure, always label them clearly, so that they can be correctly reassembled. Masking tape and/or a touch-up paint applicator work well for marking items **(see illustrations)**. Take instant photos, or sketch the locations of components and brackets.

6   Unplug the two electrical connectors, disconnect the vacuum hose (where fitted) and disconnect the crankcase breather hose from the cylinder head cover, then remove the complete air cleaner assembly, with the air mass meter, the resonator and the plenum chamber (see Chapter 4).

7   Equalise the pressure in the fuel tank by removing the filler cap, then undo the fuel feed and return lines connecting the engine to the chassis (see Chapter 4). Plug or cap all open fittings **(see illustration)**.

8   Disconnect the accelerator cable from the throttle linkage as described in Chapter 4 - where fitted, also disconnect the cruise control actuator cable (see Chapter 12). Secure the cable(s) clear of the engine/transmission.

9   Releasing its wire clip, unplug the power steering pressure switch electrical connector, then unbolt the power steering high-pressure pipe and the earth lead from the cylinder head rear support plate/engine lifting eye **(see illustrations)**.

10   Marking or labelling all components as they are disconnected (see paragraph 5 above), disconnect the vacuum hoses as follows:

(a)   One from the rear of the throttle housing (only the one hose - there is no need to disconnect the second hose running to the fuel pressure regulator) **(see illustration)**.

(b)   One from the union on the inlet manifold's left-hand end **(see illustration)**.

(c)   The braking system vacuum servo unit hose - from the inlet manifold (see Chapter 9 for details).

(d)   Also disconnect the vacuum hoses from the Exhaust Gas Recirculation system components - one from the EGR valve, two from the EGR pipe (note that these last two are of different sizes, as are their pipe stubs, so that they can only be connected the correct way round).

(e)   While you are there, trace the vacuum line from the pulse-air filter housing over the top of the transmission, and disconnect it by pulling the plastic pipe out of the rubber hose just beneath the bulkhead-mounted pulse-air solenoid valve **(see illustration)**.

(f)   Secure all these hoses so that they won't get damaged as the engine/transmission is removed.

11   Unbolt the engine/transmission-to-body earth lead from the transmission's top surface **(see illustration)**. Disconnect the speedometer drive cable (see Chapter 12) and secure it clear of the engine/transmission.

12   Where the vehicle is fitted with manual transmission, disconnect the clutch cable (see Chapter 8). Where automatic transmission is fitted, disconnect the selector cable (see Chapter 7, Part B). Secure the cable clear of the engine/transmission.

13   Marking or labelling all components as they are disconnected (see paragraph 5 above), disconnect the engine wiring loom from the body as follows:

(a)   Starting at the left-hand side of the engine compartment, release and unplug the three large electrical connectors clipped to the suspension mounting - note the wire clips fitted to some connectors **(see illustration)**.

4.13B . . . unplug engine wiring loom from battery wiring and bulkhead components (arrows) . . .

4.13C . . . and disconnect ECU wiring and earth lead (arrows) to release engine wiring loom from vehicle body

4.25A Use split pins as shown to secure radiator in its raised position . . .

(b) Disconnect and/or release the battery-to-starter motor wiring, noting the single connector which must be unplugged.

(c) Unplug the electrical connector(s) to disconnect the vehicle speed sensor, oxygen sensor and, where fitted, the oil level sensor wiring - unclip the connectors to release the wiring where necessary.

(d) Work along the loom to the bulkhead, unclipping the loom and unplugging the various bulkhead-mounted components connected into it, until you reach the right-hand side of the engine compartment **(see illustration)**.

(e) Carefully prise the power steering fluid reservoir upwards out of its clip on the suspension mounting, then unscrew the ECU connector's retaining bolt and unplug the connector **(see illustration)**.

(f) Unbolt the earth lead from the right-hand inner wing panel, release the engine wiring loom and refit the power steering fluid reservoir.

(g) Secure the engine wiring loom neatly to the engine/transmission so that it cannot be damaged as the unit is removed from the vehicle.

14 Unbolt both parts of the exhaust manifold heat shield; unclip the coolant hose to allow the upper part to be withdrawn.

15 Remove the auxiliary drivebelt (see Chapter 1).

16 Unbolt the power steering pump (see Chapter 10); secure it as far as possible (without disconnecting the system's hoses) clear of the engine/transmission.

17 Raise the vehicle and support it securely on axle stands, then remove the front roadwheels. Drain the cooling system and (if the engine is to be dismantled) drain the engine oil and remove the oil filter (see Chapter 1). Also drain the transmission as described in the relevant Part of Chapter 7.

18 Withdraw the lower part of the exhaust manifold heat shield.

19 Unscrew the nuts to disconnect the exhaust system front downpipe from the manifold, then unhook all the system's rubber mountings and withdraw the complete exhaust system from under the vehicle (see Chapter 4 for details).

20 Where the vehicle is fitted with manual transmission, mark their positions, then disconnect the gearchange linkage and transmission support rods from the rear of the transmission. Unscrew the retaining nuts, and withdraw the gear linkage heat shield from the underbody. Unbolt the rear end of the linkage from the underbody, swivel the linkage around to the rear, and tie it to the underbody (see Chapter 7, Part A, for details).

21 Disconnect both anti-roll bar links from their respective suspension strut - note the flexible brake hose bracket attached to each link stud - and both track rod ends from their steering knuckles. Unfasten the clamp bolt securing each front suspension lower arm balljoint to its steering knuckle (see Chapter 10 for details). Check that both balljoints can be released from the knuckle assemblies when required, but leave them in place for the time being, secured by the clamp bolts if necessary.

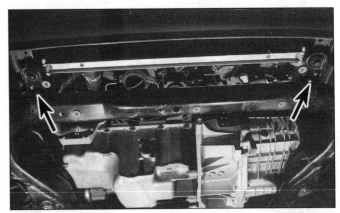

4.25B . . . while you unbolt the bottom mountings (arrowed) - note that the mountings are handed, and do not lose the mounting rubbers

22 Where the vehicle is fitted with air conditioning, unbolt the accumulator/dehydrator from the subframe; secure it as far as possible (without disconnecting the system's hoses) clear of the engine/transmission. **Warning:** *Do not disconnect the refrigerant hoses.*

23 Unbolt the steering gear from the subframe; if the bolts are not accessible from above, a Ford service tool will be required to reach them from underneath the vehicle (see Chapter 10 for details).

24 Unscrew the two bolts securing the power steering system pipes to the right-hand side of the subframe.

25 Hold the radiator in its raised position, by inserting split pins through the holes in the rear of the engine compartment front crossmember and into the radiator's upper mounting extensions. Unbolt the radiator mounting brackets from the subframe; note that they are handed, and are marked to ensure correct refitting **(see illustrations)**. Collect and store the bottom mounting rubbers for safekeeping, noting which way up they are fitted.

26 Unbolt the engine/transmission rear mounting from the subframe - where the vehicle is fitted with automatic transmission, a separate damper may be fitted beneath the subframe, which must be unbolted to reach the mounting's fasteners. Where the vehicle is fitted with manual transmission, also unscrew the mounting centre bolt, and unbolt the mounting bracket from the transmission.

27 Unscrew the engine/transmission front mounting centre bolt, and unbolt the mounting from the subframe, noting the location of the wiring connector bracket.

28 Use white paint or similar (do not use a sharp-pointed scriber, which might break the underbody protective coating and cause rusting) to mark the exact relationship of the subframe to the underbody. Unscrew the four mounting bolts from the subframe (note their different-sized washers - see also illustration 4.47A) and allow the subframe

4.30 Unscrew bolts (arrowed) to release air conditioning compressor from engine

4.35 Lowering the engine/transmission unit out of the vehicle

to hang down on the suspension lower arm balljoints. Disconnect the balljoints one at a time from the steering knuckle assemblies (see Chapter 10) and lower the subframe to the ground; withdraw the subframe from under the vehicle.

29 Marking or labelling all components as they are disconnected (see paragraph 5 above) and catching as much as possible of the escaping coolant in the drain tray, disconnect the cooling system hoses and pipes as follows - refer to Chapter 3 for further details, if required:

(a) Remove the radiator top hose.
(b) Remove the (heater) hose running from the thermostat to the engine compartment bulkhead union.
(c) Disconnect from the thermostat the hose running to the expansion tank - secure the hose clear of the working area.
(d) Disconnect from the thermostat the coolant hose/pipe which runs to the radiator bottom hose.
(e) Disconnect the radiator bottom hose from the radiator union, from the (sump) heater coolant pipe and from the water pump union - secure the hose clear of the working area.
(f) Unbolt the (heater) coolant pipe from the sump, trace the pipe/hose round to the engine compartment bulkhead union, disconnecting (where fitted) the oil cooler hoses from the cooler unions, then remove it.
(g) Unless the vehicle has air conditioning fitted, secure the radiator as far forwards as possible while it is in its raised position; if air conditioning is fitted, remove the radiator completely (see Chapter 3).

30 Where the vehicle is fitted with air conditioning, unplug the compressor's electrical connector, and unbolt the compressor from the engine **(see illustration)**. Secure it as far as possible (without disconnecting the system's hoses) clear of the engine/transmission. **Warning:** *Do not disconnect the refrigerant hoses.*

31 Where the vehicle is fitted with manual transmission, disconnect the driveshafts from the transmission as follows, referring to Chapter 8 for further details when required:

(a) Unscrew the nuts securing the right-hand driveshaft support bearing, and withdraw the heat shield.
(b) Pull the right-hand driveshaft out of the transmission; be prepared to catch any spilt oil.
(c) Secure the driveshaft clear of the engine/transmission - remember that the unit is to be lowered out of the vehicle - and ensure that the inner joint is not turned through more than 18°.
(d) Prise the left-hand driveshaft out of the transmission - again, be prepared for oil spillage. Secure the driveshaft clear of the engine/transmission, and ensure that its inner joint is not turned through more than 18°.

32 Where the vehicle is fitted with automatic transmission, proceed as follows, referring to Chapter 7, Part B and to Chapter 8 for further details when required:

(a) Unscrew its centre bolt, then unbolt the engine/transmission rear mounting bracket from the transmission.
(b) Disconnect the fluid cooler pipe from the rear of the transmission, and secure it clear of the unit.
(c) Prise the left-hand driveshaft out of the transmission; be prepared to catch any spilt oil.
(d) Secure the driveshaft clear of the engine/transmission - remember that the unit is to be lowered out of the vehicle - and ensure that the inner joint is not turned through more than 18°.
(e) Unscrew the nuts securing the right-hand driveshaft support bearing, and withdraw the heat shield.
(f) Pull the right-hand driveshaft out of the transmission - again, be prepared for oil spillage. Secure the driveshaft clear of the engine/transmission, and ensure that its inner joint is not turned through more than 18°.
(g) Disconnect the fluid cooler pipe from the front of the transmission, and secure it clear of the unit.

33 The engine/transmission unit should now be hanging on the right- and left-hand mountings only, with all components which connect it to the rest of the vehicle disconnected or removed and secured well clear of the unit. Make a final check that this is the case, then ensure that the body is securely supported, high enough to permit the withdrawal of the engine/transmission unit from underneath; allow for the height of the engine dolly, if used.

34 Take the weight of the engine/transmission unit, using the lifting eyes provided on the cylinder head. Unscrew the six nuts securing the right-hand mounting bracket, then the three nuts securing the left-hand bracket. **Warning:** *Do not put any part of your body under the vehicle, or under the engine/transmission unit, when they are supported only by a hoist or other lifting equipment.*

35 Lower the engine/transmission to the ground, and withdraw it from under the vehicle **(see illustration)**.

36 Referring to the relevant part of Chapter 7, separate the transmission from the engine.

37 While the engine/transmission is removed, check the mountings; renew them if they are worn or damaged. Similarly, check the condition of all coolant and vacuum hoses and pipes (see Chapter 1); components that are normally hidden can now be checked properly, and should be renewed if there is any doubt at all about their condition. Where the vehicle is fitted with manual transmission, take the opportunity to overhaul the clutch components (see Chapter 8). It is regarded by many as good working practice to renew the clutch assembly as a matter of course, whenever major engine overhaul work is carried out. Check also the condition of all components (such as the transmission oil seals) disturbed on removal, and renew any that are damaged or worn.

Refitting

38 Refitting is the reverse of the removal procedure, noting the following points. Tighten all fasteners to the torque wrench settings

2B

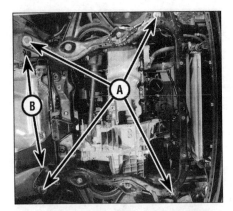

4.47A Tighten subframe mounting bolts (A) while ensuring that alignment remains correct - Ford service tools (B) shown in use here . . .

4.47B . . . but alternative methods using ordinary hand tools can achieve acceptable alignment, with care

4.49 Special tool required to hold engine/transmission unit precisely, so that mountings can be tightened into correct position

given; where settings are not quoted in the Specifications Sections of the two Parts of this Chapter, refer to the Specifications Section of the relevant Chapter of this manual.

39   In addition to the points noted in paragraph 37 above, always re-new any circlips and self-locking nuts disturbed on removal.

40   Where wiring, etc, was secured by cable ties which had to be cut on removal, ensure that it is secured with new ties on refitting.

41   With all overhaul operations completed, refit the transmission to the engine as described in Chapter 7.

42   Manoeuvre the engine/transmission unit under the vehicle, attach the hoist, and lift the unit into position until the right- and left-hand mountings can be reassembled; tighten the (new) nuts only lightly at this stage. Do not yet release the hoist; the weight of the engine/transmission unit must not be taken by the mountings until all are correctly aligned.

43   Using new circlips, and ensuring that the inner joints are not twisted through too great an angle (see Chapter 8), refit the driveshafts. Where the vehicle is fitted with manual transmission, the procedure is the reverse of that outlined in paragraph 31 above. Where the vehicle is fitted with automatic transmission, proceed as follows, referring to Chapter 7, Part B and to Chapter 8 for further details when required:

(a) Refit the left-hand driveshaft.

(b) Using the clips provided to ensure that they are correctly routed, and tightening the couplings to the specified torque wrench setting where possible, reconnect the fluid cooler pipes, first to the rear, then to the front, of the transmission.

(c) Refit the right-hand driveshaft to the transmission, refit the heat shield, and tighten the support bearing nuts to the specified torque wrench setting.

(d) Refit the engine/transmission rear mounting bracket to the transmission, tightening the bolts to the torque wrench setting specified, then refit the mounting, tightening the centre bolt only lightly at this stage.

44   Where the vehicle is fitted with air conditioning, do not forget to refit the compressor; tighten the bolts to the specified torque wrench setting, and plug in its electrical connector.

45   Using the marks and notes made on removal, refit the cooling system hoses. Where they are left disconnected or unclipped for the time being, do not forget to secure them at the appropriate moment during the reassembly procedure. Refit the radiator (if removed), using split pins to secure it in the raised position.

46   Offer up the subframe one side at a time, and hold it by securing the suspension lower arm balljoints to the steering knuckle assemblies. Refit the subframe bolts, ensuring that the washers are refitted correctly, and tightening the bolts only lightly at this stage.

47   The subframe must now be aligned on the underbody. Ford specify the use of service tool 15-097, which is a pair of tapered guides, with attachments to hold them in the subframe as it is refitted. However, since the working diameter of these tools is 20.4 mm, and since the corresponding aligning holes in the subframe and underbody are

4.50A Do not allow the left-hand mounting to twist as its nuts (arrowed) are tightened

respectively 21 mm and 22 mm in diameter, there is a significant in-built tolerance possible in the subframe's alignment, even if the correct tools are used. If these tools are not available, you can align the sub-frame by eye, centring the subframe aligning holes on those of the un-derbody, and using the marks made on removal for assistance. Alter-natively, you can align the subframe using a tapered drift (such as a clutch-aligning tool), or even a deep socket spanner of suitable size **(see illustrations)**.

48   Once the subframe is aligned as precisely as possible, tighten its bolts to the specified torque wrench setting without disturbing its posi-tion. Recheck the alignment once all the bolts are securely tightened.

49   With the subframe aligned and securely fastened, the engine/transmission unit must now be positioned precisely, before the mountings can be reassembled. Ford specify the use of service tool 21-172; this is a fixture bolted to the subframe in place of the en-gine/transmission front mounting, so that when the mounting's centre bolt is refitted, it is held 60 mm above the subframe's top surface, and offset 20 mm to the rear of the mounting's subframe bolt holes (cen-tres). DIY mechanics are advised to obtain the Ford tool; the only alter-native is to have a copy fabricated **(see illustration)**.

50   Fasten the tool to the subframe in place of the engine/transmis-sion front mounting, and lightly tighten the mounting's centre bolt. Re-fit the engine/transmission mountings in the following sequence:

(a) Tighten the left-hand mounting's nuts to the specified torque wrench setting - do not allow the mounting to twist as it is tightened **(see illustration)**.

(b) Tighten the right-hand mounting's four bracket-to-engine nuts to the specified torque wrench setting.

4.50B Tighten the right-hand mounting's four bracket-to-engine nuts (two shown at A), release the hoist, then tighten the two bracket-to-mounting nuts (B). Do not allow mounting to twist

4.50C Unbolt special tool . . .

4.50D . . . then refit front mounting - do not forget wiring connector bracket - tighten the mounting's nuts first, then its centre bolt

(c) Slowly release the hoist so that the weight of the engine/transmission unit is taken by the mountings.

(d) Tighten the right-hand mounting's two bracket-to-mounting nuts to the specified torque wrench setting - do not allow the mounting to twist as it is tightened **(see illustration)**.

(e) Reassemble the engine/transmission rear mounting, tightening the fasteners to the specified torque wrench settings; tighten the centre bolt last.

(f) Refit the steering gear to the subframe; if the Ford service tool is used to tighten the bolts from underneath the vehicle (see Chapter 10 for details), note that a torque wrench which can tighten in an anti-clockwise direction will be required.

(g) Unbolt the special tool from the front mounting, refit the mounting - do not forget the wiring connector bracket - and tighten first the mounting's bolts/nuts, then its centre bolt, to their respective specified torque wrench settings **(see illustrations)**.

51   Refit the bottom mounting rubbers to the radiator - ensure that both are the correct way up - then refit the radiator mounting brackets to the subframe, ensuring that each is returned to its correct (marked) location, and tightening the bolts to the torque wrench setting specified. Remove the split pins, and secure the coolant hose connections (where necessary).

52   Refit the air conditioning accumulator/dehydrator (where appropriate) to the subframe.

53   Tighten the two bolts securing the power steering system pipes to the right-hand side of the subframe.

54   Fasten each front suspension lower arm balljoint and track rod end to their respective steering knuckles, and both anti-roll bar links to their respective suspension strut. Note the flexible brake hose bracket attached to each link stud (see Chapter 10 for details).

55   Where the vehicle is fitted with manual transmission, swivel the linkage around to the front, tighten its rear fasteners, then refit the gear linkage heat shield. Reconnect the gearchange linkage and transmission support rods to the transmission, adjusting the linkage using the marks made on removal (see Chapter 7, Part A, for details).

56   Re-install the remaining components and fasteners in the reverse order of removal.

57   Add coolant, engine oil and transmission fluids as needed (see Chapter 1).

58   Run the engine, and check for proper operation and the absence of leaks. Shut off the engine, and recheck the fluid levels.

59   Remember that, since the front suspension subframe and steering gear have been disturbed, the wheel alignment and steering angles must be checked fully and carefully as soon as possible, with any necessary adjustments being made. This operation is best carried out by an experienced mechanic, using proper checking equipment; the vehicle should therefore be taken to a Ford dealer or similarly-qualified person for attention.

5   Engine overhaul - dismantling sequence

1   It is much easier to dismantle and work on the engine if it is mounted on a portable engine stand. These stands can often be hired from a tool hire shop. Before the engine is mounted on a stand, the flywheel/driveplate should be removed (Part A of this Chapter, Section 21) so that the stand bolts can be tightened into the end of the cylinder block/crankcase.

2   If a stand is not available, it is possible to dismantle the engine with it mounted on blocks, on a sturdy workbench or on the floor. Be extra-careful not to tip or drop the engine when working without a stand.

3   If you are going to obtain a reconditioned engine, all external components must be removed first, to be transferred to the replacement engine (just as they will if you are doing a complete engine overhaul yourself). **Note:** *When removing the external components from the engine, pay close attention to details that may be helpful or important during refitting. Note the fitted position of gaskets, seals, spacers, pins, washers, bolts and other small items.* These external components include the following:

(a) Alternator and brackets (Chapter 5).
(b) HT leads and spark plugs (Chapter 1).
(c) Thermostat and housing (Chapter 3).
(d) Dipstick tube.
(e) Fuel injection system components (Chapter 4).
(f) All electrical switches and sensors - refer to the appropriate Chapter.
(g) Inlet and exhaust manifolds (Part A of this Chapter).
(h) Oil filter (Chapter 1).
(i) Engine/transmission mounting brackets (Part A of this Chapter, Section 22).
(j) Flywheel/driveplate (Part A of this Chapter, Section 21).

4   If you are obtaining a "short" engine (which consists of the engine cylinder block/crankcase, crankshaft, pistons and connecting rods all assembled), then the cylinder head, sump, oil pump, and timing belt will have to be removed also.

5   If you are planning a complete overhaul, the engine can be dismantled and the internal components removed in the following order.

(a) Inlet and exhaust manifolds (Part A of this Chapter).
(b) Timing belt, toothed pulleys and tensioner, and timing belt inner cover (Part A of this Chapter).
(c) Cylinder head (Part A of this Chapter, Section 14).
(d) Flywheel/driveplate (Part A of this Chapter, Section 21).
(e) Sump (Part A of this Chapter, Section 15).
(f) Oil pump (Part A of this Chapter, Section 16).
(g) Piston/connecting rod assemblies (Section 9).
(h) Crankshaft (Section 10).

2B

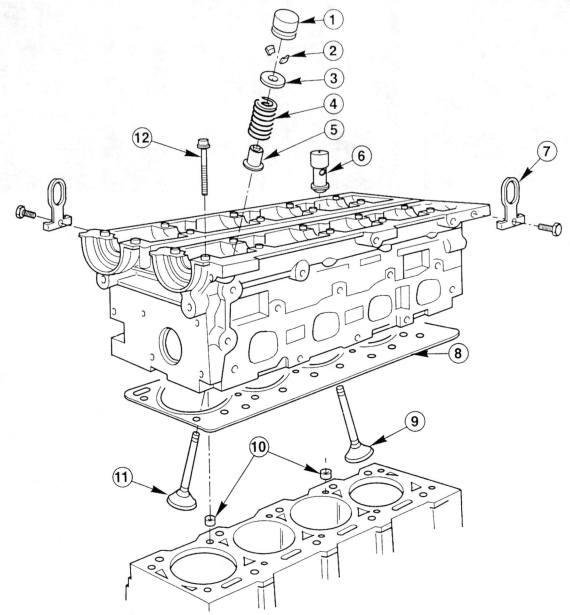

6.1 Cylinder head components

1	Hydraulic tappet
2	Valve collets
3	Valve spring upper seat
4	Valve spring
5	Valve spring lower seat/stem oil seal
6	Oil-retaining valve

7	Engine lifting eye
8	Cylinder head gasket
9	Inlet valve
10	Locating dowels
11	Exhaust valve
12	Cylinder head bolt

6   Before beginning the dismantling and overhaul procedures, make sure that you have all of the correct tools necessary. Refer to the introductory pages at the beginning of this manual for further information.

6   Cylinder head - dismantling

Note: *New and reconditioned cylinder heads are available from the manufacturers, and from engine overhaul specialists. Due to the fact that some specialist tools are required for the dismantling and inspection procedures, and new components may not be readily available (refer to Section 1 of this Part), it may be more practical and economical for the home mechanic to purchase a reconditioned head, rather than*

to dismantle, inspect and recondition the original head.

1   Remove the camshafts and hydraulic tappets (Part A of this Chapter, Section 13), being careful to store the hydraulic tappets as described **(see illustration)**.

2   Remove the cylinder head (Part A of this Chapter, Section 14).

3   Using a valve spring compressor, compress each valve spring in turn until the split collets can be removed. A special valve spring compressor will be required, to reach into the deep wells in the cylinder head without risk of damaging the hydraulic tappet bores; such compressors are now widely available from most good motor accessory shops. Release the compressor, and lift off the spring upper seat and spring **(see illustrations)**.

4   If, when the valve spring compressor is screwed down, the spring

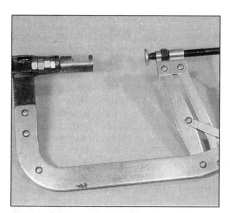

6.3A Standard valve spring compressor modified as shown . . .

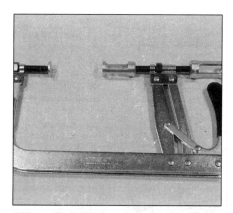

6.3B . . . or purpose-built special version, is required to compress valve springs without damaging cylinder head . . .

6.3C . . . so that both valve split collets can be removed from the valve's stem - small magnetic pick-up tool prevents loss of small metal components on removal and refitting

6.6A Ford service tool in use to remove valve spring lower seat/stem oil seals . . .

6.6B . . . can be replaced by home-made tool if suitable spring can be found

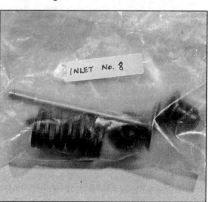

6.7 Use clearly-marked containers to identify components and to keep matched assemblies together

2B

6.8 Cylinder head oil-retaining valve (arrowed)

upper seat refuses to free and expose the split collets, gently tap the top of the tool, directly over the upper seat, with a light hammer. This will free the seat.

5   Withdraw the valve through the combustion chamber. If it binds in the guide (won't pull through), push it back in, and de-burr the area around the collet groove with a fine file or whetstone; take care not to mark the hydraulic tappet bores.

6   Ford recommend the use of their service tool 21-160 to extract the valve spring lower seat/stem oil seals; while this is almost indis-

pensable if the seals are to be removed without risk of (extremely expensive) damage to the cylinder head, we found that a serviceable substitute can be made from a strong spring of suitable size. Screw on the tool or spring so that it bites into the seal, then draw the seal off the valve guide **(see illustrations)**.

7   It is essential that the valves are kept together with their collets, spring seats and springs, and in their correct sequence (unless they are so badly worn that they are to be renewed). If they are going to be kept and used again, place them in a labelled polythene bag or similar small container **(see illustration)**. Note that No 1 valve is nearest to the timing belt end of the engine.

8   If the oil-retaining valve is to be removed (to flush out the cylinder head oil galleries thoroughly), seek the advice of a Ford dealer as to how it can be extracted; it may be that the only course of action involves destroying the valve as follows. Screw a self-tapping screw into its ventilation hole, and use the screw to provide purchase with which the valve can be drawn out; a new valve must be purchased and pressed into place on reassembly **(see illustration)**.

7   Cylinder head and valve components - cleaning and inspection

Note: *Always check first what replacement parts are available before planning any overhaul operation; refer to Section 1 of this Part. A Ford dealer, or a good engine reconditioning specialist/automotive parts supplier, may be able to suggest alternatives which will enable you to overcome the lack of replacement parts.*

1   Thorough cleaning of the cylinder head and valve components,

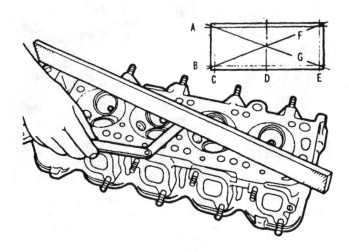

7.6 Check the cylinder head gasket surfaces for warpage, in the planes indicated (A to G). Try to slip a feeler gauge under the precision straight edge (see the Specifications for the maximum distortion allowed, and use a feeler blade of that thickness)

followed by a detailed inspection, will enable you to decide how much valve service work must be carried out during the engine overhaul. **Note:** *If the engine has been severely overheated, it is best to assume that the cylinder head is warped, and to check carefully for signs of this.*

Cleaning

2   Scrape away all traces of old gasket material and sealing compound from the cylinder head (see Part A of this Chapter, Section 14 for details).
3   Scrape away the carbon from the combustion chambers and ports, then wash the cylinder head thoroughly with paraffin or a suitable solvent.
4   Scrape off any heavy carbon deposits that may have formed on the valves, then use a power-operated wire brush to remove deposits from the valve heads and stems.

Inspection

Note: *Be sure to perform all the following inspection procedures before concluding that the services of a machine shop or engine overhaul specialist are required. Make a list of all items that require attention.*

Cylinder head

5   Inspect the head very carefully for cracks, evidence of coolant leakage, and other damage. If cracks are found, a new cylinder head should be obtained.
6   Use a straight edge and feeler blade to check that the cylinder head gasket surface is not distorted **(see illustration)**. If it is, it may be possible to re-surface it.
7   Examine the valve seats in each of the combustion chambers. If they are severely pitted, cracked or burned, then they will need to be renewed or re-cut by an engine overhaul specialist. If they are only slightly pitted, this can be removed by grinding-in the valve heads and seats with fine valve-grinding compound, as described below.
8   If the valve guides are worn, indicated by a side-to-side motion of the valve, new guides must be fitted. Measure the diameter of the existing valve stems (see below) and the bore of the guides, then calculate the clearance, and compare the result with the specified value; if the clearance is excessive, renew the valves or guides as necessary.
9   The renewal of valve guides is best carried out by an engine overhaul specialist.
10   If the valve seats are to be re-cut, this must be done *only after* the guides have been renewed.

Valves

11   Examine the head of each valve for pitting, burning, cracks and general wear, and check the valve stem for scoring and wear ridges. Rotate the valve, and check for any obvious indication that it is bent. Look for pits and excessive wear on the tip of each valve stem. Renew any valve that shows any such signs of wear or damage.
12   If the valve appears satisfactory at this stage, measure the valve stem diameter at several points, using a micrometer **(see illustration)**. Any significant difference in the readings obtained indicates wear of the valve stem. Should any of these conditions be apparent, the valve(s) must be renewed.
13   If the valves are in satisfactory condition, they should be ground (lapped) into their respective seats, to ensure a smooth gas-tight seal. If the seat is only lightly pitted, or if it has been re-cut, fine grinding compound *only* should be used to produce the required finish. Coarse valve-grinding compound should *not* be used unless a seat is badly burned or deeply pitted; if this is the case, the cylinder head and valves should be inspected by an expert, to decide whether seat re-cutting, or even the renewal of the valve or seat insert, is required.
14   Valve grinding is carried out as follows. Place the cylinder head upside-down on a bench, with a block of wood at each end to give clearance for the valve stems.
15   Smear a trace of (the appropriate grade of) valve-grinding compound on the seat face, and press a suction grinding tool onto the valve head. With a semi-rotary action, grind the valve head to its seat, lifting the valve occasionally to redistribute the grinding compound **(see illustration)**. A light spring placed under the valve head will greatly ease this operation.
16   If coarse grinding compound is being used, work only until a dull, matt even surface is produced on both the valve seat and the valve, then wipe off the used compound, and repeat the process with fine compound. When a smooth unbroken ring of light grey matt finish is produced on both the valve and seat, the grinding operation is complete. *Do not* grind in the valves any further than absolutely necessary, or the seat will be prematurely sunk into the cylinder head.
17   When all the valves have been ground-in, carefully wash off *all* traces of grinding compound, using paraffin or a suitable solvent, before reassembly of the cylinder head.

Valve components

18   Examine the valve springs for signs of damage and discolouration, and also measure their free length by comparing each of the existing springs with a new component.
19   Stand each spring on a flat surface, and check it for squareness **(see illustration)**. If any of the springs are damaged, distorted, or have lost their tension, obtain a complete set of new springs.
20   Check the spring upper seats and collets for obvious wear and cracks. Any questionable parts should be renewed, as extensive damage will occur if they fail during engine operation. Any damaged or excessively-worn parts must be renewed; the valve spring lower seat/stem oil seals must be renewed as a matter of course whenever they are disturbed.
21   Check the hydraulic tappets as described in Part A of this Chapter, Section 13.

8   Cylinder head - reassembly

1   Regardless of whether or not the head was sent away for repair work of any sort, make sure that it is clean before beginning reassembly. Be sure to remove any metal particles and abrasive grit that may still be present from operations such as valve grinding or head resurfacing. Use compressed air, if available, to blow out all the oil holes and passages.
2   Beginning at one end of the head, lubricate and install the first valve. Apply molybdenum disulphide-based grease or clean engine oil to the valve stem, and refit the valve. Where the original valves are being re-used, ensure that each is refitted in its original guide. If new valves are being fitted, insert them into the locations to which they have been ground.

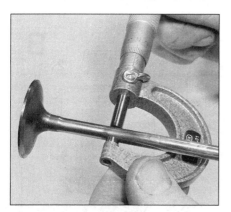

7.12 Measuring the diameter of a valve stem - if any significant difference is found in the readings obtained, excessive valve stem wear is indicated

7.15 Grinding-in a valve seat - do not grind in the valves any more than absolutely necessary, or their seats will be prematurely sunk into the cylinder head

7.19 Check each valve spring for squareness

8.3 Valve spring pressure is sufficient to seat lower seat/stem oil seals on reassembly

8.5 Apply a small dab of grease to each collet before installation - it will hold them in place on the valve stem until the spring is released

9.4 Removing the oil baffle to provide access to crankshaft and bearings

2B

3   Fit the plastic protector supplied with new valve spring lower seat/stem oil seals to the end of the valve stem, then put the new seal squarely on top of the guide, and leave it there; the action of refitting the valve spring presses the lower seat/stem oil seal into place **(see illustration)**.

4   Refit the valve spring and upper seat.

5   Compress the spring with a valve spring compressor, and carefully install the collets in the stem groove. Apply a small dab of grease to each collet to hold it in place if necessary **(see illustration)**. Slowly release the compressor, and make sure the collets seat properly.

6   When the valve is installed, place the cylinder head flat on the bench and, using a hammer and interposed block of wood, tap the end of the valve stem gently, to settle the components.

7   Repeat the procedure for the remaining valves. Be sure to return the components to their original locations - don't mix them up!

8   Refit the hydraulic tappets (Part A of this Chapter, Section 13).

9   Piston/connecting rod assemblies - removal

Note: *Always check first what replacement parts are available before planning any overhaul operation; refer to Section 1 of this Part. A Ford dealer, or a good engine reconditioning specialist/automotive parts supplier, may be able to suggest alternatives which will enable you to overcome the lack of replacement parts.*

Note: *While this task is theoretically possible when the engine is in place in the vehicle, in practice, it requires so much preliminary dis-*

mantling, and is so difficult to carry out due to the restricted access, that owners are advised to remove the engine from the vehicle first. In addition to the new gaskets and other replacement parts required, a hoist will be needed. Alternatively, an adjustable engine support bar, fitting into the water drain channels on each side of the bonnet aperture, and having a hook which will engage the engine lifting eyes and allow the height of the engine to be adjusted, could be used. Lifting equipment such as this can be hired from most tool hire shops - be sure that any such equipment is rated well in excess of the combined weight of the engine/transmission unit.

1   Remove the cylinder head (Part A of this Chapter, Section 14).

2   Bolt lifting eyes to suitable points on the engine and transmission, then attach the lifting equipment so that the engine/transmission unit is supported securely.

3   Remove the sump (Part A of this Chapter, Section 15).

4   Undo the screws securing the oil pump pick-up/strainer pipe to the pump, then unscrew the four nuts, and withdraw the oil pump pick-up/strainer pipe and oil baffle **(see illustration)**.

5   Temporarily refit the crankshaft pulley, so that the crankshaft can be rotated. Note that each piston/connecting rod assembly can be identified by its cylinder number (counting from the timing belt end of the engine) etched into the flat-machined surface of both the connecting rod and its cap. The numbers are visible from the front (exhaust side) of the engine. Furthermore, each piston has an arrow stamped into its crown, pointing towards the timing belt end of the engine. If no marks can be seen, make your own before disturbing any of the components, so that you can be certain of refitting each piston/connecting rod assembly the right way round, to its correct (original) bore, with the

9.5A Each connecting rod and big-end bearing cap will have a flat-machined surface visible from the front (exhaust) side of the engine, with the cylinder number etched in it

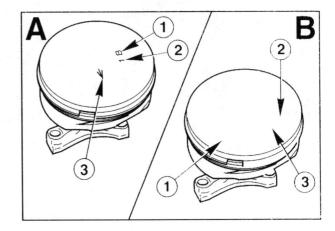

9.5B Piston crown markings

    A   *1.6 and 1.8 litre engines*
    B   *2.0 litre engines*
    1   *Gudgeon pin diameter grade - when used*
    2   *Piston skirt diameter grade*
    3   *Arrow mark - pointing to timing belt end of engine*

cap also the right way round **(see illustrations)**.

6   Use your fingernail to feel if a ridge has formed at the upper limit of ring travel (about a quarter-inch down from the top of each cylinder). If carbon deposits or cylinder wear have produced ridges, they must be completely removed with a special tool **(see illustration)**. Follow the manufacturer's instructions provided with the tool. Failure to remove the ridges before attempting to remove the piston/connecting rod assemblies may result in piston ring breakage.

7   Slacken each of the big-end bearing cap bolts half a turn at a time, until they can be removed by hand. Remove the No 1 cap and bearing shell. Don't drop the shell out of the cap.

8   Remove the upper bearing shell, and push the connecting rod/piston assembly out through the top of the engine. Use a wooden hammer handle to push on the connecting rod's bearing recess. If resistance is felt, double-check that all of the ridge was removed from the cylinder.

9   Repeat the procedure for the remaining cylinders.

10   After removal, reassemble the big-end bearing caps and shells on their respective connecting rods, and refit the bolts finger-tight. Leaving the old shells in place until reassembly will help prevent the bearing recesses from being accidentally nicked or gouged. New shells should be used on reassembly.

11   Don't attempt to separate the pistons from the connecting rods - see Section 12.

10 Crankshaft - removal

Note: *The crankshaft can be removed only after the engine/transmission has been removed from the vehicle. It is assumed that the transmission and flywheel/driveplate, timing belt, cylinder head, sump, oil pump pick-up/strainer pipe and oil baffle, oil pump, and piston/connecting rod assemblies, have already been removed. The crankshaft left-hand oil seal carrier must be unbolted from the cylinder block/crankcase before proceeding with crankshaft removal.*

1   Before the crankshaft is removed, check the endfloat. Mount a DTI (Dial Test Indicator, or dial gauge) with the stem in line with the crankshaft and just touching the crankshaft **(see illustration)**.

2   Push the crankshaft fully away from the gauge, and zero it. Next, lever the crankshaft towards the gauge as far as possible, and check the reading obtained. The distance that the crankshaft moved is its endfloat; if it is greater than specified, check the crankshaft thrust surfaces for wear. If no wear is evident, new thrustwashers should correct the endfloat; these are part of the No 3 (centre) main bearing upper shell **(see illustration)**.

3   If no dial gauge is available, feeler gauges can be used. Gently lever or push the crankshaft all the way towards the right-hand end of the engine. Slip feeler gauges between the crankshaft and the right-hand face of the No 3 (centre) main bearing to determine the clearance

9.6 A ridge reamer may be required, to remove the ridge from the top of each cylinder - do this before removing the pistons!

10.1 Checking crankshaft endfloat with a dial gauge

10.2 Thrustwashers integral with No 3 (centre) main bearing upper shell control crankshaft endfloat

10.3 Checking crankshaft endfloat with a feeler gauge

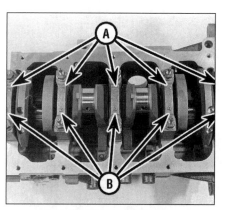

10.4 Before unbolting crankshaft main bearing caps, note arrows pointing to timing belt end of engine (A), and bearing numbers (B) consecutive from timing belt end

11.1A Remove water pump . . .

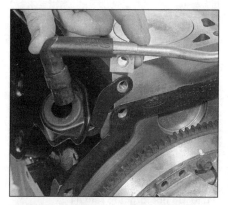

11.1B . . . crankcase breather pipe and PCV valve . . .

11.1C . . . unbolt crankcase ventilation system oil separator . . .

11.1D . . . remove electrical switches/sensors such as crankshaft speed/position sensor . . .

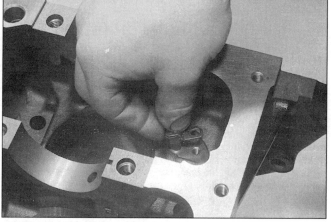

11.1E . . . unbolt blanking plugs (where fitted) to clean out oilways . . .

(see illustration).

4   Check the main bearing caps, to see if they are marked to indicate their locations **(see illustration)**. They should be numbered consecutively from the timing belt end of the engine - if not, mark them with number-stamping dies or a centre-punch. The caps will also have an embossed arrow pointing to the timing belt end of the engine. Noting the different fasteners (for the oil baffle nuts) used on caps 2 and 4, slacken the cap bolts a quarter-turn at a time each, starting with the left- and right-hand end caps and working toward the centre, until they

can be removed by hand.
5   Gently tap the caps with a soft-faced hammer, then separate them from the cylinder block/crankcase. If necessary, use the bolts as levers to remove the caps. Try not to drop the bearing shells if they come out with the caps.
6   Carefully lift the crankshaft out of the engine. It may be a good idea to have an assistant available, since the crankshaft is quite heavy. With the bearing shells in place in the cylinder block/crankcase and main bearing caps, return the caps to their respective locations on the block, and tighten the bolts finger-tight. Leaving the old shells in place until reassembly will help prevent the bearing recesses from being accidentally nicked or gouged. New shells should be used on reassembly.

11 Cylinder block/crankcase - cleaning and inspection

Note: *Always check first what replacement parts are available before planning any overhaul operation; refer to Section 1 of this Part. A Ford dealer, or a good engine reconditioning specialist/automotive parts supplier may be able to suggest alternatives which will enable you to overcome the lack of replacement parts.*

Cleaning

1   For complete cleaning, remove the water pump, all external components, and all electrical switches/sensors. Unbolt the piston-cooling oil jets or blanking plugs (as applicable); note that Ford state that the piston-cooling oil jets (where fitted) must be renewed whenever the engine is dismantled for full overhaul **(see illustrations)**.

2B

11.1F ... but note that piston-cooling oil jets (where fitted) must be renewed as a matter of course whenever engine is overhauled

11.2 Felt marker pens can be used as shown to identify bearing shells without damaging them

11.4 The core plugs should be removed with a puller - if they're driven into the block, they may be impossible to retrieve

11.8 All bolt holes in the block - particularly the main bearing cap and head bolt holes - should be cleaned and restored with a tap (be sure to remove debris from the holes after this is done)

11.9 A large socket on an extension can be used to drive the new core plugs into their bores

11.10 Do not forget to refit all components - such as oilway blanking plugs (three of four arrowed) - tighten fasteners to torque wrench settings specified

2   Remove the main bearing caps, and separate the bearing shells from the caps and the cylinder block/crankcase. Mark or label the shells, indicating which bearing they were removed from, and whether they were in the cap or the block, then set them aside **(see illustration)**. Wipe clean the block and cap bearing recesses, and inspect them for nicks, gouges and scratches.

3   Scrape all traces of gasket from the cylinder block/crankcase, taking care not to damage the sealing surfaces.

4   Remove all oil gallery plugs (where fitted). The plugs are usually very tight - they may have to be drilled out and the holes re-tapped. Use new plugs when the engine is reassembled. Drill a small hole in the centre of each core plug, and pull them out with a car bodywork dent puller **(see illustration)**. Caution: *The core plugs (also known as freeze or soft plugs) may be difficult or impossible to retrieve if they are driven into the block coolant passages.*

5   If any of the castings are extremely dirty, all should be steam-cleaned.

6   After the castings are returned from steam-cleaning, clean all oil holes and oil galleries one more time. Flush all internal passages with warm water until the water runs clear, then dry thoroughly, and apply a light film of oil to all machined surfaces, to prevent rusting. If you have access to compressed air, use it to speed the drying process, and to blow out all the oil holes and galleries. **Warning:** *Wear eye protection when using compressed air!*

7   If the castings are not very dirty, you can do an adequate cleaning job with hot soapy water (as hot as you can stand!) and a stiff brush. Take plenty of time, and do a thorough job. Regardless of the cleaning method used, be sure to clean all oil holes and galleries very

thoroughly, and to dry all components completely; protect the machined surfaces as described above, to prevent rusting.

8   All threaded holes must be clean and dry, to ensure accurate torque readings during reassembly; now is also a good time to clean and check the threads of all principal bolts - however, note that some, such as the cylinder head and flywheel/driveplate bolts, are to be renewed as a matter of course whenever they are disturbed. Run the proper-size tap into each of the holes, to remove rust, corrosion, thread sealant or sludge, and to restore damaged threads **(see illustration)**. If possible, use compressed air to clear the holes of debris produced by this operation; a good alternative is to inject aerosol-applied water-dispersant lubricant into each hole, using the long spout usually supplied. **Warning:** *Wear eye protection when cleaning out these holes in this way, and be sure to dry out any excess liquid left in the holes.*

9   When all inspection and repair procedures are complete (see below) and the block is ready for reassembly, apply suitable sealant to the new oil gallery plugs, and insert them into the holes in the block. Tighten them securely. After coating the sealing surfaces of the new core plugs with suitable sealant, install them in the cylinder block/crankcase **(see illustration)**. Make sure they are driven in straight and seated properly, or leakage could result. Special tools are available for this purpose, but a large socket with an outside diameter that will just slip into the core plug, used with an extension and hammer, will work just as well.

10   Refit the blanking plugs or (new) piston-cooling oil jets (as applicable), tightening their Torx screws to the torque wrench setting specified **(see illustration)**. Refit also all other external components

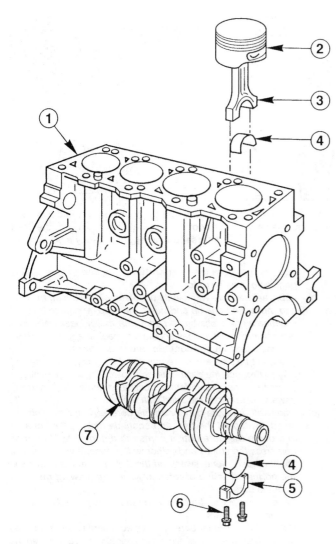

11.12 Cylinder block, piston/connecting rod and crankshaft details

1 Cylinder block/crankcase
2 Piston
3 Connecting rod
4 Big-end bearing shell
5 Big-end bearing cap
6 Big-end bearing cap bolts
7 Crankshaft

removed, referring to the relevant Chapter of this manual for further details where required. Refit the main bearing caps, and tighten the bolts finger-tight.
11 If the engine is not going to be reassembled right away, cover it with a large plastic bag to keep it clean; protect the machined surfaces as described above, to prevent rusting.

Inspection

12 Visually check the castings for cracks and corrosion. Look for stripped threads in the threaded holes. If there has been any history of internal coolant leakage, it may be worthwhile having an engine overhaul specialist check the cylinder block/crankcase for cracks with special equipment. If defects are found, have them repaired, if possible, or renew the assembly **(see illustration)**.
13 Check each cylinder bore for scuffing and scoring.
14 Noting that the cylinder bores must be measured with all the crankshaft main bearing caps bolted in place (without the crankshaft and bearing shells), to the specified torque wrench settings, measure the diameter of each cylinder at the top (just under the ridge area),

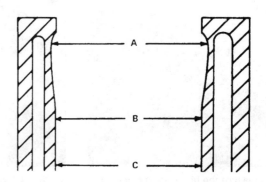

11.14A Measure the diameter of each cylinder just under the wear ridge (A), at the centre (B) and at the bottom (C)

11.14B The ability to "feel" when the telescoping gauge is at the correct point will be developed over time, so work slowly, and repeat the check until you're satisfied that the bore measurement is accurate

2B

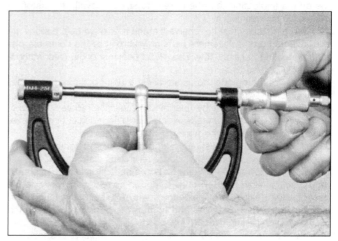

11.14C The gauge is then measured with a micrometer to determine the bore size

centre and bottom of the cylinder bore, parallel to the crankshaft axis. Next, measure each cylinder's diameter at the same three locations across the crankshaft axis **(see illustrations)**. Note the measurements obtained.
15 Measure the piston diameter at right-angles to the gudgeon pin

11.15 Measure the piston skirt diameter at right-angles to the gudgeon pin axis, just above the base of the skirt

11.23A A "bottle-brush" hone will produce better results if you have never honed cylinders before

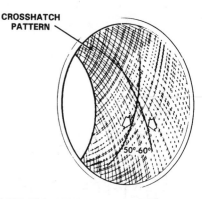

11.23B The cylinder hone should leave a smooth, cross-hatch pattern with the lines intersecting at approximately a 60° angle

axis, just above the bottom of the skirt; again, note the results **(see illustration)**.

16   If it is wished to obtain the piston-to-bore clearance, measure the bore and piston skirt as described above, and subtract the skirt diameter from the bore measurement. If the precision measuring tools shown are not available, the condition of the pistons and bores can be assessed, though not quite as accurately, by using feeler gauges as follows. Select a feeler gauge of thickness equal to the specified piston-to-bore clearance, and slip it into the cylinder along with the matching piston. The piston must be positioned exactly as it normally would be. The feeler gauge must be between the piston and cylinder on one of the thrust faces (at right-angles to the gudgeon pin bore). The piston should slip through the cylinder (with the feeler gauge in place) with moderate pressure; if it falls through or slides through easily, the clearance is excessive, and a new piston will be required. If the piston binds at the lower end of the cylinder, and is loose toward the top, the cylinder is tapered. If tight spots are encountered as the piston/feeler gauge is rotated in the cylinder, the cylinder is out-of-round (oval).

17   Repeat these procedures for the remaining pistons and cylinder bores.

18   Compare the results with the Specifications at the beginning of this Chapter; if any measurement is beyond the dimensions specified for that class (check the piston crown marking to establish the class of piston fitted), or if any bore measurement is significantly different from the others (indicating that the bore is tapered or oval), the piston or bore is excessively-worn.

19   Worn pistons must be renewed; at the time of writing, pistons are available as Ford replacement parts only as part of the complete piston/connecting rod assembly. See a Ford dealer or engine reconditioning specialist for advice.

20   If any of the cylinder bores are badly scuffed or scored, or if they are excessively-worn, out-of-round or tapered, the usual course of action would be to have the cylinder block/crankcase rebored, and to fit new, oversized, pistons on reassembly. See a Ford dealer or engine reconditioning specialist for advice.

21   If the bores are in reasonably good condition and not excessively-worn, then it may only be necessary to renew the piston rings.

22   If this is the case (and if new rings can be found), the bores should be honed, to allow the new rings to bed in correctly and provide the best possible seal; before honing the bores, refit the main bearing caps (without the bearing shells), and tighten the bolts to the specified torque wrench setting. **Note:** *If you don't have the tools, or don't want to tackle the honing operation, most engine reconditioning specialists will do it for a reasonable fee.*

23   Two types of cylinder hones are commonly available - the flex hone or "bottle-brush" type, and the more traditional surfacing hone with spring-loaded stones. Both will do the job and are used with a power drill, but for the less-experienced mechanic, the "bottle-brush" hone will probably be easier to use. You will also need some paraffin or honing oil, and rags. Proceed as follows:

(a)   Mount the hone in the drill, compress the stones, and slip it

into the first bore **(see illustration)**. *Be sure to wear safety goggles or a face shield!*

(b)   *Lubricate the bore with plenty of honing oil, switch on the drill, and move the hone up and down the bore, at a pace that will produce a fine cross-hatch pattern on the cylinder walls. Ideally, the cross-hatch lines should intersect at approximately a 60° angle* **(see illustration)**. *Be sure to use plenty of lubricant, and don't take off any more material than is absolutely necessary to produce the desired finish.* **Note:** *Piston ring manufacturers may specify a different crosshatch angle - read and follow any instructions included with the new rings.*

(c)   *Don't withdraw the hone from the bore while it's running. Instead, switch off the drill, and continue moving the hone up and down the bore until it comes to a complete stop, then compress the stones and withdraw the hone. If you're using a "bottle-brush" hone, switch off the drill, then turn the chuck in the normal direction of rotation while withdrawing the hone from the bore.*

(d)   *Wipe the oil out of the bore, and repeat the procedure for the remaining cylinders.*

(e)   *When all the cylinder bores are honed, chamfer the top edges of the bores with a small file, so the rings won't catch when the pistons are installed. Be very careful not to nick the cylinder walls with the end of the file.*

(f)   *The entire cylinder block/crankcase must be washed very thoroughly with warm, soapy water, to remove all traces of the abrasive grit produced during the honing operation.* **Note:** *The bores can be considered clean when a lint-free white cloth - dampened with clean engine oil - used to wipe them out doesn't pick up any more honing residue, which will show up as grey areas on the cloth. Be sure to run a brush through all oil holes and galleries, and flush them with running water.*

(g)   *When the cylinder block/crankcase is completely clean, rinse it thoroughly and dry it, then lightly oil all exposed machined surfaces, to prevent rusting.*

24   The cylinder block/crankcase should now be completely clean and dry, with all components checked for wear or damage, and repaired or overhauled as necessary. Refit as many ancillary components as possible, for safekeeping (see paragraphs 9 and 10 above). If reassembly is not to start immediately, cover the block with a large plastic bag to keep it clean, and protect the machined surfaces as described above to prevent rusting.

12 Piston/connecting rod assemblies - inspection

Note: *Always check first what replacement parts are available before planning any overhaul operation; refer to Section 1 of this Part. A Ford dealer, or a good engine reconditioning specialist/automotive parts supplier may be able to suggest alternatives which will enable you to overcome the lack of replacement parts.*

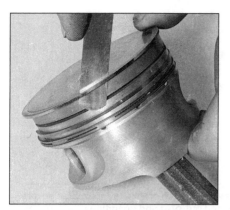

12.2 Using feeler gauge blades to remove piston rings

12.4A The piston ring grooves can be cleaned with a special tool, as shown here . . .

12.4B . . . or a section of a broken ring, if available

1   Before the inspection process can be carried out, the piston/connecting rod assemblies must be cleaned, and the original piston rings removed from the pistons. The rings should have smooth, polished working surfaces, with no dull or carbon-coated sections (showing that the ring is not sealing correctly against the bore wall, so allowing combustion gases to blow by) and no traces of wear on their top and bottom surfaces. The end gaps should be clear of carbon, but not polished (indicating a too-small end gap), and all the rings (including the elements of the oil control ring) should be free to rotate in their grooves, but without excessive up-and-down movement. If the rings appear to be in good condition, they are probably fit for further use; check the end gaps (in an unworn part of the bore) as described in Section 16. If any of the rings appears to be worn or damaged, or has an end gap significantly different from the specified value, the usual course of action is to renew all of them as a set. **Note:** *While it is usual always to renew piston rings when an engine is overhauled, this of course assumes that rings are available separately - if not, it follows that great care must be taken not to break or damage any of the rings during the following procedures, and to ensure that each ring is marked on removal so that it is refitted **only** the original way up, and **only** to the same groove.*

2   Using a piston ring installation tool, carefully remove the rings from the pistons. If such a tool is not available, the rings can be removed by hand, expanding them over the top of the pistons. The use of two or three old feeler blades will be helpful in preventing the rings dropping into empty grooves **(see illustration)**. Be careful not to nick or gouge the pistons in the process, and mark or label each ring as it is removed, so that its original top surface can be identified on reassembly, and so that it can be returned to its original groove. Take care also with your hands - piston rings are sharp!

3   Scrape all traces of carbon from the top of the piston. A handheld wire brush or a piece of fine emery cloth can be used, once the majority of the deposits have been scraped away. *Do not*, under any circumstances, use a wire brush mounted in a drill motor to remove deposits from the pistons - the piston material is soft, and may be eroded away by the wire brush.

4   Use a piston ring groove-cleaning tool to remove carbon deposits from the ring grooves. If a tool isn't available, but replacement rings have been found, a piece broken off the old ring will do the job. Be very careful to remove only the carbon deposits - don't remove any metal, and do not nick or scratch the sides of the ring grooves **(see illustrations)**. Protect your fingers - piston rings are sharp!

5   Once the deposits have been removed, clean the piston/rod assemblies with solvent, and dry them with compressed air (if available). Make sure the oil return holes in the back sides of the ring grooves, and the oil hole in the lower end of each rod, are clear.

6   If the pistons and cylinder walls aren't damaged or worn excessively - refer to Section 11 for details of inspection and measurement procedures - and if the cylinder block/crankcase is not rebored, new pistons won't be necessary. Normal piston wear appears as even vertical wear on the piston thrust surfaces, and slight looseness of the top ring in its groove.

7   Carefully inspect each piston for cracks around the skirt, at the pin bosses, and at the ring lands (between the ring grooves).

8   Look for scoring and scuffing on the thrust faces of the skirt, holes in the piston crown, and burned areas at the edge of the crown. If the skirt is scored or scuffed, the engine may have been suffering from overheating and/or abnormal combustion, which caused excessively-high operating temperatures. The cooling and lubrication systems should be checked thoroughly. A hole in the piston crown is an indication that abnormal combustion (pre-ignition) was occurring. Burned areas at the edge of the piston crown are usually evidence of spark knock (detonation). If any of the above problems exist, the causes must be corrected, or the damage will occur again. The causes may include intake air leaks, incorrect fuel/air mixture, incorrect ignition timing, or EGR system malfunctions.

9   Corrosion of the piston, in the form of small pits, indicates that coolant is leaking into the combustion chamber and/or the crankcase. Again, the cause must be corrected, or the problem may persist in the rebuilt engine.

10   Check the piston-to-rod clearance by twisting the piston and rod in opposite directions. Any noticeable play indicates excessive wear, which must be corrected. The piston/connecting rod assemblies should be taken to a Ford dealer or engine reconditioning specialist to have the pistons, gudgeon pins and rods checked, and new components fitted as required.

11   *Don't* attempt to separate the pistons from the connecting rods (even if non-genuine replacements are found elsewhere). This is a task for a Ford dealer or similar engine reconditioning specialist, due to the special heating equipment, press, mandrels and supports required to do the job. If the piston/connecting rod assemblies do require this sort of work, have the connecting rods checked for bend and twist, since only such engine repair specialists will have the facilities for this purpose.

12   Check the connecting rods for cracks and other damage. Temporarily remove the big-end bearing caps and the old bearing shells, wipe clean the rod and cap bearing recesses, and inspect them for nicks, gouges and scratches. After checking the rods, replace the old shells, slip the caps into place, and tighten the bolts finger-tight.

13 Crankshaft - inspection

Note: *Always check first what replacement parts are available before planning any overhaul operation; refer to Section 1 of this Part. A Ford dealer, or a good engine reconditioning specialist/automotive parts supplier, may be able to suggest alternatives which will enable you to overcome the lack of replacement parts.*

1   Clean the crankshaft, and dry it with compressed air if available. **Warning:** *Wear eye protection when using compressed air! Be sure to clean the oil holes with a pipe cleaner or similar probe.*

2   Check the main and crankpin (big-end) bearing journals for uneven wear, scoring, pitting and cracking.

2B

13.3 Rubbing a penny lengthwise along each journal will reveal its condition - if copper rubs off and is embedded in the crankshaft, the journals should be reground

3   Rub a penny across each journal several times **(see illustration)**. If a journal picks up copper from the penny, it is too rough.
4   Remove all burrs from the crankshaft oil holes with a stone, file or scraper.
5   Using a micrometer, measure the diameter of the main bearing and crankpin (big-end) journals, and compare the results with the Specifications at the beginning of this Chapter **(see illustration)**.
6   By measuring the diameter at a number of points around each journal's circumference, you will be able to determine whether or not the journal is out-of-round. Take the measurement at each end of the journal, near the webs, to determine if the journal is tapered.
7   If the crankshaft journals are damaged, tapered, out-of-round, or worn beyond the limits specified in this Chapter, the crankshaft must be taken to an engine overhaul specialist, who will regrind it, and who can supply the necessary undersize bearing shells.
8   Check the oil seal journals at each end of the crankshaft for wear and damage. If either seal has worn an excessive groove in its journal, consult an engine overhaul specialist, who will be able to advise whether a repair is possible, or whether a new crankshaft is necessary.

14 Main and big-end bearings - inspection

Note: *Always check first what replacement parts are available before planning any overhaul operation; refer to Section 1 of this Part. A Ford dealer, or a good engine reconditioning specialist/automotive parts supplier, may be able to suggest alternatives which will enable you to overcome the lack of replacement parts.*
1   Even though the main and big-end bearing shells should be re-newed during the engine overhaul, the old shells should be retained for close examination, as they may reveal valuable information about the condition of the engine **(see illustration)**.
2   Bearing failure occurs because of lack of lubrication, the pres-ence of dirt or other foreign particles, overloading the engine, and cor-rosion. Regardless of the cause of bearing failure, it must be corrected before the engine is reassembled, to prevent it from happening again.
3   When examining the bearing shells, remove them from the cylin-der block/crankcase and main bearing caps, and from the connecting rods and the big-end bearing caps, then lay them out on a clean sur-face in the same general position as their location in the engine. This will enable you to match any bearing problems with the corresponding crankshaft journal. *Do not* touch any shell's bearing surface with your fingers while checking it, or the delicate surface may be scratched.
4   Dirt or other foreign matter gets into the engine in a variety of ways. It may be left in the engine during assembly, or it may pass through filters or the crankcase ventilation system. It may get into the oil, and from there into the bearings. Metal chips from machining oper-ations and normal engine wear are often present. Abrasives are some-times left in engine components after reconditioning, especially when parts are not thoroughly cleaned using the proper cleaning methods. Whatever the source, these foreign objects often end up embedded in the soft bearing material, and are easily recognized. Large particles will

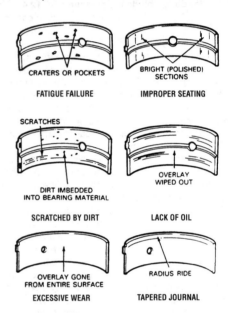

13.5 Measure the diameter of each crankshaft journal at several points, to detect taper and out-of-round conditions

14.1 When inspecting the main and big-end bearings, look for these problems

not embed in the material, and will score or gouge the shell and journal. The best prevention for this cause of bearing failure is to clean all parts thoroughly, and to keep everything spotlessly-clean during en-gine assembly. Frequent and regular engine oil and filter changes are also recommended.
5   Lack of lubrication (or lubrication breakdown) has a number of inter-related causes. Excessive heat (which thins the oil), overloading (which squeezes the oil from the bearing face) and oil leakage (from ex-cessive bearing clearances, worn oil pump or high engine speeds) all contribute to lubrication breakdown. Blocked oil passages, which usu-ally are the result of misaligned oil holes in a bearing shell, will also starve a bearing of oil, and destroy it. When lack of lubrication is the cause of bearing failure, the bearing material is wiped or extruded from the shell's steel backing. Temperatures may increase to the point where the steel backing turns blue from overheating.
6   Driving habits can have a definite effect on bearing life. Full-throttle, low-speed operation (labouring the engine) puts very high loads on bearings, which tends to squeeze out the oil film. These loads cause the shells to flex, which produces fine cracks in the bearing face (fatigue failure). Eventually, the bearing material will loosen in pieces, and tear away from the steel backing. Short-distance driving leads to corrosion of bearings, because insufficient engine heat is produced to drive off condensed water and corrosive gases. These products collect in the engine oil, forming acid and sludge. As the oil is carried to the engine bearings, the acid attacks and corrodes the bearing material.
7   Incorrect shell refitting during engine assembly will lead to bearing failure as well. Tight-fitting shells leave insufficient bearing running

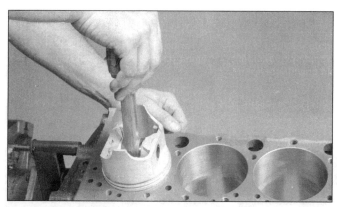

16.2 When checking piston ring end gap, the ring must be square in the cylinder bore (this is done by pushing the ring down with the top of a piston, as shown)

clearance, and will result in oil starvation. Dirt or foreign particles trapped behind a bearing shell result in high spots on the bearing, which lead to failure. *Do not* touch any shell's bearing surface with your fingers during reassembly; there is a risk of scratching the delicate surface, or of depositing particles of dirt on it.

15 Engine overhaul - reassembly sequence

1   Before reassembly begins, ensure that all new parts have been obtained, and that all necessary tools are available. Read through the entire procedure, to familiarise yourself with the work involved, and to ensure that all items necessary for reassembly of the engine are at hand. In addition to all normal tools and materials, suitable sealant will be required for two of the joint faces (Ford recommend Hylosil 102 for the cylinder block/crankcase-to-sump/oil pump/oil seal carrier joints, and Loctite 518 for the camshaft right-hand bearing caps). In all other cases, provided the relevant mating surfaces are clean and flat, new gaskets will be sufficient to ensure joints are oil-tight. *Do not* use any kind of silicone-based sealant on any part of the fuel system or inlet manifold, and *never* use exhaust sealants upstream of the catalytic converter.
2   In order to save time and avoid problems, engine reassembly can be carried out in the following order:

   (a)   *Crankshaft (Section 17).*
   (b)   *Piston/connecting rod assemblies (Section 18).*
   (c)   *Oil pump (Part A of this Chapter, Section 16).*
   (d)   *Sump (Part A of this Chapter, Section 15).*
   (e)   *Flywheel/driveplate (Part A of this Chapter, Section 21).*
   (f)   *Cylinder head (Part A of this Chapter, Section 14).*
   (g)   *Timing belt inner cover, tensioner and toothed pulleys, and timing belt (Part A of this Chapter).*
   (h)   *Engine external components.*

3   At this stage, all engine components should be absolutely clean and dry, with all faults repaired; they should be laid out (or in individual containers) on a completely-clean work surface.

16 Piston rings - refitting

1   Before installing new piston rings, check the end gaps. Lay out each piston set with a piston/connecting rod assembly, and keep them together as a matched set from now on.
2   Insert the top compression ring into the first cylinder, and square it up with the cylinder walls by pushing it in with the top of the piston **(see illustration)**. The ring should be near the bottom of the cylinder, at the lower limit of ring travel.
3   To measure the end gap, slip feeler gauges between the ends of the ring, until a gauge equal to the gap width is found **(see illustration)**. The feeler gauge should slide between the ring ends with a slight amount of drag. Compare the measurement to the value given in the Specifications Section of this Chapter; if the gap is larger or smaller than specified, double-check to make sure you have the correct rings before proceeding. If you are assessing the condition of used rings, have the cylinder bores checked and measured by a Ford dealer or similar engine reconditioning specialist, so that you can be sure of exactly which component is worn, and seek advice as to the best course of action to take.
4   If the end gap is still too small, it must be opened up by careful filing of the ring ends using a fine file. If it is too large, this is not as serious, unless the specified limit is exceeded, in which case very careful checking is required of the dimensions of all components, as well as of the new parts.
5   Repeat the procedure for each ring that will be installed in the first cylinder, and for each ring in the remaining cylinders. Remember to keep rings, pistons and cylinders matched up.
6   Refit the piston rings as follows. Where the original rings are being refitted, use the marks or notes made on removal, to ensure that each ring is refitted to its original groove and the same way up. New rings generally have their top surfaces identified by markings (often an indication of size, such as "STD", or the word "TOP") - the rings must be fitted with such markings uppermost **(see illustration)**. **Note:** *Always follow the instructions printed on the ring package or box - different manufacturers may require different approaches. Do not mix up the top and second compression rings, as they usually have different cross-sections.*
7   The oil control ring (lowest one on the piston) is usually installed first. It is composed of three separate elements. Slip the spacer/expander into the groove **(see illustration)**. If an anti-rotation tang is used, make sure it is inserted into the drilled hole in the ring groove. Next, install the lower side rail. Don't use a piston ring installation tool on the oil ring side rails, as they may be damaged. Instead, place one end of the side rail into the groove between the spacer/expander and the ring land, hold it firmly in place, and slide a finger around the piston while pushing the rail into the groove **(see illustration)**. Next, install the upper side rail in the same manner.

2B

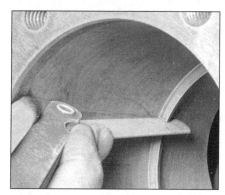

16.3 With the ring square in the bore, measure the end gap with a feeler gauge

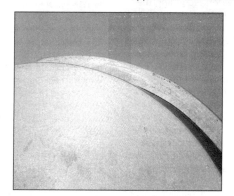

16.6 Look for etched markings ("STD" - indicating a standard-sized ring - shown here) identifying piston ring top surface

16.7A Installing the spacer/expander in the oil control ring groove

16.7B DO NOT use a piston ring installation tool when installing the oil ring side rails

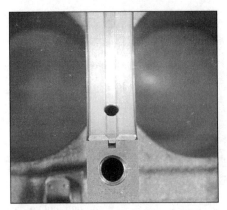

17.4 Tab on each bearing shell must engage with notch in block or cap, and oil holes in upper shells must align with block oilways

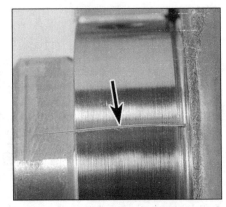

17.6 Lay the Plastigage strips (arrowed) on the main bearing journals, parallel to the crankshaft centre-line

8   After the three oil ring components have been installed, check that both the upper and lower side rails can be turned smoothly in the ring groove.

9   The second compression (middle) ring is installed next, followed by the top compression ring - ensure their marks are uppermost, and be careful not to confuse them. Don't expand either ring any more than necessary to slide it over the top of the piston.

10   With all the rings in position, space the ring gaps (including the elements of the oil control ring) uniformly around the piston at 120 intervals. Repeat the procedure for the remaining pistons and rings.

17 Crankshaft - refitting and main bearing running clearance check

1   Crankshaft refitting is the first major step in engine reassembly. It is assumed at this point that the cylinder block/crankcase and crankshaft have been cleaned, inspected and repaired or reconditioned as necessary. Position the engine upside-down.

2   Remove the main bearing cap bolts, and lift out the caps. Lay the caps out in the proper order, to ensure correct installation.

3   If they're still in place, remove the old bearing shells from the block and the main bearing caps. Wipe the bearing recesses of the block and caps with a clean, lint-free cloth. They must be kept spotlessly-clean!

Main bearing running clearance check

4   Clean the backs of the new main bearing shells. Fit the shells with an oil groove in each main bearing location in the block; note the thrustwashers integral with the No 3 (centre) main bearing upper shell. Fit the other shell from each bearing set in the corresponding main bearing cap. Make sure the tab on each bearing shell fits into the notch in the block or cap. Also, the oil holes in the block must line up with the oil holes in the bearing shell **(see illustration)**. **Caution:** *Don't hammer the shells into place, and don't nick or gouge the bearing faces. No lubrication should be used at this time.*

5   Clean the bearing surfaces of the shells in the block and the crankshaft main bearing journals with a clean, lint-free cloth. Check or clean the oil holes in the crankshaft, as any dirt here can go only one way - straight through the new bearings.

6   Once you're certain the crankshaft is clean, carefully lay it in position in the main bearings. Trim several pieces of the appropriate-size Plastigage (they must be slightly shorter than the width of the main bearings), and place one piece on each crankshaft main bearing journal, parallel with the crankshaft centre-line **(see illustration)**.

7   Clean the bearing surfaces of the cap shells, and install the caps in their respective positions (don't mix them up) with the arrows pointing to the timing belt end of the engine. Don't disturb the Plastigage **(see illustration)**.

8   Working on one cap at a time, from the centre main bearing outwards (and ensuring that each cap is tightened down squarely and evenly onto the block), tighten the main bearing cap bolts to the specified torque wrench setting. Don't rotate the crankshaft at any time during this operation!

9   Remove the bolts, and carefully lift off the main bearing caps. Keep them in order. Don't disturb the Plastigage or rotate the crankshaft. If any of the main bearing caps are difficult to remove, tap them gently from side-to-side with a soft-faced mallet to loosen them.

10   Compare the width of the crushed Plastigage on each journal with the scale printed on the Plastigage envelope to obtain the main bearing running clearance **(see illustration)**. Check the Specifications to make sure that the clearance is correct.

11   If the clearance is not as specified, seek the advice of a Ford dealer or similar engine reconditioning specialist - if the crankshaft journals are in good condition (see Section 13), it may be possible simply to renew the shells to achieve the correct clearance. If this is not possible, the crankshaft must be reground by a specialist who can supply the necessary undersized shells. First though, make sure that no dirt or oil was between the bearing shells and the caps or block when the clearance was measured. If the Plastigage is noticeably wider at one end than the other, the journal may be tapered (see Section 13).

12   Carefully scrape all traces of the Plastigage material off the main bearing journals and the bearing surfaces. Be very careful not to scratch the bearing - use your fingernail or the edge of a credit card.

Final refitting

13   Carefully lift the crankshaft out of the engine. Clean the bearing surfaces of the shells in the block, then apply a thin, uniform layer of clean molybdenum disulphide-based grease, engine assembly lubricant, or clean engine oil to each surface **(see illustration)**. Coat the thrustwasher surfaces as well.

14   Lubricate the crankshaft oil seal journals with molybdenum disulphide-based grease, engine assembly lubricant, or clean engine oil.

15   Make sure the crankshaft journals are clean, then lay the crankshaft back in place in the block **(see illustration)**. Clean the bearing surfaces of the shells in the caps, then lubricate them. Install the caps in their respective positions, with the arrows pointing to the timing belt end of the engine.

16   Working on one cap at a time, from the centre main bearing outwards (and ensuring that each cap is tightened down squarely and evenly onto the block), tighten the main bearing cap bolts to the specified torque wrench setting.

17   Rotate the crankshaft a number of times by hand, to check for any obvious binding.

18   Check the crankshaft endfloat (see Section 10). It should be correct if the crankshaft thrust faces aren't worn or damaged, and if the No 3 (centre) main bearing's upper shell has been renewed.

19   Refit the crankshaft left-hand oil seal carrier, and install a new seal (see Part A of this Chapter, Section 20).

17.7 Refit the main bearing caps and tighten the bolts as specified

17.10 Compare the width of the crushed Plastigage to the scale on the envelope to determine the main bearing oil clearance (always take the measurement at the widest point of the Plastigage). Be sure to use the correct scale; Imperial and metric scales are included

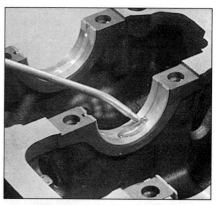

17.13 Ensure bearing shells are absolutely clean, lubricate liberally . . .

17.15 . . . and refit the crankshaft

18.3 Tab on each big-end bearing shell must engage with notch in connecting rod or cap

18.9 The piston can be driven gently into the cylinder bore with the end of a wooden or plastic hammer handle

2B

18 Piston/connecting rod assemblies - refitting and big-end bearing running clearance check

1   Before refitting the piston/connecting rod assemblies, the cylinder bores must be perfectly clean, the top edge of each cylinder must be chamfered, and the crankshaft must be in place.

2   Remove the big-end bearing cap from No 1 cylinder connecting rod (refer to the marks noted or made on removal). Remove the original bearing shells, and wipe the bearing recesses of the connecting rod and cap with a clean, lint-free cloth. They must be kept spotlessly-clean!

Big-end bearing running clearance check

3   Clean the back of the new upper bearing shell, fit it to the connecting rod, then fit the other shell of the bearing set to the big-end bearing cap. Make sure the tab on each shell fits into the notch in the rod or cap recess **(see illustration)**. **Caution:** *Don't hammer the shells into place, and don't nick or gouge the bearing face. Don't lubricate the bearing at this time.*

4   It's critically important that all mating surfaces of the bearing components are perfectly clean and oil-free when they're assembled.

5   Position the piston ring gaps as described in Section 16, lubricate the piston and rings with clean engine oil, and attach a piston ring compressor to the piston. Leave the skirt protruding about a quarter-inch, to guide the piston into the cylinder bore. The rings must be compressed until they're flush with the piston.

6   Rotate the crankshaft until No 1 crankpin (big-end) journal is at BDC (Bottom Dead Centre), and apply a coat of engine oil to the cylinder walls.

7   Arrange the No 1 piston/connecting rod assembly so that the arrow on the piston crown points to the timing belt end of the engine. The cylinder number (counting from the timing belt end of the engine) is etched into the flat-machined surface of the connecting rod and its cap, and must be visible from the front (exhaust side) of the engine (see illustrations 9.5A and 9.5B). Gently insert the assembly into the No 1 cylinder bore, and rest the bottom edge of the ring compressor on the engine block.

8   Tap the top edge of the ring compressor to make sure it's contacting the block around its entire circumference.

9   Gently tap on the top of the piston with the end of a wooden hammer handle **(see illustration)**, while guiding the connecting rod's big-end onto the crankpin. The piston rings may try to pop out of the ring compressor just before entering the cylinder bore, so keep some pressure on the ring compressor. Work slowly, and if any resistance is felt as the piston enters the cylinder, stop immediately. Find out what's binding, and fix it before proceeding. *Do not*, for any reason, force the piston into the cylinder - you might break a ring and/or the piston.

10   To check the big-end bearing running clearance, cut a piece of the appropriate-size Plastigage slightly shorter than the width of the connecting rod bearing, and lay it in place on the No 1 crankpin (big-end) journal, parallel with the crankshaft centre-line (see illustration 17.6).

11   Clean the connecting rod-to-cap mating surfaces, and refit the

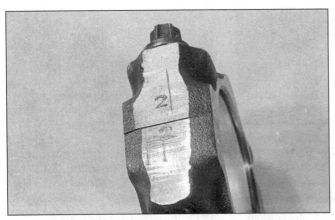

18.11 The connecting rod and big-end bearing cap of each assembly must share the same etched cylinder number, visible from the same (front/exhaust) side of the engine

big-end bearing cap. Make sure the etched number on the cap is on the same side as that on the rod **(see illustration)**. Tighten the cap bolts evenly - first use a torque wrench to tighten the bolts to the specified (first stage) torque setting, then use an ordinary socket extension bar and an angle gauge to tighten the bolts further through the specified (second stage) angle. Use a thin-wall socket, to avoid erroneous torque readings that can result if the socket is wedged between the cap and nut. If the socket tends to wedge itself between the nut and the cap, lift up on it slightly until it no longer contacts the cap. Don't rotate the crankshaft at any time during this operation!

12   Unscrew the bolts and detach the cap, being very careful not to disturb the Plastigage.

13   Compare the width of the crushed Plastigage to the scale printed on the Plastigage envelope, to obtain the running clearance (see illustration 17.10). Compare it to the Specifications, to make sure the clearance is correct.

14   If the clearance is not as specified, seek the advice of a Ford dealer or similar engine reconditioning specialist - if the crankshaft journals are in good condition (see Section 13), it may be possible simply to renew the shells to achieve the correct clearance. If this is not possible, the crankshaft must be reground by a specialist, who can also supply the necessary undersized shells. First though, make sure that no dirt or oil was trapped between the bearing shells and the connecting rod or cap when the clearance was measured. Also, recheck the crankpin diameter. If the Plastigage was wider at one end than the other, the crankpin journal may be tapered (see Section 13).

15   Carefully scrape all traces of the Plastigage material off the journal and the bearing surface. Be very careful not to scratch the bearing - use your fingernail or the edge of a credit card.

Final piston/connecting rod refitting

16   Make sure the bearing surfaces are perfectly clean, then apply a uniform layer of clean molybdenum disulphide-based grease, engine assembly lubricant, or clean engine oil, to both of them. You'll have to push the piston into the cylinder to expose the bearing surface of the shell in the connecting rod.

17   Slide the connecting rod back into place on the crankpin (big-end) journal, refit the big-end bearing cap, and then tighten the bolts in two stages, as described above.

18   Repeat the entire procedure for the remaining piston/connecting rod assemblies.

19   The important points to remember are:

(a)   *Keep the backs of the bearing shells and the recesses of the connecting rods and caps perfectly clean when assembling them.*

(b)   *Make sure you have the correct piston/rod assembly for each cylinder - use the etched cylinder numbers to identify the front-facing side of both the rod and its cap.*

(c)   *The arrow on the piston crown must face the timing belt end of the engine.*

(d)   *Lubricate the cylinder bores with clean engine oil.*

(e)   *Lubricate the bearing surfaces when refitting the big-end bearing caps after the running clearance has been checked.*

20   After all the piston/connecting rod assemblies have been properly installed, rotate the crankshaft a number of times by hand, to check for any obvious binding.

19   Engine - initial start-up after overhaul

1   With the engine refitted in the vehicle, double-check the engine oil and coolant levels. Make a final check that everything has been reconnected, and that there are no tools or rags left in the engine compartment.

2   With the spark plugs removed and the ignition system disabled by unplugging the ignition coil's electrical connector, remove fuse 14 to disconnect the fuel pump. Turn the engine on the starter until the oil pressure warning light goes out.

3   Refit the spark plugs, and connect all the spark plug (HT) leads (Chapter 1). Reconnect the ignition coil wiring, refit the fuel pump fuse, then switch on the ignition and listen for the fuel pump; it will run for a little longer than usual, due to the lack of pressure in the system.

4   Start the engine, noting that this also may take a little longer than usual, due to the fuel system components being empty.

5   While the engine is idling, check for fuel, coolant and oil leaks. Don't be alarmed if there are some odd smells and smoke from parts getting hot and burning off oil deposits. If the hydraulic tappets have been disturbed, some valve gear noise may be heard at first; this should disappear as the oil circulates fully around the engine, and normal pressure is restored in the tappets.

6   Keep the engine idling until hot water is felt circulating through the top hose, check that it idles reasonably smoothly and at the usual speed, then switch it off.

7   After a few minutes, recheck the oil and coolant levels, and top-up as necessary (Chapter 1).

8   If they were tightened as described, there is no need to re-tighten the cylinder head bolts once the engine has first run after reassembly - in fact, Ford state that the bolts *must not* be re-tightened.

9   If new components such as pistons, rings or crankshaft bearings have been fitted, the engine must be run-in for the first 500 miles (800 km). Do not operate the engine at full-throttle, or allow it to labour in any gear during this period. It is recommended that the oil and filter be changed at the end of this period.

Chapter 3 Cooling, heating, and air conditioning systems

Contents

3

Specifications

Coolant
Mixture type	See Chapter 1
Cooling system capacity	See Chapter 1

System pressure
Pressure test	1.2 bars - should hold this pressure for at least 10 seconds

Expansion tank filler cap
Pressure rating	1.2 bars approximately - see cap for actual value

Thermostat
Starts to open	88°C

Radiator electric cooling fan
Switches on at:

Single-speed fans, two-speed fans - first stage	100°C
Two-speed fans - second stage	103°C

Switches off at:

Single-speed fans, two-speed fans - first stage	93°C
Two-speed fans - second stage	100°C

Coolant temperature sensor
Resistance:

At -40°C	860.0 to 900.0 kilohms
At 20°C	35.0 to 40.0 kilohms
At 100°C	1.9 to 2.5 kilohms
At 120°C	1.0 to 1.3 kilohms

Air conditioning system

	Nm	lbf ft
Refrigerant	R134a	

Torque wrench settings

	Nm	lbf ft
Radiator mounting bracket-to-subframe bolts..	23	17
Fluid cooler pipe unions - automatic transmission.................................	23	17
Thermostat housing-to-cylinder head bolts	20	15
Water outlet-to-thermostat housing bolts	8 to 11	6 to 8
Coolant temperature sensor..	23	17
Coolant temperature gauge sender..	8	6
Water pump bolts	18	13
Water pump pulley bolts..	See Chapter 2A	
Air conditioning compressor mounting bolts	25	18

1 General information

Engine cooling system

All vehicles covered by this manual employ a pressurised engine cooling system with thermostatically-controlled coolant circulation. A water pump mounted on the drivebelt end of the cylinder block/crankcase pumps coolant through the engine. The coolant flows around each cylinder and toward the transmission end of the engine. Cast-in coolant passages direct coolant around the inlet and exhaust ports, near the spark plug areas and close to the exhaust valve guides.

A wax pellet type thermostat is located in a housing at the transmission end of the engine. During warm-up, the closed thermostat prevents coolant from circulating through the radiator. Instead, it returns through the coolant metal pipe running across the front of the engine to the radiator bottom hose and the water pump. The supply to the heater is made from the rear of the thermostat housing. As the engine nears normal operating temperature, the thermostat opens and allows hot coolant to travel through the radiator, where it is cooled before returning to the engine.

The cooling system is sealed by a pressure-type filler cap in the expansion tank. The pressure in the system raises the boiling point of the coolant, and increases the cooling efficiency of the radiator. When the engine is at normal operating temperature, the coolant expands, and the surplus is displaced into the expansion tank. When the system cools, the surplus coolant is automatically drawn back from the tank into the radiator.

Warning: *DO NOT attempt to remove the expansion tank filler cap, or to disturb any part of the cooling system, while it or the engine is hot, as there is a very great risk of scalding. If the expansion tank filler cap must be removed before the engine and radiator have fully cooled down (even though this is not recommended) the pressure in the cooling system must first be released. Cover the cap with a thick layer of cloth, to avoid scalding, and slowly unscrew the filler cap until a hissing sound can be heard. When the hissing has stopped, showing that pressure is released, slowly unscrew the filler cap further until it can be removed; if more hissing sounds are heard, wait until they have stopped before unscrewing the cap completely. At all times, keep well away from the filler opening.*

Warning: *Do not allow antifreeze to come in contact with your skin, or with the painted surfaces of the vehicle. Rinse off spills immediately with plenty of water. Never leave antifreeze lying around in an open container, or in a puddle in the driveway or on the garage floor. Children and pets are attracted by its sweet smell, but antifreeze is fatal if ingested.*

Warning: *If the engine is hot, the electric cooling fan may start rotating even if the engine is not running, so be careful to keep hands, hair and loose clothing well clear when working in the engine compartment.*

Heating system

The heating system consists of a blower fan and heater matrix (radiator) located in the heater unit, with hoses connecting the heater matrix

to the engine cooling system. Hot engine coolant is circulated through the heater matrix. When the heater temperature control on the facia is operated, a flap door opens to expose the heater box to the passenger compartment. When the blower control is operated, the blower fan forces air through the unit according to the setting selected.

Air conditioning system

See Section 11.

2 Antifreeze - general information

Warning: *Do not allow antifreeze to come in contact with your skin, or with the painted surfaces of the vehicle. Rinse off spills immediately with plenty of water. Antifreeze is highly toxic if ingested. Never leave antifreeze lying around in an open container, or in puddles on the floor; children and pets are attracted by its sweet smell, and may drink it. Check with local authorities about disposing of used antifreeze - many have collection centres which will see that antifreeze is disposed of safely.*

The cooling system should be filled with a water/ethylene glycol-based antifreeze solution, of a strength which will prevent freezing down to at least -25°C, or lower if the local climate requires it. Antifreeze also provides protection against corrosion, and increases the coolant boiling point.

The cooling system should be maintained according to the schedule described in Chapter 1. If antifreeze is used that is not to Ford's specification, old or contaminated coolant mixtures are likely to cause damage, and encourage the formation of corrosion and scale in the system. Use distilled water with the antifreeze, if available - if not, be sure to use only soft water. Clean rainwater is suitable.

Before adding antifreeze, check all hoses and hose connections, because antifreeze tends to leak through very small openings. Engines don't normally consume coolant, so if the level goes down, find the cause and correct it.

The exact mixture of antifreeze-to-water which you should use depends on the relative weather conditions. The mixture should contain at least 40% antifreeze, but not more than 70%. Consult the mixture ratio chart on the antifreeze container before adding coolant. Hydrometers are available at most automotive accessory shops to test the coolant. Use antifreeze which meets the vehicle manufacturer's specifications.

3 Cooling system hoses - disconnection and renewal

Note: *Refer to the warnings given in Section 1 of this Chapter before starting work.*

1   If the checks described in Chapter 1 reveal a faulty hose, it must be renewed as follows **(see illustration)**.

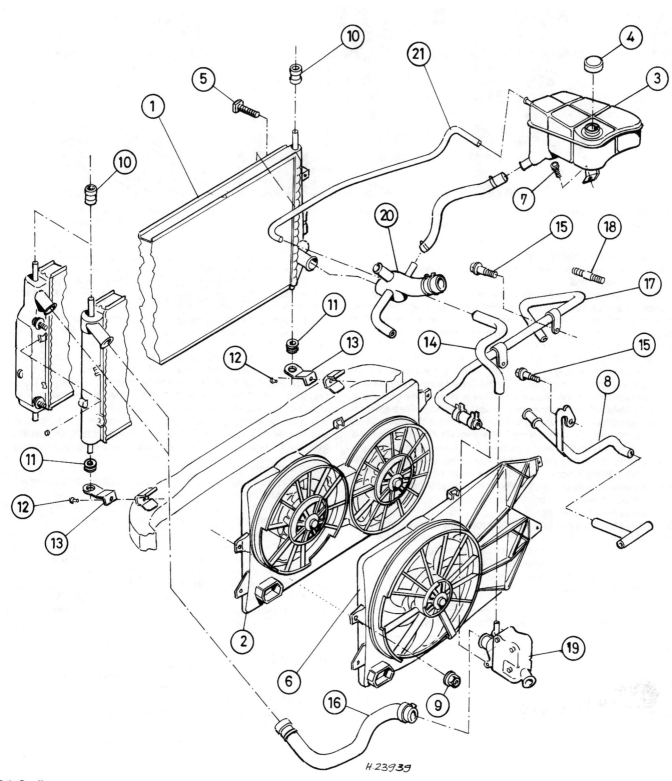

H.23939

3.1 Cooling system components

1	Radiator	7	Bolt	15	Bolt
2	(Twin) electric cooling fan and shroud	8	Coolant pipe	16	Radiator top hose
3	Expansion tank	9	Nut	17	Coolant pipe/hose
4	Filler/pressure cap	10	Top mounting rubber	18	Stud
5	Bolt	11	Bottom mounting rubber	19	Thermostat housing
6	(Single) electric cooling fan and shroud	12	Bolt	20	Radiator bottom hose
		13	Radiator mounting bracket		
		14	Coolant hose		

3

4.5 Unbolt water outlet to withdraw thermostat

4.14 Ensure thermostat is refitted as shown

5.10A Fan shroud is secured at top by mounting nut (A), at bottom by clip (B) . . .

2   First drain the cooling system (see Chapter 1); if the antifreeze is not due for renewal, the drained coolant may be re-used, if it is collected in a clean container.

3   To disconnect any hose, use a pair of pliers to release the spring clamps (or a screwdriver to slacken screw-type clamps), then move them along the hose clear of the union. Carefully work the hose off its stubs. The hoses can be removed with relative ease when new - on an older car, they may have stuck.

4   If a hose proves stubborn, try to release it by rotating it on its unions before attempting to work it off. Gently prise the end of the hose with a blunt instrument (such as a flat-bladed screwdriver), but do not apply too much force, and take care not to damage the pipe stubs or hoses. Note in particular that the radiator hose unions are fragile; do not use excessive force when attempting to remove the hoses. If all else fails, cut the hose with a sharp knife, then slit it so that it can be peeled off in two pieces. While expensive, this is preferable to buying a new radiator. Check first, however, that a new hose is readily available.

5   When refitting a hose, first slide the clamps onto the hose, then work the hose onto its unions. If the hose is stiff, use soap (or washing-up liquid) as a lubricant, or soften it by soaking it in boiling water, but take care to prevent scalding.

6   Work each hose end fully onto its union, then check that the hose is settled correctly and is properly routed. Slide each clip along the hose until it is behind the union flared end, before tightening it securely.

7   Refill the system with coolant (see Chapter 1).

8   Check carefully for leaks as soon as possible after disturbing any part of the cooling system.

4 Thermostat - removal, testing and refitting

Note: *Refer to the warnings given in Section 1 of this Chapter before starting work.*

Removal

1   Disconnect the battery negative (earth) lead (see Chapter 5, Section 1).

2   Unbolt the resonator support bracket from the engine compartment front crossmember. Slacken the two clamp screws securing the resonator to the air mass meter and plenum chamber hoses, then swing the resonator up clear of the thermostat housing (see Chapter 4).

3   Drain the cooling system (see Chapter 1). If the coolant is relatively new or in good condition, drain it into a clean container and re-use it.

4   Disconnect the expansion tank coolant hose and the radiator top hose from the thermostat housing's water outlet.

5   Unbolt the water outlet and withdraw the thermostat **(see illustration)**. Note the position of the air bleed valve, and how the thermostat is installed (which end is facing outwards).

Testing

General check

6   Before assuming the thermostat is to blame for a cooling system

problem, check the coolant level, auxiliary drivebelt tension and condition (see Chapter 1) and temperature gauge operation.

7   If the engine seems to be taking a long time to warm up (based on heater output or temperature gauge operation), the thermostat is probably stuck open. Renew the thermostat.

8   If the engine runs hot, use your hand to check the temperature of the radiator top hose. If the hose isn't hot, but the engine is, the thermostat is probably stuck closed, preventing the coolant inside the engine from escaping to the radiator - renew the thermostat. **Caution:** *Don't drive the vehicle without a thermostat. The lack of a thermostat will slow warm-up time. The engine management system's ECU will then stay in warm-up mode for longer than necessary, causing emissions and fuel economy to suffer.*

9   If the radiator top hose is hot, it means that the coolant is flowing and the thermostat is open. Consult the *"Fault diagnosis"* section at the front of this manual to assist in tracing possible cooling system faults.

Thermostat test

10   If the thermostat remains in the open position at room temperature, it is faulty, and must be renewed as a matter of course.

11   To test it fully, suspend the (closed) thermostat on a length of string in a container of cold water, with a thermometer beside it; ensure that neither touches the side of the container.

12   Heat the water, and check the temperature at which the thermostat begins to open; compare this value with that specified. Continue to heat the water until the thermostat is fully open; the temperature at which this should happen is stamped in the unit's end. Remove the thermostat and allow it to cool down; check that it closes fully.

13   If the thermostat does not open and close as described, if it sticks in either position, or if it does not open at the specified temperature, it must be renewed.

Refitting

14   Refitting is the reverse of the removal procedure. Clean the mating surfaces carefully, renew the thermostat's sealing ring if it is worn or damaged, then refit the thermostat with its air bleed valve uppermost **(see illustration)**. Tighten the water outlet bolts to the specified torque wrench setting.

15   Refill the cooling system (see Chapter 1).

16   Start the engine and allow it to reach normal operating temperature, then check for leaks and proper thermostat operation.

5 Radiator electric cooling fan(s) - testing, removal and refitting

Note: *Refer to the warnings given in Section 1 of this Chapter before starting work.*

Testing

1   The radiator cooling fan is controlled by the engine management

5.10B . . . and is hooked over radiator top edge (one point arrowed)

5.11 Removing radiator electric cooling fan and shroud assembly

6.9 Location (arrowed) of coolant temperature gauge sender

system's ECU, acting on the information received from the coolant temperature sensor. Where twin fans or two-speed fans are fitted, control is through a resistor assembly, secured to the bottom left-hand corner of the fan shroud - this can be renewed separately if faulty.

2   First, check the relevant fuses and relays (see Chapter 12).

3   To test the fan motor, unplug the electrical connector, and use fused jumper wires to connect the fan directly to the battery. If the fan still does not work, renew the motor.

4   If the motor proved sound, the fault lies in the coolant temperature sensor (see Section 6 for testing details), in the wiring loom (see Chapter 12 for testing details) or in the engine management system (see Chapter 6).

Removal and refitting

5   Disconnect the battery negative (earth) lead (see Chapter 5, Section 1).

6   Unbolt the resonator support bracket from the engine compartment front crossmember. Slacken the two clamp screws securing the resonator to the air mass meter and plenum chamber hoses, then swing the resonator up clear of the thermostat housing (see Chapter 4).

7   Drain the cooling system (see Chapter 1).

8   Remove the radiator top hose completely. Disconnect the metal coolant pipe/hose from the thermostat, and unbolt the coolant pipe from the exhaust manifold heat shield.

9   Unplug the cooling fan electrical connector(s), then release all wiring and hoses from the fan shroud.

10   Unscrew the two nuts securing the fan shroud, then lift the assembly to disengage it from its bottom mountings and from the radiator top edge **(see illustrations)**.

11   Withdraw the fan and shroud as an assembly **(see illustration)**.

12   At the time of writing, the fan, motor and shroud are available only as a complete assembly, and must be renewed together if faulty.

13   Refitting is the reverse of the removal procedure. Ensure that the shroud is settled correctly at all four mounting points before refitting and tightening the nuts.

---

6   Cooling system electrical switches and sensors - testing, removal and refitting

Note: *Refer to the warnings given in Section 1 of this Chapter before starting work.*

Coolant temperature gauge sender

Testing

1   If the coolant temperature gauge is inoperative, check the fuses first (see Chapter 12).

2   If the gauge indicates Hot at any time, consult the *"Fault diagnosis"* section at the front of this manual, to assist in tracing possible cooling system faults.

3   If the gauge indicates Hot shortly after the engine is started from cold, unplug the coolant temperature sender's electrical connector. If the gauge reading now drops, renew the sender. If the reading remains high, the wire to the gauge may be shorted to earth, or the gauge is faulty.

4   If the gauge fails to indicate after the engine has been warmed up (approximately 10 minutes) and the fuses are known to be sound, switch off the engine. Unplug the sender's electrical connector, and use a jumper wire to connect the white/red wire to a clean earth point (bare metal) on the engine. Switch on the ignition without starting the engine. If the gauge now indicates Hot, renew the sender.

5   If the gauge still does not work, the circuit may be open, or the gauge may be faulty. See Chapter 12 for additional information.

Removal

6   Unbolt the resonator support bracket from the engine compartment front crossmember. Slacken the two clamp screws securing the resonator to the air mass meter and plenum chamber hoses, then swing the resonator up clear of the thermostat housing (see Chapter 4).

7   Drain the cooling system (see Chapter 1).

8   Disconnect the expansion tank coolant hose and the radiator top hose from the thermostat housing's water outlet, then disconnect the metal coolant pipe/hose from the thermostat.

9   Unplug the electrical connector from the sender **(see illustration)**.

10   Unscrew the sender and withdraw it.

Refitting

11   Clean as thoroughly as possible the opening in the thermostat housing, then apply a light coat of sealant to the sender's threads. Screw in the sender and tighten it to the specified torque wrench setting, and plug in its electrical connector.

12   Reconnect the hoses and refit the resonator, top-up the cooling system (see Chapter 1) and run the engine. Check for leaks and proper gauge operation.

Coolant temperature sensor

Testing

13   Disconnect the battery negative (earth) lead (see Chapter 5, Section 1).

14   Unbolt the resonator support bracket from the engine compartment front crossmember. Slacken the two clamp screws securing the resonator to the air mass meter and plenum chamber hoses, then swing the resonator up clear of the thermostat housing (see Chapter 4).

3

6.15 Location (arrowed) of coolant temperature sensor

7.5 Radiator mounting bracket-to-subframe bolts (A), air conditioning system condenser mounting bolt (B)

8.8 Power steering system pump should be removed to reach water pump hose union (arrowed)

15   Unplug the electrical connector from the sensor **(see illustration)**.

16   Using an ohmmeter, measure the resistance between the sensor terminals. Depending on the temperature of the sensor tip, the resistance measured will vary, but should be within the broad limits given in the Specifications Section of this Chapter. If the sensor's temperature is varied - by removing it (see below) and placing it in a freezer for a while, or by warming it gently - its resistance should alter accordingly.

17   If the results obtained show the sensor to be faulty, renew it.

18   On completion, plug in the connector and refit the resonator.

Removal

19   Disconnect the battery negative (earth) lead (see Chapter 5, Section 1).

20   Unbolt the resonator support bracket from the engine compartment front crossmember. Slacken the two clamp screws securing the resonator to the air mass meter and plenum chamber hoses, then swing the resonator up clear of the thermostat housing (see Chapter 4).

21   With the engine *completely cool*, remove the expansion tank filler cap to release any pressure, then refit the cap. Provided you work swiftly and plug the opening as soon as the sensor is unscrewed, coolant loss will thus be minimised; this will avoid the draining of the complete cooling system which would otherwise be necessary (see Chapter 1).

22   Unplug the electrical connector from the sensor.

23   Unscrew the sensor and withdraw it. If the cooling system has not been drained, plug the opening as quickly as possible.

Refitting

24   Clean as thoroughly as possible the opening in the thermostat housing, then apply a light coat of sealant to the sensor's threads. Remove the material used to plug the sensor hole (where applicable), and quickly install the sensor to prevent coolant loss. Tighten the sensor to the specified torque wrench setting, and plug in its electrical connector.

25   Refit the resonator, top-up the cooling system (see Chapter 1) and run the engine, checking for leaks.

Coolant low level switch

Testing

26   The switch is a reed-type unit mounted in the bottom of the cooling system expansion tank, activated by a magnetic float. If the coolant level falls to the "MIN" level or less, the appropriate bulb lights in the warning display.

27   If the bulb fails to light during the 5-second bulb test, check the bulb, and renew if necessary as described in Chapter 12.

28   To check the switch itself, unplug its electrical connector, and use an ohmmeter to measure the resistance across the switch terminals. With the float up, a resistance of 90 ohms should be measured; when it is down, the resistance should increase to approximately 150 kilohms.

29   If the results obtained from the check are significantly different from those expected, the switch is faulty, and must be renewed.

30   If the switch and bulb are proven to be sound, the fault must be in the wiring or in the auxiliary warning control assembly (see Chapter 12).

Removal

31   Disconnect the battery negative (earth) lead (see Chapter 5, Section 1).

32   Remove the expansion tank (see Section 7).

33   Unplug the switch electrical connector.

34   Release the switch by twisting its retainer anti-clockwise, then withdraw it.

Refitting

35   Refitting is the reverse of the removal procedure. Refill the cooling system (see Chapter 1). Start the engine, and check for coolant leaks when it is fully warmed-up.

---

7   Radiator and expansion tank - removal, inspection and refitting

Note: *Refer to the warnings given in Section 1 of this Chapter before starting work.*

Radiator

Removal

Note: *If leakage is the reason for removing the radiator, bear in mind that minor leaks can often be cured using a radiator sealant such as Holts Radweld, with the radiator in situ.*

1   Remove the radiator fan and shroud assembly (see Section 5).

2   Disconnect the bottom hose from the radiator.

3   If the vehicle has automatic transmission, disconnect the fluid cooler lines, and plug the lines and fittings.

4   If the vehicle has air conditioning, unscrew the condenser mounting nuts or bolts, detach the condenser from the radiator, and tie it to the engine compartment front crossmember. **Warning:** *Do not disconnect any of the refrigerant hoses.*

5   Unbolt the radiator mounting brackets from the subframe; note that they are handed, and are marked to ensure correct refitting **(see illustration)**. Collect the bottom mounting rubbers, noting which way up they are fitted, and store them carefully.

6   Carefully lower the radiator from the vehicle, and withdraw it.

7   With the radiator removed, it can be inspected for leaks and damage. If it needs repair, have a radiator specialist or dealer service department perform the work, as special techniques are required.

8   Insects and dirt can be removed from the radiator with a garden hose or a soft brush. Don't bend the cooling fins as this is done.

8.9 Unscrew bolts (arrowed) . . .

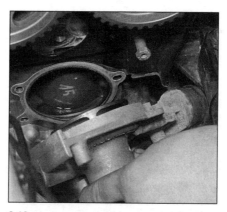

8.10 . . . to remove water pump - always renew gasket and clean all mating surfaces carefully

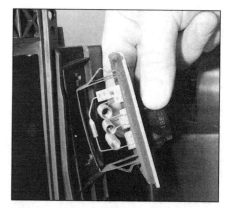

9.5 Heater blower motor control resistor can be prised out of heater unit

Refitting

9   Refitting is the reverse of the removal procedure. Be sure the mounting rubbers are seated properly at the base of the radiator.

10   After refitting, refill the cooling system with the proper mixture of antifreeze and water (see Chapter 1).

11   Start the engine, and check for leaks. Allow the engine to reach normal operating temperature, indicated by the radiator top hose becoming hot. Recheck the coolant level, and add more if required.

12   If working on a vehicle with automatic transmission, check and add transmission fluid as needed (see Chapter 1).

Expansion tank

13   With the engine *completely cool*, remove the expansion tank filler cap to release any pressure, then refit the cap.

14   Disconnect the hoses from the tank, upper hose first. As each hose is disconnected, drain the tank's contents into a clean container. If the antifreeze is not due for renewal, the drained coolant may be re-used, if it is kept clean.

15   Unscrew the tank's two mounting bolts and withdraw it, unplugging the coolant low level switch electrical connector (where fitted).

16   Wash out the tank, and inspect it for cracks and chafing - renew it if damaged.

17   Refitting is the reverse of the removal procedure. Refill the cooling system with the proper mixture of antifreeze and water (see Chapter 1), then start the engine and allow it to reach normal operating temperature, indicated by the radiator top hose becoming hot. Recheck the coolant level and add more if required, then check for leaks.

8   Water pump - check, removal and refitting

Note: *Refer to the warnings given in Section 1 of this Chapter before starting work.*

Check

1   A failure in the water pump can cause serious engine damage due to overheating.

2   There are three ways to check the operation of the water pump while it's installed on the engine. If the pump is defective, it should be replaced with a new or rebuilt unit.

3   With the engine running at normal operating temperature, squeeze the radiator top hose. If the water pump is working properly, a pressure surge should be felt as the hose is released. **Warning:** *Keep your hands away from the radiator electric cooling fan blades!*

4   Remove the timing belt covers (see Chapter 2, Part A). Water pumps are equipped with weep or vent holes. If a failure occurs in the pump seal, coolant will leak from the hole. In most cases you'll need an electric torch to find the hole on the water pump from underneath to check for leaks.

5   If the water pump shaft bearings fail, there may be a howling sound at the drivebelt end of the engine while it's running. Shaft wear can be felt if the water pump pulley is rocked up and down. Don't mistake drivebelt slippage, which causes a squealing sound, for water pump bearing failure.

Removal and refitting

6   Remove the timing belt and tensioner (see Chapter 2, Part A). As noted in Chapter 2, if the belt is fouled with coolant, it must be renewed as a matter of course.

7   Drain the cooling system (see Chapter 1).

8   Disconnect the radiator bottom hose from the pump union. It is easier to reach this union if the power steering pump is unbolted and moved aside as described in Chapter 10 **(see illustration)**. There is no need to disconnect any of the power steering system hoses.

9   Unbolt and remove the water pump **(see illustration)**. If the pump is to be renewed, unbolt the timing belt guide pulleys, and transfer them to the new pump.

10   Clean the mating surfaces carefully; the gasket must be renewed whenever it is disturbed **(see illustration)**.

11   On refitting, use grease to stick the new gasket in place, refit the pump, and tighten the pump bolts to the specified torque wrench setting.

12   The remainder of the reassembly procedure is the reverse of dismantling. Note that a new tensioner spring and retaining pin must be fitted if the timing belt has been removed for the first time. Tighten all fasteners to the specified torque wrench settings, and refill the system with coolant as described in Chapter 1.

9   Heater/ventilation components - removal and refitting

Heater blower motor

Removal

1   Disconnect the battery negative (earth) lead (see Chapter 5, Section 1).

2   Release the four clips (by pulling them out) securing the passenger side footwell upper trim panel, then withdraw the panel.

3   Unplug the motor's electrical connector.

4   Lift the motor's retaining lug slightly, twist the motor anti-clockwise (seen from beneath) through approximately 30°, then withdraw the assembly.

5   The motor's control resistor can be removed by sliding a slim screwdriver into the slot provided in one end. Press the screwdriver in approximately 5 mm against spring pressure, and prise the resistor out **(see illustration)**.

Refitting

6   Refitting is the reverse of the removal procedure. Refit the motor,

3

9.6 Ensure blower motor retaining lug (arrowed) engages securely in heater unit on reassembly

9.9A Coolant pipes to heater matrix must be disconnected . . .

9.9B . . . but can be reached best from beneath vehicle (arrowed)

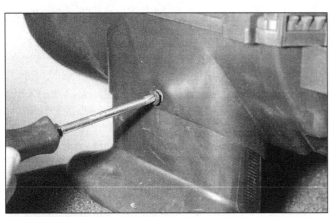

9.11 Remove screw to allow air duct to be retracted into air distributor at base of heater unit . . .

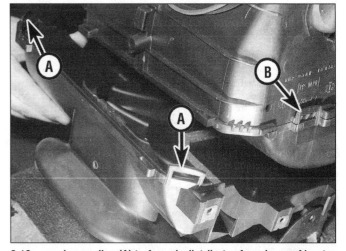

9.12 . . . release clips (A) to free air distributor from base of heater unit - note clips (B) securing . . .

and twist it clockwise until the retaining lug engages securely **(see illustration)**.

Heater matrix

Removal

7   Disconnect the battery negative (earth) lead (see Chapter 5, Section 1).

8   Drain the cooling system (see Chapter 1).

9   Disconnect the coolant hoses from the heater matrix unions protruding through the engine compartment bulkhead **(see illustrations)**.

10   Working inside the passenger compartment, remove the trim panels from each footwell, just in front of the centre console. Each panel is secured by two screws. If additional clearance is required, the centre console can be removed as well (see Chapter 11), but this is not essential.

11   Remove the single screw to release the air duct in the base of the heater unit **(see illustration)**.

12   Remove the three Torx-type screws (size T20) securing the air distributor to the heater unit bottom cover, then release the clips. There is a single plastic clip on each side, and additional metal clips may be found. Push the duct up to retract it, and withdraw the air distributor **(see illustration)**.

13   Release the clips - there are two plastic clips on each side, and additional metal clips may be found - then withdraw the heater unit's bottom cover, complete with the matrix **(see illustration)**.

14   Undo the screw and withdraw the clamp to separate the matrix from the bottom cover **(see illustration)**.

Refitting

15   Refitting is the reverse of the removal procedure. Additional metal

9.13 . . . heater unit's bottom cover, complete with matrix

clips may be required to secure the heater unit's bottom cover and the air distributor. Ensure that the duct is lowered from the air distributor and secured with its screw.

16   Refill the cooling system with the proper mixture of antifreeze and water (see Chapter 1). Start the engine and allow it to reach normal operating temperature, indicated by the radiator top hose becoming hot. Recheck the coolant level and add more if required, then check for leaks. Check the operation of the heater.

9.14 Remove clamp (one screw) to separate matrix from heater unit's bottom cover

10.4 Remove screws (arrowed) securing each end of heater control unit

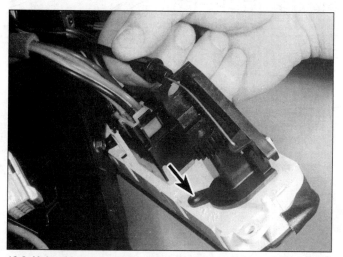

10.8 Unhooking operating cable from temperature control - note retaining screw (arrowed)

10.10 Unplugging electrical connectors from rear of heater control unit

3

Pollen filter
17   Refer to Chapter 1.

10 Heater/air conditioning controls - removal and refitting

Blower/air conditioning control
Removal
1   Disconnect the battery negative (earth) lead (see Chapter 5, Section 1).
2   Remove the ashtray. Referring to the relevant Sections of Chapter 11, undo the two upper screws from the centre console and pull out the cassette storage compartment, then remove the radio/cassette player.
3   Pull the heater control/radio bezel out of the three clips securing its top edge, pull it forwards and unplug the switch electrical connector (where fitted).
4   Pull off the heater control knobs, and remove the screw securing each end of the heater control unit **(see illustration)**. Pull the control unit out of the facia.
5   Unplug the two electrical connectors from the blower/air conditioning control. Remove the retaining screw and withdraw the control, twisting it to release it from the panel.

Refitting
6   Refitting is the reverse of the removal procedure. Check the operation of the control on completion.

Temperature control
Removal
7   Remove the heater control unit as described in paragraphs 1 to 4 above.
8   On vehicles without air conditioning, unhook the operating cable from the temperature control **(see illustration)**; where air conditioning is fitted, unplug the control's electrical connector. Undo the retaining screw, and withdraw the control.

Refitting
9   Refitting is the reverse of the removal procedure; check the operation of the control on completion.

Air distribution control
Removal
10   Remove the heater control unit as described in paragraphs 1 to 4 above. Unplug the electrical connectors, and unhook the operating cable (where fitted) to withdraw the unit **(see illustration)**.
11   Use a pair of slim screwdrivers to release the clips on each side of the control, then withdraw the control from the unit.

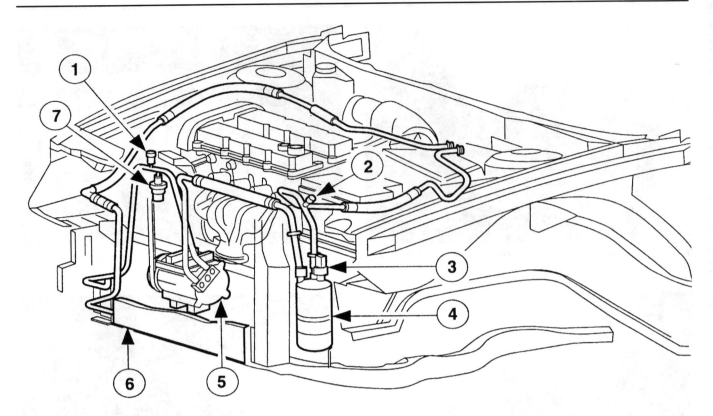

11.1 Air conditioning system components

1	Quick-release Schrader valve-type coupling - high-pressure side	4	Accumulator/dehydrator
2	Quick-release Schrader valve-type coupling - low-pressure side	5	Compressor
		6	Condenser
3	Pressure-cycling switch - low-pressure side	7	Pressure-regulating switch - high-pressure side

Refitting

12   Refitting is the reverse of the removal procedure. Check the operation of the controls on completion.

11 Air conditioning system - general information and precautions

General information

The air conditioning system consists of a condenser mounted in front of the radiator, an evaporator mounted adjacent to the heater matrix, a compressor mounted on the engine, an accumulator/dehydrator, and the plumbing connecting all of the above components - this contains a choke (or "venturi") mounted in the inlet to the evaporator, which creates the drop in pressure required to produce the cooling effect **(see illustration)**.

A blower fan forces the warmer air of the passenger compartment through the evaporator core (rather like a radiator in reverse), transferring the heat from the air to the refrigerant. The liquid refrigerant boils off into low-pressure vapour, taking the heat with it when it leaves the evaporator.

Precautions

Warning: *The air conditioning system is under high pressure. Do not loosen any fittings or remove any components until after the system has been discharged. Air conditioning refrigerant should be properly discharged into an approved type of container, at a dealer service department or an automotive air conditioning repair facility capable of handling R134a refrigerant. Always wear eye protection when discon-*

necting air conditioning system fittings.

When an air conditioning system is fitted, it is necessary to observe the following special precautions whenever dealing with any part of the system, its associated components, and any items which necessitate disconnection of the system:

(a) *While the refrigerant used - R134a - is less damaging to the environment than the previously-used R12, it is still a very dangerous substance. It must not be allowed into contact with the skin or eyes, or there is a risk of frostbite. It must also not be discharged in an enclosed space - while it is not toxic, there is a risk of suffocation. The refrigerant is heavier than air, and so must never be discharged over a pit.*

(b) *The refrigerant must not be allowed to come in contact with a naked flame, otherwise a poisonous gas will be created - under certain circumstances, this can form an explosive mixture with air. For similar reasons, smoking in the presence of refrigerant is highly dangerous, particularly if the vapour is inhaled through a lighted cigarette.*

(c) *Never discharge the system to the atmosphere - R134a is not an ozone-depleting ChloroFluoroCarbon (CFC) as is R12, but is instead a hydrofluorocarbon, which causes environmental damage by contributing to the "greenhouse effect" if released into the atmosphere.*

(d) *R134a refrigerant must **not** be mixed with R12; the system uses different seals (now green-coloured, previously black) and has different fittings requiring different tools, so that there is no chance of the two types of refrigerant becoming mixed accidentally.*

(e) *If for any reason the system must be disconnected, entrust this task to your Ford dealer or a refrigeration engineer.*

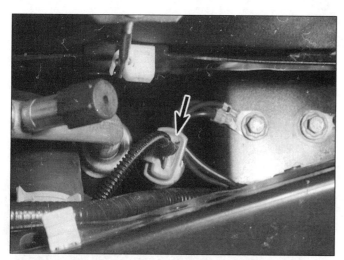

12.23 Unplug pressure-cycling switch electrical connector (arrowed)

12.33 Unplug pressure-regulating switch electrical connector (arrowed)

(f) *It is essential that the system be professionally discharged prior to using any form of heat - welding, soldering, brazing, etc - in the vicinity of the system, before having the vehicle oven-dried at a temperature exceeding 70°C after repainting, and before disconnecting any part of the system.*

12 Air conditioning system components - removal and refitting

Warning: *The air conditioning system is under high pressure. Do not loosen any fittings or remove any components until after the system has been discharged. Air conditioning refrigerant should be properly discharged into an approved type of container, at a dealer service department or an automotive air conditioning repair facility capable of handling R134a refrigerant. Cap or plug the pipe lines as soon as they are disconnected, to prevent the entry of moisture. Always wear eye protection when disconnecting air conditioning system fittings.*
Note: *This Section refers to the components of the air conditioning system itself - refer to Sections 9 and 10 for details of components common to the heating/ventilation system.*

Condenser

1 Have the refrigerant discharged at a dealer service department or an automotive air conditioning repair facility.
2 Disconnect the battery negative (earth) lead (see Chapter 5, Section 1).
3 Remove the radiator undershield (see Chapter 1).
4 Using the Ford service tool 34-001, disconnect the refrigerant lines from the condenser. Immediately cap the open fittings, to prevent the entry of dirt and moisture.
5 Unbolt the condenser (see illustration 7.5) and lift it out of the vehicle. Store it upright, to prevent oil loss.
6 Refitting is the reverse of removal.
7 If a new condenser was installed, add 20 cc of refrigerant oil to the system.
8 Have the system evacuated, charged and leak-tested by the specialist who discharged it.

Evaporator

9 The evaporator is mounted with the heater matrix. Apart from the need to have the refrigerant discharged, and to use Ford service tools 34-001 and 34-003 to disconnect the lines, the procedure is as described in Section 9 of this Chapter.
10 On reassembly, if a new evaporator was installed, add 20 cc of refrigerant oil to the system.

11 Have the system evacuated, charged and leak-tested by the specialist who discharged it.

Compressor

12 Have the refrigerant discharged at a dealer service department or an automotive air conditioning repair facility.
13 Disconnect the battery negative (earth) lead (see Chapter 5, Section 1).
14 Remove the radiator undershield (see Chapter 1).
15 Remove the auxiliary drivebelt (see Chapter 1).
16 Unbolt the compressor from the cylinder block/crankcase, press it to one side, and unscrew the clamping bolt to disconnect the refrigerant lines. Plug the line connections, swing the compressor upright, unplug its electrical connector, then withdraw the compressor from the vehicle. **Note:** *Keep the compressor level during handling and storage. If the compressor has seized, or if you find metal particles in the refrigerant lines, the system must be flushed out by an air conditioning technician, and the accumulator/dehydrator must be renewed.*
17 Prior to installation, turn the compressor clutch centre six times, to disperse any oil that has collected in the head.
18 Refit the compressor in the reverse order of removal; renew all seals disturbed.
19 If you are installing a new compressor, refer to the compressor manufacturer's instructions for adding refrigerant oil to the system.
20 Have the system evacuated, charged and leak-tested by the specialist that discharged it.

Accumulator/dehydrator

21 Have the refrigerant discharged at a dealer service department or an automotive air conditioning repair facility.
22 Disconnect the battery negative (earth) lead (see Chapter 5, Section 1).
23 The accumulator/dehydrator, which acts as a reservoir and filter for the refrigerant, is located in the left-hand front corner of the engine compartment. Using the Ford service tool 34-003, disconnect the refrigerant line next to the accumulator/dehydrator from the compressor. Immediately cap the open fittings, to prevent the entry of dirt and moisture, then unplug the pressure-cycling switch electrical connector **(see illustration)**.
24 Remove the radiator undershield (see Chapter 1).
25 Unbolt the accumulator/dehydrator from the front suspension subframe.
26 Using the Ford service tool 34-003, disconnect the lower refrigerant line from the accumulator/dehydrator. It may be necessary to unscrew the pressure-cycling switch to allow the use of the tool. Immediately cap the open fittings, to prevent the entry of dirt and moisture.
27 Withdraw the accumulator/dehydrator.
28 Refit the accumulator/dehydrator in the reverse order of removal;

3

renew all seals disturbed.

29   If you are installing a new accumulator/dehydrator, refer to the manufacturer's instructions for adding refrigerant oil to the system.

30   Have the system evacuated, charged and leak-tested by the specialist that discharged it.

Pressure-cycling and pressure-regulating switches

31   Have the refrigerant discharged at a dealer service department or an automotive air conditioning repair facility.

32   Disconnect the battery negative (earth) lead (see Chapter 5, Section 1).

33   Unplug the switch electrical connector, and unscrew it **(see illustration)**.

34   Refitting is the reverse of the removal procedure; there is no need to top-up the refrigerant oil.

35   Have the system evacuated, charged and leak-tested by the specialist that discharged it.

Chapter 4 Fuel and exhaust systems

Contents

4

Specifications

General

Idle speed:
    Regulated - nominal (± 50 rpm).. 830 to 880 rpm*
    Unregulated - base.. 1500 rpm*
Idle mixture (CO level).. Not available
Given for reference only - not adjustable.

Rev limiter operation

Fuel injectors shut off at:
    Automatic transmission, position "N" selected................................. 4100 rpm
    Automatic transmission, any other position selected .... 6800 rpm (approximately)
    Manual transmission .... 6800 to 7100 rpm

Fuel pressure

Regulated fuel pressure - engine running at idle speed:

Pressure regulator vacuum hose connected .... 2.1 ± 0.2 bars

Pressure regulator vacuum hose disconnected................................ 2.7 ± 0.2 bars

Note: *When the ignition is switched off, the system should hold 1.8 bars for 5 minutes. If the engine is hot, the pressure may rise to maximum of 2.7 bars during this check. Pressure regulator (when reconnected) should prevent any higher pressure being reached.*

Fuel injectors

Resistance .... 13.7 to 15.2 ohms

Idle speed control valve

Resistance .... 6 to 14 ohms

Idle-increase solenoid valve

Resistance .... 50 to 120 ohms

Torque wrench settings

	Nm	lbf ft
Plenum chamber-to-inlet manifold fasteners	4	3
Throttle housing-to-inlet manifold screws..	10	7
Idle speed control valve bolts...	6	4
Fuel pressure regulator bolts..	6	4
Fuel injector bolts	6	4
Fuel rail-to-inlet manifold bolts...	10	7
Fuel feed and return line threaded couplings at fuel rail	24 to 30	17 to 22
All exhaust system nuts and bolts...	40 to 45	30 to 33

---

1 General information and precautions

This Chapter is concerned with those features of the engine management system that supply clean fuel and air to the engine, meter it in the required proportions, and dispose of the results. Since the emission control sub-systems modify the functions of both the fuel and exhaust sub-systems, all of which are integral parts of the whole engine management system, there are many cross-references to Chapters 5 and 6. Information on the electronic control system, its fault diagnosis, sensors and actuators, is given in Chapter 6.

The air intake system consists of several plastics components designed to eliminate induction roar as much as possible. The air intake tube (opening behind the direction indicator/headlight assembly) is connected, via small and large resonators located under the front left-hand wing, to the air cleaner assembly in the engine compartment. Once it has passed through the filter element and the air mass meter, the air enters the plenum chamber mounted above the throttle housing and inlet manifold; the resonator mounted in the engine compartment further reduces noise levels.

The fuel system consists of a plastic tank (mounted under the body, beneath the rear seats), combined metal and plastic fuel hoses, an electric fuel pump mounted in the fuel tank, and an electronic fuel injection system.

The exhaust system consists of an exhaust manifold, the front downpipe and catalytic converter and, on production-fit systems, a rear section incorporating two or three silencers and the tailpipe assembly. The service replacement exhaust system consists of three or four sections: the front downpipe/catalytic converter, the intermediate pipe and front silencer, and the tailpipe and rear silencer. On some versions, the tailpipe is in two pieces, with two rear silencers. The system is suspended throughout its entire length by rubber mountings.

Extreme caution should be exercised when dealing with either the fuel or exhaust systems. Fuel is a primary element for combustion. Be very careful! The exhaust system is an area for exercising caution, as it operates at very high temperatures. Serious burns can result from even momentary contact with any part of the exhaust system, and the fire risk is ever-present. The catalytic converter in particular runs at very high temperatures - refer to the information in Chapter 6.

Warning: *Many of the procedures in this Chapter require the removal of fuel lines and connections, which may result in some fuel spillage. Petrol is extremely flammable, so take extra precautions when you work on any part of the fuel system. Don't smoke, or allow open flames or bare light bulbs, near the work area. Don't work in a garage where a nat-ural gas-type appliance (such as a water heater or clothes dryer) with a pilot light is present. If you spill any fuel on your skin, rinse it off immediately with soap and water. When you perform any kind of work on the fuel system, wear safety glasses, and have a Class B type fire extinguisher on hand. Before carrying out any operation on the fuel system, refer also to the precautions given in "Safety first!" at the beginning of this manual, and follow them implicitly. Petrol is a highly-dangerous and volatile liquid, and the precautions necessary when handling it cannot be overstressed.*

---

2 Fuel system - depressurisation

Warning: *The fuel system will remain pressurised for long periods of time after the engine is switched off - this pressure must be released before any part of the system is disturbed. Petrol is extremely flammable, so take extra precautions when you work on any part of the fuel system. Don't smoke, or allow open flames or bare light bulbs, near the work area. Don't work in a garage where a natural gas-type appliance (such as a water heater or clothes dryer) with a pilot light is present. If you spill any fuel on your skin, rinse it off immediately with soap and water. When you perform any kind of work on the fuel system, wear safety glasses, and have a Class B type fire extinguisher on hand.*

1   The fuel system referred to in this Chapter is defined as the fuel tank and tank-mounted fuel pump/fuel gauge sender unit, the fuel filter, the fuel injectors and the pressure regulator in the injector rail, and the metal pipes and flexible hoses of the fuel lines between these components. All these contain fuel, which will be under pressure while the engine is running and/or while the ignition is switched on.

2   The pressure will remain for some time after the ignition has been switched off, and must be relieved before any of these components is disturbed for servicing work.

3   The simplest method is simply to disconnect the fuel pump's electrical supply while the engine is running - either by removing the fuel pump fuse (number 14), or by lifting the red button on the fuel cut-off switch (see Section 13) - and to allow the engine to idle until it dies through lack of fuel pressure. Turn the engine over once or twice on the starter to ensure that all pressure is released, then switch off the ignition; do not forget to refit the fuse (or depress the red button, as appropriate) when work is complete.

4   The Ford method of depressurisation is to use service tool 29-033 fitted to the fuel rail pressure test/release fitting - a Schrader-type valve with a blue plastic cap, located on the union of the fuel feed line and the fuel rail - to release the pressure, using a suitable container and

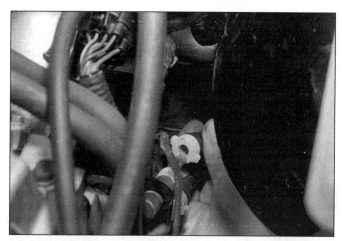

3.3 Disconnect fuel line quick-release couplings by squeezing together protruding locking lugs and pulling coupling apart

wads of rag to catch the spilt fuel. *Do not* simply depress the valve core to release fuel pressure - droplets of fuel will spray out, with a consequent risk of fire, and of personal injury through fuel getting into your eyes. **Warning:** *Either procedure will merely relieve the increased pressure necessary for the engine to run. Remember that fuel will still be present in the system components, and take precautions accordingly before disconnecting any of them.*

5   Note that, once the fuel system has been depressurised and drained (even partially), it will take significantly longer to restart the engine - perhaps several seconds of cranking - before the system is refilled and pressure restored.

---

3   Fuel lines and fittings - general information

Warning: *The fuel system pressure must be released before any part of the system is disturbed - see Section 2. Petrol is extremely flammable, so take extra precautions when you work on any part of the fuel system. Don't smoke, or allow open flames or bare light bulbs, near the work area. Don't work in a garage where a natural gas-type appliance (such as a water heater or clothes dryer) with a pilot light is present. If you spill any fuel on your skin, rinse it off immediately with soap and water. When you perform any kind of work on the fuel system, wear safety glasses, and have a Class B type fire extinguisher on hand.*

Disconnecting and connecting quick-release couplings

1   Quick-release couplings are employed at all unions in the fuel feed and return lines.
2   Before disconnecting any fuel system component, relieve the residual pressure in the system (see Section 2), and equalise tank

pressure by removing the fuel filler cap. **Warning:** *This procedure will merely relieve the increased pressure necessary for the engine to run - remember that fuel will still be present in the system components, and take precautions accordingly before disconnecting any of them.*
3   Release the protruding locking lugs on each union, by squeezing them together and carefully pulling the coupling apart. Use rag to soak up any spilt fuel. Where the unions are colour-coded, the pipes cannot be confused. Where both unions are the same colour, note carefully which pipe is connected to which, and ensure that they are correctly reconnected on refitting **(see illustration)**.
4   To reconnect one of these couplings, press them together until the locking lugs snap into their groove. Switch the ignition on and off five times to pressurise the system, and check for any sign of fuel leakage around the disturbed coupling before attempting to start the engine.

Checking
5   Checking procedures for the fuel lines are included in Chapter 1.

Component renewal
6   If you must renew any damaged sections, use original-equipment replacement hoses or pipes, constructed from exactly the same material as the section you are replacing. Do not install substitutes constructed from inferior or inappropriate material, or you could cause a fuel leak or a fire.
7   Before detaching or disconnecting any part of the fuel system, note the routing of all hoses and pipes, and the orientation of all clamps and clips. Replacement sections must be installed in exactly the same manner.
8   Before disconnecting any part of the fuel system, be sure to relieve the fuel system pressure (see Section 2), and equalise tank pressure by removing the fuel filler cap. Also disconnect the battery negative (earth) lead - see Chapter 5, Section 1. Cover the fitting being disconnected with a rag, to absorb any fuel that may spray out.

---

4   Air cleaner assembly and air intake components - removal and refitting

Air cleaner assembly
1   Disconnect the battery negative (earth) lead - see Chapter 5, Section 1.
2   Unclip the air mass meter from the air cleaner cover (see Chapter 6).
3   Disconnect the crankcase breather hose, either from the air cleaner housing or from the cylinder head cover union **(see illustration)**.
4   Remove the rubber retaining band **(see illustration)**. Withdraw the air cleaner assembly, lifting it upwards out of its grommets, and releasing it from the rubber connector sleeve in the inner wing panel.
5   Refitting is the reverse of the removal procedure. Ensure that the housing pegs seat correctly in their grommets, and that the intake mouth is fully engaged inside the connector sleeve **(see illustration)**.

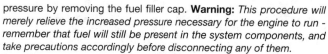

4

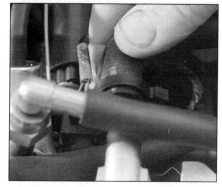

4.3 Disconnecting the crankcase breather hose from the cylinder head union

4.4 Remove rubber retaining band to withdraw air cleaner assembly

4.5 Ensure air filter housing intake mouth is fully engaged inside connector sleeve

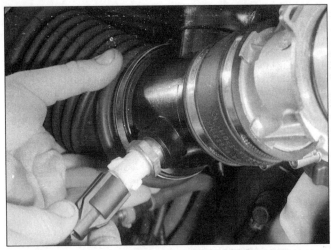

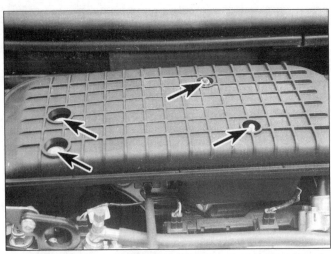

4.7 Unplugging intake air temperature sensor's electrical connector

4.9 Plenum chamber fasteners (arrowed) - four shown here, some vehicles may only have three

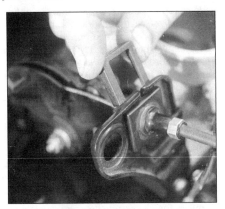

4.10A Lift plenum chamber and (where fitted) disconnect the vacuum hose - note the two rubber spacers (arrowed) . . .

4.10B . . . and the sealing O-ring (arrowed) in the chamber's mouth

5.3 Removing clip securing accelerator cable to throttle housing bracket

Air intake components

Note: *Depending on the reason for removal, these components can be removed either individually, or as one assembly. For example, unplugging the two electrical connectors and disconnecting the vacuum hose (where fitted), will allow the air cleaner assembly cover to be removed with the air mass meter, the resonator and the plenum chamber.*

Air mass meter

6   Refer to Section 4 of Chapter 6.

Resonator (engine compartment)

7   Unbolt the resonator support bracket from the engine compartment front crossmember. Slacken the two clamp screws securing the resonator to the air mass meter and plenum chamber hoses. Swing the resonator clear of the thermostat housing, and unplug the intake air temperature sensor's electrical connector **(see illustration)**. Withdraw the resonator.

8   Refitting is the reverse of the removal procedure.

Plenum chamber

9   Prising out the rubber plugs covering them, undo the chamber's fasteners **(see illustration)**. Slacken the clamp screw securing the chamber to the resonator hose.

10   Lift the chamber and (where fitted) disconnect the vacuum hose from its underside. Withdraw the chamber - note the two rubber spacers (one on each throttle housing stud) and the sealing O-ring in the chamber's mouth **(see illustrations)**.

11   Refitting is the reverse of the removal procedure. Ensure that the O-ring and spacers are correctly seated.

Underwing components

12   Remove the left-hand wheel arch liner (see Chapter 11).

13   Unbolt and withdraw the air intake tube and both resonators as required.

14   Refitting is the reverse of the removal procedure.

5   Accelerator cable (models without traction control) - removal, refitting and adjustment

Removal

1   Disconnect the battery negative (earth) lead - see Chapter 5, Section 1.

2   Remove the plenum chamber (see Section 4).

3   Remove the clip securing the cable to the throttle housing bracket **(see illustration)**. Disconnect the cable end nipple from the throttle linkage, and release the cable from any securing clips or ties.

4   Working in the passenger compartment, reach up to the top of the accelerator pedal. Pull the end fitting and collar out of the pedal, then release the cable inner wire through the slot in the pedal **(see illustration)**. Tie a length of string to the end of the cable.

5   Returning to the engine compartment, pull the cable through the bulkhead until the string can be untied and the cable removed.

Refitting

6   Refitting is the reverse of the removal procedure; use the string to draw the cable through the bulkhead.

7   Adjust the cable as described below.

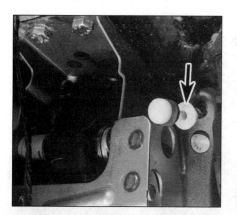

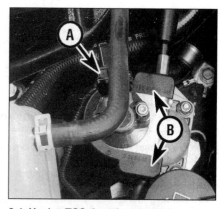

5.4 Pull the accelerator cable end fitting (arrowed) out of the pedal

5.9 Location of accelerator cable adjuster - remove metal clip (arrowed) to enable adjustment to be made

6.4 Unplug TCS throttle actuator's electrical connector (A), and prise off its cover at two points (B)

1   Disconnect the battery negative (earth) lead - see Chapter 5, Section 1.
2   Remove the plenum chamber (see Section 4).
3   Remove the clip securing the cable to the throttle housing bracket, then pull the cable's grommet out of the bracket. Disconnect the cable end nipple from the throttle linkage, and release the cable from any securing clips or ties.
4   Unplug the TCS throttle actuator's electrical connector, and prise off its cover (see illustration).
5   Noting which cable section is connected to which pulley, disconnect the first cable end nipple from the throttle actuator's upper pulley, then slide the cable outer upwards out of the actuator housing. Disconnect the second cable in the same way from the actuator's lower pulley.
6   Working in the passenger compartment, reach up to the top of the accelerator pedal. Pull the end fitting and collar out of the pedal, then release the cable inner wire through the slot in the pedal. Tie a length of string to the end of the cable.
7   Returning to the engine compartment, pull the cable through the bulkhead until the string can be untied and the pedal-to-actuator cable removed.

6.11 Location of TCS throttle actuator-to-throttle housing cable adjuster (arrowed)

Refitting

8   Refitting is the reverse of the removal procedure. Use the string to draw the pedal-to-actuator cable through the bulkhead. Ensure that each cable end is connected to the correct actuator pulley.
9   Adjust both cables as described below.

Adjustment

Note: *Both sections of the cable must be adjusted together, even if only one has been disturbed.*
10 Remove the plenum chamber (see Section 4).
11 Remove the metal clip from the adjuster of each cable section (see illustration), and lubricate the adjusters' grommets with soapy water.
12 Remove any slack by pulling both cable outers as far as possible out of their respective adjusters.
13 Unplug the TCS throttle actuator's electrical connector, and prise off its cover. Lock both pulleys together by pushing a locking pin (a pin punch or a similar tool of suitable size) into their alignment holes. Disconnect the actuator-to-throttle housing cable's end nipple from the throttle linkage.
14 Have an assistant depress the accelerator pedal fully. The pedal-to-actuator cable outer will move back into the adjuster; hold it there, and refit the clip.
15 Connect the actuator-to-throttle housing cable end nipple to the throttle linkage, and check that the cable outer's grommet is correctly secured in the housing bracket.
16 Again have the assistant depress the accelerator pedal fully. The actuator-to-throttle housing cable outer will move back into the adjuster; hold it there, and refit the clip.

Adjustment

8   Remove the plenum chamber (see Section 4).
9   Find the cable adjuster - this is either at the throttle housing bracket, or two-thirds along the length of the cable, clipped to the front suspension right-hand mounting (see illustration). Remove the metal clip and lubricate the adjuster's grommet with soapy water.
10 Remove any slack by pulling the cable outer as far as possible out of the adjuster. Have an assistant depress the accelerator pedal fully - the cable outer will move back into the adjuster - and hold it there while the clip is refitted.
11 Check that the throttle valve moves smoothly and easily from the fully-closed to the fully-open position and back again, as the assistant depresses and releases the accelerator pedal. Re-adjust the cable if required.
12 When the setting is correct, refit the plenum chamber (see Section 4).

6 Accelerator cable (models with traction control) - removal, refitting and adjustment

Removal

Note: *While the following procedure deals with the complete cable, the pedal-to-actuator and actuator-to-throttle housing sections of the cable are available separately, and can be removed and refitted individually. If doing this, modify the procedure as required.*

17   Remove the locking pin from the pulleys. Check that the throttle valve moves smoothly and easily from the fully-closed to the fully-open position and back again, as the assistant depresses and releases the accelerator pedal. Re-adjust the cable(s) if required.

18   When the setting is correct, refit the TCS throttle actuator's cover and electrical connector, then refit the plenum chamber (see Section 4).

7   Accelerator pedal - removal and refitting

1   Disconnect the cable inner wire from the pedal - see Section 5 or 6, as appropriate.

2   Undo the retaining nuts and bolt, then withdraw the pedal assembly **(see illustration)**.

3   Refitting is the reverse of the removal procedure. Adjust the cable(s) as described in the relevant Section of this Chapter.

8   Fuel pump/fuel pressure - check

Warning: *Petrol is extremely flammable, so take extra precautions when you work on any part of the fuel system. Don't smoke, or allow open flames or bare light bulbs, near the work area. Don't work in a garage where a natural gas-type appliance (such as a water heater or clothes dryer) with a pilot light is present. If you spill any fuel on your skin, rinse it off immediately with soap and water. When you perform any kind of work on the fuel system, wear safety glasses, and have a Class B type fire extinguisher on hand.*

Fuel pump operation check

1   Switch on the ignition and listen for the fuel pump (the sound of an electric motor running, audible from beneath the rear seats). Assuming there is sufficient fuel in the tank, the pump should start and run for approximately one or two seconds, then stop, each time the ignition is switched on. **Note:** *If the pump runs continuously all the time the ignition is switched on, the electronic control system is running in the backup (or "limp-home") mode referred to by Ford as "Limited Operation Strategy" (LOS). This almost certainly indicates a fault in the ECU itself, and the vehicle should therefore be taken to a Ford dealer for a full test of the complete system, using the correct diagnostic equipment; do not waste time trying to test the system without such facilities.*

2   Listen for fuel return noises from the fuel pressure regulator. It should be possible to feel the fuel pulsing in the regulator and in the feed hose from the fuel filter.

3   If the pump does not run at all, check the fuse, relay and wiring (see Chapter 6).

Fuel pressure check

3   A fuel pressure gauge, equipped with an adaptor to suit the

7.2 Removing the accelerator pedal assembly

Schrader-type valve on the fuel rail pressure test/release fitting (identifiable by its blue plastic cap, and located on the union of the fuel feed line and the fuel rail) is required for the following procedure. If the Ford special tool 29-033 is available (see Section 2), the tool can be attached to the valve, and a conventional-type pressure gauge attached to the tool.

4   If using the service tool, ensure that its tap is turned fully anti-clockwise, then attach it to the valve. Connect the pressure gauge to the service tool. If using a fuel pressure gauge with its own adaptor, connect it in accordance with its maker's instructions **(see illustration)**.

5   Start the engine and allow it to idle. Note the gauge reading as soon as the pressure stabilises, and compare it with the pressure listed in this Chapter's Specifications.

(a)   *If the pressure is high, check for a restricted fuel return line. If the line is clear, renew the pressure regulator.*

(b)   *If the pressure is low, pinch the fuel return line. If the pressure now goes up, renew the fuel pressure regulator. If the pressure does not increase, check the fuel feed line, the fuel pump and the fuel filter.*

6   Detach the vacuum hose from the fuel pressure regulator; the pressure shown on the gauge should increase. Note the increase in pressure, and compare it with that listed in this Chapter's Specifications. If the pressure increase is not as specified, check the vacuum hose and pressure regulator.

7   Reconnect the regulator vacuum hose, and switch off the engine. Verify that the fuel pressure stays at the specified level for five minutes after the engine is turned off.

8   Carefully disconnect the fuel pressure gauge. Be sure to cover the

8.4 A fuel pressure gauge, equipped with an adaptor to suit the Schrader-type valve on the fuel rail pressure test/release fitting, is needed to check fuel pressure

9.4 Unplugging the fuel pump/fuel gauge sender unit electrical connector (arrowed)

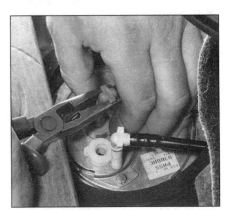

9.5 If fuel couplings are difficult to release, use pliers and a block of wood as shown to prise pipe end out of union - be careful not to damage pipes or unions

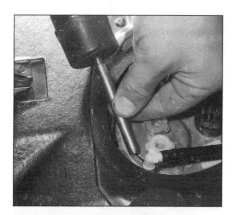

9.6 Fuel pump/fuel gauge sender unit's retaining ring can be released using ordinary tools as shown. Correct service tool will probably be required on refitting

9.7A Removing fuel pump/fuel gauge sender unit - take care not to bend float arm, and note how it is fitted on spring-loaded extension

9.7B Fuel pump/fuel gauge sender unit's sealing ring must be renewed whenever it is disturbed

fitting with a rag before slackening it. Mop up any spilt petrol.
9   Run the engine, and check that there are no fuel leaks.

9 Fuel pump/fuel gauge sender unit - removal and refitting

Warning: *Petrol is extremely flammable, so take extra precautions when you work on any part of the fuel system. Don't smoke, or allow open flames or bare light bulbs, near the work area. Don't work in a garage where a natural gas-type appliance (such as a water heater or clothes dryer) with a pilot light is present. If you spill any fuel on your skin, rinse it off immediately with soap and water. When you perform any kind of work on the fuel system, wear safety glasses, and have a Class B type fire extinguisher on hand.*

Note: *Ford specify the use of their service tool 23-038 (a large box spanner with projecting teeth to engage the fuel pump/sender unit retaining ring's slots) for this task. While alternatives are possible, as shown below, in view of the difficulty experienced in removing and refitting the pump/sender unit, owners are strongly advised to obtain this tool before starting work. The help of an assistant will be required.*

1   Relieve the residual pressure in the fuel system (see Section 2), and equalise tank pressure by removing the fuel filler cap. **Warning:** *This procedure will merely relieve the increased pressure necessary for the engine to run - remember that fuel will still be present in the system components, and take precautions accordingly before disconnecting any of them.*

2   Disconnect the battery negative (earth) lead - see Chapter 5, Section 1.

3   Unbolt or fold forwards (as appropriate) the rear seat base cushion (see Chapter 11). Withdraw from the vehicle's floor the grommet covering the fuel pump/sender unit. Wash off any dirt from the tank's top surface, and dry it; use a vacuum cleaner to clean the immediate surroundings of the vehicle's interior, to reduce the risk of introducing water, dirt and dust into the tank while it is open.

4   Unplug the fuel pump/sender unit's electrical connector **(see illustration)**.

5   To disconnect the fuel feed and return pipes from the unit, release each pipe's coupling, by squeezing together the protruding locking lugs on each union and carefully pulling the coupling apart. Use rag to soak up any spilt fuel. Where the couplings are difficult to separate, use a pair of pliers and a block of wood as shown, to lever the pipe out of the union. Considerable force may be required, but be as careful as possible to avoid damaging any of the components **(see illustration)**.

6   Release the fuel pump/sender unit's retaining ring by turning it anti-clockwise. As noted above, Ford recommend the use of service tool 23-038. For those without access to such equipment, a hammer and drift, or a pair of slip-jointed pliers, will serve as an adequate substitute - at least for removal **(see illustration)**.

7   Withdraw the fuel pump/fuel gauge sender unit, taking care not to bend the float arm. The float arm is mounted on a spring-loaded extension, to hold it closely against the bottom of the tank. Note the sealing ring; this must be renewed whenever it is disturbed **(see illustrations)**.

8   On refitting, use a new sealing ring, and ensure that the gauze filter over the base of the pump pick-up is clean.

9   Align the pump/sender unit with the tank opening, and refit it, ensuring that the float arm is not bent. Insert the unit so that the float arm slides correctly up the extension, until the unit's top mounting plate can be aligned with the tank opening and pressed onto the sealing ring. This may require a considerable amount of pressure; if so, be careful to avoid damaging any of the components. The Ford service tool provides the best way of holding the ring square to the tank and turning it at the same time.

10   Maintain the pressure while an assistant refits and engages the retaining ring. When the ring is engaged in the tank lugs, turn it clockwise to tighten it until it is secured.

11   The remainder of the refitting procedure is the reverse of removal. Observe the colour-coding to ensure that the fuel pipes are reconnected to the correct unions.

10 Fuel tank - removal and refitting

Warning: *The fuel system pressure must be released before any part of the system is disturbed - see Section 2. Petrol is extremely flammable, so take extra precautions when you work on any part of the fuel system. Don't smoke, or allow open flames or bare light bulbs, near the work area. Don't work in a garage where a natural gas-type appliance (such as a water heater or clothes dryer) with a pilot light is present. If you spill any fuel on your skin, rinse it off immediately with soap and water. When you perform any kind of work on the fuel system, wear safety glasses, and have a Class B type fire extinguisher on hand.*

1   A fuel tank drain plug is not provided; it is therefore preferable to carry out the removal operation when the tank is nearly empty. Before proceeding, disconnect the battery negative (earth) lead, and syphon or hand-pump the remaining fuel from the tank. Alternatively, disconnect the feed pipe from the fuel filter (see Chapter 1), and connect a spare length of hose to this so that when the ignition is switched on, the fuel pump will empty the tank into a clean container. If this approach is adopted, ensure that the container is large enough to take all the fuel in the tank, and be careful to take all suitable precautions to prevent the risk of fire. **Note:** *Before disconnecting or opening any part of the fuel system, relieve the residual pressure (see Section 2), and equalise tank pressure by removing the fuel filler cap. Also disconnect the battery negative (earth) lead - see Chapter 5, Section 1.*

2   Unbolt or fold forwards (as appropriate) the rear seat base cushion (see Chapter 11). Withdraw from the vehicle's floor the grommet covering the fuel pump/sender unit. Unplug the fuel pump/sender

4

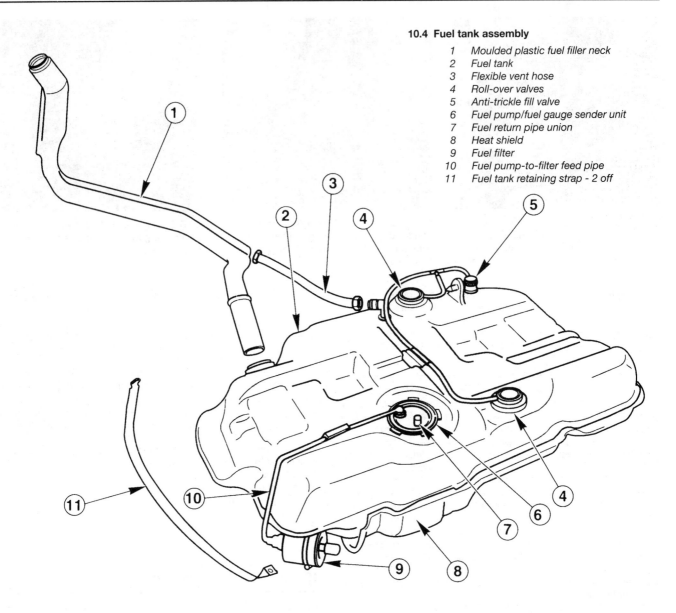

10.4 Fuel tank assembly

1	Moulded plastic fuel filler neck
2	Fuel tank
3	Flexible vent hose
4	Roll-over valves
5	Anti-trickle fill valve
6	Fuel pump/fuel gauge sender unit
7	Fuel return pipe union
8	Heat shield
9	Fuel filter
10	Fuel pump-to-filter feed pipe
11	Fuel tank retaining strap - 2 off

unit's electrical connector, and disconnect the fuel return pipe (coded red) from the unit (see Section 9).

3   Raise the rear of the vehicle, and support it securely on axle stands. Get underneath and familiarise yourself with the layout of the fuel tank assembly before proceeding **(see illustration)**. **Warning:** *Do not place any part of your body under a vehicle when it's supported only by a jack!*

4   Either remove the fuel filter, or disconnect its outlet pipe (see Chapter 1).

5   Unhook the exhaust system rubber mountings. Lower the system onto a suitable support, so that the front downpipe-to-exhaust manifold joint is not strained, or remove it completely (see Section 17).

6   Unbolt the rear suspension anti-roll bar mounting clamps **(see illustration)**. Swing the bar down as far as possible - if clearance is very restricted, it is advisable to remove the bar completely (see Chapter 10).

7   Disconnect the flexible vent hose from the moulded plastic fuel tank filler neck as follows:

(a)   *On Saloon and Hatchback models, reach up into the right-hand side aperture in the rear suspension crossmember, slacken the clamp, and work the hose off the filler neck stub. This is a job for someone with small hands, good tools and a lot of patience!* **(see illustration)**.

(b)   *On Estate models, slacken the clamp immediately above the*

rear anti-roll bar, and work the hose off the filler neck stub **(see illustration)**.

8   Unscrew the six retaining nuts, and withdraw the exhaust system's rear heat shield from the underbody **(see illustration)**.

9   Support the tank with a trolley jack or similar. Place a sturdy plank between the support and the tank, to protect the tank.

10   Unscrew the bolt at the front of each retaining strap, and pivot them down until they are hanging out of the way. Note the earth lead under the left-hand strap's bolt - clean the mating surfaces before the tank is refitted, so that clean, metal-to-metal contact is ensured.

11   Lower the tank enough to unclip the fuel return pipe (coded red) from its top surface, then disconnect the charcoal canister's vapour hose from the union at the top rear of the tank **(see illustration)**. If you have any doubts, clearly label the fuel lines and hoses, and their respective unions. Plug the hoses, to prevent leakage and contamination of the fuel system.

12   Remove the tank from the vehicle, releasing it from the filler neck stub. While the tank is removed, unhook the retaining straps (twist them through 90° to do so), and check that they and their locations in the underbody are in good condition.

13   With the fuel tank removed, the filler neck can be withdrawn. It is secured by a single screw in the filler opening, and by two bolts to the underbody.

14   Refitting is the reverse of the removal procedure.

10.6 Unbolt rear anti-roll bar mounting clamps (one arrowed) when preparing to remove the fuel tank

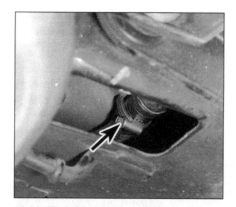

10.7A Fuel filler vent hose clamp (arrowed) is accessible through right-hand side aperture in rear suspension crossmember on Saloon and Hatchback models ...

10.7B ... on Estate models, it is immediately above rear suspension anti-roll bar

10.8 Exhaust system must be lowered and heat shield removed to enable fuel tank removal - arrow shows location of retaining strap front bolt

10.11 Lower fuel tank - do not distort filler neck stub (A) - and unclip (red-coded) fuel return pipe (B), then disconnect charcoal canister's vapour hose (C)

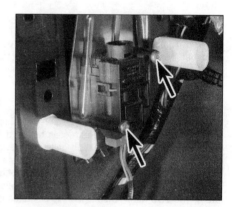

13.3 Fuel cut-off switch retaining screws (arrowed)

11 Fuel tank cleaning and repair - general information

Warning: *Petrol is extremely flammable, so take extra precautions when you work on any part of the fuel system. Don't smoke, or allow open flames or bare light bulbs, near the work area. Don't work in a garage where a natural gas-type appliance (such as a water heater or clothes dryer) with a pilot light is present. If you spill any fuel on your skin, rinse it off immediately with soap and water. When you perform any kind of work on the fuel system, wear safety glasses, and have a Class B type fire extinguisher on hand.*

1   Any repairs to the fuel tank or filler neck should be carried out by a professional who has experience in this critical and potentially-dangerous work. Even after cleaning and flushing of the fuel system, explosive fumes can remain and ignite during repair of the tank.

2   If the fuel tank is removed from the vehicle, it should not be placed in an area where sparks or open flames could ignite the fumes coming out of the tank. Be especially careful inside garages where a natural gas-type appliance is located, because the pilot light could cause an explosion.

12 Roll-over valves - removal and refitting

Warning: *The fuel system pressure must be released before any part of the system is disturbed - see Section 2. Petrol is extremely flammable, so take extra precautions when you work on any part of the fuel system. Don't smoke, or allow open flames or bare light bulbs, near the work*

area. Don't work in a garage where a natural gas-type appliance (such as a water heater or clothes dryer) with a pilot light is present. If you spill any fuel on your skin, rinse it off immediately with soap and water. When you perform any kind of work on the fuel system, wear safety glasses, and have a Class B type fire extinguisher on hand.*

Note: *Refer to illustrations 10.4 and 10.11 for details.*

1   Remove the fuel tank (see Section 10).

2   Prise the two valves out of the tank, and remove the anti-trickle fill valve from its mounting. Take care not to damage the valves or the tank. Prise out the rubber seals from the tank openings, and renew then if they are worn, distorted, or if either has been leaking.

3   If either valve is thought to be faulty, seek the advice of a Ford dealer as to whether they can be renewed individually. If not, the complete valve and pipe assembly must be renewed.

4   Refitting is the reverse of the removal procedure. Ensure that both roll-over valves are pressed securely into their seals, so that there can be no fuel leaks.

13 Fuel cut-off switch - removal and refitting

1   Disconnect the battery negative (earth) lead - see Chapter 5, Section 1.

2   Remove the trim panel from the left-hand footwell.

3   Peel back the sound-insulating material from the switch, and undo its two retaining screws **(see illustration)**.

4   Unplug the switch electrical connector, and withdraw the switch.

5   Refitting is the reverse of the removal procedure. Ensure that the switch is reset by depressing its red button.

14 Fuel injection system/engine management system - general information

These models are equipped with a Sequential Electronically-controlled Fuel Injection (SEFI) system. The system is composed of three basic sub-systems: fuel system, air induction system and electronic control system. **Note:** *Refer to illustrations 2.1A and 2.1B of Chapter 6 for further information on the components of the system.*

Fuel system

An electric fuel pump located inside the fuel tank supplies fuel under pressure to the fuel rail, which distributes fuel evenly to all injectors. A filter between the fuel pump and the fuel rail protects the components of the system. A pressure regulator controls the system pressure in relation to inlet tract depression. From the fuel rail, fuel is injected into the inlet ports, just above the inlet valves, by four fuel injectors. The system also includes features such as the flushing of fresh (ie, cold) fuel around each injector on start-up, thus improving hot starts.

The amount of fuel supplied by the injectors is precisely controlled by an Electronic Control Unit (ECU). The ECU uses the signals derived from the engine speed/crankshaft position sensor and the camshaft position sensor, to trigger each injector separately in cylinder firing order (sequential injection), with benefits in terms of better fuel economy and lower exhaust emissions.

Air induction system

The air system consists of an air filter housing, an air mass meter, an intake resonator and plenum chamber, and a throttle housing. The air mass meter is an information-gathering device for the ECU; it uses a "hot-wire" system to send the ECU a constantly-varying (analogue) voltage signal corresponding to the volume of air passing into the engine. Another sensor in the air mass meter measures intake air temperature. The ECU uses these signals to calculate the mass of air entering the engine.

The throttle valve inside the throttle housing is controlled by the driver, through the accelerator pedal. As the valve opens, the amount of air that can pass through the system increases. The throttle potentiometer opens further, the air mass meter's signal alters, and the ECU opens each injector for a longer duration, to increase the amount of fuel delivered to the inlet ports.

Electronic control system

The ECU controls the fuel injection system, as well as the other sub-systems which make up the entire engine management system. It receives signals from a number of information sensors, which monitor such variables as intake air mass and temperature, coolant temperature, engine speed and position, acceleration/deceleration, and exhaust gas oxygen content. These signals help the ECU determine the injection duration necessary for the optimum air/fuel ratio. These sensors and associated ECU-controlled relays are located throughout the engine compartment. For further information regarding the ECU and its control of the engine management system, see Chapter 6.

Idle speed and mixture adjustment - general

Both the idle speed and mixture are under the control of the ECU, and cannot be adjusted. Not only can they not be adjusted, they cannot even be checked, except with the use of special diagnostic equipment (see Chapter 6) - this makes it a task for a Ford dealer service department. *Do not* attempt to "adjust" these settings in any way without such equipment.

If the idle speed and mixture are thought to be incorrect, take the vehicle to a Ford dealer for the complete system to be tested.

On models equipped with a heated windscreen, an idle-increase solenoid valve is fitted, which raises the idle speed to compensate for the increased load on the engine when the heated windscreen is switched on. When the valve is open, air from the plenum chamber bypasses the throttle housing and idle speed control valve, passing directly into the inlet manifold through the union on its left-hand end. The system is active only for the four minutes that the heated windscreen circuit is live, and is supplementary to the main (ECU-controlled) idle speed regulation.

15 Fuel injection system/engine management system - check

Warning: *Petrol is extremely flammable, so extra precautions must be taken when working on any part of the fuel system. Do not smoke, or allow open flames or bare light bulbs, near the work area. Don't work in a garage if a natural gas-type appliance with a pilot light is present. While performing any work on the fuel system, wear safety glasses, and have a dry chemical (Class B) fire extinguisher on hand. If you spill any fuel on your skin, rinse it off immediately with soap and water.*
Note: *This is an initial check of the fuel delivery and air induction sub-systems of the engine management system, to be carried out in conjunction with the operational check of the fuel pump (see Section 8), and as part of the preliminary checks of the complete engine management system (see Section 3 of Chapter 6).*

1   Check the earth wire connections for tightness. Check all wiring and electrical connectors that are related to the system. Loose electrical connectors and poor earths can cause many problems that resemble more serious malfunctions.
2   Check to see that the battery is fully-charged. The ECU and sensors depend on an accurate supply voltage to properly meter the fuel.
3   Check the air filter element - a dirty or partially-blocked filter will severely impede performance and economy (see Chapter 1).
4   If a blown fuse is found, renew it and see if it blows again. If it does, search for a short-circuited wire in the harness related to the system (see Chapter 6).
5   Check the air intake duct from the intake to the inlet manifold for leaks, which will result in an excessively-lean mixture. Also check the condition of the vacuum hoses connected to the inlet manifold.
6   Remove the plenum chamber from the throttle housing. Check the throttle valve for dirt, carbon or other residue build-up. If it's dirty, seek the advice of a Ford dealer - since the electronic control system is designed to compensate for factors such as the build-up of dirt in the throttle housing, it may well be best to leave it dirty, unless the deposits are extensive. **Note:** *A warning label on the housing states specifically that the housing bore and the throttle valve have a special coating, and must **not** be cleaned using carburettor cleaner, as this may damage it.*
7   With the engine running, place a screwdriver or a stethoscope against each injector, one at a time. Listen through the screwdriver handle or stethoscope for a clicking sound, indicating operation.
8   If an injector isn't operating (or sounds different from the others), turn off the engine, and unplug the electrical connector from the injector. Check the resistance across the terminals of the injector, and compare your reading with the resistance value listed in this Chapter's Specifications. If the resistance isn't as specified, renew the injector.
9   A rough idle, diminished performance and/or increased fuel consumption could also be caused by clogged or fouled fuel injectors. Fuel additives that can sometimes clean fouled injectors are available at car accessory shops.
10   The remainder of the system checks should be left to a dealer service department or other qualified repair specialist, as there is a chance that the ECU may be damaged if tests are not performed properly.

16 Fuel system components - check and renewal

Warning: *The fuel system pressure must be released before any part of the system is disturbed - see Section 2. Petrol is extremely flammable, so take extra precautions when you work on any part of the fuel system. Don't smoke, or allow open flames or bare light bulbs, near the work area. Don't work in a garage where a natural gas-type appliance (such as a water heater or clothes dryer) with a pilot light is present. If you spill any fuel on your skin, rinse it off immediately with soap and water.*

16.8 Undo screws (arrowed) to remove throttle housing

16.12A Fuel injectors can be unbolted (arrowed) . . .

16.12B . . . and removed individually if required, but it is better to remove them with the fuel rail, if servicing is necessary. O-ring seals (arrowed) must be renewed whenever injector is removed

When you perform any kind of work on the fuel system, wear safety glasses, and have a Class B type fire extinguisher on hand.

Throttle housing

Check

1   Remove the plenum chamber (see Section 4), and verify that the throttle linkage operates smoothly.
2   If the housing bore and valve are dirty enough for you to think that this might be the cause of a fault, seek the advice of a Ford dealer. *Do not* clean the housing (see the notes in the checking procedure given in Section 15).

Renewal

3   Disconnect the battery negative (earth) lead - see Chapter 5, Section 1.
4   Remove the plenum chamber (see Section 4).
5   Disconnect the accelerator cable from the throttle linkage (see Section 5 or 6, as appropriate). Where fitted, also disconnect the cruise control actuator cable (see Chapter 12).
6   Releasing its wire clip, unplug the large electrical connector (next to the fuel pressure regulator). Similarly release and unplug the throttle potentiometer's electrical connector.
7   Clearly label, then detach, all vacuum hoses from the throttle housing.
8   Remove the throttle housing mounting screws **(see illustration)**, then detach the throttle housing and gasket from the inlet manifold. Discard the gasket - this must be renewed whenever it is disturbed.
9   Using a soft brush and carburettor cleaner, thoroughly clean the exterior of the throttle housing, then blow out all passages with compressed air. **Caution:** *Do not clean the throttle housing's bore, the throttle valve, or the potentiometer, either by scraping or with a solvent. Just wipe them over carefully with a clean soft cloth.*
10   Refitting is the reverse of the removal procedure. Fit a new gasket, and tighten the housing screws to the specified torque.

Fuel rail and injectors

Check

11   Refer to the procedure in the fuel system check (see Section 15).

Renewal

Note: *For simplicity, and to ensure the necessary absolute cleanliness on reassembly, the following procedure describes the removal of the fuel rail assembly, complete with the injectors and pressure regulator, so that the injectors can be serviced individually on a clean work surface.*

It is also possible to remove and refit an individual injector once the fuel system has been depressurised and the battery has been disconnected. If this approach is followed, read through the complete procedure, and work as described in the relevant paragraphs, depending on the amount of preliminary dismantling required. Be careful not to

allow any dirt to enter the system **(see illustrations)**.
12   Relieve the residual pressure in the fuel system (see Section 2), and equalise tank pressure by removing the fuel filler cap. **Warning:** *This procedure will merely relieve the increased pressure necessary for the engine to run - remember that fuel will still be present in the system components, and take precautions accordingly before disconnecting any of them.*
13   Disconnect the battery negative (earth) lead - see Chapter 5, Section 1.
14   Remove the plenum chamber (see Section 4).
15   If the additional clearance is required, disconnect the accelerator cable from the throttle linkage (see Section 5 or 6, as appropriate). Where fitted, also disconnect the cruise control actuator cable (see Chapter 12).
16   Releasing the wire clips, unplug the four fuel injector electrical connectors.
17   Disconnect the fuel feed and return lines at the quick-release couplings next to the braking system vacuum servo unit, then unclip the fuel hoses from the inlet manifold; use rag to soak up any spilt fuel. **Note:** *Do not disturb the threaded couplings at the fuel rail unions unless absolutely necessary; these are sealed at the factory. The quick-release couplings will suffice for all normal service operations.*
18   Disconnect the crankcase breather hose from the cylinder head cover union, and the vacuum hose from the fuel pressure regulator **(see illustration)**.

4

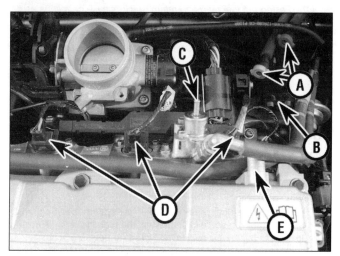

16.18 Injector removal - disconnect fuel lines at quick-release couplings (A), unclip hoses (B), disconnect vacuum hose from regulator (C), unplug electrical connectors (D) - three of four shown - and disconnect breather hose from union (E)

16.19A Unscrew bolts (arrowed) . . .

16.19B . . . and withdraw fuel rail with injectors and pressure regulator - renew nose seals (arrowed) whenever rail is disturbed

19   Unscrew the three bolts securing the fuel rail, and withdraw the rail, carefully prising it out of the inlet manifold, and draining any remaining fuel into a suitable clean container **(see illustrations)**. Note the seals between the rail noses and the manifold; these must be renewed whenever the rail is removed.

20   Clamping the rail carefully in a vice fitted with soft jaws, unscrew the two bolts securing each injector, and withdraw the injectors. Place each in a clean, clearly-labelled storage container.

21   If you are renewing the injector(s), discard the old injector, the nose seal and the O-rings. If you are simply renewing leaking injector O-rings, and intend to re-use the same injectors, remove the old nose seal and O-rings, and discard them.

22   Further testing of the injector(s) is beyond the scope of the home mechanic. If you are in doubt as to the status of any injector(s), it can be tested at a dealer service department.

23   Refitting is the reverse of the removal procedure, noting the following points:

(a)   *Lubricate each nose seal and O-ring with clean engine oil on installation.*

(b)   *Locate each injector carefully in the fuel rail recess, ensuring that the locating tab on the injector head fits into the slot provided in the rail. Tighten the bolts to the specified torque.*

(c)   *Fit a new seal to each fuel rail nose, and ensure that the seals are not displaced as the rail is refitted. Ensure that the fuel rail is settled fully in the manifold before tightening the three bolts evenly and to the torque wrench setting specified.*

(d)   *Fasten the fuel feed and return quick-release couplings as described in Section 3.*

(e)   *Ensure that the breather hose, vacuum hose and wiring are routed correctly, and secured on reconnection by any clips or ties provided.*

(f)   *On completion, switch the ignition on and off five times, to activate the fuel pump and pressurise the system, without cranking the engine. Check for signs of fuel leaks around all disturbed unions and joints before attempting to start the engine.*

Fuel pressure regulator

Check

24   Refer to the fuel pump/fuel pressure check procedure (see Section 8).

Renewal

25   Relieve the residual pressure in the fuel system (see Section 2), and equalise tank pressure by removing the fuel filler cap. **Warning:** *This procedure will merely relieve the increased pressure necessary for the engine to run - remember that fuel will still be present in the system components, and take precautions accordingly before disconnecting any of them.*

26   Disconnect the battery negative (earth) lead - see Chapter 5, Section 1.

27   Remove the plenum chamber (see Section 4).

28   Disconnect the vacuum hose from the regulator.

29   Unscrew the two regulator retaining bolts, place a wad of clean rag to soak up any spilt fuel, and withdraw the regulator **(see illustration)**.

30   Refitting is the reverse of the removal procedure, noting the following points:

(a)   *Renew the regulator sealing O-ring whenever the regulator is disturbed. Lubricate the new O-ring with clean engine oil on installation.*

(b)   *Locate the regulator carefully in the fuel rail recess, and tighten the bolts to the specified torque wrench setting.*

(c)   *On completion, switch the ignition on and off five times, to activate the fuel pump and pressurise the system, without cranking the engine. Check for signs of fuel leaks around all disturbed unions and joints before attempting to start the engine.*

Idle speed control valve

Check

31   Disconnect the battery negative (earth) lead - see Chapter 5, Section 1.

32   Raise the front of the vehicle, and support it securely on axle stands. **Warning:** *Do not place any part of your body under a vehicle when it's supported only by a jack!*

33   Unplug the valve's electrical connector **(see illustration)**.

34   Connect a 12-volt battery across the valve's terminals - positive (+) to terminal 37 (the green/yellow wire) and negative (-) to terminal 21 (the black/yellow). **Caution:** *It is essential that the correct polarity is observed, or the diode incorporated in the valve may be damaged.*

35   A distinct click should be heard each time contact is made and broken. If not, measure the resistance between the terminals. If the resistance is as specified, the valve is okay (but there may be a problem with the wiring or the ECU). If the resistance is not as specified, renew the valve (see below).

36   Plug in the valve's electrical connector.

Renewal

37   Disconnect the battery negative (earth) lead - see Chapter 5, Section 1.

38   Raise the front of the vehicle, and support it securely on axle stands. **Warning:** *Do not place any part of your body under a vehicle when it's supported only by a jack!*

39   Unplug the valve's electrical connector.

40   Unscrew the two retaining bolts, and withdraw the valve from the inlet manifold **(see illustration)**.

41   Since the valve's individual components are not available separately, and the complete assembly must be renewed if it is thought to be faulty, there is nothing to be lost by attempting to flush out the passages, using carburettor cleaner or similar solvent. This won't take much time or effort, and may well cure the fault.

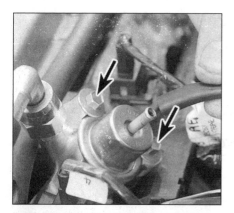

16.29 Disconnect vacuum hose, and unscrew bolts (arrowed) to withdraw fuel pressure regulator

16.33 Access to idle speed control valve is from underneath vehicle - unplug electrical connector (arrowed) to check valve

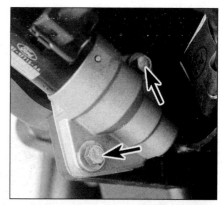

16.40 Unscrew bolts (arrowed) to remove idle speed control valve

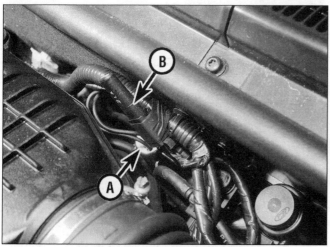

16.43 Location of idle-increase solenoid valve (A) and diode (B)

42   Refitting is the reverse of the removal procedure, noting the following points:

(a) Clean the mating surfaces carefully, and always fit a new gasket whenever the valve is disturbed.
(b) Tighten the bolts evenly and to the specified torque wrench setting.
(c) Once the wiring and battery are reconnected, start the engine and allow it to idle. When it has reached normal operating temperature, check that the idle speed is stable, and that no induction (air) leaks are evident. Switch on all electrical loads (headlights, heated rear window, etc), and check that the idle speed is still correct.

Idle-increase solenoid valve

Check

43   If this valve is thought to be faulty, unplug its electrical connector and disconnect its vacuum hoses, then connect a battery directly across the valve's terminals. Check that air can flow through the valve's passages when the solenoid is energised, and that nothing can pass when the solenoid is not energised. Alternatively, connect an ohmmeter to measure the resistance between the valve's terminals, and compare this reading to that listed in the Specifications Section at the beginning of this Chapter. Renew the valve if it is faulty **(see illustration)**.

44   The solenoid's diode is fitted to control any voltage "spikes" which might occur as the solenoid is switched off. A faulty diode would not, therefore, necessarily interfere with the operation of the valve. If the diode is thought to be faulty, however, it can be checked by un-

plugging it and connecting an ohmmeter across its terminals, to check that continuity exists in one direction only. If continuity is found in both directions, or in neither, the diode is faulty, and must be renewed.

Renewal

45   If better access is required, remove the plenum chamber (see Section 4).
46   Disconnect the battery negative (earth) lead - see Section 1 of Chapter 5.
46   Unplug the valve's electrical connector. Unclip the valve from the bulkhead, then disconnect its vacuum hoses and withdraw it.
47   Refitting is the reverse of the removal procedure.

17 Exhaust system - general information and component renewal

Warning: *Inspection and repair of exhaust system components should be done only after enough time has elapsed after driving the vehicle to allow the system components to cool completely. This applies particularly to the catalytic converter, which runs at very high temperatures. Also, when working under the vehicle, make sure it is securely supported on axle stands.*

1   The exhaust system is composed of an exhaust manifold, the front downpipe and catalytic converter, and a rear section incorporating two silencers (three on some versions) and the tailpipe assembly. The service replacement exhaust system consists of three or four sections: the front downpipe/catalytic converter, the intermediate pipe and front silencer, and the tailpipe and rear silencer. On some versions, the tailpipe is in two pieces, with two rear silencers. The system is suspended throughout its entire length by rubber mountings.
2   If any of these parts are damaged or deteriorated, excessive noise and vibration will occur.
3   Conduct regular inspections of the exhaust system, to keep it safe and quiet. Look for any damaged or bent parts, open seams, holes, loose connections, excessive corrosion, or other defects which could allow exhaust fumes to enter the vehicle. Deteriorated exhaust system components should not be repaired - they should be replaced with new parts.
4   If the exhaust system components are extremely corroded or rusted together, they will probably have to be cut from the exhaust system. The most convenient way of accomplishing this is to have a quick-fit exhaust repair specialist remove the corroded sections. If, however, you want to save money by doing it yourself (and you don't have an oxy/acetylene welding outfit with a cutting torch), simply cut off the old components with a hacksaw. If you have compressed air, special pneumatic cutting chisels can also be used. If you do decide to tackle the job at home, be sure to wear eye protection, to protect your eyes from metal chips, and work gloves, to protect your hands. If the production-fit system is still fitted, it must be cut at the points shown

4

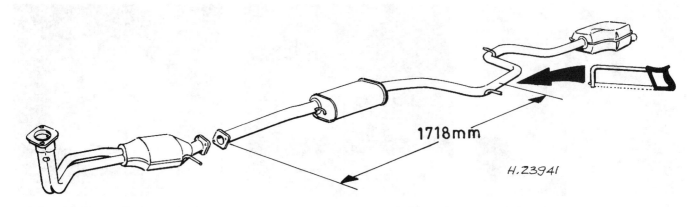

17.4A Cutting point for renewal of production-fit exhaust system - 1.6 and 1.8 models

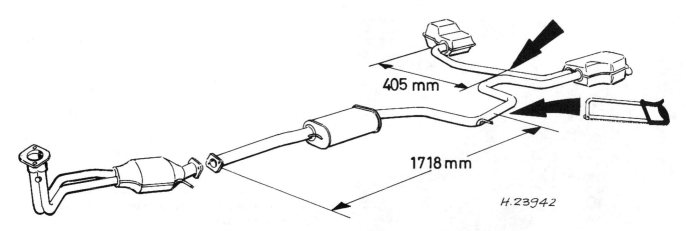

17.4B Cutting points for renewal of production-fit exhaust system - 2.0 models

(see illustrations) for the service-replacement system sections to fit.

5   Here are some simple guidelines to apply when repairing the exhaust system:

(a)   *Work from the back to the front when removing exhaust system components.*

(b)   ***Warning:*** *The catalytic converter operates at very high temperatures, and takes a long time to cool. Wait until it's completely cool before attempting to remove the converter. Failure to do so could result in serious burns.*

(c)   *Apply penetrating fluid to the exhaust system component fasteners, to make them easier to remove.*

(d)   *Use new gaskets, rubber mountings and clamps when installing exhaust system components.*

(e)   *Apply anti-seize compound to the threads of all exhaust system fasteners during reassembly.*

(f)   *Note that the downpipe is secured to the manifold by two bolts, with a coil spring, spring seat and self-locking nut on each. On refitting, tighten the nuts until they stop on the bolt shoulders; the pressure of the springs will then suffice to make a leakproof joint* **(see illustration)**. *Do not overtighten the nuts to cure a leak - the bolts will shear. Renew the gasket and the springs if a leak is found (also see Chapter 2, Part A).*

(g)   *Be sure to allow sufficient clearance between newly-installed parts and all points on the underbody, to avoid overheating the floorpan, and possibly damaging the interior carpet and insulation. Pay particularly close attention to the catalytic converter and its heat shield.*

17.5 Tighten exhaust system front downpipe-to-manifold nuts as described - do not overtighten them

Chapter 5   Engine electrical systems

Contents

Specifications

Battery

Type..	Lead-acid
Rating - Cold cranking/Reserve capacity	500 A/75 RC, 590 A/95 RC, or 650 A/130 RC

Ignition timing

Nominal...	10° ± 2° BTDC

Note: *Ignition timing is under control of ECU - it may vary constantly at idle speed, and is not adjustable.*

Ignition coil

Output..	37.0 kilovolts (minimum)
Primary resistances - measured at coil connector terminal pins	0.50 ± 0.05 ohms

Alternator
Type:

	Model	Rated output
Bosch unit	NC 14V 60-90A	90A
Mitsubishi unit	A004T	90A
Minimum brush length - all types	5.0 mm	
Regulated voltage @ 4000 (engine) rpm		
and 3 to 7 amp load - all types..	13.5 to 14.6 volts	

Starter motor
Type:

	Model	Rated output
Bosch unit	DW	1.1 or 1.4 kW
Lucas/Magneti Marelli unit	M79	1.0 kW
Minimum brush length - all types	8.0 mm	
Commutator minimum diameter:		
Bosch units	32.8 mm	
Lucas/Magneti Marelli unit	Not available	
Armature endfloat:		
Bosch units	0.30 mm	
Lucas/Magneti Marelli unit	0.25 mm	

Torque wrench settings

	Nm	lbf ft
Crankshaft speed/position sensor:		
Sensor-to-bracket screw	6 to 9	4 to 6
Bracket-to-cylinder block crankcase screw....................	21	15
Ignition coil bracket-to-cylinder head screws	21	15
Alternator mounting bolts	50	37
Starter motor mounting bolts	35	26

1 General information, precautions and battery disconnection

General information

The engine electrical systems include all ignition, charging and starting components. Because of their engine-related functions, these components are discussed separately from body electrical devices such as the lights, the instruments, etc (which are included in Chapter 12).

Precautions

Always observe the following precautions when working on the electrical system:

(a) Be extremely careful when servicing engine electrical components. They are easily damaged if checked, connected or handled improperly.

(b) Never leave the ignition switched on for long periods of time when the engine is not running.

(c) Don't disconnect the battery leads while the engine is running.

(d) Maintain correct polarity when connecting a battery lead from another vehicle during jump starting - see the "Booster battery (jump) starting" section at the front of this manual.

(e) Always disconnect the negative lead first, and reconnect it last, or the battery may be shorted by the tool being used to loosen the lead clamps **(see illustration)**.

It's also a good idea to review the safety-related information regarding the engine electrical systems located in the "Safety first!" section at the front of this manual, before beginning any operation included in this Chapter.

Battery disconnection

Several systems fitted to the vehicle require battery power to be available at all times, either to ensure their continued operation (such as the clock) or to maintain control unit memories (such as that in the engine management system's ECU) which would be wiped if the battery were to be disconnected. Whenever the battery is to be disconnected therefore, first note the following, to ensure that there are no unforeseen consequences of this action:

(a) First, on any vehicle with central locking, it is a wise precaution to remove the key from the ignition, and to keep it with you, so that it does not get locked in if the central locking should engage accidentally when the battery is reconnected!

(b) The engine management system's ECU will lose the information stored in its memory - referred to by Ford as the "KAM" (Keep-Alive Memory) - when the battery is disconnected. This includes idling and operating values, and any fault codes detected - in the case of the fault codes, if it is thought likely that the system has developed a fault for which the corresponding code has been logged, the vehicle must be taken to a Ford dealer for the codes to be read, using the special diagnostic equipment necessary for this (see Chapter 6). Whenever the battery is disconnected, the information relating to idle speed control and other operating values will have to be re-programmed into the unit's memory. The ECU does this by itself, but until then, there may be surging, hesitation, erratic idle and a generally inferior level of performance. To allow the ECU to relearn these values, start the engine and run it as close to idle speed as possible until it reaches its normal operating temperature, then run it for approximately two minutes at 1200 rpm. Next, drive the vehicle as far as necessary - approximately 5 miles of varied driving conditions is usually sufficient - to complete the relearning process.

(c) If the battery is disconnected while the alarm system is armed or activated, the alarm will remain in the same state when the battery is reconnected. The same applies to the engine immobiliser system (where fitted).

(d) If a trip computer is in use, any information stored in memory will be lost.

(e) If a Ford "Keycode" audio unit is fitted, and the unit and/or the battery is disconnected, the unit will not function again on reconnection until the correct security code is entered. Details of this procedure, which varies according to the unit and model year, are given in the "Ford Audio Systems Operating Guide" supplied with the vehicle when new, with the code itself being given in a "Radio Passport" and/or a "Keycode Label" at the same time. Ensure you have the correct code before you disconnect the battery. For obvious security reasons, the procedure is not given in this manual. If you do not have the code or details of the correct procedure, but can supply proof of ownership and a legitimate reason for wanting this information, the vehicle's selling dealer may be able to help.

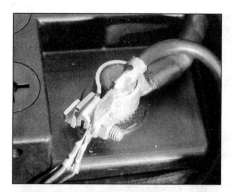

1.2 Always disconnect battery - negative (earth) lead first - to prevent the possibility of short-circuits

2.2A Unscrew hold-down nuts (one of two arrowed) . . .

2.2B . . . and withdraw hold-down clamp to release battery

Devices known as "memory-savers" (or "code-savers") can be used to avoid some of the above problems. Precise details vary according to the device used. Typically, it is plugged into the cigarette lighter, and is connected by its own wires to a spare battery; the vehicle's own battery is then disconnected from the electrical system, leaving the "memory-saver" to pass sufficient current to maintain audio unit security codes and ECU memory values, and also to run permanently-live circuits such as the clock, all the while isolating the battery in the event of a short-circuit occurring while work is carried out. **Warning:** *Some of these devices allow a considerable amount of current to pass, which can mean that many of the vehicle's systems are still operational when the main battery is disconnected. If a "memory-saver" is used, ensure that the circuit concerned is actually "dead" before carrying out any work on it!*

2 Battery - removal and refitting

Note: *See also the relevant Sections of Chapter 1.*
1   Disconnect the battery leads, negative (earth) lead first - see Section 1.
2   Remove the battery hold-down clamp **(see illustrations)**.
3   Lift out the battery. Be careful - it's heavy.
4   While the battery is out, inspect the tray for corrosion (see Chapter 1).
5   If you are renewing the battery, make sure that you get one that's identical, with the same dimensions, amperage rating, cold cranking rating, etc. Dispose of the old battery in a responsible fashion. Most local authorities have facilities for the collection and disposal of such items - batteries contain sulphuric acid and lead, and should not be simply thrown out with the household rubbish!
6   Refitting is the reverse of the removal procedure.

3 Battery leads - check and renewal

Note: *See also the relevant Sections of Chapter 1.*
1   Periodically inspect the entire length of each battery lead for damage, cracked or burned insulation, and corrosion. Poor battery lead connections can cause starting problems and decreased engine performance.
2   Check the lead-to-terminal connections at the ends of the leads for cracks, loose wire strands and corrosion. The presence of white, fluffy deposits under the insulation at the lead terminal connection is a sign that the lead is corroded and should be renewed. Check the terminals for distortion, missing clamp bolts, and corrosion.
3   When removing the leads, always disconnect the negative lead first, and reconnect it last (see Section 1). Even if only the positive lead is being renewed, be sure to disconnect the negative lead from the battery first (see Chapter 1 for further information regarding battery lead removal).
4   Disconnect the old leads from the battery, then trace each of

them to their opposite ends, and detach them from the starter solenoid and earth terminals. Note the routing of each lead, to ensure correct installation.
5   If you are renewing either or both of the old leads, take them with you when buying new parts. It is vitally important that you replace the leads with identical parts. Leads have characteristics that make them easy to identify: positive leads are usually red, larger in cross-section, and have a larger-diameter battery post clamp; earth leads are usually black, smaller in cross-section and have a slightly smaller-diameter clamp for the negative post.
6   Clean the threads of the solenoid or earth connection with a wire brush to remove rust and corrosion. Apply a light coat of battery terminal corrosion inhibitor, or petroleum jelly, to the threads, to prevent future corrosion.
7   Attach the lead to the solenoid or earth connection, and tighten the mounting nut/bolt securely.
8   Before connecting a new lead to the battery, make sure that it reaches the battery post without having to be stretched.
9   Connect the positive lead first, followed by the negative lead.

4 Ignition system - general information and precautions

General
The ignition system includes the ignition switch, the battery, the crankshaft speed/position sensor, the coil, the primary (low tension/LT) and secondary (high tension/HT) wiring circuits, and the spark plugs. On models with automatic transmission, a separate ignition module is also fitted, its functions being incorporated in the ECU on models with manual transmission. The ignition system is controlled by the engine management system's Electronic Control Unit (ECU). Using data provided by information sensors which monitor various engine functions (such as engine speed and piston position, intake air mass and temperature, engine coolant temperature, etc.), the ECU ensures a perfectly-timed spark under all conditions (see Chapter 6). **Note:** *The ignition timing is under the full control of the ECU, and cannot be adjusted - see Section 8 for further details.*

Precautions
When working on the ignition system, take the following precautions:
(a)   *Do not keep the ignition switch on for more than 10 seconds if the engine will not start.*
(b)   *If a separate tachometer is ever required for servicing work, consult a dealer service department before buying a tachometer for use with this vehicle - some tachometers may be incompatible with this ignition system - and always connect it in accordance with the equipment manufacturer's instructions.*
(c)   *Never connect the ignition coil terminals to earth. This could result in damage to the coil and/or the ECU or ignition module (whichever is fitted).*

5

(d)   Do not disconnect the battery when the engine is running.

(e)   Make sure that the ignition module (where fitted) is properly earthed.

(f)   Refer to the warning at the beginning of the next Section concerning HT voltage.

5   Ignition system - testing

Warning: *Because of the high voltage generated by the ignition system, extreme care should be taken whenever an operation is performed involving ignition components. This not only includes the ignition module/ECU, coil and spark plug (HT) leads, but related components such as electrical connectors, tachometer and other test equipment also.*

Note: *This is an initial check of the "ignition part" of the main engine management system, to be carried out as part of the preliminary checks of the complete engine management system (see Chapter 6).*

1   If the engine turns over but won't start, disconnect the (HT) lead from any spark plug, and attach it to a calibrated tester (available at most automotive accessory shops). Connect the clip on the tester to a good earth - a bolt or metal bracket on the engine. If you're unable to obtain a calibrated ignition tester, have the check carried out by a Ford dealer service department or similar. Any other form of testing (such as jumping a spark from the end of an HT lead to earth) is not recommended, because of the risk of personal injury, or of damage to the ECU/ignition module (see notes above and in Section 4).

2   Crank the engine and watch the end of the tester to see if bright blue, well-defined sparks occur.

3   If sparks occur, sufficient voltage is reaching the plug to fire it. Repeat the check at the remaining plugs, to ensure that all leads are sound and that the coil is serviceable. However, the plugs themselves may be fouled or faulty, so remove and check them as described in Chapter 1.

4   If no sparks or intermittent sparks occur, the spark plug lead(s) may be defective - check them as described in Chapter 1.

5   If there's still no spark, check the coil's electrical connector, to make sure it's clean and tight. Check for full battery voltage to the coil at the connector's centre terminal. The coil is earthed through the ECU - *do not* attempt to check this. Check the coil itself (see Section 6). Make any necessary repairs, then repeat the check again.

6   The remainder of the system checks should be left to a dealer service department or other qualified repair facility, as there is a chance that the ECU may be damaged if tests are not performed properly.

6   Ignition coil - removal and refitting

Warning: *Because of the high voltage generated by the ignition system, extreme care should be taken whenever an operation is performed involving ignition components. This not only includes the ignition module/ECU, coil and spark plug (HT) leads, but related components such as electrical connectors, tachometer and other test equipment also.*

Check

1   Having checked that full battery voltage is available at the centre terminal of the coil's electrical connector (see Section 5), disconnect the battery negative (earth) lead - see Section 1.

2   Unplug the coil's electrical connector, if not already disconnected.

3   Using an ohmmeter, measure the resistance of the coil's primary windings, connecting the meter between the coil's terminal pins as follows. Measure first from one outer pin to the centre pin, then from the other outer pin to the centre. Compare your readings with the coil primary resistance listed in the Specifications Section at the beginning of this Chapter.

4   Disconnect the spark plug (HT) leads - note their connections or label them carefully, as described in Chapter 1. Use the meter to check that there is continuity (ie, a resistance corresponding to that of the coil secondary winding) between each pair of (HT) lead terminals; Nos 1 and 4 terminals are connected by their secondary winding, as

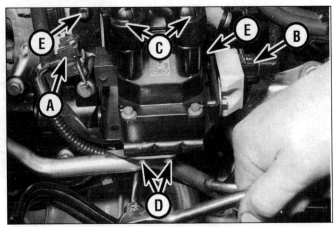

6.9 Unplug coil electrical connector (A), suppressor connector (B), and spark plug/HT leads (C), remove screws (D), then undo Torx-type screws (E) to release ignition coil assembly

are Nos 2 and 3. Now switch to the highest resistance scale, and check that there is no continuity between either pair of terminals and the other - ie, there should be infinite resistance between terminals 1 and 2, or 4 and 3 - and between any terminal and earth.

5   If either of the above tests yield resistance values outside the specified amount, or results other than those described, renew the coil. Any further testing should be left to a dealer service department or other qualified repair facility.

Removal and refitting

6   Disconnect the battery negative (earth) lead - see Section 1.

7   Remove the air mass meter and resonator - refer to Chapter 4.

8   Unplug the electrical connector from each side of the coil, then disconnect the spark plug (HT) leads - note their connections or label them carefully, as described in Chapter 1.

9   Undo the two screws securing the EGR pipe to the coil bracket, then remove the coil mounting (Torx-type) screws. Withdraw the coil assembly from the cylinder head **(see illustration)**.

10   The suppressor can be unbolted from the mounting bracket, if required; note that the coil and bracket are only available as a single unit.

11   Refitting is the reverse of the removal procedure. Ensure that the spark plug (HT) leads are correctly reconnected, and tighten the coil screws securely.

7   Ignition module (automatic transmission models only) - removal and refitting

Note: *See Chapter 6 for component location illustrations.*

1   Disconnect the battery negative (earth) lead - see Section 1.

2   If better access is required, remove the resonator (see Chapter 4).

3   Unplug the electrical connector from the module **(see illustration)**.

4   Remove the retaining screws, and detach the module from the bulkhead mounting bracket.

5   Refitting is the reverse of the removal procedure.

8   Ignition timing - checking

As noted in Section 4, the ignition timing is controlled entirely by the ECU (acting with the ignition module, on models with automatic transmission), and cannot be adjusted. The value quoted in the Specifications Section of this Chapter is for reference only, and may vary significantly if "checked" by simply connecting a timing light to the system and running the engine at idle speed.

Not only can the ignition timing not be adjusted, it cannot be checked either, except with the use of special diagnostic equipment

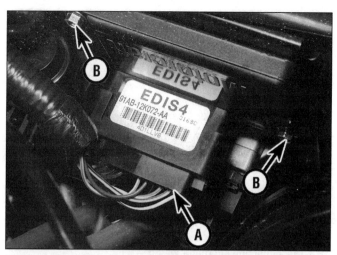

7.3 Separate ignition module is fitted to automatic transmission models only - note electrical connector (A) and retaining screws (B)

(see Chapter 6) - this makes it a task for a Ford dealer service department.

Owners who are taking their vehicles abroad should note that the ignition system is set for the engine to use petrol of 95 RON octane rating by fitting a "plug-in bridge" to the service connector on the engine compartment bulkhead **(see illustration)**. Removing the "plug-in bridge" retards the ignition timing - by an unspecified value - to allow the engine to run on 91 RON fuel. This grade of fuel is the "Regular" or "Normal" widely used abroad, but not at present available in the UK. If you are taking the vehicle abroad, seek the advice of a Ford dealer (or of one of the motoring organisations). This will ensure that you are familiar with the grades of fuel you are likely to find (and the sometimes confusing names for those grades), and that the vehicle is set correctly at all times for the fuel used. **Note:** *The octane ratings mentioned above are both, of course, for **unleaded** petrol. Do not use leaded petrol at any time in a vehicle equipped with a catalytic converter.*

9 Crankshaft speed/position sensor - checking, removal and refitting

Checking
1   See Section 4 of Chapter 6.

Removal and refitting
2   Disconnect the battery negative (earth) lead - see Section 1.
3   Raise the front of the vehicle, and support it securely on axle

stands. **Warning:** *Do not place any part of your body under a vehicle when it's supported only by a jack!*
4   Unplug the sensor's electrical connector **(see illustration)**.
5   Undo the sensor's retaining screw and withdraw the sensor. The sensor's bracket cannot be unbolted from the cylinder block/crankcase unless the transmission and flywheel/driveplate have been removed (see Chapter 2).
6   Refitting is the reverse of the removal procedure.

10 Charging system - general information and precautions

General information
The charging system includes the alternator, an internal voltage regulator, a no-charge (or "ignition") warning light, the battery, and the wiring between all the components. The charging system supplies electrical power for the ignition system, the lights, the radio, etc. The alternator is driven by the auxiliary drivebelt at the front (right-hand end) of the engine.

The purpose of the voltage regulator is to limit the alternator's voltage to a preset value. This prevents power surges, circuit overloads, etc., during peak voltage output.

The charging system doesn't ordinarily require periodic maintenance. However, the drivebelt, battery and wires and connections should be inspected at the intervals outlined in Chapter 1.

The dashboard warning light should come on when the ignition key is turned to positions "II" or "III", then should go off immediately the engine starts. If it remains on, or if it comes on while the engine is running, there is a malfunction in the charging system (see Section 11). If the light does not come on when the ignition key is turned, and the bulb is sound (see Chapter 12), there is a fault in the alternator.

Precautions
Be very careful when making electrical circuit connections to a vehicle equipped with an alternator, and note the following:

(a)   *When reconnecting wires to the alternator from the battery, be sure to note the polarity.*

(b)   *Before using arc-welding equipment to repair any part of the vehicle, disconnect the wires from the alternator and the battery terminals.*

(c)   *Never start the engine with a battery charger connected.*

(d)   *Always disconnect both battery leads before using a battery charger.*

(e)   *The alternator is driven by an engine drivebelt which could cause serious injury if your hand, hair or clothes become entangled in it with the engine running.*

(f)   *Because the alternator is connected directly to the battery, it could arc or cause a fire if overloaded or shorted-out.*

5

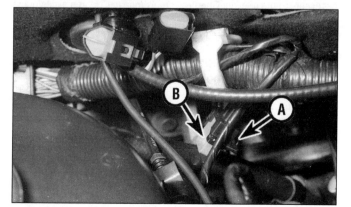

8.0 Service connector (A) mounted on engine compartment bulkhead is fitted with "plug-in bridge" (B) to set engine to use (unleaded) petrol of 95 RONoctane rating

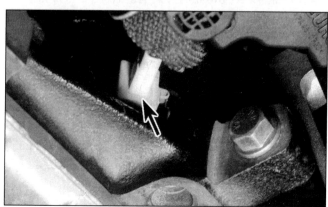

9.4 Location of crankshaft speed/position sensor - connector arrowed - in front of cylinder block/crankcase

(g) *Wrap a plastic bag over the alternator, and secure it with rubber bands, before steam-cleaning or pressure-washing the engine.*

(h) *Never disconnect the alternator terminals while the engine is running.*

11 Charging system - testing

1   If a malfunction occurs in the charging circuit, don't automatically assume that the alternator is causing the problem. First check the following items:

(a) *Check the tension and condition of the auxiliary drivebelt - renew it if it is worn or deteriorated (see Chapter 1).*

(b) *Ensure the alternator mounting bolts and nuts are tight.*

(c) *Inspect the alternator wiring harness and the electrical connections at the alternator; they must be in good condition, and tight.*

(d) *Check the large main fuses in the engine compartment (see Chapter 12). If any is blown, determine the cause, repair the circuit and renew the fuse (the vehicle won't start and/or the accessories won't work if the fuse is blown).*

(e) *Start the engine and check the alternator for abnormal noises - for example, a shrieking or squealing sound may indicate a badly-worn bearing or brush.*

(f) *Make sure that the battery is fully-charged - one bad cell in a battery can cause overcharging by the alternator.*

(g) *Disconnect the battery leads (negative first, then positive). Inspect the battery posts and the lead clamps for corrosion. Clean them thoroughly if necessary (see Section 3 and Chapter 1). Reconnect the lead to the negative terminal.*

(h) *With the ignition and all accessories switched off, insert a test light between the battery negative post and the disconnected negative lead clamp:*

   (1) If the test light does not come on, re-attach the clamp and proceed to the next step.

   (2) If the test light comes on, there is a short in the electrical system of the vehicle. The short must be repaired before the charging system can be checked.

   (3) To find the short, disconnect the alternator wiring harness:

      (a) If the light goes out, the alternator is at fault.

      (b) If the light stays on, remove each fuse until it goes out - this will tell you which component is short-circuited.

2   Using a voltmeter, check the battery voltage with the engine off. It should be approximately 12 volts.

3   Start the engine and check the battery voltage again. Increase engine speed until the voltmeter reading remains steady; it should now be approximately 13.5 to 14.6 volts.

4   Switch on as many electrical accessories (eg the headlights, heated rear window and heater blower) as possible, and check that the alternator maintains the regulated voltage at around 13 to 14 volts. The voltage may drop and then come back up; it may also be necessary to increase engine speed slightly, even if the charging system is working properly.

5   If the voltage reading is greater than the specified charging voltage, renew the voltage regulator (see Section 13).

6   If the voltmeter reading is less than that specified, the fault may be due to worn brushes, weak brush springs, a faulty voltage regulator, a faulty diode, a severed phase winding, or worn or damaged slip rings. The brushes and slip rings may be checked (see Section 13), but if the fault persists, the alternator should be renewed or taken to an auto-electrician for testing and repair.

12 Alternator - removal and refitting

1   Disconnect the battery negative (earth) lead - see Section 1.

2   Remove the plenum chamber (see Chapter 4).

3   Unscrew the nuts to disconnect the wiring from the alternator

12.3 Disconnecting alternator wiring

(see illustration). If additional working clearance is required, undo the right-hand of the three screws securing the wiring "rail" to the rear of the inlet manifold.

4   Jack up and support the front right-hand corner of the vehicle. Remove the auxiliary drivebelt and the engine oil filter - place a wad of rag to soak up the spilled oil (see Chapter 1). Rather than refit a used filter, you are advised to drain the engine oil, and then to fit a new filter and refill the engine with clean oil on reassembly. Where an engine oil cooler is fitted, it may prove necessary to remove this as well, to provide the clearance necessary to remove the alternator (see Chapter 2, Part A).

5   Unscrew the two bolts securing the power steering system pipes to the right-hand side of the front suspension subframe. With the front wheels in the straight-ahead position, disconnect the right-hand track rod end from the steering knuckle (see Chapter 10).

6   Remove the mounting bolts and nuts (one at the top, two at the bottom). Withdraw the alternator from the engine, and manoeuvre it out through the wheel arch **(see illustration)**. Do not drop it, it is fragile.

7   If you are renewing the alternator, take the old one with you when purchasing a replacement unit. Make sure that the new or rebuilt unit is identical to the old alternator. Look at the terminals - they should be the same in number, size and location as the terminals on the old alternator. Finally, look at the identification markings - they will be stamped in the housing, or printed on a tag or plaque affixed to the housing. Make sure that these numbers are the same on both alternators.

8   Many new/rebuilt alternators do not have a pulley installed, so you may have to switch the pulley from the old unit to the new/rebuilt one. When buying an alternator, ask about the installation of pulleys - some auto-electrical specialists will perform this service free of charge.

9   Refitting is the reverse of the removal procedure, referring where necessary to the relevant Chapters of this manual. Tighten all fasteners to the specified torque wrench settings.

10   Check the charging voltage to verify proper operation of the alternator (see Section 11).

13 Alternator brushes and voltage regulator - renewal

Note: *This procedure assumes that replacement parts of the correct type have been obtained. At the time of writing, no individual alternator components were available as separate replacement Ford parts. An auto electrical specialist should be able to supply parts such as brushes.*

The following procedure is for the Bosch unit fitted to the project vehicle - details may vary for other alternator types.

1   Remove the alternator from the vehicle (see Section 12) and place it on a clean workbench.

2   Remove the three screws, and withdraw the plastic end cover

12.6 Alternator must be withdrawn through right-hand front wheel arch

13.2 Renewing voltage regulator/brush holder - Bosch alternator. Remove three screws and withdraw end cover ...

13.4 ... then remove regulator/brush holder assembly (secured by two screws)

(see illustration).

3   Remove the two voltage regulator/brush holder mounting screws.
4   Remove the regulator/brush holder from the end frame **(see illustration)**. If you are renewing the assembly, proceed to paragraph 8, install the new unit, reassemble the alternator, and refit it to the engine (see Section 12). If you are going to check the brushes, proceed to the next paragraph.
5   Measure the exposed length of each brush, and compare it to the minimum length listed in this Chapter's Specifications. If the length of either brush is less than the specified minimum, renew the assembly.
6   Make sure that each brush moves smoothly in the brush holder.
7   Check that the slip rings - the ring of copper on which each brush bears - are clean. Wipe them with a solvent-moistened cloth; if either appears scored or blackened, take the alternator to a repair specialist for advice.
8   Refit the voltage regulator/brush holder, ensuring that the brushes bear correctly on the slip rings, and that they compress into their holders. Tighten the screws securely.
9   Install the rear cover, and tighten the screws securely.
10   Refit the alternator (see Section 12).

14 Starting system - general information and precautions

General information

The sole function of the starting system is to turn over the engine quickly enough to allow it to start.

The starting system consists of the battery, the starter motor, the starter solenoid, and the wires connecting them. The solenoid is mounted directly on the starter motor.

The solenoid/starter motor assembly is installed on the rear upper part of the engine, next to the transmission bellhousing.

When the ignition key is turned to position "III", the starter solenoid is actuated through the starter control circuit. The starter solenoid then connects the battery to the starter. The battery supplies the electrical energy to the starter motor, which does the actual work of cranking the engine.

The starter motor on a vehicle equipped with automatic transmission can be operated only when the selector lever is in Park or Neutral ("P" or "N").

If the alarm system is armed or activated, the starter motor cannot be operated. The same applies with the engine immobiliser system (where fitted).

Precautions

Always observe the following precautions when working on the starting system:

(a)   Excessive cranking of the starter motor can overheat it, and

cause serious damage. Never operate the starter motor for more than 15 seconds at a time without pausing to allow it to cool for at least two minutes. Excessive starter operation will also risk unburned fuel collecting in the catalytic converter's element, causing it to overheat when the engine does start (see Chapter 6).
(b)   The starter is connected directly to the battery, and could arc or cause a fire if mishandled, overloaded or shorted-out.
(c)   Always detach the lead from the negative terminal of the battery before working on the starting system (see Section 1).

15 Starting system - testing

Note: *Before diagnosing starter problems, make sure that the battery is fully-charged, and ensure that the alarm/engine immobiliser system is not activated.*

1   If the starter motor does not turn at all when the switch is operated, make sure that, on automatic transmission models, the selector lever is in Park or Neutral ("P" or "N").
2   Make sure that the battery is fully-charged, and that all leads, both at the battery and starter solenoid terminals, are clean and secure.
3   If the starter motor spins but the engine is not cranking, the over-running clutch or (when applicable) the reduction gears in the starter motor may be slipping, in which case the starter motor must be overhauled or renewed. (Other possibilities are that the starter motor mounting bolts are very loose, or that teeth are missing from the flywheel/driveplate ring gear.)
4   If, when the switch is actuated, the starter motor does not operate at all but the solenoid clicks, then the problem lies with either the battery, the main solenoid contacts, or the starter motor itself (or the engine is seized).
5   If the solenoid plunger cannot be heard to click when the switch is actuated, the battery is faulty, there is a fault in the circuit, or the solenoid itself is defective.
6   To check the solenoid, connect a fused jumper lead between the battery (+) and the ignition switch terminal (the small terminal) on the solenoid. If the starter motor now operates, the solenoid is OK, and the problem is in the ignition switch, selector lever position sensor (automatic transmission) or in the wiring.
7   If the starter motor still does not operate, remove it (see Section 16). The brushes and commutator may be checked (see Section 17), but if the fault persists, the motor should be renewed, or taken to an auto-electrician for testing and repair.
8   If the starter motor cranks the engine at an abnormally-slow speed, first make sure that the battery is charged, and that all terminal connections are tight. If the engine is partially seized, or has the wrong viscosity oil in it, it will crank slowly.
9   Run the engine until normal operating temperature is reached, then switch off and disable the ignition system by unplugging the igni-

5

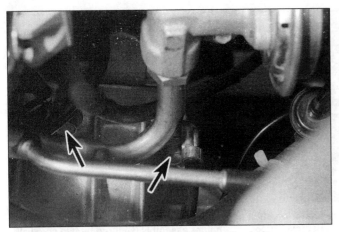

16.3 Unscrew upper two starter motor mounting bolt (arrowed) from above

16.6 Disconnect starter motor wiring (A), then unscrew remaining mounting bolt (B), and remove starter motor from beneath vehicle

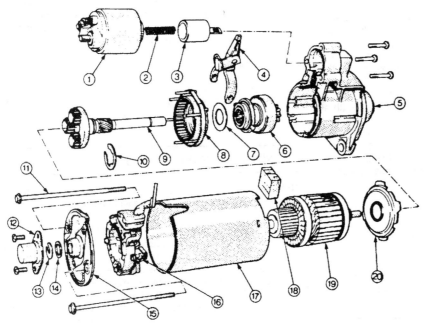

17.1A Exploded view of the Bosch DW starter motor

1   Solenoid
2   Spring
3   Plunger
4   Engaging lever
5   Drive end housing
6   Drive pinion and clutch
7   Spacer
8   Ring gear and carrier
9   Output shaft and planet gear unit
10 Circlip
11 Screw
12 End cap
13 C-clip
14 Shim
15 Commutator end housing
16 Brushplate
17 Yoke
18 Rubber block
19 Armature
20 Retaining plate

tion coil's electrical connector; remove fuse 14 to disconnect the fuel pump.

10   Connect a voltmeter positive lead to the battery positive terminal, and connect the negative lead to the negative terminal.

11   Crank the engine, and take the voltmeter readings as soon as a steady figure is indicated. Do not allow the starter motor to turn for more than 15 seconds at a time. A reading of 10.5 volts or more, with the starter motor turning at normal cranking speed, is normal. If the reading is 10.5 volts or more but the cranking speed is slow, the solenoid contacts are burned, the motor is faulty, or there is a bad connection. If the reading is less than 10.5 volts and the cranking speed is slow, the starter motor is faulty or there is a problem with the battery.

16 Starter motor - removal and refitting

1   Disconnect the battery negative (earth) lead - see Section 1.
2   Remove the air mass meter and resonator - refer to Chapter 4.
3   Unscrew the upper two starter motor mounting bolts, noting that one also secures an engine/transmission earth lead **(see illustration)**.
4   Raise the front of the vehicle, and support it securely on axle stands. **Warning:** *Do not place any part of your body under a vehicle when it's supported only by a jack!*

5   Unscrew the nuts to disconnect the wiring from the starter/solenoid terminals.
6   Remove the remaining starter motor mounting bolt **(see illustration)**. Remove the starter.
7   Refitting is the reverse of the removal procedure. Tighten the bolts to the specified torque wrench settings.

17 Starter motor - brush and solenoid renewal

Note: *This procedure assumes that replacement brushes of the correct type have been obtained - at the time of writing, no individual starter motor components were available as separate replacement Ford parts. An auto electrical specialist should be able to supply parts such as brushes.*

The following procedures are for the Lucas/Magneti Marelli unit fitted to the project vehicle - the procedure is essentially the same for the Bosch unit that may be found on other models.

1   Remove the starter motor from the vehicle (Section 16) **(see illustrations)**.

Brush renewal

2   Remove the brushes as shown **(see illustrations)**.

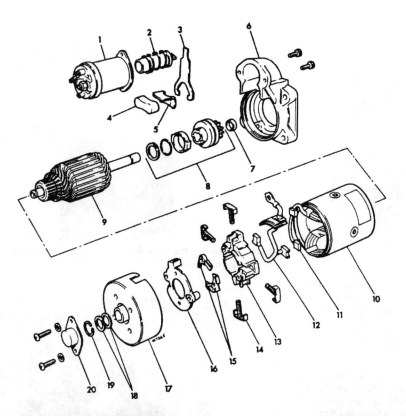

17.1B Exploded view of the Lucas/Magneti Marelli starter motor

1 Solenoid
2 Plunger
3 Engaging lever
4 Rubber pad
5 Plastic support block
6 Drive end housing
7 Thrust collar
8 Drive pinion and clutch
9 Armature
10 Yoke
11 Negative brushes
12 Positive brushes and bus bar
13 Brushbox
14 Brush holder and spring
15 Insulators
16 Plastic insulating plate
17 Commutator end housing
18 Shims
19 C-clip
20 End cap

5

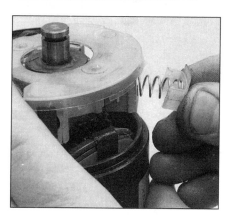

17.2A Remove the two screws to release the end cap. Withdraw the gasket and prise out the C-clip, noting any shims fitted to control armature endfloat . . .

17.2B . . . unscrew the two screws . . .

17.2C . . . and withdraw the end housing . . .

17.2D . . . then unclip the brush holders and springs . . .

17.2E . . . unscrew the nut securing the solenoid link . . .

17.2F . . . withdraw the negative brushes . . .

17.2G . . . lift off the plastic insulating plate . . .

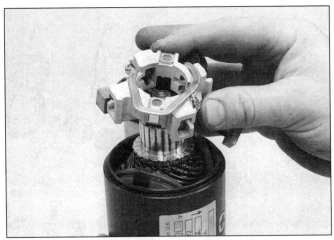

17.2H . . . remove the brushbox and remove the positive brushes complete with the bus bar . . .

3   In some cases, the brushes will have wear limit marks, in the form of a groove etched along one face of each brush; when the brushes are worn down to these marks, they must be renewed. If no marks are provided, measure the length of each brush, and compare it with the minimum length given in the Specifications Section of this Chapter. If any brush is worn below this limit, renew the brushes as a set. If the brushes are still serviceable, clean them with a petrol-moistened cloth. Check that the spring pressure is equal for all brushes, and holds the brushes securely against the commutator. If in doubt about the condition of the brushes and springs, compare them with new components.
4   Clean the commutator with a petrol-moistened cloth, then check for signs of scoring, burning, excessive wear or severe pitting. If worn or damaged, the commutator should be attended to by an auto-electrician.
5   Refitting is the reverse of the removal procedure.

Solenoid renewal

6   Unscrew the nut, noting the lockwasher(s), and disconnect the motor link from the solenoid terminal.
7   Unscrew the two bolts securing the solenoid to the motor drive end housing.
8   Release the solenoid plunger from the starter engaging lever, then withdraw the solenoid, noting the spring.
9   Refitting is the reverse of the removal procedure. Clean the solenoid, its plunger and the motor/solenoid mating surfaces carefully, and lubricate the plunger/starter engaging lever surfaces with a smear of grease.

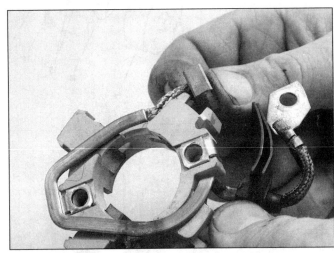

17.2I . . . note how the bus bar is engaged on the brushbox before removing it

Chapter 6   Emissions control systems

Contents

Specifications

Crankshaft speed/position sensor
Resistance .... 200 to 450 ohms

Camshaft position sensor
Resistance .... 200 to 900 ohms

Intake air temperature sensor
Resistance:
At -40° C...	860 to 900 kilohms
At 20° C...	35 to 40 kilohms
At 100° C...	1.9 to 2.5 kilohms
At 120° C...	1.0 to 1.3 kilohms

Throttle potentiometer

Resistance - see text	400 to 6000 ohms

Power steering pressure switch

Operating pressure - green switch body:

Contacts open - infinite resistance	31.5 ± 3.5 bars
Contacts close - 0 to 2.5 ohms resistance	Between 13.5 and 24.0 bars

Charcoal canister-purge solenoid valve

Resistance	50 to 120 ohms

Pulse-air solenoid valve

Resistance	50 to 120 ohms

Torque wrench settings

	Nm	lbf ft
Camshaft position sensor screw	18 to 23	13 to 17
Intake air temperature sensor...	23	17
Oxygen sensor...	60	44
Exhaust Gas Recirculation (EGR) system components:		
Valve-to-inlet manifold bolts	9	6
Pipe-to-ignition coil screws...	10	7
Pulse-air system components:		
Filter housing mounting bolt...	47	35
Piping-to-exhaust manifold		
sleeve nuts	32	24

1   General information

To minimise pollution of the atmosphere from incompletely-burned and evaporating gases, and to maintain good driveability and fuel economy, a number of emission control systems are used on these vehicles. They include the following:

(a) *The engine management system (comprising both fuel and ignition sub-systems) itself.*

(b) *Positive Crankcase Ventilation (PCV) system.*

(c) *Evaporative Emissions Control (EVAP) system.*

(d) *Exhaust Gas Recirculation (EGR) system.*

(e) *Catalytic converter.*

The Sections of this Chapter include general descriptions, checking procedures within the scope of the home mechanic, and component renewal procedures (when possible) for each of the systems listed above.

Before assuming an emissions control system is malfunctioning, check the fuel and ignition systems carefully (see Chapters 4 and 5). The diagnosis of some emission control devices requires specialised tools, equipment and training. If checking and servicing become too difficult, or if a procedure is beyond the scope of your skills, consult your dealer service department or other specialist.

This doesn't mean, however, that emission control systems are particularly difficult to maintain and repair. You can quickly and easily perform many checks, and do most of the regular maintenance, at home with common tune-up and hand tools. **Note:** *The most frequent cause of emissions problems is simply a loose or broken electrical connector or vacuum hose, so always check the electrical connectors and vacuum hoses first.*

Pay close attention to any special precautions outlined in this Chapter. It should be noted that the illustrations of the various systems may not exactly match the system installed on your vehicle, due to changes made by the manufacturer during production or from year-to-year.

Vehicles sold in some areas will carry a Vehicle Emissions Control Information (VECI) label, and a vacuum hose diagram located in the engine compartment. These contain important specifications and setting procedures for the various emissions control systems, with the vacuum hose diagram identifying emissions control components. When servicing the engine or emissions systems, the VECI label in your particular vehicle should always be checked for up-to-date information.

2   Electronic control system - description and precautions

Description

The EEC-IV (Ford's fourth-generation Electronic Engine Control system) engine management system controls fuel injection by means of a microcomputer known as the ECU (Electronic Control Unit) **(see illustrations)**.

The ECU receives signals from various sensors, which monitor changing engine operating conditions such as intake air mass (ie, intake air volume and temperature), coolant temperature, engine speed, acceleration/deceleration, exhaust oxygen content, etc. These signals are used by the ECU to determine the correct injection duration.

The system is analogous to the central nervous system in the human body - the sensors (nerve endings) constantly relay signals to the ECU (brain), which processes the data and, if necessary, sends out a command to change the operating parameters of the engine (body) by means of the actuators (muscles).

Here's a specific example of how one portion of this system operates. An oxygen sensor, located in the exhaust downpipe, constantly monitors the oxygen content of the exhaust gas. If the percentage of oxygen in the exhaust gas is incorrect, an electrical signal is sent to the ECU. The ECU processes this information, and then sends a command to the fuel injection system, telling it to change the air/fuel mixture; the end result is an air/fuel mixture ratio which is constantly maintained at a predetermined ratio, regardless of driving conditions. This happens in a fraction of a second, and goes on almost all the time while the engine is running - the exceptions are that the ECU cuts out the system and runs the engine on values pre-programmed ("mapped") into its memory both while the oxygen sensor is reaching its normal operating temperature after the engine has been started from cold, and when the throttle is fully open for full acceleration.

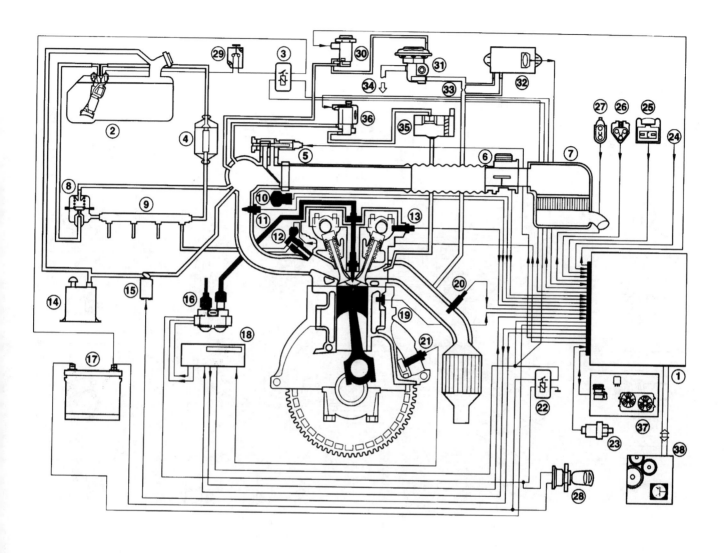

2.1A Engine management system, showing fuel injection, ignition and emissions control sub-systems

1	ECU (Electronic Control Unit)	22	Power supply relay
2	Fuel pump/fuel gauge sender unit	23	Power steering pressure switch
3	Fuel pump relay	24	Air conditioning compressor clutch solenoid
4	Fuel filter	25	Service connector - for octane adjustment
5	Idle speed control valve	26	Self-test connector - for Ford STAR tester
6	Air mass meter		diagnostic equipment
7	Air cleaner assembly	27	Diagnosis connector - for Ford diagnostic
8	Fuel pressure regulator		equipment FDS 2000
9	Fuel rail	28	Ignition switch
10	Throttle potentiometer	29	Fuel cut-off switch
11	Intake air temperature sensor	30	Exhaust Gas Recirculation (EGR) solenoid valve
12	Fuel injector	31	Exhaust Gas Recirculation (EGR) valve
13	Camshaft position sensor	32	Exhaust Gas Recirculation (EGR) exhaust gas
14	Charcoal canister		pressure differential sensor
15	Charcoal canister-purge solenoid valve	33	Exhaust Gas Recirculation (EGR) pressure
16	Ignition coil		differential measuring point
17	Battery	34	To inlet manifold
18	Ignition module - only separate (from ECU)	35	Pulse-air filter housing
	on vehicles with automatic transmission	36	Pulse-air solenoid valve
19	Coolant temperature sensor	37	Air conditioning/radiator electric cooling fan control
20	Oxygen sensor	38	Automatic transmission control system -
21	Crankshaft speed/position sensor		where applicable

6

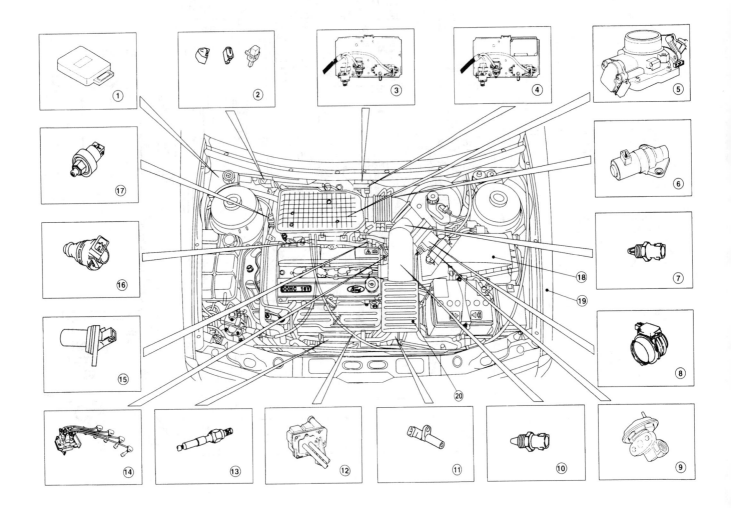

2.1B Location of principal fuel injection, ignition and emissions control system components

1   ECU (Electronic Control Unit)
2   Self-test, diagnosis and service connectors (left to right)
3   Bulkhead component mounting bracket - manual transmission - showing from left to right, (EGR) solenoid valve, pulse-air solenoid valve and (EGR) exhaust gas pressure differential sensor
4   Bulkhead component mounting bracket - automatic transmission - showing from left to right, (EGR) solenoid valve, pulse-air solenoid valve and (EGR) exhaust gas pressure differential sensor, with separate ignition module above
5   Throttle housing, including potentiometer
6   Idle speed control valve

7   Intake air temperature sensor
8   Air mass meter
9   Exhaust Gas Recirculation (EGR) valve
10 Coolant temperature sensor
11 Crankshaft speed/position sensor
12 Pulse-air filter housing
13 Oxygen sensor
14 Ignition coil and spark plug (HT) leads
15 Camshaft position sensor
16 Fuel injector(s)
17 Power steering pressure switch
18 Air cleaner assembly
19 Air intake tube and resonators - under left-hand front wing
20 Resonator

In the event of a sensor malfunction, a back-up circuit will take over, to provide driveability until the problem is identified and fixed.

Precautions

(a) *Always disconnect the power by uncoupling the battery terminals - see Section 1 of Chapter 5 - before removing any of the electronic control system's electrical connectors.*

(b) *When installing a battery, be particularly careful to avoid reversing the positive and negative battery leads.*

(c) *Do not subject any components of the system (especially the ECU) to severe impact during removal or installation.*

(d) *Do not be careless during fault diagnosis. Even slight terminal contact can invalidate a testing procedure, and damage one of the numerous transistor circuits.*

(e) *Never attempt to work on the ECU, to test it (with any kind of test equipment), or to open its cover.*

(f) *If you are inspecting electronic control system components during rainy weather, make sure that water does not enter any part. When washing the engine compartment, do not spray these parts or their electrical connectors with water.*

3 Diagnosis system - general information

General

The various components of the fuel, ignition and emissions control systems (not forgetting the same ECU's control of sub-systems such as the radiator cooling fan, air conditioning and automatic transmission, where appropriate) are so closely interlinked that diagnosis of a fault in any one component is virtually impossible using traditional methods. Working on simpler systems in the past, the experienced mechanic may well have been able to use personal skill and knowledge immediately to pinpoint the cause of a fault, or quickly to isolate the fault, by elimination; however, with an engine management system integrated to this degree, this is not likely to be possible in most instances, because of the number of symptoms that could arise from even a minor fault.

So that the causes of faults can be quickly and accurately traced and rectified, the ECU is provided with a built-in self-diagnosis facility, which detects malfunctions in the system's components. When a fault occurs, three things happen: the ECU identifies the fault, stores a corresponding code in its memory, and (in most cases) runs the system using back-up values pre-programmed ("mapped") into its memory; some form of driveability is thus maintained, to enable the vehicle to be driven to a garage for attention.

Any faults that may have occurred are indicated in the form of three-digit codes when the system is connected (via the built-in diagnosis or self-test connectors, as appropriate) to special diagnostic equipment - this points the user in the direction of the faulty circuit, so that further tests can pinpoint the exact location of the fault.

Given below is the procedure that would be followed by a Ford technician to trace a fault from scratch. Should your vehicle's engine management system develop a fault, read through the procedure and decide how much you can attempt, depending on your skill and experience and the equipment available to you, or whether it would be simpler to have the vehicle attended to by your local Ford dealer. If you are concerned about the apparent complexity of the system, however, remember the comments made in the fourth paragraph of Section 1 of this Chapter; the preliminary checks require nothing but care, patience and a few minor items of equipment, and may well eliminate the majority of faults.

(a) *Preliminary checks*
(b) *Fault code read-out **
(c) *Check ignition timing and base idle speed. Recheck fault codes to establish whether fault has been cured or not **
(d) *Carry out basic check of ignition system components. Recheck fault codes to establish whether fault has been cured or not **

(e) *Carry out basic check of fuel system components. Recheck fault codes to establish whether fault has been cured or not **
(f) *If fault is still not located, carry out system test **

Note: *Operations marked with an asterisk require special test equipment.*

Preliminary checks

Note: *When carrying out these checks to trace a fault, remember that if the fault has appeared only a short time after any part of the vehicle has been serviced or overhauled, the first place to check is where that work was carried out, however unrelated it may appear, to ensure that no carelessly-refitted components are causing the problem.*

If you are tracing the cause of a "partial" engine fault, such as lack of performance, in addition to the checks outlined below, check the compression pressures (see Part A of Chapter 2) and bear in mind the possibility that one of the hydraulic tappets might be faulty, producing an incorrect valve clearance. Check also that the fuel filter has been renewed at the recommended intervals.

If the system appears completely dead, remember the possibility that the alarm/inhibitor system may be responsible.

1   The first check for anyone without special test equipment is to switch on the ignition, and to listen for the fuel pump (the sound of an electric motor running, audible from beneath the rear seats); assuming there is sufficient fuel in the tank, the pump should start and run for approximately one or two seconds, then stop, each time the ignition is switched on. If the pump runs continuously all the time the ignition is switched on, the electronic control system is running in the back-up (or "limp-home") mode referred to by Ford as "Limited Operation Strategy" (LOS). This almost certainly indicates a fault in the ECU itself, and the vehicle should therefore be taken to a Ford dealer for a full test of the complete system using the correct diagnostic equipment; do not waste time trying to test the system without such facilities.

2   If the fuel pump is working correctly (or not at all), a considerable amount of fault diagnosis is still possible without special test equipment. Start the checking procedure as follows.

3   Open the bonnet and check the condition of the battery connections - remake the connections or renew the leads if a fault is found (Chapter 5). Use the same techniques to ensure that all earth points in the engine compartment provide good electrical contact through clean, metal-to-metal joints, and that all are securely fastened. (In addition to the earth connection at the engine lifting eye and that from the transmission to the body/battery, there is one earth connection behind each headlight assembly, and one below the power steering fluid reservoir.)

4   Referring to the information given in Chapter 12 and in the wiring diagrams at the back of this manual, check that all fuses protecting the circuits related to the engine management system are in good condition. Fit new fuses if required; while you are there, check that all relays are securely plugged into their sockets.

5   Next work methodically around the engine compartment, checking all visible wiring, and the connections between sections of the wiring loom. What you are looking for at this stage is wiring that is obviously damaged by chafing against sharp edges, or against moving suspension/transmission components and/or the auxiliary drivebelt, by being trapped or crushed between carelessly-refitted components, or melted by being forced into contact with hot engine castings, coolant or EGR pipes, etc. In almost all cases, damage of this sort is caused in the first instance by incorrect routing on reassembly after previous work has been carried out (see the note at the beginning of this sub-Section).

6   Obviously wires can break or short together inside the insulation so that no visible evidence betrays the fault, but this usually only occurs where the wiring loom has been incorrectly routed so that it is stretched taut or kinked sharply; either of these conditions should be obvious on even a casual inspection. If this is thought to have happened and the fault proves elusive, the suspect section of wiring should be checked very carefully during the more detailed checks which follow.

7   Depending on the extent of the problem, damaged wiring may be repaired by rejoining the break or splicing-in a new length of wire, us-

6

ing solder to ensure a good connection, and remaking the insulation with adhesive insulating tape or heat-shrink tubing, as desired. If the damage is extensive, given the implications for the vehicle's future reliability, the best long-term answer may well be to renew that entire section of the loom, however expensive this may appear.

8   When the actual damage has been repaired, ensure that the wiring loom is rerouted correctly, so that it is clear of other components, is not stretched or kinked, and is secured out of harm's way using the plastic clips, guides and ties provided.

9   Check all electrical connectors, ensuring that they are clean, securely fastened, and that each is locked by its plastic tabs or wire clip, as appropriate. If any connector shows external signs of corrosion (accumulations of white or green deposits, or streaks of "rust"), or if any is thought to be dirty, it must be unplugged and cleaned using electrical contact cleaner. If the connector pins are severely corroded, the connector must be renewed; note that this may mean the renewal of that entire section of the loom - see your local Ford dealer for details.

10   If the cleaner completely removes the corrosion to leave the connector in a satisfactory condition, it would be wise to pack the connector with a suitable material which will exclude dirt and moisture, and prevent the corrosion from occurring again; a Ford dealer may be able to recommend a suitable product. **Note:** The system's connectors use gold-plated pins, which must **not** be mixed with the older tin-plated types (readily identifiable from the different colour) if a component is renewed, nor must the lithium grease previously used to protect tin-plated pins be used on gold-plated connectors.

11   Following the accompanying schematic diagram, and working methodically around the engine compartment, check carefully that all vacuum hoses and pipes are securely fastened and correctly routed, with no signs of cracks, splits or deterioration to cause air leaks, or of hoses that are trapped, kinked, or bent sharply enough to restrict air flow **(see illustrations)**. Check with particular care at all connections and sharp bends, and renew any damaged or deformed lengths of hose.

12   Working from the fuel tank, via the filter, to the fuel rail (and including the feed and return), check the fuel lines, and renew any that are found to be leaking, trapped or kinked.

13   Check that the accelerator cable is correctly secured and adjusted; renew the cable if there is any doubt about its condition, or if it appears to be stiff or jerky in operation. Refer to the relevant Sections of Chapter 4 for further information, if required.

14   If there is any doubt about the operation of the throttle, remove the plenum chamber from the throttle housing, and check that the throttle valve moves smoothly and easily from the fully-closed to the fully-open position and back again, as an assistant depresses the accelerator pedal. If the valve shows any sign of stiffness, sticking or otherwise-inhibited movement (and the accelerator cable is known from the previous check to be in good condition), spray the throttle linkage with penetrating lubricant, allow time for it to work, and repeat the check; if no improvement is obtained, the complete throttle housing must be renewed (Chapter 4).

15   Unclip the air cleaner cover, and check that the air filter element and the crankcase ventilation system filter are not clogged or soaked. (A clogged air filter will obstruct the intake air flow, causing a noticeable effect on engine performance; a clogged crankcase ventilation system filter will inhibit crankcase "breathing"). Renew or clean the filter(s) as appropriate; refer to the relevant Sections of Chapter 1 for further information, if required. Before refitting the air cleaner cover, check that the air intake (located under the front left-hand wing, opening behind the direction indicator/headlight assembly) is clear. It should be possible to blow through the intake, or to probe it (carefully) as far as the rear of the direction indicator light. **Note:** Working in the engine compartment while the engine is running requires great care if the risk of personal injury is to be avoided; among the dangers are burns from contact with hot components, or contact with moving components such as the radiator cooling fan or the auxiliary drivebelt. Refer to "Safety first!" at the front of this manual before starting, and ensure that your hands, and long hair or loose clothing, are kept well clear of hot or moving components at all times.

17   Working from the air intake junction at the inner wing panel, via

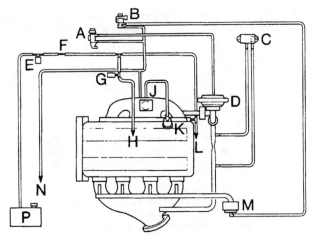

3.11A Vacuum hose routing schematic diagram

A   Exhaust Gas Recirculation (EGR) solenoid valve
B   Pulse-air solenoid valve
C   Exhaust Gas Recirculation (EGR) exhaust gas
      pressure differential sensor
D   Exhaust Gas Recirculation (EGR) valve
E   Charcoal canister-purge solenoid valve
F   Restrictor
G   Idle-increase solenoid valve - where fitted
H   Connection to plenum chamber
J   Connection to inlet manifold
K   Fuel pressure regulator
L   Connection to Positive Crankcase Ventilation
      (PCV) valve
M   Pulse-air filter housing
N   Connection to heating/air conditioning system controls
P   Charcoal canister

the air cleaner assembly and air mass meter, to the resonator, plenum chamber, throttle housing and inlet manifold (and including the various vacuum hoses and pipes connected to these), check for air leaks. Usually, these will be revealed by sucking or hissing noises, but minor leaks may be traced by spraying a solution of soapy water on to the suspect joint; if a leak exists, it will be shown by the change in engine note and the accompanying air bubbles (or sucking-in of the liquid, depending on the pressure difference at that point). If a leak is found at any point, tighten the fastening clamp and/or renew the faulty components, as applicable.

18   Similarly, work from the cylinder head, via the manifold (and not forgetting the related EGR and pulse-air system components) to the tailpipe, to check that the exhaust system is free from leaks. The simplest way of doing this, if the vehicle can be raised and supported safely and with complete security while the check is made, is to temporarily block the tailpipe while listening for the sound of escaping exhaust gases; any leak should be evident. If a leak is found at any point, tighten the fastening clamp bolts and/or nuts, renew the gasket, and/or renew the faulty section of the system, as necessary, to seal the leak.

19   It is possible to make a further check of the electrical connections by wiggling each electrical connector of the system in turn as the engine is idling; a faulty connector will be immediately evident from the engine's response as contact is broken and remade. A faulty connector should be renewed to ensure the future reliability of the system; note that this may mean the renewal of that entire section of the loom - see your local Ford dealer for details.

20   Switch off the engine. If the fault is not yet identified, the next step is to check the ignition voltages, using an engine analyser with an oscilloscope - without such equipment, the only tests possible are to remove and check each spark plug in turn, to check the spark plug (HT) lead connections and resistances, and to check the connections and resistances of the ignition coil. Refer to the relevant Sections of Chapters 1 and 5.

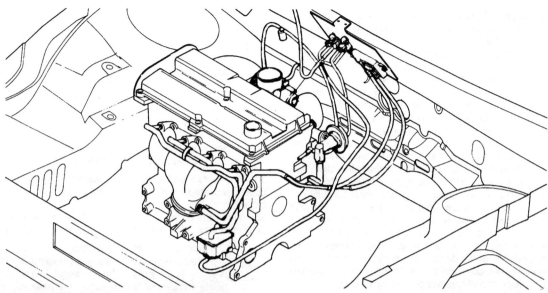

3.11B Installation of vacuum hoses in engine compartment

21   The final step in these preliminary checks would be to use an exhaust gas analyser to measure the CO level at the exhaust tailpipe. This check cannot be made without special test equipment - see your local Ford dealer for details.

Fault code read-out

22   As noted in the general comments at the beginning of this Section, the preliminary checks outlined above should eliminate the majority of faults from the engine management system. If the fault is not yet identified, the next step is to connect a fault code reader to the ECU, so that its self-diagnosis facility can be used to identify the faulty part of the system; further tests can then be made to identify the exact cause of the fault.

23   In their basic form, fault code readers are simply hand-held electronic devices, which take data stored within an ECU's memory and display it when required as two- or three-digit fault codes. The more sophisticated versions now available can also control sensors and actuators, to provide more effective testing; some can store information, so that a road test can be carried out, and any faults encountered during the test can be displayed afterwards.

24   Ford specify the use of their STAR (Self-Test Automatic Readout) tester; most Ford dealers should have such equipment, and the staff trained to use it effectively. The only alternatives are as follows:

(a)   To obtain one of those proprietary readers which can interpret EEC-IV three-digit codes - at present, such readers are too expensive for the DIY enthusiast, but are becoming more popular with smaller specialist garages.

(b)   To use an analogue voltmeter, whereby the stored codes are displayed as sweeps of the voltmeter needle. This option limits the operator to a read-out of any codes stored - ie, there is no control of sensors and/or actuators - but can still be useful in pinpointing the faulty part of the engine management system. The display is interpreted as follows. Each code (whether fault code or command/separator) is marked by a three-to-four second pause - code "538" would therefore be shown as long (3 to 4 seconds) pause, five fast sweeps of the needle, slight (1 second) pause, three fast sweeps, slight pause, eight fast sweeps, long pause.

(c)   Owners without access to such equipment must take the vehicle to a Ford dealer, or to an expert who has similar equipment and the skill to use it.

25   Because of the variations in the design of fault code readers, it is not possible to give exact details of the sequence of tests; the manufacturer's instructions must be followed, in conjunction with the codes given below. The following ten paragraphs outline the procedure to be

followed using a version of the Ford STAR tester, to illustrate the general principles, as well as notes to guide the owner using only a voltmeter.

26   The vehicle must be prepared by applying the handbrake, switching off the air conditioning (where fitted) and any other electrical loads (lights, heated rear window, etc), then selecting neutral (manual transmission) or the "P" position (automatic transmission). Where the engine is required to be running, it must be fully warmed-up to normal operating temperature before the test is started. Using any adaptors required,

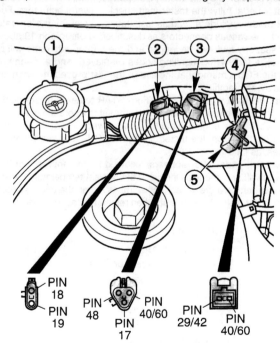

3.26 Location and terminal identification of engine management system self-test, diagnosis and service connectors

1   Power steering fluid reservoir
2   Diagnosis connector - for Ford diagnostic equipment FDS 2000
3   Self-test connector - for fault code read-out - pin 17 is output terminal, pin 48 is input terminal, pin 40/60 is earth
4   Service connector - for octane adjustment
5   Plug-in bridge - to suit 95 RON fuel

connect the fault code reader to the system via the (triangular, three-pin) self-test connector on the right-hand end of the engine compartment bulkhead **(see illustration)**. If a voltmeter is being used, connect its positive lead to the battery positive terminal, and its negative lead to the self-test connector's output terminal, pin 17. Have a pen and paper ready to write down the codes displayed.

27   Set the tester in operation. For the Ford STAR tester, a display check will be carried out and the test mode requirements must be entered. If a voltmeter is being used, connect a spare length of wire to earth the self-test connector's input terminal, pin 48. Be very careful to ensure that you earth the correct terminal - the one with the white/green wire. The first part of the test starts, with the ignition switched on, but with the engine off. On pressing the "Mem/test" button, the tester displays "TEST" and the ready code "000", followed by a command code "010" - the accelerator pedal must be fully depressed within 10 seconds of the command code appearing, or fault codes "576" or "577" will appear when they are called up later. If a voltmeter is being used, code "000" will not appear (except perhaps as a flicker of the needle) and "010" will appear as a single sweep - to ensure correct interpretation of the display, watch carefully for the interval between the end of one code and the beginning of the next, otherwise you will become confused and misinterpret the read-out.

28   The tester will then display the codes for any faults in the system at the time of the test. Each code is repeated once; if no faults are present, code "111" will be displayed. If a voltmeter is being used, the pause between repetitions will vary according to the equipment in use and the number of faults in the system, but was found to be approximately 3 to 4 seconds - it may be necessary to start again, and to repeat the read-out until you are familiar with what you are seeing.

29   Next the tester will display code "010" (now acting as a separator), followed by the codes for any faults stored in the ECU's memory; if no faults were stored, code "111" will be displayed.

30   When prompted by the tester, the operator must next depress the accelerator pedal fully; the tester then checks several actuators. Further test modes include a "wiggle test" facility, whereby the operator can check the various connectors as described in paragraph 19 above (in this case, any fault will be logged and the appropriate code will be displayed), a facility for recalling codes displayed, and a means for clearing the ECU's memory at the end of the test procedure when any faults have been rectified.

31   The next step when using the Ford STAR tester is to conduct a test with the engine running. With the tester set in operation (see paragraph 26 above) the engine is started and allowed to idle. On pressing the "Mem/test" button, the tester displays "TEST", followed by one of two codes, as follows.

32   If warning code "998" appears, followed by the appropriate fault code, switch off and check as indicated the coolant temperature sensor, the intake air temperature sensor, the air mass meter, the throttle potentiometer and/or their related circuits, then restart the test procedure.

33   If command code "020" appears, carry out the following procedure within ten seconds:

(a)   *Depress the brake pedal fully.*

(b)   *Turn the steering to full-lock (either way) and centre it again, to produce a signal from the power steering pressure switch - if no signal is sent, fault code "521" will be displayed.*

(c)   *If automatic transmission is fitted, switch the overdrive cancel button on and off, then do the same for the "Economy/Sport" mode switch.*

(d)   *Wait for separator code "010" to be displayed, then within 10 seconds, depress the accelerator pedal fully, increasing engine speed rapidly above 3000 rpm - release the pedal.*

34   Any faults found in the system will be logged and displayed. Each code is repeated once; if no faults are present, code "111" will be displayed.

35   When the codes have been displayed for all faults logged, the ECU enters its "Service Adjustment Programme", as follows:

(a)   *The programme lasts for 2 minutes.*

(b)   *The idle speed control valve is deactivated, and the idle speed is set to its pre-programmed (unregulated) value. If the appropriate equipment is connected, the base idle speed can be checked (note, however, that it is not adjustable).*

(c)   *The ignition timing can be checked if a timing light is connected (note, however, that it is not adjustable).*

(d)   *Pressing the accelerator pedal fully at any time during this period will execute a cylinder balance test. Each injector in turn is switched off, and the corresponding decrease in engine speed is logged - code "090" will be displayed if the test is successful.*

(e)   *At the end of the 2 minutes, the completion of the programme is shown by the engine speed briefly rising, then returning to normal idling speed as the idle speed control valve is reactivated.*

36   As with the engine-off test, further test modes include a "wiggle test" facility, whereby the operator can check the various connectors as described in paragraph 19 above (in this case, any fault will be logged and the appropriate code will be displayed), a facility for recalling codes displayed, and a means for clearing the ECU's memory at the end of the test procedure when any faults have been rectified. If equipment other than the Ford STAR tester is used, the ECU's memory can be cleared by disconnecting the battery - if this is not done, the code will reappear with any other codes in the event of subsequent trouble, but remember that other systems with memory (such as the clock and audio equipment) will also be affected. Should it become necessary to disconnect the battery during work on any other part of the vehicle, first check to see if any fault codes have been logged.

37   Given below are the possible codes, their meanings, and where relevant, the action to be taken as a result of a code being displayed.

Code	Meaning	Action
000	Ready for test	-
010	Command/separator code	Depress accelerator pedal fully, then release
020	Command code	Depress brake pedal fully, then release
10	Cylinder No 1 low	During cylinder balance test
20	Cylinder No 2 low	During cylinder balance test
30	Cylinder No 3 low	During cylinder balance test
40	Cylinder No 4 low	During cylinder balance test
90	Cylinder balance test successful	-
111	No faults found	-
112-114	Intake air temperature sensor	Check component (Section 4 of this Chapter)
116-118	Coolant temperature sensor - normal operating temperature not reached	If fault still exists on reaching normal operating temperature, check component (Chapter 3)
121-125	Throttle potentiometer	Check component (Section 4 of this Chapter)
129	Incorrect response from air mass meter while conducting test	Repeat test
136, 137	Oxygen sensor	Check component (Section 4 of this Chapter)

Code	Meaning	Action
139	Oxygen sensor	Check component (Section 4 of this Chapter)
144	Oxygen sensor	Check component (Section 4 of this Chapter)
157-159	Air mass meter	Check component (Section 4 of this Chapter)
167	Incorrect response from throttle potentiometer while conducting test	Repeat test
171	Oxygen sensor	Check component (Section 4 of this Chapter)
172	Oxygen sensor - mixture too weak	Check component (Section 4 of this Chapter)
173	Oxygen sensor - mixture too rich	Check component (Section 4 of this Chapter)
174, 175	Oxygen sensor	Check component (Section 4 of this Chapter)
176	Oxygen sensor - mixture too weak	Check component (Section 4 of this Chapter)
177	Oxygen sensor - mixture too rich	Check component (Section 4 of this Chapter)
178	Oxygen sensor	Check component (Section 4 of this Chapter)
179	Fuel system - mixture too weak	Check EGR valve (Section 6 of this Chapter)
181	Fuel system - mixture too rich	Check EGR valve (Section 6 of this Chapter)
182	Idle mixture too weak	Check idle speed control valve (Chapter 4)
183	Idle mixture too rich	If mixture OK, check fuel system (see below)
184, 185	Air mass meter	Check component (Section 4 of this Chapter)
186	Injector opening time (pulse width) too long	Carry out system test (see below)
187	Injector opening time (pulse width) too short	Carry out system test (see below)
188	Oxygen sensor - mixture too weak	Check component (Section 4 of this Chapter)
189	Oxygen sensor - mixture too rich	Check component (Section 4 of this Chapter)
191	Idle mixture too weak	Check EGR valve (Section 6 of this Chapter) and idle speed control valve (Chapter 4)
192	Idle mixture too rich	Check EGR valve (Section 6 of this Chapter) and idle speed control valve (Chapter 4)
194, 195	Oxygen sensor	Check component (Section 4 of this Chapter)
211	No ignition signal to ECU	Carry out system test (see below)
212	Tachometer circuit	Carry out system test (see below)
213	No ignition signal from ECU	Carry out system test (see below)
214	Camshaft position sensor	Check component (Section 4 of this Chapter)
215-217	Ignition coil	Carry out system test (see below)
218, 222	Tachometer circuit	Carry out system test (see below)
226	ECU/ignition module pulse	Carry out system test (see below)
227	Crankshaft speed/position sensor	Check component (Chapter 5)
228	Ignition module/ignition coil winding 1	Carry out system test (see below)
229	Ignition module/ignition coil winding 1	Carry out system test (see below)
231	Ignition module/ignition coil winding 3	Carry out system test (see below)
232	Ignition coil primary windings	Carry out system test (see below)
233	Ignition module	Carry out system test (see below)
234 to 237	Ignition coil primary windings	Carry out system test (see below)
238	Ignition module/ignition coil primary windings	Carry out system test (see below)
239	No ignition signal to ECU on cranking	Carry out system test (see below)
241	Incorrect response from ECU and/or ignition module while conducting test	Repeat test
243	Ignition coil failure	Carry out system test (see below)
311-316	Pulse-air system	Carry out system test (see below)
326	EGR system exhaust gas pressure differential sensor	Check component (Section 6 of this Chapter)
327	EGR system exhaust gas pressure differential sensor or solenoid valve	Check components (Section 6 of this Chapter)
328	EGR system solenoid valve	Check component (Section 6 of this Chapter)
332	EGR valve not opening	Check component (Section 6 of this Chapter)
334	EGR system solenoid valve	Check component (Section 6 of this Chapter)
335	EGR system exhaust gas pressure differential sensor	Check component (Section 6 of this Chapter)
336	Exhaust gas pressure too high	Check system (Section 6 of this Chapter)
337	EGR system exhaust gas pressure differential sensor or solenoid valve	Check components (Section 6 of this Chapter)
338, 339	Coolant temperature sensor	Carry out system test (see below)
341	Service connector earthed	Unplug connector and repeat test - reconnect on completion

6

Code	Meaning	Action
411	Engine speed too low during test	Check for air leaks, then repeat test
412	Engine speed too high during test	Check for air leaks, then repeat test
413-416	Idle speed control valve	Check component (Chapter 4, Section 16)
452	Vehicle speed sensor	Check component (Section 4 of this Chapter)
511, 512	ECU memory	Check whether battery was disconnected, then check fuse 11 - if fault still exists, renew ECU (Section 6 of this Chapter)
513	ECU reference voltage	Carry out system test (see below)
519, 521	Power steering pressure switch not operated during test	Check component is fitted and connected, then repeat test - if fault still exists, carry out system test (see below)
522, 523	Selector lever position sensor	Check component (Chapter 7, Part B)
536	Brake on/off switch not activated during test	Repeat test
538	Operator error during test	Repeat test
539	Air conditioning switched on during test	Switch off and repeat test
542, 543	Fuel pump circuit	Carry out system test (see below)
551	Idle speed control valve circuit	Carry out system test (see below)
552	Pulse-air system circuit	Carry out system test (see below)
556	Fuel pump circuit	Check fuel pump relay - if fault still exists, carry out system test (see below)
558	EGR system solenoid valve circuit	Carry out system test (see below)
563	Radiator (high-speed) electric cooling fan relay and/or circuit	Carry out system test (see below)
564	Radiator electric cooling fan relay and/or circuit	Carry out system test (see below)
565	Charcoal canister-purge solenoid valve	Check component (Section 5 of this Chapter)
573	Radiator electric cooling fan relay and/or circuit	Carry out system test (see below)
574	Radiator (high-speed) electric cooling fan relay and/or circuit	Carry out system test (see below)
575	Fuel pump and/or fuel cut-off switch circuits	Carry out system test (see below)
576, 577	Accelerator pedal not depressed fully during test procedure - kickdown not activated (A/T)	Repeat test
621	A/T shift solenoid 1 circuit	Refer to Chapter 7, Part B
622	A/T shift solenoid 2 circuit	Refer to Chapter 7, Part B
624	A/T pressure control solenoid electronic	Refer to Chapter 7, Part B
625	A/T electronic pressure control solenoid circuit	Refer to Chapter 7, Part B
629	A/T torque converter clutch solenoid	Refer to Chapter 7, Part B
634	Selector lever position sensor circuit	Check component (Chapter 7, Part B)
635, 637	A/T fluid temperature sensor	Refer to Chapter 7, Part B
639	Automatic transmission speed sensor	Refer to Chapter 7, Part B
645	Automatic transmission 1st speed	Refer to Chapter 7, Part B
646	Automatic transmission 2nd speed	Refer to Chapter 7, Part B
647	Automatic transmission 3rd speed	Refer to Chapter 7, Part B
648	Automatic transmission 4th speed	Refer to Chapter 7, Part B
653	A/T overdrive cancel button and "Economy/Sport" mode switch not operated during test	Repeat test
998	Warning code	Check fault(s) indicated by subsequent code(s)

Ignition timing and base idle speed check

Note: *The following procedure is a check only, essentially of the ECU. Both the ignition timing and the base idle speed are controlled by the ECU. The ignition timing is not adjustable at all; the base idle speed is set in production, and should not be altered.*

38   If the fault code read-out (with any checks resulting from it) has not eliminated the fault, the next step is to check the ECU's control of the ignition timing and the base idle speed. This task requires the use of a Ford STAR tester (a proprietary fault code reader can be used only if it is capable of inducing the ECU to enter its "Service Adjustment Programme"), coupled with an accurate tachometer and a good-quality timing light. Without this equipment, the task is not possible; the vehicle must be taken to a Ford dealer for attention.

39   To make the check, apply the handbrake, switch off the air conditioning (where fitted) and any other electrical loads (lights, heated rear window, etc), then select neutral (manual transmission) or the "P" position (automatic transmission). Start the engine, and warm it up to normal operating temperature. The radiator electric cooling fan must be running continuously while the check is made; this should be activated by the ECU, when prompted by the tester. Switch off the engine, and connect the test equipment as directed by the manufacturer - refer to paragraph 26 above for details of STAR tester connection.

40   Raise and support the front of the vehicle securely, and remove

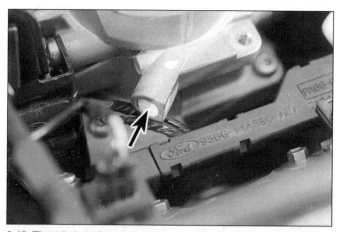

3.45 Throttle housing air bypass screw is sealed on production with a white tamperproof plug (arrowed)

the auxiliary drivebelt cover (see Chapter 1). Emphasise the two pairs of notches in the inner and outer rims of the crankshaft pulley, using white paint. Note that an ignition timing reference mark is not provided on the pulley - in the normal direction of crankshaft rotation (clockwise, seen from the right-hand side of the vehicle) the first pair of notches are irrelevant to the vehicles covered in this manual, while the second pair indicate Top Dead Centre (TDC) when aligned with the rear edge of the raised mark on the sump; when checking the ignition timing, therefore, the (rear edge of the) sump mark should appear just before the TDC notches (see Part A of Chapter 2, Section 4, for further information if required).

41   Start the engine and allow it to idle. Work through the engine-running test procedure until the ECU enters its "Service Adjustment Programme" - see paragraph 35 above.

42   Use the timing light to check that the timing marks appear approximately as outlined above at idle speed. Do not spend too much time on this check; if the timing appears to be incorrect, the system may have a fault, and a full system test must be carried out (see below) to establish its cause.

43   Using the tachometer, check that the base idle speed is as given in the Specifications Section of Chapter 4.

44   If the recorded speed differs significantly from the specified value, check for air leaks, as described in the preliminary checks (paragraphs 15 to 18 above), or any other faults which might cause the discrepancy.

45   The base idle speed is set in production by means of an air bypass screw (located in the front right-hand corner of the throttle housing) which controls the amount of air that is allowed to pass through a bypass passage, past the throttle valve when it is fully closed in the idle position; the screw is then sealed with a white tamperproof plug **(see illustration)**. In service, the idle speed is controlled by the ECU, which has the ability to compensate for engine wear, build-up of dirt in the throttle housing, and other factors which might require changes in idle speed. The air bypass screw setting should not, therefore, be altered. If any alterations are made, a blue tamperproof plug must be fitted, and the engine should be allowed to idle for at least five minutes on completion, so that the ECU can re-learn its idle values.

46   When both checks have been made and the "Service Adjustment Programme" is completed, follow the tester instructions to return to the fault code read-out, and establish whether the fault has been cured or not.

Basic check of ignition system

47   If the checks so far have not eliminated the fault, the next step is to carry out a basic check of the ignition system components, using an engine analyser with an oscilloscope - without such equipment, the only tests possible are to remove and check each spark plug in turn, to check the spark plug (HT) lead connections and resistances, and to check the connections and resistances of the ignition coil. Refer to the relevant Sections of Chapters 1 and 5.

Basic check of fuel system

48   If the checks so far have not eliminated the fault, the next step is to carry out a basic check of the fuel system components.

49   Assuming that the preliminary checks have established that the fuel pump is operating correctly, that the fuel filter is unlikely to be blocked, and also that there are no leaks in the system, the next step is to check the fuel pressure (see Chapter 4). If this is correct, check the injectors (see Chapter 4) and the Positive Crankcase Ventilation system (see Chapter 1).

System test

50   The final element of the Ford testing procedure is to carry out a system test, using a break-out box - this is a device that is connected between the ECU and its electrical connector, so that the individual circuits indicated by the fault code read-out can be tested while connected to the system, if necessary with the engine running. In the case of many of the system's components, this enables their output voltages to be measured - a more accurate means of testing.

51   In addition to the break-out box and the adaptors required to connect it, several items of specialist equipment are needed to complete these tests. This puts them quite beyond the scope of many smaller dealers, let alone the DIY owner; the vehicle should be taken to a Ford dealer for attention.

4   Information sensors - general information, testing, removal and refitting

Note: *This Section is concerned principally with the sensors which give the ECU the information it needs to control the various engine management sub-systems - for further details of those systems and their other components, refer to the relevant Chapter of this manual.*

General

ECU (Electronic Control Unit)

1   This component is the heart of the entire engine management system, controlling the fuel injection, ignition and emissions control systems. It also controls sub-systems such as the radiator cooling fan, air conditioning and automatic transmission, where appropriate. Refer to Section 2 of this Chapter for an illustration of how it works.

Air mass meter

2   This uses a "hot-wire" system, sending the ECU a constantly-varying (analogue) voltage signal corresponding to the mass of air passing into the engine. Since air mass varies with temperature (cold air being denser than warm), measuring air mass provides the ECU with a very accurate means of determining the correct amount of fuel required to achieve the ideal air/fuel mixture ratio.

Crankshaft speed/position sensor

3   This is an inductive pulse generator bolted (in a separate bracket) to the cylinder block/crankcase, to scan the ridges between 36 holes machined in the inboard (right-hand) face of the flywheel/driveplate. As each ridge passes the sensor tip, a signal is generated, which is used by the ECU to determine engine speed.

4   The ridge between the 35th and 36th holes (corresponding to 90 BTDC) is missing - this step in the incoming signals is used by the ECU to determine crankshaft (ie, piston) position.

Camshaft position sensor

5   This is bolted to the rear left-hand end of the cylinder head, to register with a lobe on the inlet camshaft. It functions in the same way as the crankshaft speed/position sensor, producing a series of pulses (corresponding to No 1 cylinder at 46 ATDC); this gives the ECU a reference point, to enable it to determine the firing order, and operate the injectors in the appropriate sequence.

Coolant temperature sensor

6   This component, which is screwed into the top of the thermostat housing, is an NTC (Negative Temperature Coefficient) thermistor -

6

that is, a semi-conductor whose electrical resistance decreases as its temperature increases. It provides the ECU with a constantly-varying (analogue) voltage signal, corresponding to the temperature of the engine coolant. This is used to refine the calculations made by the ECU, when determining the correct amount of fuel required to achieve the ideal air/fuel mixture ratio.

Intake air temperature sensor

7   This component, which is screwed into the underside of the air intake resonator, is also an NTC thermistor - see the previous paragraph - providing the ECU with a signal corresponding to the temperature of air passing into the engine. This is used to refine the calculations made by the ECU, when determining the correct amount of fuel required to achieve the ideal air/fuel mixture ratio.

Throttle potentiometer

8   This is mounted on the end of the throttle valve spindle, to provide the ECU with a constantly-varying (analogue) voltage signal corresponding to the throttle opening. This allows the ECU to register the driver's input when determining the amount of fuel required by the engine.

Vehicle speed sensor

9   This component is a Hall-effect generator, mounted on the transmission's speedometer drive. It supplies the ECU with a series of pulses corresponding to the vehicle's road speed, enabling the ECU to control features such as the fuel shut-off on the overrun, and to provide information for the trip computer, adaptive damping and cruise control systems (where fitted).

Power steering pressure switch

10   This is a pressure-operated switch, screwed into the power steering system's high-pressure pipe. Its contacts are normally closed, opening when the system reaches the specified pressure - on receiving this signal, the ECU increases the idle speed, to compensate for the additional load on the engine.

Exhaust gas pressure differential sensor

11   This component measures the difference in pressure of the exhaust gases across a venturi (restriction) in the Exhaust Gas Recirculation (EGR) system's pipe, and sends the ECU a voltage signal corresponding to the pressure difference.

Oxygen sensor

12   The oxygen sensor in the exhaust system provides the ECU with constant feedback - "closed-loop" control - which enables it to adjust the mixture to provide the best possible conditions for the catalytic converter to operate.
13   The sensor has a built-in heating element which is controlled by the ECU, in order to bring the sensor's tip to an efficient operating temperature as rapidly as possible. The sensor's tip is sensitive to oxygen, and sends the ECU a varying voltage depending on the amount of oxygen in the exhaust gases. If the intake air/fuel mixture is too rich, the exhaust gases are low in oxygen, so the sensor sends a low-voltage signal, the voltage rising as the mixture weakens and the amount of oxygen in the exhaust gases rises. Peak conversion efficiency of all major pollutants occurs if the intake air/fuel mixture is maintained at the chemically-correct ratio for the complete combustion of petrol, of 14.7 parts (by weight) of air to 1 part of fuel (the "stoichiometric" ratio). The sensor output voltage alters sharply around this point, the ECU using the signal change as a reference point, and correcting the air/fuel mixture by altering the fuel injector pulse width.

Air conditioning system

14   Two pressure-operated switches and the compressor clutch solenoid are connected to the ECU, to enable it to determine how the system is operating. The ECU can increase idle speed or switch off the system, as necessary, so that normal vehicle operation and driveability are not impaired. See Chapter 3 for further details, but note that diagnosis and repair should be left to a dealer service department or air conditioning specialist.

Automatic transmission

15   In addition to the driver's controls, the transmission has a speed sensor, a fluid temperature sensor (built into the solenoid valve unit), and a selector lever position sensor. All of these are connected to the ECU, to enable it to control the transmission through the solenoid valve unit. See Part B of Chapter 7 for further details.

Testing

ECU (Electronic Control Unit)

16   **Do not** attempt to "test" the ECU with any kind of equipment. If it is thought to be faulty, take the vehicle to a Ford dealer for the entire electronic control system to be checked using the proper diagnostic equipment. Only if all other possibilities have been eliminated should the ECU be considered at fault, and replaced.

Air mass meter

17   Testing of this component is beyond the scope of the DIY mechanic, and should be left to a Ford dealer.

Crankshaft speed/position sensor

18   Unplug the electrical connector from the sensor.
19   Using an ohmmeter, measure the resistance between the sensor terminals. Compare this reading to the one listed in the Specifications Section at the beginning of this Chapter. If the indicated resistance is not within the specified range, renew the sensor.
20   Plug in the sensor's electrical connector on completion.

Camshaft position sensor

21   The procedure is as described in paragraphs 18 to 20 above.

Coolant temperature sensor

22   Refer to Chapter 3.

Intake air temperature sensor

23   Unplug the electrical connector from the sensor.
24   Using an ohmmeter, measure the resistance between the sensor terminals. Depending on the temperature of the sensor tip, the resistance measured will vary, but it should be within the broad limits given in the Specifications Section of this Chapter. If the sensor's temperature is varied - by placing it in a freezer for a while, or by warming it gently - its resistance should alter accordingly.
25   If the results obtained show the sensor to be faulty, renew it.

Throttle potentiometer

26   Remove the plenum chamber (see Chapter 4) and unplug the potentiometer's electrical connector.
27   Using an ohmmeter, measure the resistance between the unit's terminals - first between the centre terminal and one of the outer two, then from the centre to the remaining outer terminal. The resistance should be within the limits given in the Specifications Section of this Chapter, and should alter *smoothly* as the throttle valve is moved from the fully-closed (idle speed) position to fully open and back again.
28   If the resistance measured is significantly different from the specified value, if there are any breaks in continuity, or if the reading fluctuates erratically as the throttle is operated, the potentiometer is faulty, and must be renewed.

Vehicle speed sensor

29   Testing of this component is beyond the scope of the DIY mechanic, and should be left to a Ford dealer.

Power steering pressure switch

30   Unplug the electrical connector from the sensor.
31   Using an ohmmeter, measure the resistance between the switch terminals. With the engine switched off, or idling with the roadwheels in the straight-ahead position, little or no resistance should be measured. With the engine running and the steering on full-lock, the pressure increase in the system should open the switch contacts, so that infinite resistance is now measured.
32   If the results obtained show the switch to be faulty, renew it.

Exhaust gas pressure differential sensor

33   Testing of this component is beyond the scope of the DIY mechanic, and should be left to a Ford dealer.

Oxygen sensor

34   Testing of this component can be done only by attaching special diagnostic equipment to the sensor wiring, and checking that the volt-

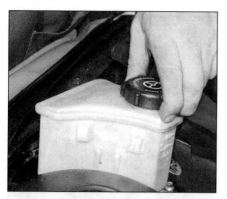

4.36A Unclip and lift power steering fluid reservoir - take care not to spill fluid . . .

4.36B . . . unscrew bolt (arrowed) to release ECU's electrical connector

4.37 Unscrew retaining bolt and withdraw ECU's mounting bracket . . .

4.38 . . . then lift ECU to disengage it, and withdraw it

4.40 Unplugging the air mass meter's electrical connector . . .

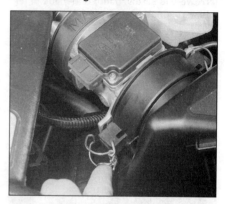

4.41 . . . release clips to separate meter from air cleaner cover

age varies from low to high values when the engine is running; *do not attempt to "test"* any part of the system with anything other than the correct test equipment. This is beyond the scope of the DIY mechanic, and should be left to a Ford dealer.

Removal and refitting

General
35 Before disconnecting any of these components, always disconnect the power by uncoupling the battery terminals, negative (earth) lead first - see Section 1 of Chapter 5.

ECU (Electronic Control Unit)
Note: *The ECU is fragile. Take care not to drop it or subject it to any other kind of impact, and do not subject it to extremes of temperature, or allow it to get wet.*
36 Carefully prise the power steering fluid reservoir upwards out of its clip on the suspension mounting. Unscrew the ECU connector's retaining bolt, and unplug the connector **(see illustrations)**.
37 Working in the passenger compartment, unscrew the retaining bolt and withdraw the mounting bracket **(see illustration)**.
38 Lifting the ECU to release it from the bulkhead carrier bracket, withdraw the unit **(see illustration)**.
39 Refitting is the reverse of the removal procedure. Whenever the ECU (or battery) is disconnected, the information relating to idle speed control and other operating values will be lost from its memory until the unit has re-programmed itself; until then, there may be surging, hesitation, erratic idle and a generally-inferior level of performance. To allow the ECU to re-learn these values, start the engine and run it as close to idle speed as possible until it reaches its normal operating temperature, then run it for approximately two minutes at 1200 rpm. Next, drive the vehicle as far as necessary - approximately 5 miles of varied driving conditions is usually sufficient - to complete the re-learning process.

Air mass meter
40 Releasing its wire clip, unplug the meter's electrical connector

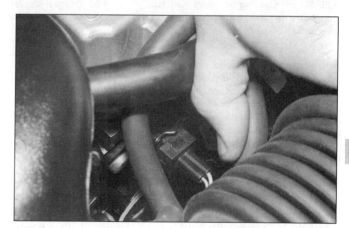

4.45 Camshaft position sensor is located at left-hand rear end of cylinder head

(see illustration).
41 Release the clips and lift the air cleaner cover, then release the two smaller clips and detach the meter from the cover **(see illustration)**.
42 Slacken the clamp securing the meter to the resonator hose, and withdraw the meter.
43 Refitting is the reverse of the removal procedure. Ensure that the meter and air cleaner cover are seated correctly and securely fastened, so that there are no air leaks.

Crankshaft speed/position sensor
44 Refer to Chapter 5.

Camshaft position sensor
45 Remove the air mass meter and resonator (refer to Chapter 4) to gain access to the sensor **(see illustration)**. Release the fuel feed and

4.49 Intake air temperature sensor (arrowed) is screwed into underside of air intake resonator

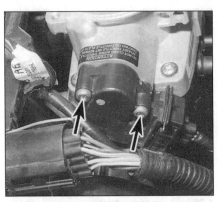

4.53 Throttle potentiometer is secured by two screws (arrowed)

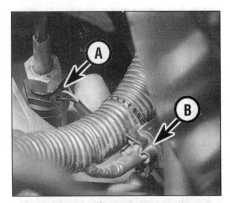

4.55 Vehicle speed sensor "A", with its electrical connector "B"

4.56 Power steering pressure switch is screwed into pipe at right-hand rear end of engine

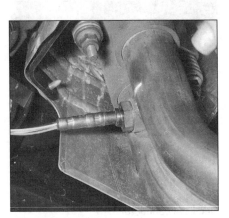

4.62 Oxygen sensor is screwed into exhaust system front downpipe . . .

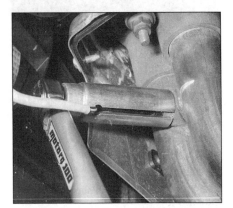

4.64 . . . slotted socket will be required to tighten sensor with a torque wrench

return hoses from their clip.

46   Releasing its wire clip, unplug the sensor's electrical connector. Remove the retaining screw, and withdraw the sensor from the cylinder head; be prepared for slight oil loss.

47   Refitting is the reverse of the removal procedure, noting the following points:

(a)   *Apply petroleum jelly or clean engine oil to the sensor's sealing O-ring.*

(b)   *Locate the sensor fully in the cylinder head, and wipe off any surplus lubricant before securing it.*

(c)   *Tighten the screw to the specified torque wrench setting.*

Coolant temperature sensor

48   Refer to Chapter 3, Section 6.

Intake air temperature sensor

49   Remove the air mass meter and resonator (refer to Chapter 4) to gain access to the sensor **(see illustration)**.

50   Releasing its clip, unplug the sensor's electrical connector, then unscrew the sensor from the resonator.

51   Refitting is the reverse of the removal procedure. Tighten the sensor to the specified torque wrench setting; if it is overtightened, its tapered thread may crack the resonator.

Throttle potentiometer

52   Remove the plenum chamber (see Chapter 4). Releasing its wire clip, unplug the large electrical connector (next to the fuel pressure regulator).

53   Releasing its wire clip, unplug the potentiometer's electrical connector. Remove the retaining screws, and withdraw the unit from the throttle housing **(see illustration)**. *Do not* force the sensor's centre to rotate past its normal operating sweep; the unit will be seriously damaged.

54   Refitting is the reverse of the removal procedure, noting the following points:

(a)   *Ensure that the potentiometer is correctly orientated, by locating its centre on the D-shaped throttle shaft (throttle closed), and aligning the potentiometer body so that the bolts pass easily into the throttle housing.*

(b)   *Tighten the screws evenly and securely (but do not overtighten them, or the potentiometer body will be cracked).*

Vehicle speed sensor

55   The sensor is mounted at the base of the speedometer drive cable, and is removed with the speedometer drive pinion **(see illustration)**. Refer to the relevant Section of Chapter 7, Part A or B, as applicable.

Power steering pressure switch

56   Releasing its clip, unplug the switch's electrical connector, then unscrew the switch **(see illustration)**. Place a wad of rag underneath, to catch any spilt fluid. If a sealing washer is fitted, renew it if it is worn or damaged.

57   Refitting is the reverse of the removal procedure; tighten the switch securely, then top-up the fluid reservoir (see Chapter 1) to replace any fluid lost from the system, and bleed out any trapped air (see Chapter 10, Section 33).

Exhaust gas pressure differential sensor

Note: *See also Section 6, illustration 6.21.*

58   If better access is required, remove the resonator (see Chapter 4).

59   Releasing its wire clip, unplug the sensor's electrical connector. Remove the two retaining screws, withdraw the unit from the bulkhead mounting bracket, then disconnect the two vacuum hoses. Note that the hoses are of different sizes, to ensure that they cannot be mixed up on reconnection.

5.10 Charcoal canister-purge solenoid valve (arrowed) is clipped to bulkhead behind engine

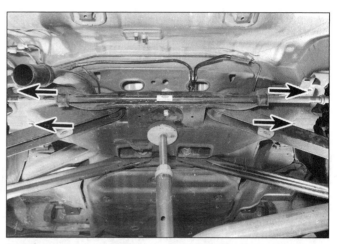

5.14 Support rear suspension crossmember on jack, and remove mounting bolts (arrowed) . . .

60   Check the condition of both hoses, and renew them if necessary (see Chapter 1).
61   Refitting is the reverse of the removal procedure. Ensure that the hoses are securely connected to the correct unions.

Oxygen sensor
Note: *The sensor is delicate, and will not work if it is dropped or knocked, if its power supply is disrupted, or if any cleaning materials are used on it.*
62   Release the sensor's electrical connector from its bracket on the engine/transmission front mounting, and unplug it to disconnect the sensor **(see illustration)**.
63   Raising and supporting the front of the vehicle if required to re-move the sensor from underneath, unscrew the sensor from the ex-haust system front downpipe; collect the sealing washer (where fitted).
64   On refitting, clean the sealing washer (where fitted) and renew it if it is damaged or worn. Apply a smear of anti-seize compound to the sensor's threads, to prevent them from welding themselves to the downpipe in service. Refit the sensor, tightening it to its specified torque wrench setting; a slotted socket will be required to do this **(see illustration)**. Reconnect the wiring and refit the connector plug.

---

5   EVAPorative emissions control (EVAP) system - general information, checking and component renewal

General description

1   This system is fitted to minimise the escape of unburned hydro-carbons into the atmosphere. The fuel tank filler cap is sealed, and a charcoal canister is mounted underneath the tank, to collect and store petrol vapours generated in the tank when the vehicle is parked. When the engine is running, the vapours are cleared from the canister (under the control of the ECU via the canister-purge solenoid valve) into the inlet tract, to be burned by the engine during normal combustion - see illustration 2.1A.
2   To ensure that the engine runs correctly when it is cold and/or idling, and to protect the catalytic converter from the effects of an over-rich mixture, the canister-purge solenoid valve is not opened by the ECU until the engine is fully warmed-up and running under part-load; the solenoid valve is then switched on and off, to allow the stored vapour to pass into the inlet.

Checking

3   Poor idle, stalling and poor driveability can be caused by an inop-erative canister-purge solenoid valve, a damaged canister, split or cracked hoses, or hoses connected to the wrong fittings. Check the

fuel filler cap for a damaged or deformed gasket.
4   Fuel loss or fuel odour can be caused by liquid fuel leaking from fuel lines, a cracked or damaged canister, an inoperative canister-purge solenoid valve, and disconnected, misrouted, kinked or dam-aged vapour or control hoses.
5   Inspect each hose attached to the canister for kinks, leaks and cracks along its entire length. Repair or renew as necessary.
6   Inspect the canister. If it is cracked or damaged, renew it. Look for fuel leaking from the bottom of the canister. If fuel is leaking, renew the canister, and check the hoses and hose routing.
7   If the canister-purge solenoid valve is thought to be faulty, unplug its electrical connector and disconnect its vacuum hoses. Connect a battery directly across the valve terminals. Check that air can flow through the valve passages when the solenoid is thus energised, and that nothing can pass when the solenoid is not energised. Alternatively, connect an ohmmeter to measure the resistance across the solenoid terminals, and compare this reading to the one listed in the Specifica-tions Section at the beginning of this Chapter. Renew the solenoid valve if it is faulty.
8   Further testing should be left to a dealer service department.

Component renewal

Charcoal canister-purge solenoid valve
9   If better access is required, remove the plenum chamber (see Chapter 4). Disconnect the battery negative (earth) lead - see Section 1 of Chapter 5.
10   Unplug the valve's electrical connector **(see illustration)**. Unclip the valve from the bulkhead, then disconnect its vacuum hoses and withdraw it.
11   Refitting is the reverse of the removal procedure.

Charcoal canister - Saloon and Hatchback models
Note: *Read through this procedure carefully before starting work, and ensure that the equipment is available that is required to carry it out safely and with minimum risk of damage, and to align the crossmember with sufficient accuracy on reassembly.*
12   Remove the fuel tank (see Chapter 4).
13   Ensure that the rear of the vehicle's body is supported securely on axle stands, then support the rear suspension crossmember with a jack. Remove the roadwheels and unscrew the rear suspension strut top mounting bolts (two per side - see Chapter 10).
14   Use white paint or similar (do not use a sharp-pointed scriber, which might break the underbody protective coating and cause rust-ing) to mark the exact relationship of the crossmember to the under-body. Unscrew the four mounting bolts **(see illustration)**. Lower the crossmember approximately 3 inches (75 mm) on the jack, and sup-port it securely. **Warning:** *DO NOT place any part of your body under the vehicle when it is supported only by a jack!*

6

15   Unscrew the two rearmost canister assembly retaining bolts **(see illustration)**.
16   Unplug the two hoses from the canister assembly, noting which way round they are fitted **(see illustration)**.
17   Unscrew the canister assembly's front retaining bolt **(see illustration)**. Withdraw the canister assembly.
18   Release the clip, and drive out the pin to separate the canister from its bracket **(see illustration)**.
19   On reassembly, refit the canister to its bracket and refit the assembly to the vehicle, tightening the retaining bolts securely, and ensuring that the two hoses are securely reconnected to their original unions.
20   Offer up the crossmember and refit the crossmember bolts, tightening them only lightly at this stage.
21   The crossmember must now be aligned on the underbody. Ford specify the use of service tool 15-097, which is a pair of tapered guides, with attachments to hold them in the crossmember as it is refitted **(see illustration)**. However, since the working diameter of these tools is 20.4 mm, and since the corresponding aligning holes in the crossmember and underbody are 21 mm and 22 mm in diameter, there is a significant in-built tolerance possible in the crossmember's alignment, even if the correct tools are used. If these tools are not available, align the crossmember by eye, centring the crossmember aligning holes on those of the underbody, and using the marks made on removal for assistance. Alternatively, use a tapered drift such as a clutch-aligning tool, or a deep socket spanner of suitable size.
22   Once the crossmember is aligned as precisely as possible, tighten its bolts to the specified torque (see Chapter 10 Specifications) without disturbing its position **(see illustration)**. Recheck the alignment once all the bolts are securely tightened.
23   The remainder of the refitting procedure is the reverse of removal.
24   Remember that, since the rear suspension crossmember has been disturbed, the wheel alignment and steering angles must be checked fully and carefully as soon as possible, with any necessary adjustments being made. This operation is best carried out by an experienced mechanic using proper checking equipment; the vehicle should therefore be taken to a Ford dealer or similar for attention.

Charcoal canister - Estate models
25   Disconnect the battery negative (earth) lead - see Section 1 of Chapter 5.
26   Raise the rear of the vehicle, and support it securely on axle stands. **Warning:** *DO NOT place any part of your body under the vehicle when it is supported only by a jack!*
27   Disconnect the two hoses from the canister assembly, noting which way round they are fitted.
28   Unscrew the canister assembly retaining bolt and withdraw the assembly, unclipping it from the front mounting.
29   Remove the plastic cover, and drive out the pin to separate the canister from its bracket **(see illustration)**.
30   On refitting, secure the canister to its bracket, and refit the assembly to the vehicle. Tighten the retaining bolt securely, and ensure that the two hoses are securely reconnected to their original unions.

5.15 ... lower crossmember by 3 inches, and unscrew charcoal canister assembly rear retaining bolts (arrowed) ...

6   Exhaust Gas Recirculation (EGR) system - general information, checking and component renewal

General information
1   To reduce oxides of nitrogen (NO_X) emissions, some of the exhaust gases are recirculated through the EGR valve to the inlet manifold. This has the effect of lowering combustion temperatures.
2   The system consists of the EGR valve, the EGR exhaust gas pressure differential sensor, the EGR solenoid valve, the ECU, and various sensors - see illustration 2.1A. The ECU is programmed to produce the ideal EGR valve lift for each operating condition.

Checking
EGR valve
3   Start the engine and allow it to idle.
4   Detach the vacuum hose from the EGR valve, and attach a hand vacuum pump in its place.
5   Apply vacuum to the EGR valve. Vacuum should remain steady, and the engine should run poorly.
   (a)   If the vacuum doesn't remain steady and the engine doesn't run poorly, renew the EGR valve and recheck it.
   (b)   If the vacuum remains steady but the engine doesn't run poorly, remove the EGR valve, and check the valve and the inlet manifold for blockage. Clean or renew parts as necessary, and recheck.

EGR system
6   Any further checking of the system requires special tools and test equipment. Take the vehicle to a dealer service department for checking.

5.16 ... unplug hoses (arrowed) from canister assembly ...

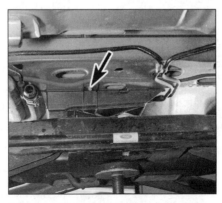

5.17 ... and remove front retaining bolt (arrowed) to release canister assembly - Saloon and Hatchback models

5.18 Release clip and drive out pin to separate canister from mounting bracket

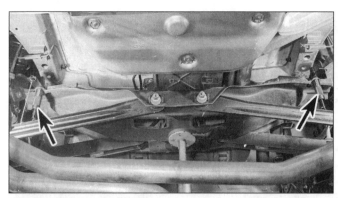

5.21 Refitting rear suspension crossmember with Ford service tools (arrowed) in place to align it with underbody . . .

5.22 . . . ensure aligned crossmember does not move - Ford tools used here - while mounting bolts are tightened

Component renewal

Note: *These components will be very hot when the engine is running. Always allow the engine to cool down fully before starting work, to prevent the possibility of burns.*

EGR valve

7   Disconnect the battery negative (earth) lead - see Section 1 of Chapter 5.

8   Remove the air mass meter and resonator - refer to Chapter 4.

9   Detach the vacuum hose, unscrew the sleeve nut securing the EGR pipe to the valve, remove the two valve mounting bolts, and withdraw the valve from the inlet manifold **(see illustrations)**. Ensure that the end of the pipe is not damaged or distorted as the valve is withdrawn, and note the valve's gasket; this must be renewed whenever the valve is disturbed.

10   Note that the metal pipe from the valve to the manifold itself should not be disturbed - it is not available separately from the manifold. However, check whenever the manifold is removed that the pipe's end fitting is securely fastened **(see illustration)**.

11   Check the valve for sticking and heavy carbon deposits. If such is found, clean the valve or renew it.

12   Refitting is the reverse of the removal procedure. Apply a smear of anti-seize compound to the sleeve nut threads, fit a new gasket, and tighten the valve bolts to the specified torque wrench setting.

EGR pipe

13   Disconnect the battery negative (earth) lead - see Section 1 of Chapter 5.

14   Remove the air mass meter and resonator - refer to Chapter 4.

15   Unbolt the exhaust manifold heat shield and remove both parts,

5.29 Charcoal canister assembly - Estate models - showing plastic cover (arrowed) and pin securing canister to mounting bracket

6.9A Disconnecting vacuum hose from Exhaust Gas Recirculation (EGR) valve . . .

6.9B . . . unscrew EGR pipe sleeve nut and remove bolts (arrowed) to release valve from inlet manifold

6

6.10 Check end fitting of EGR pipe into inlet manifold whenever manifold is removed, but do not disturb

6.15 Unbolt exhaust manifold heat shield, and unscrew sleeve nut (arrowed) securing EGR pipe to exhaust manifold . . .

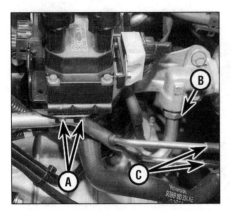

6.16 . . . undo screws "A" and sleeve nut "B", then disconnect hoses "C" - note different sizes - to release EGR pipe

6.21 EGR solenoid valve "A" and EGR exhaust gas pressure differential sensor "B", located on bulkhead mounting bracket

7.10 Pulse-air solenoid valve (arrowed) is located on bulkhead mounting bracket. It can be identified by its smaller top and its clip fastening - do not confuse it with the adjacent EGR solenoid valve

or move them aside as required to reach the end of the EGR pipe. Unscrew the sleeve nut securing the pipe to the exhaust manifold **(see illustration)**.

16　Undo the two screws securing the pipe to the ignition coil bracket, then disconnect the two vacuum hoses - note that these are of different sizes, to ensure that they cannot be mixed up on reconnection. Unscrew the sleeve nut securing the EGR pipe to the valve **(see illustration)**. Withdraw the pipe.

17　Check the condition of both hoses, and renew them if necessary (see Chapter 1). Note that if the exhaust gases have been backfiring excessively - eg, due to a blocked exhaust system - both hoses must be renewed, and their connections on the pipe must be cleaned thoroughly.

18　Refitting is the reverse of the removal procedure; ensure that the hoses are securely connected to the correct unions. Apply a smear of anti-seize compound to the sleeve nut threads, tighten the nuts securely, and tighten the two screws to their specified torque wrench setting.

EGR exhaust gas pressure differential sensor
19　Refer to Section 4 of this Chapter.

EGR solenoid valve
Note: *This component can be identified by its larger top and its two fastening screws. Do not confuse it with the adjacent pulse-air solenoid valve, especially when reconnecting vacuum hoses.*

20　Disconnect the battery negative (earth) lead - see Section 1 of Chapter 5.

21　Remove the air mass meter and resonator - refer to Chapter 4. If better access is required, remove the plenum chamber also **(see illustration)**.

22　Releasing its wire clip, unplug the electrical connector from the valve. Remove the two retaining screws, and withdraw the valve from the bulkhead mounting bracket, then label and disconnect the two vacuum hoses.

23　Refitting is the reverse of the removal procedure; ensure that the hoses are correctly reconnected.

7　Pulse-air system - general information

General information

1　This system consists of the pulse-air solenoid valve, the pulse-air valve itself, contained in the filter housing, and the piping - see illustration 2.1A. It injects filtered air directly into the exhaust ports, using the pressure variations in the exhaust gases to draw air through from the filter housing; air will flow into the exhaust only when its pressure is below atmospheric. The pulse-air valve can allow gases to flow only one way, so there is no risk of hot exhaust gases flowing back into the filter.

2　The system's primary function is raise exhaust gas temperatures on start-up, thus reducing the amount of time taken for the oxygen sensor and catalytic converter to reach operating temperature. Until this happens, the system reduces emission of unburned hydrocarbon particles (HC) and carbon monoxide (CO) by ensuring that a considerable proportion of these substances remaining in the exhaust gases after combustion are burned up, either in the manifold itself or in the catalytic converter.

3　To ensure that the system does not upset the smooth running of the engine under normal driving conditions, it is linked by the pulse-air solenoid valve to the ECU, so that it only functions during engine warm-up, when the oxygen sensor is not influencing the fuel/air mixture ratio.

Checking

4　Poor idle, stalling, backfiring and poor driveability can be caused by a fault in the system.

5　Inspect the vacuum pipe/hose connected between the filter housing and the solenoid valve for kinks, leaks and cracks along its entire length. Repair or renew as necessary.

6　Inspect the filter housing and piping. If either is cracked or damaged, renew it.

7　If the pulse-air solenoid valve is thought to be faulty, unplug its electrical connector and disconnect its vacuum hoses. Connect a battery directly across the valve terminals, and check that air can flow through the valve passages when the solenoid is thus energised, and that nothing can pass when the solenoid is not energised. Alternatively, connect an ohmmeter to measure the resistance across the valve terminals, and compare this reading to the one listed in the Specifications Section at the beginning of this Chapter. Renew the solenoid valve if it is faulty.

8　Further testing should be left to a dealer service department.

Component renewal

Pulse-air solenoid valve
Note: *This component can be identified by its smaller top and its clip fastening. Do not confuse it with the adjacent EGR solenoid valve, especially when reconnecting vacuum hoses.*

9　Disconnect the battery negative (earth) lead - see Section 1 of Chapter 5.

10　Remove the air mass meter and resonator - refer to Chapter 4. If better access is required, remove the plenum chamber also **(see illustration)**.

11　Releasing its wire clip, unplug the electrical connector, then use a small screwdriver to release the clip securing the valve to the bulkhead mounting bracket. Withdraw the valve, then label and disconnect the two vacuum hoses.

12　Refitting is the reverse of the removal procedure; ensure that the hoses are correctly reconnected.

7.13 Disconnect vacuum hose from base of pulse-air filter housing . . .

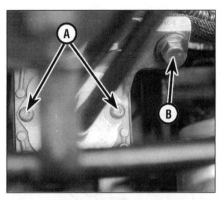

7.16 . . . undo screws "A" to disconnect piping from housing, and mounting bolt "B" to release housing

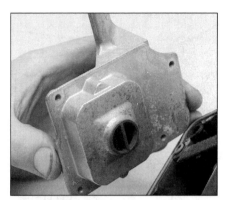

7.17A Remove four screws to release filter housing top from base . . .

7.17B . . .and withdraw foam filter for cleaning, if required - note valve in base of housing

7.23 Removing pulse-air piping - take care not to bend or distort it

7.31 Remove mounting bolt (arrowed) to remove complete pulse-air assembly - again, take care not to bend or distort piping

Pulse-air filter housing

Note: *This component, and those around it, will be very hot when the engine is running. Always allow the engine to cool down fully before starting work, to prevent the possibility of burns.*

13　Raise the front of the vehicle, and support it securely on axle stands. Disconnect the vacuum hose from the base of the filter housing **(see illustration)**.

14　Disconnect the battery negative (earth) lead - see Section 1 of Chapter 5.

15　Unbolt the resonator support bracket from the engine compartment front crossmember, slacken the two clamp screws securing the resonator to the air mass meter and plenum chamber hoses, then swing the resonator up clear of the thermostat housing (see Chapter 4).

16　Remove the screws securing the filter housing to the piping, unscrew the mounting bolt, then withdraw the housing **(see illustration)**.

17　To dismantle the filter housing, undo the four screws and separate the top from the base of the housing; extract the foam filter, and clean it in a suitable solvent **(see illustrations)**. If any of the housing's components are worn or damaged, the assembly must be renewed.

18　Refitting is the reverse of the removal procedure.

Pulse-air piping

Note: *This component, and those around it, will be very hot when the engine is running. Always allow the engine to cool down fully before starting work, to prevent the possibility of burns.*

19　Disconnect the battery negative (earth) lead - see Section 1 of Chapter 5.

20　Remove the air mass meter and resonator - refer to Chapter 4.

21　Unbolt the exhaust manifold heat shield; unclip the coolant hose to allow the upper part to be withdrawn. Apply penetrating oil to the EGR pipe sleeve nut, and to the pulse-air system sleeve nuts.

22　Remove the EGR pipe (see Section 6).

23　Remove the screws securing the filter housing to the piping - see illustration 7.16. Unscrew the four sleeve nuts securing the pipes into the exhaust manifold, and remove the piping as an assembly, taking care not to distort it **(see illustration)**.

24　Carefully clean the piping, particularly its threads and those of the manifold, removing all traces of corrosion, which might prevent them seating properly, causing air leaks when the engine is restarted.

25　On refitting, insert the piping carefully into the cylinder head ports, taking care not to bend or distort it. Apply anti-seize compound to the threads, and tighten the retaining sleeve nuts while holding each pipe firmly in its port; if a suitable spanner is available, tighten the sleeve nuts to the specified torque wrench setting.

26　The remainder of the refitting procedure is the reverse of removal.

Pulse-air filter housing and piping assembly

Note: *These components, and those around them, will be very hot when the engine is running. Always allow the engine to cool down fully before starting work, to prevent the possibility of burns.*

27　Disconnect the battery negative (earth) lead - see Chapter 5, Section 1. Unbolt the resonator support bracket from the engine compartment front crossmember. Slacken the two clamp screws securing the resonator to the air mass meter and plenum chamber hoses, then swing the resonator up clear of the thermostat housing (see Chapter 4).

28　Drain the cooling system (see Chapter 1) and disconnect the coolant hose and the coolant pipe/hose from the thermostat housing.

29　Unbolt the exhaust manifold heat shield. Apply penetrating oil to the EGR pipe sleeve nut, and to the pulse-air system sleeve nuts.

30　Remove the EGR pipe (see Section 6).

31　Unscrew the filter housing mounting bolt. Unscrew the four sleeve nuts securing the pipes into the exhaust manifold and remove the assembly, taking care not to distort it **(see illustration)**.

32　Clean the piping, particularly its threads and those of the mani-

6

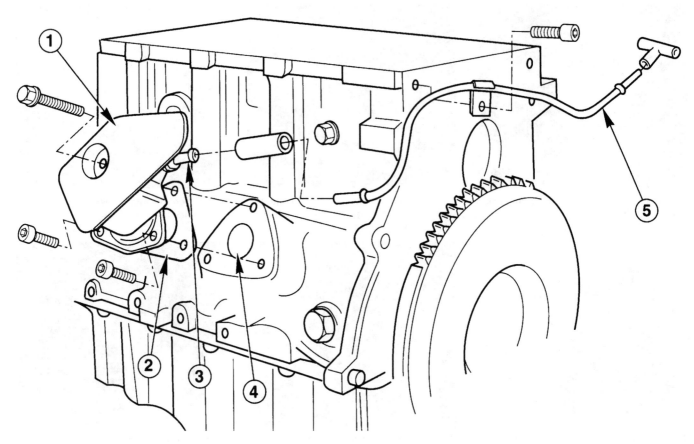

8.1 Positive Crankcase Ventilation system

1   Oil separator
2   Gasket
3   Positive Crankcase Ventilation (PCV) valve

4   Cylinder block/crankcase opening
5   Crankcase breather pipe and flexible hoses

fold, removing all traces of corrosion, which might prevent them seating properly, causing air leaks when the engine is restarted.

33   On refitting, insert the piping carefully into the cylinder head ports, taking care not to bend or distort it. Apply anti-seize compound to the threads, and tighten the retaining sleeve nuts while holding each pipe firmly in its port; if a suitable spanner is available, tighten the sleeve nuts to the specified torque wrench setting.

34   The remainder of the refitting procedure is the reverse of removal. Refill the cooling system (see Chapter 1). Run the engine, check for exhaust leaks, and check the coolant level when it is fully warmed-up.

8   Positive Crankcase Ventilation (PCV) system - general information

General information

1   The crankcase ventilation system main components are the oil separator mounted on the front (radiator) side of the cylinder block/crankcase, and the Positive Crankcase Ventilation (PCV) valve set in a rubber grommet in the separator's left-hand upper end. The associated pipework consists of a crankcase breather pipe and two flexible hoses connecting the PCV valve to a union on the left-hand end of the inlet manifold, and a crankcase breather hose connecting the cylinder head cover to the air cleaner assembly **(see illustration)**. A small foam filter in the air cleaner prevents dirt from being drawn directly into the engine.

2   The function of these components is to reduce the emission of unburned hydrocarbons from the crankcase, and to minimise the formation of oil sludge. By ensuring that a depression is created in the crankcase under most operating conditions, particularly at idle, and by positively inducing fresh air into the system, the oil vapours and "blow-by" gases collected in the crankcase are drawn from the crankcase, through the oil separator, into the inlet tract, to be burned by the engine during normal combustion.

Checking

3   Checking procedures for the system components are included in Chapter 1.

Component renewal

Cylinder head-to-air cleaner hose

4   See Chapter 1.

Positive Crankcase Ventilation (PCV) valve

5   The valve is plugged into the oil separator. Depending on the tools available, access to the valve may be possible once the pulse-air assembly has been removed (see Section 7). If this is not feasible, proceed as outlined in paragraph 6 below.

Oil separator

6   Remove the exhaust manifold (see Chapter 2, Part A). The Positive Crankcase Ventilation (PCV) valve can now be unplugged and flushed, or renewed, as required, as described in Chapter 1.

7   Unbolt the oil separator from the cylinder block/crankcase, and withdraw it; remove and discard the gasket.

8   Flush out or renew the oil separator, as required (see Chapter 1).
9   On reassembly, fit a new gasket, and tighten the fasteners to the torque wrench settings given in the Specifications Section of Chapter 2, Part B.
10 The remainder of the refitting procedure is the reverse of removal. Refill the cooling system (see Chapter 1). Run the engine, check for exhaust leaks, and check the coolant level when it is fully warmed-up.

9 Catalytic converter - general information, checking and component renewal

General information

1   The exhaust gases of any petrol engine (however efficient or well-tuned) consist largely (approximately 99 %) of nitrogen (N_2), carbon dioxide (CO_2), oxygen (O_2), other inert gases and water vapour (H_2O). The remaining 1 % is made up of the noxious materials which are currently seen (CO_2 apart) as the major polluters of the environment: carbon monoxide (CO), unburned hydrocarbons (HC), oxides of nitrogen (NO_x) and some solid matter, including a small lead content.
2   Left to themselves, most of these pollutants are thought eventually to break down naturally (CO and NO_x, for example, break down in the upper atmosphere to release CO_2) having first caused ground-level environmental problems. The massive increase world-wide in the use of motor vehicles, and the current popular concern for the environment has caused the introduction in most countries of legislation, in varying degrees of severity, to combat the problem.
3   The device most commonly used to clean up vehicle exhausts is the catalytic converter. It is fitted into the vehicle's exhaust system, and uses precious metals (platinum and palladium or rhodium) as catalysts to speed up the reaction between the pollutants and the oxygen in the vehicle's exhaust gases, CO and HC being oxidised to form H_2O and CO_2 and (in the three-way type of catalytic converter) NO_x being reduced to N_2. **Note:** *The catalytic converter is not a filter in the physical sense; its function is to promote a chemical reaction, but it is not itself affected by that reaction.*
4   The converter consists of an element (or "substrate") of ceramic honeycomb, coated with a combination of precious metals in such a way as to produce a vast surface area over which the exhaust gases must flow; the whole being mounted in a stainless-steel box. A simple "oxidation" (or "two-way") catalytic converter can deal with CO and HC only, while a "reduction" (or "three-way") catalytic converter can deal with CO, HC and NO_x. Three-way catalytic converters are further sub-divided into "open-loop" (or "uncontrolled") converters which can remove 50 to 70 % of pollutants and "closed-loop" (also known as "controlled" or "regulated") converters which can remove over 90 % of pollutants.
5   The catalytic converter fitted to the Mondeo models covered in this manual is of the three-way closed-loop type.
6   The catalytic converter is a reliable and simple device, which needs no maintenance in itself, but there are some facts of which an owner should be aware if the converter is to function properly for its full service life.

(a)   *DO NOT use leaded petrol in a vehicle equipped with a catalytic converter - the lead will coat the precious metals, reducing their converting efficiency, and will eventually destroy the converter; it will also affect the operation of the oxygen sensor, requiring its renewal if lead-fouled. Opinions vary as to how much leaded fuel is necessary to affect the converter's performance, and whether it can recover even if only unleaded petrol is used afterwards; the best course of action is, therefore, to assume the worst, and to ensure that NO leaded petrol is used at any time.*

(b)   *Always keep the ignition and fuel systems well-maintained in accordance with the manufacturer's schedule (Chapter 1) - particularly, ensure that the air filter element, the fuel filter and the spark plugs are renewed at the correct intervals. If the intake air/fuel mixture is allowed to become too rich due to ne-*

glect, the unburned surplus will enter and burn in the catalytic converter, overheating the element and eventually destroying the converter.

(c)   *If the engine develops a misfire, do not drive the vehicle at all (or at least as little as possible) until the fault is cured - the misfire will allow unburned fuel to enter the converter, which will result in its overheating, as noted above. For the same reason, do not persist if the engine refuses to start - either trace the problem and cure it yourself, or have the vehicle checked immediately by a qualified mechanic.*

(d)   *Avoid allowing the vehicle to run out of petrol.*

(e)   *DO NOT push- or tow-start the vehicle unless no other alternative exists, especially if the engine and exhaust are at normal operating temperature. Starting the engine in this way may soak the catalytic converter in unburned fuel, causing it to overheat when the engine does start - see (b) above.*

(f)   *DO NOT switch off the ignition at high engine speeds, in particular, do not "blip" the throttle immediately before switching off. If the ignition is switched off at anything above idle speed, unburned fuel will enter the (very hot) catalytic converter, with the possible risk of its igniting on the element and damaging the converter.*

(g)   *Avoid repeated successive cold starts followed by short journeys. If the converter is never allowed to reach its proper working temperature, it will gather unburned fuel, allowing some to pass into the atmosphere and the rest to soak in the element, causing it to overheat when a long journey is made - see (b) above.*

(h)   *DO NOT use fuel or engine oil additives - these may contain substances harmful to the catalytic converter. Similarly, DO NOT use silicone-based sealants on any part of the engine or fuel system, and do not use exhaust sealants on any part of the exhaust system upstream of the catalytic converter. Even if the sealant itself does not contain additives harmful to the converter, pieces of it may break off and foul the element, causing local overheating.*

(i)   *DO NOT continue to use the vehicle if the engine burns oil to the extent of leaving a visible trail of blue smoke. Unburned carbon deposits will clog the converter passages and reduce its efficiency; in severe cases, the element will overheat.*

(j)   *Remember that the catalytic converter operates at very high temperatures - hence the heat shields on the vehicle underbody - and the casing will become hot enough to ignite combustible materials which brush against it. DO NOT, therefore, park the vehicle in dry undergrowth, over long grass or piles of dead leaves.*

(k)   *Remember that the catalytic converter is FRAGILE. Do not strike it with tools during servicing work, and take great care when working on the exhaust system (see Chapter 4). Ensure that the converter is well clear of any jacks or other lifting gear used to raise the vehicle. Do not drive the vehicle over rough ground, road humps, etc, in such a way as to "ground" the exhaust system.*

(l)   *In some cases, particularly when the vehicle is new and/or is used for stop/start driving, a sulphurous smell (like that of rotten eggs) may be noticed from the exhaust. This is common to many catalytic converter-equipped vehicles, and seems to be due to the small amount of sulphur found in some petrols reacting with hydrogen in the exhaust, to produce hydrogen sulphide (H_2S) gas; while this gas is toxic, it is not produced in sufficient amounts to be a problem. Once the vehicle has covered a few thousand miles, the problem should disappear - in the meanwhile, a change of driving style, or of the brand of petrol used, may effect a solution.*

(m)   *The catalytic converter on a well-maintained and well-driven vehicle should last for between 50 000 and 100 000 miles. From this point on, careful checks should be made at regular intervals to ensure that the converter is still operating efficiently. If the converter is no longer effective, it must be renewed.*

6

Checking

7   Checking the operation of a catalytic converter requires expensive and sophisticated diagnostic equipment, starting with a high-quality exhaust gas analyser. If the level of CO in the exhaust gases is too high, a full check of the engine management system must be carried out (see Section 3 of this Chapter) to eliminate all other possibilities before the converter is suspected of being faulty.

8   The vehicle should be taken to a Ford dealer for this work to be carried out using the correct diagnostic equipment; do not waste time trying to test the system without such facilities.

Component renewal

9   The catalytic converter is part of the exhaust system front downpipe - see Chapter 4 for details of removal and refitting.

Chapter 7 Part A Manual transmission

Contents

Specifications

Manufacturer's code

Manual transmission...	MTX-75

Gear ratios

	Gear set A	Gear set B
1st...	3.417:1	3.231:1
2nd	2.136:1	2.136:1
3rd	1.448:1	1.483:1
4th	1.028:1	1.114:1
5th	0.767:1	0.854:1
Reverse	3.46:1	3.46:1

Gear set application

1.6 and 1.8 - all models	A
2.0 models	B

Final drive ratios

1.6 Hatchback and Estate	4.06:1
1.6 Saloon...	3.82:1
1.8 Hatchback and Estate	4.06:1
1.8 Saloon...	3.41:1
2.0 Hatchback and Estate	4.06:1

Torque wrench settings

	Nm	lbf ft
Transmission to engine..	40	30
Gearchange support rod	55	41
Gearchange linkage clamp bolt...	16	12
Gearchange assembly rear mounting...	44	32
Gearchange linkage to selector shaft	23	17

7A

3.1 View of the top of the gearchange assembly with the centre console removed

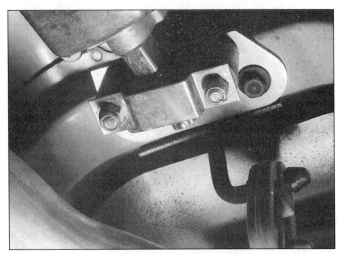

3.6 Gearchange linkage assembly rear mounting

1   General information

The vehicles covered by this manual are equipped with either a 5-speed manual or a 4-speed automatic transmission. This Part of Chapter 7 contains information on the manual transmission. Service procedures for the automatic transmission are contained in Part B.

The manual transmission is a compact, two-piece, lightweight aluminium alloy housing, containing both the transmission and differential assemblies. The manual transmission code name is MTX-75, MT standing for *M*anual *T*ransmission, X for transa*X*le (front-wheel-drive), and 75 being the distance between the input and output shafts in mm.

Because of the complexity, possible unavailability of replacement parts and special tools necessary, internal repair procedures for the manual transmission are not recommended for the home mechanic. For readers who wish to tackle a transmission rebuild, exploded views and brief notes on overhaul are provided. The bulk of the information in this Chapter is devoted to removal and refitting procedures.

2   Gearchange linkage - adjustment

Note: *The special Ford tool 16-073 will be required in order to carry out the following adjustment. This tool is simply a slotted ring which locks the gear lever in the neutral position during adjustment. If the tool is not available, adjustment is still possible by proceeding on a trial-and-error basis, preferably with the help of an assistant to hold the gear lever in the neutral position.*

1   Remove the centre console as described in Chapter 11.
2   Apply the handbrake, jack up the front of the vehicle and support it on axle stands. Move the gear lever to the neutral position.
3   Working beneath the vehicle, loosen the clamp bolt on the gearchange linkage located behind the transmission.
4   With the gear lever still in neutral, fit the special Ford tool 16-073 over the gear lever, and locate it in the recess in the lever retaining housing on top of the transmission. Twist the tool clockwise to lock the lever in the neutral position. Take care during the adjustment not to move the gear lever or displace the adjustment tool.
5   Check that the front part of the gearchange linkage from the transmission is in neutral. It will be necessary to move the linkage slightly forwards and backwards to determine that it is in the correct position.
6   Recheck that the adjustment tool is still correctly fitted to the gear lever, then tighten the clamp bolt on the gearchange linkage.
7   Remove the adjustment tool from the gear lever.
8   Lower the vehicle to the ground, then refit the centre console with reference to Chapter 11.

3   Gearchange linkage and gear lever - removal and refitting

Removal

1   Remove the centre console as described in Chapter 11 **(see illustration)**.
2   Apply the handbrake, jack up the front of the vehicle and support it on axle stands. Move the gear lever to its neutral position.
3   Working beneath the vehicle, unscrew the bolt and disconnect the gearchange linkage from the selector shaft on the rear of the transmission.
4   Mark the position of the gearchange linkage front and rear sections in relation to each other. Loosen the clamp bolt and remove the front section.
5   Unscrew the bolt securing the gearchange support rod to the bracket on the rear of the transmission.
6   Remove the heat shield. Support the weight of the gearchange linkage assembly, unscrew the nuts from the rear mounting bracket, and lower the assembly from the underbody **(see illustration)**.
7   Remove the insulator rubber from the rear of the assembly.
8   Examine the insulator rubber and the stabiliser bar mounting rubber for wear and deterioration, and if necessary obtain new ones.

Refitting

9   Refitting is a reversal of the removal procedure, but adjust the linkage as described in Section 2.

4   Speedometer drive pinion - removal and refitting

Removal

1   Access to the speedometer drive pinion may be gained from the top of the engine (after removing the air mass meter and air trunking - see Chapter 4), or from below by raising the front of the vehicle and reaching up over the top of the transmission. If the latter method is used, make sure that the vehicle is supported adequately on axle stands.
2   Unscrew the nut and disconnect the speedometer cable from the vehicle speed sensor on the transmission. Use two spanners to loosen the nut - one to counterhold the sensor, and the other to unscrew the cable nut.
3   Disconnect the wiring from the vehicle speed sensor, then unscrew the sensor from the top of the drive pinion.
4   Using a pair of grips, pull out the drive pinion retaining roll pin from the transmission casing.
5   Withdraw the speedometer drive pinion and bearing from the top of the transmission.

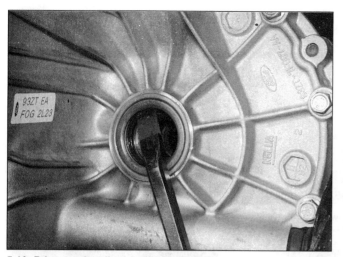

5.4A Prise out the oil seal with a suitable lever

5.4B Removing the oil seal from the transmission casing

6   Using a small screwdriver, prise the O-ring from the groove in the bearing; obtain a new one for reassembly.
7   Wipe clean the drive pinion and bearing, also the seating bore in the transmission casing.

Refitting

8   Refitting is a reversal of the removal procedure, but lightly oil the new O-ring before inserting the assembly in the transmission casing. Drive in the retaining roll pin using a hammer.

5   Oil seals - renewal

1   Oil leaks frequently occur due to wear or deterioration of the differential side gear seals and/or the gearchange selector shaft oil seal and speedometer drive pinion O-ring. Renewal of these seals is relatively easy, since the repairs can be performed without removing the transmission from the vehicle.

Differential side gear oil seals

2   The differential side gear oil seals are located at the sides of the transmission, where the driveshafts enter the transmission. If leakage at the seal is suspected, raise the vehicle and support it securely on axle stands. If the seal is leaking, oil will be found on the side of the transmission below the driveshaft.
3   Refer to Chapter 8 and remove the appropriate driveshaft. If removing the right-hand driveshaft, it will be necessary to remove the intermediate shaft as well.
4   Using a large screwdriver or lever, carefully prise the oil seal out of the transmission casing, taking care not to damage the transmission casing **(see illustrations)**. If the oil seal is reluctant to move, it is sometimes helpful to carefully drive it *into* the transmission a little way, applying the force at one point only. This will have the effect of swivelling the seal out of the casing, and it can then be pulled out. If the oil seal is particularly difficult to remove, an oil seal removal tool may be obtained from a garage or accessory shop.
5   Wipe clean the oil seal seating in the transmission casing.
6   Dip the new oil seal in clean oil, then press it a little way into the casing by hand, making sure that it is square to its seating.
7   Using suitable tubing or a large socket, carefully drive the oil seal fully into the casing until it contacts the seating.
8   Refit the driveshaft with reference to Chapter 8.

Gearchange selector shaft oil seal

9   Apply the handbrake, jack up the front of the vehicle and support it on axle stands.
10   Unscrew the bolt securing the gearchange linkage to the shaft on the rear of the transmission. Pull off the linkage and remove the rubber boot.

11   Using a suitable tool or grips, pull the oil seal out of the transmission casing. Ford technicians use a slide hammer, with an end fitting which locates over the oil seal extension. In the absence of this tool, if the oil seal is particularly tight, drill one or two small holes in the oil seal, and screw in self-tapping screws. The oil seal can then be removed from the casing by pulling on the screws.
12   Wipe clean the oil seal seating in the transmission.
13   Dip the new oil seal in clean oil, then press it a little way into the casing by hand, making sure that it is square to its seating.
14   Using suitable tubing or a large socket, carefully drive the oil seal fully into the casing.
15   Locate the rubber boot over the selector shaft.
16   Refit the gearchange linkage to the shaft on the rear of the transmission, and tighten the bolt.
17   If necessary, adjust the gearchange linkage as described in Section 2 of this Chapter.

Speedometer drive pinion oil seal

18   The procedure is covered in Section 4 of this Chapter.

6   Reversing light switch - removal and refitting

Removal

1   Remove the air cleaner and the air mass meter as described in Chapter 4.
2   Disconnect the wiring leading to the reversing light switch on the top of the transmission.
3   Unscrew the mounting bolts, and remove the reversing light switch from the cover housing on the transmission.

Refitting

4   Refitting is a reversal of the removal procedure.

7   Manual transmission - removal and refitting

Note: *Read through this procedure before starting work to see what is involved, particularly in terms of lifting equipment. Depending on the facilities available, the home mechanic may prefer to remove the engine and transmission together, then separate them on the bench, as described in Chapter 2.*

Removal

1   Disconnect the battery negative (earth) lead (refer to Chapter 5, Section 1). For better access, the battery may be removed completely.
2   If necessary, the bonnet may be removed as described in

7A

7.3 Use split pins to hold the radiator in its raised position

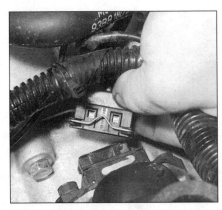

7.6 Disconnecting the wiring multi-plug from the reversing light switch

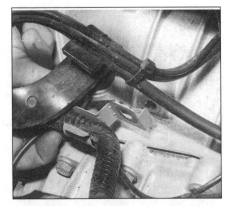

7.7 Removing the wiring loom bracket from the top of the transmission

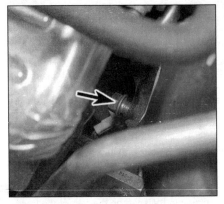

7.10 Mounting bolt with earth lead located beneath the exhaust manifold

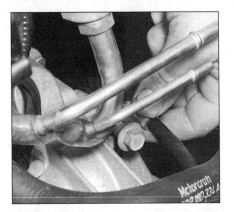

7.11 Removing the starter motor bolt with the earth cable

7.13 Radiator front lower cover removal

Chapter 11, Section 8 for better access, and for fitting the engine lifting hoist.

3   Hold the radiator in its raised position by inserting split pins through the holes in the upper mounting extensions **(see illustration)**. This is necessary to retain the radiator when the subframe is removed.

4   Remove the air mass meter and air inlet duct with reference to Chapter 4.

5   Remove the air cleaner assembly as described in Chapter 4.

6   Disconnect the wiring from the reversing light switch on the transmission **(see illustration)**.

7   Unscrew the bolt, and remove the wiring loom bracket from the top of the transmission **(see illustration)**.

8   Detach the earth cable located between the transmission and the body.

9   Disconnect the clutch cable from the release lever on the transmission, with reference to Chapter 8.

10   Unscrew and remove the three upper bolts securing the transmission to the engine. Also unscrew the mounting bolt with the earth lead, located beneath the exhaust manifold **(see illustration)**.

11   Unscrew and remove the starter motor upper mounting bolt, noting that an earth cable is attached to it **(see illustration)**.

12   Apply the handbrake, jack up the front of the vehicle and support it on axle stands. Remove the front wheels.

13   Remove the front lower cover from under the radiator by prising out the side clips and unscrewing the retaining bolts **(see illustration)**.

14   Remove the wheel arch liner from the right-hand side of the vehicle as described in Chapter 11.

15   Unscrew the bolts and remove the auxiliary drivebelt cover.

16   Working on each side of the vehicle in turn, unscrew the nut and disconnect the anti-roll bar link from the strut, noting that the flexible brake hose bracket is attached to the link stud.

17   Extract the split pins, then unscrew the nuts securing the track rod ends to the steering knuckles on each side. Release the balljoints

7.23 Unscrew the bolt securing the gearchange linkage rod to the shaft on the rear of the transmission

from the steering knuckle arms, using a balljoint separator tool.

18   Working on each side in turn, note which way round the front suspension lower arm balljoint clamp bolt is fitted, then unscrew and remove it from the knuckle assembly. Lever the balljoint down from the knuckle - if it is tight, prise the joint open carefully using a large flat-bladed tool. Take care not to damage the balljoint seal during the separation procedure.

19   Disconnect the cooling fan multi-plug on the subframe behind the radiator, and unclip the plug from the bracket.

20   Disconnect the multi-plug from the wiring leading to the oxygen

7.24 Removing the gearchange linkage front section

7.25 Unscrewing the bolt securing the gearchange support rod to the bracket on the rear of the transmission

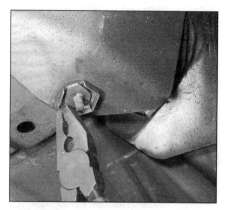

7.26 Removing the gear linkage heat shield

7.27A Unscrew the gear linkage rear mounting bolts (arrowed) . . .

7.27B . . . swivel the linkage around, and tie it to the underbody

7.30A Remove the centre bolt (arrowed) from the rear mounting . . .

7.30B . . . then unbolt the mounting from the subframe and remove it

7.31A Unscrew the nut and bolt (arrowed) . . .

7.31B . . . and remove the transmission support rod bracket

sensor, then unclip the wiring from the engine rear mounting.

21 Disconnect the vacuum hose from the pulse-air system filter.

22 Remove the complete exhaust system as described in Chapter 4.

23 Unscrew the bolt securing the gearchange linkage to the selector shaft on the rear of the transmission (see illustration).

24 Mark the position of the gearchange linkage front and rear sections, then unscrew the clamp bolt. Disconnect the linkage from the selector shaft on the rear of the transmission, and separate the front and rear sections of the linkage (see illustration).

25 Unscrew the mounting bolt, and disconnect the gearchange support rod from the bracket on the rear of the transmission (see illustration).

26 Remove the gear linkage heat shield from the underbody by unscrewing the nuts (see illustration).

27 Unscrew and remove the gear linkage rear mounting bolts, swivel the linkage around to the rear, and tie it to the underbody (see illustrations).

28 On models fitted with air conditioning, unscrew and remove the mounting bolts securing the dehydrator to the subframe, and tie it to one side.

29 Unscrew and remove the bolts securing the steering gear to the subframe. The bolts are difficult to reach using normal spanners; if possible, the special cranked Ford tool should be obtained (see Chapter 10).

30 Unscrew and remove the centre bolt from the engine/transmission rear mounting (roll restrictor), then unbolt the mounting from the subframe (see illustrations).

31 Unscrew the nut and bolt, and remove the support rod bracket

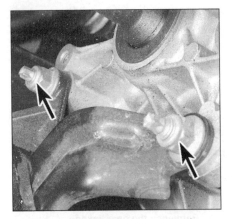

7.32A Nuts securing the rear mounting bracket to the transmission

7.32B Removing the rear mounting bracket

7.33 Removing the bolt from the engine front mounting bracket

7.34A Removing the power steering fluid cooler pipes from the subframe

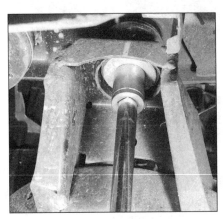

7.34B Unscrewing the subframe front . . .

7.34C . . . and rear mounting bolts

from the rear of the transmission **(see illustrations)**.
32   Unscrew the nuts and bolts, and remove the engine/transmission rear mounting bracket from the transmission **(see illustrations)**.
33   Unscrew and remove the centre bolt from the engine front mounting, and detach the pulse-air filter from the bracket on the mounting **(see illustration)**.
34   With the help of an assistant, support the weight of the subframe, using trolley jacks if possible. Unscrew the bolts securing the power steering fluid cooler pipes to the subframe, then unscrew the subframe mounting bolts, and lower the subframe to the ground **(see illustrations)**.
35   Position a suitable container beneath the transmission, then unscrew the drain plug and drain the oil **(see illustration)**. Refit and tighten the plug on completion.
36   Unscrew the bolts securing the right-hand driveshaft centre bearing to the cylinder block. Remove the heat shield, then pull out the right-hand strut so that the intermediate shaft is removed from the transmission differential gears. Be prepared for oil spillage.
37   Support the right-hand driveshaft on axle stands, making sure that the inner tripod joint is not turned through more than 18 (damage may occur if the joint is turned through too great an angle).
38   Insert a suitable lever between the left-hand driveshaft inner joint and the transmission case (with a thin piece of wood against the case), then prise free the joint from the differential. If it proves reluctant to move, strike the lever firmly with the palm of the hand. Be careful not to damage the adjacent components, and be prepared for oil spillage. As the right-hand driveshaft has already been removed, it is possible to release the left-hand driveshaft by inserting a forked drift from the right-hand side, but care must be taken to prevent damage to the dif-

ferential gears.
39   Support the left-hand driveshaft on axle stands, making sure that the inner tripod joint is not turned through more than 18 (damage may occur if the joint is turned through too great an angle).
40   Disconnect the multi-plug from the wiring leading to the vehicle speed sensor.
41   Unscrew the cable nut, and disconnect the speedometer cable from the top of the vehicle speed sensor. Hold the sensor with a spanner while the cable nut is loosened.
42   If necessary, the vehicle may be lowered to the ground at this stage, in order to connect an engine hoist. If an engine support bar which locates over the engine compartment is to be used, then the vehicle may be left in its raised position.
43   Attach the hoist to diagonally-opposite positions on the engine, and take the weight of the engine and transmission **(see illustration)**.
44   Unscrew the nuts from the engine right-hand mounting bracket. Note that, where a hydraulic mounting is fitted (see Chapter 2A, Section 22), the mounting must never be tilted by more than 5 .
45   Unscrew the retaining nuts, and remove the engine/transmission left-hand mounting from the transmission.
46   On models fitted with air conditioning, lower the engine until the compressor is below the right-hand side member.
47   On models without air conditioning, lower the transmission until it is opposite the aperture on the left-hand side of the engine compartment.
48   Support the weight of the transmission on a trolley jack. Use safety chains or a cradle to steady the transmission on the jack.
49   Remove the remaining starter motor mounting bolts.
50   Unscrew and remove the lower bolts securing the transmission to

7.35 Unscrewing the transmission oil drain plug

7.43 Supporting the engine with a hoist

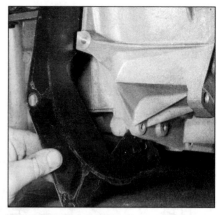

7.51 Removing the lower cover plate

the engine. Also unscrew the bolts securing the lower cover plate to the transmission.

51   With the help of an assistant, withdraw the transmission squarely from the engine, taking care not to allow its weight to hang on the clutch friction disc. As the transmission is being withdrawn, remove the lower cover plate sandwiched between the transmission and engine **(see illustration)**. Lower the transmission to the ground.

52   The clutch components can now be inspected with reference to Chapter 8, and renewed if necessary. (Unless they are virtually new, it is worth renewing the clutch components as a matter of course, even if the transmission has been removed for some other reason.)

Refitting

53   If removed, refit the clutch components (see Chapter 8).

54   With the transmission secured to the trolley jack as on removal, raise it into position, and then carefully slide it onto the rear of the engine, at the same time engaging the input shaft with the clutch friction disc splines. Do not use excessive force to refit the transmission - if the input shaft does not slide into place easily, readjust the angle of the transmission so that it is level, and/or turn the input shaft so that the splines engage properly with the disc. If problems are still experienced, check that the clutch friction disc is correctly centred (Chapter 8).

55   Refit the lower bolts securing the transmission to the engine, and tighten moderately at this stage.

56   Insert and tighten the starter mounting bolts, noting that an earth cable is attached to one of them.

57   Raise the transmission to its normal position.

58   Refit the engine/transmission left-hand mounting, and tighten the nuts.

59   Refit the engine right-hand mounting bracket, and tighten the nuts.

60   If previously lowered, raise the front of the vehicle, and support on axle stands.

61   Refit the speedometer cable to the vehicle speed sensor, and tighten the cable nut.

62   Reconnect the wiring to the speed sensor.

63   Insert the left-hand driveshaft into the transmission, making sure that it is fully engaged with the internal circlip.

64   Refit the right-hand driveshaft and intermediate shaft, and tighten the bolts.

65   Refit and align the subframe, with reference to Chapter 2B, Section 4. Tighten the mounting bolts to the specified torque.

66   Refit the pulse-air filter. Tighten the centre bolt in the engine front mounting.

67   Refit the engine rear mounting bracket, and tighten the bolts.

68   Refit the transmission support rod and bracket, and tighten the bolts and nut.

69   Refit the engine rear mounting to the subframe, and tighten the bolts.

70   Refit the steering gear to the subframe, and tighten the mounting bolts.

71   On models with air conditioning, refit the dehydrator to the subframe, and tighten the mounting bolts.

72   Refit the gear linkage and heat shield with reference to Section 3.

73   Refit the transmission gearchange support rod to the rear of the transmission, and tighten the bolt. Adjust the gear linkage if necessary, with reference to Section 2.

74   Refit the exhaust system, with reference to Chapter 4.

75   Reconnect the vacuum hose to the pulse-air system filter.

76   Reconnect the oxygen sensor wiring.

77   Reconnect and secure the cooling fan multi-plug.

78   Refit the front suspension lower arm balljoints to the knuckle assemblies, with reference to Chapter 10.

79   Refit the track rod ends to the steering knuckles on each side, with reference to Chapter 10.

80   Refit the anti-roll bar links to the struts, and tighten the nuts.

81   Refit the auxiliary drivebelt cover and the wheel arch liner.

82   Refit the front lower cover beneath the radiator.

83   Refit the wheels, and lower the vehicle to the ground.

84   Insert the upper bolts securing the transmission to the engine.

85   Reconnect the clutch cable with reference to Chapter 8.

86   Refit the earth cable between the transmission and the body.

87   Refit the wiring loom bracket to the top of the transmission.

88   Reconnect the wiring to the reversing light switch.

89   Tighten all transmission mounting bolts fully.

90   Refit the air cleaner assembly, air mass meter and air inlet duct, with reference to Chapter 4.

91   Remove the split pins holding the radiator in its raised position.

92   If removed, refit the bonnet.

93   If removed, refit the battery and reconnect the leads.

94   Fill the transmission with oil, and check the level as described in Chapter 1.

95   Make a final check that all connections have been made, and all bolts tightened fully.

96   Road test the vehicle to check for proper transmission operation, then check the transmission visually for leakage of oil.

7A

8   Manual transmission mounting - checking and renewal

This procedure is covered in Chapter 2A, Section 22.

9   Manual transmission overhaul - general

1   Overhauling a manual transmission is a difficult job for the do-it-yourselfer. It involves the dismantling and reassembly of many small

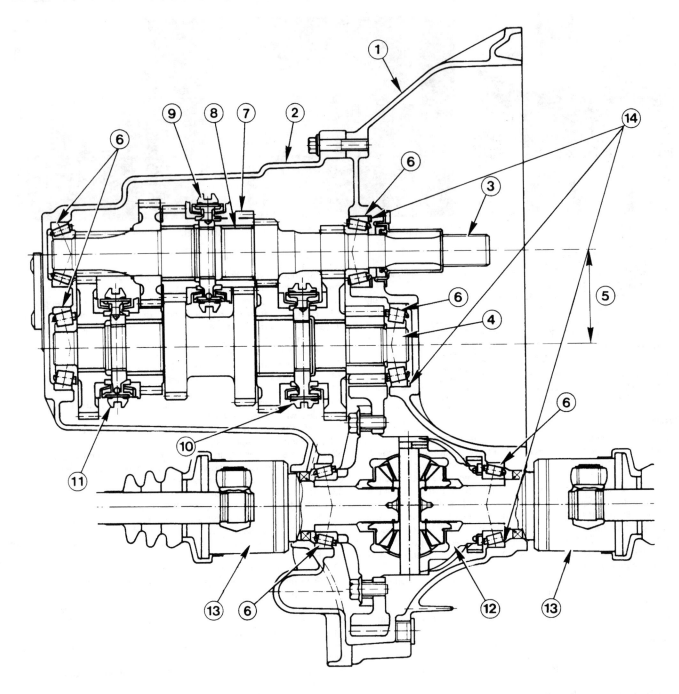

9.4A Sectional diagram of the manual transmission

1	Clutch housing	6	Taper roller bearings	12	Differential
2	Transmission housing	7	4th gear	13	Driveshafts
3	Input shaft	8	Needle roller bearing	14	Shims
4	Output shaft	9	3rd/4th synchro		
5	Distance between shaft	10	1st/2nd synchro		
	centres = 75 mm	11	5th/reverse synchro		

parts. Numerous clearances must be precisely measured and, if necessary, changed with selected spacers and circlips. As a result, if
transmission problems arise, while the unit can be removed and refitted by a competent do-it-yourselfer, overhaul should be left to a transmission specialist. Rebuilt transmissions may be available - check with
your dealer parts department, motor factors, or transmission specialists. At any rate, the time and money involved in an overhaul is almost

sure to exceed the cost of a rebuilt unit.
2   Nevertheless, it's not impossible for an inexperienced mechanic
to rebuild a transmission, providing the special tools are available, and
the job is done in a deliberate step-by-step manner so nothing is over-
looked.
3   The tools necessary for an overhaul include: internal and external
circlip pliers, a bearing puller, a slide hammer, a set of pin punches, a

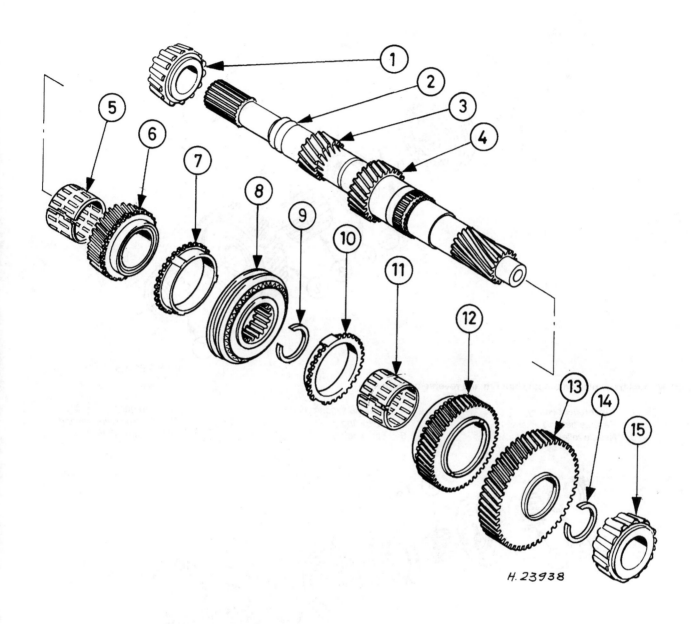

H.23938

9.4B Manual transmission input shaft components

1	Taper roller bearing	6	3rd gear	11	Needle roller bearing
2	Input shaft	7	3rd/4th synchro ring	12	4th gear
3	1st gear	8	3rd/4th synchro hub	13	5th gear
4	2nd gear	9	Snap-ring	14	Snap-ring
5	Needle roller bearing	10	4th/5th synchro ring	15	Taper roller bearing

dial test indicator, and possibly a hydraulic press. In addition, a large, sturdy workbench and a vice or transmission stand will be required.

4   During dismantling of the transmission, make careful notes of how each part comes off, where it fits in relation to other parts, and what holds it in place. Exploded views are included **(see illustrations)** to show where the parts go - but actually noting how they are fitted when you remove the parts will make it much easier to get the trans-

mission back together.

5   Before taking the transmission apart for repair, it will help if you have some idea what area of the transmission is malfunctioning. Certain problems can be closely tied to specific areas in the transmission, which can make component examination and replacement easier. Refer to the *"Fault diagnosis"* section at the front of this manual for information regarding possible sources of trouble.

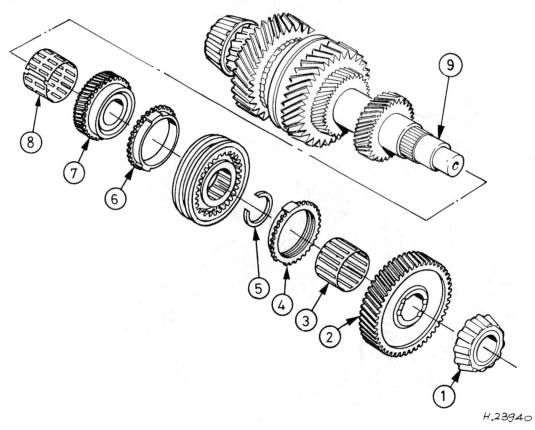

H.23940

9.4C Manual transmission output shaft 5th and reverse components

1	Taper roller bearing	4	Reverse synchro ring	7	5th gear
2	Reverse gear	5	Snap-ring	8	Needle roller bearing
3	Needle roller bearing	6	5th synchro ring	9	Output shaft

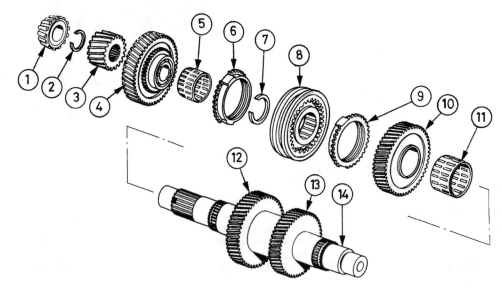

H.23937

9.4D Manual transmission output shaft 1st/2nd components

1	Taper roller bearing	6	1st synchro ring	11	Needle roller bearing
2	Snap-ring	7	Snap-ring	12	4th gear
3	Output pinion	8	1st/2nd synchro hub	13	3rd gear
4	1st gear	9	2nd synchro ring	14	Output shaft
5	Needle roller bearing	10	2nd gear		

Chapter 7 Part B Automatic transmission

Contents

7B

Specifications

Torque wrench settings

	Nm	lbf ft
Selector cable support bracket	19	14
Torque converter to driveplate	36	27
Automatic transmission to engine	40	30
Driveplate to crankshaft	112	83
Oil cooler pipes	23	17
Selector lever to floor	9	7
Speed sensor	5	4
Transmission drain plug	21	15
Selector lever position sensor	10	7

3.6 Selector lever (arrowed) on the side of the transmission

3.7 Cable support bracket bolts (arrowed)

1   General information

The CD4E automatic transmission is controlled electronically by the engine management electronic control unit. There are two operational modes (Economy and Sport), and a driver-operated overdrive inhibit switch prevents the 4th gear from operating when required during certain conditions. With the Economy mode selected, gear changes occur at low engine speeds, whereas with the Sport mode selected, the changes occur at high engine speeds.

The transmission incorporates a chain drive between the planetary gearsets and the final drive. The transmission fluid is cooled by a cooler located within the radiator.

There is no kickdown switch, as kickdown is controlled by the throttle position sensor in the engine management system.

The electronic control system has a failsafe mode, which gives the transmission limited operation in order to drive the vehicle home or to a Ford garage.

The gear selection includes the normal P, R, N, D, 2, and 1 positions. As a safety measure, it is necessary for the ignition to be switched on and for the brake pedal to be depressed in order to move the selector from position P. If the vehicle battery is discharged, the selector lever release solenoid will not function; if it is required to move the vehicle in this state, insert a pen or a similar small instrument into the aperture on the left-hand side of the centre console. Push the locking lever rearwards to allow the selector lever to be moved.

2   Fault diagnosis - general

1   In the event of a fault occurring on the transmission, first check that the fluid level is correct (see Chapter 1). If there has been a loss of fluid, check the oil seals as described in Section 7. Also check the hoses to the fluid cooler in the radiator for leaks. The only other checks possible for the home mechanic are the adjustment of the selector cable (Section 3) and the selector lever position sensor (Section 6).

2   If the fault still persists, it is necessary to determine whether it is of an electrical, mechanical or hydraulic nature; to do this, special test equipment is required. It is therefore essential to have the work carried out by an automatic transmission specialist or Ford dealer if a transmission fault is suspected.

3   Do not remove the transmission from the vehicle for possible repair before professional fault diagnosis has been carried out, since most tests require the transmission to be in the vehicle.

3   Selector cable - removal, refitting and adjustment

Removal

1   Apply the handbrake, jack up the front of the vehicle and support

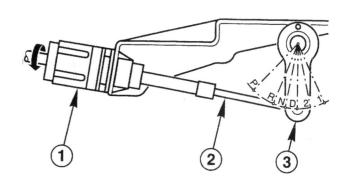

3.11 Selecting position "D" at the transmission

1 *Locking ring*	3 *Transmission lever*
2 *Cable*	

it on axle stands. Remove the left-hand front wheel.

2   Remove the air mass meter and trunking (Chapter 4) in order to gain access to the selector cable, which is located on the left-hand side of the transmission.

3   Working beneath the vehicle, remove the heat shield for access to the bottom of the selector lever assembly.

4   Disconnect the inner cable from the bottom of the selector lever assembly.

5   Turn the outer cable locking ring anti-clockwise by 90° to unlock it from the selector lever plate on the bottom of the selector lever assembly. Hold the collar while turning the locking ring.

6   Working in the engine compartment, pull the inner cable end fitting outwards from the lever on the side of the transmission **(see illustration)**.

7   Unbolt the cable support bracket from the transmission **(see illustration)**.

8   Detach the remaining cable supports, and withdraw the cable assembly from the vehicle.

Refitting and adjustment

9   Refitting is a reversal of the removal procedure, but adjust the cable as follows.

10   Inside the vehicle, move the selector lever to position "D".

11   With the inner cable disconnected from the lever on the side of the transmission, check that the lever is in the "D" position. To do this, it will be necessary to move the lever slightly up and down until it is po-

6.2 Multi-plug (arrowed) for the selector lever position sensor

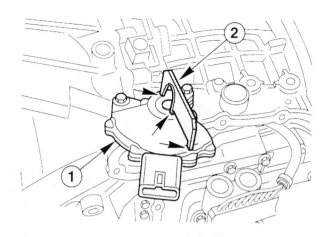

6.6 Alignment tool for the selector lever position sensor (selector in position "N")

1   *Sensor*
2   *Alignment tool (pegs arrowed)*

sitioned correctly. A further check can be made by observing that the "D" mark on the selector lever position sensor is correctly aligned **(see illustration)**.

12   Check that the cable locking ring beneath the vehicle is still unlocked (ie turned anti-clockwise by 90°).

13   With both the selector levers inside the vehicle and on the side of the transmission in position "D", refit the cable end fitting to the transmission lever, then turn the locking ring 90° cockwise to lock it.

14   Refit the heat shield to the underbody.

15   Refit the air mass meter and trunking.

16   Refit the left-hand front wheel, then lower the vehicle to the ground.

17   Road test the vehicle to check the operation of the transmission.

4   Selector assembly - removal and refitting

Removal

1   Remove the centre console as described in Chapter 11, Section 30.

2   Apply the handbrake, then jack up the front of the vehicle and support on axle stands.

3   Working beneath the vehicle, remove the heat shield, then disconnect the selector cable end fitting from the bottom of the selector lever assembly.

4   Unscrew the mounting nuts securing the selector cable plate to the bottom of the lever assembly.

5   Disconnect the wiring multi-plugs, then withdraw the selector lever assembly from inside the vehicle. Recover the gasket.

6   If necessary, the selector lever and position indicator may be unbolted from the top of the assembly.

Refitting

7   Refitting is a reversal of the removal procedure, but adjust the selector cable as described in Section 3.

5   Speedometer drive pinion - removal and refitting

Removal

1   The speedometer drive pinion is located on the rear right-hand side of the transmission. First apply the handbrake, then jack up the front of the vehicle and support it on axle stands.

2   Unscrew the nut, and disconnect the speedometer cable from the vehicle speed sensor on the transmission. Use two spanners to loosen

the nut - one to counterhold the sensor, and the other to unscrew the cable nut.

3   Disconnect the wiring from the vehicle speed sensor.

4   Unscrew the clamp bolt, and remove the clamp plate securing the drive pinion and vehicle speed sensor in the transmission.

5   Pull out the speedometer drive pinion and bearing assembly, together with the vehicle speed sensor.

6   Unscrew the vehicle speed sensor from the drive pinion bearing.

7   Remove the pinion from the bearing.

8   Using a small screwdriver, prise the rubber O-ring from the groove in the bearing; obtain a new one for reassembly.

9   Wipe clean the drive pinion and bearing, also the seating bore in the transmission casing.

Refitting

10   Refitting is a reversal of the removal procedure. Lightly oil the new O-ring before inserting the assembly in the transmission casing. Tighten the clamp bolt.

6   Selector lever position sensor - removal, refitting and adjustment

Removal

1   Remove the air mass meter and trunking (Chapter 4) in order to gain access to the selector lever position sensor, which is located on top of the transmission.

2   Disconnect the wiring multi-plug **(see illustration)**.

3   Unscrew the mounting bolts, and remove the sensor.

Refitting and adjustment

4   Refitting is a reversal of the removal procedure, but check the alignment of the sensor as follows before fully tightening the mounting bolts.

5   Move the selector lever to position "N".

6   The Ford tool for aligning the sensor consists of a metal plate, with pegs to engage with the cut-outs in the sensor and shaft **(see illustration)**. A similar tool may be made up, or alternatively, a straight edge may be used to check the alignment.

7   Twist the sensor on the shaft until the slots in the sensor housing and the plastic insert in the shaft are correctly aligned. With the sensor correctly aligned, tighten the bolts, then remove the alignment tool. As a further check, move the selector lever to position "D", and check that

7B

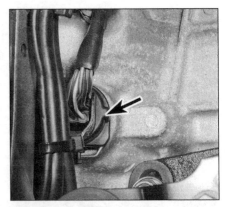

**6.7 With "D" selected, "D" mark (A) on the
selector lever position sensor should align
with cut-outs (B) in shaft's plastic insert
(shown here with "P" selected)**

**8.6 Earth lead attachment (arrowed) on
the transmission**

**8.7A Inhibitor switch multi-plug (arrowed)
on the top of the transmission**

the "D" mark on the sensor is aligned with the slots in the shaft's plastic insert **(see illustration)**.

7 Oil seals - renewal

Differential side gear oil seals

1   The procedure is the same as that for the manual transmission (refer to Chapter 7A, Section 5).

Speedometer drive pinion oil seal

2   The procedure is covered in Section 5 of this Chapter.

8 Automatic transmission - removal and refitting

Note: *Read through this procedure before starting work, to see what is involved, particularly in terms of lifting equipment. Depending on the facilities available, the home mechanic may prefer to remove the engine and transmission together, then separate them on the bench, as described in Chapter 2.*

Removal

1   Disconnect the battery negative (earth) lead (refer to Chapter 5, Section 1). For better access, the battery may be removed completely.
2   If necessary, remove the bonnet (Chapter 11) for better access, and for fitting the engine lifting hoist.
3   Raise the radiator, and hold it in the raised position by inserting split pins through the holes in the upper mounting extensions. This is necessary to retain the radiator when the subframe is removed.
4   Remove the air mass meter and trunking (Chapter 4).
5   Remove the air cleaner assembly (Chapter 4).
6   Detach the battery earth lead from the transmission **(see illustration)**.
7   Disconnect the wiring multi-plugs from the inhibitor switch, control unit and transmission speed sensor **(see illustrations)**.
8   Pull the selector cable end fitting from the lever on the side of the transmission, then unbolt the support bracket.
9   Apply the handbrake, jack up the front of the vehicle and support it on axle stands. Remove the front wheels.
10   Remove the wheel arch liner from the right-hand side of the vehicle (Chapter 11).
11   Remove the auxiliary drivebelt cover (see Chapter 1).
12   Working on each side of the vehicle in turn, unscrew the nut and disconnect the anti-roll bar link from the strut, noting that the flexible brake hose bracket is attached to the link stud.
13   Extract the split pins, then unscrew the nuts securing the track rod ends to the steering knuckles on each side. Release the balljoints

from the steering knuckle arms, using a balljoint separator tool.
14   Working on each side in turn, note which way round the front suspension lower arm balljoint clamp bolt is fitted, then unscrew and remove it from the knuckle assembly. Lever the balljoint down from the knuckle - if it is tight, prise the joint open carefully using a large flat-bladed tool. Take care not to damage the balljoint seal during the separation procedure.
15   Remove the front lower cover from under the radiator, by prising out the side clips and unscrewing the retaining bolts.
16   Drain the cooling system as described in Chapter 1.
17   Disconnect the multi-plug from the wiring leading to the oxygen sensor, then unclip the wiring from the engine rear mounting.
18   Disconnect the vacuum hose from the pulse-air system filter.
19   Remove the complete exhaust system (Chapter 4).
20   On models fitted with air conditioning, unscrew and remove the mounting bolts securing the dehydrator to the subframe, and tie it to one side.
21   Unscrew and remove the bolts securing the steering gear to the subframe. The bolts are difficult to reach using normal spanners, and if possible the special cranked Ford tool should be obtained (see Chapter 10).
22   Unbolt the engine/transmission rear mounting from the subframe.
23   Unscrew and remove the centre bolt from the engine front mounting, and detach the pulse-air filter from the bracket on the mounting.
24   Unbolt the radiator bracket from the subframe.
25   With the help of an assistant, support the weight of the subframe, using trolley jacks if possible. Unscrew the bolts securing the power steering fluid cooler pipes to the subframe, then unscrew and remove the subframe mounting bolts, and lower the subframe to the ground.
26   Unscrew and remove the centre bolt from the engine/transmission rear mounting, then unbolt the mounting from the transmission.
27   Unscrew the union nut securing the automatic transmission fluid cooler pipe to the left-hand side of the transmission. Unclip the pipe, and move it to one side. Plug the end of the pipe, to prevent dust and dirt entering the hydraulic system.
28   Position a suitable container beneath the transmission, then unscrew the drain plug and drain the fluid **(see illustration)**. Refit and tighten the plug on completion.
29   Insert a lever between the left-hand driveshaft inner joint and the transmission case (with a thin piece of wood against the case), then prise free the joint from the differential. If it proves reluctant to move, strike the lever firmly with the palm of the hand. Be careful not to damage the adjacent components, and be prepared for fluid spillage.
30   Support the left-hand driveshaft on axle stands, making sure that the inner joint is not turned through more than 18° (damage may occur if the joint is turned through too great an angle).
31   Unscrew the bolts securing the right-hand driveshaft centre bearing to the cylinder block, remove the heat shield, then pull out the right-hand strut so that the intermediate shaft is removed from the

8.7B Transmission speed sensor multi-plug on the side of the transmission

8.28 Automatic transmission fluid drain plug

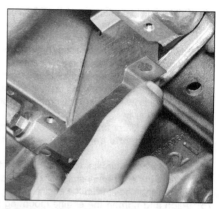

8.34 Removing the cover plate from the bottom of the transmission

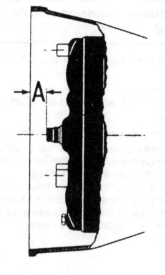

8.52 Torque converter spigot must be at least 10 mm below the transmission flange (dimension A)

transmission differential gears. Be prepared for fluid spillage.

32   Support the right-hand driveshaft on axle stands, again making sure that the inner joint is not turned through more than 18° (damage may occur if the joint is turned through too great an angle).

33   At the front of the transmission, unscrew the union nut and disconnect the fluid cooler pipe. Plug the end of the pipe, to prevent dust and dirt entering the hydraulic system.

34   Unscrew the bolts and remove the cover plate from the bottom of the transmission, for access to the torque converter retaining bolts **(see illustration)**.

35   Unscrew and remove the torque converter retaining bolts. It will be necessary to turn the engine, using the crankshaft pulley bolt, so that each of the four bolts can be unscrewed through the aperture.

36   If necessary, the vehicle may be lowered to the ground at this stage, in order to connect an engine support hoist. If an engine support bar which locates over the engine compartment is to be used, then the vehicle may be left in its raised position.

37   Attach the hoist or engine support bar to diagonally-opposite positions on the engine, and take the weight of the engine and transmission.

38   At the top of the engine, disconnect the two wiring multi-plugs from the thermostat housing.

39   Disconnect the radiator hoses from the thermostat housing.

40   Unscrew the mounting bolts, and remove the thermostat housing.

41   Unscrew and remove the upper mounting bolts securing the automatic transmission to the engine.

42   Unscrew the nuts from the engine right-hand mounting bracket.

Note that, where a hydraulic mounting is fitted (see Chapter 2A, Section 22), the mounting must never be tilted by more than 5 .

43   Unscrew the retaining nuts, and remove the engine/transmission left-hand mounting from the transmission.

44   On models fitted with air conditioning, lower the engine until the compressor is below the right-hand side member.

45   On models without air conditioning, lower the transmission until it is opposite the aperture on the left-hand side of the engine compartment.

46   Support the weight of the transmission on a trolley jack. Use safety chains or make up a cradle to steady the transmission on the jack.

47   Unscrew and remove the starter motor mounting bolts.

48   Unscrew and remove the lower bolts securing the transmission to the engine.

49   With the help of an assistant, withdraw the transmission squarely from the engine, making sure that the torque converter comes away with the transmission, and does not stay in contact with the driveplate. If this precaution is not taken, there is a risk of the torque converter falling out and being damaged.

50   Lower the transmission to the ground.

Refitting

51   Clean the contact surfaces of the driveplate and torque converter.

52   Check that the torque converter is fully entered in the transmission. To do this, place a straight-edge on the transmission flange, and check that the torque converter spigot is at least 10 mm below the straight-edge **(see illustration)**. **Caution:** *This procedure is important, to ensure that the torque converter is engaged with the fluid pump. If it is not fully engaged, serious damage will occur.*

53   With the help of an assistant, raise the transmission, and locate it on the rear of the driveplate. The torque converter must remain in full engagement during the fitting procedure.

54   Refit and tighten the transmission-to-engine bolts.

55   Refit and tighten the starter motor mounting bolts.

56   Remove the trolley jack.

57   Refit the engine/transmission left-hand and right-hand mountings, but do not fully tighten them at this stage.

58   Refit the thermostat housing, and tighten the bolts.

59   Reconnect the radiator hoses to the thermostat housing.

60   Reconnect the two wiring multi-plugs to the thermostat housing.

61   Insert and tighten all of the torque converter retaining bolts to the specified torque. Turn the engine as required to bring each of the bolts into view.

62   Refit the cover plate to the bottom of the transmission, and tighten the bolts.

63   Refit the fluid cooler pipe to the front of the transmission, and tighten the union nut.

64   Refit the right-hand driveshaft and intermediate shaft, together with the heat shield (refer to Chapter 8 if necessary).

65   Refit the left-hand driveshaft (refer to Chapter 8 if necessary).

7B

66   Refit the fluid cooler pipe to the left-hand side of the transmission, making sure that it engages with the clips correctly. Tighten the union nut.

67   Refit the engine/transmission rear mounting to the transmission, but do not fully tighten the centre bolt at this stage.

68   Refit the subframe, and align it as described in Chapter 2B, Section 4. Tighten the mounting bolts to the specified torque.

69   Refit the power steering fluid cooler pipes to the subframe, and tighten the bolts.

70   Refit the radiator bracket to the subframe, and tighten the bolts.

71   Insert the centre bolt in the engine front mounting, and hand-tighten it.

72   Refit the pulse-air filter to the engine front mounting bracket.

73   Secure the engine/transmission rear mounting to the subframe.

74   Remove the hoist from the engine.

75   Align and tighten the engine mounting bolts, with reference to Chapter 2A, Section 22.

76   Refit the steering gear to the subframe, and tighten the bolts.

77   On models fitted with air conditioning, refit the dehydrator to the subframe, and tighten the bolts.

78   Refit the complete exhaust system, with reference to Chapter 4.

79   Reconnect the vacuum hose to the pulse-air system filter.

80   Reconnect the oxygen sensor multi-plug, then clip the wiring to the engine rear mounting.

81   Refit the front lower cover under the radiator.

82   Refit both of the front suspension lower arm balljoints, and tighten the clamp bolts. Refer to Chapter 10 if necessary.

83   Refit the track rod ends to the steering knuckles on both sides. Refer to Chapter 10 if necessary.

84   Refit the anti-roll bar links to the struts on both sides.

85   Refit the auxiliary drivebelt cover and the right-hand side wheel arch liner.

86   Refit the front wheels, and lower the vehicle to the ground. Tighten the wheel nuts.

87   Refit the selector cable and bracket, and tighten the bolts.

88   Reconnect the wiring multi-plugs for the inhibitor switch and control switch.

89   Refit the battery earth lead to the transmission, and tighten the bolt.

90   Refit the air cleaner assembly as described in Chapter 4.

91   Refit the air mass meter and air inlet duct, with reference to Chapter 4.

92   Remove the split pins holding the radiator in its raised position.

93   If removed, refit the bonnet with reference to Chapter 11.

94   Reconnect the battery negative (earth) lead.

95   Adjust the selector cable as described in Section 3.

96   Adjust the selector lever position sensor as described in Section 6.

97   Fill the transmission with the correct quantity of fluid, through the dipstick/filler tube.

98   Refill the cooling system with reference to Chapter 1.

99   After running the engine, recheck the transmission fluid level, and top-up if necessary (refer to Chapter 1).

100 Road test the vehicle to check the transmission for correct operation.

9   Automatic transmission mountings - checking and renewal

This procedure is covered in Chapter 2A, Section 22.

10 Automatic transmission overhaul - general information

1   Overhaul of the automatic transmission should be left to an automatic transmission specialist or a Ford dealer. Refer to the information given in Section 2 before removing the unit.

2   Note that, if the vehicle is still within the warranty period, in the event of a fault it is important to take it to a Ford dealer, who will carry out a comprehensive diagnosis procedure using specialist equipment. Failure to do this will invalidate the warranty.

Chapter 8   Clutch and driveshafts

Contents

8

Specifications

Clutch

Disc diameter...	240 mm
Lining thickness (new)	8.84 mm
Pedal stroke:	
Right-hand-drive models	155 ± 5.0 mm
Left-hand-drive models...	145 ± 5.0 mm

Torque wrench settings	Nm	lbf ft
Clutch pressure plate to flywheel	25 to 34	18 to 25
Clutch release lever clamp bolt	21 to 27	15 to 20
Driveshaft support bearing bracket-to-cylinder block bolts	48	35
Driveshaft/hub retaining nut	340	251

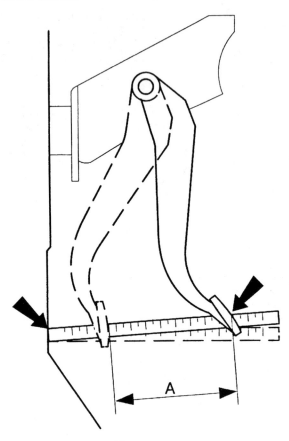

3.4 Clutch pedal stroke (A)

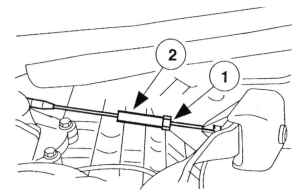

3.7 Locknut (1) and adjustment sleeve (2) for the clutch pedal stroke adjustment

1   General information

The information in this Chapter deals with the components from the engine flywheel to the front wheels, except for the transmission, which is dealt with in Chapter 7, Parts A and B. For the purposes of this Chapter, these components are grouped into the two categories, clutch (for manual transmission models) and driveshafts (for manual and automatic transmission models). Separate Sections within this Chapter offer general descriptions and checking procedures for each group.

Since many of the procedures covered in this Chapter involve working under the vehicle, make sure that it is securely supported on axle stands placed on a firm, level floor.

2   Clutch - description and check

1   All manual transmission models are equipped with a cable-operated single dry plate diaphragm spring clutch assembly. The cover assembly consists of a steel cover (dowelled and bolted to the rear face of the flywheel), the pressure plate, and a diaphragm spring.

2   The clutch disc is free to slide along the splines of the gearbox input shaft, and is held in position between the flywheel and the pressure plate by the pressure of the diaphragm spring. Friction lining material is riveted to the clutch disc (driven plate), which has a spring-cushioned hub, to absorb transmission shocks and help ensure a smooth take-up of the drive.

3   The clutch is actuated by a cable, controlled by the clutch pedal. The clutch release mechanism consists of a release arm, and a bearing which contacts the fingers of the diaphragm spring. Depressing the clutch pedal actuates the release arm by means of the cable. The arm pushes the release bearing against the diaphragm fingers, so moving the centre of the diaphragm spring inwards. As the centre of the spring is pushed inwards, the outside of the spring pivots outwards, so mov-

ing the pressure plate backwards and disengaging its grip on the clutch disc.

4   When the pedal is released, the diaphragm spring forces the pressure plate back into contact with the friction linings on the clutch disc. The disc is now firmly held between the pressure plate and the flywheel, thus transmitting engine power to the gearbox.

5   Unlike some other models in the Ford range, the clutch pedal is not of the self-adjusting type, although it uses the same serrated segment fitted to models with a self-adjusting pedal. The normal self-adjusting spring-tensioned pawl is not fitted to the segment, although the pedal moves the segment when it contacts the end stops. This arrangement means that pedal adjustment must be carried out manually.

6   The following checks may be performed to diagnose a clutch problem.

(a) First check the entire length of the clutch release cable in the engine compartment for obvious damage. Check also that it is located correctly, without any sharp turns.

(b) To check "clutch spin down time", run the engine at normal idle speed with the transmission in Neutral (clutch pedal up). Disengage the clutch (pedal down), wait several seconds, then engage reverse. No grinding noise should be heard. A grinding noise would most likely indicate a problem in the pressure plate or the clutch disc. Remember, however, that the transmission reverse gear has synchromesh fitted to it, so the probable symptom of a clutch fault would be a slight rearwards movement (or attempted movement) of the vehicle. If the check is made on level ground with the handbrake released, the movement would be more noticeable.

(c) To check for complete clutch release, run the engine at idle, and hold the clutch pedal approximately half an inch from the floor. Shift between 1st gear and reverse several times. If the shift is not smooth, or if the vehicle attempts to move forwards or backwards, component failure is indicated. Check the clutch cable and the pedal adjustment.

(d) Check the clutch pedal for excessive wear of the bushes, and for any obstructions which may restrict the pedal movement.

3   Clutch adjustment - check

1   If this check is being made after fitting a new clutch cable, the pedal should be depressed fully 10 times first.

2   Fully depress and hold down the clutch pedal, then place a steel rule against the bulkhead, and measure and record the distance to the middle of the rubber pad (dimension "C").

3   Release the pedal, and measure the distance from the bulkhead to the middle of the rubber pad again (dimension "B"). Do not lift the pedal when making the measurement.

4   Subtract dimension "C" from dimension "B" to determine the clutch pedal stroke (dimension "A") **(see illustration)**.

"A" (stroke) = "B" (released dimension) minus "C" (depressed dimension)

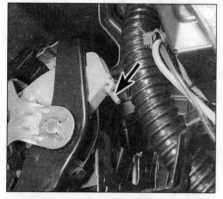

4.3 Rubber cushion (arrowed) on the end of the outer cable

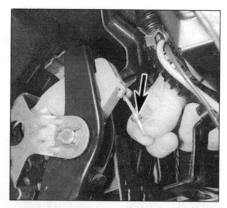

4.6 Unhooking the clutch inner cable (arrowed) from the pedal segment

4.7 Clutch cable support stay (arrowed) located next to the brake servo unit

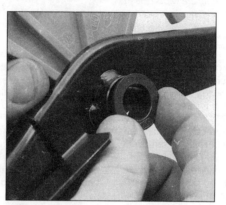

4.8 Inner cable (arrowed) fitted to the pedal segment

5.8A Removing the clutch pedal bushes

5.8B Removing the segment from the clutch pedal

5   Check that the dimension is within the tolerance given in the Specifications. If adjustment is required, proceed as follows.
6   Remove the air cleaner assembly as described in Chapter 4.
7   Loosen the locknut on the clutch cable adjuster sleeve near the release arm on the transmission. Turn the sleeve until the correct clutch pedal stroke is obtained (see illustration).
8   On completion, tighten the locknut.

4   Clutch cable - removal and refitting

Removal

1   Remove the air cleaner assembly as described in Chapter 4.
2   Disengage the clutch cable from the release arm, by gripping the inner cable with pliers and pulling it forwards to disengage the cable nipple from the release arm. Take care not to damage the cable, if it is to be re-used.
3   Disengage the outer cable from the support lug on top of the gearbox bellhousing. Note the rubber cushion on the end of the outer cable (see illustration).
4   Working inside the vehicle, remove the facia lower trim panel from beneath the steering column for access to the clutch pedal. Refer to Chapter 11 if necessary.
5   Disconnect the clutch pedal return spring from the pedal and bracket. Note where the spring is attached to the bracket, as the small hole is not easy to see.
6   Unhook the inner cable from the pedal segment (see illustration).
7   Pull the cable through the aperture in the bulkhead. Detach the cable from the support stay near the brake servo unit, and withdraw it from the engine compartment (see illustration).

Refitting

8   To refit the cable, thread it through the bulkhead from the engine

compartment side. Fit the inner cable over the segment, engaging the end stop to secure it (see illustration).
9   Reconnect the pedal return spring, making sure that it is correctly fitted in the small hole.
10   Reconnect the cable at the transmission end, passing it through the support lug on the top of the transmission, and engaging it with the release arm.
11   Locate the rubber grommet in the clutch cable support stay. Renew the grommet if necessary.
11   Adjust the pedal stroke as described in Section 3 of this Chapter.
12   Check the operation of the clutch.
13   Refit the trim panel under the steering column.
14   Refit the air cleaner assembly as described in Chapter 4.

5   Clutch pedal - removal and refitting

Removal

1   Remove the brake pedal as described in Chapter 9.
2   Remove the blue nylon spacer from the pedal pivot shaft.
3   Unhook and remove the clutch pedal return spring.
4   Remove the air cleaner assembly as described in Chapter 4.
5   Disconnect the clutch cable from the release arm as described in the previous Section.
6   Working inside the vehicle, release the inner cable from the pedal segment on the clutch pedal.
7   Withdraw the pedal pivot shaft through the mounting bracket, and remove the pedal together with the blue nylon spacer. Note that this spacer is additional to the spacer located next to the brake pedal.
8   With the pedal removed, prise out the bushes from each side, and remove the segment (see illustrations). Also remove the rubber pad. Renew the components as necessary.

8

Refitting

9   Prior to refitting the pedal, apply a little grease to the pivot shaft and pedal bushes.

10   Refitting is a reversal of the removal procedure, making sure that the bushes and spacers are correctly located.

11   Adjust the clutch pedal stroke as described in Section 3.

6   Clutch components - removal, inspection and refitting

Warning: *Dust created by clutch wear and deposited on the clutch components may contain asbestos, which is a health hazard. DO NOT blow it out with compressed air, and do not inhale any of it. DO NOT use petrol or petroleum-based solvents to clean off the dust. Brake system cleaner or methylated spirit should be used to flush the dust into a suitable receptacle. After the clutch components are wiped clean with rags, dispose of the contaminated rags and cleaner in a sealed, marked container.*

Removal

1   Access to the clutch may be gained in one of two ways. The engine/transmission unit can be removed, as described in Chapter 2B, and the transmission separated from the engine on the bench. Alternatively, the engine may be left in the vehicle and the transmission removed independently, as described in Chapter 7A. If the latter course of action is taken, note that the transmission need only be moved to the left of the engine compartment - it is not necessary to remove it completely **(see illustration)**.

2   Having separated the transmission from the engine, check if there are any marks identifying the relation of the clutch cover to the flywheel. If not, make your own marks using a dab of paint or a scriber **(see illustration)**. These marks will be used if the original cover is refitted, and will help to maintain the balance of the unit. A new cover may be fitted in any position allowed by the locating dowels.

3   Unscrew and remove the six clutch cover retaining bolts, working in a diagonal sequence, and slackening the bolts only a turn at a time **(see illustration)**. If necessary, the flywheel may be held stationary using a wide-bladed screwdriver, inserted in the teeth of the starter ring gear and resting against part of the cylinder block.

4   Ease the clutch cover off its locating dowels. Be prepared to catch the clutch disc, which will drop out as the cover is removed **(see illustration)**. Note which way round the disc is fitted.

Inspection

5   The most common problem which occurs in the clutch is wear of the clutch disc (driven plate). However, all the clutch components should be inspected at this time, particularly if the engine has covered a high mileage. Unless the clutch components are known to be virtually new, it is worth renewing them all as a set (disc, pressure plate and

6.1 Clutch is accessible with the transmission moved to one side

release bearing). Renewing a worn clutch disc by itself is not always satisfactory, especially if the old disc was slipping and causing the pressure plate to overheat.

6   Examine the linings of the clutch disc for wear and loose rivets, and the disc hub and rim for distortion, cracks, broken torsion springs, and worn splines. The surface of the friction linings may be highly glazed, but as long as the friction material pattern can be clearly seen, and the rivet heads are at least 1 mm below the lining surface, this is satisfactory. If there is any sign of oil contamination, indicated by shiny black discoloration, the disc must be renewed, and the source of the contamination traced and rectified. This will be a leaking crankshaft oil seal or gearbox input shaft oil seal. The renewal procedure for the former is given in Chapter 2; renewal of the gearbox input shaft oil seal should be entrusted to a Ford dealer, as it involves dismantling the gearbox, and the renewal of the clutch release bearing guide tube, using a press. The disc must also be renewed if the lining thickness has worn down to, or just above, the level of the rivet heads.

7   Check the machined faces of the flywheel and pressure plate. If either is grooved, or heavily scored, renewal is necessary. The pressure plate must also be renewed if any cracks are apparent, or if the diaphragm spring is damaged or its pressure suspect. Pay particular attention to the tips of the spring fingers, where the release bearing acts upon them.

8   With the gearbox removed, it is also advisable to check the condition of the release bearing, as described in Section 7. Having got this far, it is almost certainly worth renewing it.

Refitting

9   It is important that no oil or grease is allowed to come into contact with the friction material of the clutch disc or the pressure plate and

6.2 Marking the clutch cover and flywheel with a dab of paint (arrowed)

6.3 Unscrewing the clutch cover bolts

6.4 Removing the clutch cover and disc

6.11 "FLYWHEEL-SIDE" marking on the clutch disc

6.15 Using a clutch-aligning tool to centralise the clutch disc

7.2A Clutch release bearing in place on the guide sleeve

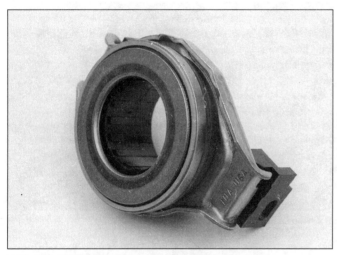

7.2B Release bearing removed from the transmission

flywheel faces. To ensure this, it is advisable to refit the clutch assembly with clean hands, and to wipe down the pressure plate and flywheel faces with a clean dry rag before assembly begins.

10 Ford technicians use a special tool for centralising the clutch disc at this stage. The tool holds the disc centrally on the pressure plate, and locates in the middle of the diaphragm spring fingers. If the tool is not available, it will be necessary to centralise the disc after assembling the cover loosely on the flywheel, as described in the following paragraphs.

11 Place the clutch disc against the flywheel, ensuring that it is the right way round. It should be marked "FLYWHEEL SIDE", but if not, position it so that the raised hub with the cushion springs is facing away from the flywheel **(see illustration)**.

12 Place the clutch cover over the dowels. Refit the retaining bolts, and tighten them finger-tight so that the clutch disc is gripped lightly, but can still be moved.

13 The clutch disc must now be centralised so that, when the engine and transmission are mated, the splines of the gearbox input shaft will pass through the splines in the centre of the clutch disc hub.

14 Centralisation can be carried out by inserting a round bar through the hole in the centre of the clutch disc, so that the end of the bar rests in the hole in the rear end of the crankshaft. Move the bar sideways or up and down, to move the clutch disc in whichever direction is necessary to achieve centralisation. Centralisation can then be checked by removing the bar and viewing the clutch disc hub in relation to the diaphragm spring fingers, or by viewing through the side apertures of the cover, and checking that the disc is central in relation to the outer edge of the pressure plate.

15 An alternative and more accurate method of centralisation is to use a commercially-available clutch-aligning tool, obtainable from most accessory shops (see *Tools and working facilities* at the beginning of this manual) **(see illustration)**.

16 Once the clutch is centralised, progressively tighten the cover bolts in a diagonal sequence to the torque setting given in the Specifications.

17 Ensure that the input shaft splines, clutch disc splines and release bearing guide sleeve are clean. Apply a thin smear of high melting-point grease to the input shaft splines and the release bearing guide sleeve.

18 Refit the transmission to the engine.

7 Clutch release bearing - removal, inspection and refitting

Removal

1 Separate the engine and transmission as described in the previous Section.

2 Withdraw the release bearing from its guide sleeve by turning the release arm **(see illustrations)**.

Inspection

3 Check the bearing for smoothness of operation, and renew it if there is any sign of harshness or roughness as the bearing is spun. Do not attempt to dismantle, clean or lubricate the bearing.

4 As mentioned earlier, it is worth renewing the release bearing as a matter of course, unless it is known to be in perfect condition.

Refitting

5 Refitting of the clutch release bearing is a reversal of the removal procedure, making sure that it is correctly located on the release arm fork. It is helpful to slightly lift the release arm while locating the bearing on its guide sleeve. Keep the fork in contact with the plastic shoulders on the bearing as the bearing is being located.

8 Clutch release shaft and bush - removal and refitting

Removal

1 Remove the clutch release bearing as described in the previous Section.

2 Unscrew the clamp bolt securing the release arm to the shaft. Mark the relative position of the shaft to the arm, then withdraw the arm from the shaft. The shaft has a master spline, to ensure that the

8

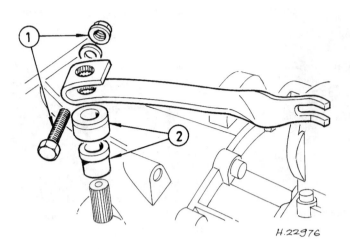

H.22976

8.2A Clutch release arm removal

    1   Clamp bolt
    2   Protective cap and bearing bush

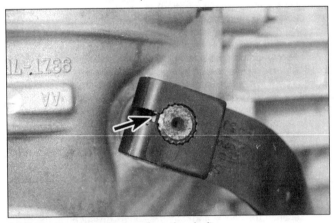

8.2C Master spline (arrowed) on the shaft

8.2B Removing the clamp bolt

8.4 Removing the bush using grips

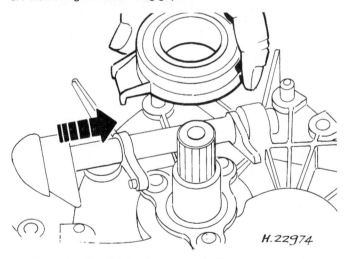

H.22974

8.5 Removing the clutch release arm shaft

arm is fitted correctly **(see illustrations)**.
3   Remove the protective cap from around the top of the release
shaft splines, to allow access to the bush.
4   Extract the bush by gently levering it from the housing, using grips
or a pair of screwdrivers, then lift it out over the splines of the shaft
(see illustration).
5   With the bush removed, the release shaft can be removed by lifting it from its lower bearing bore, manoeuvring it sideways and withdrawing it **(see illustration)**.

Refitting

6   Refitting is a reversal of the removal procedure. Apply a little
grease to the bearing surfaces, both in the transmission and in the
bush.

9   Driveshafts - description

        Drive is transmitted from the transmission differential to the front
wheels by means of two driveshafts. The right-hand driveshaft is in two
sections, and incorporates a support bearing.
        Each driveshaft consists of three main components: the sliding
(tripod type) inner joint, the actual driveshaft, and the outer CV (constant velocity) joint. The inner (male) end of the left-hand tripod joint is
secured in the differential side gear by the engagement of a circlip. The
inner (female) end of the right-hand driveshaft is held on the intermediate shaft by the engagement of a circlip. The intermediate shaft is held

in the transmission by the support bearing, which in turn is supported
by a bracket bolted to the rear of the cylinder block. The outer CV joint
on both driveshafts is of ball-bearing type, and is secured in the front
hub by the hub nut **(see illustration)**.

10   Driveshafts - removal and refitting

Removal

1   Remove the wheel cover from the wheel, apply the handbrake,

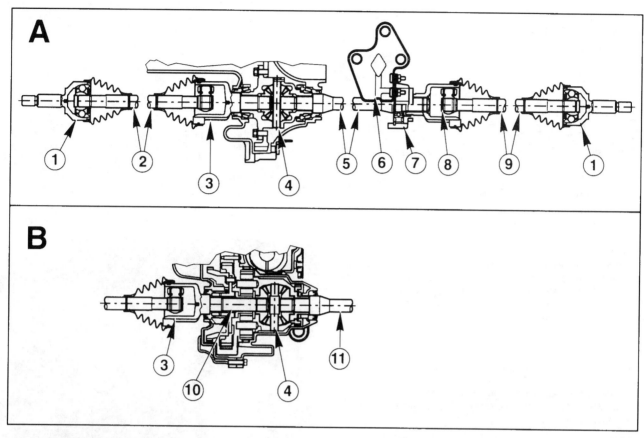

9.0 Cross-section of the driveshafts

A	Manual (MTX 75) transmission
B	Automatic (CD4E) transmission
1	Outer CV joint
2	Left-hand side driveshaft
3	Left-hand side inner tripod joint with external spline
4	Differential
5	Intermediate shaft

6	Intermediate shaft bearing support bracket
7	Intermediate shaft bearing
8	Right-hand side inner tripod joint with internal spline
9	Right-hand driveshaft
10	Long stub shaft (CD4E)
11	Short intermediate shaft (CD4E)

and engage 1st gear or "P". Loosen the hub nut about half a turn. This nut is very tight.

2   Loosen the front wheel retaining nuts.

3   Apply the handbrake, jack up the front of the vehicle and support it on axle stands. Remove the wheel.

4   Remove the front brake disc as described in Chapter 9.

5   Completely unscrew and remove the hub/driveshaft retaining nut. Note that the nut is of special laminated design, and should only be re-used a maximum of 5 times. (It is a good idea to file a small notch in the nut every time it is removed.) Obtain a new nut if necessary.

6   Where applicable, detach the ABS wiring loom bracket from the front suspension strut.

7   Unscrew the nut securing the anti-roll bar link to the front suspen-sion strut, and position the link to one side.

8   Extract the split pin from the track rod end balljoint nut. Unscrew the nut, and detach the rod from the arm on the steering knuckle using a conventional balljoint removal tool. Take care not to damage the balljoint seal.

9   Note which way round the front suspension lower arm balljoint clamp bolt is fitted, then unscrew and remove it from the knuckle as-sembly. Lever the balljoint down from the knuckle; if it is tight, carefully prise the clamp open using a large flat-bladed tool. Take care not to damage the balljoint seal during the separation procedure.

10   Using a universal puller located on the hub flange, press the driveshaft through the front hub and steering knuckle by pulling the

10.10A Using a puller on the hub flange . . .

knuckle outwards **(see illustrations)**. When the driveshaft is free, support it on an axle stand, making sure that the inner tripod joint is not turned through more than 18° (damage may occur if the joint is turned through too great an angle).

8

10.10B . . . to press the driveshaft out of the front hub and steering knuckle

10.11 Removing the left-hand driveshaft from the transmission

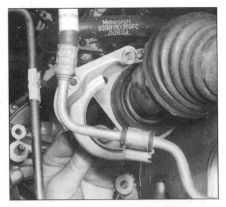

10.16 Removing the heat shield from the right-hand driveshaft support bearing

Left-hand side

11   Insert a lever between the inner driveshaft joint and the transmission case, with a thin piece of wood against the case. Prise free the inner joint from the differential **(see illustration)**. If it proves reluctant to move, strike the lever firmly with the palm of the hand. Be careful not to damage the adjacent components, and be prepared for oil spillage. Note that if the right-hand driveshaft has already been removed, it is possible to release the left-hand driveshaft by inserting a forked drift from the right-hand side. However, care must be taken to prevent damage to the differential gears, particularly if the special Ford tool is not used.

12   Withdraw the driveshaft from under the vehicle.

13   Extract the circlip from the groove on the inner end of the driveshaft, and obtain a new one.

Right-hand side

14   The right-hand driveshaft may either be removed complete with the intermediate shaft from the transmission, or it may be disconnected from the outer end of the intermediate shaft. If the latter course of action is taken, use a soft-faced mallet to sharply tap the inner CV joint housing from the intermediate shaft. The internal circlip will be released, and the driveshaft may be withdrawn from the splines.

15   Extract the circlip from the groove on the outer end of the intermediate shaft. Obtain a new circlip for use when refitting.

16   If the complete driveshaft is to be removed, proceed as follows. Unscrew the bolts securing the driveshaft support bearing bracket to the rear of the cylinder block, and remove the heat shield **(see illustration)**.

17   Withdraw the complete driveshaft from the transmission and from the bearing bracket, and remove it from under the vehicle **(see illustration)**. Be prepared for oil spillage.

Both sides

18   Check the condition of the transmission oil seals, and if necessary renew them as described in Chapter 7A (manual transmission) or Chapter 7B (automatic transmission). Check the support bearing, and if necessary renew it as described in Section 13 of this Chapter.

Refitting

Right-hand side

19   If the intermediate shaft has not been removed, proceed to paragraph 22. Otherwise, proceed as follows.

20   Carefully refit the complete driveshaft in the support bearing and into the transmission, taking care not to damage the oil seal. Turn the driveshaft until it engages the splines on the differential gears.

21   Tighten the bolts securing the support bearing to the bracket on the cylinder block to the specified torque. Proceed to paragraph 26.

22   Locate the new circlip in the groove on the outer end of the intermediate shaft, then smear 6 to 8 g of grease (to Ford specification SQM1C-9004-A) over the entire circumference of the intermediate shaft splines. This grease prevents frictional corrosion.

23   Locate the right-hand driveshaft on the intermediate shaft splines,

10.17 Removing the complete right-hand driveshaft

and push it on until the internal circlip is heard to engage with the groove in the shaft.

Left-hand side

24   Locate the new circlip in the groove on the inner end of the driveshaft.

25   Insert the driveshaft into the transmission, making sure that the circlip is fully engaged.

Both sides

26   Pull the knuckle outwards, and insert the outer end of the driveshaft through the hub. Turn the driveshaft to engage the splines in the hub, and fully push on the hub. Ford use a special tool to draw the driveshaft into the hub, but it is unlikely that the splines will be tight. However, if they are, it will be necessary to obtain the tool, or to use a similar home-made tool.

27   Screw on the hub nut finger-tight.

28   Locate the front suspension lower arm balljoint stub in the bottom of the knuckle. Insert the clamp bolt in the previously-noted position, screw on the nut, and tighten it to the specified torque.

29   Refit the track rod end balljoint to the steering knuckle, and screw on the nut. Tighten the nut to the specified torque.

30   Check that the balljoint nut split pin holes are aligned. If not, reposition the nut, but make sure that it is still tightened within the tolerance of the torque wrench setting. Insert a new split pin, and bend its legs back to secure it.

31   Locate the anti-roll bar link on the front suspension strut, and tighten the nut to the specified torque.

32   Where applicable, refit the ABS wiring loom bracket to the front suspension strut.

33   Refit the front brake disc with reference to Chapter 9.

10.36 Torque-tightening the hub nut

11.29 Removing the gaiter from the inner joint housing

11.31 Removing the support ring from the joint housing

34   Check the transmission oil level, and top-up if necessary as described in Chapter 1.
35   Refit the wheel, and lower the vehicle to the ground. Tighten the wheel retaining nuts to the specified torque.
36   Fully tighten the hub nut to the specified torque **(see illustration)**. Finally, refit the wheel cover.

11 Driveshaft inner CV joint gaiter - renewal

1   The inner CV joint gaiter is renewed by disconnecting the driveshaft from the inner CV joint housing at the transmission (left-hand side) or intermediate shaft (right-hand side). The work can be carried out either with the driveshaft removed from the vehicle, or with it *in situ*. If it is wished to fully remove the driveshaft, refer to Section 10 first. Note that if both the inner and outer gaiters are being renewed at the same time, the outer gaiter can be removed from the inner end of the driveshaft.

Renewal without removing the driveshaft

2   Loosen the front wheel nuts on the appropriate side. Apply the handbrake, jack up the front of the vehicle and support it on axle stands. Remove the wheel.
3   Unscrew the nut securing the anti-roll bar link to the front suspension strut, and position the link to one side.
4   Extract the split pin from the track rod end balljoint nut. Unscrew the nut, and detach the rod from the arm on the steering knuckle using a conventional balljoint removal tool. Take care not to damage the balljoint seal.
5   Note which way round the front suspension lower arm balljoint clamp bolt is fitted, then unscrew and remove it from the knuckle assembly. Lever the balljoint down from the knuckle; if it is tight, prise the clamp open carefully using a large flat-bladed tool. Take care not to damage the balljoint seal during the separation procedure.
6   Mark the driveshaft in relation to the joint housing, to ensure correct refitting.
7   Note the fitted location of both of the inner joint gaiter retaining clips. Release the clips from the gaiter, and slide the gaiter back along the driveshaft (away from the transmission) a little way.
8   Pull the front suspension strut outwards, while guiding the tripod joint out of the joint housing. As the joint tripod is being withdrawn from the housing, be prepared for some of the bearing rollers to fall out. Identify them for position with a dab of paint. Support the inner end of the driveshaft on an axle stand.
9   Remove the support ring from the joint housing.
10   Remove the remaining bearing rollers from the tripod, and identify them for position with a dab of paint.
11   Check that the inner end of the driveshaft is marked in relation to the splined tripod hub. If not, carefully centre-punch the two items, to ensure correct refitting. Alternatively, use dabs of paint on the driveshaft and one end of the tripod.

12   Extract the circlip retaining the tripod on the driveshaft.
13   Using a suitable puller, remove the tripod from the end of the driveshaft, and slide off the gaiter.
14   If the outer gaiter is also to be renewed, remove it with reference to Section 12.
15   Clean the driveshaft, and obtain a new tripod retaining circlip. The gaiter retaining clips and the steering track rod end split pin must also be renewed.
16   Slide the new gaiter on the driveshaft, together with new clips. Also locate the support ring on the joint housing.
17   Refit the tripod on the driveshaft splines, if necessary using a soft-faced mallet to drive it fully onto the splines. It must be fitted with the chamfered edge leading (towards the driveshaft), and with the previously-made marks aligned. Secure it in position using the new circlip. Ensure that the circlip is fully engaged in its groove.
18   Locate the bearing rollers on the tripod in their previously-noted positions, using grease to hold them in place.
19   With the front suspension strut pulled outwards, guide the tripod joint into the joint housing, making sure that the previously-made marks are aligned. Pack the joint with 180 g of CV joint grease.
20   Slide the gaiter along the driveshaft, and locate it on the support ring located on the joint housing. The small-diameter end of the gaiter must be located in the groove on the driveshaft.
21   Ensure that the gaiter is not twisted or distorted, then insert a small screwdriver under the lip of the gaiter at the housing end. This will allow trapped air to escape during the next step.
22   Push the tripod fully into the housing, then pull it out by 20 mm. Remove the screwdriver, then fit the retaining clips and tighten them.
23   Reconnect the front suspension lower arm balljoint to the knuckle assembly. Refit and tighten the clamp nut and bolt.
24   Reconnect the track rod end balljoint to the steering knuckle, and tighten the nut to the specified torque. Check that the split pin holes are correctly aligned; if necessary, reposition the nut, making sure that it is still tightened within the torque tolerance. Insert a new split pin, and bend its legs back to secure it.
25   Refit the anti-roll bar link to the front suspension strut, and tighten the nut to the specified torque.
26   Refit the wheel, and lower the vehicle to the ground. Tighten the wheel nuts.

With the driveshaft on the bench

27   Mount the driveshaft in a vice.
28   Mark the driveshaft in relation to the joint housing, to ensure correct refitting.
29   Note the fitted location of both of the inner joint gaiter retaining clips, then release the clips from the gaiter, and slide the gaiter back along the driveshaft a little way **(see illustration)**.
30   Remove the inner joint housing from the tripod. As the housing is being removed, be prepared for some of the bearing rollers to fall out. Identify them for position with a dab of paint.
31   Remove the support ring from the joint housing **(see illustration)**.

8

11.32 Removing the bearing rollers

11.34 Circlip (arrowed) retaining the tripod on the driveshaft

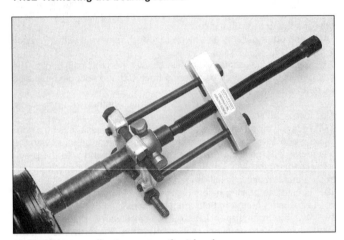

11.35 Using a puller to remove the tripod

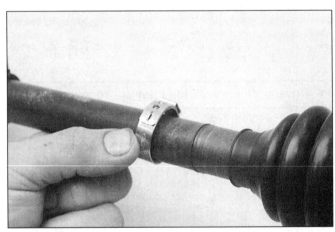

11.38 Slide the gaiter and clips onto the driveshaft

11.40A Locate the tripod on the splines . .
.

11.40B . . . and drive it fully onto the
driveshaft

11.45 Using pincers to tighten the
retaining clips

32   Remove the remaining bearing rollers from the tripod, and identify them for position with a dab of paint **(see illustration)**.
33   Check that the inner end of the driveshaft is marked in relation to the splined tripod hub. If not, carefully centre-punch the two items, to ensure correct refitting. Alternatively, use dabs of paint on the drive-shaft and one end of the tripod.
34   Extract the circlip retaining the tripod on the driveshaft **(see illus-tration)**.
35   Using a puller, remove the tripod from the end of the driveshaft, and slide off the gaiter **(see illustration)**.
36   If the outer gaiter is also to be renewed, remove it with reference

to Section 12.
37   Clean the driveshaft, and obtain a new joint retaining circlip. The gaiter retaining clips must also be renewed.
38   Slide the new gaiter on the driveshaft, together with new clips **(see illustration)**.
39   Locate the support ring on the CV joint housing.
40   Refit the tripod on the driveshaft splines, if necessary using a soft-faced mallet and a suitable socket to drive it fully onto the splines. It must be fitted with the chamfered edge leading (towards the drive-shaft), and with the previously-made marks aligned. Secure it in posi-tion using a new circlip. Ensure that the circlip is fully engaged in its

12.4A Release the clips . . .

12.4B . . . and remove the gaiter

12.5A Drive off the outer CV joint hub . . .

12.5B . . . and remove the joint from the driveshaft

12.6 Circlips fitted on the outer end of the driveshaft

12.9 Fitting the new gaiter and clips on the driveshaft

12.11 Packing the outer CV joint with new grease

groove **(see illustrations)**.

41   Locate the bearing rollers on the tripod in their previously-noted positions, using grease to hold them in place.

42   Guide the joint housing onto the tripod joint, making sure that the previously-made marks are aligned. Scoop out all of the old grease, then pack the joint with 180 g of new CV joint grease.

43   Slide the gaiter along the driveshaft, and locate it on the support ring on the CV joint housing. The small-diameter end of the gaiter must be located in the groove on the driveshaft.

44   Ensure that the gaiter is not twisted or distorted, then insert a small screwdriver under the lip of the gaiter at the housing end. This will allow trapped air to escape during the next step.

45   Push the housing fully on the tripod, then pull it out by 20 mm.

Remove the screwdriver, then fit the retaining clips and tighten them **(see illustration)**.

12 Driveshaft outer CV joint gaiter - renewal

1   The outer CV joint gaiter can be renewed by removing the inner gaiter first as described in Section 11, or after removing the driveshaft complete as described in Section 10. If the driveshaft is removed, then the inner gaiter need not necessarily be removed. It is impractical to renew the outer gaiter by dismantling the outer joint with the driveshaft in position in the vehicle. The following paragraphs describe renewal of the gaiter on the bench.

2   Mount the driveshaft in a vice.

3   Mark the driveshaft in relation to the CV joint housing, to ensure correct refitting.

4   Note the fitted location of both of the outer joint gaiter retaining clips, then release the clips from the gaiter, and slide the gaiter back along the driveshaft a little way **(see illustrations)**.

5   Using a brass drift or a copper mallet, carefully drive the outer CV joint hub from the splines on the driveshaft. Initial resistance will be felt until the internal circlips are released. Take care not to damage the bearing cage **(see illustrations)**.

6   Extract the outer circlip from the end of the driveshaft **(see illustration)**.

7   Slide the gaiter over the remaining circlip, and remove it together with the clips.

8   Clean the driveshaft, and obtain new joint retaining circlips. The gaiter retaining clips must also be renewed.

9   Slide the new gaiter (together with new clips) onto the driveshaft and over the inner circlip **(see illustration)**.

10   Fit a new outer circlip to the groove in the driveshaft.

11   Scoop out all of the old grease, then pack the joint with 100 g of new CV joint grease **(see illustration)**.

8

12   Locate the CV joint on the driveshaft so that the splines are aligned, then push the joint until the internal circlips are fully engaged.

13   Move the gaiter along the driveshaft, and locate it over the joint and onto the outer CV joint housing. The small-diameter end of the gaiter must be located in the groove on the driveshaft.

14   Ensure that the gaiter is not twisted or distorted, then insert a small screwdriver under the lip of the gaiter at the housing end, to allow any trapped air to escape.

15   Remove the screwdriver, fit the retaining clips in their previously-noted positions, and tighten them.

13 Driveshafts - inspection and joint renewal

1   If any of the checks described in Chapter 1 reveal apparent excessive wear or play in any driveshaft joint, first remove the wheel cover, and check that the hub nut (driveshaft outer nut) is tightened to the specified torque. Repeat this check on the hub nut on the other side.

2   Road test the vehicle, and listen for a metallic clicking from the front, as the vehicle is driven slowly in a circle on full-lock. If a clicking noise is heard, this indicates wear in the outer constant velocity joint, which means that the joint must be renewed; reconditioning is not possible.

3   To renew an outer CV joint, remove the driveshaft as described in Section 10, then separate the joint from the driveshaft with reference to Section 12. In principle, the gaiter can be left on the driveshaft, provided that it is in good condition; in practice, it makes sense to renew the gaiter in any case, having got this far.

4   If vibration, consistent with road speed, is felt through the car when accelerating, there is a possibility of wear in the inner tripod joints.

5   To renew an inner joint, remove the driveshaft as described in Section 10, then separate the joint from the driveshaft with reference to Section 11.

6   Continual noise from the right-hand driveshaft, increasing with road speed, may indicate wear in the support bearing. To renew this bearing, the driveshaft and intermediate shaft must be removed, and the bearing extracted using a puller.

7   Remove the bearing dust cover, and obtain a new one.

8   Drive or press on the new bearing, applying the pressure to the inner race only. Similarly drive or press on the new dust cover.

Chapter 9 Braking system

Contents

Specifications

Front brakes

Type..	Ventilated disc, with single-piston floating caliper
Disc diameter...	260.0 mm
Disc thickness:	
New	24.15 mm
Minimum..	22.20 mm
Maximum disc run-out (fitted)	0.15 mm
Maximum disc thickness variation	0.015 mm
Front hub face maximum run-out..	0.05 mm

Rear drum brakes

Type..	Leading and trailing shoes, with automatic adjusters
Drum diameter:	
New:	
1.6 Saloon/Hatchback	203.0 mm
1.8 and 2.0 Saloon/Hatchback	228.6 mm
Estate..	228.6 mm
Maximum diameter:	
1.6 Saloon/Hatchback	204.2 mm
1.8 and 2.0 Saloon/Hatchback	229.6 mm
Estate..	229.6 mm

Rear disc brakes

Type..	Solid disc, with single-piston floating caliper
Disc diameter...	252.0 mm
Disc thickness:	
New	20.0 mm
Minimum..	18.0 mm
Maximum disc run-out (fitted)	0.15 mm
Maximum disc thickness variation	0.015 mm
Rear hub face maximum run-out...	0.05 mm

Torque wrench settings

	Nm	lbf ft
Front caliper bracket..	120	89
Rear caliper bracket	59	44
Front caliper guide bolts..	28	21
Rear caliper guide bolts...	41	30
Rear drum brake backplate	50	37
Vacuum servo unit	40	30
Master cylinder	23	17
ABS hydraulic unit to bracket	20	15
Roadwheel nuts	85	63

9

1 General information

The braking system is of diagonally-split, dual-circuit design, with ventilated discs at the front, and drum or disc brakes (according to model) at the rear. The front calipers are of floating single-piston design, using asbestos-free pads. The rear drum brakes are of the leading and trailing shoe type. They are self-adjusting during footbrake operation. The rear brake shoe linings are of different thicknesses, in order to allow for the different proportional rates of wear.

Pressure-control relief (PCR) valves are fitted to the rear brakes, to prevent rear wheel lock-up under hard braking. The valves are sometimes referred to as pressure-conscious reducing valves. On non-ABS models, they are fitted in the master cylinder rear brake outlet ports; on ABS models, they are located on the ABS unit.

When rear disc brakes are fitted, the rear brake caliper is located on the front of the knuckle on Saloon and Hatchback models, and on the rear of the knuckle on Estate models **(see illustration)**.

The handbrake is cable-operated, and acts on the rear brakes. On rear drum brake models, the cables operate on the rear trailing brake shoe operating levers, and on rear disc brake models, they operate on levers on the rear calipers. The handbrake lever incorporates an automatic adjuster, which removes any slack from the cables when the lever is disengaged **(see illustration)**. Handbrake lever movement remains consistent at all times, and no adjustment is necessary or possible.

Where fitted, the anti-lock braking system (ABS) is of the four-channel low-pressure type **(see illustration)**. It uses the basic conventional brake system, together with a Bendix ABS hydraulic unit fitted between the master cylinder and the four wheel brakes. The hydraulic unit consists of a hydraulic actuator, an ABS brake pressure pump, an ABS module with built-in relay box, and two pressure-control relief valves. Braking at each of the four wheels is controlled by separate solenoid valves in the hydraulic actuator. If wheel lock-up is detected on a wheel when the vehicle speed is above 3 mph, the valve opens, releasing pressure to the relevant brake, until the wheel regains a rotational speed corresponding to the speed of the vehicle. The cycle can

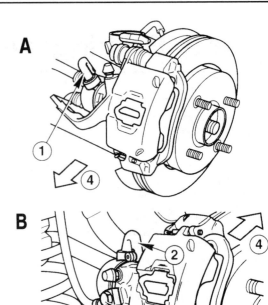

1.1 Rear disc brake location on Saloon/Hatchback models (A) and Estate models (B)

1   Handbrake cable lever facing away from caliper
2   Handbrake cable lever facing towards caliper
3   Brake hose banjo bolt
4   Front of vehicle

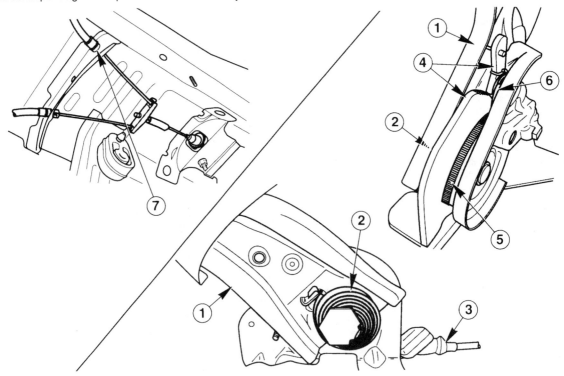

1.2 Handbrake lever and associated components

1   Handbrake lever
2   Clock spring
3   Handbrake cable
4   Toothed segment and pawl to lock the handbrake lever
5   Fine-toothed segment for the clock spring
6   Pawl for the clock spring
7   Underbody bracket

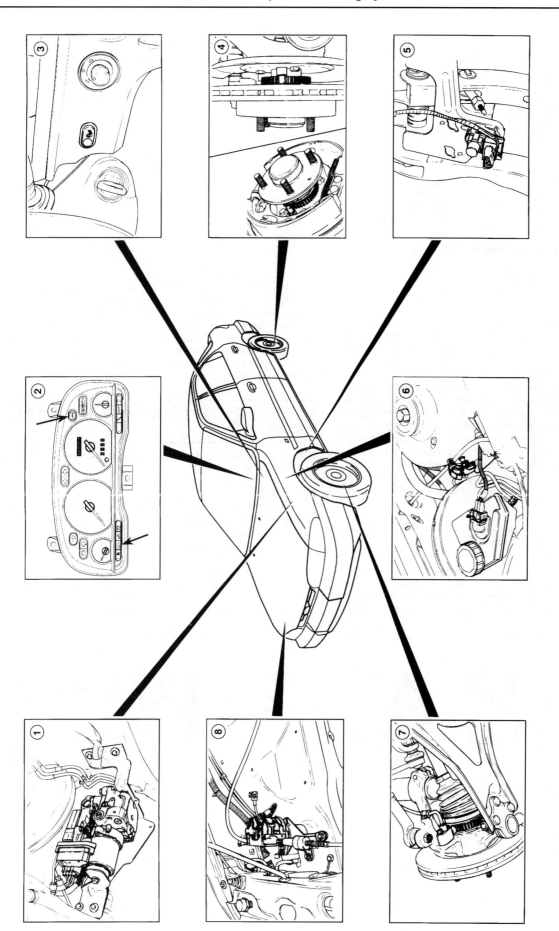

1.3 Anti-lock Braking System (ABS) and Traction Control System (TCS) component locations (left-hand-drive shown, right-hand-drive similar)

1   ABS/TCS unit
2   ABS/TCS warning lights
3   TCS switch
4   Rear wheel sensor ring location (drum brakes left, disc brakes right)

5   Stop-light switch
6   Self-test/diagnosis connectors
7   Front wheel sensor and ring
8   Throttle actuator

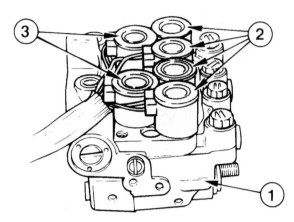

1.4 Solenoid valves fitted to the ABS/TCS hydraulic actuator

1   ABS/TCS actuator
2   ABS solenoid valves
3   TCS solenoid valves

be repeated many times a second. In the event of a fault in the ABS system, the conventional braking system is not affected. Diagnosis of a fault in the ABS system requires the use of special equipment, and this work should therefore be left to a Ford dealer. Diagnostic connectors are located on the side of the left-hand front suspension turret.

The traction control system (TCS) is fitted as an option to some models, and uses the basic ABS system, with an additional pump and valves fitted to the hydraulic actuator **(see illustration)**. If wheelspin is detected at a speed below 30 mph, one of the valves opens, to allow the pump to pressurise the relevant brake, until the spinning wheel slows to a rotational speed corresponding to the speed of the vehicle. This has the effect of transferring torque to the wheel with most traction. At the same time, the throttle plate is closed slightly, to reduce the torque from the engine. At speeds above 30 mph, the TCS operates by throttle plate adjustment only.

2   Front brake pads - renewal

Warning: *Disc brake pads must be renewed on both front wheels at the same time - never renew the pads on only one wheel, as uneven braking may result. Although genuine Ford linings are asbestos-free, the dust created by wear of non-genuine pads may contain asbestos, which is a health hazard. Never blow it out with compressed air, and don't inhale any of it. DO NOT use petroleum-based solvents to clean brake parts; use brake cleaner or methylated spirit only. DO NOT allow*

any brake fluid, oil or grease to contact the brake pads or disc. Also refer to the warning at the start of Section 15 concerning brake fluid.

1   Apply the handbrake. Loosen the front wheel nuts, jack up the front of the vehicle and support it on axle stands.
2   Remove the front wheels. Work on one brake assembly at a time, using the assembled brake for reference if necessary.
3   Follow the accompanying photos, beginning with **illustration 2.3A**, for the pad removal procedure. Be sure to stay in order, and read the caption under each illustration.
4   Inspect the front brake disc for scoring and cracks. If a detailed inspection is necessary, refer to Section 4.
5   The piston must be pushed back into the caliper bore, to provide room for the new brake pads. A C-clamp can be used to accomplish this. As the piston is depressed to the bottom of the caliper bore, the fluid in the master cylinder will rise slightly. Make sure that there is sufficient space in the brake fluid reservoir to accept the displaced fluid, and if necessary, syphon some off first.
6   Fit the new pads using a reversal of the removal procedure, but tighten the guide bolts to the torque wrench setting given in the Specifications at the beginning of this Chapter.
7   On completion, firmly depress the brake pedal a few times, to bring the pads to their normal working position. Check the level of the brake fluid in the reservoir, and top-up if necessary.
8   Give the vehicle a short road test, to make sure that the brakes are functioning correctly, and to bed-in the new linings to the contours of the disc. New linings will not provide maximum braking efficiency until they have bedded-in; avoid heavy braking as far as possible for the first hundred miles or so.

3   Front brake caliper - removal, overhaul and refitting

Note: *Refer to the warning at the beginning of the previous Section before proceeding.*

Removal

1   Apply the handbrake. Loosen the front wheel nuts, jack up the front of the vehicle and support it on axle stands. Remove the appropriate front wheel.
2   Fit a brake hose clamp to the flexible hose leading to the front brake caliper. This will minimise brake fluid loss during subsequent operations **(see illustration)**.
3   Loosen (but do not completely unscrew) the union on the caliper end of the flexible brake hose **(see illustration)**.
4   Remove the front brake pads as described in Section 2.
5   Support the caliper in one hand, and prevent the hydraulic hose from turning with the other hand. Unscrew the caliper from the hose, making sure that the hose is not twisted unduly or strained. Once the

2.3A Prise the retaining clip from the caliper. Hold it with a pair of pliers, to avoid personal injury. On models fitted with pad wear sensors, it will be necessary to disconnect the wiring

2.3B Prise the plastic covers from the ends of the two guide pins

2.3C Using a 7 mm Allen key, unscrew . . .

2.3D . . . and remove the guide bolts securing the caliper to the carrier bracket

2.3E Withdraw the caliper from the disc, and support it on an axle stand to avoid straining the hydraulic hose. The outer pad will normally remain in position against the disc, but the inner pad will stay attached to the piston in the caliper

2.3F Pull the inner pad from the piston in the caliper

2.3G Remove the outer pad from the caliper frame. Brush all dust and dirt from the caliper, pads and disc, but do not inhale it, as it may be harmful to health. Scrape any corrosion from the disc.

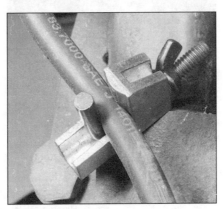

3.2 Brake hose clamp fitted to the front flexible brake hose

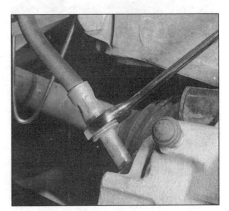

3.3 Loosening the flexible brake hose at the caliper

caliper is detached, plug the open hydraulic unions in the caliper and hose, to keep out dust and dirt.

6   If required, the caliper carrier bracket can be unbolted and re-moved from the steering knuckle **(see illustration)**.

Overhaul

7   With the caliper on the bench, brush away all traces of dust and dirt, but take care not to inhale any dust, as it may be injurious to health.

8   Pull the dust-excluding rubber seal from the end of the piston.

9   Apply low air pressure to the fluid inlet union, and eject the piston. Only low air pressure is required for this, such as is produced by a foot-operated tyre pump. Position a thin piece of wood between the piston and the caliper body, to prevent damage to the end face of the piston, in the event of its being ejected suddenly. **Caution:** *The piston may be ejected with some force.*

10   Using a suitable blunt instrument (for instance a knitting needle or a crochet hook), prise the piston seal from the groove in the cylinder bore. Take care not to scratch the surface of the bore.

11   Clean the piston and caliper body with methylated spirit, and al-low to dry. Examine the surfaces of the piston and cylinder bore for wear, damage and corrosion. If the piston alone is unserviceable, a new piston must be obtained, along with seals. If the cylinder bore is unserviceable, the complete caliper must be renewed. The seals must be renewed, regardless of the condition of the other components.

12   Coat the piston and seals with clean brake fluid, then manipulate

3.6 Removing the caliper carrier bracket

the piston seal into the groove in the cylinder bore.

13   Push the piston squarely into its bore.

14   Fit the dust-excluding rubber seal onto the piston and caliper, then depress the piston fully.

9

3.15 Tightening the carrier bracket mounting bolts

4.4A Using a micrometer to measure the thickness of the front brake disc

4.4B Disc minimum thickness marking

4.5 Measuring the disc run-out with a dial gauge

4.10A Remove the special washers . . .

4.10B . . . and withdraw the disc

Refitting

15   Refit the caliper, and where applicable the carrier bracket, by reversing the removal operations. Make sure that the flexible brake hose is not twisted. Tighten the mounting bolts and wheel nuts to the specified torque **(see illustration)**.

16   Bleed the brake circuit according to the procedure given in Section 15, remembering to remove the brake hose clamp from the flexible hose. Make sure there are no leaks from the hose connections. Test the brakes carefully before returning the vehicle to normal service.

4   Front brake disc - inspection, removal and refitting

Note: *To prevent uneven braking, BOTH front brake discs should be renewed or reground at the same time.*

Inspection

1   Apply the handbrake. Loosen the relevant wheel nuts, jack up the front of the vehicle and support it on axle stands. Remove the wheel.

2   Remove the front brake caliper and carrier bracket with reference to Section 3, but do not disconnect the flexible hose. Support the caliper on an axle stand, or suspend it out of the way with a piece of wire, taking care to avoid straining the flexible hose.

3   Temporarily refit two of the wheel nuts to diagonally-opposite studs, with the flat sides of the nuts against the disc. Tighten the nuts progressively, to hold the disc firmly.

4   Scrape any corrosion from the disc. Rotate the disc, and examine it for deep scoring, grooving or cracks. Using a micrometer, measure the thickness of the disc in several places. The minimum thickness is stamped on the disc hub **(see illustrations)**. Light wear and scoring is normal, but if excessive, the disc should be removed, and either reground by a specialist, or renewed. If regrinding is undertaken, the minimum thickness must be maintained. Obviously, if the disc is cracked, it must be renewed.

5   Using a dial gauge or a flat metal block and feeler gauges, check that the disc run-out 10 mm from the outer edge does not exceed the limit given in the Specifications. To do this, fix the measuring equipment, and rotate the disc, noting the variation in measurement as the disc is rotated **(see illustration)**. The difference between the minimum and maximum measurements recorded is the disc run-out.

6   If the run-out is greater than the specified amount, check for variations of the disc thickness as follows. Mark the disc at eight positions 45° apart, then using a micrometer, measure the disc thickness at the eight positions, 15 mm in from the outer edge. If the variation between the minimum and maximum readings is greater than the specified amount, the disc should be renewed.

7   The hub face run-out can also be checked in a similar way. First remove the disc as described later in this Section, fix the measuring equipment, then slowly rotate the hub, and check that the run-out does not exceed the amount given in the Specifications. If the hub face run-out is excessive, this should be corrected (by renewing the hub bearings - see Chapter 10) before rechecking the disc run-out.

Removal

8   With the wheel and caliper removed, remove the wheel nuts which were temporarily refitted in paragraph 3.

9   Mark the disc in relation to the hub, if it is to be refitted.

10   Remove the two special washers (where fitted), and withdraw the disc over the wheel studs **(see illustrations)**.

Refitting

11   Make sure that the disc and hub mating surfaces are clean, then locate the disc on the wheel studs. Align the previously-made marks if the original disc is being refitted.

12   Refit the two special washers, where fitted.

13   Refit the brake caliper and carrier bracket with reference to Section 3.

5.2A Releasing the automatic adjuster mechanism with a screwdriver inserted through the small hole in the backplate

5.2B Removing a rear brake drum

6.2A Note the fitted position of the springs and the adjuster strut, then clean the components with brake cleaner, and allow to dry. Position a tray beneath the backplate, to catch the fluid and residue

6.2B Remove the two shoe hold-down springs, using a pair of pliers to depress the upper ends so that they can be withdrawn downwards off the pins

6.2C Remove the hold-down pins from the backplate

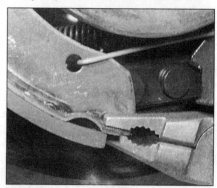

6.2D Pull the bottom end of the leading (front) brake shoe from the bottom anchor (use pliers or an adjustable spanner over the edge of the shoe to lever it away)

14   Refit the wheel, and lower the vehicle to the ground.
15   Test the brakes carefully before returning the vehicle to normal service.

5   Rear brake drum - removal, inspection and refitting

Note: *To prevent uneven braking, BOTH rear brake drums should be renewed at the same time.*

Removal

1   Chock the front wheels, release the handbrake and engage 1st gear (or "P"). Loosen the relevant wheel nuts, jack up the rear of the vehicle and support it on axle stands. Remove the wheel.
2   Remove the two special clips (where fitted), and withdraw the brake drum over the wheel studs. If the drum will not pass over the shoes, it is possible to release the automatic adjuster mechanism by prising out the small rubber grommet near the centre of the backplate, and inserting a screwdriver through the small hole. The self-adjusting ratchet can then be rotated, so that the brake shoes move to their lowest setting **(see illustrations)**. Refit the rubber grommet before proceeding.
3   With the brake drum removed, clean the dust from the drum, brake shoes, wheel cylinder and backplate, using brake cleaner or methylated spirit. *Take care not to inhale the dust, as it may contain asbestos.*

Inspection

4   Clean the inside surfaces of the brake drum, then examine the internal friction surface for signs of scoring or cracks. If it is cracked, deeply scored, or has worn to a diameter greater than the maximum

given in the Specifications, then it should be renewed, together with the drum on the other side.
5   Regrinding of the brake drum is not recommended.

Refitting

6   Locate the brake drum over the wheel studs, and (where fitted) refit the special clips. Make sure that the drum contacts the hub flange.
7   Refit the wheel, then check the remaining rear drum.
8   Lower the vehicle to the ground, and tighten the wheel nuts to the specified torque. Depress the brake pedal several times, in order to operate the self-adjusting mechanism and set the shoes at their normal operating position.
9   Test the brakes carefully before returning the vehicle to normal service.

6   Rear brake shoes - renewal

Warning: *Drum brake shoes must be renewed on both rear wheels at the same time - never renew the shoes on only one wheel, as uneven braking may result. Also, the dust created by wear of the shoes may contain asbestos, which is a health hazard. Never blow it out with compressed air, and don't inhale any of it. An approved filtering mask should be worn when working on the brakes. DO NOT use petroleum-based solvents to clean brake parts; use brake cleaner or methylated spirit only.*

1   Remove the rear brake drums as described in Section 5. Work on one brake assembly at a time, using the assembled brake for reference if necessary.
2   Follow the accompanying illustrations for the brake shoe renewal

9

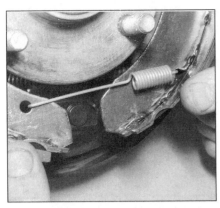

6.2E Release the trailing (rear) brake shoe from the anchor, then move the bottom ends of both shoes towards each other

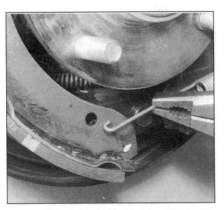

6.2F Unhook the lower return spring from the shoes, noting the location holes

6.2G Move the bottom ends of the brake shoes together, and disconnect the top ends of the shoes from the wheel cylinder, taking care not to damage the rubber boots

6.2H Unhook the upper return spring from the shoes . . .

6.2I . . . and withdraw the leading shoe from the backplate

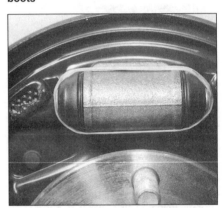

6.2J To prevent the wheel cylinder pistons from being accidentally ejected, fit a suitable elastic band or wire lengthwise over the cylinder/pistons. Don't press the brake pedal while the shoes are removed

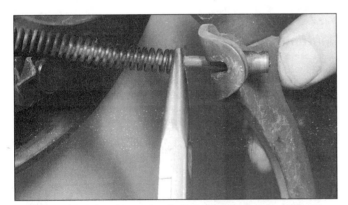

6.2K Using a pair of long-nosed pliers, pull the handbrake cable spring back from the operating lever on the rear of the trailing shoe, and hold it there. (Resistance will be felt from the handbrake lever automatic adjuster inside the vehicle.) Unhook the cable end from the cut-out in the lever, and remove the trailing shoe

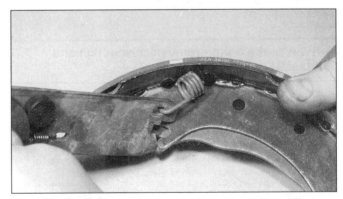

6.2L Unhook the automatic adjustment strut from the trailing brake shoe . . .

procedure **(see illustrations 6.2A to 6.2O)**. Be sure to stay in order, and read the caption under each illustration.

3   If the wheel cylinder shows signs of fluid leakage, or if there is any reason to suspect it of being defective, inspect it now, as described in the next Section.

4   Fit the new brake shoes using a reversal of the removal proce-

dure, but set the eccentric cam at its lowest position before assembling it to the trailing shoe.

5   Before refitting the brake drum, it should be checked as described in Section 5.

6   With the drum in position, refit the wheel, then carry out the renewal procedure on the remaining rear brake.

7   Lower the vehicle to the ground, and tighten the wheel nuts.

8   Depress the brake pedal several times, in order to operate the self-adjusting mechanism and set the shoes at their normal operating position.

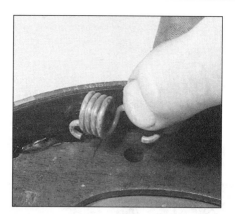

6.2M . . . and remove the small spring

6.2N Clean the backplate, and apply small amounts of high-melting-point brake grease to the brake shoe contact points. Be careful not to get grease on any friction surfaces

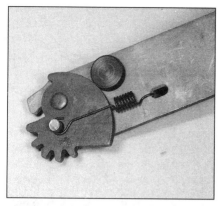

6.2O Lubricate the sliding components of the automatic adjuster with a little high-melting-point brake grease, but leave the serrations on the eccentric cam shown here clean

7.5 Bolts securing the wheel cylinder to the backplate. Hydraulic union nut and bleed screw cover are also visible

9   Make several forward and reverse stops, and operate the hand-brake fully two or three times. Give the vehicle a road test, to make sure that the brakes are functioning correctly, and to bed-in the new linings to the contours of the disc. Remember that the new linings will not give full braking efficiency until they have bedded-in.

7   Rear wheel cylinder - removal, overhaul and refitting

Note: *Before starting work, check on the availability of parts (overhaul kit of seals). Also bear in mind that if the brake shoes have been contaminated by fluid leaking from the wheel cylinder, they must be renewed. In principle, the shoes on BOTH sides of the vehicle must be renewed, even if they are only contaminated on one side.*

Removal
1   Remove the brake drum as described in Section 5.
2   Using a brake hose clamp (or a self-locking wrench with protected jaws), clamp the flexible hose leading to the wheel cylinder (the hose is looped from the side of the wheel arch to a bracket on the rear suspension strut). This will minimise brake fluid loss during subsequent operations.
3   Pull the brake shoes apart at their top ends, so that they are just clear of the wheel cylinder. The automatic adjuster will hold the shoes in this position, so that the cylinder can be withdrawn.
4   Wipe away all traces of dirt around the hydraulic union at the rear

of the wheel cylinder, then undo the union nut.
5   Unscrew the two bolts securing the wheel cylinder to the back-plate **(see illustration)**.
6   Withdraw the wheel cylinder from the backplate so that it is clear of the brake shoes. Plug the open hydraulic unions, to prevent the entry of dirt, and to minimise further fluid loss whilst the cylinder is detached.

Overhaul
7   Clean the external surfaces of the cylinder, and unscrew the bleed screw.
8   Carefully prise off the dust cover from each end of the cylinder.
9   Tap the wheel cylinder on a block of wood to eject the pistons and seals, keeping them identified for location. Finally remove the spring.
10   Clean the pistons and the cylinder by washing in methylated spirit or fresh hydraulic fluid. Do not use petrol, paraffin or any other mineral-based fluid. Remove and discard the old seals, noting which way round they are fitted.
11   Examine the surfaces of the pistons and the cylinder bores, and look for any signs of rust or scoring. If such damage is evident, the complete wheel cylinder must be renewed.
12   Reassemble by lubricating the first piston in clean hydraulic fluid, then manipulating a new seal into position, so that its raised lip faces away from the brake shoe bearing face of the piston.
13   Insert the piston into the cylinder. As the seal enters the bore, twist the piston back and forth so that the seal lip is not trapped.
14   Insert the spring, then refit the remaining piston and seal, again making sure that the seal lip is not trapped as it enters the bore.
15   Fit new dust covers to the grooves in the pistons and wheel cylinder body.
16   Refit the bleed screw.

Refitting
17   Wipe clean the backplate, and remove the plug from the end of the hydraulic pipe. Fit the cylinder onto the backplate, and screw in the hydraulic union nut by hand, being careful not to cross-thread it.
18   Tighten the mounting bolts, then fully tighten the hydraulic union nut.
19   Retract the automatic brake adjuster mechanism, so that the brake shoes engage with the pistons of the wheel cylinder. To do this, prise the shoes apart slightly, turn the automatic adjuster to its minimum position, and release the shoes.
20   Remove the clamp from the flexible brake hose.
21   Refit the brake drum with reference to Section 5.
22   Bleed the brake hydraulic system as described in Section 15. Providing suitable precautions were taken to minimise loss of fluid, it should only be necessary to bleed the relevant rear brake.
23   Test the brakes carefully before returning the vehicle to normal service.

9

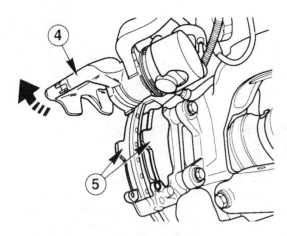

8.5A Rear brake pad removal on Saloon and Hatchback models

    4   *Brake caliper*
    5   *Brake pads*

8   Rear brake pads - renewal

Warning: *Disc brake pads must be renewed on BOTH rear wheels at the same time - never renew the pads on only one wheel, as uneven braking may result. Although genuine Ford linings are asbestos-free, the dust created by wear of non-genuine pads may contain asbestos, which is a health hazard. Never blow it out with compressed air, and don't inhale any of it. DO NOT use petroleum-based solvents to clean brake parts; use brake cleaner or methylated spirit only. DO NOT allow any brake fluid, oil or grease to contact the brake pads or disc.*

1   Chock the front wheels, and engage 1st gear (or "P"). Loosen the rear wheel nuts, jack up the rear of the vehicle and support it on axle stands.

2   Remove the rear wheels. Work on one brake assembly at a time, using the assembled brake for reference if necessary.

3   Inspect the rear brake disc as described in Section 10.

4   Extract the spring clip, and pull out the retaining pin securing the caliper to the carrier bracket. Note that on Saloon and Hatchback models, the pin is at the bottom of the caliper, whereas on Estate models, it is at the top.

5   Swivel the caliper away from the carrier bracket, to expose the brake pads **(see illustrations)**.

6   Disconnect the pad wear warning light wire (when fitted) at the connector. Also unbolt the brake hose bracket from the rear suspension strut, to avoid straining the flexible hose.

7   If necessary, the caliper may be completely removed by prising off the cap and unscrewing the pivot guide bolt. Support the caliper on an axle stand, or tie it to one side with wire.

8   Remove the pads from the carrier bracket.

9   Brush all dust and dirt from the caliper, pads and disc, but do not inhale it, as it may be harmful to health. Scrape any corrosion from the disc.

10   Before fitting the new pads, screw the caliper piston fully into its bore, at the same time pressing the piston fully to the bottom of the bore. Proprietary tools are available for this operation - at a pinch, it may be possible to use long-nosed pliers engaged with the cut-outs in the piston. Brake fluid will be displaced into the master cylinder reservoir, so check first that there is enough space to accept the fluid. If necessary, syphon off some of the fluid.

11   Fit the new pads using a reversal of the removal procedure. On completion, firmly depress the brake pedal a few times, to bring the pads to their normal working position. Check the level of the brake fluid in the reservoir, and top-up if necessary.

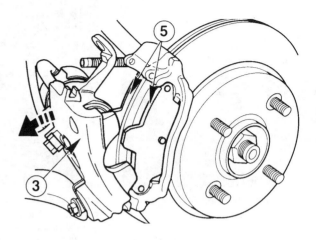

8.5B Rear brake pad removal on Estate models

    3   *Brake caliper*
    5   *Brake pads*

12   Give the vehicle a road test, to make sure that the brakes are functioning correctly, and to bed-in the new linings to the contours of the disc. Remember that full braking efficiency will not be obtained until the new linings have bedded-in.

9   Rear brake caliper - removal, overhaul and refitting

Removal

1   Chock the front wheels, and engage 1st gear (or "P"). Loosen the rear wheel nuts, jack up the rear of the vehicle and support it on axle stands. Remove the appropriate rear wheel.

2   Fit a brake hose clamp to the flexible hose leading to the rear brake caliper. This will minimise brake fluid loss during subsequent operations.

3   Loosen (but do not completely unscrew) the union on the caliper end of the flexible hose.

4   Remove the rear brake pads, and free the caliper as described in Section 8.

5   Disconnect the handbrake cable from the caliper. On Saloon and Hatchback models, the handbrake lever faces away from the caliper, whereas on Estate models, it faces towards the caliper **(see illustrations)**.

6   Support the caliper and disconnect the hydraulic hose, making sure that the hose is not twisted or strained unduly. Once the caliper is detached, place it to one side, and plug the open hydraulic unions to keep dust and dirt out.

7   If necessary, unbolt the carrier bracket from the knuckle.

Overhaul

8   No overhaul procedures were available at the time of writing. In principle, the overhaul information given for the front brake caliper will apply, but check first that spares are available. Do not attempt to dismantle the handbrake mechanism inside the caliper.

Refitting

9   Refit the caliper, and where applicable the carrier bracket, by reversing the removal operations. Tighten the mounting bolts and wheel nuts to the specified torque, and do not forget to remove the brake hose clamp from the flexible brake hose.

10   Bleed the brake circuit according to the procedure given in

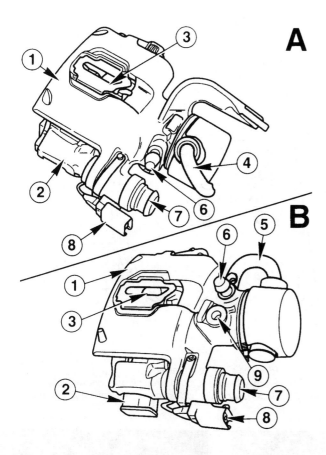

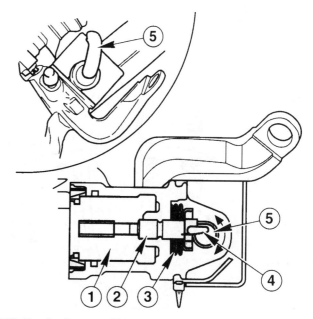

9.5B Handbrake operation on the rear brake caliper

1   Piston
2   Automatic adjusting screw
3   Spring washers
4   Cam
5   Handbrake cable lever

9.5A Rear brake caliper on Saloon/Hatchback models (A) and Estate models (B)

1   Caliper body
2   Frame
3   Brake pad spring clip
4   Handbrake cable lever facing away from caliper
5   Handbrake cable lever facing towards caliper
6   Bleed screw
7   Guide pin protective cap
8   Pad wear warning light connector
9   Flexible hydraulic hose connection

Section 15. Make sure there are no leaks from the hose connections. Test the brakes carefully before returning the vehicle to normal service.

10 Rear brake disc - inspection, removal and refitting

Refer to Section 4 (front disc inspection). Once the rear caliper is removed, the procedure is the same.

11 Master cylinder - removal and refitting

Removal

1   Disconnect the low fluid level warning light multi-plug from the fluid reservoir filler cap **(see illustration)**. Unscrew and remove the cap (note that the filler cap should not be inverted). Draw off the hydraulic fluid from the reservoir, using an old battery hydrometer or a poultry baster. *Do not* syphon the fluid by mouth; it is poisonous. Any brake fluid spilt on paintwork should be washed off with clean water, without

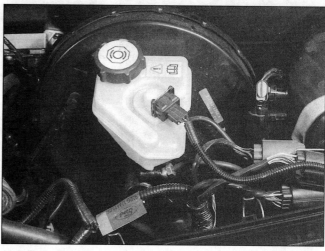

11.1 Brake fluid reservoir and low level warning light multi-plug

delay - *brake fluid is also a highly-effective paint-stripper!*
2   Identify the locations of each brake pipe on the master cylinder. On non-ABS models, there are four pipes; the two rear brake pipes are attached to PCR (pressure-conscious relief) valves on the master cylinder. On ABS models, there are only two pipes, which lead to the ABS hydraulic unit **(see illustration)**.
3   Place rags beneath the master cylinder to catch spilt hydraulic fluid.
4   Clean around the hydraulic union nuts. Unscrew the nuts, and disconnect the hydraulic lines from the master cylinder.
5   Unscrew the mounting nuts, and withdraw the master cylinder from the studs on the front of the servo unit. If the nuts are tight, a split ring spanner should be used in preference to an open-ended spanner. Plug or cap open unions, to keep dust and dirt out.
6   Recover the gasket from the master cylinder.

9

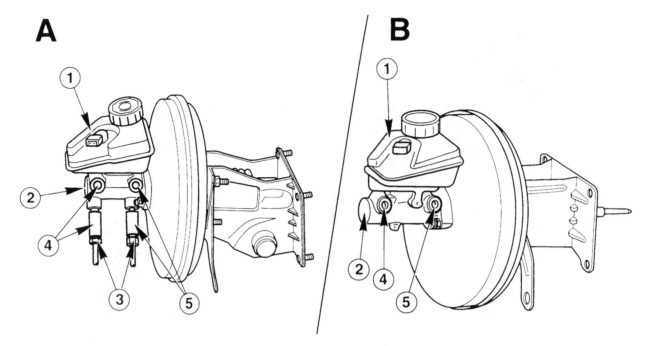

11.2 Master cylinder connections

A   Non-ABS models
B   ABS models
1   Brake fluid reservoir
2   Master cylinder

3   PCR valves for rear brakes
4   Primary brake hydraulic circuit (front right/rear left)
5   Secondary brake hydraulic circuit (front left/rear right)

12.3 Removing the hairpin clip from the right-hand end of the brake pedal pivot shaft

12.4A Unscrew the nut securing the pedal trunnion to the pushrod . . .

12.4B . . . and remove the tube from the pushrod

7   If the master cylinder is faulty, it must be renewed. At the time of writing, no overhaul kits were available.

Refitting

8   Clean the contact surfaces of the master cylinder and servo.
9   Locate a new gasket on the master cylinder.
10   Position the master cylinder on the studs on the servo unit. Refit and tighten the nuts to the specified torque.
11   Carefully insert the hydraulic lines in the apertures in the master cylinder, then tighten the union nuts. Make sure that the nuts enter their threads correctly.
12   Fill the reservoir with fresh brake fluid.
13   Bleed the hydraulic system as described in Section 15.
14   Refit the reservoir filler cap, and reconnect the multi-plug for the low fluid level warning light.
15   Test the brakes carefully before returning the vehicle to normal service.

12 Brake pedal - removal and refitting

Removal

1   Working inside the vehicle, move the driver's seat fully to the rear, to allow maximum working area.
2   Remove the ashtray, then unscrew the screws and remove the lower facia panel.
3   Prise the hairpin clip from the right-hand end of the pedal pivot shaft, and remove the washer **(see illustration)**.
4   Unscrew the nut securing the pedal trunnion to the pushrod. The nut is located near the top of the pedal **(see illustrations)**.
5   Press the pedal pivot shaft to the left, through the mounting bracket, just far enough to allow the pedal to be withdrawn. On manual transmission models, leave the blue nylon spacer (located between the clutch and brake pedals) on the pivot shaft **(see illustration)**. On automatic transmission models, the shaft can be removed completely **(see**

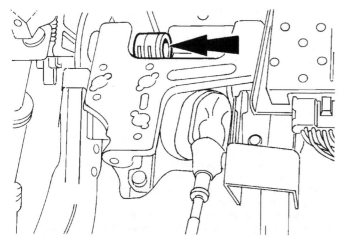

12.5A Leave the nylon spacer (arrowed) in position on the pivot shaft (left-hand-drive model shown, right-hand-drive similar)

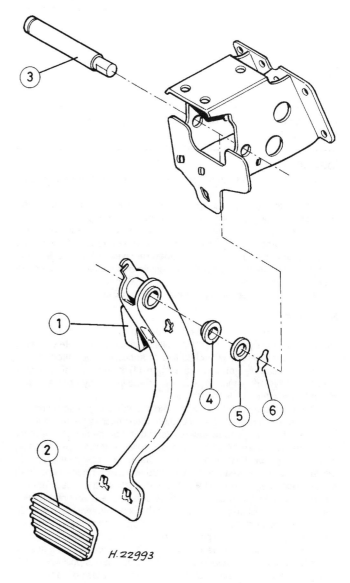

illustration).

6   With the pedal removed, prise out the bushes from each side. If necessary, also remove the pushrod trunnion and the rubber pad. Renew the components as necessary **(see illustrations)**.

Refitting

7   Prior to refitting the pedal, apply a little grease to the pivot shaft, pedal bushes and trunnion.

8   Refitting is a reversal of the removal procedure, but make sure that the pedal bushes are correctly located, and that the pedal shaft "D" section locates in the right-hand side of the pedal bracket. Also make sure that the hairpin clip is correctly located.

13 Brake pedal-to-servo cross-link (right-hand-drive models only) - removal and refitting

Removal

1   Disconnect the battery negative (earth) lead (Chapter 5, Section 1).
2   Remove the master cylinder and the vacuum servo unit as described in Sections 11 and 16. If wished, the master cylinder may be left attached to the servo unit.
3   Working inside the passenger compartment, fold down the covering from the front of both front footwells.
4   Have an assistant support the cross-link assembly from inside the engine compartment.
5   Unscrew and remove the nuts and bolts on each side of the bulkhead, and remove the link assembly from inside the engine compartment. If necessary, have the assistant hold the bolt heads

12.5B Brake pedal components - automatic transmission models

1	Pedal	4	Bush
2	Rubber pad	5	Washer
3	Pivot shaft	6	Hairpin clip

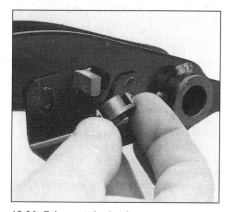

12.6A Prise out the bushes . . .

12.6B . . . from each side of the pedal . . .

12.6C . . . and remove the pushrod trunnion

9

from inside the engine compartment while the nuts are being loosened.

6   Clean the cross-link components, and examine the bushes for wear. Renew the bushes if necessary.

Refitting

7   Refitting is a reversal of the removal procedure. Refer to Sections 11 and 16 when refitting the master cylinder and vacuum servo unit.

14 Hydraulic pipes and hoses - inspection, removal and refitting

Inspection

1   Jack up the front and rear of the vehicle, and support on axle stands.

2   Check for signs of leakage at the pipe unions, then examine the flexible hoses for signs of cracking, chafing and fraying.

3   The brake pipes should be examined carefully for signs of dents, corrosion or other damage. Corrosion should be scraped off, and if the depth of pitting is significant, the pipes renewed. This is particularly likely in those areas underneath the vehicle body where the pipes are exposed and unprotected.

4   Renew any defective brake pipes and/or hoses.

Removal

5   If a section of pipe or hose is to be removed, loss of brake fluid can be reduced by unscrewing the filler cap, and completely sealing the top of the reservoir with cling film or adhesive tape. Alternatively, the reservoir can be emptied (see Section 11). If any brake fluid is spilt onto the bodywork, it must be washed off without delay - *brake fluid is also a highly-effective paint-stripper!*

6   To remove a section of pipe, hold the adjoining hose union nut with a spanner to prevent it from turning, then unscrew the union nut at the end of the pipe, and release it. Repeat the procedure at the other end of the pipe, then release the pipe by pulling out the clips attaching it to the body **(see illustrations)**. Where the union nuts are exposed to the full force of the weather, they can sometimes be quite tight. If an open-ended spanner is used, burring of the flats on the nuts is not uncommon, and for this reason, it is preferable to use a split ring (brake) spanner, which will engage all the flats. If such a spanner is not available, self-locking grips may be used as a last resort; these may well damage the nuts, but if the pipe is to be renewed, this does not matter.

7   To further minimise the loss of fluid when disconnecting a flexible brake line from a rigid pipe, clamp the hose as near as possible to the pipe to be detached, using a brake hose clamp or a pair of self-locking grips with protected jaws.

8   To remove a flexible hose, first clean the ends of the hose and the surrounding area, then unscrew the union nuts from the hose ends. Recover the spring clip, and withdraw the hose from the serrated mounting in the support bracket. Where applicable, unscrew the hose from the caliper.

9   Brake pipes supplied with flared ends and union nuts can be obtained individually or in sets from Ford dealers or accessory shops. The pipe is then bent to shape, using the old pipe as a guide, and is ready for fitting. Be careful not to kink or crimp the pipe when bending it; ideally, a proper pipe-bending tool should be used.

Refitting

10   Refitting of the pipes and hoses is a reversal of removal. Make sure that all brake pipes are securely supported in their clips, and ensure that the hoses are not kinked. Check also that the hoses are clear of all suspension components and underbody fittings, and will remain clear during movement of the suspension and steering.

11   On completion, bleed the brake hydraulic system as described in Section 15.

15 Hydraulic system - bleeding

Warning: *Brake fluid is poisonous. Take care to keep it off bare skin,*

and in particular not to get splashes in your eyes. The fluid also attacks paintwork - wash off spillages immediately with cold water.

1   If the master cylinder has been disconnected and reconnected, then the complete system (both circuits) must be bled of air. If a component of one circuit has been disturbed, then only that particular circuit need be bled.

2   Bleeding should commence on one front brake, followed by the diagonally-opposite rear brake. The remaining front brake should then be bled, followed by its diagonally-opposite rear brake.

3   There are a variety of do-it-yourself "one-man" brake bleeding kits available from motor accessory shops, and it is recommended that one of these kits be used wherever possible, as they greatly simplify the brake bleeding operation. Follow the kit manufacturer's instructions in conjunction with the following procedure. If a pressure-bleeding kit is obtained, then it will not be necessary to depress the brake pedal in the following procedure.

4   During the bleeding operation, do not allow the brake fluid level in the reservoir to drop below the minimum mark. If the level is allowed to fall so far that air is drawn in, the whole procedure will have to be started again from scratch. Only use new fluid for topping-up, preferably from a freshly-opened container. *Never re-use fluid bled from the system.*

5   Before starting, check that all rigid pipes and flexible hoses are in good condition, and that all hydraulic unions are tight. Take great care not to allow hydraulic fluid to come into contact with the vehicle paintwork, otherwise the finish will be seriously damaged. Wash off any spilt fluid immediately with cold water.

6   If a brake bleeding kit is not being used, gather together a clean jar, a length of plastic or rubber tubing which is a tight fit over the bleed screw, and a new can of the specified brake fluid (see Chapter 1 Specifications). The help of an assistant will also be required.

7   Clean the area around the bleed screw on the front brake unit to be bled (it is important that no dirt be allowed to enter the hydraulic system), and remove the dust cap. Connect one end of the tubing to the bleed screw, and immerse the other end in the jar, which should be filled with sufficient brake fluid to keep the end of the tube submerged.

8   Open the bleed screw by one or two turns, and have the assistant depress the brake pedal to the floor. Tighten the bleed screw at the end of the downstroke, then have the assistant release the pedal. Continue this procedure until clean brake fluid, free from air bubbles, can be seen flowing into the jar. Finally tighten the bleed screw with the pedal in the fully-depressed position.

9   Remove the tube, and refit the dust cap. Top-up the master cylinder reservoir if necessary, then repeat the procedure on the diagonally-opposite rear brake.

10   Repeat the procedure on the remaining circuit, starting with the front brake, and followed by the diagonally-opposite rear brake.

11   Check the feel of the brake pedal - it should be firm. If it is spongy, there is still some air in the system, and the bleeding procedure should be repeated.

12   When bleeding is complete, top-up the master cylinder reservoir and refit the cap.

16 Vacuum servo unit - testing, removal and refitting

Testing

1   To test the operation of the servo unit, depress the footbrake four or five times to dissipate the vacuum, then start the engine while keeping the footbrake depressed. As the engine starts, there should be a noticeable "give" in the brake pedal as vacuum builds up. Allow the engine to run for at least two minutes, and then switch it off. If the brake pedal is now depressed again, it should be possible to hear a hiss from the servo when the pedal is depressed. After four or five applications, no further hissing should be heard, and the pedal should feel harder.

2   Before assuming that a problem exists in the servo unit itself, inspect the non-return valve as described in the next Section.

Removal

3   Refer to Section 11 and remove the master cylinder.

14.6A Unscrewing a brake pipe union nut using a split ring spanner

14.6B Pulling out a brake pipe mounting clip

17.2 Removing the plastic adaptor from the servo unit

4 Disconnect the vacuum hose adaptor at the servo unit by pulling it free from the rubber grommet. If it is reluctant to move, prise it free, using a screwdriver with its blade inserted under the flange.
5 Unscrew the four nuts securing the servo unit to the mounting brackets on the bulkhead in the engine compartment.
6 On right-hand drive models, withdraw the servo unit so that its studs are just clear of the brackets. Have an assistant hold the brake pedal depressed, then extract the spring clip and remove the clevis pin securing the servo unit pushrod to the pedal cross-link arm.
7 On left-hand drive models, unscrew the nut securing the pedal trunnion to the servo unit pushrod inside the passenger compartment. The nut is located near the top of the pedal, and is accessible through an access hole. For improved access, remove the lower facia panel first.
8 Withdraw the servo unit from the bulkhead, and remove it from the engine compartment. On left-hand drive models, take care not to damage the bulkhead rubber grommet as the pushrod passes through it.
9 Note that the servo unit cannot be dismantled for repair or overhaul and, if faulty, must be renewed.

Refitting

10 Refitting is a reversal of the removal procedure. Refer to Section 11 for details of refitting the master cylinder.

17 Vacuum servo unit vacuum hose and non-return valve - removal, testing and refitting

Removal

1 Depress the brake pedal four or five times, to dissipate any remaining vacuum from the servo unit.
2 Disconnect the vacuum hose adaptor at the servo unit, by pulling it free from the rubber grommet **(see illustration)**. If it is reluctant to move, prise it free, using a screwdriver with its blade inserted under the flange.
3 Detach the vacuum hose from the inlet manifold connection, pressing in the collar to disengage the tabs, then withdrawing the collar slowly.
4 If the hose or the fixings are damaged or in poor condition, they must be renewed.

Testing

5 Examine the non-return valve for damage and signs of deterioration, and renew it if necessary. The valve may be tested by blowing through its connecting hoses in both directions. It should only be possible to blow from the servo end towards the inlet manifold.

Refitting

6 Refitting is a reversal of the removal procedure. If fitting a new non-return valve, ensure that it is fitted the correct way round.

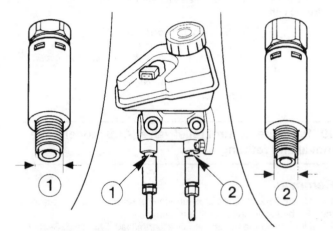

18.6 Pressure-control relief valve locations

1 *Primary PCR valve (12 mm)*
2 *Secondary PCR valve (10 mm)*

18 Pressure-control relief valve (non-ABS models) - removal and refitting

Removal

1 On non-ABS models, the two pressure-control relief valves (sometimes referred to as pressure-conscious reducing valves) are located on the master cylinder outlets to the rear brake line circuits.
2 Unscrew and remove the fluid reservoir filler cap, and draw off the fluid - see Section 11.
3 Position some rags beneath the master cylinder, to catch any spilled fluid.
4 Clean around the valve to be removed. Hold the PCR valve stationary with one spanner, and unscrew the hydraulic pipe union nut with another spanner. Pull out the pipe, and bend it slightly away from the valve.
5 Unscrew the PCR valve from the master cylinder.
6 Note that the primary and secondary PCR valves have different thread diameters, to prevent incorrect fitment. The primary valve has a 12 mm diameter thread, and the secondary valve has a 10 mm diameter thread **(see illustration)**.

Refitting

7 Refitting is a reversal of the removal procedure. On completion, bleed the hydraulic system as described in Section 15.

9

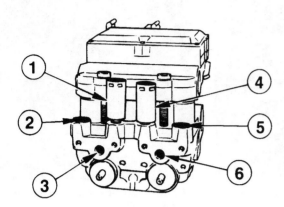

19.1 Pressure-control relief valve locations on the ABS hydraulic unit

- *1   PCR valve, rear right brake circuit*
- *2   Outlet, front left brake circuit*
- *3   Inlet, from brake master cylinder secondary circuit*
- *4   PCR valve, rear left brake circuit*
- *5   Outlet, front right brake circuit*
- *6   Inlet, from brake master cylinder primary circuit*

19 Pressure-control relief valve (ABS models) - removal and refitting

Removal

1   On ABS models, the pressure-control relief valves are located on the ABS hydraulic unit **(see illustration)**.
2   Disconnect the battery negative (earth) lead (Chapter 5, Section 1).
3   Remove the air cleaner assembly as described in Chapter 4.
4   Remove the engine air inlet duct and air plenum chamber.
5   Disconnect the low fluid level warning multi-plug from the brake fluid reservoir.
6   Unscrew and remove the brake fluid reservoir filler cap, and completely seal the top of the reservoir using cling film or adhesive tape. This will reduce loss of fluid when the PCR valve is removed.
7   Unscrew the master cylinder mounting nuts, and carefully withdraw the cylinder from the servo unit, leaving the brake pipes still connected to it. Move the master cylinder over to the left-hand side of the engine compartment, to rest against the left-hand suspension turret. (Throughout this manual, left- and right-hand are as seen from the driver's seat.)
8   Unscrew the servo unit mounting nuts, and move the unit to one side.
9   Position some rags beneath the ABS unit, to catch spilled fluid.
10   Clean around the valve to be removed. Hold the PCR valve stationary with one spanner, and unscrew the hydraulic pipe union nut with another spanner. Pull out the pipe, and bend it slightly away from the valve.
11   Unscrew the PCR valve from the ABS unit.

Refitting

12   Refitting is a reversal of the removal procedure. On completion, bleed the hydraulic system as described in Section 15.

20 ABS hydraulic unit - removal and refitting

Note: *If any part of the ABS hydraulic unit is defective, it must be renewed as an assembly. Apart from the relay box (Section 22), individual spare parts are not available.*

Removal

1   Remove both pressure-control relief valves as described in Section 19.
2   Identify the location of the remaining brake hydraulic pipes on the ABS hydraulic unit, then unscrew the union nuts and pull out the pipes. Carefully bend the pipes away from the hydraulic unit, to allow the unit to be removed.
3   Disconnect the multi-plugs from the hydraulic unit. To disconnect the main 22-pin multi-plug, push the locktab, then swivel the multi-plug outwards and unhook it.

Right-hand drive models

4   Have an assistant hold the brake pedal depressed, then extract the spring clip and remove the clevis pin securing the servo unit pushrod to the pedal cross-link arm.
5   Remove the vacuum servo unit from the engine compartment.

Left-hand drive models

6   Unscrew the nut securing the pedal trunnion to the servo unit pushrod inside the passenger compartment. The nut is located near the top of the pedal, and is accessible through an access hole. For improved access, remove the lower facia panel first.
7   Remove the vacuum servo unit, together with the pushrod, from the engine compartment. Take care not to damage the rubber grommet in the bulkhead.

All models

8   Unscrew the pump mounting nut.
9   Raise the left-hand side of the ABS hydraulic unit, then swivel the unit out of the right-hand mounting. Take care not to lose the bracket studs and insulator ring.

Refitting

10   Locate the insulator ring on the pump end, and fit the stud cap to the insulator ring.
11   Lower the ABS hydraulic unit into position, right-hand end first.
12   Fit the right-hand bracket studs onto the insulators.
13   Lower the left-hand end of the ABS hydraulic unit onto the bracket, then fit and tighten the pump mounting nut.

Left-hand drive models

14   Locate the vacuum servo unit and pushrod on the bulkhead bracket, taking care not to damage the rubber grommet.
15   Insert the pushrod in the pedal trunnion, and tighten the nut.
16   Refit the lower facia panel if it was removed.

Right-hand drive models

17   Locate the vacuum servo unit and pushrod on the bulkhead bracket.
18   Refit the clevis pin and spring clip securing the servo unit pushrod to the pedal cross-link arm.

All models

19   Reconnect the multi-plugs to the hydraulic unit.
20   Reconnect the brake pipes to the hydraulic unit, and tighten the union nuts.
21   Refit both pressure-control relief valves, with reference to Section 20.

21 ABS wheel sensor - testing, removal and refitting

Testing

1   Checking of the sensors is done before removal, connecting a voltmeter to the disconnected sensor multi-plug. Using an analogue (moving coil) meter is not practical, since the meter does not respond quickly enough. A digital meter having an AC facility may be used to check that the sensor is operating correctly. To do this, raise the relevant wheel then disconnect the wiring to the ABS sensor and connect the meter to it. Spin the wheel and check that the output voltage is between 1.5 and 2.0 volts, depending on how fast the wheel is spun.

21.4A Unscrew the mounting bolt . . .

21.4B . . . and remove the ABS sensor

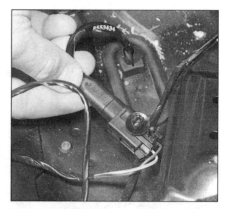

21.12 Rear ABS sensor wiring multi-plug located beneath the rear seat

Alternatively, an oscilloscope may be used to check the output of the sensor - an alternating current will be traced on the screen, of magnitude depending on the speed of the rotating wheel.

2   If the sensor output is low or zero, renew the sensor.

Removal

Front wheel sensor

3   Apply the handbrake, jack up the front of the vehicle and support it on axle stands. Remove the relevant wheel.

4   Unscrew the sensor mounting bolt located on the steering knuckle, and withdraw the sensor **(see illustrations)**.

5   Remove the sensor wiring loom from the support brackets on the front suspension strut and wheel arch.

6   Prise out the stud clips, and remove the Torx screws and screw clips holding the wheel arch liner in position. Withdraw the liner.

7   Disconnect the multi-plug, and withdraw the sensor and wiring loom.

Rear wheel sensor

8   Chock the front wheels, and engage 1st gear (or "P"). Jack up the rear of the vehicle and support it on axle stands. Remove the relevant wheel.

9   Unscrew the sensor mounting bolt, located on the brake back-plate (drum brakes) or rear suspension knuckle (disc brakes), and withdraw the sensor.

10   On disc brake models, prise out the stud clips, and remove the Torx screws and screw clips holding the wheel arch liner in position. Withdraw the liner.

11   Disconnect the sensor wiring loom from the supports on the rear suspension strut (or knuckle) and wheel arch.

12   Working inside the vehicle, lift the rear seat cushion, then disconnect the multi-plug for the sensor wiring loom **(see illustration)**.

13   Withdraw the sensor and wiring loom through the rubber grommet in the rear floor.

Refitting

Front and rear wheel sensors

14   Refitting is a reversal of the removal procedure.

22 ABS relay box - removal and refitting

Removal

1   Disconnect the battery negative (earth) lead (Chapter 5, Section 1).

2   Remove the ABS hydraulic unit as described in Section 20.

3   Unscrew the Torx mounting bolts, and withdraw the relay box from the hydraulic unit **(see illustration)**.

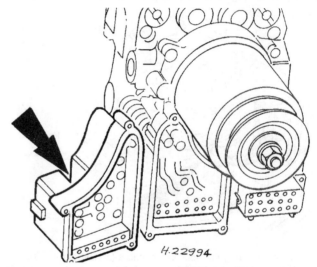

H.22994

22.3 Removing the ABS relay box (arrowed)

Refitting

4   Refitting is a reversal of the removal procedure.

23 TCS inhibitor switch - removal and refitting

Removal

1   Disconnect the battery negative (earth) lead (Chapter 5, Section 1).

2   Using a small screwdriver and a suitable pad (to protect the facia), prise out the TCS inhibitor switch from the facia.

3   Disconnect the multi-plug from the switch, and withdraw the switch.

Refitting

4   Refitting is a reversal of the removal procedure.

24 TCS throttle actuator - removal and refitting

Removal

1   The TCS throttle actuator is located in the front right-hand corner of the engine compartment. First disconnect the battery negative (earth) lead (Chapter 5, Section 1).

9

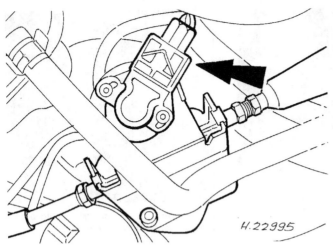

24.2 Disconnecting the multi-plug (arrowed) at the TCS actuator

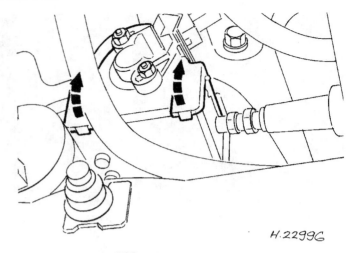

24.3 Removing the TCS motor cover

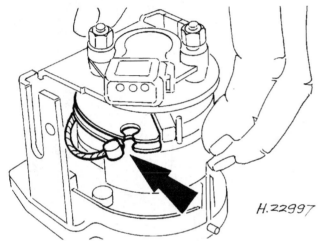

24.4A Disconnecting the accelerator cable (arrowed) from the upper throttle control segment

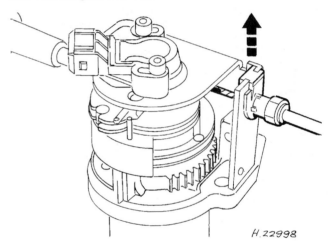

24.4B Releasing the cable from the motor housing support

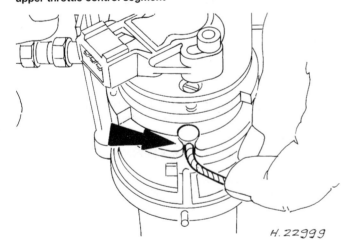

24.5 Disconnecting the accelerator cable (arrowed) from the lower throttle control segment

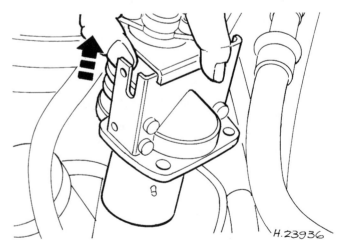

24.6 Removing the TCS actuator

2   Disconnect the wiring multi-plug at the TCS actuator **(see illustration)**.
3   Prise off the motor cover **(see illustration)**.
4   Turn the upper throttle control segment, to provide some play in the accelerator cable leading to the throttle housing, then disconnect the cable by unhooking the end stop. Release the cable from the motor

housing support **(see illustrations)**.
5   Turn the lower accelerator control segment, to provide play in the accelerator cable from the accelerator pedal, then disconnect the cable by unhooking the end stop. Release the cable from the motor housing support **(see illustration)**.
6   Unscrew the mounting bolts, and lift out the TCS throttle actuator **(see illustration)**.

25.3 Disconnecting the wiring multi-plug from the stop-light switch

25.4 Removing the stop-light switch

26.6 Handbrake lever mounting bolts

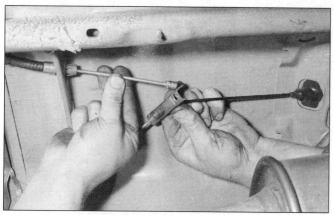

27.7 Unhooking a handbrake cable from the equaliser bar

27.8 Using a ring spanner to compress the retaining lugs securing the outer cable to the backplate

Refitting

7   Refitting is a reversal of the removal procedure. Adjust the accelerator cables as described in Chapter 4.

25 Stop-light switch - removal and refitting

Removal

1   Disconnect the battery negative (earth) lead (Chapter 5, Section 1).
2   Remove the lower facia panel, with reference to Chapter 11.
3   Disconnect the wiring multi-plug from the switch (see illustration).
4   Rotate the switch anti-clockwise by a quarter-turn, and withdraw it from the pedal bracket (see illustration).

Refitting

5   Refitting is a reversal of the removal procedure.

26 Handbrake lever - removal and refitting

Removal

1   Raise the front and rear of the vehicle, and support it on axle stands. Fully release the handbrake lever.
2   Remove the centre console as described in Chapter 11.
3   Working beneath the vehicle, release the exhaust system from the rubber mountings. Lower the exhaust system as far as possible, supporting it on blocks or more axle stands.
4   Detach the exhaust heat shield from the underbody.
5   Unhook the secondary (rear) handbrake cables from the equaliser bar.
6   Working inside the vehicle, unscrew and remove the two mounting bolts securing the handbrake lever to the floor (see illustration).

7   Turn the handbrake lever upsidedown, then disconnect the primary cable end from the segment.
8   Withdraw the handbrake from inside the vehicle.

Refitting

9   Refitting is a reversal of the removal procedure, making sure that the primary cable is correctly located in the segment. Check the operation of the handbrake before returning the vehicle to normal service.

27 Handbrake cables - removal and refitting

Removal

Primary (front)
1   Remove the handbrake lever as described in Section 26.
2   Prise the grommet from the underbody, and withdraw the cable from beneath the vehicle.

Secondary (rear)
3   Chock the front wheels, and engage 1st gear (or "P"). Jack up the rear of the vehicle and support it on axle stands. Fully release the handbrake lever.
4   Remove the relevant rear wheel.
5   Working beneath the vehicle, release the exhaust system from the rubber mountings. Lower the exhaust system as far as possible, supporting it on blocks or more axle stands.
6   Unbolt the exhaust heat shield from the underbody.
7   Unhook the relevant cable from the equaliser bar (see illustration).
8   On drum brake models, remove the rear brake shoes on the relevant side as described in Section 6, then remove the outer cable from the backplate by compressing the three retaining lugs (use a suitable ring spanner) and pushing the cable through (see illustration).

9

27.10A Release the lugs using a ring spanner . . .

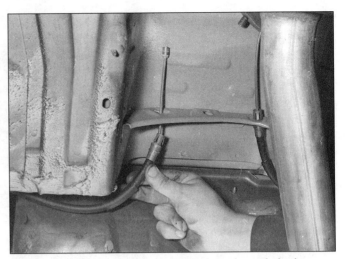

27.10B . . . and remove the outer cable from the underbody brackets

9   On disc brake models, unhook the end of the cable from the handbrake operating arm on the rear caliper.

10   Release the lugs securing the outer cable to the underbody brackets, then release the cable from the clips, and withdraw it from under the vehicle **(see illustrations)**.

Refitting

All cables

11   Refitting is a reversal of the removal procedure, but make sure that the cable end fittings are correctly located. Check the operation of the handbrake before returning the vehicle to normal service.

Chapter 10
Suspension and steering systems

Contents

10

Specifications

Front wheel alignment

Toe setting:
Tolerance allowed before resetting required.................................... -0.5 mm to -3.5 mm toe-out (-0°05' to -0°35' toe-out)
Adjustment setting (ifrequired) .... -2.0 mm ± 1.0 mm toe-out (-0°20' ± 0°10' toe-out)

Rear wheel alignment

Toe setting:
Tolerance allowed before resetting required:
Saloon/Hatchback .... 3.9 mm toe-in to -0.1 mm toe-out (0°38' toe-in to 0°02' toe-out)
Estate .... 2.7 mm toe-in to -1.3 mm toe-out (0°27' toe-in to -0°13' toe-out)
Adjustment setting (if required):
Saloon/Hatchback .... 1.9 mm ± 1.2 mm toe-in (0°18' ± 0°12' toe-in)
Estate .... 0.7 mm ± 1.2 mm toe-in (0°07' ± 0°12' toe-in)

Roadwheels and tyres

Wheel sizes:
Steel 14x5-1/2
Alloy .... 14x5-1/2 or 15x6
Tyre sizes:
Wheel size 14x5-1/2... 185/65/14 or 195/60VR/14
Wheel size 15x6.. 205/55VR/15
Tyre pressures .... See Chapter 1 Specifications

Torque wrench settings

Front suspension

	Nm	lbf ft
Front subframe	110 to 150	81 to 111
Lower arm balljoint to lower arm (service replacement, bolted on)........	58	43
Lower arm balljoint-to-steering knuckle clamp bolt	48 to 60	35 to 44
Lower arm to subframe:		
Stage 1 (used components)	50	37
Stage 1 (new components)	70	52
Stage 2	Slacken completely	
Stage 3	50	37
Stage 4	Tighten through further 90°	
Anti-roll bar...	24	18
Anti-roll bar link..	41 to 58	30 to 43
Suspension strut-to-steering knuckle pinch-bolt	84	62
Suspension strut uppermounting nut	46	34
Suspension strut thrustbearing retaining nut	59	44
Driveshaft/hub retaining nut	340	251

Rear suspension (Saloon/Hatchback)

	Nm	lbf ft
Crossmember mounting bolts.............................	102 to 138	75 to 102
Front lower arm to knuckle and to crossmember	70 to 98	52 to 72
Rear lower arm to knuckle...............................	102 to 138	75 to 102
Rear lower arm to crossmember	70 to 98	52 to 72
Anti-roll bar...	19 to 26	14 to 19
Anti-roll bar link..	30 to 40	22 to 30
Suspension strut to knuckle	70 to 98	52 to 72
Drum brake backplate	45 to 54	33 to 40
Disc brake splash shield..................................	90	66
Hub nut	290	181
Tie-bar and tie-bar bracket...............................	102 to 138	75 to 102
Suspension strut upper mounting bolts	23 to 30	17 to 22
Suspension strut upper nut	41 to 58	30 to 43

Rear suspension (Estate)

Same as for Saloon/Hatchback, except for the following.

	Nm	lbf ft
Crossmember mounting bolts.............................	120	89
Front lower arm to knuckle and to crossmember	120	89
Upper arm to knuckle	120	89
Upper arm to crossmember	84	62
Rear lower arm to knuckle and to crossmember	84	62
Anti-roll bar...	25	19
Anti-roll bar link..	35	26
Hub assembly-to-knuckle retaining bolts.................	65	48

Torque wrench settings (continued)

	Nm	lbf ft
Tie-bar to bracket	120	89
Tie-bar bracket to underbody	120	89
Tie-bar to knuckle	84	62
Shock absorber upper mounting bolt	84	62
Shock absorber lower mounting bolt	120	89

Steering

	Nm	lbf ft
Steering gear mounting bolts	114 to 159	84 to 117
Track rod end to steering knuckle	25 to 30	18 to 22
Track rod end locknut	34 to 47	25 to 35
Steering wheel	45 to 55	33 to 41
Flexible coupling-to-pinion shaft clamp bolt	23 to 32	17 to 24
Power steering pipe unions to valve body	27 to 35	20 to 26
Steering column-to-coupling clamp bolt	20 to 27	14 to 20
Steering column mounting bolts	20 to 27	14 to 20
Steering pump mounting bolts	21 to 28	15 to 21
Steering pump pressure line	57 to 73	42 to 54

	Nm	lbf ft
Roadwheel nuts	85	63

1 General information

The independent front suspension is of MacPherson strut type, incorporating coil springs, integral telescopic shock absorbers, and an anti-roll bar. The struts are attached to steering knuckles at their lower ends, and the knuckles are in turn attached to the lower suspension arm by balljoints. The anti-roll bar is bolted to the rear of the subframe, and is connected to the front suspension struts by links **(see illustration)**.

On Saloon/Hatchback models, the independent rear suspension is of "Quadralink" type, having four mounting points on each side of

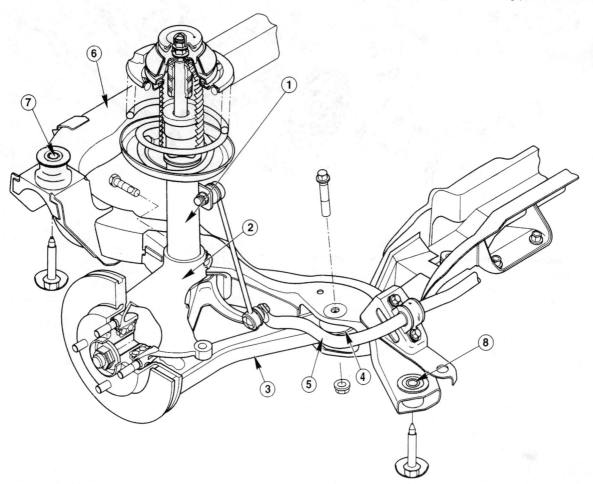

1.1 Front suspension components

1 MacPherson strut	5 Anti-roll bar
2 Steering knuckle	6 Front subframe
3 Lower arm	7 Front subframe rubber bush
4 Vertical silent bush on lower arm	8 Rear subframe rubber bush

10

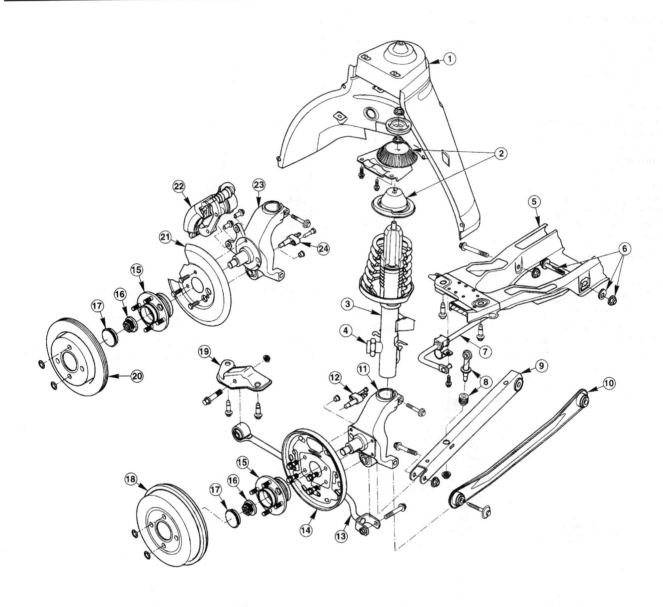

1.2 Rear suspension components on Saloon/Hatchback models

1	Wheel housing	9	Front lower arm	17	Grease cap
2	Upper mounting bracket and coil spring seat	10	Rear lower arm	18	Brake drum
3	Strut	11	Knuckle (drum brake models)	19	Tie-bar mounting bracket
4	Solenoid valve for adaptive damping	12	ABS wheel sensor (drum brake models)	20	Brake disc
5	Rear suspension crossmember	13	Tie-bar	21	Splash shield (disc brake models)
6	Eccentric bolt for rear toe setting	14	Backplate	22	Brake caliper (disc brake models)
7	Anti-roll bar	15	Hub and bearing assembly	23	Knuckle (disc brake models)
8	Link	16	Hub nut	24	ABS wheel sensor (disc brake models)

the vehicle. The two lower arms are attached to the rear suspension knuckle at their outer ends, and to the rear crossmember at their inner ends. A tie-bar, located between the bottom of the knuckle and the floor, counteracts braking and acceleration forces on each side **(see illustration)**.

On Estate models, the independent rear suspension is of "SLA" (Short and Long Arm) type. This allows a larger load area, since there are no suspension points projecting into the luggage area. There are three side arms on each side: one forged upper arm, and two pressed-steel lower side arms. A tie-bar on each side supports the rear suspension knuckles. The coil springs are separate from the shock absorbers **(see illustration)**.

A rear anti-roll bar is fitted to all models. On SI models, the front and rear shock absorbers are gas-filled; on other models, they are filled with fluid. Self-levelling rear shock absorbers are fitted as standard to Ghia Estate models.

A variable-ratio type rack-and-pinion steering gear is fitted, together with a conventional column and telescopic coupling, incorporating two universal joints. Power-assisted steering is fitted to all models. A power steering system fluid cooler is fitted, in front of the cooling system radiator on the crossmember **(see illustration)**. On models with adaptive damping, a steering position sensor with sensor disc is located above the upper universal joint.

On models with adaptive damping, it is possible to select a hard

1.3 Rear suspension components on Estate models

1	Tie-bar bracket	8	Rear lower arm	14	Splash guard (disc brake models)
2	Short front lower arm	9	Stub axle (part of hub and bearing	15	Brake disc
3	Long front upper arm		assembly)	16	Hub and bearing assembly
4	Shock absorber	10	Knuckle	17	Backplate (drum brake models)
5	Crossmember	11	Brake caliper (disc brake models)	18	ABS wheel sensor
6	Anti-roll bar	12	Hub nut	19	Tie-bar
7	Coil spring	13	Brake drum		

or soft setting for the front and rear shock absorbers. The system is computer-controlled; a switch is provided near the handbrake lever for selection of "Sport" or "Normal" mode. With this system, a solenoid valve is fitted to each suspension strut. When the valve is open, the hydraulic oil inside the shock absorber is routed through a bypass channel, making the action "softer". When the solenoid valve is closed, the shock absorber action becomes "harder". The system takes into consideration the roadspeed of the vehicle; at high speeds, the shock absorbers are automatically set to "hard". The adaptive damping computer module is located in the luggage compartment, behind the rear seat, and incorporates a self-test function. Adaptive damping is not available on Estate models **(see illustrations)**.

When working on the suspension or steering, you may come across nuts or bolts which seem impossible to loosen. These nuts and bolts on the underside of the vehicle are continually subjected to water, road grime, mud, etc, and can become rusted or seized, making them extremely difficult to remove. In order to unscrew these stubborn

1.5 The power steering system fluid cooler is located in front of the radiator

10

1.6A Adaptive damping switch located near the handbrake lever

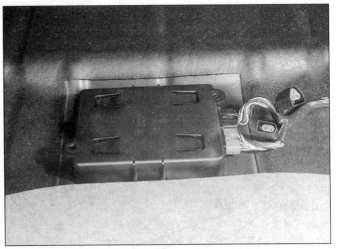

1.6B Adaptive damping computer module located in the luggage compartment

nuts and bolts without damaging them (or other components), use lots of penetrating oil, and allow it to soak in for a while. Using a wire brush to clean exposed threads will also ease removal of the nut or bolt, and will help to prevent damage to the threads. Sometimes, a sharp blow with a hammer and punch will break the bond between a nut and bolt, but care must be taken to prevent the punch from slipping off and ruining the threads. Heating the nut or bolt and surrounding area with a blow lamp sometimes helps too, but this is not recommended, because of the obvious dangers associated with fire. Extension bars or pipes will increase leverage, but never use one on a ratchet, as the internal mechanism could be damaged. Actually *tightening* the nut or bolt first may help to break it loose. Nuts or bolts which have required drastic measures to remove them should always be renewed.

Since most of the procedures dealt with in this Chapter involve jacking up the vehicle and working underneath it, a good pair of axle stands will be needed. A hydraulic trolley jack is the preferred type of jack to lift the vehicle, and it can also be used to support certain components during removal and refitting operations. **Warning:** *Never, under any circumstances, rely on a jack to support the vehicle while working beneath it. When jacking up the vehicle, do not lift or support it beneath the front or rear subframes.*

2 Steering knuckle and hub assembly - removal and refitting

Removal

1   Apply the handbrake. Remove the wheel cover from the relevant front wheel, and loosen (but do not remove) the driveshaft/hub nut. This nut is very tight.
2   Loosen the front wheel nuts, jack up the front of the vehicle and support it on axle stands. Remove the front wheel.
3   Extract the split pin from the track rod end balljoint nut. Unscrew the nut, and detach the rod from the arm on the steering knuckle using a conventional balljoint removal tool. Take care not to damage the balljoint seal.
4   Remove the ABS sensor (when fitted) as described in Chapter 9.
5   Remove the brake caliper and brake disc as described in Chapter 9, but do not disconnect the flexible hose from the caliper. Suspend the caliper from a suitable point under the wheel arch, taking care not to strain the hose.
6   Unscrew and remove the driveshaft/hub nut. Note that the nut is of special laminated design, and should only be re-used a maximum of 5 times. (It is a good idea to file a small notch on the nut every time it is removed.) Obtain a new nut if necessary.
7   Note which way round the lower arm balljoint clamp bolt is fitted, then unscrew and remove it from the knuckle assembly. Lever the

balljoint down from the knuckle; if it is tight, prise the clamp open using a large flat-bladed tool. Take care not to damage the balljoint seal during the separation procedure.
8   Unscrew and remove the pinch-bolt securing the steering knuckle assembly to the front suspension strut, noting which way round it is fitted. Prise open the clamp using a wedge-shaped tool, and release the knuckle from the strut. If necessary, tap the knuckle downwards with a soft-headed mallet to separate the two components. Support the knuckle on an axle stand.
9   Pull the steering knuckle and hub assembly from the driveshaft splines. If it is tight, connect a universal puller to the hub flange, and withdraw it from the driveshaft. When the driveshaft is free, support it on an axle stand, or suspend it from a suitable point under the wheel arch, making sure that the inner constant velocity joint is not turned through more than 18°. (Damage may occur if the joint is turned through too great an angle.)

Refitting

10   Lift the steering knuckle and hub assembly onto the driveshaft splines, and support the assembly on an axle stand.
11   Locate the assembly on the front suspension strut. Insert the pinch-bolt with its head facing forwards. Fit the nut and tighten it to the specified torque.
12   Refit the lower arm balljoint to the knuckle assembly, and insert the clamp bolt with its head facing forwards. Refit the nut and tighten it to the specified torque.
13   Refit the driveshaft/hub nut, and tighten it moderately at this stage. Final tightening of the nut is made with the vehicle lowered to the ground.
14   Refit the brake caliper and brake disc as described in Chapter 9.
15   Where fitted, refit the ABS sensor as described in Chapter 9.
16   Reconnect the track rod end balljoint to the steering arm, and tighten the nut to the specified torque. Check that the split pin holes are aligned; if necessary, turn the nut to the nearest alignment, making sure that the torque wrench setting is still within the specified range. Insert a new split pin, and bend it back to secure.
17   Refit the front wheel, and lower the vehicle to the ground. Tighten the wheel nuts to the specified torque.
18   Tighten the driveshaft/hub nut to the specified torque, and refit the wheel cover.

3 Front hub and bearings - inspection and renewal

Inspection

1   The front hub bearings are non-adjustable, and are supplied already greased.

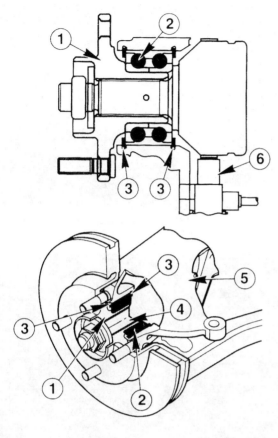

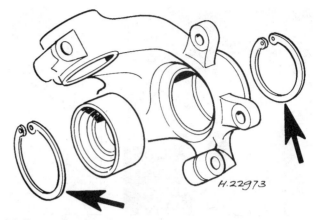

3.8 Front wheel bearing retaining circlips (arrowed)

3.5 Front hub and bearing

1	Hub	4	Stub axle
2	Double-row ball-bearing	5	Steering knuckle
3	Circlips	6	ABS sensor

2   To check the bearings for excessive wear, apply the handbrake, jack up the front of the vehicle and support it on axle stands.

3   Grip the front wheel at top and bottom, and attempt to rock it. If excessive movement is noted, it may be that the hub bearings are worn. Do not confuse wear in the driveshaft outer joint or front suspension lower arm balljoint with wear in the bearings. Hub bearing wear will show up as roughness or vibration when the wheel is spun; it will also be noticeable as a rumbling or growling noise when driving.

Renewal

4   Remove the steering knuckle and hub assembly as described in Section 2.

5   The hub must now be removed from the bearing inner races. It is preferable to use a press to do this, but it is possible to drive out the hub using a length of metal tube of suitable diameter **(see illustration)**.

6   Part of the inner race will remain on the hub, and this should be removed using a puller.

7   Note that if this procedure is being used to renew the hub only (ie it is not intended to renew the bearings), then it is important to check the condition of the bearing balls and races, to see if they are fit for re-use. It is difficult to be sure that no damage has occurred, especially if makeshift methods have been used during removal; in practice, it is probably false economy not to renew the bearings in any case, having got this far.

8   Using circlip pliers, extract the inner and outer circlips securing the hub bearing in the steering knuckle **(see illustration)**.

9   Press or drive out the bearing, using a length of metal tubing of diameter slightly less than the bearing outer race.

10   Clean the bearing seating faces in the steering knuckle.

4.2 Removing the brake hose support bracket from the front of the front suspension strut

11   Locate one of the circlips in the outer groove of the knuckle.

12   Press or drive the new bearing into the knuckle until it contacts the circlip, using a length of metal tube of diameter slightly less than the outer race. Do not apply any pressure to the inner race.

13   Locate the remaining circlip in the inner groove of the knuckle.

14   Support the inner race on a length of metal tube, then press or drive the hub fully into the bearing.

15   Refit the steering knuckle and hub assembly as described in Section 2.

4   Front suspension strut - removal and refitting

Removal

1   Apply the handbrake, then jack up the front of the vehicle and support it on axle stands. Remove the appropriate front wheel.

2   Unbolt the brake hose support bracket from the front of the suspension strut **(see illustration)**.

3   Remove the brake caliper as described in Chapter 9, but do not disconnect the flexible hydraulic hose from the caliper. Suspend the caliper from a suitable point under the wheel arch, taking care not to strain the hose.

4   Extract the split pin from the track rod end balljoint nut. Unscrew the nut, and detach the rod from the arm on the steering knuckle using a conventional balljoint removal tool. Take care not to damage the balljoint seal.

10

4.7 Removing the anti-roll bar link and ABS sensor wiring bracket

4.10 Front suspension strut upper mounting nut

4.12A Steering knuckle-to-strut pinch-bolt

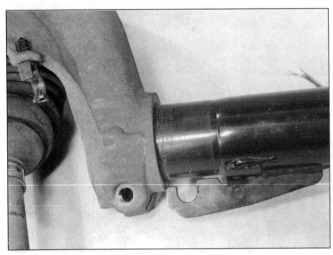

4.12B Releasing the knuckle from the strut

4.24 Final tightening of the front suspension strut upper mounting nut

5   Remove the ABS sensor (when fitted) from the steering knuckle, as described in Chapter 9.

6   Remove the clip securing the driveshaft inner gaiter to the inner CV joint. Disconnect the gaiter from the CV joint housing.

7   Remove the nut and disconnect the anti-roll bar link from the strut. Note that, on models fitted with ABS, the ABS wheel sensor wiring support bracket is located beneath the nut **(see illustration)**.

8   Note which way round the lower arm balljoint clamp bolt is fitted, then unscrew and remove it from the knuckle assembly. Lever the balljoint down from the knuckle; if it is tight, prise the clamp open carefully using a large flat-bladed tool. Take care not to damage the balljoint seal during the separation procedure.

9   Where applicable, disconnect the adaptive damping wiring multi-plug at the strut, and unclip the wire.

10   Support the strut and steering knuckle on an axle stand. Working inside the engine compartment, remove the strut cap (if fitted). Unscrew and remove the front suspension strut upper mounting nut, holding the piston rod stationary with an 8 mm Allen key **(see illustration)**.

11   Lower the suspension strut, together with the driveshaft and steering knuckle, from under the wheel arch, withdrawing the tripod on the inner end of the driveshaft from the CV joint housing.

12   Unscrew and remove the pinch-bolt securing the steering knuckle assembly to the front suspension strut, noting which way round it is fitted. Prise open the clamp using a wedge-shaped tool, and release the knuckle from the strut **(see illustrations)**.

Refitting

13   With the clamp prised open, locate the front suspension strut on

the steering knuckle, and refit the pinch-bolt with its head facing forwards. Tighten the bolt to the specified torque.

14   Locate the suspension strut (together with the driveshaft and steering knuckle) in its upper mounting, and loosely screw on the nut.

15   Locate the tripod on the inner end of the driveshaft in the CV joint housing, then manipulate the gaiter onto the housing, and fit a new clip.

16   Where applicable, reconnect the adaptive damping multi-plug, and fit the wire in the clip.

17   Locate the lower arm balljoint fully in the bottom of the steering knuckle. Refit the clamp bolt and tighten it to the specified torque.

18   Reconnect the anti-roll bar link to the strut, and tighten the nut to the specified torque. On models fitted with ABS, do not forget to locate the sensor wiring support bracket beneath the nut.

19   Where fitted, refit the ABS sensor as described in Chapter 9.

20   Refit the track rod end balljoint to the steering knuckle, and tighten the nut to the specified torque. Check that the split pin holes are aligned; if necessary, turn the nut to the nearest alignment, making sure that the torque wrench setting is still within the specified range. Insert a new split pin, and bend it back to secure.

21   Refit the brake caliper as described in Chapter 9.

22   Refit the brake hose support bracket to the strut, and tighten the bolt.

23   Refit the wheel, and lower the vehicle to the ground. Tighten the wheel nuts to the specified torque.

24   Tighten the suspension strut upper mounting nut to the specified torque, while holding the piston rod with an 8 mm Allen key. If the adaptor needed to do this is not available, the nut can be tightened ini-

5.3 Coil spring compressor tools fitted to the coil spring

5.4 Unscrewing the nut from the top of the strut

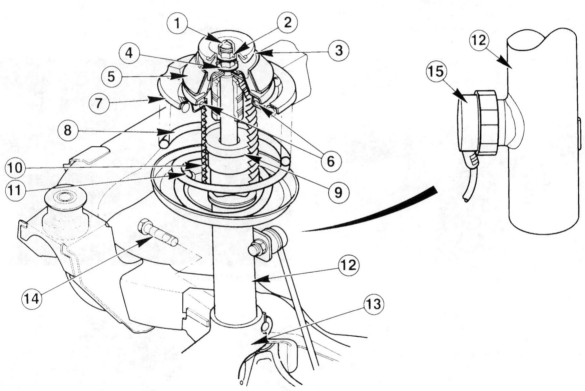

5.5A Front suspension strut components

1	Cap	5	Top mounting	9	Bump stop	13	Steering knuckle
2	Nut	6	Thrust bearing	10	Gaiter	14	Clamp bolt
3	Retainer	7	Upper spring seat	11	Lower spring seat	15	Solenoid valve for models
4	Nut	8	Spring	12	Strut		with adaptive damping

tially with a ring spanner while the piston rod is held. Final tightening can then be carried out using a torque wrench and a conventional socket **(see illustration)**.

5   Front suspension strut - overhaul

Warning: *Before attempting to dismantle the front suspension strut, a tool to hold the coil spring in compression must be obtained.* **Do not** *attempt to use makeshift methods. Uncontrolled release of the spring could cause damage and personal injury. Use a high-quality spring compressor, and carefully follow the tool manufacturer's instructions provided with it. After removing the coil spring with the compressor still fitted, place it in a safe, isolated area.*

1   If the front suspension struts exhibit signs of wear (leaking fluid,

loss of damping capability, sagging or cracked coil springs) then they should be dismantled and overhauled as necessary. The struts themselves cannot be serviced, and should be renewed if faulty, but the springs and related components can be renewed. To maintain balanced characteristics on both sides of the vehicle, the components on both sides should be renewed at the same time.

2   With the strut removed from the vehicle, clean away all external dirt, then mount it in a vice.

3   Fit the coil spring compressor tools (ensuring that they are fully engaged), and compress the spring until all tension is relieved from the upper mounting **(see illustration)**.

4   Hold the strut piston with an Allen key, and unscrew the thrust bearing retaining nut with a ring spanner **(see illustration)**.

5   Withdraw the top mounting, thrust bearing, upper spring seat and spring, followed by the gaiter and the bump stop **(see illustrations)**.

10

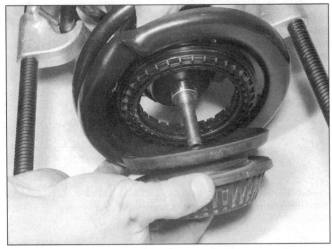

5.5B Removing the top mounting from the strut

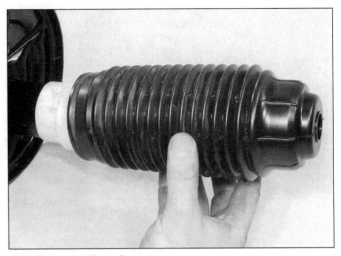

5.5C Removing the gaiter

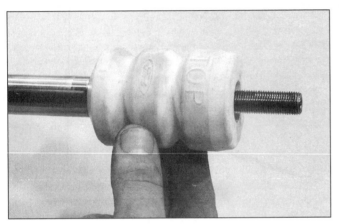

5.5D Removing the bump stop

6.2A Unscrew the nut . . .

6   If a new spring is to be fitted, the original spring must now be carefully released from the compressor. If it is to be re-used, the spring can be left in compression.

7   With the strut assembly now completely dismantled, examine all the components for wear and damage, and check the bearing for smoothness of operation. Renew components as necessary.

8   Examine the strut for signs of fluid leakage. Check the strut piston for signs of pitting along its entire length, and check the strut body for signs of damage. Test the operation of the strut, while holding it in an upright position, by moving the piston through a full stroke, and then through short strokes of 50 to 100 mm. In both cases, the resistance felt should be smooth and continuous. If the resistance is jerky, un-even, or if there is any visible sign of wear or damage to the strut, re-newal is necessary.

9   Reassembly is a reversal of dismantling, noting the following points:

(a) *Make sure that the coil spring ends are correctly located in the upper and lower seats before releasing the compressor.*

(b) *Check that the bearing is correctly fitted to the piston rod seat.*

(c) *Tighten the thrust bearing retaining nut to the specified torque.*

6   Front anti-roll bar and links - removal and refitting

Removal

1   Apply the handbrake, jack up the front of the vehicle and support it on axle stands. Remove both front wheels.

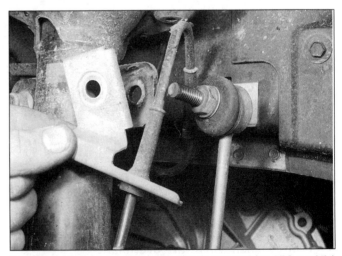

6.2B . . . and disconnect the anti-roll bar link and (on ABS models) the sensor wiring support bracket

2   Unscrew the nuts, and disconnect the anti-roll bar links from the front suspension struts on both sides of the vehicle. Note that, on models with ABS, the wheel sensor wiring support brackets are lo-cated beneath the nuts **(see illustrations)**.

3   Unscrew and remove the anti-roll bar mounting bolts from the en-

7.3 One of the nuts and bolts securing the lower arm to the subframe

7.7A Unscrew the lower arm balljoint clamp bolt . . .

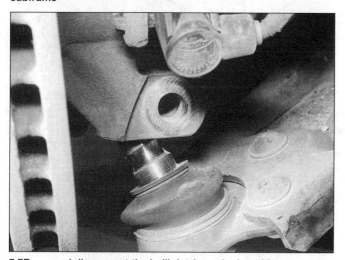

7.7B . . . and disconnect the balljoint from the knuckle

gine subframe on both sides of the vehicle.
4   Withdraw the anti-roll bar from one side of the vehicle, taking care not to damage the surrounding components.
5   If necessary, unscrew the nuts and remove the links from the anti-roll bar.

Refitting
6   Refitting is a reversal of the removal procedure.

7   Front suspension lower arm - removal, overhaul and refitting

Removal
1   Apply the handbrake, jack up the front of the vehicle and support it on axle stands. Remove the appropriate wheel.
2   If removing the right-hand side lower arm, remove the auxiliary drivebelt cover where necessary.
3   Unscrew and remove the nuts and bolts securing the lower arm to the subframe (see illustration).
4   Unscrew the nuts and disconnect the anti-roll bar links from the anti-roll bar on both sides. Swivel the anti-roll bar upwards away from the lower arm.
5   Extract the split pin from the track rod end balljoint nut. Unscrew the nut, and detach the rod from the arm on the steering knuckle using a conventional balljoint removal tool. Take care not to damage the

balljoint seal.
6   Remove the clip securing the driveshaft inner gaiter to the inner CV joint, and disconnect the gaiter from the CV joint housing. This is necessary to prevent damage to the gaiter when the steering knuckle is moved outwards to remove the lower arm.
7   Note which way round the front suspension lower arm balljoint clamp bolt is fitted, then unscrew and remove it from the knuckle assembly. Lever the balljoint down from the knuckle; if it is tight, prise the joint open carefully using a large flat-bladed tool. Take care not to damage the balljoint seal during the separation procedure. Support the inner end of the driveshaft on an axle stand (see illustrations).
8   Remove the lower arm from the subframe, and withdraw it from the vehicle.

Overhaul
9   Examine the rubber bushes and the suspension lower balljoint for wear and damage. The balljoint may be renewed as described in Section 8. The rubber bushes may be removed using a press, or a length of metal tubing together with a long bolt, washers and nut.
10   Note that the front and rear bushes are different. The front one has a solid rubber bush with a cylindrical inner tube, whereas the rear one has a voided rubber bush with a barrel-shaped inner tube (see illustration).
11   Press the new bushes into the lower arm, using the same method as used for removal. Note that, when fitting the rear bush, the voids must be in line with the front bush location. On later models, a pip on the rear bush must be aligned with a triangular alignment mark on the arm.

Refitting
12   Locate the lower arm on the subframe, and insert the mounting bolts. Fit the nuts and tighten them in stages, first to the specified torque and then through the angle specified.
13   If removed, locate the tripod on the inner end of the driveshaft in the CV joint housing, then refit the gaiter, together with a new clip.
14   Refit the front suspension lower arm balljoint to the knuckle assembly, and insert the clamp bolt with its head facing forwards. Refit the nut and tighten to the specified torque.
15   Refit the track rod end balljoint to the steering knuckle, and tighten the nut to the specified torque. Check that the split pin holes are aligned; if necessary, turn the nut to align the holes, making sure that the torque wrench setting is still within the specified range. Insert a new split pin, and bend it back to secure.
16   Swivel the anti-roll bar down, then reconnect the links to the bar and tighten the nuts to the specified torque.
17   If working on the right-hand side, refit the auxiliary drivebelt cover where necessary.
18   Refit the wheel, and lower the vehicle to the ground.

10

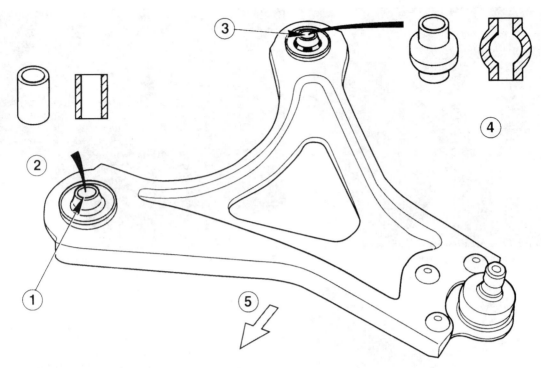

7.10 Front suspension lower arm bushes

1	Front bush	3	Rear bush	5	Front of vehicle
2	Cylindrical inner tube	4	Barrel-shaped inner tube		

8.0 Original riveted front suspension lower arm balljoint

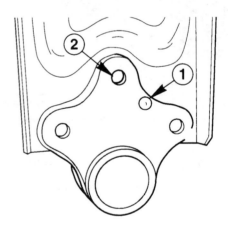

8.5 Location lug (1) and bolt hole (2) in the front suspension lower arm balljoint

8   Front suspension lower arm balljoint - renewal

Note: *If the lower arm balljoint is worn, either the complete lower arm or the balljoint alone can be renewed. If the balljoint has already been renewed, it will be bolted in position; if the original balljoint is being renewed, then it will be riveted in position (see illustration). This Section describes the renewal of a riveted balljoint.*

1   Remove the front suspension lower arm as described in Section 7. It is not recommended that the balljoint be replaced with the lower arm in position on the vehicle; the accurate drilling necessary may not be possible, and the holes in the arm may be enlarged.

2   With the lower arm on the bench, use a 3 mm drill to make a pilot hole through each of the three rivets. Now use a 9 mm drill to drill the rivets to a depth of 12 mm, then use a 7 or 8 mm drift to drive the rivets out of the arm.

3   Clean any rust or dirt from the rivet holes.

4   The new balljoint is supplied with a protective plastic cover over the rubber boot and stub, and it is recommended that this remains in position until it is time to connect the balljoint to the steering knuckle.

5   Locate the new balljoint on the lower arm, and use three new bolts to secure it, inserting the bolts *from the top* of the arm. Tighten the nuts to the specified torque. Make sure that the location lug on the balljoint engages the hole in the lower arm **(see illustration)**.

6   Refit the front suspension lower arm as described in Section 7.

9   Rear hub and bearings (Saloon/Hatchback models) - inspection and renewal

Note: *Removal of the rear hub damages the bearings, and renders them unserviceable for future use. The hub and bearing assembly **must** always be renewed if it is removed.*

10.5 Two of the bolts securing the brake backplate to the rear suspension knuckle

Inspection

1   The rear hub bearings are non-adjustable, and are supplied complete with the hub. It is not possible to renew the bearings separately from the hub.
2   To check the bearings for excessive wear, chock the front wheels, then jack up the rear of the vehicle and support it on axle stands. Fully release the handbrake.
3   Grip the rear wheel at the top and bottom, and attempt to rock it. If excessive movement is noted, or if there is any roughness or vibration felt when the wheel is spun, it is indicative that the hub bearings are worn.

Renewal

4   Remove the rear wheel.
5   On models fitted with rear brake drums, remove the rear brake drum as described in Chapter 9.
6   On models fitted with rear brake discs, remove the rear brake disc as described in Chapter 9.
7   On all models, tap off the dust cap and unscrew the hub nut. Note that the nut is of special laminated design, and should only be re-used a maximum of 5 times. It is a good idea to mark the nut with a file every time it is removed. Obtain a new one if necessary.
8   Using a suitable puller, draw the hub and bearing assembly off the stub axle. Note that this procedure renders the bearings unserviceable for future use.
9   Locate the new rear hub and bearing assembly on the stub axle, then refit the hub nut and tighten it to the specified torque.
10   Tap the dust cap fully onto the hub.
11   Refit the rear brake disc or drum as applicable, as described in Chapter 9.
12   Refit the rear wheel, and lower the vehicle to the ground.

10   Rear suspension knuckle (Saloon/Hatchback models) - removal and refitting

Note: *Removal of the rear hub from the knuckle damages the bearings, and renders them unserviceable for future use. The hub and bearing assembly **must** always be renewed if it is removed.*

Removal

1   Chock the front wheels, then jack up the rear of the vehicle and support it on axle stands. Remove the appropriate rear wheel.
2   When applicable, remove the ABS sensor from the knuckle as described in Chapter 9.

3   Remove the rear hub and bearing assembly as described in Section 9.

Drum brake models
4   Fit a brake hose clamp to the flexible brake hose, then release the clip and detach the flexible hose from the strut. Unscrew the union nut, and detach the rigid brake pipe from the wheel cylinder. If preferred (to eliminate any bleeding procedure during refitting) the rigid brake pipe may remain attached to the wheel cylinder, provided that care is taken to prevent damage to both the rigid and flexible brake pipes.
5   Unbolt the backplate from the rear suspension knuckle **(see illustration)**, and support it to one side on an axle stand. The brake shoes and handbrake cable can remain attached.

Disc brake models
6   Unbolt the splash shield from the rear suspension knuckle.

All models
7   Unscrew and remove the bolt securing the tie-bar to the bottom of the knuckle, and move the tie-bar downwards.
8   Unscrew and remove the bolts securing the front and rear lower arms to the knuckle, and move the arms to one side.
9   Support the knuckle on an axle stand, then unscrew and remove the clamp bolt securing the knuckle to the strut.
10   Prise the top of the knuckle apart carefully using a large flat-bladed tool, and withdraw the knuckle downwards from the strut. Withdraw the knuckle from under the rear wheel arch.

Refitting

11   Locate the knuckle fully on the strut, then insert the clamp bolt and tighten to the specified torque.
12   Refit the front and rear lower arms to the knuckle, and insert the bolts finger-tight at this stage.
13   Refit the tie-bar to the bottom of the knuckle, and insert the bolt finger-tight at this stage.
14   Refit the backplate (or splash shield, as applicable) to the rear suspension knuckle, and tighten the bolts to the specified torque.

Drum brake models
15   Reconnect the rigid brake pipe to the wheel cylinder (if disconnected), and tighten the union nut.
16   Attach the flexible hose to the strut, refit the clip, and remove the hose clamp.

All models
17   Fit a new rear hub and bearing assembly as described in Section 9.
18   Where applicable, refit the ABS sensor as described in Chapter 9.
19   Refit the wheel, and lower the vehicle to the ground.
20   With the weight of the vehicle on the suspension, fully tighten the mounting bolts for the tie-bar and lower arms.
21   Where applicable, bleed the hydraulic brake circuit as described in Chapter 9.

11   Rear suspension strut (Saloon/Hatchback models) - removal and refitting

Note: *Before attempting to remove the rear suspension strut, a tool to hold the coil spring in compression must be obtained. Careful use of conventional coil spring compressors will prove satisfactory.*

Removal

1   In order to remove the rear suspension strut, the coil spring must be temporarily compressed. This will enable the piston rod to be retracted into the strut, and will provide additional room for releasing the strut from the bump stop on top of the rear suspension crossmember.
Warning: *It is important to only use a high-quality spring compressor; carefully follow the tool manufacturer's instructions provided with it.*
2   Chock the front wheels, then jack up the rear of the vehicle and support it on axle stands. Remove the appropriate wheel.

10

11.3 Unclipping the ABS sensor wiring from the strut

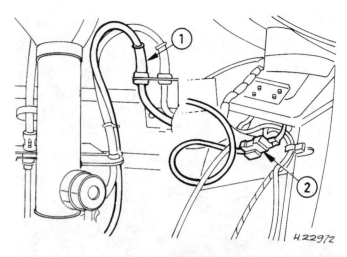

11.4 Location of the adaptive damping lead (1) and multi-plug (2)

11.8A Tie-bar mounting bolt on knuckle

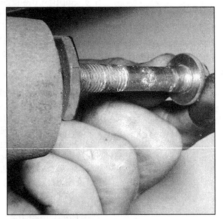

11.8B Remove the bolt . . .

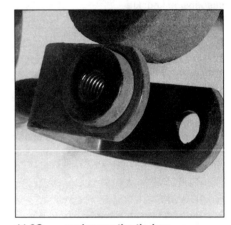

11.8C . . . and move the tie-bar downwards

11.9A Unscrew the bolt . . .

11.9B . . . and remove the rear lower arm from the knuckle

3   Where fitted, unclip the ABS sensor wiring from the strut, and re-move the sensor from the knuckle as described in Chapter 9 (see illus-tration).
4   On models fitted with adaptive damping, unclip the wiring from the strut and disconnect the multi-plug (see illustration).
5   On drum brake models, fit a brake hose clamp to the rear flexible brake hose, then unscrew the union nut securing the rigid brake pipe to the flexible hose on the strut. Extract the clip, and disconnect the flexible hose from the strut.
6   On models fitted with rear disc brakes, unbolt the caliper from the knuckle as described in Chapter 9, but leave the hydraulic hose at-

tached. Support the caliper on an axle stand, making sure that the flex-ible hose is not strained.
7   Unscrew the nut securing the rear anti-roll bar link to the front lower arm on the appropriate side. Hold the actual link with an ad-justable spanner or grips while unscrewing the nut, to prevent damage to the link joint.
8   Unscrew and remove the bolt securing the tie-bar to the bottom of the knuckle. Move the tie-bar downwards (see illustrations).
9   Unscrew and remove the bolts securing the front and rear lower arms to the knuckle, and move the arms to one side (see illustra-tions).

11.10A Support the knuckle on a trolley jack . . .

11.10B . . . and remove the knuckle-to-strut clamp bolt

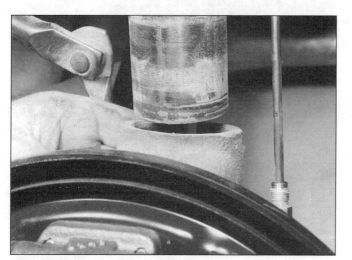

11.11 Separating the knuckle from the strut

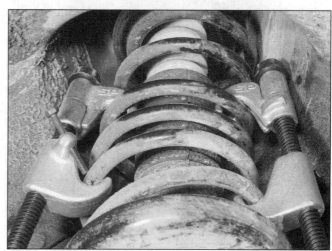

11.12 Compressor tools fitted to the rear coil spring

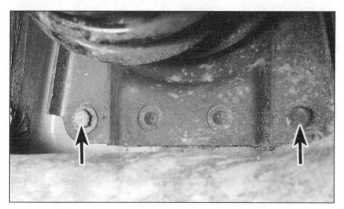

11.13 Bolts (arrowed) securing the strut upper mounting to the underbody

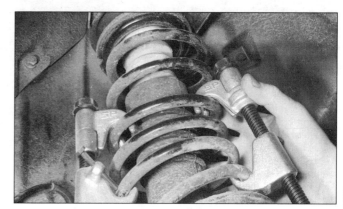

11.14 Removing the rear suspension strut

10 Support the knuckle on a trolley jack, then unscrew and remove the clamp bolt securing the knuckle to the strut **(see illustrations)**.

11 Prise the clamp on the knuckle apart using a large flat-bladed tool. Disconnect the knuckle from the strut, and lower it on the trolley jack as far as possible, taking care not to damage the handbrake cable **(see illustration)**.

12 Fit the coil spring compressor tool (ensuring that it is fully engaged), and compress the coil spring until all tension is relieved from the upper and lower mountings **(see illustration)**. This will also release

the bracket on the strut from the bump stop rubber on the top of the rear crossmember.

13 Support the strut, then reach up under the wheel arch, and unscrew the two bolts securing the upper mounting to the underbody **(see illustration)**.

14 Slightly lift the strut, to force the piston into the shock absorber and release the strut bracket from the bump stop on the crossmember. Lower the strut assembly and withdraw it from under the vehicle **(see illustration)**.

10

12.1A Rear strut dismantling - unscrew the upper mounting nut . . .

12.1B . . . remove the cup . . .

12.1C . . . upper mounting bracket and seat . . .

12.1D . . . gaiter and bump stop . . .

12.1E . . . and coil spring

Refitting

15 Locate the strut assembly (together with the coil spring compressor tool) under the wheel arch, and locate the bracket on the bump stop on the rear suspension crossmember. Insert the two bolts securing the upper mounting to the underbody tower, and tighten them to the specified torque.

16 Carefully release the coil spring compressor tool, making sure that the spring locates correctly in the upper and lower seats, and that the strut bracket locates on the crossmember bump stop. The bump stop is tapered inwards, and the strut bracket should be fully engaged with it before releasing the coil spring.

17 Raise the knuckle and engage it with the strut, then insert the clamp bolt and tighten to the specified torque.

18 Reconnect the front and rear lower arms to the knuckle, and finger-tighten the bolts at this stage.

19 Reconnect the tie-bar to the bottom of the knuckle, and finger-tighten the bolt at this stage.

20 Refit the anti-roll bar link to the lower arm, and tighten the nut to the specified torque.

21 On disc brake models, refit the caliper bracket to the knuckle, and tighten the mounting bolts to the specified torque (see Chapter 9). Make sure that the flexible brake hose is not twisted.

22 On drum brake models, connect the flexible hose to the strut, insert the clip, then insert the rigid brake line and tighten the union nut. Remove the brake hose clamp, then bleed the hydraulic brake circuit as described in Chapter 9.

23 Where applicable, reconnect the wiring multi-plug for the adap-

tive damping, and clip the wiring to the strut.

24 Where applicable, refit the ABS sensor as described in Chapter 9, and clip the wiring to the strut.

25 Refit the wheel, and lower the vehicle to the ground.

26 With the weight of the vehicle on the rear suspension, fully tighten the lower arm and tie-bar mounting bolts.

12 Rear suspension strut (Saloon/Hatchback models) - overhaul

1 The procedure is similar to that for the front suspension strut, and reference should be made to Section 5. Note that the spring compressor tools will already be in position on the coil spring following the removal operation. Refer also to the accompanying illustrations for details of the separate components **(see illustrations)**.

13 Rear anti-roll bar and links (Saloon/Hatchback models) - removal and refitting

Removal

1 Chock the front wheels, then jack up the rear of the vehicle and support it on axle stands. Remove both rear wheels.

2 Unscrew the nuts securing the anti-roll bar links to the front lower

13.2A Loosen the nut . . .

13.2B . . . remove the nut and rubber bush . . .

13.2C . . . and remove the anti-roll bar link from the lower arm

13.3 Rear anti-roll bar mounting clamp

14.9 Bolt securing the rear lower arm to the crossmember

arms on both sides. Hold the upper part of the links with a spanner while loosening the nuts. Recover the rubber bushes **(see illustrations)**.

3   Unscrew the bolts securing the anti-roll bar mounting clamps to the rear suspension crossmember, then unhook the clamps and withdraw the anti-roll bar from under the vehicle **(see illustration)**.

4   Examine the rubber bushes for the mounting clamps and links, and if necessary renew them. The links are available individually.

Refitting

5   Locate the anti-roll bar on the rear crossmember, hook the mounting clamps in position, and insert the bolts. Tighten the bolts to the specified torque.

6   Locate the anti-roll bar links in the front lower arms on both sides, making sure that the rubber bushes are in position. Refit the nuts and tighten them to the specified torque.

7   Refit the rear wheels, and lower the vehicle to the ground.

14 Rear suspension lower arms (Saloon/Hatchback models) - removal and refitting

Removal

1   Chock the front wheels, then jack up the rear of the vehicle and support it on axle stands. Remove the appropriate rear wheel.

Front lower arm

2   To remove the front lower arm, it is necessary to remove the fuel tank first. Refer to Chapter 4 for details.

3   Unscrew the nut and disconnect the anti-roll bar link from the lower arm. Hold the actual link with an adjustable spanner or grips while unscrewing the nut, to prevent damage to the link joint. Recover the rubber bush.

4   Unscrew and remove the bolt securing the front lower arm to the knuckle.

5   Unscrew and remove the bolt securing the front lower arm to the crossmember.

6   Withdraw the front lower arm from under the vehicle.

Rear lower arm

7   Unscrew and remove the bolt securing the rear lower arm to the knuckle.

8   The bolt securing the rear lower arm to the crossmember has an eccentric head and spacer, which are used to adjust the rear toe setting. Before removing this bolt, mark its position, using a scriber or similar sharp instrument through the aperture in the crossmember.

9   Unscrew and remove the bolt securing the rear lower arm to the crossmember **(see illustration)**. The bolt may be removed through the aperture in the crossmember. Recover the eccentric spacer.

10   Withdraw the rear lower arm from under the vehicle.

Refitting

11   Refitting is a reversal of the removal procedure, but the arm mounting bolts should be finger-tightened initially, and only fully tight-

10

14.11 "TOP" marking on the rear lower arm

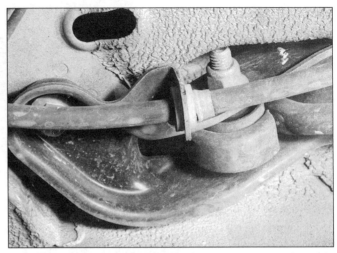

15.4 Tie-bar bracket on the underbody

ened after the vehicle is lowered to the ground, so that its weight is on the rear suspension. Note that the rear lower arm is marked "TOP" for correct refitting **(see illustration)**. The rear toe setting should be checked, and if necessary adjusted, at the earliest opportunity.

15 Rear suspension tie-bar (Saloon/Hatchback models) - removal and refitting

Removal

1   Chock the front wheels, then jack up the rear of the vehicle and support it on axle stands. Remove the appropriate rear wheel.
2   Disconnect the handbrake cable from the tie-bar bracket on the underbody.
3   Unscrew and remove the bolt securing the tie-bar bracket to the rear suspension knuckle.
4   Unscrew the bolts securing the tie-bar bracket to the underbody, and withdraw the bracket from the vehicle **(see illustration)**.
5   Mount the bracket in a vice, then unscrew and remove the bolt, and remove the tie-bar from the bracket.
6   It is not possible to renew the rubber bushes - if they are worn excessively, the tie-bar should be renewed complete.

Refitting

7   Refitting is a reversal of the removal procedure. The bracket-to-underbody bolts should be fully tightened to the specified torque before lowering the vehicle. The bolts securing the tie-bar to the bracket and knuckle should be finger-tightened initially, and only fully tightened after the vehicle is lowered to the ground, so that its weight is on the rear suspension.

16 Rear suspension crossmember (Saloon/Hatchback models) - removal and refitting

Note: *Before attempting to remove the rear suspension crossmember, tools to hold the coil springs in compression must be obtained. Careful use of conventional coil spring compressors will prove satisfactory.*

Removal

1   Chock the front wheels, then jack up the rear of the vehicle and support it on axle stands. Remove both rear wheels.
2   Remove the complete exhaust system as described in Chapter 4.
3   Unscrew and remove the bolts securing the tie-bars to the rear suspension knuckles, and disconnect the tie-bars.

16.8 One of the rear suspension crossmember mounting bolts

4   Unscrew the nuts securing the rear anti-roll bar links to the front lower arms. Hold the actual links stationary while the nuts are being unscrewed, to prevent damage to the joints. Swivel the anti-roll bar upwards, and recover the rubber bushes.
5   Where applicable, remove the ABS wheel sensor from the rear suspension knuckle as described in Chapter 9.
6   Unscrew and remove the bolts, and disconnect both lower arms from the rear suspension knuckle.
7   To allow the rear suspension struts to be released from the rubber stops on the top of the crossmember, it is necessary to fit coil spring compressor tools to both of the rear coil springs, and compress them until all tension is removed from the upper and lower mountings. **Warning:** *It is important to only use high-quality spring compressors, and to carefully follow the tool manufacturer's instructions provided with them.* With the compressor tools fitted, support the struts to one side.
8   Support the rear suspension crossmember on a trolley jack, then unscrew the four mounting bolts from the underbody **(see illustration)**.
9   Lower the crossmember to the ground.
10   Unscrew the bolts securing the anti-roll bar clamps to the crossmember, then remove the clamps and withdraw the anti-roll bar.
11   Remove the lower arms from the crossmember as described in Section 14.

Refitting

12   Refitting is a reversal of the removal procedure. Ford specify the use of a special tool (tool number 15-097) to accurately align the cross-

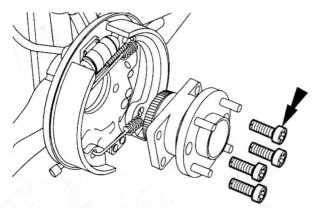

17.7 Mounting bolts (arrowed) for the rear hub on Estate models

19.3 Rear shock absorber lower mounting bolt (Estate)

member onto the underbody before tightening the mounting bolts. This tool should be obtained if possible, since inaccurate alignment would result in bad handling and excessive tyre wear. The tie-bar and arm mounting bolts should be finger-tightened initially, and only fully tightened after the vehicle is lowered to the ground, so that its weight is on the rear suspension. The rear toe setting should be checked, and if necessary adjusted, at the earliest opportunity.

17 Rear hub and bearings (Estate models) - inspection and renewal

Inspection
1   The rear hub bearings are non-adjustable, and are supplied complete with the hub. It is not possible to renew the bearings separately from the hub.
2   To check the bearings for excessive wear, chock the front wheels, then jack up the rear of the vehicle and support it on axle stands. Fully release the handbrake.
3   Grip the rear wheel at the top and bottom, and attempt to rock it. If excessive movement is noted, or if there is any roughness or vibration felt when the wheel is spun, it is indicative that the hub bearings are worn.

Renewal
4   Remove the rear wheel.
5   On drum brake models, remove the rear brake drum as described in Chapter 9.
6   On disc brake models, remove the rear brake disc as described in Chapter 9.
7   Turning the hub as necessary, line up the hole in the flange with the each of the bolts securing the hub assembly to the rear suspension knuckle; unscrew and remove the bolts **(see illustration)**.
8   Withdraw the hub and bearing assembly. Refit two of the hub mounting bolts, to hold the backplate/splash shield in place.
9   If necessary, the stub shaft may be removed from the hub for inspection of the bearing, by unscrewing the hub nut. Note that the hub nut is of special laminated design, and may only be re-used a maximum of five times. (It is a good idea to file a small notch on the nut every time it is removed; obtain a new nut if necessary.) Tighten the nut on reassembly.
10   Fit the new hub and bearing assembly using a reversal of the removal procedure. Tighten all nuts and bolts to the specified torque.

18 Rear suspension knuckle (Estate models) - removal and refitting

Removal
1   Chock the front wheels, then jack up the rear of the vehicle and

support it on axle stands. Remove the appropriate rear wheel, and release the handbrake.
2   Position a trolley jack or axle stand beneath the rear suspension lower arm, to keep the coil spring in compression.
3   Where applicable, remove the ABS sensor as described in Chapter 9.

Drum brake models
4   Remove the rear brake drum as described in Chapter 9.
5   Disconnect the flexible hydraulic brake hose at the bracket on the rear suspension crossmember as described in Chapter 9.

Disc brake models
6   Remove the rear brake disc as described in Chapter 9.

All models
7   Remove the rear hub as described in Section 17.
8   Remove the backplate or splash shield, as applicable. On drum brake models, support the backplate assembly on an axle stand, to prevent damage to the handbrake cable.
9   Unscrew and remove the shock absorber lower mounting bolt.
10   Unscrew and remove the three bolts securing the tie-bar to the knuckle.
11   Unscrew and remove the bolt securing the front lower arm to the knuckle.
12   Unscrew and remove the bolt securing the upper arm to the knuckle.
13   Support the knuckle, then unscrew and remove the bolt securing the rear lower arm to the knuckle, and withdraw the knuckle.

Refitting
14   Refitting is a reversal of the removal procedure, but delay fully tightening the rubber bush mounting bolts until the weight of the vehicle is on the suspension. Tighten all bolts to the specified torque. Where the flexible rear brake hose was disconnected, bleed the hydraulic system as described in Chapter 9. Finally check, and if necessary adjust, the rear wheel toe setting as described in Section 36.

19 Rear shock absorber (Estate models) - removal, testing and refitting

Removal
1   Chock the front wheels, then jack up the rear of the vehicle and support it on axle stands. Remove the appropriate wheel.
2   Position a trolley jack under the coil spring area of the rear lower suspension arm, to keep the coil spring in compression.
3   Unscrew and remove the shock absorber lower mounting bolt **(see illustration)**.
4   Unscrew and remove the upper mounting bolt, and withdraw the shock absorber from under the vehicle.

10

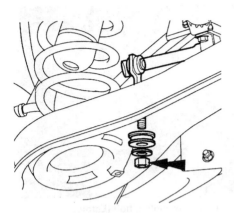

20.2A Mounting nut (arrowed) and rubber bush securing the rear anti-roll bar link to the rear lower arm

20.2B View of the anti-roll bar link nut through the rear lower arm

20.3 Anti-roll bar mounting clamp on the rear suspension crossmember

21.5 Rear lower arm-to-knuckle mounting bolt

21.6 Front lower arm-to-knuckle mounting bolt

Testing

5   Check the mounting rubbers for damage and deterioration. If they are worn, they may be renewed separately from the shock absorber body.
6   Mount the shock absorber in a vice, gripping it by the lower mounting. Examine the shock absorber for signs of fluid leakage. Test the operation of the shock absorber by moving it through a full stroke, and then through short strokes of 50 to 100 mm. In both cases, the resistance felt should be smooth and continuous. If the resistance is jerky or uneven, the shock absorber should be renewed.

Refitting

7   Refitting is a reversal of the removal procedure, but tighten the mounting bolts to the specified torque.

20 Rear anti-roll bar and links (Estate models) - removal and refitting

Removal

1   Chock the front wheels, then jack up the rear of the vehicle and support it on axle stands. Remove both rear wheels.
2   Unscrew the nuts, and remove the washers and bushes securing the anti-roll bar links to the rear lower arms **(see illustrations)**.
3   Using a Torx key, unscrew the bolts securing the anti-roll bar mounting clamps to the rear suspension crossmember; release the clamps, and withdraw the anti-roll bar from under the vehicle **(see illustration)**.
4   Examine the rubber bushes for the mounting clamps and links, and if necessary renew them. The links are available individually.

Refitting

5   Locate the anti-roll bar on the rear crossmember, then refit the clamps and tighten the bolts to the specified torque.
6   Refit the anti-roll bar links to the rear lower arms, together with the bushes and washers. Tighten the nuts to the specified torque, while holding the actual links stationary in their central position.
7   Refit the rear wheels, and lower the vehicle to the ground.

21 Rear coil spring (Estate models) - removal and refitting

Note: *Before attempting to remove the rear suspension coil spring, a tool to hold the coil spring in compression must be obtained. Careful use of conventional coil spring compressors will prove satisfactory.*

Removal

1   Chock the front wheels, then jack up the rear of the vehicle and support it on axle stands. Remove the appropriate wheel.
2   Support the weight of the rear lower arm beneath the coil spring position with a trolley jack.
3   Fit the coil spring compressor tool (ensuring that it is fully engaged), and compress the coil spring until all tension is relieved from the upper mounting.
4   Unscrew the nut, and remove the washer and bush attaching the anti-roll bar link to the rear lower arm.
5   Unscrew and remove the bolt securing the rear lower arm to the knuckle **(see illustration)**.
6   Unscrew and remove the bolt securing the front lower arm to the knuckle **(see illustration)**.

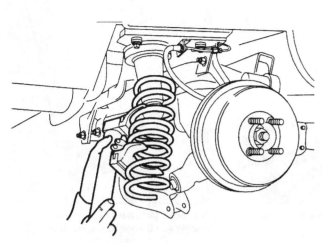

21.7 Removing the coil spring, with compressor tool attached, from under the vehicle

21.9 Correct location of the coil spring in the upper seat (arrowed)

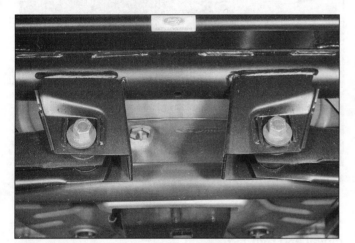

22.3 Bolts securing the rear lower arms to the crossmember - note the eccentric spacers

23.2 Front lower arm-to-crossmember securing bolt

7   Lower the rear lower arm, and withdraw the coil spring from under the vehicle. Take care to keep the compressor tool in full engagement with the coil spring **(see illustration)**.

8   If a new coil spring is to be fitted, the original coil spring must be released from the compressor. If it is to be re-used, the coil spring can be left in compression.

Refitting

9   Refitting is a reversal of the removal procedure, but make sure that the coil spring is located correctly in the upper and lower seats **(see illustration)**. Delay fully tightening the two lower arm mounting bolts until the weight of the vehicle is on the rear suspension. Finally check, and if necessary adjust, the rear wheel toe setting as described in Section 36.

22 Rear suspension rear lower arm (Estate models) - removal and refitting

Removal

1   Remove the rear suspension coil spring as described in Section 21.

2   The bolt securing the rear lower arm to the crossmember has an eccentric head and spacer, which are used to adjust the rear toe set-

ting. Before removing this bolt, mark its position, using a scriber or similar sharp instrument through the aperture in the crossmember.

3   Unscrew and remove the bolt securing the rear lower arm to the crossmember. The bolt may be removed through the aperture in the crossmember. Recover the eccentric spacer **(see illustration)**.

4   Withdraw the rear lower arm from under the vehicle.

Refitting

5   Refitting is a reversal of the removal procedure, but delay fully tightening the lower arm mounting bolts until the weight of the vehicle is on the rear suspension. Finally check, and if necessary adjust, the rear wheel toe setting as described in Section 36.

23 Rear suspension front lower arm (Estate models) - removal and refitting

Removal

1   Chock the front wheels, then jack up the rear of the vehicle and support it on axle stands. Remove the appropriate wheel.

2   Unscrew and remove the bolt securing the front lower arm to the crossmember **(see illustration)**.

3   Unscrew and remove the bolt securing the front lower arm to the

10

23.3 Front lower arm (arrowed)

24.3 Bolt (arrowed) securing the upper arm to the knuckle

25.7 Bolts (arrowed) securing the rear suspension tie-bar to the knuckle

25.8A Tie-bar bracket front bolt (arrowed) on the underbody

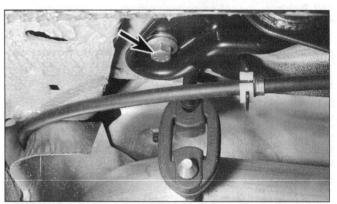

25.8B Tie-bar bracket rear bolt (arrowed) on the underbody

knuckle, and withdraw the arm from under the vehicle **(see illustration)**.

Refitting

4   Refitting is a reversal of the removal procedure, but delay fully tightening the mounting bolts until the weight of the vehicle is on the rear suspension.

24 Rear suspension upper arm (Estate models) - removal and refitting

Removal

1   Chock the front wheels, then jack up the rear of the vehicle and support it on axle stands. Remove the appropriate wheel.
2   Using a trolley jack, support the rear lower arm beneath the coil spring position.
3   Unscrew and remove the bolt securing the upper arm to the knuckle **(see illustration)**.
4   Unscrew and remove the bolt securing the upper arm to the crossmember, and withdraw the arm from under the vehicle.

Refitting

5   Refitting is a reversal of the removal procedure, but delay fully tightening the mounting bolts until the weight of the vehicle is on the rear suspension.

25 Rear suspension tie-bar (Estate models) - removal and refitting

Removal

1   Chock the front wheels, then jack up the rear of the vehicle and support it on axle stands. Remove the appropriate wheel.
2   Using a trolley jack, support the rear lower arm beneath the coil spring position.
3   Unscrew and remove the bolt securing the rear shock absorber to the knuckle.
4   Where applicable, release the ABS wheel sensor lead from the tie-bar.
5   Detach the handbrake cable from the tie-bar bracket.
6   Refer to Chapter 9, and disconnect the handbrake cable from the rear brake shoes or rear caliper, as applicable. Pass the cable through the hole in the tie-bar.
7   Unscrew and remove the three bolts securing the tie-bar to the knuckle **(see illustration)**.
8   Unbolt the tie-bar bracket from the underbody, and withdraw the assembly from under the vehicle **(see illustrations)**.
9   Mount the tie-bar in a vice, then unscrew the bolt, and separate the tie-bar from its bracket.
10   It is not possible to renew the rubber bush in the tie-bar, and if it is excessively worn, the complete tie-bar must be renewed.

Refitting

11   Refitting is a reversal of the removal procedure, but delay fully tightening the bolt which secures the arm to the bracket until the weight of the vehicle is on the rear suspension. On completion, check the operation of the handbrake.

26.7A Rear suspension crossmember rear mounting bolt

26.7B Rear suspension crossmember front mounting bolt

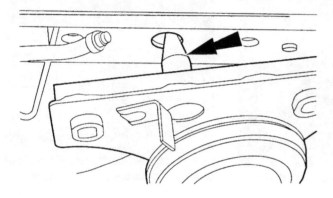

26.9 Guide pin (arrowed) for correct alignment of the rear crossmember

27.6 Removing the steering wheel retaining bolt

(a) When raising the crossmember, note that guide pins are provided to ensure correct alignment (see illustration).
(b) Delay fully tightening the suspension mounting bolts until the weight of the vehicle is on the rear suspension.
(c) Tighten all bolts to the specified torque.
(d) Bleed the brake hydraulic system as described in Chapter 9.
(e) Check, and if necessary adjust, the rear wheel toe setting as described in Section 36.

26 Rear suspension crossmember (Estate models) - removal and refitting

Removal

1   Chock the front wheels, then jack up the rear of the vehicle and support on axles stands. Remove both rear wheels. Make sure that the vehicle is supported high enough for the crossmember to be removed.
2   Disconnect the handbrake rear cables from the front primary cable, as described in Chapter 9.
3   Where applicable, remove the ABS wheel sensors from the rear knuckles, and disconnect the wiring leads from the clips as described in Chapter 9.
4   Disconnect the flexible brake hoses from the brackets on both sides of the crossmember, as described in Chapter 9.
5   Working on each side of the vehicle, unbolt the tie-bar brackets from the underbody.
6   Support the rear suspension crossmember on a trolley jack.
7   Unscrew the mounting bolts, and lower the crossmember to the ground (see illustrations).
8   If necessary, remove the suspension components from the crossmember as described in the appropriate Sections of this Chapter.

Refitting

9   Refitting is a reversal of the removal procedure, noting the following points:

27 Steering wheel - removal and refitting

Warning: All models are equipped with an air bag system. Make sure that the safety recommendations given in Chapter 12 are followed, to prevent personal injury.

Removal

1   Disconnect the battery negative (earth) lead (refer to Chapter 5, Section 1).
2   Warning: Before proceeding, wait a minimum of 15 minutes, as a precaution against accidental firing of the air bag unit. This period ensures that any stored energy in the back-up capacitor is dissipated.
3   Turn the steering wheel so that the front wheels are in the straight-ahead position.
4   Unscrew the screws, and remove the steering column upper and lower shrouds.
5   From the rear of the steering wheel, unscrew the air bag module mounting screws. Carefully lift the module from the steering wheel, and disconnect the air bag multi-plug and horn wiring connections. Warning: Position the air bag module in a safe place, with the mechanism facing downwards as a precaution against accidental operation.
6   Make sure that the steering lock is not engaged. Unscrew the retaining bolt from the centre of the steering wheel (see illustration).

10

27.7 Feeding the horn and air bag wiring through the hole in the steering wheel hub

27.9 Tightening the steering wheel retaining bolt

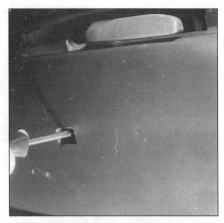

28.4A Unscrew the screws from the lower shroud . . .

28.4B . . . remove the rubber ring . . .

28.4C . . . and remove the lower shroud

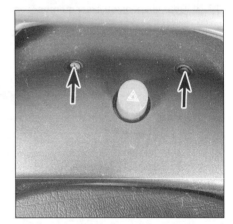

28.4D Upper shroud retaining screws (arrowed)

7   Remove the steering wheel from the top of the column, while feeding the horn and air bag wiring through the hole in the steering wheel hub **(see illustration)**.

Refitting

8   Make sure that the front wheels are still facing straight-ahead, then locate the steering wheel on the top of the steering column.
9   Refit the retaining bolt, and tighten it to the specified torque while holding the steering wheel **(see illustration)**. Do not tighten the bolt with the steering lock engaged, as this may damage the lock.
10   Reconnect the horn wiring connections and air bag multi-plug.
11   Locate the air bag module/horn contact on the steering wheel, then insert the mounting screws and tighten them.
12   Refit the steering column upper and lower shrouds. Insert and tighten the screws.
13   Reconnect the battery negative lead.

---

28 Steering column - removal, inspection and refitting

Warning: *All models are equipped with an air bag system. Make sure that the safety recommendations given in Chapter 12 are followed, to prevent personal injury.*

Removal

1   Disconnect the battery negative (earth) lead (refer to Chapter 5, Section 1).
2   **Warning:** *Before proceeding, wait a minimum of 15 minutes, as a*

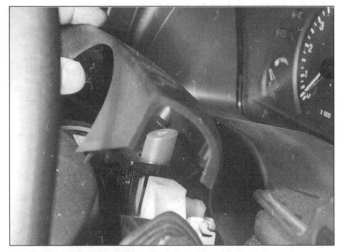

28.4E Removing the upper shroud

precaution against accidental firing of the air bag unit. This period ensures that any stored energy in the back-up capacitor is dissipated.
3   Turn the steering wheel so that the front wheels are in the straight-ahead position. Remove the ignition key, then turn the steering wheel slightly as necessary until the steering lock engages.
4   Unscrew the screws, and remove the steering column lower and upper shrouds. As the lower shroud is being removed, it will be necessary to remove the rubber ring from the ignition switch/steering lock **(see illustrations)**.

28.6A Unscrew the clamp plate bolt . . .

28.6B . . . and swivel the clamp plate around

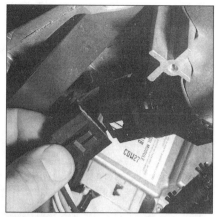

28.7A Disconnecting the multi-plug from the ignition switch

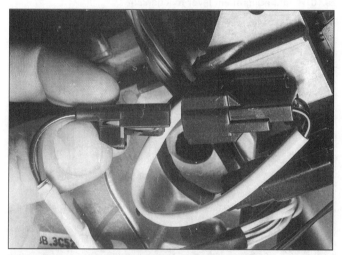

28.7B Disconnecting the small multi-plug . . .

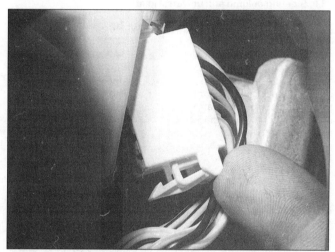

28.7C . . . and main multi-plug from the steering column

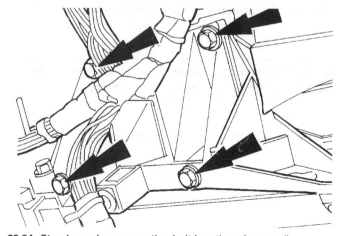

28.8A Steering column mounting bolt locations (arrowed)

28.8B Removing the steering column

5   Remove the driver's side lower facia panel (see Chapter 11).

6   Unscrew the clamp plate bolt securing the steering column shaft to the flexible coupling. Swivel the clamp plate around, and disengage it from the flexible coupling stub **(see illustrations)**.

7   Release the cable tie from the wiring loom at the steering column, and disconnect the multi-plugs **(see illustrations)**.

8   Unscrew and remove the steering column mounting bolts, then slide the column upwards to disengage the retaining tab from the

groove in the cross-beam bracket, and withdraw it from inside the vehicle **(see illustrations)**.

Inspection

9   With the steering column removed, check the universal joints for wear, and examine the column upper and lower shafts for any signs of

10

28.9 Steering column and universal joint

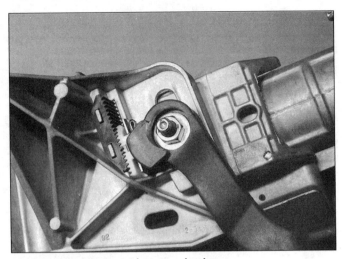

28.10 Height adjustment lever mechanism

damage or distortion **(see illustration)**. Where evident, the column should be renewed complete.
10   Examine the height adjustment lever mechanism for wear and damage **(see illustration)**.
11   With the steering lock disengaged, turn the inner column, and check the upper and lower bearings for smooth operation. The bearings are obtainable separately, and should be renewed if necessary. Dismantling and reassembly of the column assembly is a relatively easy operation.

Refitting

12   Locate the steering column on its bracket, making sure that the tab slides down into the groove correctly.
13   Insert the mounting bolts and tighten to the specified torque **(see illustration)**.
14   Reconnect the multi-plugs, and secure the wiring loom with the cable tie.
15   Locate the steering column shaft on the flexible coupling, swivel the clamp plate round, then insert the bolt and tighten to the specified torque.
16   Refit the driver's side lower trim panel.
17   Refit the steering column upper and lower shrouds.
18   Reconnect the battery negative lead.

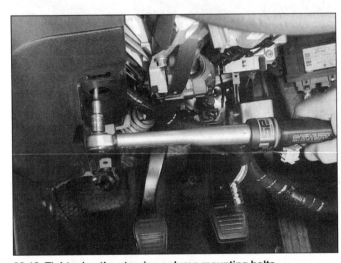

28.13 Tightening the steering column mounting bolts

29 Steering column flexible coupling - removal and refitting

Removal

1   Disconnect the battery negative (earth) lead (refer to Chapter 5, Section 1).
2   Turn the steering wheel so that the front wheels are in the straight-ahead position. Remove the ignition key, then turn the steering wheel slightly as necessary until the steering lock engages.
3   Unscrew the clamp plate bolt securing the steering column shaft to the flexible coupling. Swivel the clamp plate around, and disengage it from the flexible coupling stub.
4   Carefully prise the rubber boot from the bulkhead, and withdraw it into the passenger compartment. Take care not to damage the sealing lip of the boot.
5   Using an Allen key, unscrew the clamp bolt securing the flexible coupling to the pinion shaft on the steering gear, and withdraw the coupling from inside the vehicle.

Refitting

6   Refitting is a reversal of the removal procedure, but tighten the clamp bolts to the specified torque. Make sure that the rubber boot engages correctly in the bulkhead and on the flexible coupling.

30 Power steering gear (all except left-hand-drive models with ABS) - removal and refitting

Removal

1   Remove the steering column flexible coupling as described in Section 29.
2   Apply the handbrake, then jack up the front of the vehicle and support it on axle stands. Remove both front wheels.
3   Working beneath the vehicle, unbolt the rear engine mounting from the transmission and underbody.
4   Extract the split pins from the track rod end balljoint nuts, then unscrew the nuts, and detach the rods from the arms on the steering knuckles using a conventional balljoint removal tool. Take care not to damage the balljoint seals.
5   Position a suitable container beneath the steering gear, then unscrew the union nuts securing the power steering fluid supply, return, and cooler lines to the steering gear. Identify the lines for position, then unbolt the clamps, disconnect the lines, and allow the fluid to drain into the container. Cover the apertures in the steering gear and also the ends of the fluid pipes, to prevent the ingress of dust and dirt into the hydraulic circuit.
6   Unscrew and remove the steering gear mounting bolts. The bolts are located on top of the steering gear, and are difficult to reach. Ide-

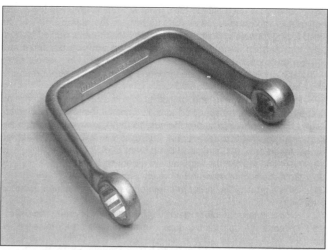

30.6 U-shaped Ford spanner for unscrewing the steering gear mounting bolts

30.9 Tightening the steering gear mounting bolts using the U-shaped spanner

ally, the special U-shaped Ford spanner should be used, but it is just possible to reach them with a normal spanner **(see illustration)**.

7   Withdraw the steering gear through the wheel arch.

Refitting

8   If the steering gear is being replaced with a new one, the new unit will be supplied together with union nuts already fitted. The new nuts must only be used with new feed and return lines - otherwise, they must be removed and discarded. If the original lines and union nuts are being used, the Teflon rings on the union nuts must be renewed. To do this, the rings must be expanded individually onto a fitting adaptor **(see illustration)**, then located in the grooves of the union nuts.

9   Locate the steering gear on the subframe, and insert the two mounting bolts. Tighten the bolts to the specified torque **(see illustration)**. Note that, if the special Ford tool is being used, the bottom of the tool must be turned anti-clockwise in order to tighten the mounting bolts.

10   Remove the covers from the apertures on the steering gear, then reconnect the fluid lines and tighten the union nuts to the specified torque. Refit the clamps and tighten the bolts.

11   Refit the track rod end balljoints to the steering knuckles, and tighten the nuts to the specified torque. Check that the split pin holes are aligned; if necessary, turn the nuts to the nearest alignment, making sure that the torque wrench setting is still within the specified

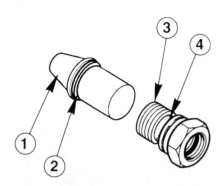

30.8 Using an adaptor to fit the Teflon rings to the union nuts

1	Adaptor	4	Groove location for
2	Teflon ring		the Teflon ring
3	Union nut		

range. Insert new split pins, and bend them back to secure.

12   Refit the rear engine mounting to the transmission and underbody, and tighten the bolts to the specified torque.

13   Refit the front wheels, and lower the vehicle to the ground.

14   Refit the steering column flexible coupling with reference to Section 29.

15   Bleed the power steering hydraulic system as described in Section 33.

16   Have the front wheel alignment checked, and if necessary adjusted, at the earliest opportunity (refer to Section 36).

31 Power steering gear (left-hand-drive models with ABS) - removal and refitting

Removal

1   Disconnect the battery negative (earth) lead (refer to Chapter 5, Section 1).

2   Working inside the vehicle, unscrew the clamp plate bolt securing the steering column shaft to the flexible coupling. Swivel the clamp plate around, and disengage it from the flexible coupling stub.

3   Apply the handbrake, then jack up the front of the vehicle and support it on axle stands. Remove both wheels.

4   On manual transmission models, disconnect the gearchange linkage and support rods from the transmission, as described in Chapter 7, Part A.

5   Remove the exhaust downpipe complete, as described in Chapter 4.

6   Remove the cover from under the radiator by unscrewing the screws and releasing the clips.

7   Support the radiator in its raised position, by inserting split pins through the small holes in the radiator mounting extensions which protrude through the upper mountings **(see illustration)**.

8   Unbolt and remove the radiator lower mounting brackets.

9   Where applicable, unscrew the bolts securing the air conditioning accumulator to the subframe.

10   Working beneath the vehicle, unbolt the engine rear mounting from the transmission and underbody.

11   Unscrew the front engine mounting-to-cylinder block bolts, and also the through-bolt.

12   Extract the split pins from the track rod end balljoint nuts, then unscrew the nuts, and detach the rods from the arms on the steering knuckles using a conventional balljoint removal tool. Take care not to damage the balljoint seals.

13   Working on each side in turn, unscrew the mounting nuts, and remove the anti-roll bar links from the front suspension struts. Note that,

10

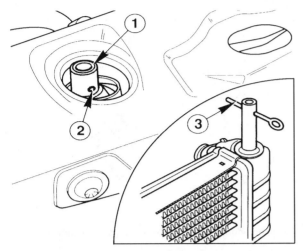

31.7 Method of supporting the radiator in its raised position

    1   Radiator upper mounting extension
    2   Small hole
    3   Pin or split pin inserted through hole

on models fitted with ABS, the ABS sensor wiring support brackets are located beneath the nuts.

14   Working on each side in turn, note which way round the front suspension lower arm balljoint clamp bolt is fitted, then unscrew and re-move it from the knuckle assembly. Lever the balljoint down from the knuckle - if it is tight, prise the joint open carefully using a large flat-bladed tool. Take care not to damage the balljoint seal during the separation procedure.

15   Support the weight of the front subframe assembly on two trolley jacks (or two scissor jacks).

16   Unscrew and remove the subframe mounting bolts, then lower the subframe sufficiently to gain access to the power steering fluid pipes on top of the steering gear. Note that the front subframe mounting bolts are gold in colour - the rear ones are silver.

17   Position a suitable container beneath the steering gear, then unscrew the union nuts securing the power steering fluid supply, return, and cooler lines to the steering gear. Identify the lines for position, then unbolt the clamps, disconnect the lines, and allow the fluid to drain into the container. Cover the apertures in the steering gear and also the ends of the fluid pipes, to prevent the ingress of dust and dirt into the hydraulic circuit.

18   Lower the subframe, together with the power steering gear, to the ground.

19   Unscrew the mounting bolts and remove the power steering gear from the subframe.

20   Using a suitable Allen key, unscrew the clamp bolt securing the flexible coupling to the pinion shaft on the steering gear, and withdraw the coupling.

21   Refer to Section 30, paragraph 8 for details of renewing the Teflon rings.

Refitting

22   Refit the flexible coupling to the pinion shaft on the steering gear, then insert and tighten the clamp bolt using an Allen key.

23   Locate the power steering gear on the subframe, then insert the mounting bolts and tighten to the specified torque.

24   Raise the subframe until it is possible to refit the fluid lines. Tighten the union nuts and clamps.

25   Raise the subframe, making sure that the alignment holes are in line with the holes in the underbody. At the same time, make sure that the flexible coupling locates correctly on the steering column. Ford technicians use a special tool to ensure that the subframe is correctly aligned - refer to Chapter 2 for more details of the alignment procedure. With the subframe aligned, insert and tighten the mounting bolts to the specified torque. Note that the front mounting bolts are gold in colour - the rear bolts are silver.

26   Working on each side in turn, refit the front suspension lower arm balljoint to the knuckle assembly, and insert the clamp bolt with its head facing forwards. Refit the nut and tighten to the specified torque.

27   Working on each side in turn, refit the anti-roll bar links and tighten the mounting nuts to the specified torque. On models fitted with ABS, don't forget to locate the wheel sensor wiring support brackets beneath the nuts.

28   Refit the track rod end balljoints to the steering knuckles, and tighten the nuts to the specified torque. Check if the split pin holes are aligned, and if necessary turn the nuts to the nearest alignment, making sure that the torque wrench setting is still within the specified range. Insert new split pins, and bend them back to secure.

29   Refit and tighten the engine front mounting bolts.

30   Refit the engine rear mounting and tighten the bolts.

31   Where applicable, insert and tighten the air conditioning accumulator bolts.

32   Refit the radiator lower mounting brackets and tighten the bolts.

33   Remove the split pins supporting the radiator in its raised position.

34   Refit the cover under the radiator.

35   Refit the exhaust downpipe as described in Chapter 4.

36   On manual transmission models, reconnect the gearchange linkage and support rods.

37   Refit the front wheels, and lower the vehicle to the ground.

38   Working inside the vehicle, reconnect the steering column clamp plate, then insert the bolt and tighten to the specified torque.

39   Reconnect the battery negative lead.

40   Bleed the power steering hydraulic system as described in Section 33.

41   Have the front wheel alignment checked, and if necessary adjusted, at the earliest opportunity (refer to Section 36).

32 Power steering gear rubber gaiters - renewal

1   Remove the track rod end and its locknut from the track rod, as described in Section 35. Make sure that a note is made of the exact position of the track rod end on the track rod, in order to retain the front wheel alignment setting on refitting.

2   Release the outer retaining clip and inner plastic clamp band, and disconnect the gaiter from the steering gear housing.

3   Disconnect the breather from the gaiter, then slide the gaiter off the track rod.

4   Scrape off all grease from the old gaiter, and apply to the track rod inner joint. Wipe clean the seating areas on the steering gear housing and track rod.

5   Slide the new gaiter onto the track rod and steering gear housing, and reconnect the breather.

6   Fit a new inner plastic clamp band and outer retaining clip.

7   Refit the track rod end as described in Section 35.

8   Have the front wheel alignment checked, and if necessary adjusted, at the earliest opportunity (refer to Section 36).

33 Power steering hydraulic system - bleeding

1   Following any operation in which the power steering fluid lines have been disconnected, the power steering system must be bled, to remove any trapped air.

2   With the front wheels in the straight-ahead position, check the power steering fluid level in the reservoir and, if low, add fresh fluid until it reaches the "MAX" or "MAX COLD" mark. Pour the fluid slowly, to prevent air bubbles forming, and use only the specified fluid (refer to Chapter 1 Specifications).

3   Start the engine, and allow it to run at a fast idle. Check the hoses and connections for leaks.

4   Stop the engine, and recheck the fluid level. Add more if necessary, up to the "MAX" or "MAX COLD" mark.

5   Start the engine again, allow it to idle, then bleed the system by

35.4 Using a balljoint separator tool to release the track rod end balljoint

slowly turning the steering wheel from side to side several times. This should purge the system of all internal air. However, if air remains in the system (indicated by the steering operation being very noisy), leave the vehicle overnight, and repeat the procedure again the next day.

6   If air still remains in the system, it may be necessary to resort to the Ford method of bleeding, which uses a vacuum pump. Turn the steering to the right until it is near the stop, then fit the vacuum pump to the fluid reservoir, and apply 0.15 bars of vacuum. Maintain the vacuum for a minimum of 5 minutes, then repeat the procedure with the steering turned to the left.

7   Keep the fluid level topped-up throughout the bleeding procedure; note that, as the fluid temperature increases, the level will rise.

8   On completion, switch off the engine, and return the front wheels to the straight-ahead position.

34 Power steering pump - removal and refitting

Removal

1   Disconnect the battery negative (earth) lead (refer to Chapter 5, Section 1).

2   Unscrew and remove the bolt securing the hydraulic fluid line support to the engine lifting bracket on the right-hand side of the engine.

3   Unscrew and remove the bolt securing the hydraulic fluid line support to the pump mounting bracket.

4   Position a suitable container beneath the power steering pump, to catch spilt fluid.

5   Loosen the clip, and disconnect the fluid supply hose from the pump inlet. Plug the hose, to prevent the ingress of dust and dirt.

6   Unscrew the union nut, and disconnect the high-pressure line from the pump. Allow the fluid to drain into the container.

7   Apply the handbrake, then jack up the front of the vehicle and support it on axle stands. Remove the right-hand front wheel.

8   Unbolt and remove the lower drivebelt cover.

9   Using a spanner, rotate the drivebelt tensioner in a clockwise direction to release the belt tension, then slip the drivebelt off the pulleys and remove from the vehicle. Refer to Chapter 1 if necessary.

10   Unscrew and remove the four mounting bolts, and withdraw the power steering pump from its bracket. Access to the bolts on the right-hand side of the engine is gained by turning the pump pulley until a hole lines up with the bolt.

Refitting

11   Locate the power steering pump on the mounting bracket, and secure with the four bolts. Tighten the bolts to the specified torque.

12   Slip the drivebelt over the pulleys, then rotate the drivebelt tensioner in a clockwise direction, and locate the drivebelt on it. Release the tensioner to tension the drivebelt.

13   Refit the lower belt cover.

14   Refit the right-hand front wheel, and lower the vehicle to the ground.

15   If necessary, the sealing ring on the high-pressure outlet should be renewed, using the same procedure as described in Section 30, paragraph 8.

16   Reconnect the high-pressure line to the pump, and tighten the union nut.

17   Reconnect the fluid supply hose to the pump inlet, and tighten the clip.

18   Refit the hydraulic fluid line support to the pump mounting bracket, and tighten the bolt.

19   Refit the hydraulic fluid line support to the engine lifting bracket on the right-hand side of the engine, and tighten the bolt.

20   Reconnect the battery negative lead.

21   Bleed the power steering hydraulic system as described in Section 33.

35 Track rod end - renewal

1   Apply the handbrake, then jack up the front of the vehicle and support it on axle stands. Remove the appropriate front roadwheel.

2   Using a suitable spanner, slacken the locknut on the track rod by a quarter-turn. Hold the track rod end stationary with another spanner engaged with the special flats while loosening the locknut.

3   Extract the split pin, then unscrew and remove the track rod end balljoint retaining nut.

4   To release the tapered shank of the balljoint from the steering knuckle arm, use a balljoint separator tool (if the balljoint is to be re-used, take care not to damage the dust cover when using the separator tool) **(see illustration)**.

5   Count the number of exposed threads visible on the inner section of the track rod, and record this figure.

6   Unscrew the track rod end from the track rod, counting the number of turns necessary to remove it. If necessary, hold the track rod stationary with grips.

Refitting

7   Screw the track rod end onto the track rod by the number of turns noted during removal, until it just contacts the locknut.

8   Engage the shank of the balljoint with the steering knuckle arm, and refit the nut. Tighten the nut to the specified torque. If the balljoint shank turns while the nut is being tightened, press down on the balljoint. The tapered fit of the shank will lock it, and prevent rotation as the nut is tightened.

9   Check that the split pin holes in the nut and balljoint shank are aligned. If necessary turn the nut to the nearest alignment, making sure that the torque wrench setting is still within the specified range. Insert a new split pin, and bend it back to secure.

10   Now tighten the locknut, while holding the track rod end as before.

11   Refit the roadwheel, and lower the vehicle to the ground.

12   Finally check, and if necessary adjust, the front wheel alignment as described in Section 29.

36 Wheel alignment and steering angles - general information

1   Accurate front wheel alignment is essential to provide positive steering, and to prevent excessive tyre wear. Before considering the steering/suspension geometry, check that the tyres are correctly inflated, that the front wheels are not buckled, and that the steering linkage and suspension joints are in good order, without slackness or wear.

10

2   Wheel alignment consists of four factors **(see illustration)**:

Camber is the angle at which the front wheels are set from the vertical, when viewed from the front of the vehicle. "Positive camber" is the amount (in degrees) that the wheels are tilted outward at the top of the vertical. *Castor* is the angle between the steering axis and a vertical line, when viewed from each side of the car. "Positive castor" is when the steering axis is inclined rearward at the top.

Steering axis inclination is the angle (when viewed from the front of the vehicle) between the vertical and an imaginary line drawn through the suspension strut upper mounting and the lower suspension arm balljoint.

Toe setting is the amount by which the distance between the front inside edges of the roadwheels (measured at hub height) differs from the diametrically-opposite distance measured between the rear inside edges of the front roadwheels.

3   With the exception of the toe setting, all other steering angles are set during manufacture, and no adjustment is possible. It can be assumed, therefore, that unless the vehicle has suffered accident damage, all the preset steering angles will be correct. Should there be some doubt about their accuracy, it will be necessary to seek the help of a Ford dealer, as special gauges are needed to check the steering angles.

4   Two methods are available to the home mechanic for checking the toe setting. One method is to use a gauge to measure the distance between the front and rear inside edges of the roadwheels. The other method is to use a scuff plate, in which each front wheel is rolled across a movable plate which records any deviation, or scuff, of the tyre from the straight-ahead position as it moves across the plate. Relatively-inexpensive equipment of both types is available from accessory outlets.

5   If, after checking the toe setting using whichever method is preferable, it is found that adjustment is necessary, proceed as follows.

6   Turn the steering wheel onto full-left lock, and record the number of exposed threads on the right-hand track rod. Now turn the steering onto full-right lock, and record the number of threads on the left-hand track rod. If there are the same number of threads visible on both sides, then subsequent adjustment can be made equally on both sides. If there are more threads visible on one side than the other, it will be necessary to compensate for this during adjustment. *After adjustment, there must be the same number of threads visible on each track rod. This is most important.*

7   To alter the toe setting, slacken the locknut on the track rod, and turn the track rod using self-locking pliers to achieve the desired setting. When viewed from the side of the car, turning the rod clockwise will increase the toe-in, turning it anti-clockwise will increase the toe-out. Only turn the track rods by a quarter of a turn each time, and then recheck the setting.

8   After adjustment, tighten the locknuts. Reposition the steering gear rubber gaiters, to remove any twist caused by turning the track rods.

9   The rear wheel toe-setting may also be checked and adjusted, but as this additionally requires alignment with the front wheels, it should be left to a Ford garage or specialist having the special equipment required.

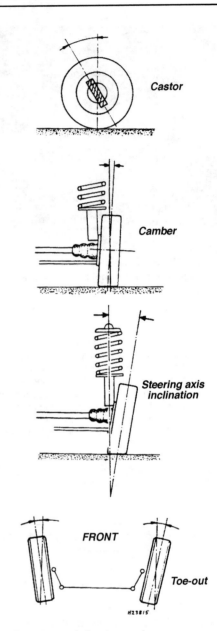

36.2 Wheel alignment and steering angles

Chapter 11   Bodywork and fittings

Contents

Specifications

Torque wrench settings

	Nm	lbf ft
Bonnet and tailgate hinges...	24	18
Boot lid	10	7
Front seat mounting bolts..	38	28
Seat belt mounting nuts and bolts	38	28
Bumper mounting nuts..	10	7

1 General information

The bodyshell and underframe on all models is of all-steel welded construction, incorporating progressive crumple zones at the front and rear, and a rigid centre safety cell. The bulkhead behind the engine compartment incorporates crash grooves which determine its energy-absorption characteristics, and special beams to prevent the intrusion of the front wheels into the passenger compartment during a serious accident. All passenger doors incorporate side impact bars.

All sheet metal surfaces which are prone to corrosion are galvanized. The painting process includes a base colour which closely matches the final topcoat, so that any stone damage is not noticeable.

Hatchback, Saloon and Estate versions are available. The front section of the vehicle up to the "B" pillar is identical on all models.

Automatic seat belts are fitted to all models, and the front seat belt stalks are mounted on automatic tensioners (also known as "grabbers") **(see illustration)**. In the event of a serious front impact, a spring mass sensor releases a coil spring which pulls the stalk buckle downwards and tensions the seat belt. It is not possible to reset the tensioner once fired, and it must therefore be renewed.

In the UK, central locking is standard on all models **(see illustration)**. In other countries, it is available on certain models only. Where double-locking is fitted, the lock mechanism is disconnected (when the system is in use) from the interior door handles, making it impossible to open any of the doors or the tailgate/bootlid from inside the vehicle. This means that, even if a thief should break a side window, he will not be able to open the door using the interior handle. Models with the double-locking system are fitted with a control module located beneath the facia on the right-hand side. In the event of a serious accident, a crash sensor unlocks all doors if they were previously locked.

Many of the procedures in this Chapter require the battery to be disconnected. Refer to Chapter 5, Section 1 first.

2 Maintenance - bodywork and underframe

1   The general condition of a vehicle's bodywork is the one thing that significantly affects its value. Maintenance is easy, but needs to be regular. Neglect, particularly after minor damage, can lead quickly to further deterioration and costly repair bills. It is important also to keep watch on those parts of the vehicle not immediately visible, for instance the underside, inside all the wheel arches, and the lower part of the engine compartment.

2   The basic maintenance routine for the bodywork is washing - preferably with a lot of water, from a hose. This will remove all the loose solids which may have stuck to the vehicle. It is important to flush these off in such a way as to prevent grit from scratching the finish. The wheel arches and underframe need washing in the same way, to remove any accumulated mud, which will retain moisture and tend to encourage rust. Paradoxically enough, the best time to clean the underframe and wheel arches is in wet weather, when the mud is thoroughly wet and soft. In very wet weather, the underframe is usually cleaned of large accumulations automatically, and this is a good time for inspection.

3   Periodically, except on vehicles with a wax-based underbody protective coating, it is a good idea to have the whole of the underframe of the vehicle steam-cleaned, engine compartment included, so that a thorough inspection can be carried out to see what minor repairs and renovations are necessary. Steam-cleaning is available at many garages, and is necessary for the removal of the accumulation of oily grime which sometimes is allowed to become thick in certain areas. If steam-cleaning facilities are not available, there are some excellent grease solvents available, such as Holts Engine Degreasant, which can be brush-applied. The dirt can then be simply hosed off. Note that these methods should not be used on vehicles with wax-based underbody protective coating, or the coating will be removed. Such vehicles should be inspected annually, preferably just prior to Winter, when the underbody should be washed down, and any damage to the wax coating repaired using Holts Undershield. Ideally, a completely fresh coat

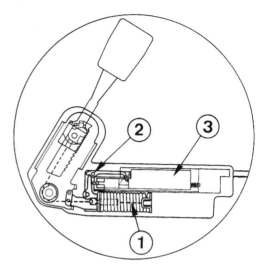

1.4 Automatic seat belt tensioner

1   Coil spring
2   Lever system
3   Spring mass sensor

should be applied. It would also be worth considering the use of such wax-based protection for injection into door panels, sills, box sections, etc, as an additional safeguard against rust damage, where such protection is not provided by the vehicle manufacturer.

4   After washing paintwork, wipe off with a chamois leather to give an unspotted clear finish. A coat of clear protective wax polish, such as the many excellent Turtle Wax polishes, will give added protection against chemical pollutants in the air. If the paintwork sheen has dulled or oxidised, use a cleaner/polisher combination such as Turtle Wax Hard Shell to restore the brilliance of the shine. This requires a little effort, but such dulling is usually caused because regular washing has been neglected. Care needs to be taken with metallic paintwork, as special non-abrasive cleaner/polisher is required, to avoid damage to the finish. Always check that the door and ventilator opening drain holes and pipes are completely clear, so that water can be drained out. Brightwork should be treated in the same way as paintwork. Windscreens and windows can be kept clear of the smeary film which often appears by the use of proprietary glass cleaner such as Holts Mixra. Never use any form of wax or other body or chromium polish on glass.

3 Maintenance - upholstery and carpets

Mats and carpets should be brushed or vacuum-cleaned regularly, to keep them free of grit. If they are badly-stained, remove them from the vehicle for scrubbing or sponging, and make quite sure they are dry before refitting. Seats and interior trim panels can be kept clean by wiping with a damp cloth and Turtle Wax Carisma. If they do become stained (which can be more apparent on light-coloured upholstery), use a little liquid detergent and a soft nail brush to scour the grime out of the grain of the material. Do not forget to keep the headlining clean in the same way as the upholstery. When using liquid cleaners inside the vehicle, do not over-wet the surfaces being cleaned. Excessive damp could get into the seams and padded interior causing stains, offensive odours, or even rot. If the inside of the vehicle gets wet accidentally, it is worthwhile taking some trouble to dry it out properly, particularly where carpets are involved. *Do not leave oil or electric heaters inside the vehicle for this purpose.*

4 Minor body damage - repair

Note: *For more detailed information about bodywork repair, Haynes Publishing produce a book by Lindsay Porter called "The Car*

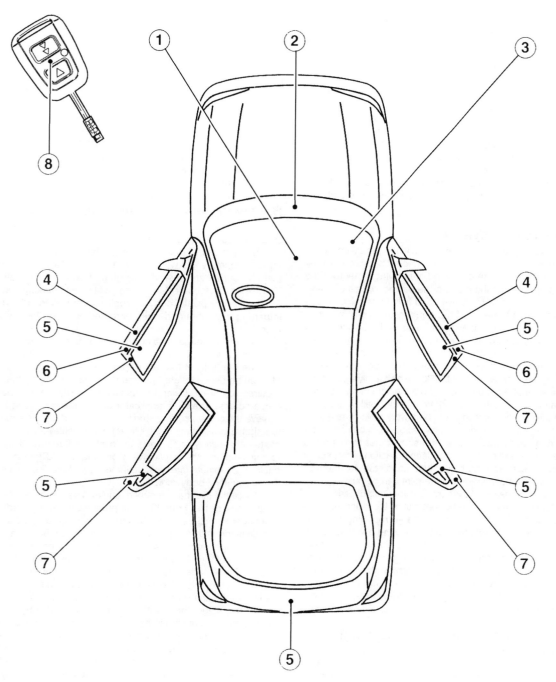

1.5 Central locking component locations

1	Indicator light	4	Infra-red receiver	7	Ajar switch
2	Buzzer	5	Lock motor	8	Infra-red transmitter
3	Central locking module	6	Set/reset switch		

Bodywork Repair Manual". This incorporates information on such aspects as rust treatment, painting and glass-fibre repairs, as well as details on more ambitious repairs involving welding and panel-beating.

The colour photographic sequence between pages 32 and 33 illustrates the operations detailed in the following sub-Sections.

Repair of minor scratches in bodywork

If the scratch is very superficial and does not penetrate to the metal of the bodywork, repair is very simple. Lightly rub the area of the scratch with a paintwork renovator, such as Turtle Wax Color Back, or

a very fine cutting paste, like Holts Body+Plus Rubbing Compound, to remove loose paint from the scratch, and to clear the surrounding bodywork of wax polish. Rinse the area with clean water.

Apply touch-up paint to the scratch, using a fine paint brush; continue to apply fine layers of paint until the surface of the paint in the scratch is level with the surrounding paintwork. Allow the new paint at least two weeks to harden, then blend it into the surrounding paintwork by rubbing the scratch area with a paintwork renovator, such as Turtle Wax Color Back, or a very fine cutting paste, like Holts Body+Plus Rubbing Compound. Finally apply wax polish from one of the Turtle

11

Wax range of wax polishes.

Where the scratch has penetrated right through to the metal of the bodywork, causing the metal to rust, a different repair technique is required. Remove any loose rust from the bottom of the scratch with a penknife, then apply rust-inhibiting paint, such as Turtle Wax Rust Master, to prevent the formation of rust in the future. Using a rubber or nylon applicator, fill the scratch with bodystopper paste, such as Holts Body+Plus Knifing Putty. If required, this paste can be mixed with cellulose thinners, such as Holts Body+Plus Cellulose Thinners, to provide a very thin paste which is ideal for filling narrow scratches. Before the stopper-paste in the scratch hardens, wrap a piece of smooth cotton rag around the top of a finger. Dip the finger in cellulose thinners, and quickly sweep it across the surface of the stopper-paste in the scratch; this will ensure that the surface of the stopper-paste is slightly hollowed. The scratch can now be painted over, as described earlier in this Section.

Repair of dents in bodywork

When deep denting of the vehicle's bodywork has taken place, the first task is to pull the dent out, until the affected bodywork almost attains its original shape. There is little point in trying to restore the original shape completely, as the metal in the damaged area will have stretched on impact, and cannot be reshaped fully to its original contour. It is better to bring the level of the dent up to a point which is about 3 mm below the level of the surrounding bodywork. In cases where the dent is very shallow anyway, it is not worth trying to pull it out at all. If the underside of the dent is accessible, it can be hammered out gently from behind, using a mallet with a wooden or plastic head. Whilst doing this, hold a suitable block of wood firmly against the outside of the panel, to absorb the impact from the hammer blows and thus prevent a large area of the bodywork from being "belled-out".

Should the dent be in a section of the bodywork which has a double skin or some other factor making it inaccessible from behind, a different technique is called for. Drill several small holes through the metal inside the area - particularly in the deeper section. Then screw long self-tapping screws into the holes, just sufficiently for them to gain a good purchase in the metal. Now the dent can be pulled out by pulling on the protruding heads of the screws with a pair of pliers.

The next stage of the repair is the removal of the paint from the damaged area, and from an inch or so of the surrounding "sound" bodywork. This is accomplished most easily by using a wire brush or abrasive pad on a power drill, although it can be done just as effectively by hand, using sheets of abrasive paper. To complete the preparation for filling, score the surface of the bare metal with a screwdriver or the tang of a file, or alternatively, drill small holes in the affected area. This will provide a really good "key" for the filler paste.

To complete the repair, see the Section on filling and respraying.

Repair of rust holes or gashes in bodywork

Remove all paint from the affected area, and from an inch or so of the surrounding "sound" bodywork, using an abrasive pad or a wire brush on a power drill. If these are not available, a few sheets of abrasive paper will do the job most effectively. With the paint removed, you will be able to judge the severity of the corrosion, and therefore decide whether to renew the whole panel (if this is possible) or to repair the affected area. New body panels are not as expensive as most people think, and it is often quicker and more satisfactory to fit a new panel than to attempt to repair large areas of corrosion.

Remove all fittings from the affected area, except those which will act as a guide to the original shape of the damaged bodywork (eg headlight shells, etc). Then, using tin snips or a hacksaw blade, remove all loose metal and any other metal badly affected by corrosion. Hammer the edges of the hole inwards, in order to create a slight depression for the filler paste.

Wire-brush the affected area, to remove the powdery rust from the surface of the remaining metal. Paint the affected area with rust-inhibiting paint, such as Turtle Wax Rust Master; if the back of the rusted area is accessible, treat this also.

Before filling can take place, it will be necessary to block the hole in some way. This can be achieved by the use of aluminium or plastic mesh, or aluminium tape.

Aluminium or plastic mesh, or glass-fibre matting, is probably the best material to use for a large hole. Cut a piece to the approximate size and shape of the hole to be filled, then position it in the hole so that its edges are below the level of the surrounding bodywork. It can be retained in position by several blobs of filler paste around its periphery.

Aluminium tape should be used for small or very narrow holes. Pull a piece off the roll, trim it to the approximate size and shape required, then pull off the backing paper (if used) and stick the tape over the hole; it can be overlapped if the thickness of one piece is insufficient. Burnish down the edges of the tape with the handle of a screwdriver or similar, to ensure that the tape is securely attached to the metal underneath.

Bodywork repairs - filling and respraying

Before using this Section, see the Sections on dents, deep scratches, rust holes and gash repairs.

Many types of bodyfiller are available, but generally speaking, those proprietary kits which contain a tin of filler paste and a tube of resin hardener, are best for this type of repair; examples are Holts Body+Plus, or Holts No-Mix, which can be used directly from the tube. A wide, flexible plastic or nylon applicator will be found invaluable for imparting a smooth and well-contoured finish to the surface of the filler.

Mix up a little filler on a clean piece of card or board - measure the hardener carefully (follow the maker's instructions on the pack), otherwise the filler will set too rapidly or too slowly. Alternatively, Holts No-Mix can be used straight from the tube without mixing, but daylight is required to cure it. Using the applicator, apply the filler paste to the prepared area; draw the applicator across the surface of the filler, to achieve the correct contour and to level the surface. As soon as a contour that approximates to the correct one is achieved, stop working the paste - if you carry on too long, the paste will become sticky and begin to "pick-up" on the applicator. Continue to add thin layers of filler paste at 20-minute intervals, until the level of the filler is just proud of the surrounding bodywork.

Once the filler has hardened, any excess can be removed using a metal plane or file. From then on, progressively-finer grades of abrasive paper should be used, starting with a 40-grade production paper, and finishing with a 400-grade wet-and-dry paper. Always wrap the abrasive paper around a flat rubber, cork, or wooden block - otherwise the surface of the filler will not be completely flat. During the smoothing of the filler surface, the wet-and-dry paper should be periodically rinsed in water. This will ensure that a very smooth finish is imparted to the filler at the final stage.

At this stage, the "dent" should be surrounded by a ring of bare metal, which in turn should be encircled by the finely "feathered" edge of the good paintwork. Rinse the repair area with clean water, until all of the dust produced by the rubbing-down operation has gone.

Spray the whole area with a light coat of primer, either Holts Body+Plus Grey or Red Oxide Primer - this will show up any imperfections in the surface of the filler. Repair these imperfections with fresh filler paste or bodystopper, and once more smooth the surface with abrasive paper. If bodystopper is used, it can be mixed with cellulose thinners to form a really thin paste which is ideal for filling small holes. Repeat this spray-and-repair procedure until you are satisfied that the surface of the filler and the feathered edge of the paintwork are perfect. Clean the repair area with clean water, and allow to dry fully.

The repair area is now ready for final spraying. Paint spraying must be carried out in a warm, dry, windless and dust-free atmosphere. This condition can be created artificially if you have access to a large indoor working area, but if you are forced to work in the open, you will have to pick your day very carefully. If you are working indoors, dousing the floor in the work area with water will help to settle the dust which would otherwise be in the atmosphere. If the repair area is confined to one body panel, mask off the surrounding panels; this will help to minimise the effects of a slight mis-match in paint colours. Bodywork fittings (eg chrome strips, door handles etc) will also need to be masked off. Use genuine masking tape and several thicknesses of

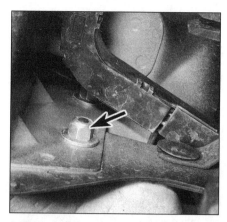

6.4 Screw (arrowed) securing the wheel arch liner to the front bumper

6.5A Front bumper mounting bolt (arrowed)

6.5B Disconnecting the front bumper from the side guides

newspaper for the masking operations.

Before commencing to spray, agitate the aerosol can thoroughly, then spray a test area (an old tin, or similar) until the technique is mastered. Cover the repair area with a thick coat of primer; the thickness should be built up using several thin layers of paint, rather than one thick one. Using 400 grade wet-and-dry paper, rub down the surface of the primer until it is really smooth. While doing this, the work area should be thoroughly doused with water, and the wet-and-dry paper periodically rinsed in water. Allow to dry before spraying on more paint.

Spray on the top coat using Holts Dupli-Color Autospray, again building up the thickness by using several thin layers of paint. Start spraying in the centre of the repair area and then, with a side-to-side motion, work outwards until the whole repair area and about 2 inches of the surrounding original paintwork is covered. Remove all masking material 10 to 15 minutes after spraying on the final coat of paint.

Allow the new paint at least two weeks to harden, then, using a paintwork renovator such as Turtle Wax Color Back, or a very fine cutting paste like Holts Body+Plus Rubbing Compound, blend the edges of the paint into the existing paintwork. Finally, apply wax polish.

Plastic components

With the use of more and more plastic body components by the vehicle manufacturers (eg bumpers, spoilers, and in some cases major body panels), rectification of more serious damage to such items has become a matter of either entrusting repair work to a specialist in this field, or renewing complete components. Repair of such damage by the DIY owner is not really feasible, owing to the cost of the equipment and materials required for effecting such repairs. The basic technique involves making a groove along the line of the crack in the plastic, using a rotary burr in a power drill. The damaged part is then welded back together, using a hot air gun to heat up and fuse a plastic filler rod into the groove. Any excess plastic is then removed, and the area rubbed down to a smooth finish. It is important that a filler rod of the correct plastic is used, as body components can be made of a variety of different types (eg polycarbonate, ABS, or polypropylene).

Damage of a less serious nature (abrasions, minor cracks etc) can be repaired by the DIY owner, using a two-part epoxy filler repair material such as Holts Body+Plus, or Holts No-Mix, which can be used directly from the tube. Once mixed in equal proportions (or applied direct from the tube in the case of Holts No-Mix), this is used in similar fashion to the bodywork filler used on metal panels. The filler is usually cured in twenty to thirty minutes, ready for sanding and painting.

If the owner is renewing a complete component himself, or if he has repaired it with epoxy filler, he will be left with the problem of finding a suitable paint for finishing which is compatible with the type of plastic used. At one time, the use of a universal paint was not possible, owing to the complex range of plastics encountered in body component applications. Standard paints, generally speaking, will not bond satisfactorily to plastic or rubber, but Holts Professional Spraymatch paints to match any plastic or rubber finish can be obtained from deal-

ers. However, it is now possible to obtain a plastic body parts finishing kit which consists of a pre-primer treatment, a primer and coloured top coat. Full instructions are normally supplied with a kit, but basically, the method is to first apply the pre-primer to the component concerned, and allow it to dry for up to 30 minutes. Then the primer is applied, and left to dry for about an hour before finally applying the special-coloured top coat. The result is a correctly-coloured component, where the paint will flex with the plastic or rubber, a property that standard paint does not normally possess.

5   Major body damage - repair

Where serious damage has occurred, or large areas need renewal due to neglect, it means that complete new panels will need welding-in; this is best left to professionals. If the damage is due to impact, it will also be necessary to check completely the alignment of the bodyshell; this can only be carried out accurately by a Ford dealer, using special jigs. If the body is left misaligned, it is primarily dangerous, as the car will not handle properly, and secondly, uneven stresses will be imposed on the steering, suspension and possibly transmission, causing abnormal wear or complete failure, particularly to items such as the tyres.

6   Bumpers - removal and refitting

Removal

Front bumper

1   Apply the handbrake, jack up the front of the vehicle and support it on axle stands.

2   Where applicable, remove the foglights from the front bumper (Chapter 12).

3   Where applicable, disconnect the tubing from the headlight washer jets.

4   Unscrew the screws securing the wheel arch liners to the front bumper **(see illustration)**.

5   Unscrew the bumper mounting nuts, and withdraw the bumper forwards from the vehicle, at the same time disconnecting the guides from the side pins **(see illustrations)**.

Rear bumper

6   Chock the front wheels, jack up the rear of the vehicle and support it on axle stands.

7   Disconnect the rear exhaust mounting rubber, and support the exhaust system on an axle stand.

8   Remove the screws securing the wheel arch liners to the rear bumper.

11

6.9 Rear bumper mounting nuts

7.2 Removing a radiator grille mounting screw

7.3 Unclipping the radiator grille from the front panel

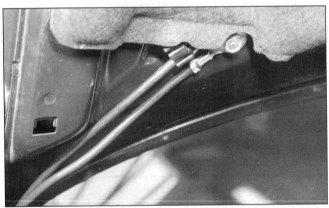

8.5 Earth lead and washer hoses on the underside of the bonnet

8.7 Mark around the bonnet hinges with a soft pencil before removal

9   Unscrew the bumper mounting nuts, and withdraw the bumper rearwards from the vehicle, at the same time disconnecting the guides from the side pins **(see illustration)**.

Refitting

Front and rear bumpers

10   Refitting is a reversal of the removal procedure. Make sure that the guides locate correctly on the side pins.

7   Radiator grille - removal and refitting

Removal

1   Support the bonnet in the open position.
2   Using a Torx key, unscrew the radiator grille mounting screws **(see illustration)**.
3   Unclip the radiator grille from the front panel **(see illustration)**.

Refitting

4   Refitting is a reversal of the removal procedure.

8   Bonnet - removal, refitting and adjustment

Removal

1   Open the bonnet, and support it in the open position using the stay.
2   Disconnect the battery negative (earth) lead (Chapter 5, Section 1).
3   Prise out the clips from the insulator on the underside of the bon-net, for access to the windscreen washer hoses and engine compart-

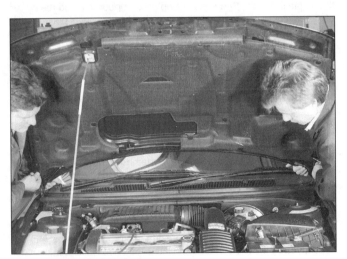

8.8 Removing the bonnet

ment light. It is not necessary to completely remove the insulator.
4   Disconnect the wiring from the engine compartment light, and un-clip the wiring from the bonnet.
5   Unbolt the earth lead from the bonnet **(see illustration)**.
6   Disconnect the windscreen washer hoses from the bottom of the jets, and unclip the hose from the bonnet.
7   To assist in correctly realigning the bonnet when refitting it, mark the outline of the hinges with a soft pencil. Loosen the two hinge re-taining bolts on each side **(see illustration)**.
8   With the help of an assistant, unscrew the four bolts, release the stay, and lift the bonnet from the vehicle **(see illustration)**.

8.9 Buffer for adjustment of the bonnet front height

9.3 Bonnet release lever

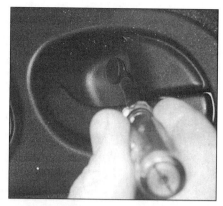

11.2A Prise out the plastic cover . . .

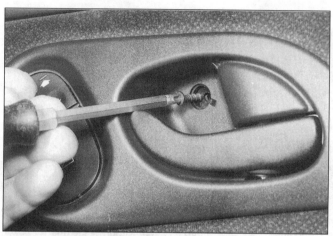

11.2B . . . remove the screw . . .

11.2C . . . and withdraw the bezel from the inner door handle

Refitting

9   Refitting is a reversal of the removal procedure. Position the bonnet hinges within the outline marks made during removal, but if necessary alter its position to provide a uniform gap all round. Adjust the rear height of the bonnet by repositioning it on the hinges. Adjust the front height by repositioning the lock (see Section 10) and turning the rubber buffers on the engine compartment front cross panel up or down to support the bonnet **(see illustration)**.

9 Bonnet release cable and lever - removal and refitting

Removal

1   With the bonnet open, disconnect the battery negative (earth) lead (Chapter 5, Section 1).
2   Working inside the vehicle, remove the trim from the "B" pillar, and pull off the door weatherstrips from the bottom of the door apertures.
3   Remove the clips and screws, and withdraw the lower side trim, to give access to the bonnet release lever **(see illustration)**.
4   Release the outer cable from the lever bracket.
5   Unscrew and remove the lever mounting screws, and turn the lever clockwise through a quarter-turn to disconnect it from the cable.
6   Remove the radiator grille (Section 7). Also remove the backing panel from the engine compartment front crossmember.
7   Release the inner and outer cables from the lock.
8   Withdraw the cable from the engine compartment, feeding it through the front crossmember, and removing the grommet from the bulkhead.

Refitting

9   Refitting is a reversal of the removal procedure.

10 Bonnet lock - removal, refitting and adjustment

Removal

1   Remove the radiator grille (Section 7).
2   Release the inner and outer cables from the bonnet lock.
3   Mark the position of the lock on the crossmember, then unscrew the mounting nuts and withdraw the lock.

Refitting and adjustment

4   Refitting is a reversal of the removal procedure, starting by positioning the lock as noted before removal.
5   If the front of the bonnet is not level with the front wings, the lock may be moved up or down within the mounting holes. After making an adjustment, raise or lower the rubber buffers to support the bonnet correctly.

11 Door inner trim panel - removal and refitting

Removal

1   Disconnect the battery negative (earth) lead (Chapter 5, Section 1).
2   Carefully prise out the plastic cover with a small screwdriver. Remove the screw, and ease the bezel off the inner door handle **(see illustrations)**.

11

11.3A Remove the window operating switch . . .

11.3B . . . and disconnect the multi-plug

11.4A Remove the cover . . .

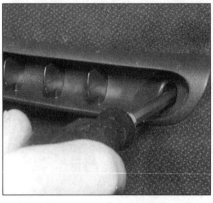

11.4B . . . then remove the screws and withdraw the door pull handle

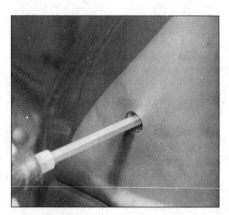

11.5A Remove the plastic cap and the screw . . .

11.5B . . . then withdraw the quarter bezel

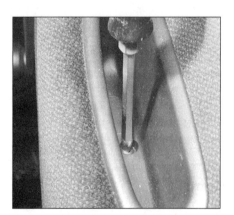

11.6A Remove the screw . . .

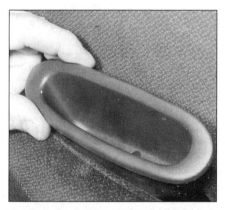

11.6B . . . and withdraw the rear door pull handle

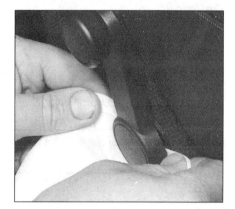

11.7A Using a clean cloth to release the spring clip from the window regulator handle

3   Where applicable, remove the window operating switch and disconnect the multi-plug **(see illustrations)**.

Front door

4   Carefully prise out the cover, remove the screws and withdraw the door pull handle **(see illustrations)**.

5   Prise off the plastic cap, remove the screw, and withdraw the quarter bezel from the front of the window opening **(see illustrations)**.

Rear door

6   Prise off the cap, then remove the screw and withdraw the door pull handle **(see illustrations)**.

Front and rear doors

7   On models fitted with manual (ie non-electric) windows, fully shut the window, and note the position of the regulator handle. Release the spring clip by inserting a clean cloth between the handle and the door trim. Pull the cloth against the open ends of the clip to release it, at the same time pulling the handle from the regulator shaft splines. Withdraw the handle (and where fitted, the spacer) and recover the clip **(see illustrations)**.

8   Prise the caps from the trim panel retaining screws, then remove the screws and lift off the panel. Where a speaker is attached to the trim panel, disconnect the multi-plug **(see illustrations)**.

11.7B Withdrawing the window regulator handle

11.7C Recover the spring clip from the window regulator handle

11.8A Prise out the caps . . .

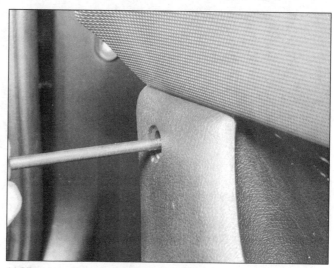

11.8B . . . remove the inner-facing screws . . .

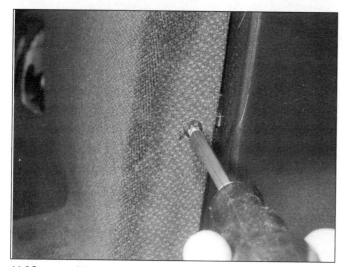

11.8C . . . and the side screws . . .

11.8D . . . then lift off the trim panel

11

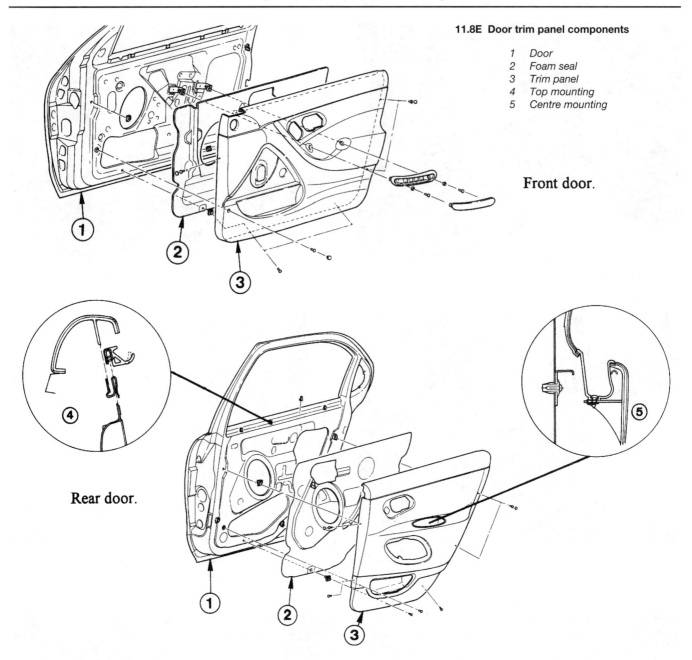

11.8E Door trim panel components

1   Door
2   Foam seal
3   Trim panel
4   Top mounting
5   Centre mounting

Front door.

Rear door.

9   If necessary, the foam insulation may be removed from the door. First remove the speaker as described in Chapter 12.

10   On models with manual windows, remove the foam spacer from the regulator spindle **(see illustration)**.

11   On the rear door, unscrew the screws and remove the door pull bracket **(see illustration)**.

12   Carefully cut the adhesive with a knife, and remove the foam insulation **(see illustration)**.

Refitting

13   Refitting is a reversal of the removal procedure.

---

12 Door window glass - removal and refitting

Removal

Front (manual/non-electric)

1   Disconnect the battery negative (earth) lead (Chapter 5, Section 1).

2   Remove the door inner trim panel (Section 11).

3   Remove the door exterior mirror (Section 16).

4   Temporarily refit the regulator handle on its splines.

5   Lower the window until the glass support bracket is visible through the holes in the door inner panel. Remove the regulator handle.

6   Carefully prise off the weatherstrip from the outside of the door.

7   Support the glass, then unscrew the bolts from the support bracket.

8   Lift the glass from the door while tilting it at the rear, and withdraw it from the outside.

Front (electric)

9   Disconnect the battery negative (earth) lead (Chapter 5, Section 1).

10   Remove the door inner trim panel (Section 11).

11   Remove the door exterior mirror (Section 16).

12   Temporarily reconnect the battery and the window operating switch. Lower the window until the support bracket and bolts are visible through the holes in the door inner panel **(see illustration)**. Disconnect the battery lead and the operating switch again.

13   Carefully prise off the weatherstrip from the outside of the door **(see illustration)**.

14   Support the glass, then unscrew the bolts from the support bracket.

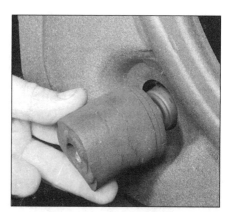

11.10 Removing the foam spacer

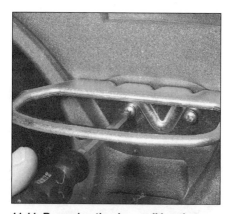

11.11 Removing the door pull bracket from a rear door

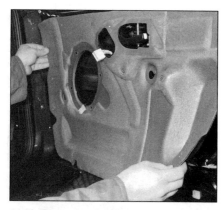

11.12 Removing the foam insulation

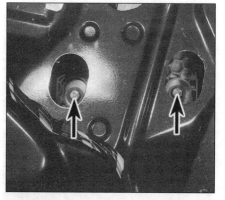

12.12 Window support bracket bolts (arrowed) viewed through the holes in the door inner panel

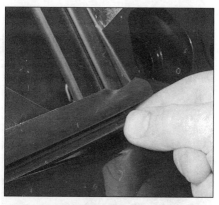

12.13 Removing the weatherstrip from the outside of the door

12.15 Lifting the glass from the front door

12.21A Unscrew the screws . . .

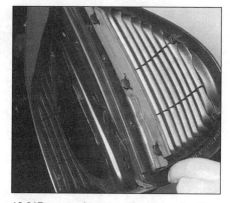

12.21B . . . and remove the air vent grilles from the rear door

12.26 Lifting the glass from the rear door

15   Lift the glass from the door while tilting it at the rear, and withdraw it from the outside **(see illustration)**.

Rear (manual/non-electric)

16   Disconnect the battery negative (earth) lead (Chapter 5, Section 1).
17   Remove the door inner trim panel (Section 11).
18   Temporarily refit the regulator handle on its splines.
19   Lower the window until the glass support bracket and bolts are visible through the holes in the door inner panel. Remove the regulator handle.
20   Support the glass, then unscrew the bolts from the support bracket.
21   Unscrew the screws, and remove the air vent grilles from the rear of the rear door **(see illustrations)**.

22   Carefully prise off the weatherstrip from the outside of the door.
23   Have an assistant raise the glass from the outside, and hold it near its shut position.
24   Loosen (but do not remove) the three regulator mounting bolts, then slide the top bolts to the right, and push them out. Slide the bottom bolt upwards, and push it out. Lower the regulator assembly inside the door.
25   Working inside the door, lower the glass until it is below the regulator position, and move the glass to the outer side of its channels.
26   With the help of an assistant, lift the glass out of the door, and withdraw it from the outside **(see illustration)**.

Rear (electric)

27   The procedure is as just described for manual windows, making allowances for the difference in the regulator mechanism.

11

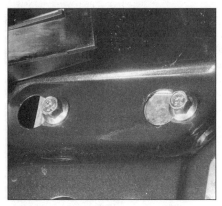

13.2A Window regulator upper mounting bolts (front door)

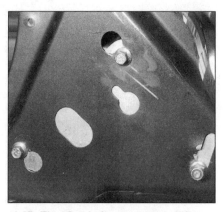

13.2B Electric window motor mounting bolts (front door)

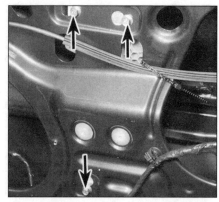

13.2C Window regulator mounting bolts - arrowed (rear door)

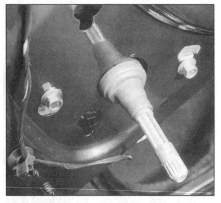

13.2D Manual winder mounting bolts (rear door)

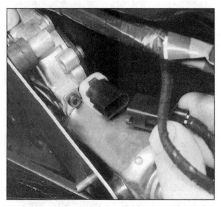

13.5 Disconnecting the wiring multi-plug from an electrically-operated window

13.6A Removing the window regulator mechanism from the front door

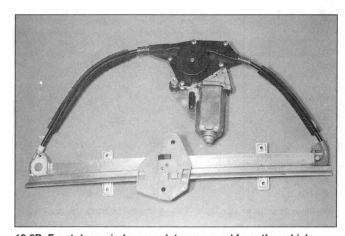

13.6B Front door window regulator removed from the vehicle

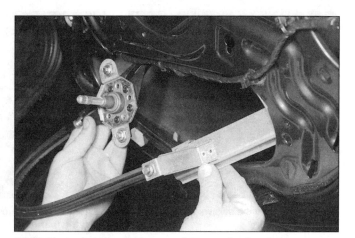

13.6C Removing the window regulator mechanism from the rear door

Refitting

All doors

28   Refitting is a reversal of the removal procedure, making sure that the glass is correctly located in the support bracket.

13   Door window regulator - removal and refitting

Removal

1   Remove the window glass (Section 12).
2   Loosen (but do not remove) the regulator and manual

winder/electric motor mounting bolts **(see illustrations)**.
3   Twist the winder or motor (as applicable) in the bolt slots, and push it inwards.
4   Slide the top bolts to the right, and push them out. Slide the bottom bolt upwards, and push it out.
5   On electric windows, disconnect the wiring multi-plug from the motor **(see illustration)**.
6   Withdraw the window regulator mechanism from inside the door, through the hole in the inner panel **(see illustrations)**.

Refitting

7   Refitting is a reversal of the removal procedure.

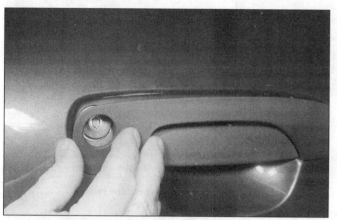

13.6D Rear door window regulator removed from the vehicle

14.3A Remove the two bolts (arrowed) . . .

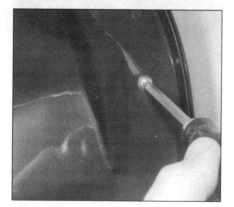

14.3B . . . followed by the exterior handle bezel

14.4A Unscrew the lock mounting bolts . . .

14.4B . . . and remove the plate

14.4C Removing the additional support screw

14.5 Disconnecting the central locking and alarm system wiring multi-plugs

14 Door handle and lock components - removal and refitting

Removal

Front door exterior handle

1   Remove the door inner trim panel (Section 11).
2   Use a knife to cut through the adhesive strip, so that the foam insulator can be peeled back locally for access to the lock. *Do not* peel back the foam insulator without first cutting through the adhesive strip, otherwise the insulator will be damaged. To ensure a good seal when the insulator is pressed back, do not touch the adhesive strip.
3   Unscrew and remove the two bolts for the exterior handle outer bezel, and remove the bezel **(see illustrations)**.
4   Unscrew and remove the lock mounting bolts on the inner rear edge of the door, and remove the plate. Also remove the additional support screw **(see illustrations)**.
5   Unclip and disconnect the wiring multi-plugs for the central locking and alarm systems **(see illustration)**.
6   Disconnect the wiring multi-plug from the door lock.
7   Disconnect the inner handle illumination light. Undo the screws and remove the inner handle. Disconnect the operating cable from the inner handle, as described later in this Section **(see illustrations)**.

11

14.7A Removing the inner handle

14.7B Disconnecting the operating cable from the inner handle

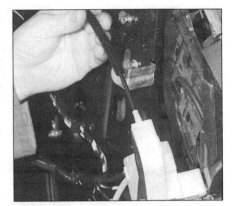

14.8A Removing the lock and exterior handle assembly from inside the door

14.8B Front door lock and exterior handle assembly removed from the vehicle

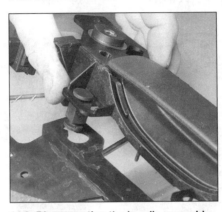

14.9 Disconnecting the handle assembly from the lock bracket

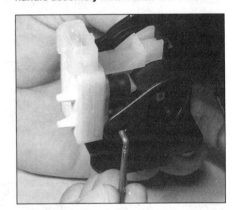

14.10 Pulling out the handle connecting rods

14.11 Removing the central locking "Set-reset" sensor

14.14A Prise out the plug . . .

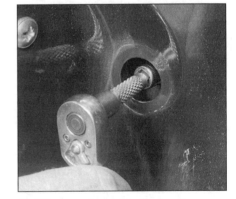

14.14B . . . and unscrew the handle mounting nuts

8   Manipulate the lock and handle assembly as necessary, and disconnect the wiring multi-plugs for the alarm sensor and central locking. Withdraw the complete assembly from inside the door **(see illustrations)**.

9   To disconnect the handle assembly from the lock bracket, slide the rubber posts inwards, and push out the assembly **(see illustration)**.

10   To remove the handle itself, twist the door handle through a quarter-turn, and pull out the connecting rods **(see illustration)**.

11   Remove the alarm sensor and the central locking "Set-reset" sensor **(see illustration)**.

Rear door exterior handle

12   Remove the door inner trim panel (Section 11).

13   Use a knife to cut through the adhesive strip, so that the foam insulator can be peeled back for access to the lock. *Do not* peel back the foam insulator without first cutting through the adhesive strip. To en-

sure a good seal when the insulator is pressed back, do not touch the adhesive strip.

14   Prise out the plug from the rear edge of the door, then unscrew the handle mounting nuts **(see illustrations)**.

15   Prise up the clip, and disconnect the operating rod from the lock **(see illustration)**.

16   Withdraw the handle from the outside of the door **(see illustration)**.

Interior handle

17   Remove the door inner trim panel (Section 11).

18   Use a knife to cut through the adhesive strip, so that the foam insulator can be peeled back for access to the lock. *Do not* peel back the foam insulator without first cutting through the adhesive strip. To ensure a good seal when the insulator is pressed back, do not touch the adhesive strip.

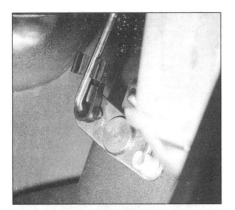

14.15 Disconnect the operating rod from the lock

14.16 Removing the rear door exterior handle

14.24 Prise out the barrel retaining tab . . .

14.25 . . . and pull out the lock barrel

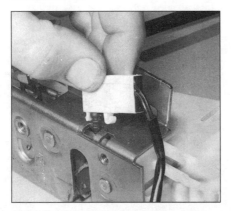

14.31 Unclipping the door-ajar sensor

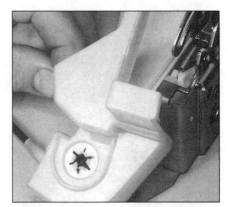

14.32 Removing the plastic shield from the locating post

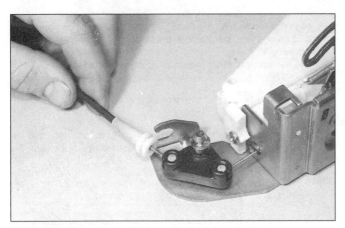

14.33 Slide the outer cable from the lock bracket

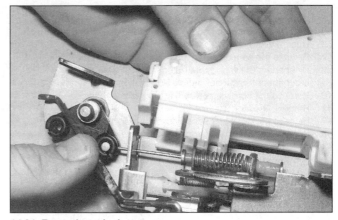

14.34 Removing a lock motor

19 Disconnect the interior handle illumination light.
20 Undo the screws and remove the interior handle.
21 To remove the cable, first pull back the plastic outer cable end and blanking piece. Apply light inward pressure to the control lever, with the lever in the locked position, until the inner cable is aligned with the release slot in the bottom of the cable holder.
22 Push down on the cable ferrule, and disconnect the inner cable. Remove the handle assembly.

Lock barrel

23 Remove the exterior handle as described earlier in this Section.
24 Prise out the barrel retaining tab from the handle body, using a small screwdriver **(see illustration)**.
25 Insert the key, turn it so that it engages the barrel, then pull out the barrel **(see illustration)**.

Lock motor - front door

26 Remove the exterior handle as described earlier in this Section.
27 Extract the clip, and pull out the operating rod.
28 Remove the operating rod from the plastic bush, by turning it through a quarter-turn.
29 Release the sensor wiring loom from the clip.
30 Detach the mounting plate from the lock.
31 Release the door-ajar sensor from the clip **(see illustration)**.
32 Prise the plastic shield from the locating post **(see illustration)**.
33 Slide the outer cable from the lock bracket **(see illustration)**, then turn the inner cable through a quarter-turn to remove it from the bell crank.
34 Unscrew the mounting screws and remove the lock motor **(see illustration)**.

11

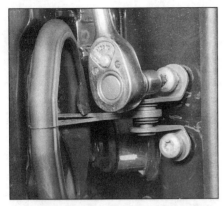

15.2A Front door check strap mounting screw removal

15.2B Front door check strap removed

15.3 Disconnecting a door wiring connector

15.4 Extract the small circlips . . .

15.5A . . . then drive out the hinge pins . . .

15.5B . . . and remove them

Lock motor - rear door

35 Remove the exterior handle as described earlier in this Section.
36 Unscrew and remove the three lock mounting screws.
37 Release the sensor wiring loom from the clip on the door.
38 Disconnect the wiring multi-plug from the door lock.
39 Disconnect the interior handle illumination light.
40 Remove the screws, and remove the interior handle.
41 Remove the lock assembly.
42 Release the door-ajar sensor from the clip.
43 Prise the plastic shield from the locating post.
44 Slide the outer cable from the lock bracket, then turn the inner cable through a quarter-turn to remove it from the bell crank.
45 Unscrew the mounting screws and remove the lock motor.

Striker

46 Using a pencil, mark the position of the striker.
47 Undo the mounting screws using a Torx key, and remove the striker.

Check strap

48 Disconnect the battery negative (earth) lead (Chapter 5, Section 1).
49 Using a Torx key, unscrew and remove the check strap mounting screw(s). On the front door, there are two screws; on the rear door, there is only one.
50 Prise the rubber grommet from the door aperture, then unscrew the mounting nuts and withdraw the check strap from the door.

Refitting

Handles (exterior and interior)

51 Refitting is a reversal of the removal procedure.

Lock barrel

52 Check that the retaining clip is fitted correctly.

53 Align the grooves on the barrel with the grooves on the body and operating lever, then carefully push the barrel into the handle until it engages the clip.
54 The remaining refitting procedure is a reversal of removal.

Lock motor

55 Refitting is a reversal of the removal procedure.

Striker

56 Refitting is a reversal of the removal procedure, but check that the door lock passes over the striker centrally. If necessary, re-position the striker before fully tightening the mounting screws.

Check strap

57 Refitting is a reversal of the removal procedure.

15 Door - removal and refitting

Removal

1 Disconnect the battery negative (earth) lead (Chapter 5, Section 1).
2 Using a Torx key, unscrew and remove the check strap mounting screw(s). On the front door, there are two screws; on the rear door, there is only one **(see illustrations)**.
3 Disconnect the wiring connector(s) by twisting them anti-clockwise. On the front door, there are two connectors; on the rear door, there is only one **(see illustration)**.
4 Extract the small circlips from the top of the upper and lower hinge pins **(see illustration)**.
5 Have an assistant support the weight of the door, then drive the hinge pins down through the hinges using a small drift **(see illustrations)**.
6 Carefully withdraw the door from the hinges.

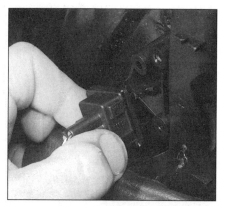
16.4 Disconnecting the wiring multi-plug from an electric exterior mirror

16.5A Unscrew the screws . . .

16.5B . . . and withdraw the mirror

Refitting

7   Refitting is a reversal of the removal procedure, but check that the door lock passes over the striker centrally. If necessary, re-position the striker.

16 Exterior mirror and glass - removal and refitting

Removal

1   Where electric mirrors are fitted, disconnect the battery negative (earth) lead (Chapter 5, Section 1).
2   Prise off the cap, unscrew the screw, and remove the quarter bezel from the front of the window opening.
3   On manual mirrors, detach the adjustment lever.
4   On electric mirrors, disconnect the wiring multi-plug **(see illustration)**.
5   On both types of mirror, use a Torx key to unscrew the mirror mounting screws, then withdraw the mirror from the outside of the door **(see illustrations)**. Recover the gasket.

Refitting

6   Refitting is a reversal of the removal procedure.

17 Interior mirror - removal and refitting

Removal

1   Using a length of strong thin cord or fishing line, break the adhesive bond between the base of the mirror and the glass. Have an assistant support and remove the mirror as it is released.
2   If the original mirror is to be refitted, thoroughly clean its base with methylated spirit and a lint-free cloth. Allow a period of one minute for the spirit to evaporate. Clean the windscreen black patch in a similar manner.

Refitting

3   During the installation of the mirror, it is important that the mirror base, windscreen black patch and the adhesive patch are not touched or contaminated in any way, otherwise poor adhesion will result.
4   Prior to fitting the mirror, the vehicle should have been at an ambient temperature of at least 20°C.
5   With the contact surfaces thoroughly cleaned, remove the protective tape from one side of the adhesive patch, and press it firmly into contact with the mirror base.
6   If fitting the mirror to a new windscreen, the protective tape must also be removed from the windscreen black patch.
7   Using a hairdryer or a hot air gun, warm the mirror base and the adhesive patch for about 30 seconds to a temperature of 50 to 70°C. Peel back the protective tape from the other side of the adhesive patch

on the mirror base. Align the mirror base and the windscreen patch, and press the mirror firmly into position. Hold the base of the mirror firmly against the windscreen for a minimum period of two minutes, to ensure full adhesion.
8   Wait at least thirty minutes before adjusting the mirror position.

18 Boot lid - removal and refitting

Removal

1   Disconnect the battery negative (earth) lead (Chapter 5, Section 1), and open the boot lid.
2   Where applicable, pull off the trim covering, and release the wiring on the hinge arm.
3   Where fitted, remove the trim from inside the boot lid.
4   Disconnect the wiring at the connectors visible through the boot lid inner skin aperture.
5   Attach a length of strong cord to the end of the wires in the aperture, to act as an aid to guiding the wiring through the lid when it is re-fitted.
6   Release the cable guide rubber grommet, and withdraw the wiring loom through it. Untie the cord, and leave it in the boot lid.
7   Mark the position of the hinge arms with a pencil.
8   Place rags beneath each corner of the boot lid, to prevent damage to the paintwork.
9   With the help of an assistant, unscrew the mounting bolts and lift the boot lid from the car.

Refitting

10   Refitting is a reversal of the removal procedure. Check that the boot lid is correctly aligned with the surrounding bodywork, with an equal clearance around its edge. Adjustment is made by loosening the hinge bolts, and moving the boot lid within the elongated mounting holes. Check that the lock enters the striker centrally when the boot lid is closed.

19 Boot lid lock components - removal and refitting

Removal

Lock barrel

1   Disconnect the battery negative (earth) lead (Chapter 5, Section 1).
2   With the boot lid open, remove the luggage space trim from the right-hand rear corner.
3   Remove the screws, and prise out the rear light trim cover from the guides.
4   Release the door-ajar sensor from the clip near the lock.
5   Slide the outer cable from the lock bracket. Raise the inner cable

11

20.6A Unclipping the upper trim panel from the tailgate

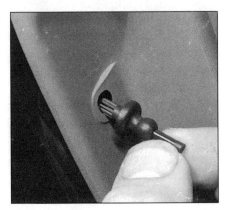

20.6B Shelf cord post removal

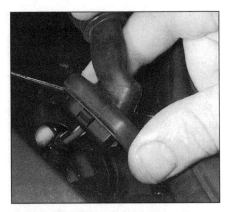

20.7 Removing the wiring loom rubber grommet

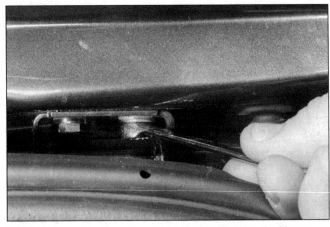

20.12 Unscrewing the bolts securing the tailgate to the hinges

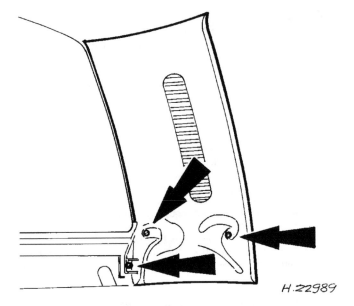

20.16 "D" pillar trim panel retaining screws (arrowed) - Estate models

until it is aligned with the slot in the barrel lever, and disconnect it.
6   Pull out the lock locating spring clip.
7   Detach the cable mounting bracket from the barrel, and remove the barrel.

Lock
8   Disconnect the battery negative (earth) lead (Chapter 5, Section 1).
9   With the boot lid open, prise out the clips and remove the trim from inside the boot lid.
10   Release the door-ajar sensor from the clip near the lock.
11   Using a Torx key, unscrew the lock mounting screws, and withdraw the lock for access to the cables.
12   Disconnect both the inner and outer cables from the lock bracket.
13   Prise open the plastic lip, and remove the central locking control rod.
14   Withdraw the lock assembly.

Refitting

Lock barrel and lock
15   Refitting is a reversal of the removal procedure.

20 Tailgate - removal and refitting

Removal

Hatchback
1   Disconnect the battery negative (earth) lead (Chapter 5, Section 1). Open the tailgate.
2   The tailgate may be unbolted from the hinges and the hinges left

in position, or the hinges may be detached from the roof panel by unscrewing the mounting nuts. In the latter case, carefully pull down the rear edge of the headlining for access to the nuts. Take care not to damage the headlining.
3   Remove the parcel shelf left-hand support bracket as follows. Fold the rear seat forwards, and disconnect the left-hand seat pull cable from the bracket and clips. Unscrew the screws and remove the bracket.
4   Pull up the rear seat side bolster, then carefully remove the side trim from the left-hand side of the luggage area. On low-series models, the bolster is retained with a screw.
5   Separate the tailgate wiring loom multi-plugs, located on the left-hand side of the luggage compartment, on top of the wheel arch.
6   Unclip and remove the upper trim panel from the inside of the tailgate. Also remove the rear shelf cord plastic post **(see illustrations)**.
7   Prise out the rubber grommet from the top of the tailgate aperture, and pull the wiring loom out through the hole in the body **(see illustration)**.
8   Disconnect the rear window washer tube from the jet.
9   Prise out the rubber grommet from the right-hand side of the tailgate aperture, and pull out the washer tube.
10   Have an assistant support the tailgate in its open position.
11   Using a small screwdriver, prise off the clips securing the struts to the tailgate. Pull the sockets from the ball-studs, and move the struts downwards.

20.24 Tailgate hinge and bolts - Estate models

21.2 Prising the spring clip from the upper end of the strut

21.3 Prising the spring clip from the lower end of the strut

22.6 Tailgate lock barrel and bracket

12 If the headlining has been pulled back, unscrew and remove the hinge nuts from the roof panel. Otherwise, unscrew the bolts securing the tailgate to the hinges **(see illustration)**.

13 Withdraw the tailgate from the body aperture, taking care not to damage the paintwork.

Estate

14 Disconnect the battery negative (earth) lead (Chapter 5, Section 1).

15 The tailgate may be unbolted from the hinges and the hinges left in position, or the hinges may be detached from the rear roof panel by unscrewing the mounting nuts. In the latter case, carefully pull down the rear edge of the headlining for access to the nuts. Take care not to damage the headlining.

16 Unscrew the retaining screws, then unclip the "D" pillar trim panels from both sides **(see illustration)**.

17 Unclip and remove the upper trim panel from inside the tailgate.

18 Carefully remove the side trim from the left-hand side of the luggage area, and separate the tailgate wiring loom multi-plugs in the rear light cluster housing.

19 Attach a strong fine cord to the end of the wiring loom, to act as an aid to guiding the wiring through the tailgate when it is refitted.

20 Prise the rubber grommet from the top left-hand side of the tailgate aperture, and pull out the wiring loom. Untie the cord, leaving it in position in the "D" pillar.

21 Disconnect the rear window washer tube from the jet. Pull out the rubber grommet, and remove the tube.

22 Have an assistant support the tailgate in its open position.

23 Using a small screwdriver, prise off the clip securing the struts to the tailgate. Pull the sockets from the ball-studs, and move the struts downwards.

24 Unscrew and remove the hinge nuts from the roof panel, or the hinge bolts from the hinge, as desired **(see illustration)**. Withdraw the tailgate from the body aperture, taking care not to damage the paintwork.

Refitting

Hatchback and Estate

25 Refitting is a reversal of the removal procedure, but check that the tailgate is located centrally in the body aperture, and that the striker enters the lock centrally. If necessary, loosen the mounting nuts and re-position the tailgate as required.

21 Tailgate support strut - removal and refitting

Removal

1 Support the tailgate in its open position.

2 Prise off the upper spring clip securing the strut to the tailgate, then pull the socket from the ball-stud **(see illustration)**.

3 Similarly prise off the bottom clip **(see illustration)**, and pull the socket from the ball-stud. Withdraw the strut.

Refitting

4 Refitting is a reversal of the removal procedure, but make sure that the piston end of the strut is fitted on the body (ie downwards).

22 Tailgate lock components - removal and refitting

Removal

Lock barrel (Hatchback)

1 Disconnect the battery negative (earth) lead (Chapter 5, Section 1).

2 With the tailgate open, pull up the weatherstrip for access to the lock. Remove the screws and clips, and remove the trim panel from the rear of the luggage compartment.

3 Unhook the parcel net, then remove the screws and clips, and remove the rear crossmember trim.

4 Remove the screws, and prise out the rear light trim cover from the guides.

5 Release the door-ajar sensor from the clip near the lock.

6 Slide the outer cable from the lock bracket. Raise the inner cable until it is aligned with the slot in the barrel lever, and disconnect it **(see illustration)**.

7 Pull out the lock barrel locating spring clip.

11

22.8A Removing the lock barrel . . .

22.8B . . . and cylinder

22.14 Removing the door-ajar sensor from the lock

22.15 Removing a lock mounting screw

22.16 Disconnecting the cables from the lock

22.21 Tailgate lock - Estate models

8   Detach the cable mounting bracket from the barrel, and remove the barrel and cylinder **(see illustrations)**.

Lock barrel (Estate)

9   Disconnect the battery negative (earth) lead (Chapter 5, Section 1).
10   Unclip and remove the tailgate trim panel. Undo the three screws and remove the lock shield, then unclip the door-ajar sensor.
11   Working through the aperture in the tailgate inner panel, pull out the lock barrel locating spring clip. Unhook the operating rod and withdraw the lock barrel.

Lock (Hatchback)

12   Disconnect the battery negative (earth) lead (Chapter 5, Section 1).
13   With the tailgate open, pull up the weatherstrip for access to the lock. Remove the screws and clips, and remove the trim panel from the rear of the luggage compartment.
14   Release the door-ajar sensor from the clip near the lock **(see illustration)**.
15   Using a Torx key, unscrew the lock mounting screws, and withdraw the lock for access to the cables **(see illustration)**.
16   Disconnect both the inner and outer cables from the lock bracket **(see illustration)**.
17   Prise open the plastic clip, and remove the central locking control rod.
18   Withdraw the lock assembly.

Lock (Estate)

19   Disconnect the battery negative (earth) lead (Chapter 5, Section 1).
20   Open the tailgate. Undo the screws and remove the inner trim.
21   Using a Torx key, unscrew the lock mounting screws, and carefully withdraw the lock **(see illustration)**.
22   Release the door-ajar sensor from the clip near the lock.
23   Disconnect the barrel operating rod, and remove the lock.
24   If necessary, the lock striker assembly may be removed by disconnecting the release cable and unscrewing the mounting bolts **(see illustration)**.

22.24 Lock striker assembly - Estate models

Refitting

Lock barrel and lock - all models

25   Refitting is a reversal of the removal procedure.

23 Central locking system components - testing, removal and refitting

Testing

1   The central locking module incorporates a service-test mode, which is activated by operating one of the lock position switches 8 times within 10 seconds. A buzzer will sound, to indicate that the service-test mode is operating, and to indicate that no faults have been

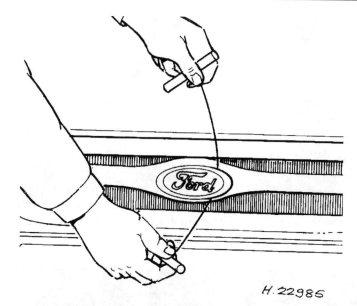

25.1 Using a length of cord to remove the emblem from the radiator grille

found in the system. If a fault has been found, the system should be checked by a Ford dealer or electrical specialist. The central locking module also incorporates the alarm system module.

Removal

Central locking/alarm module
2   To remove the module, first remove the lower right-hand facia panel (right-hand-drive models) or the glovebox (left-hand-drive models).
3   Disconnect the battery negative (earth) lead (Chapter 5, Section 1).
4   Unscrew the mounting bolts, and remove the module from the bracket beneath the facia.
5   Disconnect the wiring multi-plug, and withdraw the module from inside the vehicle.
6   Note that a different module is used for models without an anti-theft alarm.

Central locking set/reset switch
7   This procedure is covered in Section 14, under front door handle removal.

Central locking door-ajar switch
8   This procedure is covered in Section 14, under front door lock motor removal.

Refitting

Central locking/alarm module
9   Refitting is a reversal of the removal procedure.

Central locking set/reset switch
10   Refitting is a reversal of the removal procedure.

Central locking door-ajar switch
11   Refitting is a reversal of the removal procedure.

24 Windscreen and fixed windows - removal and refitting

1   The windscreen and rear window on all models are bonded in place with special mastic, as are the rear side windows on Estate models. Special tools are required to cut free the old units and fit replacements; special cleaning solutions and primer are also required. It is

therefore recommended that this work is entrusted to a Ford dealer or windscreen replacement specialist.
2   Note that the windscreen contributes towards the structural strength of the vehicle as a whole, so it is important that it is fitted correctly.

25 Body side-trim mouldings and adhesive emblems - removal and refitting

Removal

1   Insert a length of strong cord (fishing line is ideal) behind the moulding or emblem concerned. With a sawing action, break the adhesive bond between the moulding or emblem and the panel **(see illustration)**.
2   Thoroughly clean all traces of adhesive from the panel using methylated spirit, and allow the location to dry.

Refitting

3   Peel back the protective paper from the rear face of the new moulding or emblem. Carefully fit it into position on the panel concerned, but take care not to touch the adhesive. When in position, apply hand pressure to the moulding/emblem for a short period, to ensure maximum adhesion to the panel.

26 Sunroof - general information and adjustment

1   The sunroof should operate freely, without sticking or binding, as it is opened and closed. When in the closed position, check that the panel is flush with the surrounding roof panel.
2   If adjustment is required, open the sun blind, but leave the glass panel shut. Unscrew and remove the three lower frame-to-glass panel retaining screws. Slide the lower frame back into the roof.
3   Loosen the central and front securing screws. Adjust the glass roof panel so that it is flush at its front edge with the roof panel, then retighten the securing screws.
4   Pull the lower frame forwards, and insert and tighten its retaining screws to complete.

27 Seats - removal and refitting

Removal

Front seat
1   Release the seat belt, and slide the seat fully forwards.
2   Using a Torx key, undo the screws and remove the rear mounting trims, then unscrew the rear mounting bolts **(see illustrations)**.

27.2A Unscrew the Torx-headed screws . . .

27.2B ... and remove the mounting trims for access to the front seat rear mounting bolts

27.4 Disconnecting an electric seat multi-plug

27.5 Front seat front mounting bolt

27.6 Rear seat cushion hinge bolt

27.10 Rear seat backrest mounting bolts

28.2 Front seat belt reel unit lower mounting bolt

3   Slide the seat fully rearwards.
4   Where electric seats are fitted, disconnect the battery negative (earth) lead (Chapter 5, Section 1). Disconnect the seat wiring multi-plugs **(see illustration)**.
5   Unscrew the front mounting bolts, and remove the seat from the vehicle **(see illustration)**.

Rear seat cushion

6   Fold the rear seat cushion forwards. (Note that, on some models, the seat cushion is held in place by screws which must be removed first.) Using a Torx key, unscrew and remove the mounting bolts from the hinges on each side **(see illustration)**.
7   Withdraw the seat cushion from the vehicle.

Rear seat backrest

8   Fold the rear seat cushion and both backrests forwards.
9   Unclip the backrest rear trims, where fitted, and raise them.
10   Using a Torx key, unscrew the mounting bolts **(see illustration)**.
11   Withdraw the backrest from inside the vehicle.

Rear seat side bolster

12   Fold the rear seat backrest forwards.
13   On low-series models, remove the screw and pull the bolster forwards to disengage the clips. On high-series models, simply pull the bolster upwards to disengage the clips.

Refitting

14   Refitting is a reversal of the removal procedure, but tighten the mounting bolts to the specified torque.

28.3A Front seat belt guide and mounting bolt

28 Seat belts - removal and refitting

Warning: *Be careful when handling the seat belt tensioning device ("grabber"). It contains a powerful spring, which could cause injury if released in an uncontrolled fashion. Once fired, the grabber cannot be reset, and must be renewed. Note also that seat belts and associated components which have been subject to impact loads must be renewed.*

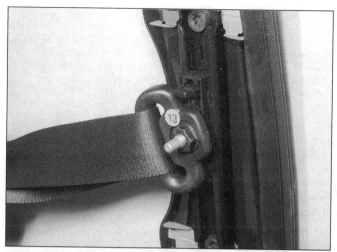

28.3B Front seat belt shackle and mounting nut

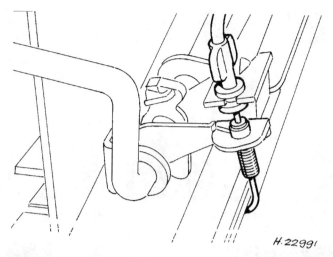

28.4A Front seat belt stalk cable

28.4B Front seat stalk mounting nut

28.5A Remove the recline adjustment knob . . .

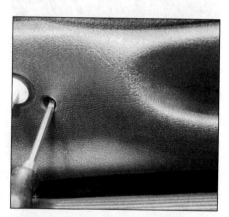

28.5B . . . unscrew the trim retaining screws . . .

28.5C . . . and unscrew the seat belt end retaining bolt

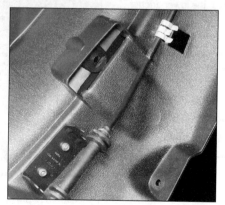

28.6A Detach the rear seat release cable

28.6B Removing the plastic cover from the rear seat lock

Removal

Front seat belt

1   Remove the trim from the "B" pillar and the scuttle.
2   Unscrew the mounting bolts and remove the seat belt reel unit **(see illustration)**.
3   Unscrew the bolt securing the seat belt guide to the "B" pillar, then unscrew the nut securing the seat belt shackle **(see illustrations)**.
4   Detach the stalk cable, then undo the mounting nut, and remove the stalk and grabber assembly from the front seat **(see illustrations)**.
Warning: *There is a potential risk of the grabber firing during removal,*

so it should be handled carefully. As an extra precaution, a spacer may be fitted on the cable before removal. Hold the adjustment lever in the "adjust" position while inserting the spacer.

5   Remove the recline adjustment knob and trim from the outer side of the front seat, then unscrew the bolt and remove the seat belt end from the seat **(see illustrations)**.

Rear side seat belt

6   Unscrew the screws and remove the trim from the "C" pillar. It will be necessary to detach the rear seat release cable, and remove the plastic cover from the rear seat lock **(see illustrations)**.

11

28.7A Rear seat belt shackle mounting bolt

28.7B Rear seat belt reel mounting bolt

28.8 Rear seat belt lower anchorage

29.10A Removing a middle screw from the lower trim

29.10B Releasing the fasteners from the cowl side trim

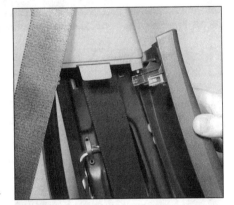

29.11 Separating the "B" pillar lower and upper trim

7   Fold the rear seat cushions forward. Unscrew the mounting bolts from the seat belt shackle and reel **(see illustrations)**.

8   Unscrew the mounting bolt securing the seat belt stalk, and withdraw the stalk. Also unscrew the mounting bolt from the lower anchorage, where applicable **(see illustration)**.

Rear centre seat belt

9   Unscrew the mounting bolts securing the seat belt and stalks to the floor. Note that the stalks are handed, and are marked Left or Right.

Refitting

10   Refitting is a reversal of the removal procedure. Tighten the mounting nuts and bolts to the specified torque.

29 Interior trim panels - removal and refitting

Removal

Sun visor

1   Disconnect the wiring for the vanity mirror light, where fitted.

2   Unscrew the mounting screws and remove the visor.

3   Prise up the cover, unscrew the inner bracket mounting screws, and remove the bracket.

Passenger grab handle

4   Prise up the covers, then unscrew the mounting screws and remove the grab handle.

"A" pillar trim

5   Pull away the door weatherstrip in the area of the trim.

6   Release the alarm and aerial wiring from the upper and middle clips.

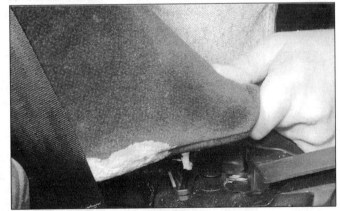

29.15A Pull up the rear seat bolster . . .

7   Carefully press the trim away from the upper and middle clips, and pull the trim upwards. Recover the lower sealing strip.

8   Remove the upper and middle clips from the pillar.

"B" pillar and cowl side trim

9   Pull away the door weatherstrip in the area of the trim.

10   Undo the screws, release the fasteners and remove the lower trim **(see illustrations)**.

11   Carefully separate the lower trim from the upper trim, using a screwdriver if necessary **(see illustration)**.

12   Unscrew the seat belt mounting bolt from under the front seat, remove the remaining trim from the "B" pillar, and feed the belt through the trim.

"C" pillar trim (Saloon and Hatchback)

13   Pull away the door weatherstrip in the area of the trim.

29.15B ... and release the upper hook

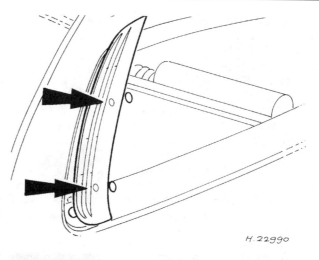

29.18 Screw locations (arrowed) for the "C" pillar upper trim - Estate models

H.22990

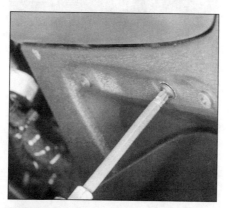

29.23A Unscrew the mounting screws from the upper corners ...

29.23B ... and above the coin tray position ...

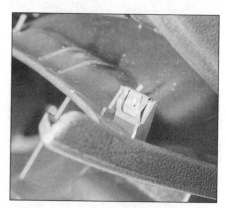

29.23C ... and withdraw the lower facia panel

30.3 Gear lever knob removal

14   Fold the rear seat cushion forwards.
15   Pull up the rear seat bolster, and release the upper hook. Note that, on low-series models, the bolster is retained with a screw (see illustrations).
16   Undo the screw, release the clips, and detach the upper trim.
17   Remove the rear seat belt lower mounting bolt, then remove the trim, and pass the seat belt through it.

"C" pillar trim (Estate)
18   Prise off the caps, unscrew the screws, and remove the upper trim from the "C" pillar (see illustration).
19   Unscrew the mounting bolt securing the rear seat belt upper shackle to the "C" pillar.
20   Unclip and remove the trim.

"D" pillar trim (Estate)
21   Remove the three mounting screws, then unclip the trim from the "D" pillar.

Lower facia panel
22   Remove the steering column top and bottom shrouds.
23   Unscrew the mounting screws from the upper corners and above the coin tray position, and withdraw the lower facia panel from the facia (see illustrations).

Refitting
24   Refitting is a reversal of the removal procedure. Where seat belt fastenings have been disturbed, make sure that they are tightened to the specified torque.

30   Centre console - removal and refitting

11

Removal
1   Disconnect the battery negative (earth) lead (Chapter 5, Section 1).
2   Pull the ashtray from the facia.
3   Pull off the gear lever (or selector lever) knob (see illustration).
4   Using a screwdriver, carefully prise out the gear lever gaiter/switch panel or selector lever panel, as applicable. When

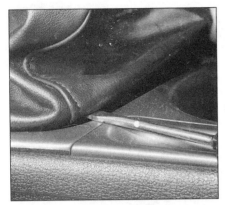

30.4 Prising out the gear lever gaiter

30.6A Prise off the plastic caps . . .

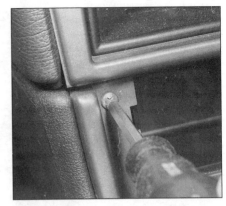

30.6B . . . and unscrew the mounting screws at the front top . . .

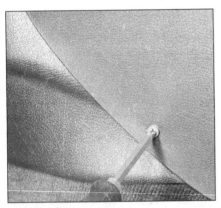

30.6C . . . at the sides . . .

30.6D . . . and inside the cassette storage box

30.7A Withdrawing the front of the console from the facia

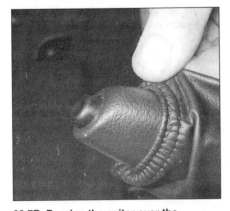

30.7B Passing the gaiter over the handbrake lever

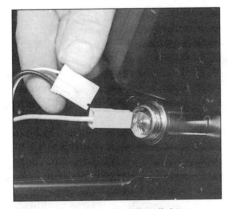

30.8 Disconnecting the cigar lighter wiring

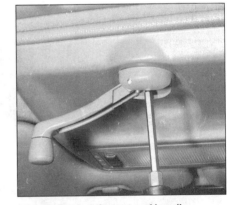

31.3 Removing the sunroof handle securing screw

necessary, disconnect the wiring multi-plugs **(see illustration)**.

5   Remove the adaptive damping switch, when fitted (Chapter 12).

6   Prise off the plastic caps, then unscrew the centre console mounting screws. These are located on each side, on the front top, and inside the cassette storage box. The screws with the washers go on the side of the console; the front screws are smaller than the others, and black in colour **(see illustrations)**.

7   Fully apply the handbrake lever. Withdraw the centre console, at the same time passing the gaiter over the handbrake lever **(see illustrations)**.

8   Disconnect the cigar lighter wiring **(see illustration)**.

Refitting

9   Refitting is a reversal of the removal procedure.

31 Overhead console - removal and refitting

Removal

1   Disconnect the battery negative (earth) lead (Chapter 5, Section 1).

2   When applicable, remove the sunroof switch (Chapter 12).

3   When applicable, remove the sunroof handle, after undoing the securing screw **(see illustration)**.

4   Push the console towards the windscreen, to disengage it from the clips.

Refitting

5   Refitting is a reversal of the removal procedure.

32.1 Glovebox removal

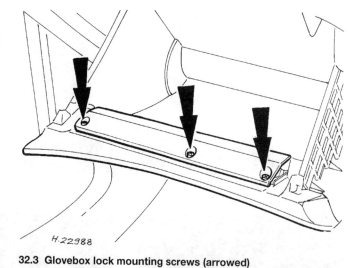

32.3 Glovebox lock mounting screws (arrowed)

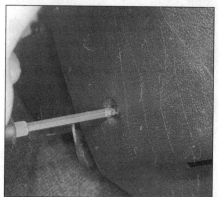

33.3A Unscrew the screws . . .

33.3B . . . and remove the heater side covers

33.18A Prise off the covers . . .

32 Glovebox - removal and refitting

Removal

1   Open the glovebox. Using a screwdriver, carefully press in one side of the glovebox near the hinge, to release it from the plastic clip (see illustration).
2   Withdraw the glovebox and, where necessary, disconnect the wiring multi-plug for the light.
3   If necessary, the lock may be removed by unscrewing the mounting screws and removing the lock plate and spring (see illustration).
4   To remove the lock barrel, depress the spring tabs.

Refitting

5   Locate the barrel in the lock plate, making sure that the clips are fully engaged.
6   Hold the latch pins together, and engage the right-hand pin of the lock plate.
7   Refit the spring, and engage the left-hand pin of the lock plate.
8   Refit the lock plate, and tighten the screws.
9   Reconnect the wiring multi-plug and refit the glovebox, making sure that it is fully inserted in the plastic clips.

33 Facia - removal and refitting

Removal

1   Disconnect the battery negative (earth) lead (Chapter 5, Section 1).
2   Remove the windscreen wiper arms (Chapter 12), then remove the cowl from just in front of the windscreen. The cowl is in two

sections, with retaining screws located along its front edge. With the cowl removed, disconnect the speedometer cable by pulling it from the intermediate inner cable extension.
3   Remove the centre console (Section 30), then unscrew the screws and remove the heater side covers (see illustrations).
4   Remove the steering column (Chapter 10).
5   Remove the instrument panel (Chapter 12).
6   Where fitted, unscrew the screws and remove the automatic warning system display.
7   Remove the radio and (if fitted) the CD player (Chapter 12).
8   Remove the heater control panel (Chapter 3).
9   Using a screwdriver, carefully prise out the headlight switch panel, and disconnect the wiring multi-plugs.
10   Remove the glovebox (Section 32).
11   Remove the small piece of carpet from under the passenger side of the facia.
12   Remove the side trim panels from the "A" and "B" pillars on each side of the vehicle (Section 29). The upper panels on the "B" pillars can be left in position.
13   At the base of the right-hand "A" pillar, disconnect the wiring multi-plugs, earth leads and aerial, noting their fitted positions.
14   Identify the position of the wiring multi-plugs on the fusebox, then disconnect them.
15   Disconnect the wiring from the footwell lights, where fitted.
16   Prise out the speedometer cable rubber grommet at the bulkhead near the pedal bracket, then release the cable from the clips.
17   Remove the screws and withdraw the glovebox side trim, for access to the side facia mounting screw.
18   Open the front doors. Prise off the trim covers, then pull away the door weatherstrip by the side mounting bolt positions on each side (see illustrations).

11

33.18B . . . and pull away the weatherstrip to reveal the facia mounting bolts

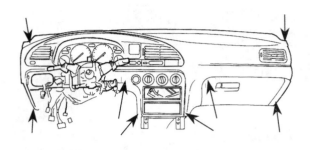

33.20A Facia mounting bolt positions (left-hand-drive shown, right-hand-drive similar)

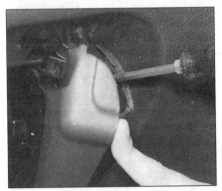

33.20B Facia mounting bolt next to the glovebox

33.20C Facia centre mounting bolt next to the heater panel

33.20D Facia mounting bolt near the heater

33.22 Disconnecting the fresh air hoses

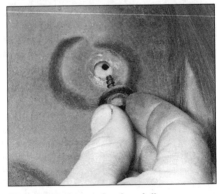

34.3 Removing a wheel arch liner retaining screw

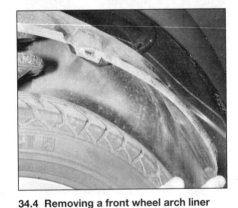

34.4 Removing a front wheel arch liner

19 Unscrew the facia side mounting bolts.

20 Unscrew the facia centre mounting bolts **(see illustrations)**.

21 Withdraw the facia from the bulkhead, far enough to be able to reach in behind it.

22 Disconnect the remaining multi-plugs and connections, noting their locations on the various components for correct refitting. It will also be necessary to release some wiring loom holders, clips and plastic ties, and the fresh air vent hoses **(see illustration)**.

23 Withdraw the facia from one side of the vehicle.

Refitting

24 Refitting is a reversal of the removal procedure. On completion, check the operation of all electrical components.

34 Wheel arch liner - removal and refitting

Removal

Front

1 Apply the handbrake, jack up the front of the vehicle and support

it on axle stands. If wished, remove the wheel to improve access.

2 Prise out the stud clip on the front lower edge of the liner.

3 Using a Torx key, unscrew the screws securing the liner to the inner wheel arch panel **(see illustration)**.

4 Remove the screws and clips securing the liner to the outer edge of the wheel arch and bumper. Withdraw the liner from under the vehicle **(see illustration)**.

Rear

5 Chock the front wheels, jack up the rear of the vehicle and support it on axle stands. If wished, remove the wheel to improve access.

6 Unscrew and remove the nuts, located on either side of the coil spring, securing the central section of the liner.

7 Using a Torx key, unscrew the screws securing the liner to the centre of the inner wheel arch panel.

8 Remove the clips securing the liner to the outer edge of the wheel arch, and withdraw the liner from under the vehicle.

Refitting

9 Refitting is a reversal of the removal procedure. If the wheels were removed, tighten the wheel nuts to the specified torque.

Chapter 12   Body electrical system

Contents

Specifications

Fuses (auxiliary fusebox in engine compartment)

Note: *Fuse ratings and circuits are liable to change from year to year. Consult the handbook supplied with the vehicle, or consult a Ford dealer, for specific information.*

Fuse No	Rating	Colour	Circuit(s) protected
1	80	Black	Power supply to main fusebox
2	60	Yellow	Radiator electric cooling fans
3	60	Yellow	Diesel engine glow plugs and/or ABS braking system
4	20	Yellow	Ignition system, or ignition and daytime running lights
5	30	Light green	Heated windscreen (left-hand side)
6	30	Light green	Heated windscreen (right-hand side)
7	30	Light green	ABS braking system
8	30	Light green	Air conditioning compressor/heated seats or air conditioning compressor/daytime running lights
9	20	Light blue	ECU (petrol), Cold start solenoid (Diesel)
10	20	Light blue	Ignition switch
11	3	Violet	ECU memory
12	15	Light blue	Horn and hazard flasher warning system
13	15	Light blue	Oxygen sensor
14	15	Light blue	Fuel pump
15	10	Red	Dipped beam headlight (right-hand side)
16	10	Red	Dipped beam headlight (left-hand side)
17	10	Red	Main beam headlight (right-hand side)
18	10	Red	Main beam headlight (left-hand side)

12

Fuses (main fusebox in passenger compartment)

Note: *Fuse ratings and circuits are liable to change from year to year. Consult the handbook supplied with the vehicle, or consult a Ford dealer, for specific information.*

Fuse	Rating	Colour	Circuit(s) protected
19	7.5	Brown	Heated door mirrors
20	10	Black	Front/rear wiper motor (circuit breaker)
21	30	Light green	Front electric windows (only)
21	40	Orange	Front and rear electric windows
22	7.5	Brown	ABS module
23	15	Light blue	Adaptive damping
24	15	Light blue	Stop-lights
25	20	Yellow	Central locking system/double-locking/anti-theft alarm
26	20	Yellow	Foglights
27	15	Light blue	Cigar lighter
28	30	Light green	Headlight washer system
29	30	Light green	Heated rear window
30	7.5	Brown	Interior lighting and auxiliary warning system.
31	7.5	Brown	Instrument panel illumination
32	7.5	Brown	Radio
33	7.5	Brown	Front and rear sidelights (left-hand side).
34	7.5	Brown	Interior lighting and digital clock
35	7.5	Brown	Front and rear sidelights (right-hand side)
36	30	Light green	Radio
37	30	Light green	Heater blower
38	7.5	Brown	Airbag

Relays (auxiliary fusebox in engine compartment)

Relay	Colour	Circuit(s) protected
R1	Green	Daytime running lights (left hand-drive, but not all countries) or dim-dip lights (UK)
R2	Black	Radiator electric cooling fan (high speed)
R3	Blue (petrol)	Air conditioning cut-out
R3	Brown (Diesel)	Air conditioning in conjunction with Diesel engine
R4	Yellow	Windscreen heater time delay
R5	Dark green (petrol)	Radiator electric cooling fan (low speed)
R5	Black (Diesel)	Radiator electric cooling fan (low speed)
R6	Yellow	Starter solenoid
R7	Brown	Horns
R8	Brown	Fuel pump
R9	White	Dipped beam headlights
R10	White	Main beam headlights
R11	Brown	ECU power supply (petrol), cold start (Diesel)

Relays (main fusebox in passenger compartment)

Relay	Colour	Circuit(s) protected
R12	White	Interior, courtesy and footwell lights
R13	Yellow	Heated rear window
R14	Yellow	Heater blower
R15	Green	Windscreen wiper motor
R16	Black	Ignition

Auxiliary relays (not in the fuseboxes)

Relay	Colour	Circuit(s) protected	Location
R17	Black	Diesel glow plug	Battery tray
R18	Black	"One-touch down" driver's window relay	Driver's door
R19	Blue	Speed control cut-off below the instrument panel	Central fuse box bracket
R20	Blue	Headlight washer system	Bulb module bracket
R21	Orange	Rear screen wiper interval	Bulb module bracket
R22	White	Foglights (left-hand-drive only)	Interface module bracket
R23	Black	Direction indicators	Steering column
R24	White	Anti-theft alarm (left-hand side)	Door lock module bracket
R25	White	Anti-theft alarm (right-hand side)	Door lock module bracket
R26	Black	Heated seats	Door lock module bracket

Bulbs

	Wattage	Type
Headlight main beam	55	Halogen
Headlight dipped beam	55	Halogen
Foglights	55	Halogen

Sidelights	5	Wedge
Direction indicator lights	21	Bayonet
Side repeater lights	5	Wedge
Stop-lights	21	Bayonet
Reversing lights	21	Bayonet
Rear fog/tail lights (Saloon and Estate)	21/4	Bayonet
Rear tail light (Saloon and Hatchback)	5	Bayonet
Number plate lights	5	Festoon
Engine compartment	10	Wedge
Interior lights	10	Festoon
Reading light..	5	Wedge

Torque wrench settings

	Nm	lbf ft
Windscreen wiper motor bolts:		
Into old motor (see text)	8	6
Into new motor (see text)...	12	9

1 General information

Warning: *Before carrying out any work on the electrical system, read through the precautions given in "Safety first!" at the beginning of this manual.*

The electrical system is of 12-volt negative earth type. Power for the lights and all electrical accessories is supplied by a lead/acid battery which is charged by the alternator.

This Chapter covers repair and service procedures for the various electrical components not associated with the engine. Information on the battery, ignition system, alternator, and starter motor can be found in Chapter 5.

All models are fitted with a driver's air bag, which is designed to prevent serious chest and head injuries to the driver during an accident. A similar bag for the front seat passenger is also available **(see illustration)**. The sensor and electronic unit for the air bag is located next to the steering column inside the vehicle, and contains a back-up

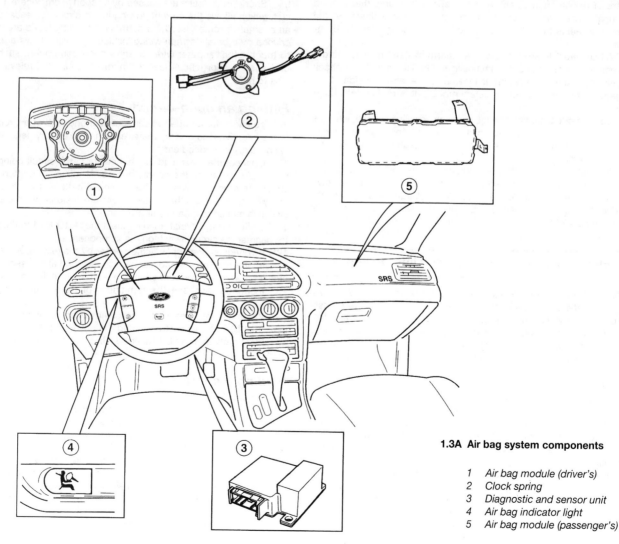

1.3A Air bag system components

1   Air bag module (driver's)
2   Clock spring
3   Diagnostic and sensor unit
4   Air bag indicator light
5   Air bag module (passenger's)

12

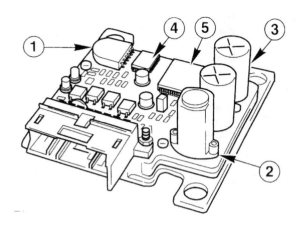

1.3B Air bag sensor and electronic unit

1	*Crash sensor*	*4*	*Application Specific*
2	*Safety sensor*		*Integrated Circuit*
3	*Voltage back-up*	*5*	*Microprocessor*

capacitor, crash sensor, decelerometer, safety sensor, integrated circuit and microprocessor **(see illustration)**. The air bag is inflated by a gas generator, which forces the bag out of the module cover in the centre of the steering wheel. A "clock spring" ensures that a good electrical connection is maintained with the air bag at all times - as the steering wheel is turned in each direction, the spring winds and unwinds.

All UK models are fitted with an alarm system incorporating a movement sensor and ignition immobiliser. On Saloon and Hatchback models, the alarm system horn is located on the left-hand side of the luggage compartment, but on Estate models, it is on the right-hand side.

Some models are fitted with a headlight levelling system, which is controlled by a knob on the facia. On position "0", the headlights are in their base position, and on position "5", the headlights are in their maximum inclined angle.

It should be noted that, when portions of the electrical system are serviced, the cable should be disconnected from the battery negative terminal, to prevent electrical shorts and fires. **Caution:** *When disconnecting the battery for work described in the following Sections, refer to Chapter 5, Section 1.*

2 Electrical fault finding - general information

Note: *Refer to the precautions given in "Safety first!" and in Section 1 of this Chapter before starting work. The following tests relate to testing of the main electrical circuits, and should not be used to test delicate electronic circuits (such as engine management systems, anti-lock braking systems, etc), particularly where an electronic control module is used. Also refer to the precautions given in Chapter 5, Section 1.*

General

1   A typical electrical circuit consists of an electrical component, any switches, relays, motors, fuses, fusible links or circuit breakers related to that component, and the wiring and connectors which link the component to both the battery and the chassis. To help to pinpoint a problem in an electrical circuit, wiring diagrams are included at the end of this manual.

2   Before attempting to diagnose an electrical fault, first study the appropriate wiring diagram, to obtain a complete understanding of the components included in the particular circuit concerned. The possible sources of a fault can be narrowed down by noting if other components related to the circuit are operating properly. If several components or circuits fail at one time, the problem is likely to be related to a shared fuse or earth connection.

3   Electrical problems usually stem from simple causes, such as loose or corroded connections, a faulty earth connection, a blown fuse, a melted fusible link, or a faulty relay (refer to Section 3 for details of testing relays). Visually inspect the condition of all fuses, wires and connections in a problem circuit before testing the components. Use the wiring diagrams to determine which terminal connections will need to be checked in order to pinpoint the trouble-spot.

4   The basic tools required for electrical fault-finding include a circuit tester or voltmeter (a 12-volt bulb with a set of test leads can also be used for certain tests); an ohmmeter (to measure resistance and check for continuity); a battery and set of test leads; and a jumper wire, preferably with a circuit breaker or fuse incorporated, which can be used to bypass suspect wires or electrical components. Before attempting to locate a problem with test instruments, use the wiring diagram to determine where to make the connections.

5   To find the source of an intermittent wiring fault (usually due to a poor or dirty connection, or damaged wiring insulation), a "wiggle" test can be performed on the wiring. This involves wiggling the wiring by hand to see if the fault occurs as the wiring is moved. It should be possible to narrow down the source of the fault to a particular section of wiring. This method of testing can be used in conjunction with any of the tests described in the following sub-Sections.

6   Apart from problems due to poor connections, two basic types of fault can occur in an electrical circuit - open-circuit, or short-circuit.

7   Open-circuit faults are caused by a break somewhere in the circuit, which prevents current from flowing. An open-circuit fault will prevent a component from working.

8   Short-circuit faults are caused by a "short" somewhere in the circuit, which allows the current flowing in the circuit to "escape" along an alternative route, usually to earth. Short-circuit faults are normally caused by a breakdown in wiring insulation, which allows a feed wire to touch either another wire, or an earthed component such as the bodyshell. A short-circuit fault will normally cause the relevant circuit fuse to blow.

Finding an open-circuit

9   To check for an open-circuit, connect one lead of a circuit tester or the negative lead of a voltmeter either to the battery negative terminal or to a known good earth.

10   Connect the other lead to a connector in the circuit being tested, preferably nearest to the battery or fuse. At this point, battery voltage should be present, unless the lead from the battery or the fuse itself is faulty (bearing in mind that some circuits are live only when the ignition switch is moved to a particular position).

11   Switch on the circuit, then connect the tester lead to the connector nearest the circuit switch on the component side.

12   If voltage is present (indicated either by the tester bulb lighting or a voltmeter reading, as applicable), this means that the section of the circuit between the relevant connector and the switch is problem-free.

13   Continue to check the remainder of the circuit in the same fashion.

14   When a point is reached at which no voltage is present, the problem must lie between that point and the previous test point with voltage. Most problems can be traced to a broken, corroded or loose connection.

Finding a short-circuit

15   To check for a short-circuit, first disconnect the load(s) from the circuit (loads are the components which draw current from a circuit, such as bulbs, motors, heating elements, etc).

16   Remove the relevant fuse from the circuit, and connect a circuit tester or voltmeter to the fuse connections.

17   Switch on the circuit, bearing in mind that some circuits are live only when the ignition switch is moved to a particular position.

18   If voltage is present (indicated either by the tester bulb lighting or a voltmeter reading, as applicable), this means that there is a short-circuit.

19   If no voltage is present during this test, but the fuse still blows with the load(s) reconnected, this indicates an internal fault in the load(s).

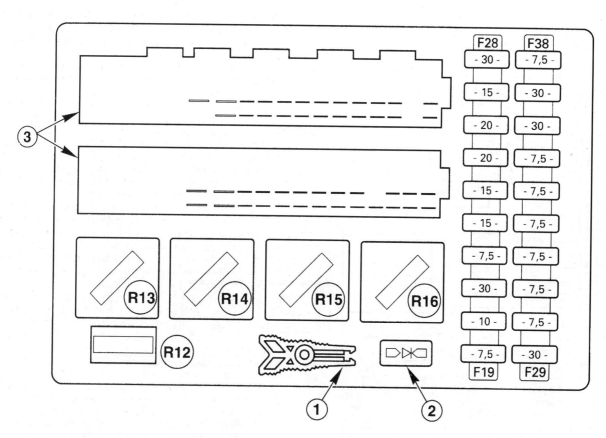

3.1 Main fusebox layout

1   *Fuse/relay removal tweezers*   2   *Diode*   3   *Multi-plug connections*

Finding an earth fault

20   The battery negative terminal is connected to "earth" - the metal of the engine/transmission unit and the vehicle body - and many systems are wired so that they only receive a positive feed, the current returning via the metal of the car body. This means that the component mounting and the body form part of that circuit. Loose or corroded mountings can therefore cause a range of electrical faults, ranging from total failure of a circuit, to a puzzling partial failure. In particular, lights may shine dimly (especially when another circuit sharing the same earth point is in operation), motors (eg wiper motors or the radiator cooling fan motor) may run slowly, and the operation of one circuit may have an apparently-unrelated effect on another. Note that on many vehicles, earth straps are used between certain components, such as the engine/transmission and the body, usually where there is no metal-to-metal contact between components, due to flexible rubber mountings, etc.

21   To check whether a component is properly earthed, disconnect the battery (refer to Chapter 5, Section 1) and connect one lead of an ohmmeter to a known good earth point. Connect the other lead to the wire or earth connection being tested. The resistance reading should be zero; if not, check the connection as follows.

22   If an earth connection is thought to be faulty, dismantle the connection, and clean both the bodyshell and the wire terminal (or the component earth connection mating surface) back to bare metal. Be careful to remove all traces of dirt and corrosion, then use a knife to trim away any paint, so that a clean metal-to-metal joint is made. On reassembly, tighten the joint fasteners securely; if a wire terminal is being refitted, use serrated washers between the terminal and the bodyshell, to ensure a clean and secure connection. When the connection is remade, prevent the onset of corrosion in the future by applying a coat of petroleum jelly or silicone-based grease, or by spraying on (at regular intervals) a proprietary ignition sealer such as Holts Damp Start, or a water-dispersant lubricant such as Holts Wet Start.

3   Fuses, relays and timer module - testing and renewal

Note: *It is important to note that the ignition switch and the appropriate electrical circuit must always be switched off before any of the fuses (or relays) are removed and renewed. In the event of the fuse/relay unit having to be removed, the battery earth lead must be disconnected. When reconnecting the battery, reference should be made to Chapter 5.*

1   Fuses are designed to break a circuit when a predetermined current is reached, in order to protect components and wiring which could be damaged by excessive current flow. Any excessive current flow will be due to a fault in the circuit, usually a short-circuit (see Section 2). The main fusebox, which also carries some relays, is located inside the vehicle below the facia panel on the passenger's side, and is accessed by a lever behind the glovebox **(see illustration)**.

2   A central timer module is located on the bottom of the main fusebox. This module contains the time control elements for the heated rear window, interior lights and intermittent wiper operation. The module also activates a warning buzzer/chime when the vehicle is left with the lights switched on, or if a vehicle fitted with automatic transmission is not parked in position "P".

3   The auxiliary fusebox is located on the front left-hand side of the engine compartment, and is accessed by unclipping and removing the

12

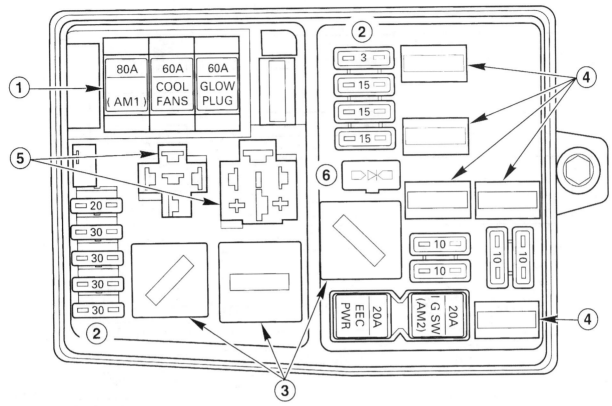

3.3 Auxiliary fusebox layout

1   Fuses 1 to 3
2   Fuses 4 to 8, 11 to 14
3   Relays R2, R5 and R6
4   Relays R7 to R11
5   Relay sockets for relays R1 and R4
6   Diode

cover. The auxiliary fusebox also contains some relays **(see illustration)**. Each circuit is identified by numbers on the main fusebox and on the inside of the auxiliary fusebox cover. Reference to the fuse chart in the Specifications at the start of this Chapter will indicate the circuits protected by each fuse. Plastic tweezers are attached to the main fusebox and to the inside face of the auxiliary fuse and block cover, to remove and fit the fuses and relays.

4   To remove a fuse, use the tweezers provided to pull it out of the holder. Slide the fuse sideways from the tweezers. The wire within the fuse is clearly visible, and it will be broken if the fuse is blown **(see illustration)**.

5   Always renew a fuse with one of an identical rating. Never substitute a fuse of a higher rating, or make temporary repairs using wire or metal foil; more serious damage, or even fire, could result. The fuse rating is stamped on top of the fuse. Never renew a fuse more than

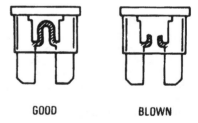

GOOD   BLOWN

3.4 The fuses can be checked visually to determine if they are blown

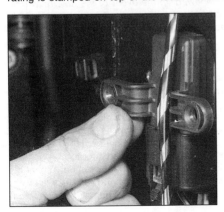

3.7 "One-touch down" window relay in the driver's door

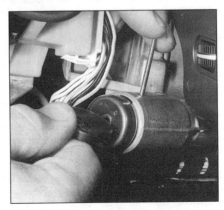

4.3A Depress the locking plunger . . .

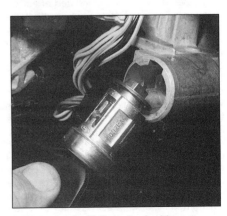

4.3B . . . and withdraw the ignition lock barrel

4.4A Release the retaining tab . . .

4.4B . . . and remove the ignition switch

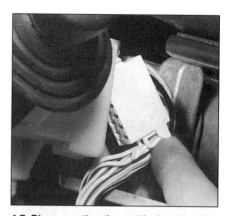

4.7 Disconnecting the multi-plug from the windscreen wiper multi-function switch

4.8A Depress the plastic tab with a screwdriver . . .

4.8B . . . and remove the windscreen wiper multi-function switch

once without tracing the source of the trouble.

6   Spare fuses of various current ratings are provided in the cover of the auxiliary fusebox. Note that if the vehicle is to be laid up for a long period, fuse 34 in the main fusebox should be removed, to prevent the ancillary electrical components from discharging the battery.

7   Relays are electrically-operated switches, which are used in certain circuits. The various relays can be removed from their respective locations by carefully pulling them from the sockets. Each relay in the fuseboxes has a plastic bar on its upper surface to enable the use of the tweezers. The locations and functions of the various relays are given in the Specifications (see illustration).

8   If a component controlled by a relay becomes inoperative and the relay is suspect, listen to the relay as the circuit is operated. If the relay is functioning, it should be possible to hear it click as it is energized. If the relay proves satisfactory, the fault lies with the components or wiring of the system. If the relay is not being energized, then either the relay is not receiving a switching voltage, or the relay itself is faulty. (Do not overlook the relay socket terminals when tracing faults.) Testing is by the substitution of a known good unit, but be careful; while some relays are identical in appearance and in operation, others look similar, but perform different functions.

9   The central timer module located on the bottom of the main fusebox incorporates its own self-diagnosis function. Note that diagnosis cannot take place if the heated rear window is defective.

10   To activate the system, press the heated rear window button while the ignition is being switched on, then release the button. Operate the light switch, washer pump switch and all of the door switches one after the other, and check that the buzzer confirms that the input signals are correct.

11   Now move the wiper lever to the intermittent wipe position, and check the output signals by operating the same switches.

12   The self-diagnosis function is turned off by switching the ignition off and on again.

4   Switches - removal and refitting

Removal

Ignition switch and lock barrel

1   Disconnect the battery negative (earth) lead (refer to Chapter 5, Section 1).

2   Remove the rubber gaiters and locking rings, then remove the securing screws and take off the steering column upper and lower shrouds.

3   Insert the ignition key, and turn it to the accessory position. Using a small screwdriver or twist drill through the hole in the side of the lock housing, depress the locking plunger and withdraw the lock barrel (see illustrations).

4   The switch may be removed from the steering column assembly by disconnecting the multi-plug, then using a screwdriver to release the switch retaining tab (see illustrations).

Windscreen wiper multi-function switch

5   Disconnect the battery negative (earth) lead (refer to Chapter 5, Section 1).

6   Remove the rubber gaiters and locking rings, then remove the securing screws and take off the steering column upper shroud.

7   Disconnect the multi-plug (see illustration).

8   Depress the plastic tab with a screwdriver, and lift the switch assembly from the steering column (see illustrations).

Main light, auxiliary foglight and rear foglight combination switch

9   Disconnect the battery negative (earth) lead (refer to Chapter 5, Section 1).

10   Carefully prise the switch panel from the facia, using a screwdriver against a cloth pad to prevent damage to the facia (see illustration).

12

4.10 Prising out the light switch

4.11 Disconnecting the multi-plugs from the light switch and rheostat

4.23 Removing the direction indicator, dipped beam and hazard flasher multi-function switch. Direction indicator relay (flasher unit) is attached

4.44 Disconnecting the multi-plug from the handbrake lever

4.49 Prising out the heated rear window switch

4.50 Disconnecting the multi-plug from the heated rear window switch

11 Disconnect the multi-plugs and withdraw the switch panel **(see illustration)**.

12 Unscrew the four mounting screws, and remove the switch from the panel.

13 Pull off the switch control knob, and remove the blanking plug and retainer.

14 Depress the plastic tabs, and remove the front cover and switch.

Instrument light rheostat

15 Disconnect the battery negative (earth) lead (refer to Chapter 5, Section 1).

16 Carefully prise the light switch panel from the facia, using a screwdriver against a cloth pad to prevent damage to the facia.

17 Disconnect the multi-plugs from the rear of the switch, then remove the screws and withdraw the instrument light rheostat from the panel.

Door mirror control switch

18 Disconnect the battery negative (earth) lead (refer to Chapter 5, Section 1).

19 Carefully prise the switch from the facia, using a screwdriver against a cloth pad to prevent damage to the facia.

20 Disconnect the multi-plug and withdraw the switch.

Direction indicator, dipped beam and hazard flasher multi-function switch

21 Disconnect the battery negative (earth) lead (refer to Chapter 5, Section 1).

22 Remove the rubber gaiters and locking rings, then remove the screws and take off the steering column upper shroud.

23 Depress the retaining lug and withdraw the switch assembly, then disconnect the multi-plug **(see illustration)**.

24 With the switch assembly removed, pull out the direction indicator relay if required.

Horn switch (steering wheel without air bag)

Note: *When an air bag is fitted, the horn switch is removed with the air bag unit. Refer to Section 28.*

25 Disconnect the battery negative (earth) lead (refer to Chapter 5, Section 1).

26 Carefully pull off the padded centre of the steering wheel which incorporates the horn switch.

27 Disconnect the wiring and remove the switch assembly.

Luggage compartment switch

28 Disconnect the battery negative (earth) lead (refer to Chapter 5, Section 1).

29 With the tailgate/bootlid open, pull the weatherstrip from the centre of the rear cross panel.

30 Carefully prise out the trim fasteners from the bottom corners of the rear trim, then unscrew the retaining screws and remove the trim panel.

31 Disconnect the wiring multi-plug, and pull out the switch.

Electrically-operated window switch (single)

32 Disconnect the battery negative (earth) lead (refer to Chapter 5, Section 1).

33 Carefully prise out the switch from the door inner trim panel, using a cloth pad to prevent damage to the trim.

34 Disconnect the multi-plug and remove the switch.

Electrically-operated window switch (multiple) and isolator

35 Disconnect the battery negative (earth) lead (refer to Chapter 5, Section 1).

36 Prise the blanking cap from inside the inner door handle cavity, and remove the screw.

37 Hold the inner door handle in its open position, then remove the bezel and withdraw it over the handle.

4.57A Unscrew the cross-head screw . . .

4.57B . . . and pull out the courtesy light switch

5.1 Removing the cover from the rear of the headlight

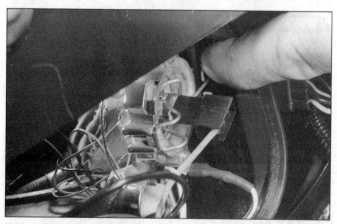

5.2A Release the spring clip . . .

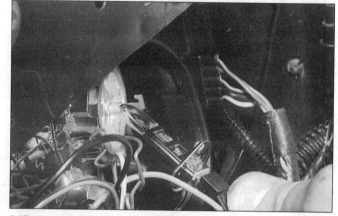

5.2B . . . and withdraw the headlight bulb

38   Depress the retaining lug and remove the switch assembly, then disconnect the multi-plug.

Electrically-operated sunroof switch and traction control switch

39   Disconnect the battery negative (earth) lead (refer to Chapter 5, Section 1).
40   Carefully prise out the switch with a screwdriver, using a cloth pad to prevent damage to the trim.
41   Disconnect the multi-plug and remove the switch.

Handbrake-on warning switch

42   Disconnect the battery negative (earth) lead (refer to Chapter 5, Section 1).
43   Remove the centre console as described in Chapter 11.
44   Disconnect the multi-plug, then remove the screw and withdraw the switch from the handbrake lever mounting bracket **(see illustration)**.

"Economy/Sport" mode switch (automatic transmission models)

45   Disconnect the battery negative (earth) lead (refer to Chapter 5, Section 1).
46   Select Neutral, then prise out the selector indicator panel, using a cloth pad to prevent damage to the surrounding trim.
47   Push the switch out of the panel, and disconnect the multi-plug.

Heated windscreen switch and heated rear window switch

48   Disconnect the battery negative (earth) lead (refer to Chapter 5, Section 1).
49   Carefully prise out the switch, using a cloth pad to prevent damage to the trim **(see illustration)**.
50   Disconnect the multi-plug and remove the switch **(see illustration)**.

Electrically-operated seat switch and heated seat switch

51   Disconnect the battery negative (earth) lead (refer to Chapter 5, Section 1).
52   Carefully prise out the switch, using a cloth pad to prevent

damage to the trim.
53   Disconnect the multi-plug and remove the switch.

Adaptive damping switch

54   Disconnect the battery negative (earth) lead (refer to Chapter 5, Section 1).
55   Carefully prise out the switch, using a cloth pad to prevent damage to the trim.
56   Disconnect the multi-plug and remove the switch.

Courtesy light door switch

57   Open the door, then unscrew the cross-head screw and carefully pull the switch from the pillar **(see illustrations)**. Take care not to force the wire from the switch terminal, otherwise it will be difficult to retrieve it from the pillar.
58   Disconnect the wire, and tie it in a loose knot to prevent it dropping back into the pillar.

Refitting

59   Refitting of all switches is a reversal of the removal procedure.

5   Bulbs (exterior lights) - renewal

Note: *Ensure that all exterior lights are switched off before disconnecting the wiring connectors from any exterior light bulbs. Do not touch the glass of halogen-type bulbs (headlights, front foglights) with the fingers; if the glass is accidentally touched, clean it with methylated spirit.*

Headlight (dipped beam)

1   Working under the bonnet, depress the plastic clips and remove the cover from the rear of the headlight unit **(see illustration)**.
2   Release the spring clip and withdraw the bulb, then disconnect the wiring lead **(see illustrations)**.

12

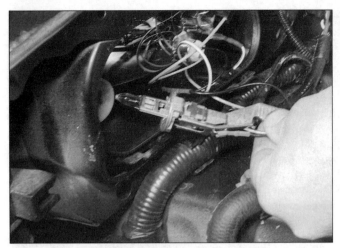

5.5 Removing the headlight (main beam) bulbholder

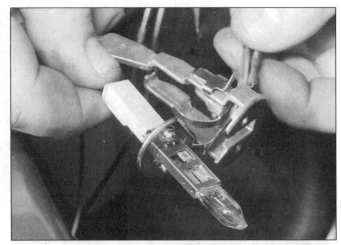

5.6 Removing the headlight (main beam) bulb from the bulbholder

3   Fit the new bulb using a reversal of the removal procedure. Have the headlight beam alignment checked as described later in this Chapter.

Headlight (main beam)
4   Working under the bonnet, depress the plastic clips and remove the cover from the rear of the headlight unit.
5   Turn the bulbholder anti-clockwise, and remove it from the rear of the headlight unit **(see illustration)**.
6   Pull out the bulb and disconnect the wiring lead **(see illustration)**.
7   Fit the new bulb using a reversal of the removal procedure, making sure that the bulbholder is correctly located in the headlight unit. Have the headlight beam alignment checked as described later in this Chapter.

Front sidelight
8   Working under the bonnet, depress the plastic clips and remove the cover from the rear of the headlight unit.
9   Pull the bulbholder from the rear of the headlight unit **(see illustration)**.
10   Pull the wedge-type bulb from the bulbholder **(see illustration)**.
11   Fit the new bulb using a reversal of the removal procedure.

Front direction indicator
12   Open the bonnet. Loosen (but do not remove) the screw located above the front direction indicator (see illustration 7.10).
13   Withdraw the front direction indicator light unit.
14   Rotate the bulbholder anti-clockwise, and withdraw it from the light unit.
15   Twist the bulb anti-clockwise, and remove it from the bulbholder **(see illustration)**.

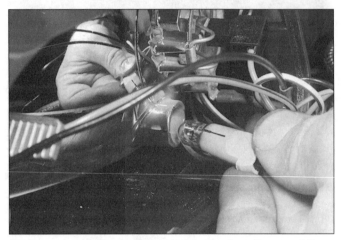

5.9 Removing the front sidelight bulbholder from the rear of the headlight unit

16   Fit the new bulb using a reversal of the removal procedure, but before refitting the light unit, first insert the holding spring in its bore.

Side repeaters
17   The side repeater light is held in position by spring pressure.
18   Depending on how the light unit was previously fitted, press it either forwards or rearwards, and remove it from the front wing **(see illustration)**.
19   Turn the bulbholder anti-clockwise, and disconnect it from the

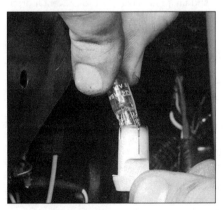

5.10 Pulling the wedge-type bulb from the bulbholder

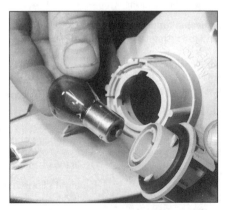

5.15 Removing the front direction indicator bulb

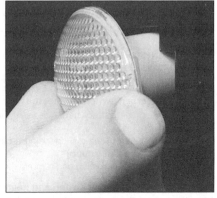

5.18 Removing the side repeater from the front wing

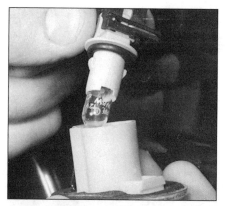

5.19 Removing the bulbholder from the side repeater lens/bulbholder

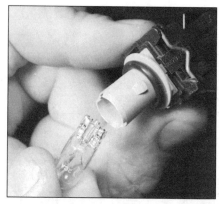

5.20 Removing the wedge-type bulb from the side repeater bulbholder

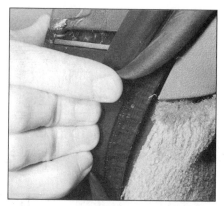

5.26A Pull back the weatherstrip . . .

5.26B . . . and unclip the trim cover

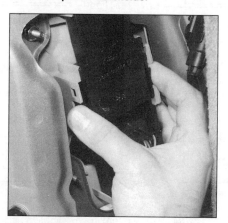

5.27A Pressing the two plastic locking tabs together (Estate)

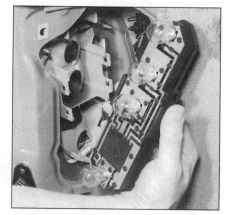

5.27B Removing the rear light cluster (Estate)

housing **(see illustration)**.

20   Pull the wedge-type bulb from the holder **(see illustration)**.

21   Fit the new bulb using a reversal of the removal procedure.

Front foglight

22   Unscrew the cross-head screws securing the front foglight unit to the valance, and withdraw the light unit.

23   Prise open the plastic clips and remove the rear cover from the light unit.

24   Release the spring clips and withdraw the bulb, then pull off the wiring connector.

25   Fit the new bulb using a reversal of the removal procedure.

Rear light cluster

26   With the tailgate or bootlid open, flip open the trim cover to reveal the bulbholder in the rear corner of the luggage compartment. On Estate models, pull back the weatherstrip and unclip the trim cover **(see illustrations)**.

27   Press the two plastic locking tabs together, and withdraw the complete rear light cluster **(see illustrations)**.

28   Depress and twist the appropriate bulb to remove it from the bulbholder **(see illustrations)**.

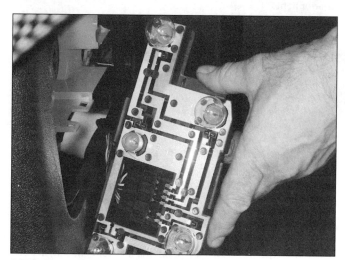

5.27C Removing the rear light cluster (Saloon)

5.28A Removing a bulb from the rear light cluster bulbholder

12

SALOON

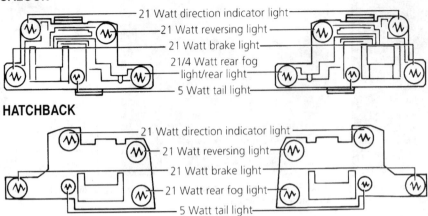

HATCHBACK

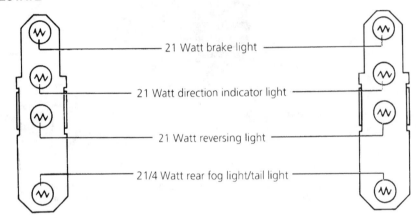

ESTATE

- 21 Watt brake light
- 21 Watt direction indicator light
- 21 Watt reversing light
- 21/4 Watt rear fog light/tail light

5.28B Bulb positions in the rear light cluster

29   Fit the new bulb using a reversal of the removal procedure. Make sure that the rear light cluster is fully inserted.

Number plate light

30   Remove the cross-head screws from the number plate light, and remove the light unit **(see illustration)**.
31   Release the festoon-type bulb from the contact springs **(see illustration)**.
32   Fit the new bulb using a reversal of the removal procedure. Make sure that the tension of the contact springs is sufficient to hold the bulb firmly.

6   Bulbs (interior lights) - renewal

Engine compartment light

1   With the bonnet open, pull the wedge-type bulb from the bulb-holder.
2   Fit the new bulb using a reversal of the removal procedure.

Interior lights

3   Switch off the interior light by locating the switch in its middle position.

5.30 Remove the cross-head screws . . .

5.31 . . . for access to the festoon-type bulb

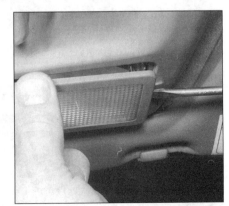

6.4 Prise out the interior light with a screwdriver

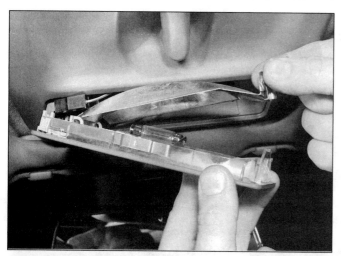

6.5 Lifting the reflector from the interior light

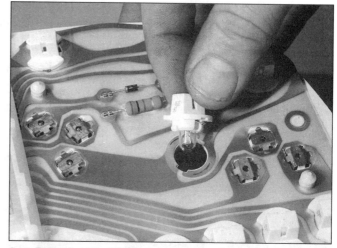

6.11 Removing a bulb from the rear of the instrument panel

4   Using a small screwdriver, carefully prise out the light or bulb cover, as applicable **(see illustration)**.
5   Lift up the reflector, then release the festoon-type bulb from the contact springs **(see illustration)**.
6   Fit the new bulb using a reversal of the removal procedure. Make sure that the tension of the contact springs is sufficient to hold the bulb firmly.

Reading light
7   With the reading light switched off, prise out the light using a small screwdriver.
8   Hinge back the contact plate, and release the festoon-type bulb from the contact springs.
9   Fit the new bulb using a reversal of the removal procedure. Make sure that the tension of the contact springs is sufficient to hold the bulb firmly.

Instrument panel illumination and warning lights
10   Remove the instrument panel as described in Section 10.
11   Twist the bulbholder anti-clockwise to remove it **(see illustration)**.
12   Fit the new bulbholder using a reversal of the removal procedure.

Foglight warning indicator
13   Using a screwdriver, prise out the indicator from the facia, and disconnect the multi-plug.
14   Twist the bulbholder anti-clockwise with the screwdriver, and remove it **(see illustration)**.
15   Fit the new bulb using a reversal of the removal procedure.

Hazard warning light
16   Pull the cover directly up from the switch, then remove the bulb **(see illustrations)**.
17   Fit the new bulb using a reversal of the removal procedure.

Glovebox light
18   Open the glovebox, then pull out the wedge-type bulb from the light located under the upper edge.

Heater fan switch illumination
19   Pull off the switch knob, then depress and twist the bulb to remove it.

Automatic transmission selector panel illumination
20   Disconnect the battery negative (earth) lead (refer to Chapter 5, Section 1).
21   Remove the ashtray.
22   Select Neutral, then prise out the panel from the centre console.
23   Disconnect the multi-plug from the overdrive control switch.
24   Disconnect the bulbholder and pull out the wedge-type bulb.
25   Fit the new bulb using a reversal of the removal procedure.

Interior door handle illumination
26   Disconnect the battery negative (earth) lead (refer to Chapter 5, Section 1).
27   Remove the door interior trim panel as described in Chapter 11.
28   Using a knife, cut free the foam watershield for access to the rear of the interior door handle.
29   Pull out the bulbholder and remove the bulb.

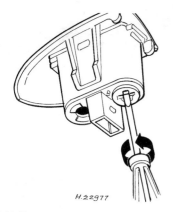

6.14 Removing the bulb from the foglight warning indicator

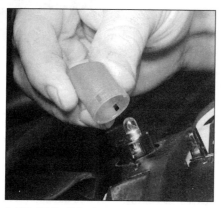

6.16A Pull off the hazard warning light cover . . .

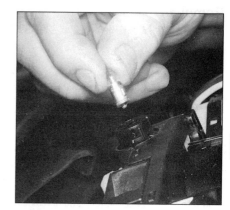

6.16B . . . and remove the bulb

12

6.32A Twist the bulbholder anti-clockwise . . .

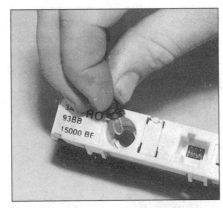

6.32B . . . and remove it from the rear of the clock

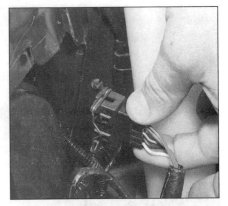

7.4 Disconnecting the headlight unit wiring multi-plug

7.8A Unscrew the outer mounting screws . . .

7.8B . . . and inner mounting screws . . .

7.8C . . . and withdraw the headlight unit assembly

Clock illumination

30   Disconnect the battery negative (earth) lead (refer to Chapter 5, Section 1).
31   Remove the clock as described in Section 13.
32   Twist the bulbholder anti-clockwise using a screwdriver, then re-move the bulbholder from the rear of the clock **(see illustrations)**.

Heater control illumination

33   Remove the heater control panel (Chapter 3), then twist the bulb-holder anti-clockwise and remove the bulb from the rear of the panel.

---

7   Exterior light units - removal and refitting

Removal

1   Disconnect the battery negative (earth) lead (refer to Chapter 5, Section 1).

Headlight unit

2   With the bonnet supported in its open position, loosen (but do not remove) the screw located above the front direction indicator.
3   Withdraw the front direction indicator unit forwards, and discon-nect the wiring multi-plug. Place the unit to one side.
4   Disconnect the wiring multi-plug for the headlight unit **(see illustration)**.
5   Remove the radiator grille as described in Chapter 11.
6   Remove the front bumper as described in Chapter 11.
7   The headlights fitted from new are a single unit, joined by a plastic back-piece running across the front of the vehicle. However, if it is re-quired to renew a headlight unit on one side only, the back-piece must first be removed complete, then cut in half on the bench.
8   Unscrew the mounting bolts from each side of the headlight unit, and withdraw the unit from the front of the vehicle **(see illustrations)**.

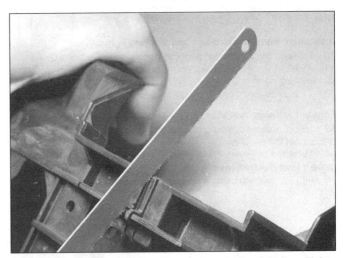

7.8D Using a hacksaw to cut through the middle of the headlight back-piece, in order to fit a new unit

Use a hacksaw to cut through the centre of the headlight unit (ie be-tween the two headlights), and obtain a connecting kit from a Ford dealer to attach the new unit.
9   If necessary, the lens may be removed separately by releasing the clips **(see illustrations)**. To remove the diffuser, release the clips, then remove the rubber seal.

Front direction indicator

10   With the bonnet supported in its open position, loosen (but do not remove) the screw located above the front direction indicator **(see illustration)**.

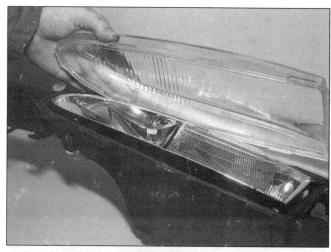

7.9A Release the clips . . .

7.9B . . . and remove the headlight lens

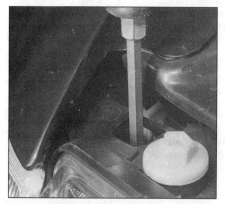

7.10 Loosen the front direction indicator retaining screw

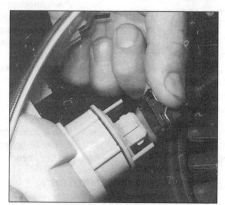

7.12 Disconnecting the wiring plug from the indicator bulbholder

7.20A Rear light cluster mounting nuts (arrowed)

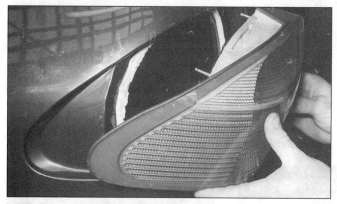

7.20B Removing the rear light cluster unit

11   Withdraw the front direction indicator light unit.
12   Rotate the bulbholder anti-clockwise, and withdraw it from the light unit. Alternatively, the wiring plug can be disconnected from the bulbholder, leaving the bulb in position **(see illustration)**. Remove the light unit.

Foglight (front)

13   Unscrew the cross-head screws securing the front foglight unit to the valance, and withdraw the light unit from the valance.
14   Prise open the plastic clips, and remove the rear cover from the light unit.
15   Release the spring clips and withdraw the bulb, then pull off the wiring connector. Remove the foglight unit.

Rear light cluster

16   With the tailgate or bootlid open, unhook the parcel net (where fitted) from the rear of the luggage compartment.
17   On Saloon and Hatchback models, remove the screws, release the clips, and remove the trim panel from the rear cross panel. On Estate models, it is sufficient to open the flap.
18   Remove the screws, and press the rear light trim cover from the guides (where applicable).
19   Disconnect the wiring multi-plug.
20   Unscrew the four mounting nuts, and withdraw the light unit from the outside of the vehicle **(see illustrations)**.

Rear number plate light assembly

21   Remove both number plate lights as described in Section 5.
22   With the tailgate or bootlid open, remove the screws and withdraw the inner trim panel.
23   Unscrew the nuts, and remove the outer cover and number plate base from the tailgate.
24   Disconnect the multi-plug and remove the light assembly.

Refitting

25   Refitting of all the external light units is a reversal of the removal procedure, noting the following points:

   (a) *When refitting the rubber seal on the headlight unit, note that it has a tapered seat.*
   (b) *If one or both headlights have been disturbed, have the beam alignment checked as described in the next Section.*
   (c) *When refitting the rear light cluster, check the condition of the sealer on the body panel, and if necessary renew it.*

12

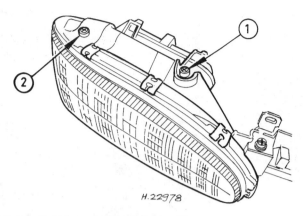

8.2 Headlight beam setting adjustment screws

1   Vertical alignment screw
2   Horizontal alignment screw

8   Headlight beam alignment - checking and adjustment

1   Accurate adjustment of the headlight beam is only possible using optical beam-setting equipment. This work should therefore be carried out by a Ford dealer, or other service station with the necessary facilities.
2   Temporary adjustment can be made after renewal of a headlight bulb or unit, or as an emergency measure if the alignment is incorrect following accident damage. Turn the adjustment screws on the top of the headlamp unit to make the adjustment **(see illustration)**.
3   Before making any adjustments to the settings, it is important that the tyre pressures are correct, and that the vehicle is standing on level ground. Bounce the front of the vehicle a few times to settle the suspension. Ideally, somebody of average size should sit in the driver's seat during the adjustment, and the vehicle should have a full tank of fuel. Where a vehicle is fitted with an electrical beam levelling system, set the switch to the "O" position before making any adjustments.
4   Whenever temporary adjustments are made, the settings must be checked and if necessary reset by a Ford dealer or other qualified person as soon as possible.

9   Headlight levelling motor - removal and refitting

Removal

1   Remove the headlight unit as described in Section 7, then remove the cover.
2   Disconnect the wiring multi-plug from the motor.

3   Rotate the motor upwards approximately 60°, then pull it forwards slightly.
4   Disconnect the adjustment spindle by pressing the ball coupling to one side, away from the socket on the reflector.
5   Withdraw the motor from the headlight unit.

Refitting

6   Refitting is a reversal of the removal procedure, but make sure that the motor is turned down until it engages the stop.

10   Instrument panel - removal and refitting

Removal

1   Disconnect the battery negative (earth) lead (refer to Chapter 5, Section 1).
2   Where fitted, remove the clock as described in Section 13.
3   Where fitted, remove the trip computer module as described in Section 18.
4   Remove the heated rear window switch as described in Section 4.
5   Where fitted, remove the heated windscreen switch.
6   Where fitted, remove the display assembly warning indicator for the foglights **(see illustration)**.
7   Remove any blanking covers from the unused switch positions **(see illustration)**.
8   Prise out the blanking covers, then unscrew the retaining screws and remove the instrument panel surround **(see illustrations)**.
9   Unscrew the mounting screws, and withdraw the instrument panel a little way from the facia **(see illustration)**.
10   Disconnect the two multi-plugs from the rear of the instrument panel **(see illustration)**.
11   Withdraw the instrument panel from the facia, at the same time releasing the speedometer intermediate cable.

Refitting

12   Refitting is a reversal of the removal procedure.

11   Instrument panel components - removal and refitting

Removal

1   Remove the warning light and illumination bulbs by twisting them anti-clockwise **(see illustration)**.
2   Carefully prise off the glass and bezel from the front of the instrument panel, noting the positions of the retaining lugs **(see illustration)**.
3   Note the positions of the five diffusers, then remove them from the instrument panel.
4   To remove the speedometer head, unscrew the three mounting screws and withdraw the head from the housing.

10.6 Removing the foglight warning indicator

10.7 Removing a switch blanking cover

10.8A With the blanking covers removed, unscrew the concealed screws . . .

10.8B . . . and the remaining screws . . .

10.8C . . . and lift out the instrument panel surround

10.9 Three of the instrument panel mounting screws (arrowed)

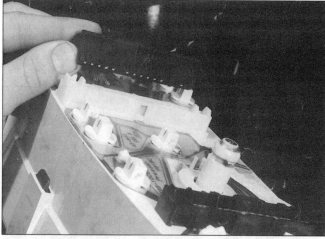

10.10 Disconnecting the multi-plugs from the rear of the instrument panel

8   Using a small punch, push in the multi-plug securing pins, and re-move the multi-plugs.
9   Carefully lift the printed circuit from the location dowels on the housing, taking care not to damage it.

Refitting

10   Refitting is a reversal of the removal procedure.

12 Speedometer drive cable - removal and refitting

Removal

1   Remove the windscreen wiper arms as described in Section 15.
2   With the bonnet closed, release the grille panel upper edge from just in front of the windscreen, by prising off the caps and unscrewing the upper retaining screws.
3   Open the bonnet, and support with the stay.
4   Pull off the sealing strip from the cross panel at the rear of the en-gine compartment.
5   Unscrew the lower screws, and remove the grille panel halves from in front of the windscreen, withdrawing first one side and then the other.
6   Disconnect the battery negative (earth) lead (refer to Chapter 5, Section 1).
7   Reach in behind the bulkhead. Squeeze the collar on the upper end of the speedometer cable, where it is attached to the intermediate cable from the rear of the speedometer head. Disconnect the cable,

5   To remove the tachometer, unscrew the single screw and withdraw it from the housing.
6   Similarly remove the fuel gauge and temperature gauge by un-screwing the single screws.
7   Remove all the pin contacts.

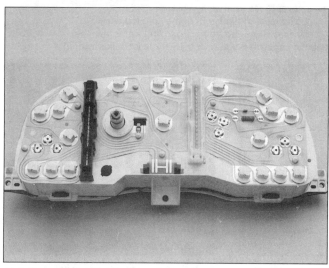

11.1 Rear view of the instrument panel, showing bulbholders

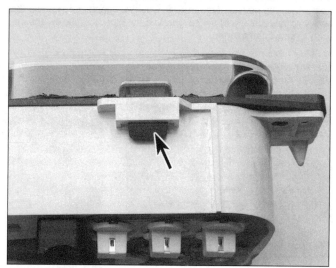

11.2 Bezel retaining lug on the instrument panel

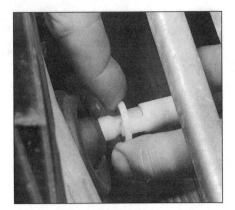

12.7A Squeeze the collar . . .

12.7B . . . and disconnect the speedometer main cable from the intermediate cable

12.9A Unscrew the cable nut . . .

12.9B . . . and disconnect the speedometer cable from the vehicle speed sensor

and withdraw it from the bulkhead inner panel, together with the rubber grommet **(see illustrations)**.
8   Apply the handbrake, jack up the front of the vehicle and support it on axle stands.
9   Unscrew the nut and disconnect the speedometer cable from the vehicle speed sensor on the transmission, then withdraw the cable from within the engine compartment. Use two spanners to loosen the nut - one to counterhold the sensor, and the other to unscrew the cable nut **(see illustrations)**.

Refitting
10   Refitting is a reversal of the removal procedure.

13 Clock - removal and refitting

Removal
1   Disconnect the battery negative (earth) lead (refer to Chapter 5, Section 1).
2   Using a small screwdriver, prise the clock out of the facia **(see illustration)**. To prevent damage to the facia, place a cloth pad beneath the screwdriver.
3   Disconnect the multi-plug from the rear of the clock, and withdraw the clock **(see illustration)**.

Refitting
4   Refitting is a reversal of the removal procedure. Reset the clock on completion.

14 Horn - removal and refitting

Removal
1   Apply the handbrake, jack up the front of the vehicle and support it on axle stands.
2   Unscrew the bolts, and release the clips securing the radiator lower cover to the front of the vehicle.
3   Disconnect the wiring from the horn terminal.
4   Unscrew the mounting bolt, and withdraw the horn with its mounting bracket from under the vehicle **(see illustration)**.

13.2 Prising the clock out of the facia

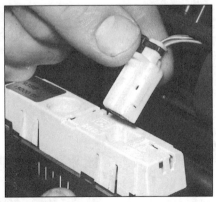

13.3 Disconnecting the multi-plug from the rear of the clock

14.4 Horn and mounting bracket (arrowed)

15.3 Loosening the wiper arm retaining nut

15.5 Removing the wiper arm from the spindle

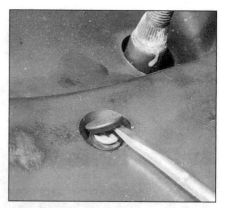

16.3A Prise off the cap . . .

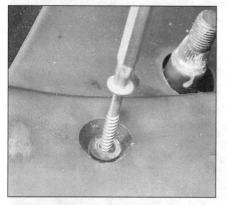

16.3B . . . and remove the upper retaining screws

16.5 Removing the bonnet sealing strip

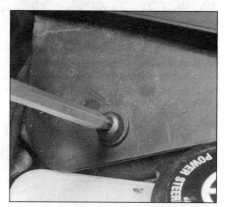

16.6A Unscrew the lower screws . . .

Refitting
5   Refitting is a reversal of the removal procedure.

15 Wiper arms - removal and refitting

Removal
1   Disconnect the battery negative (earth) lead (refer to Chapter 5, Section 1). If the windscreen wiper arms are to be removed, close the bonnet.

16.6B . . . and remove the grille panel from in front of the windscreen

2   With the wiper(s) "parked" (ie in the normal at-rest position), mark the positions of the blade(s) on the screen, using a wax crayon or strips of masking tape.
3   Lift up the plastic cap from the bottom of the wiper arm, and loosen the nut one or two turns (see illustration).
4   Lift the wiper arm, and release it from the taper on the spindle by moving it to one side.
5   Completely remove the nut, and withdraw the wiper arm from the spindle (see illustration).

Refitting
6   Refitting is a reversal of the removal procedure. Make sure that the arm is fitted in the previously-noted position.

16 Windscreen wiper motor and linkage - removal and refitting

Removal
1   Disconnect the battery negative (earth) lead (refer to Chapter 5, Section 1).
2   Remove the wiper arms as described in Section 15.
3   With the bonnet closed, release the grille panel upper edge from just in front of the windscreen, by prising off the caps and unscrewing the upper retaining screws (see illustrations).
4   Open the bonnet, and support it with the stay.
5   Pull off the bonnet sealing strip from the cross panel at the rear of the engine compartment (see illustration).
6   Unscrew the lower screws, and remove the grille panel halves from in front of the windscreen, withdrawing one side then the other side (see illustrations).

12

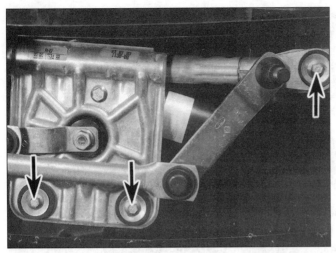

16.7 Wiper motor mounting bolt locations (right-hand-drive)

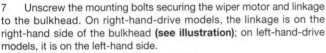

16.9 Removing the wiper motor and linkage

7   Unscrew the mounting bolts securing the wiper motor and linkage to the bulkhead. On right-hand-drive models, the linkage is on the right-hand side of the bulkhead **(see illustration)**; on left-hand-drive models, it is on the left-hand side.

8   Disconnect the wiper motor multi-plug.

9   Withdraw the wiper motor, complete with the linkage, from the bulkhead **(see illustration)**.

10   Mark the position of the motor arm on the mounting plate, then unscrew the centre nut **(see illustration)**.

11   Unscrew the motor mounting bolts, and separate the motor from the linkage assembly.

Refitting

12   Refitting is a reversal of the removal procedure. There are two tightening torques for the motor mounting bolts - the lower one for bolts that are being re-inserted into an old motor, and the higher ones for bolts that are being inserted into a new motor. Make sure that the wiper motor is in its "parked" position before fitting the motor arm, and check that the wiper linkage is in line with the motor arm.

17 Tailgate wiper motor assembly - removal and refitting

Removal

1   Disconnect the battery negative (earth) lead (refer to Chapter 5, Section 1).

16.10 Wiper motor arm and mounting plate located on the motor

2   Remove the tailgate wiper arm as described in Section 15.

3   Remove the tailgate inner trim panel by unscrewing the retaining screws.

4   Release the multi-plug from the clip, then disconnect it **(see illustration)**.

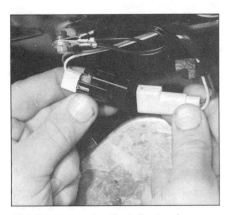

17.4 Disconnecting the tailgate wiper motor multi-plug

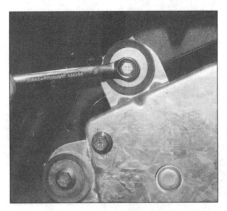

17.6A Unscrew the mounting bolts . . .

17.6B . . . and remove the tailgate wiper motor assembly (Hatchback shown - Estate similar)

17.7A Tailgate wiper motor assembly and mounting plate

17.7B A mounting rubber removed from the mounting plate

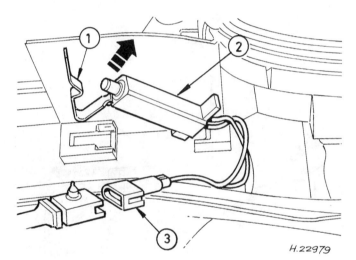

19.9 Low air temperature sender unit removal

1 Clip	*2 Sender unit*	*3 Multi-plug*

5   Disconnect the wiper motor earth lead.
6   Unscrew the mounting bolts, and remove the wiper motor from inside the tailgate **(see illustrations)**.
7   Unbolt and remove the mounting plate. If necessary, remove the mounting rubbers for renewal **(see illustrations)**.

Refitting

8   Refitting is a reversal of the removal procedure. Make sure that the wiper motor is in its "parked" position before fitting the wiper arm.

18 Trip computer module - removal and refitting

Removal

1   Disconnect the battery negative (earth) lead (refer to Chapter 5, Section 1).
2   Using a small screwdriver, prise the trip computer module out of the facia. To prevent damage to the facia, place a cloth pad beneath the screwdriver.
3   Disconnect the multi-plug from the rear of the trip computer module, and withdraw the unit.
4   If necessary, the bulb can be removed by twisting it anti-clockwise.

Refitting

5   Refitting is a reversal of the removal procedure.

19 Auxiliary warning system - general information and component renewal

1   Some models are fitted with an auxiliary warning system, which monitors brake lights, sidelights, dipped beam and tail lights, external temperature, and door/tailgate/bootlid opening. An engine oil level warning light on the instrument panel is also part of the system.
2   The auxiliary warning system module and graphic warning display are combined into one unit.

Service interval reminder

3   The system also includes a service interval reminder warning light, which is illuminated if the specified mileage (or time) since the last service has been reached.
4   To reset the service interval system and turn off the light, a switch inside the glovebox must be depressed for a minimum of 4 seconds with the ignition switched on. This should be carried out by a Ford dealer if the vehicle is still in the warranty period.

Component renewal

5   The following paragraphs describe brief removal procedures for the auxiliary warning system components. Disconnect the battery negative (earth) lead before commencing work (refer to Chapter 5, Section 1). Refitting procedures are a reversal of removal.

Display warning bulb
6   Remove the control assembly.
7   Prise off the cover, and pull out the relevant bulb and bulbholder.

Low air temperature warning sender unit
8   Remove the front bumper.
9   Unclip the sender unit and disconnect the multi-plug **(see illustration)**.

Engine oil level sensor
10   Apply the handbrake, jack up the front of the vehicle and support it on axle stands.
11   Place a container beneath the oil level sensor, to catch any spilt oil.
12   Unscrew the screws and remove the cover from the sensor.
13   Disconnect the multi-plug.
14   Unscrew and remove the sensor, and remove the seal **(see illustration)**.

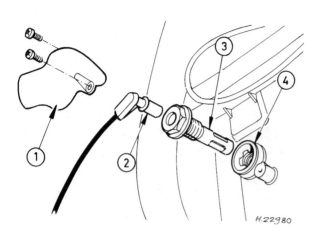

19.14 Engine oil level sensor removal

    1   Cover   *3   Sensor*
    2   Multi-plug   *4   Seal*

Door ajar sensor

15   Remove the door lock as described in Chapter 11, Section 14.
16   Unclip the sensor and disconnect the multi-plug.

Low coolant warning switch

17   Refer to Chapter 3, Section 6.

Low washer fluid switch

18   Disconnect the multi-plug from the washer fluid reservoir.
19   Drain or syphon out the fluid from the reservoir.
20   Using a screwdriver, lever out the switch from the reservoir **(see illustration)**.

Service indicator reset switch

21   Remove the glove compartment lid as described in Chapter 11, Section 32.
22   Carefully lever out the switch using a small screwdriver.
23   Remove the rear cover and disconnect the wiring **(see illustration)**.

Control assembly

24   Remove the instrument panel surround, referring to Section 10.
25   Unscrew the mounting screws, disconnect the multi-plugs and remove the assembly.

Bulb failure module

26   Remove the lower facia panel from under the steering wheel.
27   Unclip the bulb failure module and disconnect the multi-plug.

20 Anti-theft alarm system - general information

1   All UK models are fitted with an anti-theft alarm system, incorporating movement sensors and an ignition immobiliser. The system is activated when the vehicle is locked.
2   The system includes a start inhibitor circuit, which makes it impossible to start the engine with the system armed.
3   The movement sensors consist of two ultrasonic units, located in the "B" pillars, incorporating transmitters and receivers **(see illustrations)**. The receivers check that the echo frequency matches the original frequency. If there is any significant difference, the system triggers the alarm.
4   The system module is located on a bracket beneath the right-hand side of the facia. The set and reset switches are located in a housing by the lock barrel holder in the doors, tailgate or bootlid.
5   To allow temporary opening of the tailgate or bootlid, an inhibit switch is fitted to the lock barrel. This suppresses the alarm system

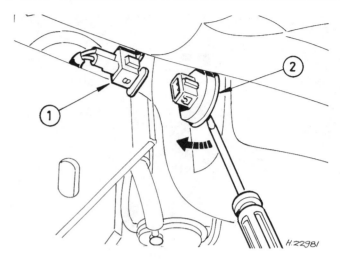

19.20 Removing the low washer fluid switch

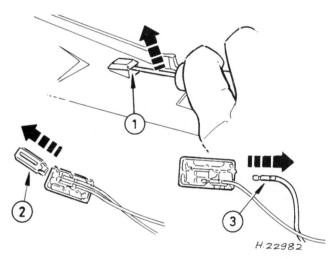

19.23 Service indicator switch removal

    1   Lever out the switch   *3   Wiring*
    2   Cover

20.3A Disconnecting a movement sensor multi-plug

20.3B Removing a movement sensor

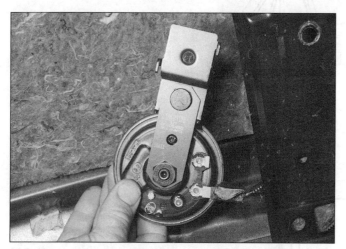

20.7 Alarm system horn location on Hatchback and Saloon models

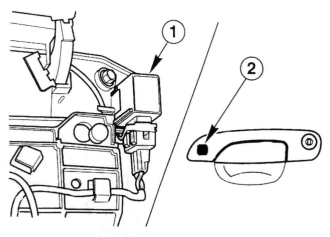

20.6 Infra-red receiver location on the door handle

1 Receiver
2 Infra-red eye on the door handle

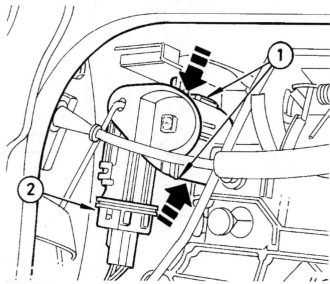

20.10 Alarm system door lock switch removal

1 Clips (arrowed) 2 Multi-plug

until the tailgate or bootlid is closed again.
6 Where remote central locking is fitted, an infra-red receiver is located on the exterior door handle (see illustration). Note that excessive heat can destroy this receiver; therefore, it should be covered with aluminium tape if (for instance) a paint-drying heat process is to be used.
7 The alarm system is fitted with its own horn. On Hatchback and Saloon models, it is located on the left-hand side of the luggage compartment; on Estate models, it is located on the right-hand side of the luggage compartment (see illustration).
8 Relays which activate the direction indicators when the alarm is triggered are located on the alarm module.
9 The alarm system incorporates a self-test function, which can be activated by operating the bonnet switch or one of the lock position switches eight times within 10 seconds. During the check, the horn or buzzer issues acoustic signals which should occur every time a door, bonnet or tailgate is opened. If the doors are double-locked, the signal will occur when something is moved within the passenger compartment. A more comprehensive test can be made using the Ford FDS 2000 diagnostic tester.
10 The door lock switches associated with the alarm system are located behind the door trim panels (see illustration).

21 Cruise control system - general information

1 Cruise control is available as an option on some models.
2 The cruise control system components are shown in the

accompanying illustration (see illustration).
3 The cruise control system is only active at road speeds between 25 mph and 125 mph.
4 The speed control unit is located on the right-hand side of the engine compartment, between the front suspension top mounting and the bulkhead. It incorporates an electronic amplifier and stepper motor with a reduction-gear train, and a control cable which is connected to the throttle housing.
5 The vehicle speed sensor uses the speedometer cable drive pinion to generate pulses which are fed to the speed control unit.
6 The stop-light switch, brake pedal switch and (when applicable) clutch pedal switch are used to disable the cruise control system. The stop-light switch is activated when the brake pedal is applied gently, and the brake pedal switch is activated when the brake pedal is applied forcibly.
7 An indicator light on the instrument panel is illuminated when the system is in operation.
8 The following paragraphs describe brief removal procedures for the cruise control system components. The battery negative (earth) lead should be disconnected before commencing work (refer to Chapter 5, Section 1). Refitting is a reversal of removal.

12

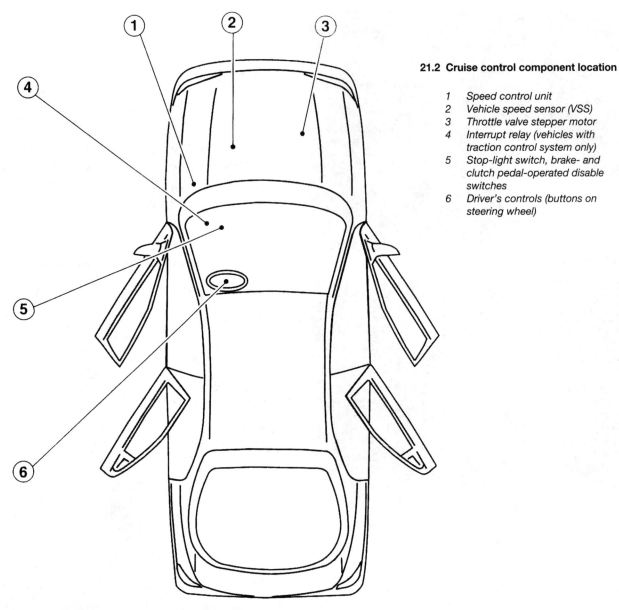

21.2 Cruise control component location

1 Speed control unit
2 Vehicle speed sensor (VSS)
3 Throttle valve stepper motor
4 Interrupt relay (vehicles with traction control system only)
5 Stop-light switch, brake- and clutch pedal-operated disable switches
6 Driver's controls (buttons on steering wheel)

Speed control switch

9   Remove the steering column upper and lower shrouds, with reference to Chapter 10.
10   Remove the air bag module as described in Section 29.
11   Disconnect the multi-plugs, then unscrew the screws and remove the switch.

Disable switches

12   Remove the lower facia panel from under the steering column.
13   Disconnect the multi-plugs from the clutch switch, brake pedal switch and stop-light switch.
14   To remove the clutch and brake pedal switches, twist them anti-clockwise. To remove the stop-light switch, twist it clockwise **(see illustration)**.
15   Before refitting the brake pedal and stop-light switches, pull out the contact rod. Adjustment occurs automatically as the switches are fitted **(see illustration)**.

Speed control actuator

16   Remove the air cleaner as described in Chapter 4, Section 3.
17   Disconnect the actuator cable from the throttle linkage on the throttle housing, by releasing the inner cable end fitting from the segment and unclipping the outer cable from the bracket.
18   Unscrew the actuator mounting bolt, then slide the actuator out of

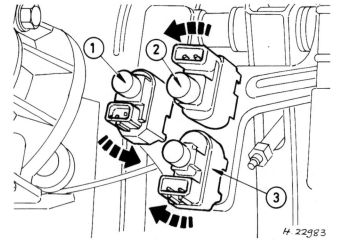

H.22983

21.14 Removal of the speed control disable switches

1 Clutch switch
2 Brake pedal switch
3 Stop-light switch

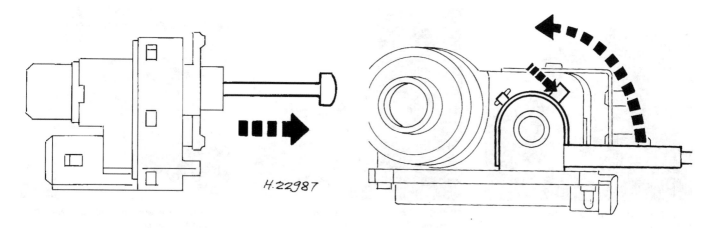

21.15 Resetting the brake pedal and stop-light switches

21.20 Removing the actuator cable locking arm

22.2 Washer reservoir mounting bolts (arrowed)

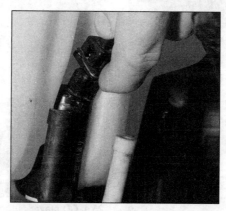

22.3 Disconnecting the washer pump and level sensor multi-plugs

22.6 Pulling the windscreen washer pump from the reservoir

the mounting pin holes.

19   Disconnect the multi-plug and remove the assembly.

20   Depress the actuating cable cap locking arm, and remove the cap by turning it anti-clockwise **(see illustration)**.

21   Using a small screwdriver, release the cable end from the pulley in the actuator. Be careful not to damage the cable retaining lugs.

22   When connecting the cable end to the pulley, rotate the pulley approximately one turn while keeping the cable taut. **Note:** *Incorrect assembly of the cable onto the pulley may result in a high idle speed. Check that the throttle lever is in its idle position after refitting the actuator.*

22 Windscreen/tailgate washer system components - removal and refitting

Removal

Washer reservoir and pump

1   Unscrew the bolts, and release the clips to remove the radiator lower cover.

2   Unscrew the mounting bolts, and pull the reservoir forwards slightly **(see illustration)**. For better access, it may be necessary to remove the front bumper.

3   Disconnect the multi-plugs for the windscreen washer pump and fluid level sensor **(see illustration)**.

4   Disconnect the hoses from the windscreen washer pump and (where applicable) from the headlamp washer pump. Anticipate some loss of fluid by placing a container beneath the reservoir.

5   Withdraw the reservoir from the vehicle.

6   Pull the level sensor, the windscreen washer pump, and (where

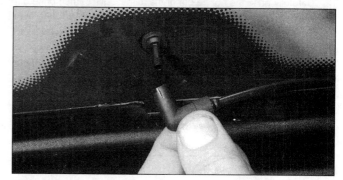

22.11 Pull the washer tube from the bottom of the nozzle

applicable) the headlamp washer pump, from the reservoir **(see illustration)**.

7   Remove the rubber seals.

Washer nozzle (windscreen)

8   With the bonnet supported in its open position, carefully disconnect the washer tube from the bottom of the nozzle.

9   Using a screwdriver and working from under the bonnet, carefully prise out the nozzle. Where necessary, disconnect the wiring for the nozzle heater.

Washer nozzle (rear window)

10   With the tailgate open, carefully pull off the inner trim panel from the top of the tailgate.

11   Pull the washer tube from the bottom of the nozzle **(see illustration)**.

12

22.12A Remove the nozzle from the tailgate glass . . .

22.12B . . . and prise out the rubber grommet

23.6 Using the special U-shaped rods to remove the radio

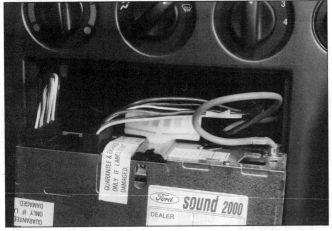

23.7 Connections to the rear of the radio

25.4 CD player autochanger

12 Carefully prise the nozzle out of the tailgate glass, then prise out the rubber grommet **(see illustrations)**. Where necessary, disconnect the wiring for the nozzle heater.

Refitting

13 Refitting is a reversal of the removal procedure. In the case of the washer nozzles, press them in until they are fully engaged. The rear window washer nozzle must rest against the rubber seal.

23 Radio/cassette player - coding, removal and refitting

Note: *Special tools are required to remove the radio.*

Coding

1 If a Ford "Keycode" unit is fitted, and the unit and/or the battery is disconnected, the unit will not function again on reconnection until the correct security code is entered. Details of this procedure are given in the "Ford Audio Systems Operating Guide" supplied with the vehicle when new, with the code itself being given in a "Radio Passport" and/or a "Keycode Label" at the same time.

2 For obvious security reasons, the re-coding procedure is not given in this manual - if you do not have the code or details of the correct procedure, but can supply proof of ownership and a legitimate reason for wanting this information, the vehicle's selling dealer may be able to help.

3 Note that these units will allow only ten attempts at entering the code - any further attempts will render the unit permanently inoperative until it has been reprogrammed by Ford themselves. At first, three consecutive attempts are allowed; if all three are incorrect, a 30-minute delay is required before another attempt can be made. Each of any

subsequent attempts (up to the maximum of ten) can be made only after a similar delay.

Removal

4 Disconnect the battery negative (earth) lead.

5 Where fitted, prise the cover/surround from the front of the radio/cassette player. Note that the cover is not fitted to all models.

6 In order to release the radio retaining clips, two U-shaped rods must be inserted into the special holes on each side of the radio **(see illustration)**. If possible, it is preferable to obtain purpose-made rods from an audio specialist, as these have cut-outs which snap firmly into the clips so that the radio can be pulled out. Pull the unit squarely from its aperture, or it may jam. If the unit proves difficult to withdraw, remove the cassette tray (or where applicable, the CD player) from beneath the unit, then reach through the aperture and ease it out from behind.

7 With the radio partly withdrawn, disconnect the feed, earth, aerial and speaker leads **(see illustration)**. Where applicable, also detach and remove the plastic support bracket from the rear of the unit.

Refitting

6 Refitting is a reversal of removal. With the leads reconnected to the rear of the unit, press it into position until the retaining clips are felt to engage. Reactivate the unit by entering the correct code in accordance with the maker's instructions.

24 Radio/cassette player power amplifier - removal and refitting

Removal

1 Disconnect the battery negative (earth) lead. See Chapter 5,

26.2 Removing a speaker retaining screw

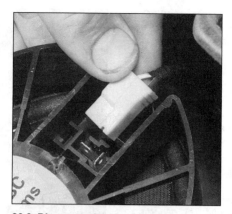

26.3 Disconnecting the wiring from a speaker

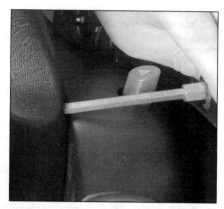

28.4 Unscrewing an air bag mounting bolt

28.5 Disconnecting the air bag wiring multi-plug (arrowed)

Section 1.
2   Unscrew the screws and remove the lower facia panel.
3   The radio/cassette player power amplifier is located beneath the facia.
4   Unscrew the cross-head screws, disconnect the wiring and re-move the amplifier.

Refitting
5   Refitting is a reversal of the removal procedure.

25 Compact disc player - removal and refitting

1   A compact disc (CD) player is available as an optional extra on most models. On some models, an autochanger version is available, which can hold a number of discs at a time.

Removal
2   The battery negative (earth) lead should be disconnected before commencing work.

CD player, or autochanger control unit
3   The procedure is identical to that for the radio/cassette player de-scribed in Section 23.

CD player autochanger
4   The CD player autochanger unit is mounted on the right-hand side of the luggage compartment **(see illustration)**. The wiring loom passes up the "C" pillar, across to the left-hand side "A" pillar, then to the centre console area.
5   Remove the trim cover from the autochanger unit.
6   Unscrew the mounting screws, and remove the autochanger unit from its mounting bracket.
7   Disconnect the multi-plug and remove the unit from inside the vehicle.

Refitting
8   Refitting is a reversal of the removal procedure.

26 Speakers - removal and refitting

Removal
1   Remove the door trim panel as described in Chapter 11.
2   Unscrew the cross-head screws, and withdraw the speaker from the door inner panel **(see illustration)**.
3   Disconnect the wiring and remove the speaker **(see illustration)**.

Refitting
4   Refitting is a reversal of the removal procedure.

27 Radio aerial - removal and refitting

Removal
1   Prise out the trim cover from the headlining immediately below the base of the aerial.
2   Unscrew the cross-head screw from the base of the aerial, and remove the aerial mast.

Refitting
3   Refitting is a reversal of the removal procedure.

28 Air bag unit (driver's side) - removal and refitting

Warning: *Handle the air bag unit with extreme care, as a precaution against personal injury, and always hold it with the cover facing away from the body. If in doubt concerning any proposed work involving the air bag unit or its control circuitry, consult a Ford dealer or other quali-fied specialist.*

Removal
1   Disconnect the battery negative (earth) lead (refer to Chapter 5, Section 1).
2   **Warning:** *Before proceeding, wait a minimum of 15 minutes, as a precaution against accidental firing of the air bag unit. This period en-sures that any stored energy in the back-up capacitor is dissipated.*
3   Rotate the steering wheel so that one of the mounting bolt holes is visible above the steering column upper shroud.
4   Unscrew and remove the first mounting bolt, then turn the steer-ing wheel as necessary and remove the remaining mounting bolts **(see illustration)**.
5   Carefully withdraw the air bag unit from the steering wheel far enough to disconnect the wiring multi-plug, then remove it from inside the vehicle **(see illustration)**. **Warning:** *Stand the unit with the cover*

12

uppermost, and do not expose it to heat sources in excess of 100°C.

6   **Warning:** *Do not attempt to open or repair the air bag unit, or apply any electrical current to it. Do not use any air bag unit which is visibly damaged or which has been tampered with.*

Refitting

7   Refitting is a reversal of the removal procedure.

29 Air bag control module - removal and refitting

Removal

1   Disconnect the battery negative (earth) lead (refer to Chapter 5, Section 1).

2   **Warning:** *Before proceeding, wait a minimum of 15 minutes, as a precaution against accidental firing of the air bag unit. This period ensures that any stored energy in the back-up capacitor is dissipated.*

3   Remove the facia panel as described in Chapter 11.

4   Disconnect the multi-plug from the module, by pressing the locking tab upwards and swivelling the retaining strap.

5   Unscrew the mounting bolts and remove the module from the vehicle.

Refitting

6   Refitting is a reversal of the removal procedure.

30 Air bag clock spring - removal and refitting

Removal

1   Remove the air bag unit as described in Section 28.

2   Disconnect the horn switch multi-plug.

3   If fitted, disconnect the multi-plugs for the cruise control.

30.6 Clock spring fitted to the steering column

4   Remove the steering wheel and shrouds.

5   Using a small screwdriver, release the retaining tabs, then remove the clock spring from the steering column.

Refitting

6   Refitting is a reversal of the removal procedure, but make sure that the steering wheel is centralised. The clock spring must be fitted in its central position, with the special alignment marks aligned and the TOP mark uppermost. To check for this position, turn the clock spring housing anti-clockwise until it is tight, then turn in the opposite direction by two-and-three-quarter turns **(see illustration)**.

KEY TO SYMBOLS

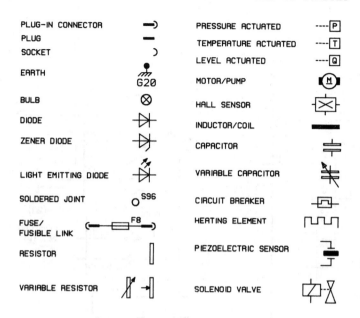

PLUG-IN CONNECTOR	PRESSURE ACTUATED	----[P]
PLUG	TEMPERATURE ACTUATED	----[T]
SOCKET	LEVEL ACTUATED	----[Q]
EARTH G20	MOTOR/PUMP	(M)
BULB	HALL SENSOR	
DIODE	INDUCTOR/COIL	
ZENER DIODE	CAPACITOR	
LIGHT EMITTING DIODE	VARIABLE CAPACITOR	
SOLDERED JOINT S96	CIRCUIT BREAKER	
FUSE/ FUSIBLE LINK F8	HEATING ELEMENT	
RESISTOR	PIEZOELECTRIC SENSOR	
VARIABLE RESISTOR	SOLENOID VALVE	

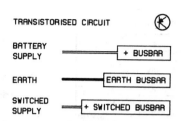

TRANSISTORISED CIRCUIT	(K)
BATTERY SUPPLY	+ BUSBAR
EARTH	EARTH BUSBAR
SWITCHED SUPPLY	+ SWITCHED BUSBAR

NOTES:

1. All diagrams are divided into numbered circuits depending on function e.g. Diagram 11 : Exterior lighting.
2. Items are arranged in relation to a plan view of the vehicle.
3. Wires may interconnect between diagrams and are located by using a grid reference e.g. 2/A1 denotes a position on diagram 2 grid location A1.
4. Complex items appear on the diagrams in sections and are shown in full on the internal connections page (see below).
5. Brackets show how the circuit may be connected in more than one way.
6. Items with a broken border have other connections shown elsewhere.
7. Not all items are fitted to all models.

INTERNAL CONNECTION DETAILS

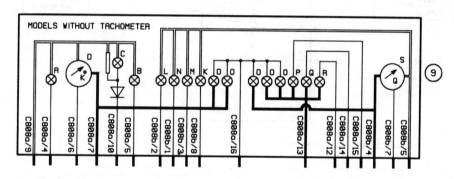

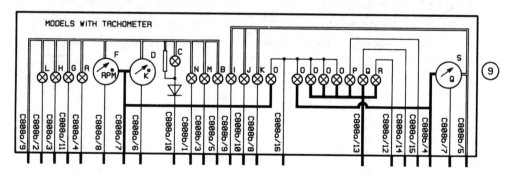

KEY TO INSTRUMENT CLUSTER (ITEM 9)

A =	Traction Control Warning Light	G =	Low Oil Level Warning Light	M =	Low Oil Pressure Warning Light
B =	Airbag Warning Light	H =	Overdrive Off Warning Light	N =	Instrument Illumination
C =	No Charge Warning Light	I =	Sport Warning Light	O =	Direction Indicator Warning Light LH
D =	Temperature Gauge	J =	Adaptive Damping Warning Light	P =	Direction Indicator Warning Light RH
E =	Tachometer	K =	Anti-lock Braking Warning Light	Q =	High Beam Warning Light
F =	Cruse Control Warning Light	L =	Low Brake Fluid Level/ Handbrake-on Warning Light	R =	Fuel Gauge

H24540

T.M.MAAKE

12

Notes, internal connection details and key to symbols

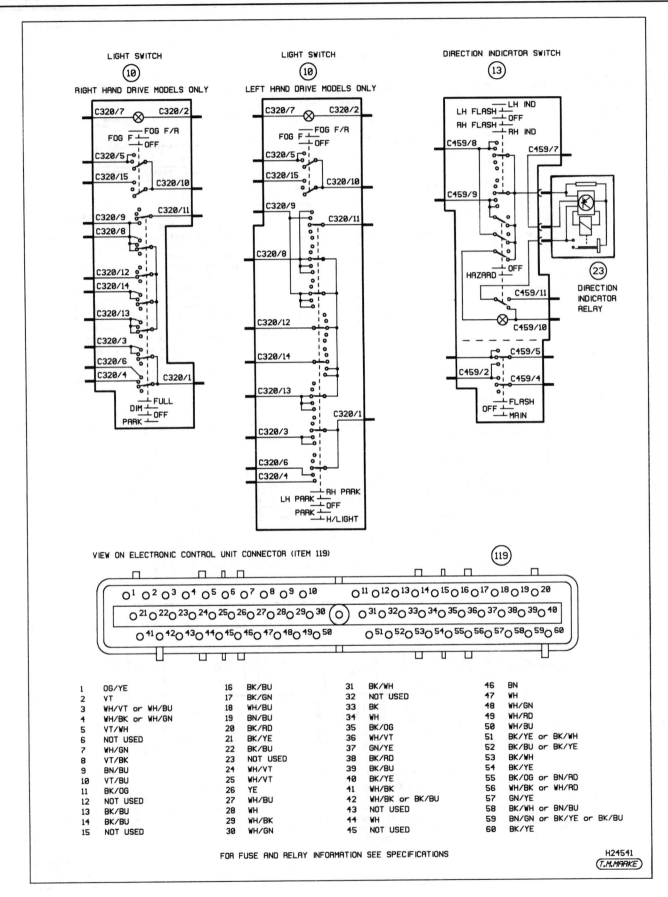

LIGHT SWITCH
(10)
RIGHT HAND DRIVE MODELS ONLY

LIGHT SWITCH
(10)
LEFT HAND DRIVE MODELS ONLY

DIRECTION INDICATOR SWITCH
(13)

VIEW ON ELECTRONIC CONTROL UNIT CONNECTOR (ITEM 119)   (119)

1	OG/YE	16	BK/BU	31	BK/WH	46	BN
2	VT	17	BK/GN	32	NOT USED	47	WH
3	WH/VT or WH/BU	18	WH/BU	33	BK	48	WH/GN
4	WH/BK or WH/GN	19	BN/BU	34	WH	49	WH/RD
5	VT/WH	20	BK/RD	35	BK/OG	50	WH/BU
6	NOT USED	21	BK/YE	36	WH/VT	51	BK/YE or BK/WH
7	WH/GN	22	BK/BU	37	GN/YE	52	BK/BU or BK/YE
8	VT/BK	23	NOT USED	38	BK/RD	53	BK/WH
9	BN/BU	24	WH/VT	39	BK/BU	54	BK/YE
10	VT/BU	25	WH/VT	40	BK/YE	55	BK/OG or BN/RD
11	BK/OG	26	YE	41	WH/BK	56	WH/BK or WH/RD
12	NOT USED	27	WH/BU	42	WH/BK or BK/BU	57	GN/YE
13	BK/BU	28	WH	43	NOT USED	58	BK/WH or BN/BU
14	BK/BU	29	WH/BK	44	WH	59	BN/GN or BK/YE or BK/BU
15	NOT USED	30	WH/GN	45	NOT USED	60	BK/YE

FOR FUSE AND RELAY INFORMATION SEE SPECIFICATIONS

H24541
(T.M.MARKE)

Internal connection details continued

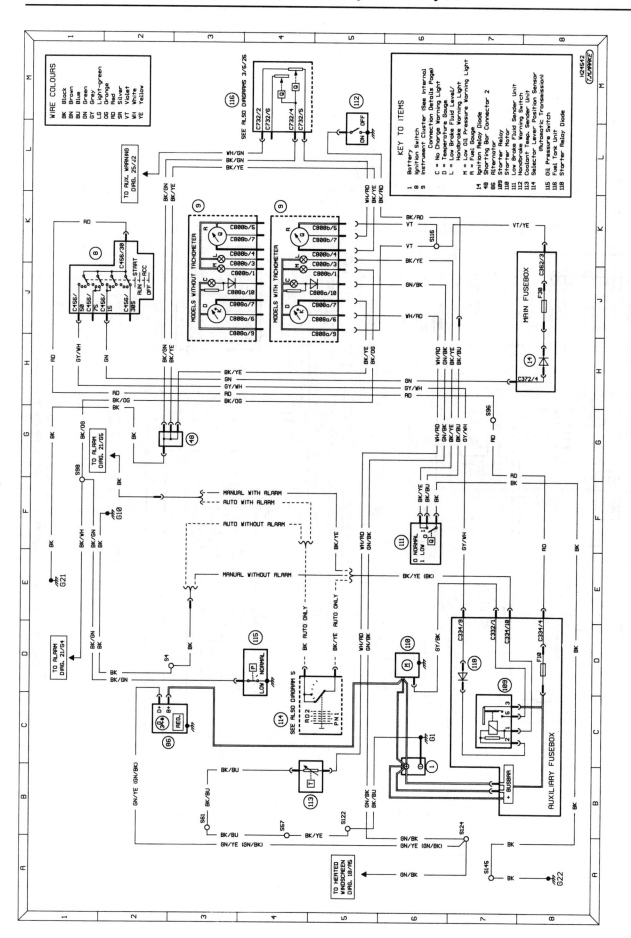

Diagram 1: Starting, charging, warning lights and gauges

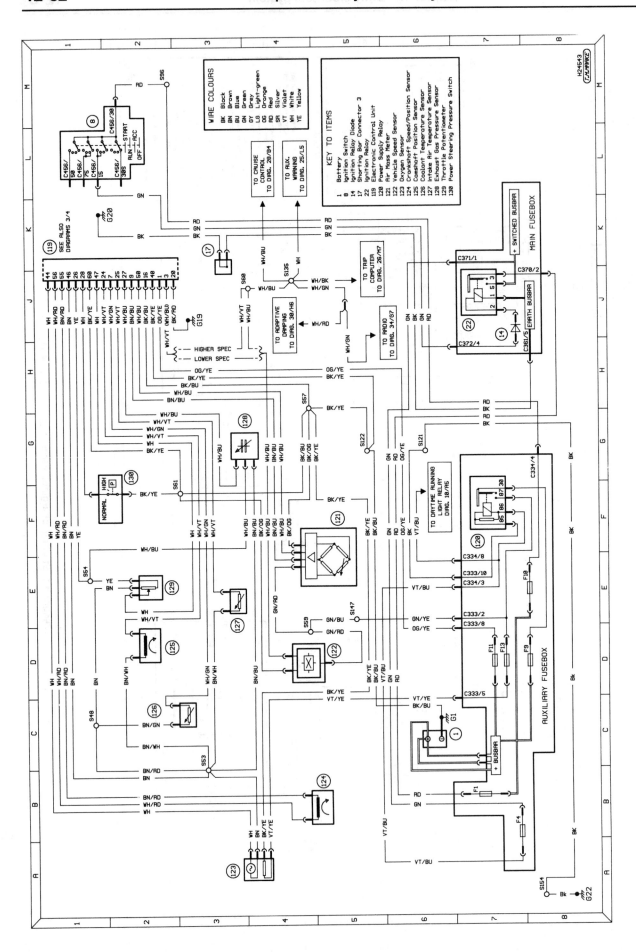

Diagram 2: Engine management - sensor inputs (manual transmission models)

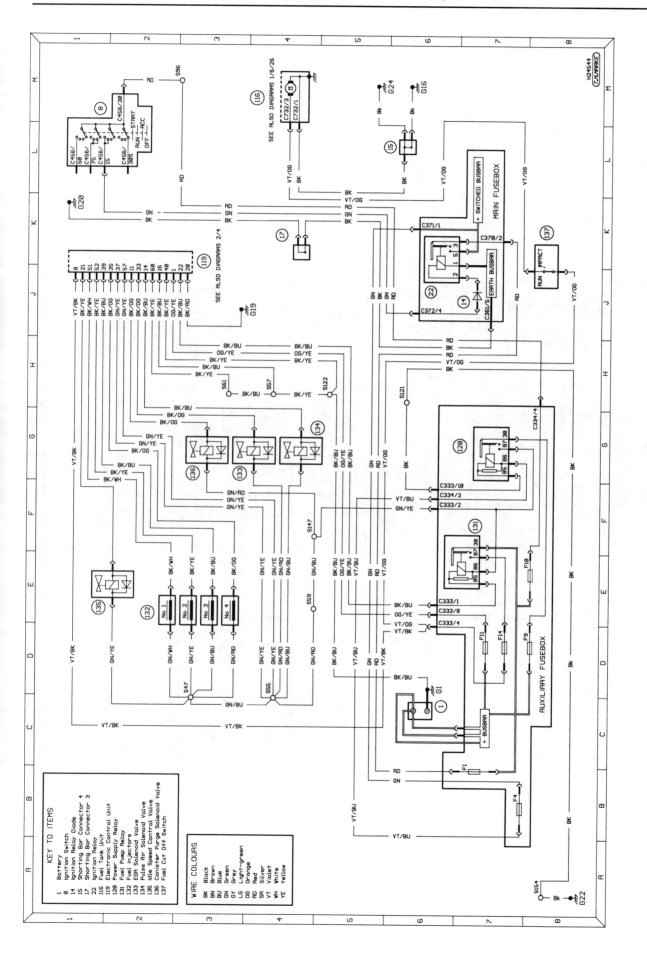

Diagram 3: Engine management - solenoid outputs and fuel pump (manual transmission models)

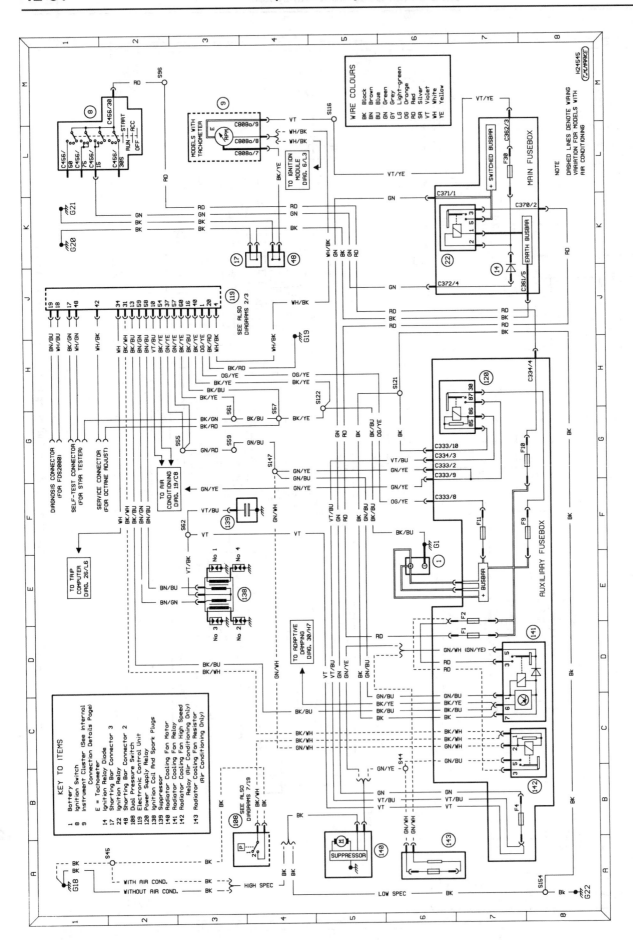

Diagram 4: Engine management - ignition, tachometer, cooling fan and diagnostic connectors (manual transmission models)

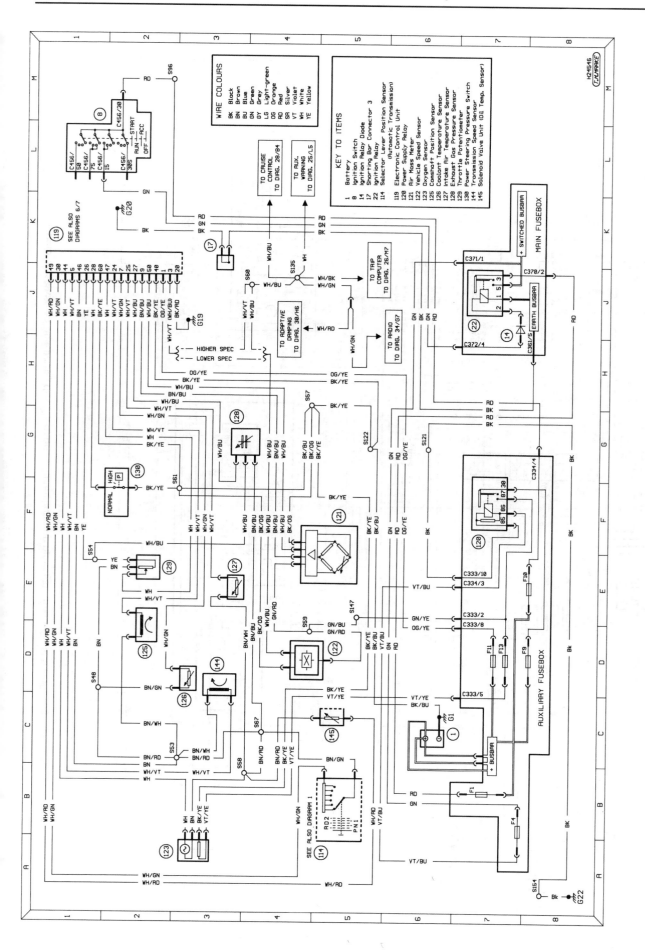

Diagram 5: Engine management - sensor inputs (automatic transmission models)

12

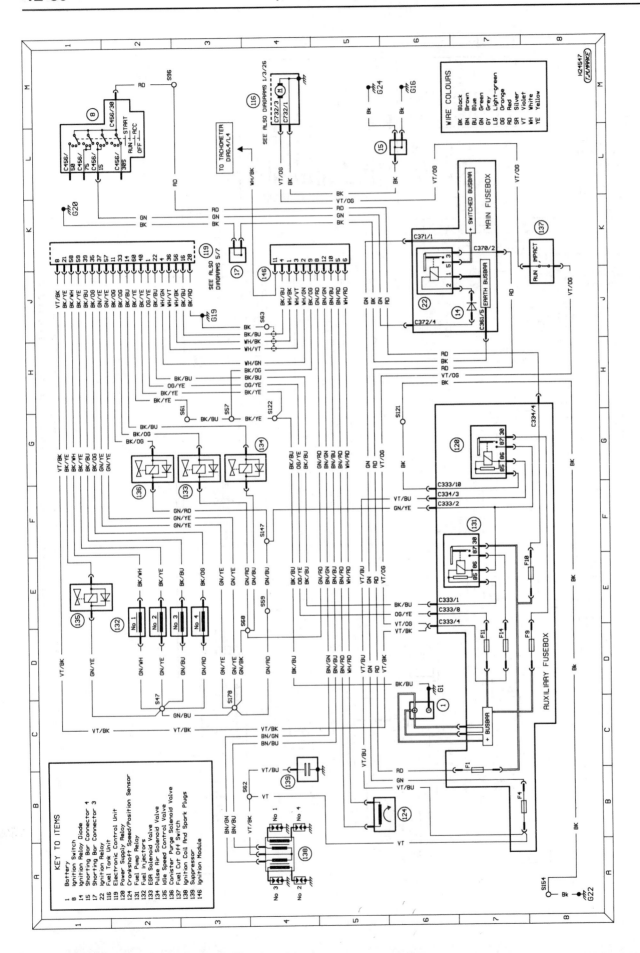

Diagram 6: Engine management - solenoid outputs, ignition and fuel pump (automatic transmission models)

KEY TO ITEMS

1   Battery
8   Ignition Switch
14   Ignition Relay Diode
15   Shorting Bar Connector 4
16   Shorting Bar Connector 3
22   Ignition Relay
116   Fuel Tank Unit
119   Electronic Control Unit
120   Power Supply Relay
124   Crankshaft Speed/Position Sensor
131   Fuel Pump Relay
132   Fuel Injectors
134   EGR Solenoid Valve
135   Pulse Air Solenoid Valve
136   Idle Speed Control Valve
137   Canister Purge Solenoid Valve
138   Ignition Coil And Spark Plugs
139   Fuel Cut Off Switch
139   Suppressor
146   Ignition Module

WIRE COLOURS

BK   Black
BN   Brown
BU   Blue
GN   Green
GY   Grey
LG   Light-green
OG   Orange
RD   Red
SR   Silver
VT   Violet
WH   White
YE   Yellow

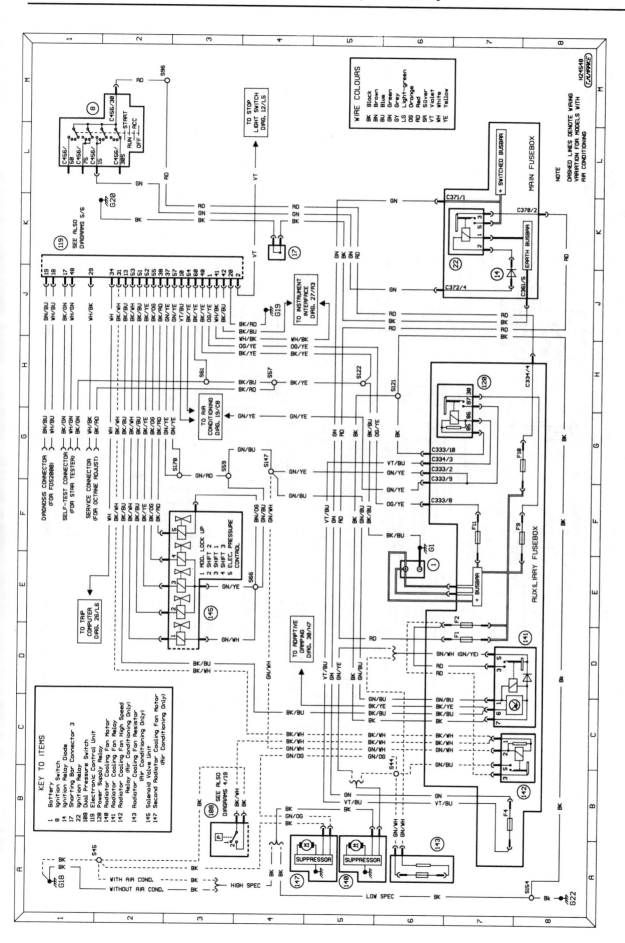

Diagram 7: Engine management - cooling fan, solenoid valve unit and diagnostic connectors (automatic transmission models)

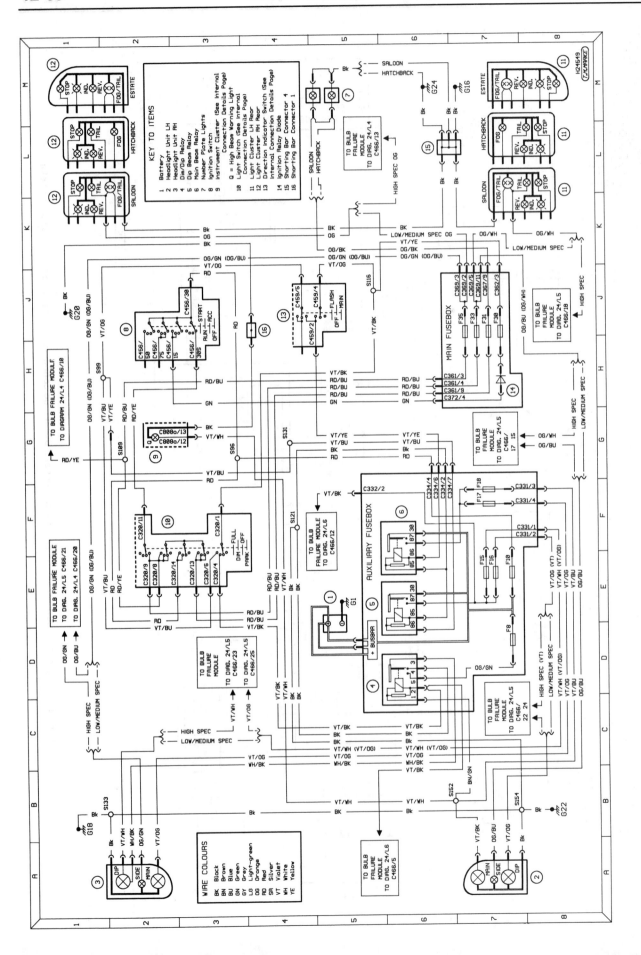

Diagram 8: Exterior lighting - side and headlights (right-hand-drive models: dim-dip)

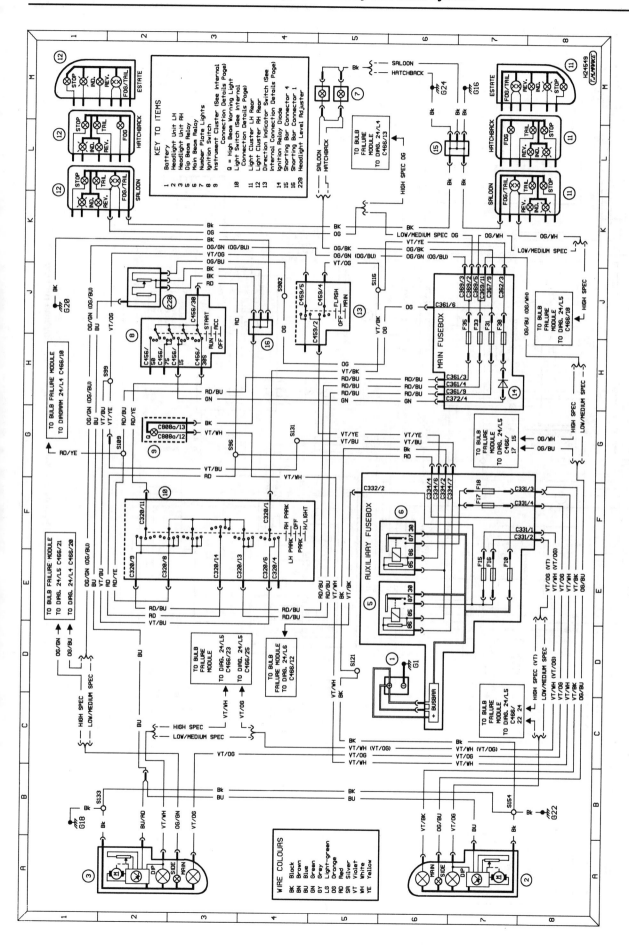

Diagram 9: Exterior lighting - side and headlights (left-hand-drive models: non-dim-dip)

12

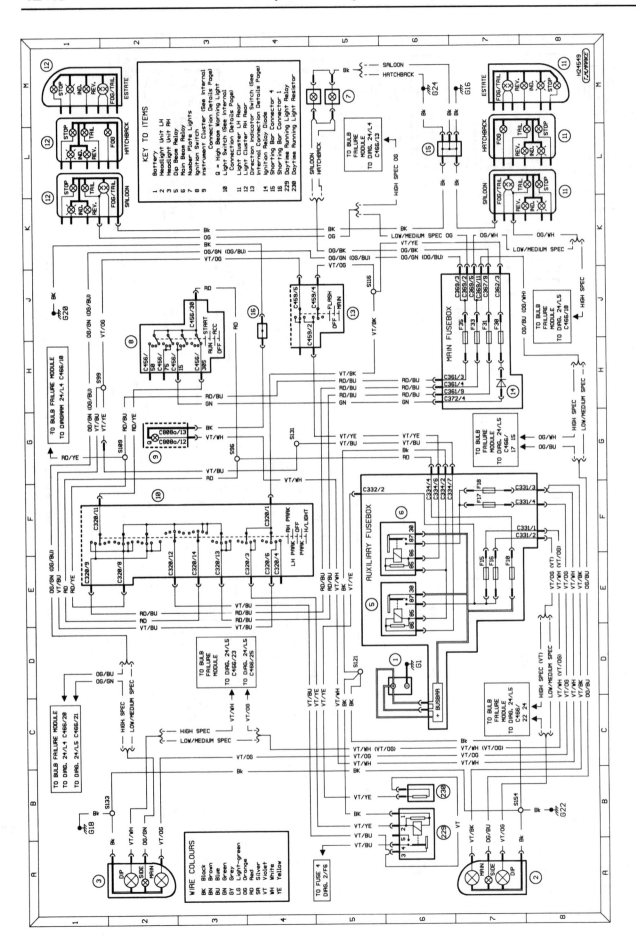

Diagram 10: Exterior lighting - side and headlights (left-hand-drive models: daytime running lights)

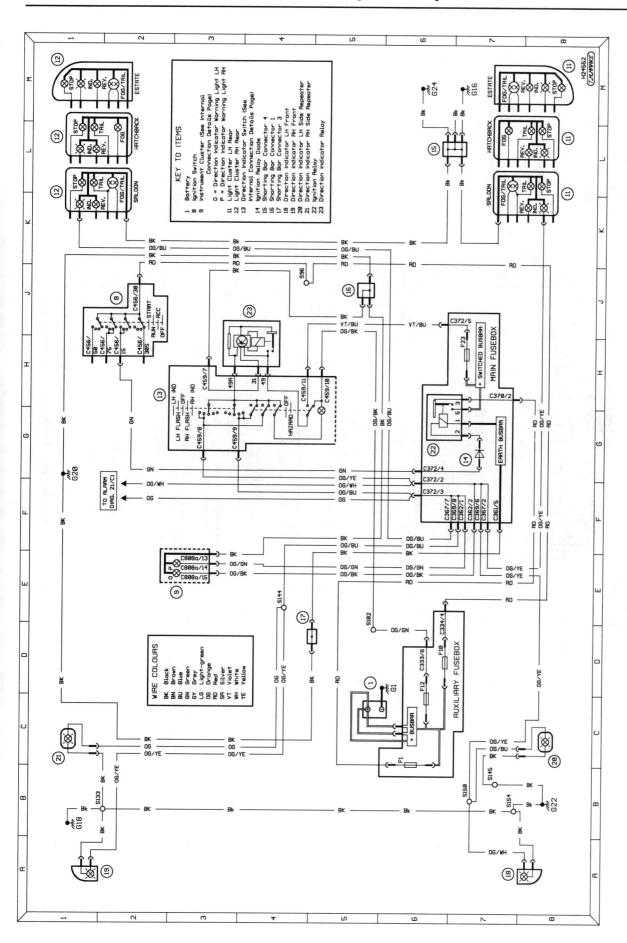

Diagram 11: Exterior lighting – hazard flasher and direction indicators

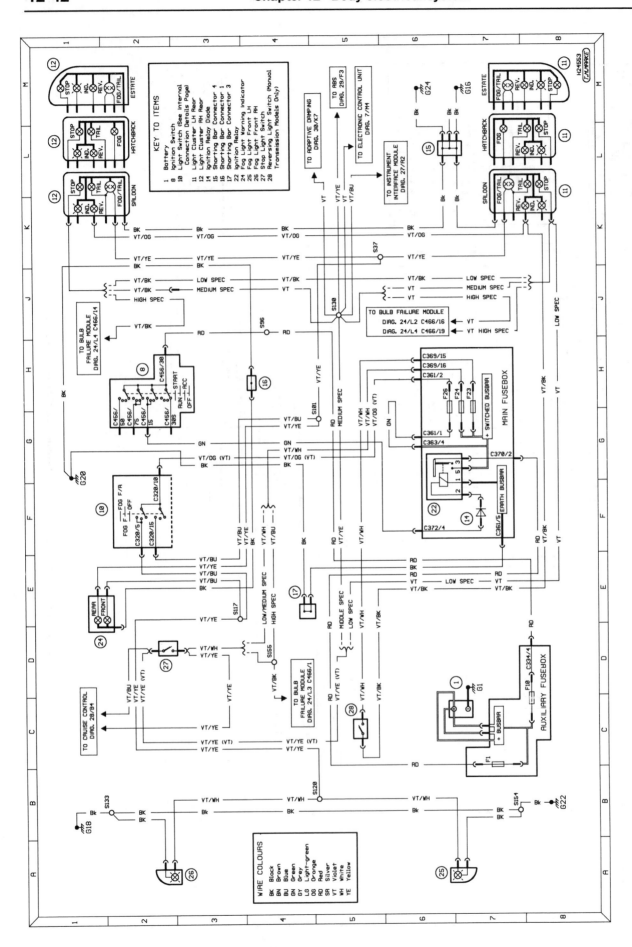

Diagram 12: Exterior lighting - foglights, stop-lights and reversing lights

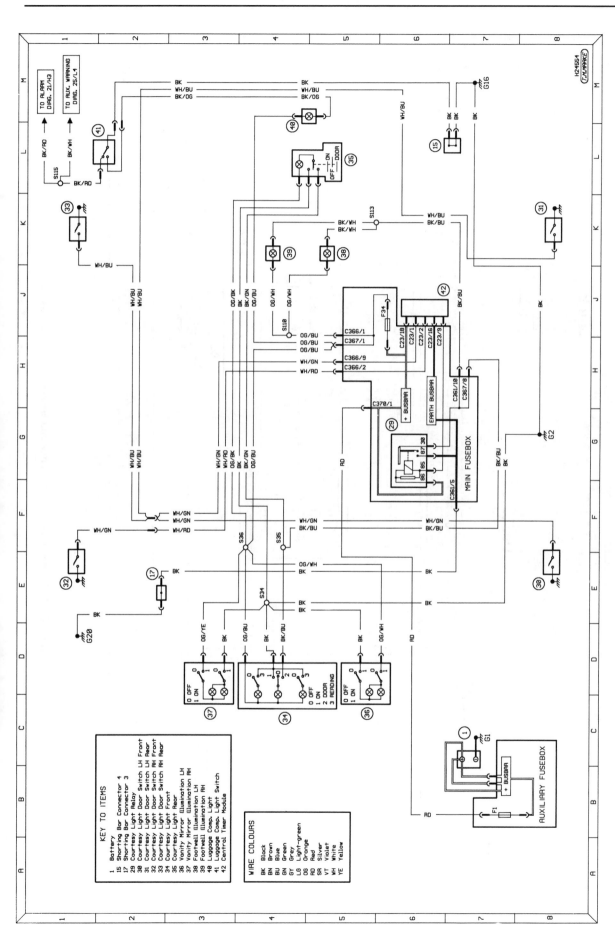

Diagram 13: Interior lighting - front and rear courtesy, footwell and luggage compartment lights

12

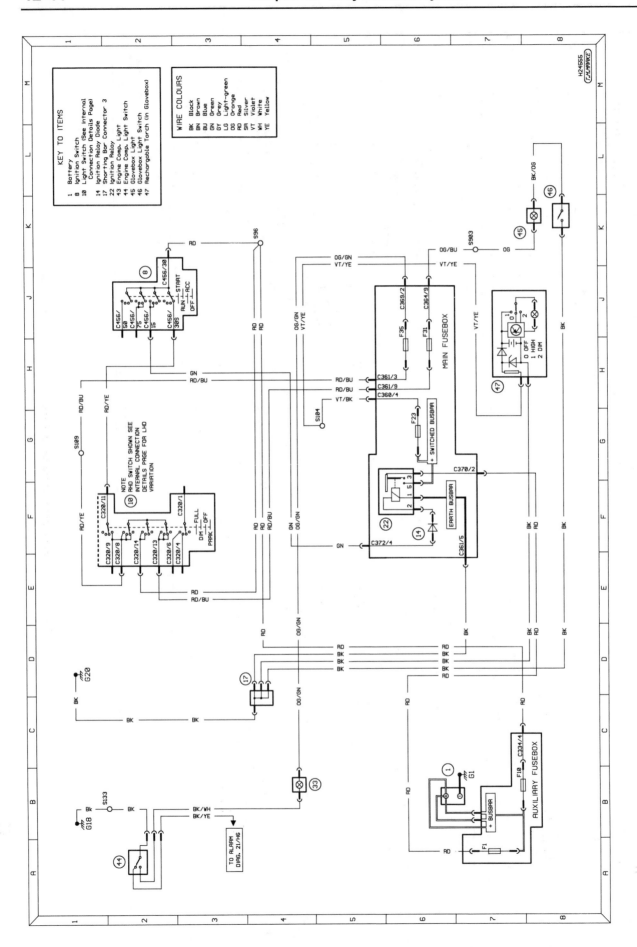

Diagram 14: Interior lighting - torch, glovebox and engine compartment lights

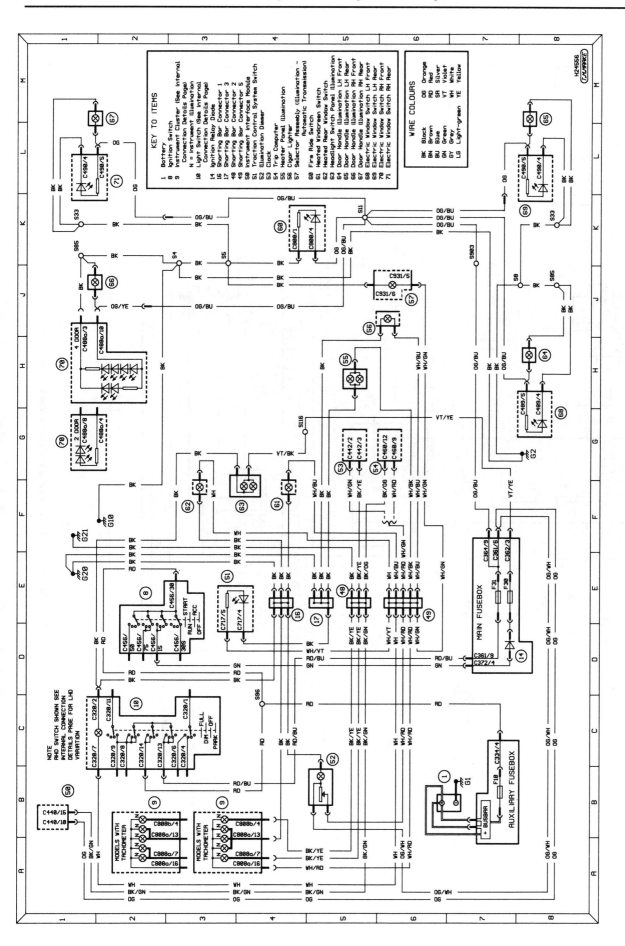

Diagram 15: Interior illumination

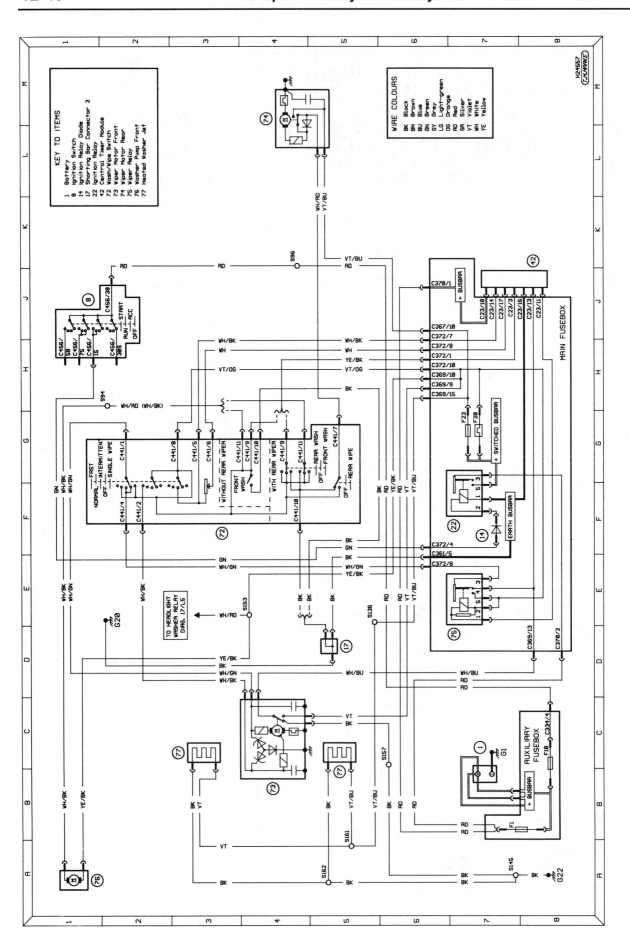

Diagram 16: Wash/wipe and heated washer jets

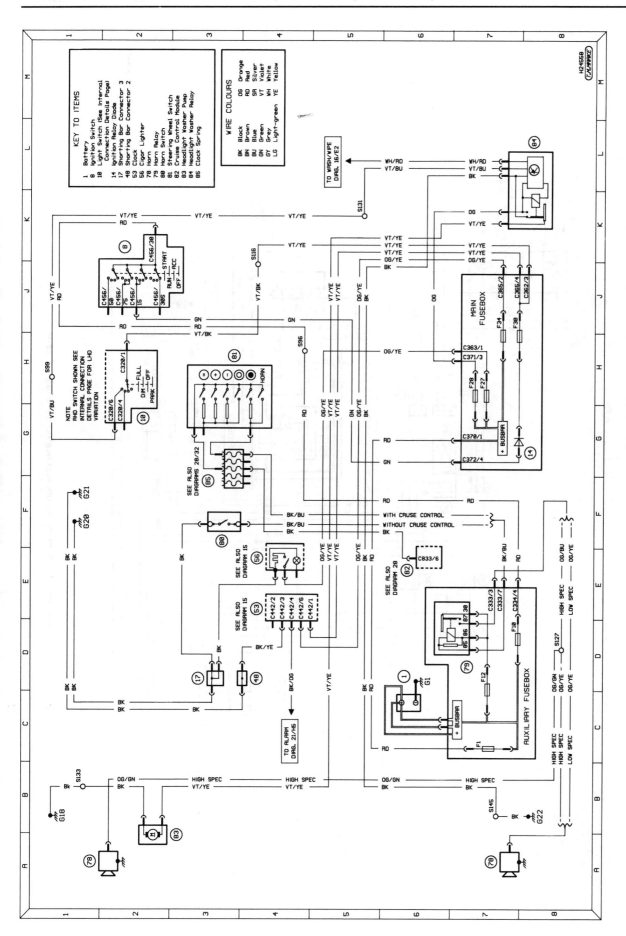

Diagram 17: Headlight washer, horn, clock and cigar lighter

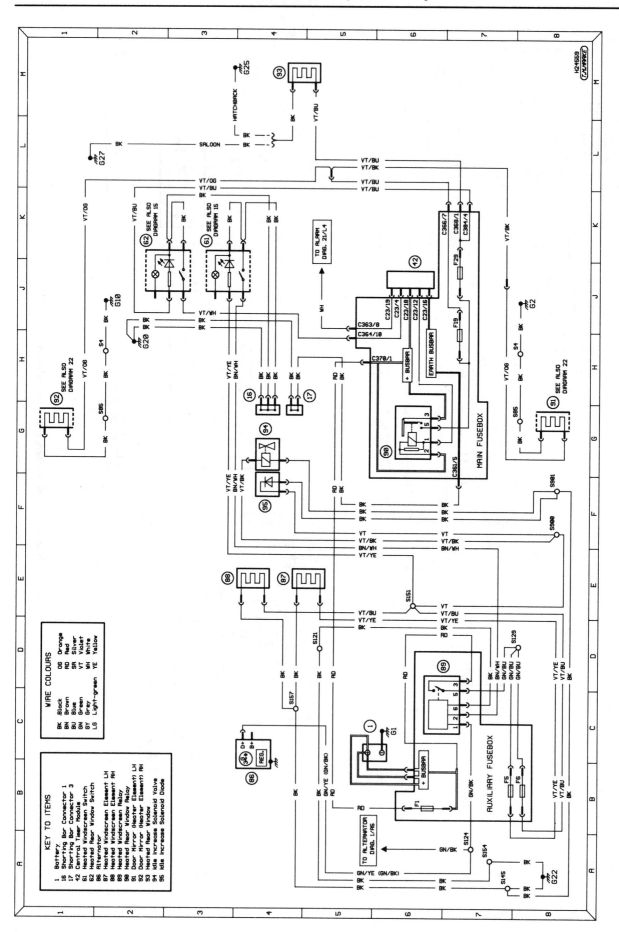

Diagram 18: Heated mirrors and heated front/rear screens

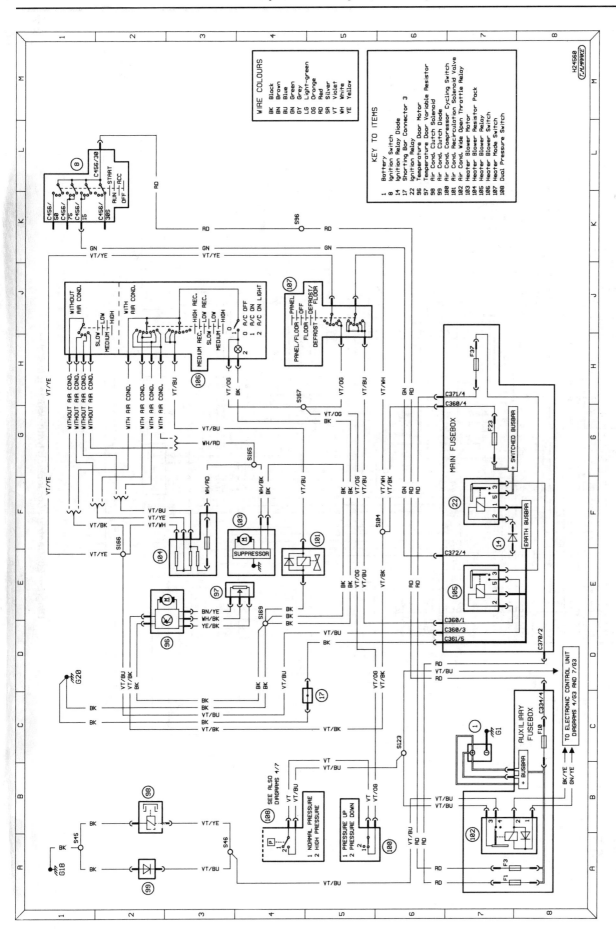

Diagram 19: Air conditioning and heater blower

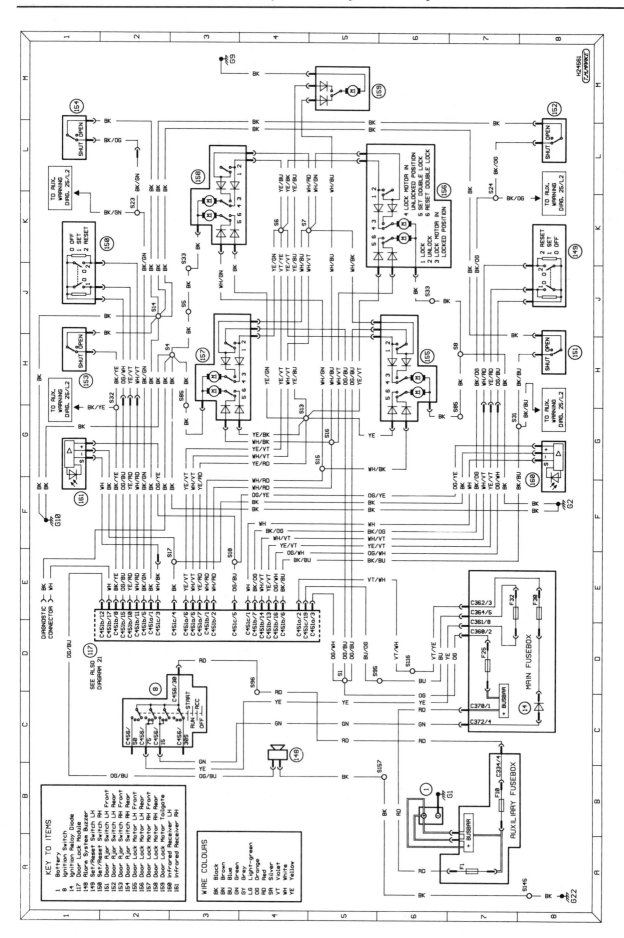

Diagram 20: Central door locking (with double locking)

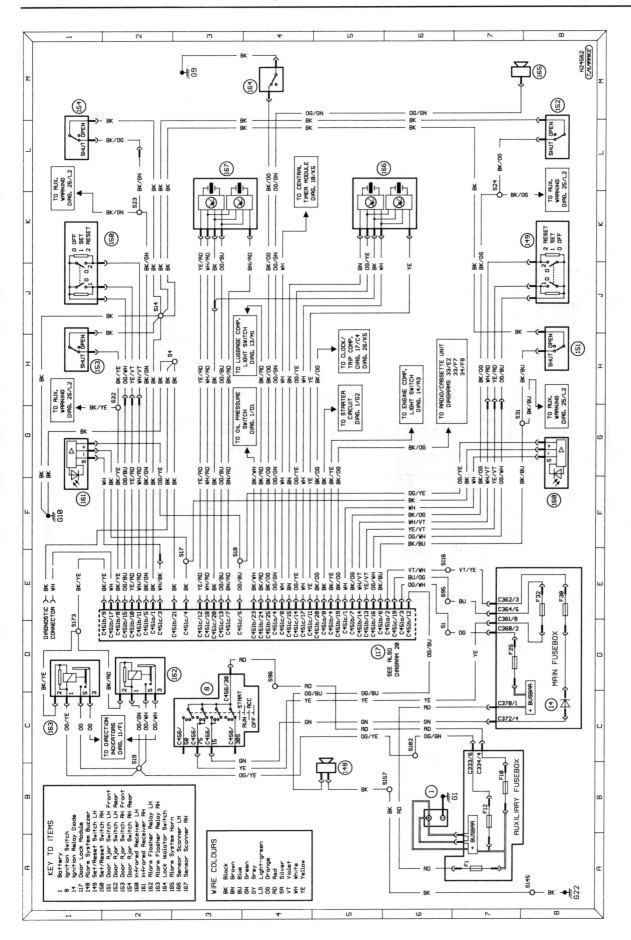

Diagram 21: Anti-theft alarm

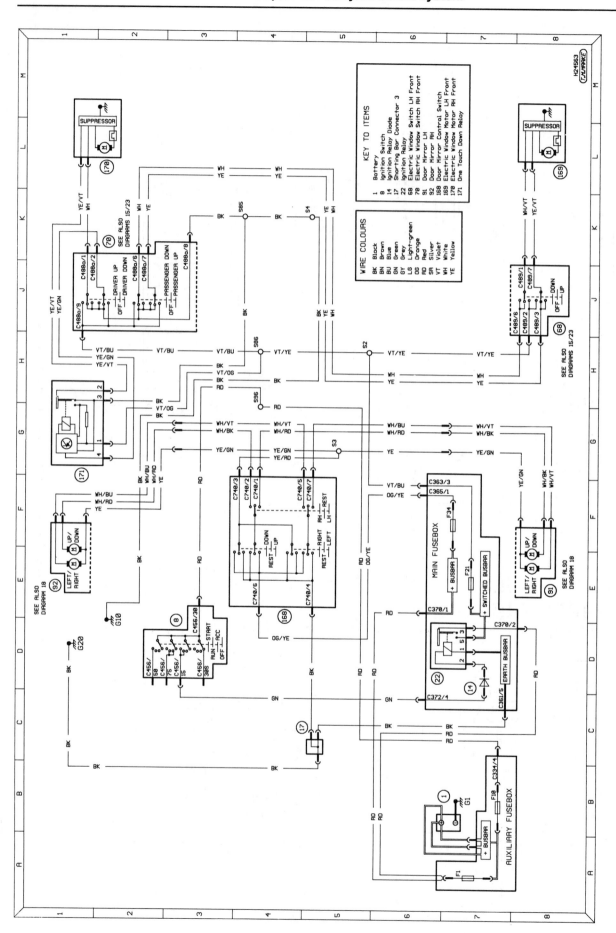

Diagram 22: Electric mirrors and (front) electric windows

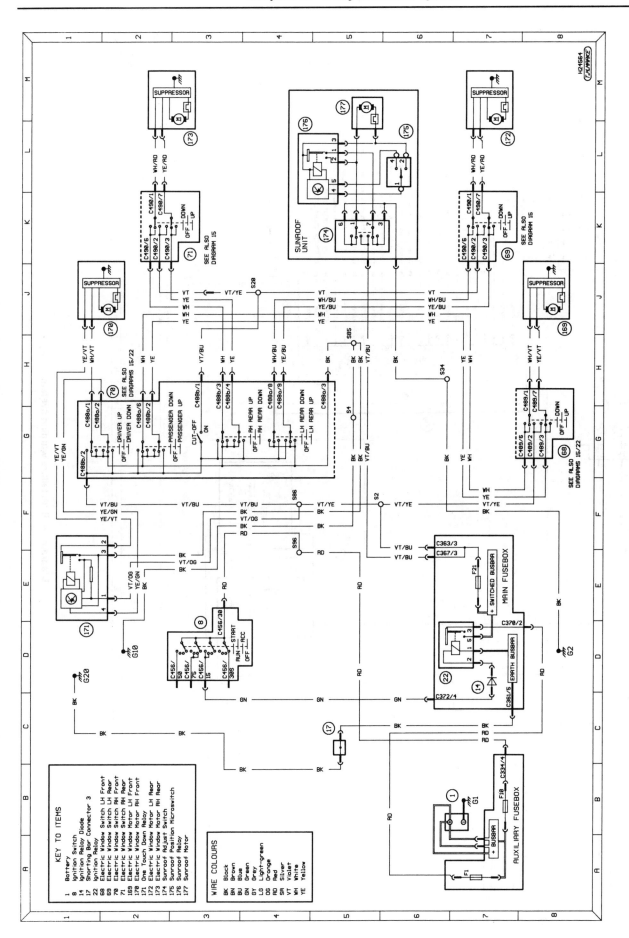

Diagram 23: Electric sunroof and (front and rear) electric windows

KEY TO ITEMS

1	Battery
8	Ignition Switch
14	Ignition Relay Diode
17	Shorting Bar Connector 3
22	Ignition Relay
68	Electric Window Switch LH Front
69	Electric Window Switch RH Front
70	Electric Window Switch LH Rear
71	Electric Window Switch RH Front
168	Electric Window Motor LH Front
169	Electric Window Motor RH Front
170	Electric Window Motor LH Rear
171	Electric Window Motor RH Rear
172	One Touch Down Relay
173	Sunroof Adjust Relay
174	Sunroof Position Microswitch
175	Sunroof Relay
176	Sunroof Relay
177	Sunroof Motor

WIRE COLOURS

BK	Black
BN	Brown
BU	Blue
GN	Green
GY	Grey
LG	Light-green
OG	Orange
RD	Red
SR	Silver
VT	Violet
WH	White
YE	Yellow

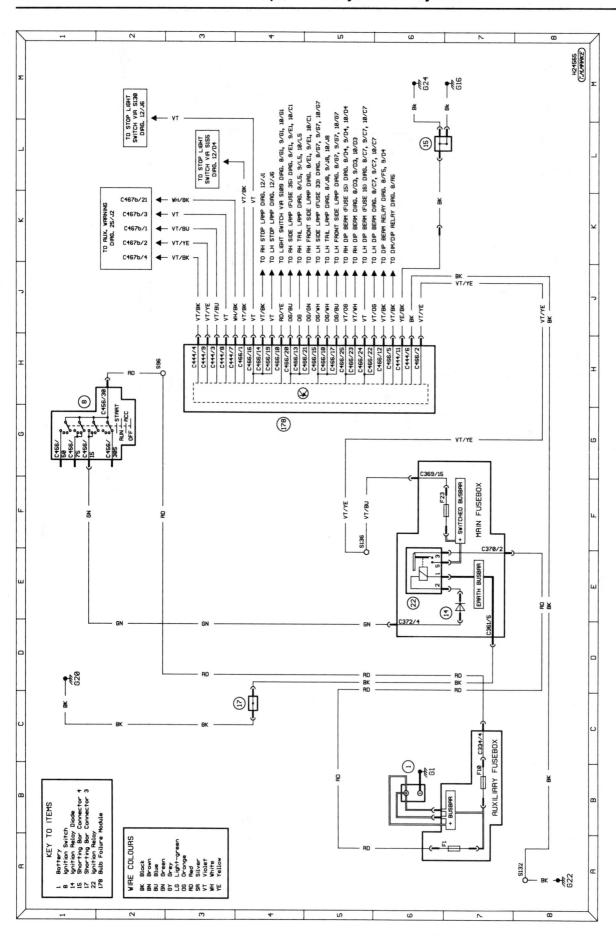

Diagram 24: Bulb failure warning system

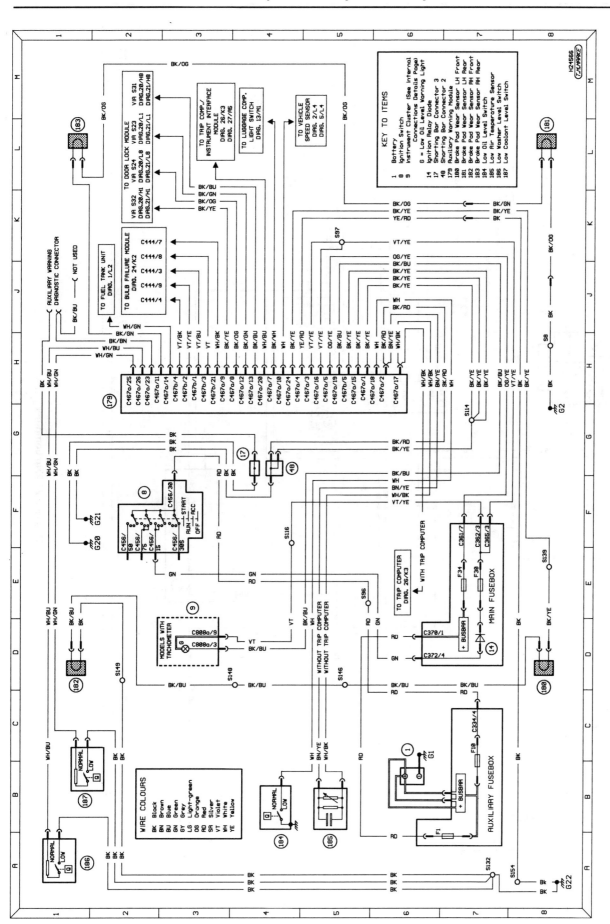

Diagram 25: Auxiliary warning system

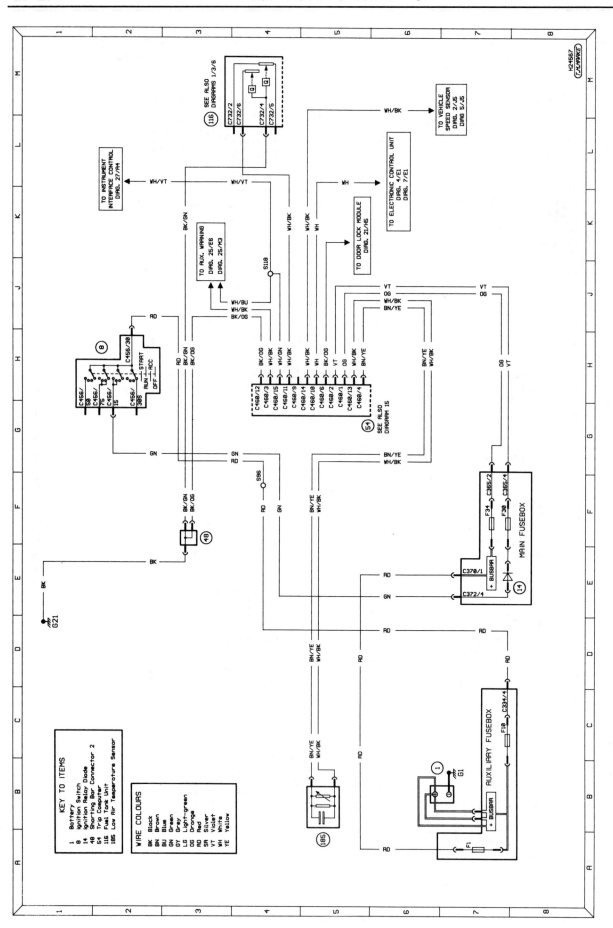

Diagram 26: Trip computer

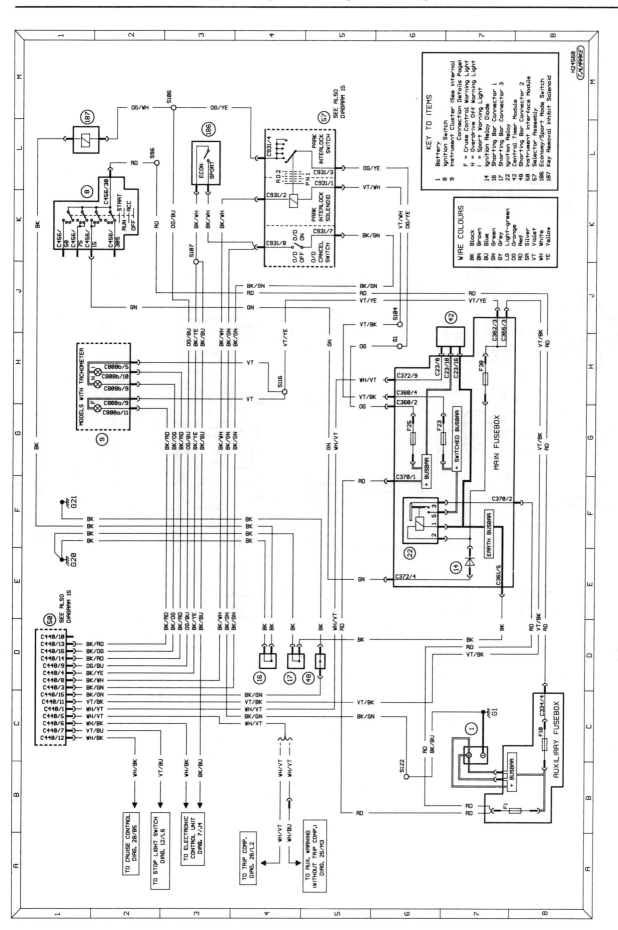

Diagram 27: Instrument interface control

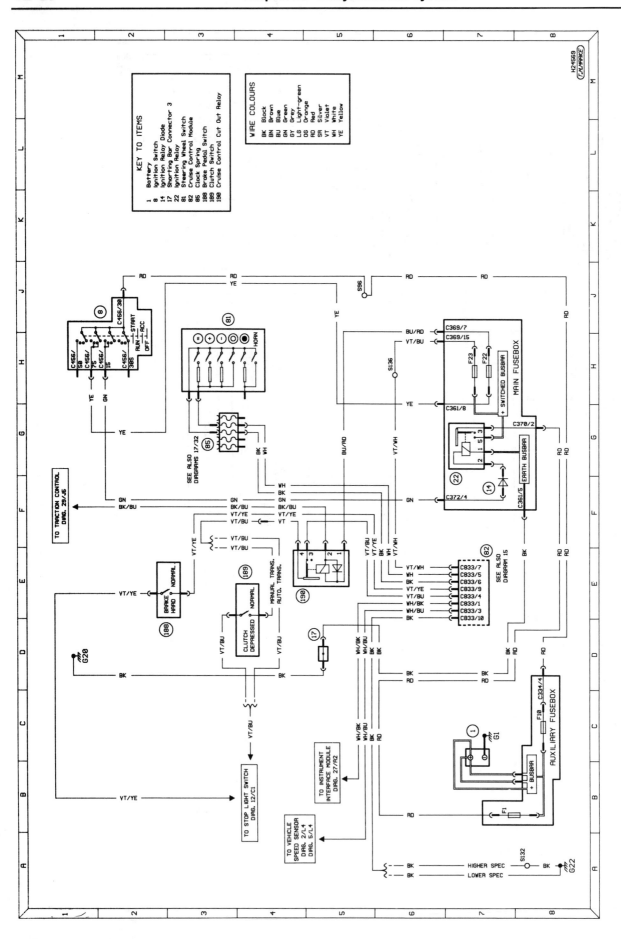

Diagram 28: Cruise control

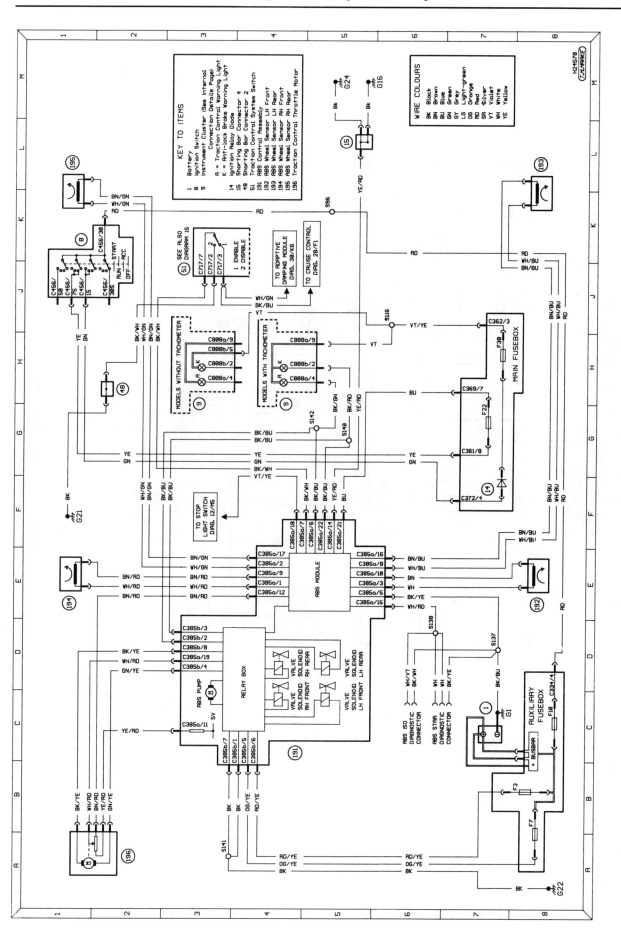

Diagram 29: ABS with traction control

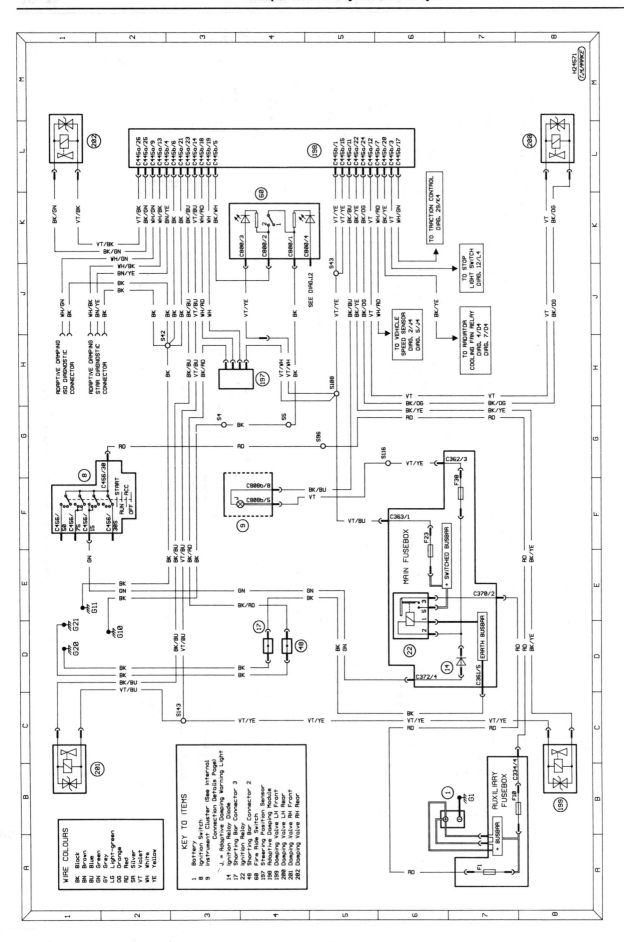

Diagram 30: Adaptive damping system

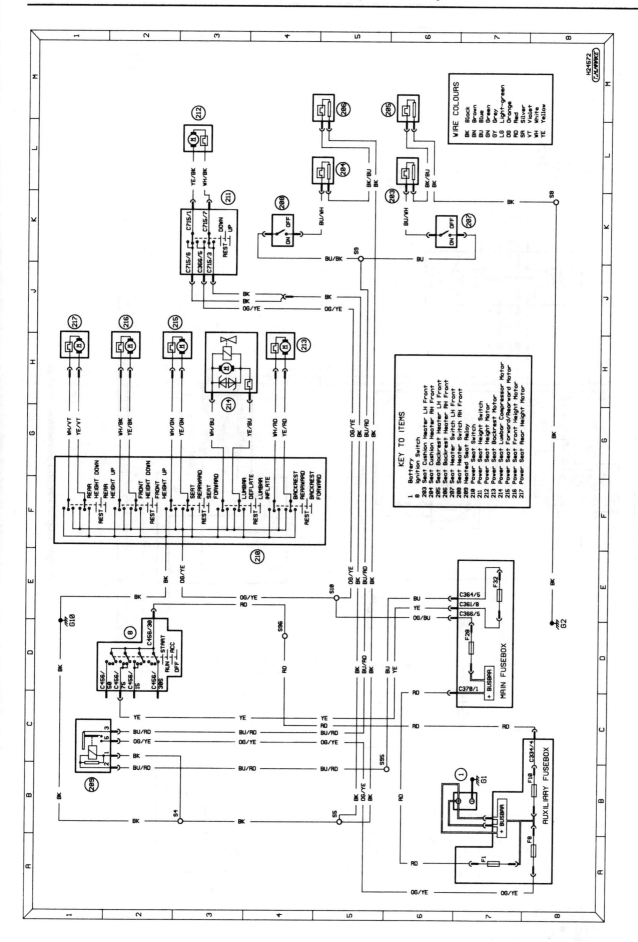

Diagram 31: Heated seats and driver's seat electric adjustment

KEY TO ITEMS

1   Battery Switch
8   Ignition Switch
203 Seat Cushion Heater LH Front
204 Seat Cushion Heater RH Front
205 Seat Backrest Heater LH Front
206 Seat Backrest Heater RH Front
207 Seat Heater Switch LH Front
208 Seat Heater Switch RH Front
209 Heated Seat Relay
210 Power Seat Switch
211 Power Seat Height Switch
212 Power Seat Height Motor
213 Power Seat Backrest Motor
214 Power Seat Lumbar Compressor Motor
215 Power Seat Forward/Rearward Motor
216 Power Seat Front Height Motor
217 Power Seat Rear Height Motor

WIRE COLOURS

BK   Black
BN   Brown
BU   Blue
GN   Green
GY   Grey
LG   Light-green
OG   Orange
RD   Red
SR   Silver
VT   Violet
WH   White
YE   Yellow

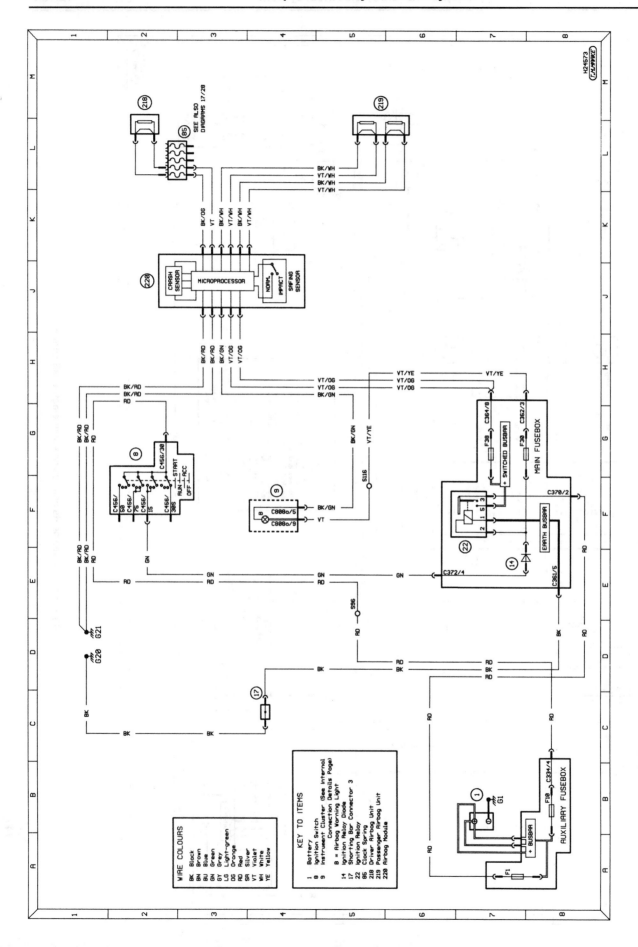

Diagram 32: Driver and passenger air bags

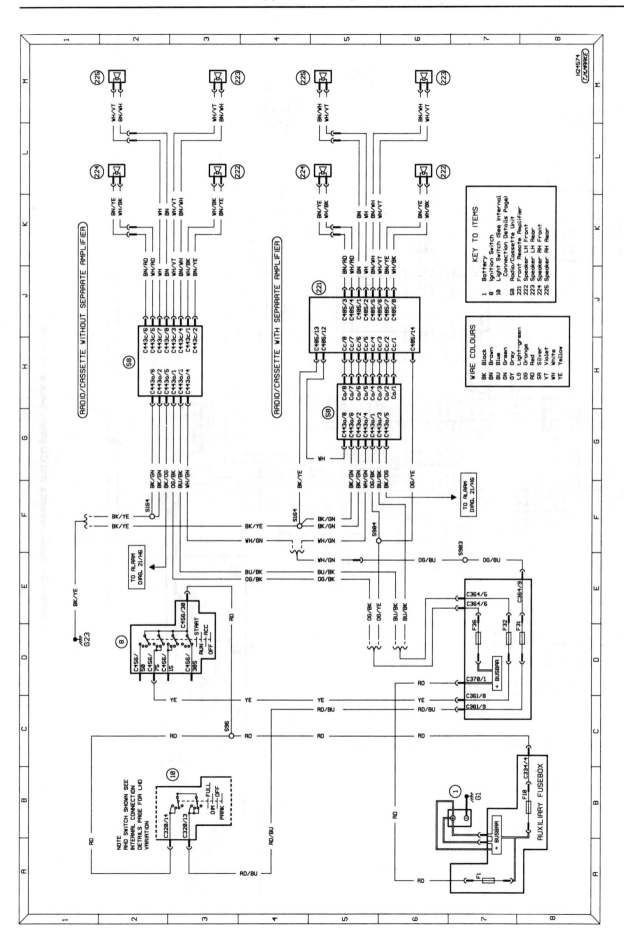

Diagram 33: Radio/cassette (with amplifier)

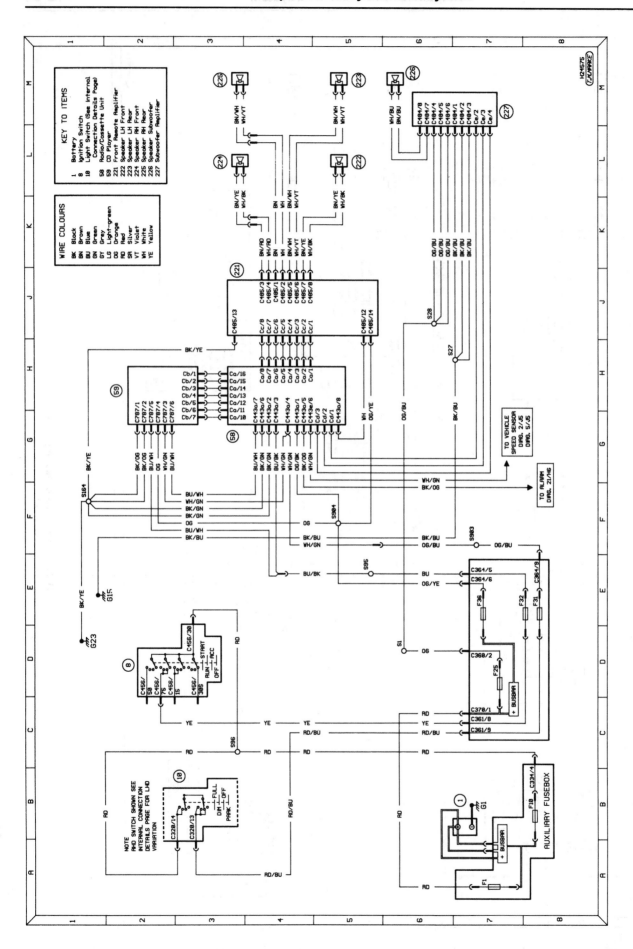

Diagram 34: Radio/cassette and CD player (with subwoofer)

Index

Note: *References throughout this index relate to Chapter and Page numbers, separated by a hyphen.*